An Architectural Guidebook to

San Francisco and the Bay Area

An Architectural Guidebook to

San Francisco and the Bay Area

Susan Dinkelspiel Cerny

CONTRIBUTING AUTHORS AND PHOTOGRAPHERS
Beth A. Armstrong, Anthony Bruce, Susan Dinkelspiel Cerny
Charlene Duval, Ward Hill, Marianne Rapalus Hurley, Judy Irvin, William Kostura
Gail G. Lombardi, Betty Marvin, Woodruff Minor, Mitchell P. Postel, Shelby Sampson

Gibbs Smith, Publisher
TO ENRICH AND INSPIRE HUMANKIND
Salt Lake City | Charleston | Santa Fe | Santa Barbara

First Edition
11 10 09 08 07   5 4 3 2 1

Text © 2007 Susan Dinkelspiel Cerny
Photographs © 2007 as noted throughout the book, and also by the following:
   Cover (front)—
      QT Luong/terragalleria.com
   Front (pp. i–xvi) and back (pp. 501–552)—
      Susan Dinkelspiel Cerny (pp. ii–iii, viii, x, xii, xvi, 551)
   Architectural Styles (pp. 503–510)—
      Beth A. Armstrong, 1
      Anthony Bruce, 7b [2]
      Susan Dinkelspiel Cerny, 2, 5c, 6, 11 [2], 14, 15a, 15b, 16c, 17a [1], 17a [2], 17b [1]
      Charlene Duval, 7a [1], 8, 9, 15d, 16a, 17b [3]
      Ward Hill, 3, 4, 10 [1], 10 [3], 13, 16b [2], 17b [2]
      Marianne Rapalus Hurley, 7a [2], 7b [1], 10 [2], 12, 16b [1]
      Betty Marvin, 5a, 5b, 15c
      Berkeley Architectural Heritage Association, 11 [1]

Published by
Gibbs Smith, Publisher
P.O. Box 667
Layton, Utah 84041

1.800.835.4993 orders
www.gibbs-smith.com

Cover design by Kurt Hauser
Maps, layout design, and production by Rudy Ramos
Printed and bound in Canada

Library of Congress Cataloging-in-Publication Data

Cerny, Susan Dinkelspiel.
An architectural guidebook to San Francisco and the Bay area / Susan Dinkelspiel Cerny ;
contributing authors and photographers, Beth A. Armstrong . . . [et al.]. — 1st ed.
    p. cm.
Includes bibliographical references and index.
ISBN-13: 978-1-58685-432-4
ISBN-10: 1-58685-432-1
1. Architecture—California—San Francisco Bay Area—Guidebooks.
2. San Francisco Bay Area (Calif.)—Guidebooks.
I. Armstrong, Beth A. II. Title.

NA735.S35C47 2007
720.9794'6—dc22
                              2007007940

In memory of my parents, who inspired me—
Miriam and Richard C. Dinkelspiel

And to my grandchildren—
Sara Coleman
Miles, Diego, and Jacob Stern
Alexander, Nicholas, Zachary, and Joshua Meurer

• • •

Ballad of the Hyde Street Grip

Oh, the lights are in the Mission, and the ships are in the Bay;
And Tamalpais is looming from the Gate, across the way;
The Presidio trees are waving, and the hills are growing brown,
And the driving fog is harried from the Ocean to the town!
How the pulleys slap and rattle! How the cables hum and whip!
Oh, they sing a gallant chorus, on the Hyde Street Grip!

Gelett Burgess, 1901

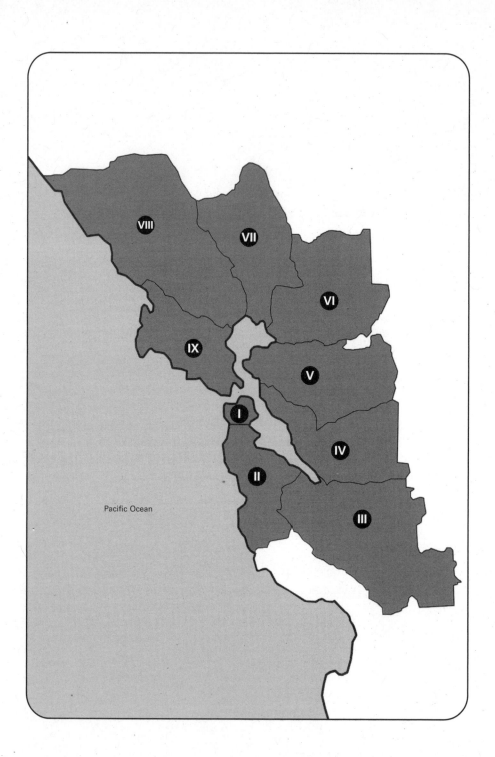

Pacific Ocean

Contents

De Young Museum, San Francisco

Acknowledgments

First, I must acknowledge and gratefully thank all the contributing authors who participated in this enormous task; even when it was evident that it would be more time consuming than any of us anticipated, they carried through to completion. Thank you Beth A. Armstrong, Anthony Bruce, Charlene Duval, Ward Hill, Marianne Rapalus Hurley, Judy Irvin, William Kostura, Gail G. Lombardi, Betty Marvin, Woodruff Minor, Mitchell P. Postel, and Shelby Sampson.

Everyone would like to thank Gary Goss, researcher extraordinaire, who has made known the identities of so many architects of so many buildings.

This guide builds and expands on previous architectural guides to the Bay Area, and is indebted to the many researchers and authors who have gone before us. Recent local cultural heritage surveys, often unpublished, are also invaluable.

Susan Cerny thanks Kathleen Steadman, Elizabeth Stern Coleman, and John McBride, who read many of the early drafts and offered editorial suggestions. Anthony Bruce, Burl Willis, Kirk Peterson (AIA), and Jerry Sulliger provided help with Contra Costa County. Kathleen Thompson Hill and Gerald Hill assisted with Napa County. Jocelyn Moss, senior librarian at the Kent History Room, Marin County Free Library, provided patient assistance as did Gordon White, chief of Cultural Resources at Point Reyes National Seashore, and historian Dewy Livingston of Inverness. Architects Robert Swatt, Steven House, and ACE Architects provided photographs and information on their work, particularly in the Oakland Fire Area.

Judy Irvin thanks Jim Kern, director of Vallejo Naval and Historical Museum, Vallejo; Randy L. Starbuck, director of Economic Development, Suisun City; and Shirley Paolini, Bird's Landing unofficial historian and bartender of Solano County.

Charlene Duval of Santa Clara County wishes to thank her co-authors: Leslie Dill, Franklin Maggi, and Bonnie Montgomery. She thanks George Espinola for information on architects Frank D. Wolfe, Charles S. McKenzie, and the firm of Wolfe & Higgins; Pat Dunning for help with Los Gatos; Michael Borbely for providing information on Palm Haven; April Halberstadt for architect attributions for the Saratoga area; Jack Douglas as a generous resource person; Bob Johnson from the California Room at the King Library; and Riley Doty of the Tile Heritage Foundation. Photographs were provided by the authors with the exception of the Palm Haven houses, which were provided by Michael Borbely, and 129 Edelen Avenue, which was provided by Pat Dunning.

Point Bonito Lighthouse, Marin County

Ward Hill thanks Wayne Gehrke, Group 4 Architecture, South San Francisco; Martha Rosman, archivist for the Burlingame Historical Society; and Robert Blunk, Blunk Demattei Associates, Burlingame.

Marianne Hurley thanks Ron Bausman, Shawn Montoya, Holly Hoods and the Healdsburg Museum and Historical Society, Bruce Kibby, the Cloverdale Historical Society, John Schubert, Prue Draper, Sonoma League for Historic Preservation, Hanna Boys Center, Glen Ellen Historical Society, Katherine Rinehart and the Sonoma County Library History Annex, and Diana Painter. For Napa County she thanks Jo Noble of Calistoga, Lesley Frederickson at Napa Landmarks, and the Napa County Historical Society.

Gibbs Smith (president), Madge Baird (managing editor), and Linda Nimori (project editor) at Gibbs Smith, Publisher, provided assistance and direction for helping fit this vast amount of information into book form.

Finally, I wish to thank my patient husband, Joseph Cerny, for accompanying me on my many "outings" and for reading the entire text.

Preface

This guide to the architecture and built environment of the San Francisco Bay Area was compiled by a group of contributors who include historians, architectural historians, city planners, and architects. The authors have chosen from a wide variety of places and types of buildings, from dense old inner-city neighborhoods to a stone amphitheater on the side of a mountain; it is crammed with information. The old favorites are here, those buildings always included in any guide to Bay Area architecture, but the scope has broadened to include towns and neighborhoods that had not been given much attention before. This guide naturally builds from previous guides and historical accounts, but also takes advantage of recent local building surveys and histories. The book could easily be twice as long, but due to the limitations of space, not every significant building could be included; "Further Reading" offers sources for more detailed information.

The San Francisco Bay Area, as defined by the Association of Bay Area Governments (ABAG), contains nine counties that comprise the nine chapters of this guidebook: 1) San Francisco, 2) San Mateo, 3) Santa Clara, 4) Alameda, 5) Contra Costa, 6) Solano, 7) Napa, 8) Sonoma, and 9) Marin. These nine counties contain 101 incorporated cities and many unincorporated communities that consider themselves towns; most are included. Towns or neighborhoods with groups of similar buildings or histories may be described within a paragraph rather than listed individually.

Every attempt has been made to produce accurate usable maps, but supplementing our maps with standard road maps is always advisable. We apologize in advance for errors or discrepancies made while marking the specific location of entries.

All buildings listed in this guide can be viewed from a public right-of-way. Please respect private property and do not venture up driveways or entrance pathways.

Introduction

Geography

The San Francisco Bay Area is a delightful place surrounded by water and framed by mountains and hills. It is also a densely populated area of nearly seven million. From the air, one is struck by a vast, continuous, unrelenting ring of buildings and freeways surrounding the bay, spilling over the hills and off into the distance. Patches of open space are the region's public parks.

The bay itself is approximately fifty miles long and averages about ten miles wide, shaped somewhat like a long oval with the Golden Gate a narrow strait that opens to the Pacific Ocean and separates the Marin and San Francisco peninsulas.

The hills that frame the bay average about 1,000 feet in height. Mt. Tamalpais, in Marin County north of the Golden Gate, rises to 2,604 feet. Mt. Diablo, at 3,849 feet, rises to the east of Walnut Creek. San Jose, at the south end of the bay, is backed by 4,206-foot Mt. Hamilton. In the far north bay, Mt. St. Helena is the tallest mountain at 4,336 feet.

The land varies from wide plains that slope from hills and mountains to the bay, to deep narrow canyons in the folds of the mountains and hills; valleys lie between. On the coast, wide sandy beaches are as common as 100-foot cliffs that rise directly above a pounding surf. Weather patterns are as varied; coastal fog and wind cool San Francisco, while hills and mountains often block the fog from moving inland.

In this vastness of built environment and altered landscape, where are the best buildings, the great streets and civic plazas, the places where history reveals itself—places of surprise and possibly intrigue, beautiful, pleasant places, dramatic places? This is a guide to "architecture" but buildings are not isolated objects. Buildings are connected to a world beyond them and exist in their particular location for geographic, economic, social, political, and historic reasons. Briefly discussed are transportation systems—freeways, bridges, ferries, trains; public parkland—national, regional, and local; and city and suburban landscape plans that include the layout of streets and the color of sidewalks.

Some places provide an interesting streetscape even though individual buildings may be ordinary. The relationship between the width of the street, the height and width of the buildings, the rhythm of windows to walls are all aspects of what make certain streets pleasant places to walk, while others are more pleasant if driven by and ignored.

The entire ensemble of built environment can provide a physical record of how a place evolved and became what it is today. Even

Oakland Bay Bridge

redeveloped areas are usually surrounded by blocks of buildings and street patterns from an earlier era, revealing a history of events that created what is standing today. Each era in the history of the Bay Area has left its mark upon the built and altered landscape.

Discovery and Settlement

The Spanish were the first non-Native Americans to settle in the Bay Area, beginning in 1776. Although Juan Rodrigues Cabrillo sailed north from San Diego along the California Coast in 1542, he did not see the Golden Gate or San Francisco Bay. For more than 200 years, ships sailed by the bay without knowing it was there. The open passage of the Golden Gate into the bay is blocked from view by Angel Island, and the bay is often filled with fog.

It was not until 1769 that Don Gasper de Portolá made an overland expedition from San Diego and became the first Spaniard to see San Francisco Bay. Spanish explorers visited the area several more times before 1776 when Juan Bautista de Anza led a group of pioneers from Mexico overland to Monterey. Anza marked the location for the presidio (fort) and the mission where the pioneers built permanent settlements. The Spanish left an imprint on the land that remains today.

The mission was named for St. Francis of Asís—San Francisco de Asís—and it was the sixth of California's twenty-one missions. The mission church that stands today, commonly called Mission Dolores, was built between 1782 and 1791, and is the oldest building standing in the San Francisco Bay Area.

Other missions and settlements were established by the Spanish: Mission Santa Clara de Asís, now the site of the Santa Clara University, and El Pueblo San José de Guadalupe, which is today's San Jose, were founded in 1777. Mission San José de Guadalupe was established in 1797, followed by San Rafael Arcángel (Archangel) in 1817 and San Francisco Solano, in Sonoma (the most northern of the missions) in 1823.

The Spanish lost control of its Mexican territories in 1821, and California and the Bay Area became part of Mexico. Between 1833 and 1835, the missions were secularized and the mission lands divided and distributed to loyal Mexicans under a Mexican Land Grant program; vast tracts of land known as ranchos were granted to just a few families.

Non-Spanish and non-Mexican pioneers had begun to arrive in California as early as 1814, but their numbers accelerated after Mexican independence. Yerba Buena Pueblo was established in 1835 by Captain William Richardson, an English pioneer who had arrived in 1822. Yerba Buena was located around what is now Portsmouth Square and would soon become the historic center of San Francisco.

Even before the Mexican-American War began in 1846, the United States government had attempted to purchase California from the Mexicans. There were several unfortunate incidents in 1846 between U.S. soldiers and Mexicans, including a revolt that briefly established the Bear Flag Republic. California officially became a possession of the United States with the signing of the Treaty of Guadalupe Hidalgo in 1848. By the end of 1848, the California Gold Rush had begun, and California became a state in 1850.

The legacy of Spanish/Mexican settlements in the Bay Area includes five missions, the Presidio of San Francisco, the location of the cities of San Francisco, San Jose, Santa Clara, San Rafael, and Sonoma; roads between the missions (El Camino Real) and between Mexican ranchos (such as San Pablo Avenue, formerly Contra Costa Road); and many place-names. The irregularity of county lines and the history of how land was subdivided over time is also a legacy of the rancho system. Several Bay Area cities originated during the transition between the Mexican rancho era and the American era.

There are few Spanish/Mexican residential buildings still standing in the Bay Area. Some of these thick-walled adobe dwellings are encased within the walls of buildings that have grown around them, while others have been reconstructed, some on their original sites and others on alternative sites. There are a few town plazas laid out by Spanish/Mexican settlers, including those in Sonoma and Concord.

With the discovery of gold and the subsequent influx of gold miners, the population of the Bay Area grew and changed, and the era of the vast Mexican ranchos ended. Some Mexican owners were able to establish title to their land, but the majority sold it, often cheaply, and some were even cheated out of their property.

Between 1849 and 1869, the year the transcontinental railroad was opened, gold and other types of mining changed the economic, political, and social structure of California. All areas of the economy supported the mining activities: agriculture, manufacturing, logging, and associated businesses were established.

In the early days of the Gold Rush, shelters were simple or even primitive, sometimes nothing more than a tent or lean-to made of logs, but soon prefabricated buildings and building materials were shipped by boat from the East Coast. By 1851, the building trades were busy cutting lumber from the plentiful forests of redwood and Douglas fir, and constructing an instant city of simple frame buildings. After fires destroyed San Francisco several times, brick and stone were preferred in the business and manufacturing districts.

Transportation

Waterways were the primary means of transportation during the Gold Rush. Early settlements were commonly established along the edge of the bay or on rivers, navigable creeks, and sloughs unless there was a strong economic incentive to settle inland.

The Bay Area's first railroad opened in 1863–1864 between San Francisco and San Jose. A railroad between Sacramento, Napa, and Vallejo was established by 1868. Initially the Central Pacific's Intercontinental Railroad avoided the watery Delta area by passing over the Altamont Pass to Sunol to its terminus in Oakland. Beginning in the 1870s and continuing through the 1890s, expanding rail lines connected lumber operations and agricultural lands to shipping ports. Towns sprang up along the tracks. Beginning in the 1930s, the smaller, more rural rail lines began to disappear.

Buses, which replaced interurban electric trains in the 1940s and 1950s, except on the Peninsula, still run. The Bay Area Rapid Transit (BART) system has augmented the buses, and some ferry service has been reestablished. Four- to eight-lane freeways, stacked freeway interchanges, seven bridges, and numerous tunnels dominate today's automobile-oriented transportation system, which just keeps getting more and more congested.

Growth in the Bay Area was steady but not dramatic in the years preceding the Second World War. According to census data compiled by the Association of Bay Area Governments, the Bay Area had a population of 1.7 million in 1940. By 1950, the population was 2.6 million; it has increased at the steady rate of almost one million in each following decade with the result that it has more than doubled in the past thirty-five years and today is nearly seven million. The astounding population increase has profoundly affected the built environment, from freeway construction to housing tracts and the loss of most local agriculture.

> . . . in 1962 Americans were just learning that they would have to fight for a decent environment. Suddenly the country was being ruined before our eyes, smashed, raped, poisoned, stunk up, and, not least, disfigured by inhumane and even hideous buildings (Allen Temko, Introduction, *No Way to Build a Ball Park,* Chronicle Books, 1993).

For thirty years, Allen Temko rallied against ugly buildings, ill-conceived freeways and, in particular, bad planning. Temko did this with clarity and wit through articles published in the *San Francisco Chronicle.* If he didn't win a battle, he brought attention to the issues. He inspired others to look at the built environment, take action, join the debate, and fight for good buildings and good planning.

The alarm voiced during the 1960s, however, especially over the loss of agricultural land, was not heeded. Huge tracts of single-family houses continue to be constructed in vast numbers on increasingly smaller lots. New residential neighborhoods are usually not within walking distance of shops and services nor convenient to public transportation. Wide boulevards surrounding and isolating them are not pedestrian friendly. The automobile remains essential to suburban life.

As the population moves farther and farther away from the older established centers of business and manufacturing, which had been located primarily in Oakland and San Francisco, new business centers have been or are being built. There is some activity in building townhouses and high-rise apartment buildings near these centers, but the single-family housing tracts continue.

The Association of Bay Area Governments was established by the state in 1962. Today it is active in transportation issues, air and water quality, gathering and disseminating statistical data, establishing minimum affordable housing quotas, but is not engaged in real land-use planning. Transportation planning such as widening freeways, building freeway exchanges, and extending BART and bus routes are regional plans and are implemented "after the fact," when congestion has become intolerable, or to provide access to new development.

Individual incorporated cities and counties create their own zoning and land-use regulations. These entities, especially cities, compete among each other for new business and housing development to increase their own tax bases. There is a disincentive to plan together and this practice results in unfortunate planning decisions.

The Embarcadero, San Francisco

There are some bright spots. Concerned over the loss of open space, voters and legislators have approved funding for creating or expanding parkland. The Golden Gate National Recreation Area contains about 75,000 acres, including the former U.S. Army installation at the Presidio and others. It is contiguous with the Pt. Reyes National Seashore, Mt. Tamalpais State Park, and watershed land in Marin and San Mateo Counties. The East Bay Regional Park District contains nearly 100,000 acres in fifty-nine separate parks. A Bay Ridge Trail and Shoreline Park Trail is evolving. Most of the lower hills and all of the mountains have hiking trails; on a clear day, one can experience vistas from the bay to the Sierra Nevada.

In the near future, all open space in the Bay Area will be public parkland or open space preserves or subsidized agricultural land. The value of Bay Area land is so high and the pressure to develop large private landholdings is so intense that undeveloped land will be preserved only through private or public intervention.

From most Bay Area freeways, unpleasant views are often mitigated by the ridges of hills, the silhouette of a mountain, or the sparkling water of the bay. Yes, the freeways are lined with the ubiquitous malls, pretentious chain hotels, auto rows, and big-box retailers, all screaming to be noticed and surrounded by acres of parking; most towns and cities have merged together to form a continuous city, but one always has the certainty that there is some open space—a park, a mountain, or a beach—not far away.

It [the San Francisco Bay Area] *is massively suburbanized, yet its heart was never cut out despite violent assaults.*

—Richard Walker

Classy City: Residential Realms of the Bay Region.
Online version: Department of Geography,
University of California–Berkeley, revised 2002.

I
San Francisco City and County

William Kostura, author

Susan Dinkelspiel Cerny, editor & photographer (1–5, 8–12, 15–18)

Ward Hill, photographer (6– 7)

John McBride, photographer (13, 14)

To understand how San Francisco developed over the past two centuries and to "read" the city through its architecture, it is useful to break the city's history down into eight broad periods.

The Spanish and Mexican Eras, 1776–1848

In 1776, when the Spanish established a religious mission and military presidio, it was the most northern of the Spanish settlements in California. Far from the government in Mexico, it was rarely provisioned and became a sleepy backwater compared to the settlements in Monterey, Carmel, and others to the south. Only the mission church, Mission Dolores, and one adobe wall of the Presidio Officer's Club remain from this period in San Francisco.

The Spanish were not interested in trading, but their Mexican successors were. Between 1835 and 1836, William Richardson and Jacob Leese built modest homes and trading posts near today's Clay Street and Grant Avenue, the Mexican pueblo, Yerba Buena. Over the next decade, about 500 others joined them. When the United States took possession of Yerba Buena in 1846, it was renamed San Francisco. The village formed the seed of the future city. It had grown to 1,000 by 1848, when gold was discovered in the Sierra foothills.

The Gold Rush, 1849–1850s

The population mushroomed during the Gold Rush of 1849 to 1853. San Francisco's waterfront was the center of shipping; large vessels transferred their goods to shallow-draft vessels that could sail to Sacramento, Marysville, and Stockton, close to the gold mines. Wharves and warehouses were built, along with wholesale houses, business offices, hotels, a U.S. Mint, and a host of secondary businesses. Residences (some of them imported from the East) were built in Gothic Revival, Greek Revival, and Italianate styles.

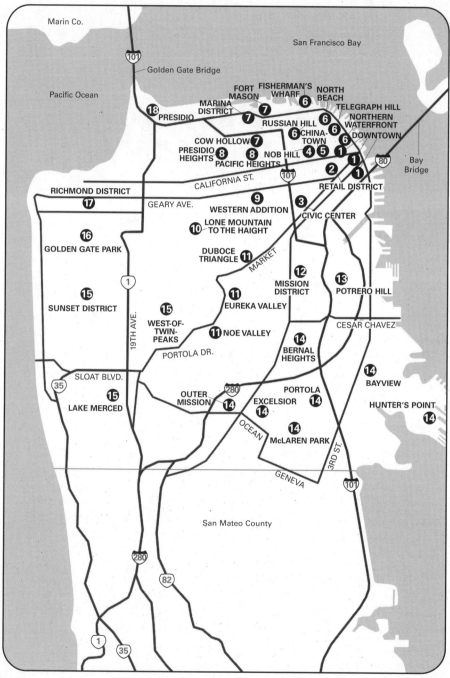

Marin Co.

San Francisco Bay

101
Golden Gate Bridge

Pacific Ocean

FORT **FISHERMAN'S** **NORTH**
MASON **WHARF** **BEACH** 6
18 **MARINA** **TELEGRAPH HILL**
PRESIDIO **DISTRICT** 7 **NORTHERN**
7 **RUSSIAN HILL** 6 **WATERFRONT**
6 6 **DOWNTOWN**
COW HOLLOW 7 **CHINA-** 6
PRESIDIO **TOWN** 1
HEIGHTS 8 8 **NOB HILL** 4 5 1 1
PACIFIC HEIGHTS 2 1
CALIFORNIA ST. 101 **RETAIL DISTRICT**
RICHMOND DISTRICT 80 **Bay**
17 **GEARY AVE.** 9 **Bridge**
WESTERN ADDITION 3
16 **LONE MOUNTAIN** **CIVIC CENTER**
GOLDEN GATE PARK 10 **TO THE HAIGHT**
DUBOCE 12
1 **TRIANGLE** 11 **MARKET**
15 13
SUNSET DISTRICT 15 11 **MISSION** **POTRERO HILL**
WEST-OF- **EUREKA VALLEY** **DISTRICT**
TWIN- **CESAR CHAVEZ**
PEAKS 11 **NOE VALLEY**
19TH AVE. **PORTOLA DR.** 14
BERNAL
SLOAT BLVD. **HEIGHTS**
35 14 **PORTOLA** 14
15 **OUTER** 280 **BAYVIEW**
LAKE MERCED **MISSION** 14 **EXCELSIOR** 14
14 **HUNTER'S POINT**
OCEAN 14 14
McLAREN PARK
GENEVA 3RD ST.
101

San Mateo County

280

82

1

35

I • San Francisco City and County

The Silver Boom, 1859–1880s

Just as the Gold Rush waned, silver was discovered in Nevada's Comstock Lode. San Francisco capitalists provided the funds needed for extracting the silver, and San Francisco foundries manufactured the necessary machinery. Money flowed into the city, which led to another building boom. Construction stimulated by the flow of silver continued, with some periods of recession, into the 1880s. Buildings from this period tended to be exuberant and the most highly ornamented of any in the city's history; they were *encrusted* with ornament. It was a wonderland of a city, and San Franciscans knew it. When it was gone, they looked back on it as "the City that Was."

A cluster of commercial buildings dating to the 1850s and 1860s still stands in Jackson Square; houses survive on Telegraph Hill, Russian Hill, and scattered outer neighborhoods. Victorian-era houses from the 1870s to the 1890s are found in abundance in the Western Addition, Mission District, Eureka Valley, Noe Valley, Haight-Ashbury, and Duboce Triangle neighborhoods.

The Earthquake and Fire, 1890s–1906

During the 1890s, construction of steel-frame skyscrapers began downtown, based on models developed in Chicago. The city was modernizing with electrical power plants, electric streetcars, and an extensive telephone system. In architecture, Victorian exuberance was being replaced by more sober styles such as Classic Revival, Mission and Spanish Colonial Revival, Tudor, and Shingle, based on historical precedence. Architects trained on the East Coast and at the École des Beaux-Arts in Paris synthesized these styles, often brilliantly, for modern needs.

The Reconstruction, 1906–1920s

Just as these trends were well under way, the earthquake and fire of April 18–21, 1906, destroyed nearly all of the city east of Van Ness Avenue, south of Market, and about a third of the Mission District. Downtown was quickly rebuilt, and by 1909, it was declared "complete." A visitor to the city would never know that a disaster had occurred here, save for one fact: the downtown was stylistically uniform—a gleaming, ordered, cohesive city of Classical ornament—built of white granite, pressed brick, and glazed terra-cotta draped over steel frames. Almost nothing from the Victorian era remained.

Reconstruction of the residential neighborhoods took longer, well into the mid-1910s. These neighborhoods—Nob Hill, Russian Hill, North Beach, the Tenderloin, and the Mission north of Twentieth Street—were built up much more densely; single-family houses were replaced with flats and apartment buildings.

The Economic Rebound, 1920s–1950s

Several years after World War I, the economy rebounded, and the city's growth was tremendous. Improvements to the infrastructure (made in the 1910s under City Engineer Michael M. O'Shaughnessy), such as the Twin Peaks Tunnel for streetcars and the extension of Market Street and Portola Boulevard to the southwestern part of the city, made possible new neighborhoods west of Twin Peaks. Neighborhoods south and west of the Mission, platted in the nineteenth century, became fully built.

The Redevelopment, 1950s–1980s

The 1950s to the 1970s were cataclysmic years regarding both the appearance of the city and the forcible removal of thousands of San Franciscans from their homes through urban renewal or eminent domain. The Bayshore Freeway (U.S. 101), Embarcadero Freeway, Central Freeway, and

The Shaklee Building (1978–1979; Skidmore, Owings & Merrill, architects) at 1 Front Street is one of the most prominent high-rises on lower Market Street.

Interstate 280 sliced through neighborhoods, uprooting and dividing communities. More freeways were planned, sparking the Freeway Revolt of 1959. The San Francisco Redevelopment Agency cleared approximately 120 blocks in the Western Addition and south of Market neighborhoods, as well as commercial buildings in the old Produce District that contained thousands of residential buildings.

A high-rise boom began in 1959. Stylistically, these buildings aggressively broke with the past. Granite, terra-cotta, cornices, window moldings, ornament, and sculpted massing were old-fashioned; glass, steel, concrete, clean lines, and boxy shapes were in. Between 1959 and 1981, thirty-three million square feet of office space was built in the downtown.

Inevitably, a reaction set in. In 1968, the Junior League published *Here Today,* a survey that documents the city's oldest buildings. Groups such as Heritage, Victorian Alliance, and San Francisco Tomorrow were founded to preserve historic architecture through education and advocacy, and to moderate growth. To a large degree these efforts have been successful.

The Changing Skyline, 1990s–present

A building boom that began in the mid-1990s is again changing the skyline of downtown. Ever-taller buildings are being constructed in the redeveloping areas south of Market for a projected increased population of 10,000.

Claus Oldenberg and Coosje van Bruggen's *Cupid's Span* (2003) livens the new Embarcadero in Rincon Park, on Herb Caen Way at Folsom Street.

1 · Downtown: Jackson Square, Financial District, Southern Waterfront

Jackson Square

Early in the Gold Rush, Jackson Square became the location of San Francisco's first downtown. Commercial buildings were built here due to the site's proximity to Portsmouth Square, which had been the center of town life during the Mexican period, and because it was close to the waterfront. The district consists mainly of brick commercial buildings from two to four stories in height. Certain blocks—the buildings on the 700 block of Montgomery Street, the 400 block of Jackson Street, and the 500 block of Washington Street—survived the earthquake and fire of 1906. These are the only commercial buildings in San Francisco dating to the 1850s–1870s. The 400 and 500 blocks of Pacific Avenue became the Barbary Coast, an entertainment district.

1. Burr Building, 1855
520–550 Washington Street

This building is in a remarkable state of preservation. Cast-iron pilasters by the Vulcan and Sutter foundries, most with Egyptian capitals, parade across the front. The cornices are dentilated brick, and windows are original four-over-four wood sash.

2. Columbus Savings Bank, 1905
700 Montgomery Street

Meyer and O'Brien, architects

One of two Italian banks founded by John F. Fugazi. It has a rounded corner entry and is constructed of carved Colusa sandstone, which is unfortunately deteriorating.

3. Canessa Printing Co., 1913
708–710 Montgomery Street

Luigi Mastropasqua, architect

The fenestration of porthole windows over Italianate window hoods is unusual.

4. 712–714 Montgomery Street, early 1850s

Although altered, this building has a great history. During the 1860s, George Hearst's real estate and mining offices, and the Comstock Lode's Savage, Best and Belcher, and North Potosi silver mines were headquartered here. During the 1910s–1920s, the building housed studios of artist Gottardo Piazzoni and sculptor Ralph Stackpole.

Next door, the building at **716–718 Montgomery** has a stucco front, dentiled cornice, and four-over-four windows typical of Gold Rush buildings. During the late 1920s, Dorothea Lange and Robert Boardman Howard had studios here.

5. Turkish Baths and Genella Building, 1868, 1851
722 and 728 Montgomery Street

Number 728 was built in 1851 as a chinaware shop; the Odd Fellows occupied the top floor in the 1850s, professional offices and Nevada silver mining offices in the 1860s–1870s. Between 1880 and 1959, an array of artists had studios here, notably Maynard Dixon, Edgar Mathews, Theodore Wores, Ralph Stackpole, Jules Tavernier, Gottardo Piazzoni, and Xavier Martinez. **722** (1868) was a financial district "health spa"—Turkish baths, physician's office, and pharmacy. Its cast-iron ornament was imported from New York City. Attorney Melvin Belli merged these buildings for his offices in 1959. He removed the original stucco facing from both buildings in order to foster an inaccurate Old West look. The

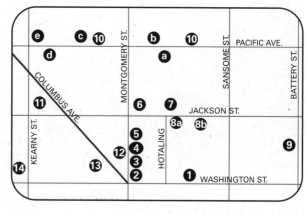

buildings are being rebuilt behind their façades.

6. Bank of Lucas, Turner and Co., 1854
800–804 Montgomery Street

Originally a three-story building, it was reduced to two by the 1906 earthquake. The rusticated granite front has a central pedimented entry, segmented arched windows, and a corner entry with two arched openings. The granite was almost certainly imported from China. Lucas, Turner and Co. was managed by William Tecumseh Sherman, of later Civil War fame.

7. Gold Rush buildings, early 1850s
468–470, 472 Jackson Street

Number 472 is especially reminiscent of primitive Gold Rush architecture. It retains the iron shutters and old window sash.

8. Cast-iron-front buildings, 1850s–1870s
407–473 Jackson Street

This is the largest collection of architectural cast iron in San Francisco. All six of these brick buildings have iron pilasters made by local foundries. Most have elaborate pedimented windows in the upper stories and

retain iron window shutters on the ground floor.

8a. Ghirardelli Chocolate Factory, circa 1857
415–431 Jackson Street

Their original factory was housed here, with offices located at 435–441 Jackson in 1861.

8b. Hotaling Building, 1866
451–455 Jackson Street

This building housed a wholesale liquor firm. The Italianate treatment is exceptional.

9. U.S. Custom House, 1906–1911
555 Battery Street
Eames and Young (St. Louis), architects

Here is a noble pile of Raymond-granite: Beaux-Arts classicism at its best. There is fine stone carving here: lions, eagles, pedimented windows above granite balustrades span the width of the second floor, and there are bronze doors, elaborate lanterns, and window grilles.

10. The Barbary Coast, 1906–1910
400 and 500 Blocks of Pacific Avenue

These two blocks of Pacific Avenue comprised the famed, or infamous, Barbary Coast. Almost every building on the 500 block, and many on the 400 block, contained a saloon and dance hall. In its heyday it was the city's busiest entertainment district. Reformers shut it down in 1917, but a tame revival, known as the International Settlement, was attempted in the 1940s.

10a. Engine Co. 1, 1909
451 Pacific Avenue
Newton J. Tharp, city architect

This is a Classic Revival–style firehouse with a rusticated sandstone front.

10b. Livery stables,
circa 1906–1907
450, 470–498 Pacific Avenue

These brick buildings also held two of Izzy Gomez's early saloons.

10c. Diana Hall & Lew Purcell's So Different,
circa 1906
544–550 Pacific Avenue

This three-story brick building housed the So Different Club, a famed African American dance hall.

10d. Hippodrome Theater,
circa 1906
551–559 Pacific Avenue

An ornate outdoor lobby with reliefs of dancing nudes recalls originals by sculptor Arthur J. Putnam. It housed the Hippodrome between 1911 and 1916, and Goman's Gay Nineties in the 1940s.

10e. The Seattle Saloon and Dance Hall, 1907
570–574 Pacific Avenue
James Francis Dunn, architect

This establishment retains its tan brick façade and much of its classical ornament.

11. Sentinel Building,
1906–1907
916 Kearny Street
Salfield and Kohlberg, architects

Only the steel frame of this seven-story building had been erected in 1906. The exterior walls are clad in glazed white brick, and the rounded and rectangular bay windows are covered with sheet copper.

12. Banco Populare Italiano Fugazi, 1908
Intersection (V-shaped gore) of Columbus Avenue and Montgomery Street
Paff and Baur, architects

This was John F. Fugazi's second bank. The terra-cotta ornamentation of fluted Ionic pilasters, arched windows, and lions' heads are lively and engaging. The third story is a 1916 addition by architect Italo Zanolini.

13. Columbo Building, 1913
1–21 Columbus Avenue
Reid Brothers, architects

Saved during a much-publicized preservation effort, the two-story building has a rounded corner entry, once recessed, held by four fluted Doric columns; engaged Doric columns along the sides separate altered storefronts.

14. Lodging house and stores, 1913
833–839 Kearny Street
Joseph Cahen, architect

The upper stories of this building are French in feeling, particularly the third-floor windows, which have women's faces on the keystones. Delicate floral ornament fills the lower portion of the pilaster fluting.

Financial District

The heart of the historic Financial District centers around California, Montgomery, and Sansome Streets. The first important building in this area was Parrott's Granite Block (1851–1852), a three-story building at the northwest corner of California and Montgomery, and an early home of Wells Fargo Bank. Not until the mid-1860s, however, did these streets become firmly entrenched as the center of finance in the city. By the mid-1870s, the district had dozens of brick buildings with fronts of cast iron, heavily ornamented in Italianate style. In 1891, the first steel-frame building, the Mills Building, was completed.

The 1906 earthquake and fire left little standing except the shells of recently constructed steel-frame skyscrapers. When the district was rebuilt, most of the new taller, steel-frame office buildings were Classical Revival in style with a three-part composition: their lower stories, corresponding to the base of a classical column, have monumental entrances; the middle stories, corresponding to the shaft, were plainer in treatment; and the upper stories, corresponding to the capital, were highly ornamental.

In the late-1920s, architects abandoned the Classic three-part composition and used a façade scheme with vertical lines that rose uninterrupted from the ground to the top. Ascending setbacks were used to break up the rectangular form and give the impression of ever-greater heights. After World War II, architects embraced the principles of Modernism and the International style; ornament and setbacks became a thing of the past. Not until the mid-1980s did a reaction set in.

15. Transamerica Pyramid, 1971
600 Montgomery Street

William Pereira and Associates, architects

No building in San Francisco deserves the adjective "soaring" more than this one does; it has become a city icon. The tapered proportions are perfect, and the jungle gym of structural supports at the base imparts a feeling of

strength but is not particularly pedestrian friendly. Bits of crushed quartz imbedded in the concrete surface give the building a pleasing surface texture and sheen. The Pyramid stands on the site of the Montgomery Block, completed in 1853 and demolished amid protest in 1959.

16. Bank of Italy, 1908
550 Montgomery Street

Shea and Lofquist, architects

This was the first permanent home of A. P. Giannini's Bank of Italy (later, Bank of America). The building features a heavily rusticated classicism, with a first story of carved granite. The sumptuous lobby is made of

plaster and marble. Founded in 1904, the bank thrived because Giannini reached out to blue-collar Italian laborers, which other Italian banks refused to do. The Bank of Italy ended up absorbing all of the other Italian banks and many others. By the 1970s, it was the world's largest bank.

17. Small brick commercial buildings, 1906–1914
Sacramento, Clay, Sansome, Leidesdorff, and Commercial Streets

This is the best collection of small early-twentieth-century commercial buildings remaining in the Financial District, which

15

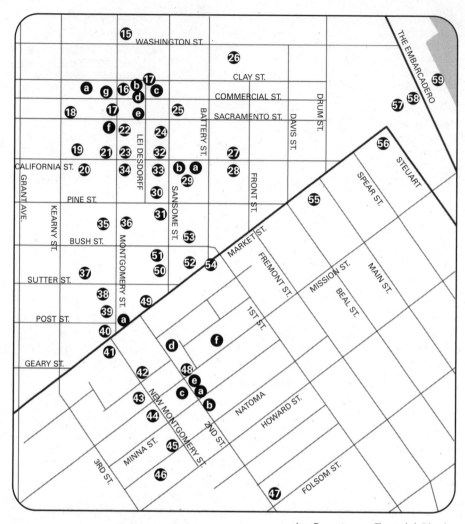

I • Downtown: Financial District

was once filled with buildings such as these. Nearly all retain their cornices, wood sash windows, and ornament; they demonstrate how carefully designed and beautifully finished they were.

17a. 643–647 Clay, 1912
Joseph Cahen, architect

This is a nicely detailed classical design.

17b. 555 Clay, 1907
C. A. Meussdorffer, architect

Here is a two-story beige brick building with simple square columns, paired second-story windows, and a projecting dentiled cornice. **559 Clay** (1906; William H. Weeks, architect) is four stories, with a façade of glazed white bricks and two pairs of three-grouped windows on the upper stories.

17c. 405 Sansome, 1906
Salfield and Kohlberg, architects

This is a four-story brick building; windows on the third story are arched. **407–411 Sansome** (1906; Albert Pissis, architect), also four stories, is similar but without the arches.

17d. 554–556 Commercial, 1908

Rousseau and Rousseau, architects

Here is a delightful brick building with an orange-and-buff checkered pattern. **565 Commercial** (1914; Frederick H. Meyer) is a Beaux-Arts-style PG&E substation. **566 Commercial** (1907; Wright, Rushforth and Cahill, architects) has a giant Gothic window.

17e. Britton and Rey Lithography Plant, 1909
560 Sacramento and 215 Leidesdorff

Albert Pissis, architect

The company, founded in 1852, was the city's largest lithography firm. This general area was the center of the city's printing industry. The building is a narrow three-bay, four-story building faced with brick.

17f. Jack's Restaurant, 1907
615 Sacramento Street

Salfield and Kohlberg, architects

19

This narrow three-story stucco-faced building has an overhanging cornice and rusticated brick window surrounds. The formal French restaurant traces its history to 1864.

17g. 608 Commercial Street, 1875–1877

The first floor and façade of the former U.S. Subtreasury Building, it was subsumed into the Bank of Canton high-rise in 1982; it houses the Pacific Heritage Museum.

18. Shirley Building, 1909
600–602 Kearny Street

C. A. Meussdorffer, architect

This is a small three-story commercial building; its upper floors are clad in glazed white terra-cotta; the second-story Palladian-type windows have arched hood moldings. **625 Kearny Street** (1907; Luigi Mastropasqua, architect) is covered with swirling Art Nouveau ornament.

19. 580 California Street, 1984

Philip Johnson and John Burgee, architects

This is kitschy postmodernism, clad in granite, with ornate lanterns in the entrance colonnade. Ghostly figures in front of the mansard roof add a note of whimsy.

20. Bank of America Building, 1968
555 California Street

Wurster, Bernardi and Emmons, architects

Skidmore, Owings & Merrill, architects

Pietro Belluschi, design consultant

Every once in a while, when light conditions are perfect, and when viewed from the right perspective, the setting sun glints off of the faceted red granite skin of this high-rise building with spectacular results. At other times, the building is dark and over-powering rather than awesome. The lobby is lifeless. The bleak windswept plaza is improved by the sculpture known as the *Banker's Heart.*

21. Financial Center Building, 1926
500 California Street

Meyer and Johnson, architects

When this office building was converted into the Omni Hotel in 2002, the remodeled base was restored to its original Florentine style and the entrance was moved from Montgomery to California Street.

22. Italian-American Bank, and A. Borel and Co., 1908
456 Montgomery

Albert Pissis, architect

Howard and Galloway, architects

Two small, very fine, granite banking-temple façades were retained as the entrance for a mid-1980s office building. This is one of the saddest examples of façadism in the city.

23. Hayward-Kohl Building, 1900–1901

400 Montgomery Street

George W. Percy, architect

The steel-frame building is clad in Colusa sandstone, is intensely decorated at the entry and upper stories with Classical ornament such as animal motifs and garlands, and has a nice marble lobby.

24. Crown Zellerbach Building, 1930, 1990

343 Sansome Street

Hyman and Appleton, architects (1930)

Johnson and Burgee, architects (1990)

The Zellerbach Paper Company began as a small business in 1875 and grew into a giant corporation with forestlands, paper mills, warehouses, and offices throughout the West Coast. Their former headquarters building is Art Deco style and is faced with terra-cotta and brick. In 1990, an addition as large as the original was built to the north and is clad in granite with terra-cotta trim.

25. Federal Reserve Bank of San Francisco, 1924

400 Sansome Street

George W. Kelham, architect

For this former Federal Reserve Bank, Kelham used a sober, formal Classicism to evoke the permanence and solid dignity of the federal government. The steel-frame building, clad in white granite, has an Ionic colonnade parading across the front, which supports an entablature where eight eagles stand with outspread wings. This is formal classicism, lacking in delicacy or whimsy.

Bronze doors and doorframes provide the only color.

26. Alcoa Building, 1964

1 Maritime Plaza, on the north side of Clay Street, opposite Front Street

Skidmore, Owings & Merrill, architects

A giant black rectangle, with exposed diagonal cross-bracing, expresses structural purity and functionality, qualities that have been much admired. The building sits upon a faceless, two-story parking garage and interrupts the street grid.

27. Tadich Grill, 1909

240–242 California Street

Ralph Warner Hart, architect

This modest two-story building is rich in green terra-cotta and sheet copper detailing. Classical pediments surmount each entrance. It is part of a splendid group including **244–252 California** (1908; Oliver Traphagen, architect) and **260 California** (1910; Lewis Hobart, architect).

28. John Hancock Building, 1959

255 California Street

Skidmore, Owings & Merrill, architects

One of a crop of modern high-rises that burst on the downtown in the late 1950s, it features a shaft of dark gray panels and smoked glass over a base of vaulted reinforced-concrete bays.

29. 300 Block of California Street

29a. Robert Dollar Building, 1919

311 California Street

Charles McCall, architect

Built as headquarters for the Dollar Steamship Line, the terra-cotta cladding is ornamented with maritime imagery along with restrained Gothic details.

29b. Balfour Building, 1920

351 California Street

George W. Kelham, architect

This was also built for a major shipper—Balfour, Guthrie and Company—and eventually came under Dollar ownership. It is richly clad in carved marble and variegated orange brick. The mid-block high-rise at **345 California Street** (1985; Skidmore, Owings & Merrill, architects) incorporates these two buildings.

30. Royal Insurance Company Building, 1907

201 Sansome Street

Howells and Stokes, architects

A New York firm designed this building for an insurance company headquartered in Liverpool, England. The first story is white marble with extremely fine carving around the entrance. The lion and unicorn above the entry was the company logo. The shaft is red brick with terra-cotta trim; the top of the building is two stories of cream terra-cotta with a double row of cornices and huge shields between paired windows, all topped by a balustrade.

31. Pacific Coast Stock Exchange, 1930

301 Pine Street and 155 Sansome Street

Miller and Pflueger, architects

This was built in 1915 as the U.S. Subtreasury Building, which moved here from 608 Commercial. When Miller and Pflueger reworked it for the Stock Exchange in 1930, they kept the Doric colonnade but slightly raised the height of the corners where the fine sculptural groups by Ralph Stackpole are standing. The adjoining Art Deco–style Stock Exchange Club (now the City Club) on Sansome Street was an addition. Its lobby of red and green Italian marbles is spectacular, and the clubrooms contain artwork by Diego Rivera, Robert Boardman Howard, and Michael Goodman.

32. Bank of California, 1906–1908
400 California Street

Bliss and Faville, architects

Built of white granite over a steel frame, this is among the finest banking temples in the city. The composition and proportions impart a feeling of majestic repose. The Corinthian capitals are intricately carved, the entablature boldly articulated, and there are Classical clathri screens over full-height windows; the interior is mostly intact. There is a museum in the basement. The high-rise addition to the west is Brutalist in style (1967; Anshen + Allen, architects). Its vertical concrete lines were intended—not very successfully—to echo the fluting of the older building's columns.

33. Insurance Exchange Building, 1913
433 California Street

Willis Polk, architect

From the first story to the cornice, this is an exercise in intensely detailed, cream terra-cotta ornament. The majestic Corinthian columns command attention, but there is also rich texturing in the middle stories.

34. Merchants' Exchange, 1903
465 California Street

D. H. Burnham and Co., architects

Designed by Willis Polk, who headed Burnham's San Francisco office at the time, this building replaced a previous Merchants' Exchange (1868) on this site. The lower stories are granite and the ornamental door and window frames are cast iron; the upper stories of buff-colored brick have six-over-six window sash. A Corinthian colonnade frames the windows in the top stories. The banking hall has marine paintings by William Coulter.

35. Russ Building, 1927
235 Montgomery Street

George W. Kelham, architect

For at least three decades this was the tallest building in San Francisco. In its use of setbacks, it was one of several 1920s skyscrapers influenced by Eliel Saarinen's Chicago Tribune competition entry. The building is notable for its exquisitely conceived Gothic ornament and terra-cotta cladding. The lobby features vaulted Gothic ceilings and a floor of patterned travertine and marble.

36. Mills Building, 1891
220 Montgomery Street

Burnham and Root, architects

Following the Chronicle Building (1888–1890), also by Burnham and Root, this was the city's second skyscraper. The building is clad in white marble

39

levels, common features of the
early 1920s. Corner setbacks in
the upper stories foreshadow
skyscrapers later in the decade.
The building is clad in terra-
cotta made by Gladding,
McBean. The entrance arch
and the lobby are both
beautifully detailed.

39. First National Bank Building, 1908
1 Montgomery Street

*D. H. Burnham and Co.,
architects*

The carefully composed Classic
bank building has a façade of
Raymond granite with a curved,
recessed corner entry flanked by
pairs of columns, and rows of
arched windows separated by
pilasters. The interior has a
lovely curved white marble
staircase; counters and benches
are carved marble; window
frames, tellers' windows, and
hardware are bronze; and the
ceiling is coffered and intensely
decorated. The bank was originally the base of an eleven-story
office tower that was demolished in 1980 when a high-rise
was built behind it. The roof of
the bank is now a garden for
the Crocker Galleria shopping
passageway.

40. Chronicle Building, 1888–1890, 1962
690 Market Street

Burnham and Root, architects

San Francisco's first skyscraper
was hidden in 1962 behind a
metal skin until 2006. The
restoration will bring back its
original blend of Romanesque
and Chicago School styling, and
perhaps the clock tower removed
during early alteration by Willis
Polk will be rebuilt.

on the lower stories and in brick
with terra-cotta ornament above.
While the fenestration is Chicago
School, the ornamental style is
Romanesque. The grand
entrance arch with receding layers of carved marble is among
the finest in the state. When two
additions were made on the east
side of the building (1914, 1918;
Willis Polk, architect) the original design concept was used. It
was built by Darius Ogden Mills,
who made a fortune as a financier in the 1860s and 1870s.

37. Hallidie Building, 1917
130–150 Sutter Street

Willis Polk, architect

This revolutionary building is
also a perplexing one in the
sense that there was nothing like
it among the architect's earlier
works, and Polk did not come

back to this model during the
remainder of his life. With its
glass curtain wall, hung from its
reinforced-concrete frame, it
presages the International style
but at the same time clings to
tradition through the use of
elaborate ornament. A cutout
pattern of bird and floral motifs
is suspended from the balconies
and the cornice. The balconies
and fire escape landings are
ornamental.

38. Hunter-Dulin Building, 1926
111 Sutter Street

*Schultze and Weaver,
architects*

This transitional building
employs historical imagery
(Romanesque, with a French
chateau roof) and a tower that is
relieved by cornices at different

40a. Native Sons' Monument, 1896–1897
Northeast corner of Montgomery and Market Streets

Willis Polk, architect

Douglas Tilden, sculptor

Commemorating California's admission to the union in 1850, a gun-toting miner waves an American flag. Behind him, a column rises to support an angel, which blesses the union. The inscription by W. H. Seward openly declares the imperialistic thrust of the country: "The unity of our empire hangs on the decision of this day."

41. Palace Hotel, 1909
633–665 Market Street

Trowbridge and Livingston, architects

The hotel evokes a feeling of restrained elegance in contrast to the bay-windowed excess of the first Palace Hotel (1875) on this site. While the façades are quite flat, the detailing and texturing are beautifully executed. The first story appears to be limestone, with elaborate cast-iron door and window frames. The upper stories are buff-colored brick with terra-cotta piers and trim. There are two great dining rooms: the lavish Garden Court, and Maxfield's, which features a large mural by Maxfield Parrish that was commissioned for the building's opening.

42. Sharon Building, 1912
39–61 New Montgomery Street

George W. Kelham, architect

This office building is distinguished by patterned brickwork, paired arched windows across the sixth story, a broad cornice, and a beautiful Classical entrance. The exterior is virtually unchanged except for the doors at the main entrance. The saloon, House of Shields, has its original 1910 wood paneling.

43. Call Building, 1914
74 New Montgomery Street

Reid Brothers, architects

Built for the offices of the *Daily Morning Call*, a newspaper founded in 1856, the seven-story building is richly decorated with Classical elements; ornamental cast iron frames both entrances; and heavy rustication in the third story recalls the architects' Fairmont Hotel. This building, the Examiner Building at 5 Third Street, and the Bulletin Building at 814 Mission are the best preserved of the city's old newspaper buildings.

44. Rialto Building, 1910
116 New Montgomery Street

Bliss and Faville, architects

Reconstructed after 1906, following the 1902 plan by architects Meyer and O'Brien, the Classic Revival–style, U-shaped building with tripartite windows admitted natural light to all offices. The triple-arched entry is set between two identical eight-story wings. Ocher-colored brick piers and spandrels are accented

45

by cream-colored window frames and decorative cornices.

45. Pacific Telephone and Telegraph Co. Building, 1925
140 New Montgomery Street
Miller and Pflueger,
with A. A. Cantin,
architects

This and the Russ Building are the best examples of Art Deco skyscrapers in the city. This one has a soaring sculpted quality that is especially evident when seen at a distance. Its tall, arched, and elaborately decorated entry bay contains a perforated golden grille that is a treasure. The building is set on a base of granite, but the upper part is clad entirely of terra-cotta glazed to resemble granite. The vertical piers are variously rounded and chamfered, imparting a scalloped quality. The ornament, especially the torch-like sculptures in the upper stories, is quite original and contributes to the building's soaring effect.

46. Underwriters' Fire Patrol Headquarters, 1909
147 Natoma Street
Clinton Day, architect

A very handsome three-story, buff-colored brick building, with terra-cotta ornament and trim, is located in one of this neighborhood's narrow alleys. Founded in 1875, Underwriters' Fire Patrol was a private, subscription-service fire-fighting firm, which operated until the late 1920s.

A 625-foot tower by Millennium Properties, which includes 120 hotel rooms and 320 residential units designed by Heller-Manus Architects, will be constructed at the southeast corner of Natoma and 2nd Streets.

47. 235 Second Street, 2001
Fee Munson Ebert
Architecture + Design

An attractive blend of seven shades of brick, with bays of steel and glass, the U-shaped five- and six-story building relates to both the historic fabric of the neighborhood and the newer buildings.

Older buildings of interest can be found in the immediate vicinity. Around the corner at **72 Tehama** is the former Brizard and Young Sheet Metal Works

(1909). Its façade is covered with sheet metal that is pressed to resemble brick and tooled sandstone. The **Marine Fireman's Union Headquarters,** 240 Second Street (1957), is attractively clad in white marble and red granite. In the entrance pavilion is a deep-relief mural by Lucienne Bloch and Stephen Dimitroff, illustrating the work of marine firemen.

48. Wells Fargo Express Building, 1897–1899
85 Second Street
Percy and Hamilton, architects

A steel-frame building clad in tan-colored brick above a two-story base of white granite, its Classical Revival style is boldly expressed in the grand entrance arch and the supporting Ionic columns. After the earthquake and fire, the building was repaired and two stories were added (1907; Meyers & Ward, architects).

Other pre-1906 buildings nearby include the following:

48a. 121 Second Street, 1908

Reid Brothers, architects

It has florid sixth-story keystones.

48b. 133 Second Street, 1906

Ralph Warner Hart, architect

This has cast-iron pilasters and round-headed windows.

48c. 142 Second Street, 1907

John C. Pelton, architect

It is red brick with tan brick quoins, piers, and window trim.

More recent skyscrapers near Second and Mission Streets can be seen:

48d. 55 Second Street, 2002

Heller-Manus Architects

Clad in sheets of glass and panels of stone aggregate that resemble granite, this has narrow setbacks that are a nod to the skyscrapers of the 1920s.

48e. 101 Second Street, 1999

Skidmore, Owings & Merrill, architects

Here is an unapologetic throwback to the International style of the 1950s; even the green-tinted glass recalls the Crown Zellerbach Building on Market Street.

48f. 560 Mission, 2002

Cesar Pelli, architect

This is the most radical design in this group, with dark-green steel window-framing members so numerous that they give the building a welcome degree of articulation.

49. Hobart Building, 1914
582–592 Market Street

Willis Polk, architect

The top six stories of the building's imposing tower of twenty-plus stories are richly decorated terra-cotta layers with curved sides. The entry is carved marble, and the bronze doors, marble lobby, and bronze elevator doors survive intact.

50. London Paris National Bank, 1910
1 Sansome Street

Albert Pissis, architect

A blatant example of "façadism" that gutted the interior of a former banking temple now serves only as an entrance foyer for a high-rise (1983; William Pereira and Associates, architects). The

façade that remains, however, is a good example of a Classical composition of alternating Ionic columns and arched window openings carved from granite.

51. Standard Oil Building, 1922
225 Bush Street

George W. Kelham, architect

Heavy Florentine Classicism was executed in granite on the first story of this building, with terra-cotta used on the stories above that. When a major addition was added in 1948, it matched the original in style and materials.

Across the street at **200 Bush** is the city's first Standard Oil Building (1912; Benjamin McDougall, architect), with carved and tooled sandstone on the lower stories.

52. Crown Zellerbach Building, 1959
1 Bush Street

Hertzka and Knowles, architects

Skidmore, Owings & Merrill, architects

This is the purest of the early International-style buildings in San Francisco. The monolithic south wall of the elevator service wing is clad with almost five million one-inch-square tiles of subtly shifting dark colors. The glass walls are tinted green. The lobby is surrounded by sheet glass and has a ceiling of about fifteen thousand small cylindrical lights. The elevator lobby is paneled in patterned marble. The travertine lobby floor continues outdoors as a platform to a circular accordion-shaped roofed and glass-walled pavilion that was originally a bank.

53. Shell Building, 1929
100 Bush Street

George W. Kelham, architect

Here is one of the great Art Deco skyscrapers of the late 1920s. Though shell motifs adorn the entrance grille, the other ornament is abstract. The detailing is as fine at the crown as at the entryway. As in Kelham's Russ Building, the terra-cotta cladding has an appealing rippling texture.

54. Mechanics' Monument, 1900
Market Street at Battery Street

Willis Polk, architect

Douglas Tilden, sculptor

This robust sculpture is dedicated to the memory of Peter Donahue, founder of the Union Iron Works and builder of early railroads and ferries. It depicts five muscular, nearly nude workers operating a drill press.

55. Matson and PG&E buildings, 1921, 1925
245 Market Street

Two great skyscrapers from the 1920s are closely matched in scale but contrasting in façade treatment. They were recently joined with a modern high-rise at 77 Beale as one property, with a general remodeling of the interiors but retention of the historic lobbies.

The **Matson Building** (1921; Bliss and Faville, architects) is clad in glazed tan terra-cotta with green accents. Nautical images relate to the Matson Steamship Lines—seashells, fish, anchors, and, of course, steamships. Monumental columns at the base, with Ionic capitals outlined by ropes, and arched windows at the top highlight the composition.

The **Pacific Gas and Electric Co. Building** (1925; Bakewell and Brown, architects) is clad in terra-cotta, textured to resemble granite. The recessed entrance arch contains idealized sculptures of PG&E field workers, a bear's head, and produce; rams' heads grace the keystone position of the window arches.

56. Southern Pacific Building, 1916
1 Market Street

Bliss and Faville, architects

The façade was retained when the interior was recently reconstructed. Faced with burnt ocher brick, an arcade graces the lower stories, with a colonnade at the top and ornamental balconies of terra-cotta. The detailing in the arches and the Ionic capitals is well executed, as one would expect in a major building from this period. There are two simple tower additions on the south (1976; Welton Beckett and Associates, architects) that lack detailing and setbacks.

57. Embarcadero Center and Environs, 1957–1983
Golden Gateway Project, Embarcadero Center, Hyatt Regency Hotel, Sidney Walton Park, and Justin Herman Plaza
East of Battery Street, from Sacramento Street to Jackson Street and south to Market Street

54

This is a complex of high-rise offices and housing set amid generous expanses of open space, much of it elevated above street level. It replaced small, early-twentieth-century brick commercial buildings and the Produce Market. The city's Redevelopment Agency condemned the old buildings and commissioned a general plan by Skidmore, Owings & Merrill in 1957. The first phase was the residential Golden Gateway Project (1959–1964; Wurster, Bernardi and Emmons; Anshen + Allen; DeMars and Reay, architects), a collection of high-rises and townhouses linked by pedestrian bridges over streets. It surrounds the Alcoa Building (see entry #26). Next was a series of office towers and elevated shops—the Embarcadero Center (1967–1981; John Portman and Associates, architects), with massing inspired by Rockefeller Center in New York—also

linked by pedestrian bridges. The Hyatt Regency Hotel (1973; John Portman and Associates, architects) has a stepped semi-pyramidal profile and a dramatic seventeen-story atrium. There are pleasant moments in this complex, such as Sidney Walton Park and the hotel atrium, but the street-level architecture is uniformly dull. In scale, style, site planning, and the interruption of the street grid, this complex represents an attitude of antiurbanism prevalent during the 1950s–1970s.

58. The Embarcadero
From Broadway to China Basin

After the 1989 Loma Prieta Earthquake damaged the elevated double-decked Embarcadero Freeway, it was demolished in 1992 to cheers. For the first time since 1959 when the freeway was completed, the street-level Embarcadero was open to the

sky, and the Ferry Building could be viewed again from lower Market Street. The redesign and completion of the various projects—including rows of palm trees, reproductions of historic streetlights, a historic streetcar line, and historical plaques and markers—has taken more than ten years, but the result is wonderful (for many, unbelievable).

59. Ferry Building, 1896–1898
The Embarcadero, opposite Market Street

A. Page Brown, architect

Edward Swain, supervising architect

For many San Franciscans, the Ferry Building is the symbol of the city. It has the commanding position at the head of Market Street, from which its sculpted tower can be seen for blocks. The western front, made of Colusa sandstone, features arcades across the full width of the lower and upper stories. Paired Corinthian columns lend a feeling of monumentality to the entrance pavilion. Until the Bay Bridge opened in 1936, this was the Bay Area's main transportation hub. Thousands of passengers riding dozens of ferryboats passed through the building each day, making it the busiest place in the city. It was nearly demolished in the 1950s, and then was altered for use as the World Trade Center. From 2001 to 2003, the grand two-story arched nave and the clathri window screens at the entrance pavilion were restored, and the bay side rebuilt when the building was renovated for use as a market hall and offices.

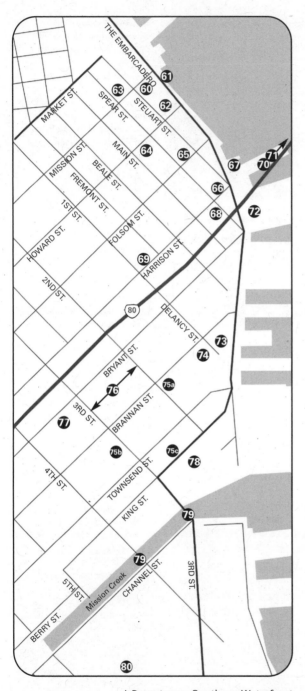

I Downtown: Southern Waterfront

Southern Waterfront

During the Gold Rush, the Southern Waterfront was less important than the waterfront north of Market Street, but by the early twentieth century, it became fully developed. After 1908, when wooden piers were rebuilt in concrete according to a City Beautiful aesthetic, most piers in the Southern Waterfront were given Mission Revival–style bulkheads, in contrast to the Classical Revival bulkheads to the north. On the landward side, a rich collection of waterfront-related warehouses and other industrial buildings survives in various states of preservation, mixed with recently built apartment and condo buildings.

60. Audiffred Building, 1889
*1 Mission Street and
100 The Embarcadero*

· One of the last nineteenth-century buildings on the waterfront, it was saved in 1906 but suffered a devastating fire in 1978. The building was rebuilt within its surviving walls, preserving the exterior details and its Victorian feeling. The first story consists of cast-iron pilasters framing storefronts, the second story is brick with Italianate window hoods, and the third story is a mansard roof with dormers. A low domed penthouse was added during the recent reconstruction.

61. U.S. Post Office Building, 1915
101 The Embarcadero

A. A. Pyle, architect

This two-story brick building has heavily rusticated corners and entrance surround. Its hipped tile roof gives it a Mediterranean feeling.

62. YMCA, 1924
166 The Embarcadero

Carl Werner, architect

Faced in terra-cotta (glazed to resemble granite) and brick, this building is a blend of Romanesque and Renaissance styles.

63. Rincon Annex Post Office, 1940
101 Spear Street

Gilbert Stanley Underwood, architect

This was the city's main post office from 1940 until the 1970s, when a new center was built at India Basin. The plain WPA Moderne exterior has some splendid Art Deco features, notably the aluminum doors and transom grilles as well as the dolphin motifs on the upper walls. The interior has Art Deco counters, window signs, and light fixtures. The greatest treasure is Anton Refugier's series of murals on themes of California history. These features were retained when two 240-foot-high office and residential towers with a covered plaza were constructed in the former delivery yard

(1989; Johnson Fain & Pereira Associates, architects).

64. Folger Coffee Company Building, 1904
101 Howard Street

Henry Schulze, architect

The handsome five-story brick building has a granite base, corbelled cornice, and deeply recessed arched windows that create architectural interest.

65. The Gap Headquarters, 2001
2 Folsom Street

Robert A. M. Stern, architect

The stepped-back exterior of Italian limestone and red brick exudes a certain degree of warmth.

66. Hills Brothers Coffee, 1924
2 Harrison Street

George W. Kelham, architect

This magnificent industrial building has many fine exterior features that were carefully preserved when it was converted into offices in 1986 and a new stepped-back office tower was constructed. The style is Roman-

esque, the cladding material is burnt ochre and tan brick, and the windows are industrial steel sash. The main entry on Harrison has a monumental entrance arch of brick and terra-cotta filled with a bronze screen and doors. The tower in the courtyard, originally used to blend varieties of green coffee, resembles a medieval Italian hill-town defensive tower; its base has been opened for a passageway. Inside the main lobby is a very interesting display illustrating the history of Hills Brothers (founded in 1881). The new office tower (1986; Whisler-Patri, architects) is clad in orange brick and gray concrete. Minimalist texturing and ornament relate to the older building.

67. Fire Station 35, 1915
Pier 22, opposite Harrison Street

A. A. Pyle, draftsman for the Harbor Commission

This has a symmetrical façade and Mission Revival–style detailing. The tile hipped roof has overhanging eaves and carved rafter ends. Other than some signage dating from the 1930s, this building has

not been altered and still functions as a waterfront firehouse.

68. Humboldt Free Warehouse, 1890
400 Spear Street

Charles Havens, architect

The well-preserved, two-story, brick former warehouse has a cornice with a corbelled-brick pattern, four-over-four wood sash second-story windows, and the first-story entrances crowned with Italianate hoods.

69. Sailors' Union of the Pacific, 1950
450 Harrison Street

William G. Merchant, architect

This Moderne-style building has a monumental, gently curved glass entrance pavilion with bold vertical fins. The lobby has green terrazzo floors and bronze doors. The Sailors' Union of the Pacific, which is still located here, is descended from the Coast Seamen's Union of the 1880s.

70. San Francisco–Oakland Bay Bridge, 1933–1936
Bryant at The Embarcadero (San Francisco Anchorage)

Charles H. Purcell, State Highway Engineer

Two very long, graceful, and silvery suspension spans connect San Francisco and Yerba Buena Island, meeting in mid-bay at a concrete Center Anchorage. Between Yerba Buena Island and Oakland is steel-truss cantilevered span that will be replaced by a single tower, self-anchored suspension bridge with a distinctive web of cables.

71. Yerba Buena and Treasure Islands
In San Francisco Bay, midway between San Francisco and Oakland

Yerba Buena is a natural hilly island through which the Bay Bridge passes. It has been occupied by the military since 1866 and access is limited; a Gothic Revival lightkeeper's house (1875) stands on the east shore. North of Yerba Buena and connected to it by a causeway is Treasure Island, a 404-acre man-made island created by filling a shoal for a municipal airport. The island was initially used for the 1939–1940 Golden Gate International Exposition. After the fair closed in 1940, the island became a Naval Reservation. Of the many Art

Deco buildings built for the fair, only an administration building and two built as future aircraft hangers were retained.

72. Piers 26 and 28, 1912–1913
The Embarcadero, between Harrison and Bryant Streets

Charles Newton Young, draftsman for the Harbor Commission

These are the last two piers with Mission Revival–style bulkheads built along the southern waterfront. Each pier has arched openings, with pent roofs over the smaller side arches and a Mission Revival parapet, or *espadana*, across the top.

73. Delancey Street, 1987–1990
600 The Embarcadero, at Delancey and Brannan Streets

Backen Arrigoni and Ross, architects

This two- to three-story apartment/workshop/retail complex for an acclaimed rehabilitation program has a gentle Mediterranean feeling to it.

74. Oriental Warehouse Live/Work Condominiums

Delancey (650 First) Street at Brannan Street

Fisher Friedman Associates, architects

Loving and Campos, architects

The sixty-six metal-sided live-work condominiums are tucked behind the brick walls of the historic Pacific Mail Steamship Company Warehouse (1867–1868).

75. South Beach Historic District

Second and Third Streets, between Brannan and King Streets

A collection of early-twentieth-century warehouses and industrial buildings was largely intact until recent years. Changes are occurring partially as a result of the economic boom spurred by Pac Bell Park (SBC) and the general gentrification of the area. While some buildings have been gutted and their industrial steel sash windows replaced, several buildings have been carefully preserved.

75a. D. N. and E. Walter Furniture Company Warehouse, 1910

601 Second Street

William D. Shea, architect

It has hardly changed at all; it retains wood sash windows, a slanted rail-spur entrance, old metal awnings, and a post-and-beam structural system.

75b. Farnsworth Building, 1906

660 Third Street

William Koenig, architect

This is possibly the most elaborate of these brick warehouses. It is tan brick with black spotting.

Decorated with elaborate brick pilasters, window hoods, sills and cornices, it retains all of its wooden windows.

75c. Garcia and Maggini Warehouse, 1913

128–136 King Street

Cunningham and Politeo, architects

A plain brick warehouse, it was the site of dramatic labor strife during the longshoremen's strike of 1934. This is a good example of how industrial buildings should be restored; old window sash was replaced with replica sash, its slanted rail-spur entrance was preserved, and even historic painted signage was restored.

76. South Park, 1854

Bounded by Second, Third, Bryant, and Brannan Streets

George Goddard, surveyor

Only the oval park remains of George Gordon's exclusive 1856 residential subdivision hidden in the center of a large city block. Gordon's London-style brick townhouses burned in 1906. Today, the park is surrounded by a mix of low-rise commercial and residential buildings.

77. Shreve Factory Lofts, 1912

539 Bryant Street

Nathaniel Blaisdell, architect

This is a great example of the attention and care that once went into making attractive industrial buildings. Although the structural system is reinforced concrete, the building is clad with buff-colored brick on two facades, with shallow recesses to create panels and chamfering. Industrial steel sash windows add further texture. The minimalist ornament consists of cornice

brackets and window keystones, and contributes to a feeling of graciousness. The building was originally used to manufacture jewelry and other products for Shreve's store at Post and Grant.

78. Pac Bell Park (SBC, now AT&T), 2000

The Embarcadero and King Street

With a nod to the past and the brick buildings of the former warehouse district, the full height of the stadium is hidden behind three-story brick walls edged in white. The façade is accented by a clock tower facing King Street and the light-rail platform.

79. Third and Fourth Street Bridges, 1932, 1913

Over Mission Creek

Joseph B. Strauss, engineer

Before Joseph B. Strauss began work on the Golden Gate Bridge, he was considered the world's leading designer of bascule drawbridges. A bascule bridge uses a heavy counterweight, usually concrete, to raise and lower its movable leaf, and was usually ungainly in appearance. In a mechanical sense, his bridges were elegant. The Third Street Bridge (1932) is a Heel Bascule type. The Fourth Street Bridge (1913) is an Overhead Bascule.

80. Mission Bay, 2004 ongoing

Third Street to I-280, Mission Creek to Mariposa Street

A huge redevelopment project on former Southern Pacific railroad yards includes the forty-acre-plus University of California medical research campus. The Campus Center, designed by Ricardo Legorreta, was completed in 2004.

2 · Retail District

The Retail District is the city's most fashionable shopping area and the location of its major hotels, theaters, and clubs. Once concentrated close to Union Square, the district has expanded and spilled across Market Street to Yerba Buena Gardens and the Moscone Convention Center, where new museums, theaters, and hotels have opened in the past decade.

Union Square's prominence as the retail and social center was assured after the St. Francis Hotel opened in 1904; after the 1906 earthquake and fire, the area was rebuilt into the district that exists today.

1. Union Square,
1860, 1942, 2002
Bounded by Geary, Post, Stockton, and Powell Streets

Michael Fotheringham and April Philips, landscape architects

The open plaza dates to the 1850s but its name recalls the meetings held here in 1860 to support the Union. In 1942, a park-over-garage by architect Timothy Pflueger was constructed. The current plaza is a complete redesign with the exception of **Dewey Monument** (1901; Newton J. Tharp, architect; Robert I. Aitken, sculptor), which commemorates Commodore Dewey's destruction of the Spanish fleet in the Philippines. The use of pink and greenish-black granite for pavers, steps, and planter boxes is the most attractive aspect of the park. Concrete for outlying elements is less fortunate but was economically necessary. Polished steel railings and benches as well as the modern concession buildings are less attractive. Only a small percentage of the area is devoted to planting, but what is there is cleverly arranged and effective. All in all, the new park is more inviting than the old one was, and in places it is prettier.

2. St. Francis Hotel,
1904–1913
335 Powell Street

Bliss and Faville, architects

The hotel was built in three stages, beginning at the south end and moving north as property became available. At twelve stories, it dwarfed the city's major nineteenth-century hotels. The building is sheathed with Colusa sandstone, which is exquisitely carved and tooled, but it needed to be completely redone in the early 1990s, a job made necessary by the spalling tendencies of the material. The tower to the west is a 1972 addition.

3. I. Magnin, 1946
Southwest corner of Geary and Stockton Streets

Timothy Pflueger, architect

This was a complete remodeling of a 1905 building for I. Magnin, a distinguished women's clothier. It has a flat façade with steel-framed windows that are flush with the white marble cladding. Black marble trim surrounds the window and door openings.

4. Neiman-Marcus, 1982
Southeast corner of Geary and Stockton Streets

Johnson and Burgee, architects

Bakewell and Brown, architects (dome and rotunda, 1907–1908)

After a contentious preservation battle to save the 1896 City of Paris building, its dome and rotunda were incorporated into the glazed corner, facing Union Square, of the 1982 Neiman-Marcus building. The art-glass dome depicts the ship *Ville de Paris*, after which Felix Verdier named his store.

5. Sachs Building, 1908
140 Geary Street
Lansburgh and Joseph, architects

The handsome commercial building, with a nicely remodeled ground-floor storefront that was inspired by the upper stories, is decorated with Classical ornament.

6. A. M. Robertson Building, 1909
218 Stockton Street
A. B. Foulkes, architect

Here is a refined traditional building in red brick with white lintels. The ground floor was built for Robertson's bookstore and publishing company; the upper floors (including the fourth, added in 1912) are still occupied by the Town and Country Club.

7. V. C. Morris Store, 1949
140 Maiden Lane
Frank Lloyd Wright, architect

The tan brick façade has a small but dramatic arched entry trimmed with four layers of radiating brick. This arch is "pulled" to the right by a belt course of cast stone and upward by a column formed by removing alternating bricks. More belt courses at the top and base help to frame the composition. Inside is a sweeping curvilinear staircase.

8. Shreve and Head Buildings, 1905, 1909
200–210, 201 Post Street
William Curlett and Son, architects

Two great classic towers of matching dimensions are by the same architect, one built just before the earthquake and fire, the other soon after. Shreve's (1905) is clad in Colusa sandstone (now painted), while the Head Building (1909) is clad in glazed terra-cotta. The main entrance is made of bronze in a florid classicism that prepares one for the shopping experience inside.

9. Lent Estate Building, 1907
214 Grant Avenue and 170–190 Post Street
Meyer and O'Brien, architects

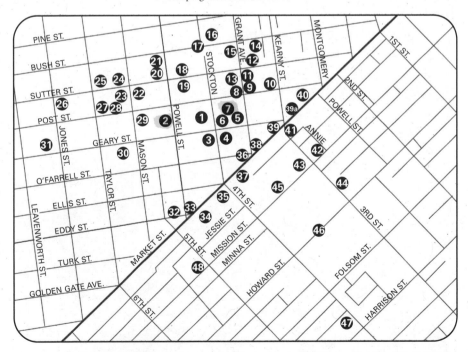

This building is notable for its inventive Art Nouveau ornament. It is one of a nice row that includes **222–228 Grant,** the Phoenix Building (1908; MacDonald and Applegarth, architects), with floral ornament around its windows, a reminder of florist Podesta-Baldocchi, whose fragrant shop was located here from 1908 to the 1980s.

10. Rochat-Cordes Building, 1909
126 Post Street

Albert Pissis, architect

A beautiful classical façade turns the corner nicely into the adjoining alley. Corinthian columns rise from the third through the fifth floors.

11. The White House, 1908
*Southeast corner of
Sutter Street and
Grant Avenue*

Albert Pissis, architect

The beautiful block-long Classical Revival façade on Sutter Street is dominated by a central bay with a monumental arched entry; Ionic pilasters on the third and fourth stories wrap around a curved corner onto Grant Avenue. The building once housed the dry goods store of Raphael Weill and Co., founded in the 1850s. After the business closed in 1965, the upper floors were converted into a parking garage. The façade, however, remains unchanged.

12. 200 Block of Sutter Street

12a. Goldberg Bowen Building, 1909
246–250 Sutter Street

Meyers and Ward, architects

Window bays are defined by Gothic ribs that rise to the cornice, where a riot of floral terracotta ornament erupts from the spandrels of the arched windows. Goldberg, Bowen and Co. was a wholesale and retail grocer of specialty foods, and a popular delicatessen.

12b. Bemiss Building, 1908
266 Sutter Street

MacDonald and Applegarth, architects

This narrow glass-front commercial building predates Polk's Hallidie Building by nine years. The architects were certainly conscious of the unusual nature of what they were doing, for on their plans they called this building "The Glass House." The only ornament is a simplified sheet-metal cornice crowned with anthemions. Wood-frame windows swivel open onto a fire escape.

13. Hammersmith Jewelry Building, 1907
301–303 Sutter Street

Lansburgh and Joseph, architects

This modest-sized building, built for a jeweler, is much loved for its spirited eclectic ornament, such as the row of Gothic arches, separated by fleur-de-lys beneath the cornice.

14. Pacific States Telephone and Telegraph Building, 1905
445 Bush Street

A. A. Cantin, architect

Headquarters for PT&T from 1907 until 1912, the building is notable for its bold second-story ornament, refined window trim, and pedimented seventh-story windows; the arched entrance and first-story windows are restrained. A former firehouse of Vancouver granite by City Architect Newton J. Tharp (1909) is found at **460 Bush Street.**

15. Home Telephone Company, 1908
333 Grant Avenue

Coxhead and Coxhead, architects

The magnificent Classical Revival building of Colusa sandstone has a central entry flanked by Corinthian columns supporting an entablature topped by a swan's neck pediment within a molded arch. Above the entry is a three-story recessed bay with two sets of paired Corinthian columns flanking the central windows. In 1924, the telephone company, now PT&T, moved to **430 Bush** (1924; Bliss and Faville, architects), and this building at 333 Grant was converted to condominiums (Huntsman Architectural Group) in 2004.

16. Notre Dame des Victoires, 1913
566 Bush Street

Louis Brouchoud, architect

This small, buff-colored brick Romanesque church, set on a high base with double staircases, has a barrel-shaped central bay flanked by polygonal towers topped by cupolas. The nave and side aisles are defined by red marble columns that support a barrel-vaulted ceiling decorated with Romanesque and Classical plaster ornament. The parish has been located here since the 1850s.

17. Stockton Street Tunnel, 1912–1914
Marsden Manson and Michael M. O'Shaughnessy, city engineers

A Classical Revival–style portal frames each end of the tunnel, with smaller arched openings for pedestrians. It was built to facilitate streetcar travel between downtown and the Panama-Pacific International Exposition of 1915.

18. Medical-Dental Office Building, 1929
450 Sutter Street

Miller and Pflueger, architects

Affectionately known simply by its address, "450 Sutter," this building and 490 Post have been the city's premier medical buildings. 450 Sutter is especially

16

notable for the Mayan imagery that is incised into the cladding. The lobby is small but spectacular, with very dark red marble walls and more Mayan ornament in the ceiling.

19. PG&E Building, 1916
447 Sutter Street

Edgar Mathews, architect

From its ornamental iron entrance to leafy window surrounds, this is an essay in delicate and intense ornament. There are paired arched windows with Romanesque columns on the upper stories. Less decorated but also important are the adjacent San Francisco Gas and Electric Company Building at **445 Sutter Street** (1909; Frederick H. Meyer, architect), and the Sir Francis Drake Hotel at **450 Powell Street** (1928; Weeks and Day, architects).

20. Physicians' Building, 1914
500 Sutter Street

Frederick H. Meyer, architect

This richly textured building is clad in buff-colored brick with cream terra-cotta trim. On the seventh and eighth stories, arched windows are supported by spiral columns.

Social and Athletic Clubs
(#s 21–25, 27, 28)

A number of social and athletic clubs were rebuilt on the northwestern edge of downtown after the 1906 earthquake. The majority, clad in brick, exhibit a refined Classic formalism, the essence of propriety.

21. The Family, 1909
545 Powell Street

C. A. Meussdorffer, architect

In form, this men's club is a modest Renaissance palazzo with monumental arched windows ranging across both façades. It is clad mainly in orange-red brick that lends a feeling of refinement to the façade. The deeply rusticated base, finished in cement, imparts a quality of strength. By the same architect, **535 Powell** (1911) was built as a residence with a decorated arched entry depicting images of fruit, and an exaggerated mansard roof sporting a Palladian dormer.

22. Francesca Club, 1919
595 Sutter Street

Edward E. Young, architect

This redbrick women's club is Georgian with the urbane feeling reminiscent of eighteenth-century London.

23. The Women's Club (now Marine's Memorial Club), 1927
609 Sutter Street

Bliss and Faville, architects

This building is notable because it departs from the formal classicism and use of color in the entrance bay. **625 Sutter** (1921–1925; Hyman and Appleton, architects) is Spanish Baroque with an intricately molded end bay.

24. The YWCA, 1918
620 Sutter Street

Lewis Hobart, architect

This seven-story brick and terra-cotta building has restrained decorative elements. On the ground floor are three arched windows and rusticated base, with arches above the top-floor windows.

25. Women's Athletic Club, 1916, 1922
640 Sutter Street

Bliss and Faville, architects

This has the feeling of an Italian Renaissance palazzo, with a band of Corinthian columns creating the effect of a loggia on the fifth and sixth stories. It is now the Metropolitan Club for women.

26. Belgravia Apartments, 1913
795 Sutter Street

Frederick H. Meyer, architect

This elegant apartment building combines Georgian and Beaux-Arts Classicism. Every detail is refined, including the entry framed by brackets, first-story arched windows with receding layers, flat arches with keystones in the upper stories, and differentiated end bays. Similar-quality apartment/hotel buildings by Meyer are located at **701 Post** (1910) and **775 Post** (1913).

27. Bohemian Club, 1934
624 Taylor Street

Lewis Hobart, architect

Will P. Day, engineer

Founded by artists and journalists in 1872, the Bohemian Club is now rather exclusive. The red-brick club is a restrained example of Art Deco; there is chamfering of the window bays, zigzag brick patterning below the cornice, and terra-cotta panels of gods. Images of the club's owl mascot are located in various places.

28. Olympic Club, 1912
524 Post Street

Paff and Baur, architects

This athletic club was founded in 1860 and is still active. The Classical Revival building has a base of white stone, middle stories of brown brick, and a top story of terra-cotta.

29. First Congregational Church, 1913
Southeast corner of Post and Mason

Reid Brothers, architects

This great Classic Revival former church is built on the site of the congregation's 1872 church that was destroyed in 1906.

30. Geary Theater, 1909
415 Geary Street

Bliss and Faville, architects

A colorful and richly textured theater building, its recessed Ionic columns, arches, and spandrels are polychrome terra-cotta and contain a wealth of imaginative detail. The main part of the façade is tan and buff-colored brick. The elaborate sheet copper marquee appears to be original. After major earthquake damage in 1989, the interior was restored. It is home to the American Conservatory Theater (ACT), whose mission is to train actors and produce plays. Next door, the **Curran Theater** at 455 Geary (1922; Alfred Henry Jacobs, architect) is a more conventional design but is still a fine building.

31. Alcazar Theater, 1917
650–656 Geary Street

T. Patterson Ross, architect

Originally a Shriners' Temple, a division of the Masons fraternal society, the building is clad in colorful terra-cotta with redbrick banding. Moorish arches of incredible complexity range across both stories, and a dome tops the composition.

32. Bank of Italy, 1920
1 Powell Street

Bliss and Faville, architects

The white granite building has a refined Classicism imparted by shallow rustication of the entire surface, monumental arched entry and windows, carved images of goddesses and gods atop the keystone volutes, and an elaborate cornice. This was the second of the bank's four headquarters.

33. Flood Building,
1902–1904
*870 Market Street and
71 Ellis Street*

Albert Pissis, architect

This grand building is twelve stories of Colusa sandstone hung on a steel frame. It is a five-part composition, with each defined by a stringcourse. The first story has six monumental entrance arches with elaborate brackets and keystones. The fifth-through-seventh stories are framed by Corinthian pavilions. The eleventh and twelfth stories are treated like a Corinthian colonnade. There is a historical exhibit in the marble lobby.

34. The Emporium,
1895–1896
835–865 Market Street

Pissis and Moore, architects

This venerable building has been reduced to its façade as part of a mammoth new retail and high-rise hotel project that extends through the block to Mission Street. The building once housed the largest dry goods store in the city. After 1906, it was rebuilt behind its surviving façade, a great example of monumental Classicism. Eighteen columns and pilasters march across the fifth-through-seventh stories, lower floors have cast-iron columns between showcase windows, and entrances are arched. The 1908 rotunda is repositioned within the new building.

35. Pacific Building, 1907
801 Market Street

Charles Whittlesey, architect

This is one of the more colorful downtown buildings, with seven floors clad in green tiles above

two of reddish brown. The ornamentation is Sullivanesque with gargoyles.

36. Phelan Building, 1908
760 Market Street

William Curlett, architect

This ten-story elegant flatiron building is sheathed in glazed white terra-cotta, with pediments at the fourth-floor level and in the upper tier within the arches.

The lobby and staircase are white marble.

37. Humboldt Bank Building, 1906
785 Market Street

Meyer and O'Brien, architects

At fifteen stories plus an elaborate dome, this building has a base clad with Colusa sandstone and the upper stories in terra-cotta. Overscaled Classical

36

ornament and rusticated piers distinguish this design.

38. Union Trust Company Building, 1910
744 Market Street and 2 Grant Avenue

Clinton Day, architect

Among a handful of grand banking temples, this one is bolder, with iron fences, bronze lanterns, and a profusion of ornament that provides a showcase of great stone carving. The **Savings Union Bank** at 1 Grant (1910; Bliss and Faville, architects) is a somber, domed Roman temple.

39. Mutual Savings Bank Building, 1902
700 Market Street

William Curlett, architect

With an exquisite broken pediment and carved foliage over the main entrance, this early skyscraper also has a Baroque dormer projecting from the red mansard roof.

39a. Lotta's Fountain, 1875
Market, Geary, and Kearny Streets

Wyneken and Townsend, architects

The High Victorian cast-iron drinking fountain was a gift to the city by Lotta Crabtree, a child singer and dancer in Gold Rush camps who became a very popular actress in adulthood. It hasn't worked in ages, but San Franciscans love it dearly. Each April 18 since 1939, crowds have gathered here at 5:18 a.m. in memory of the 1906 earthquake to honor survivors.

40. Mechanics' Institute, 1909
57–65 Post Street

Albert Pissis, architect

A second-floor arcade distinguishes this restrained Classicism. The interior treasures are the spiral iron staircase and second-floor reading room that houses a good library. The Institute was founded in 1854 to serve architects and the building trades; their first building on this site was built in 1866.

41. Hearst Building, 1909
5 Third Street

James C. Green, architect

This is a colorful potpourri of polychrome terra-cotta ornament over the entry and on the second story, depicting shields, wreaths, foliage, and a rope pattern framing the windows. Each decorative piece was hand carved and then a mold was made into which clay was hand pressed. There is a bronze grille of mythological animals over the door. Julia Morgan simplified the cornice and first story in 1937.

42. California Historical Society (CHS)
678 Mission Street

CHS was founded in 1871, became moribund in 1906 after

the earthquake, and was re-established in 1922. In 1995, the society moved to this two-story, former commercial building from a Pacific Heights mansion. Changing exhibits and a bookstore (open to the public) complement an outstanding research library. At **300 Fourth Street,** the Society of California Pioneers also has an excellent library.

43. Aronson Building, 1903
700 Mission Street

Hemenway and Miller, architects

The upper stories are clad in terra-cotta, with lush ornament filling the spandrels of the arched windows. The lower stories are in buff-colored brick, and the first floor has cast-iron pillars between altered storefronts. Diagonally across the intersection stands the tan brick Williams Building by Clinton Day (1907).

44. San Francisco Museum of Modern Art, 1994
151 Third Street

Mario Botta, architect

A study in sculpted massing, block-like units are set back from each other in terraces and are bisected by a central cylindrical tower that is sliced at an angle at the top. The building is in pre-fabricated panels of warm, richly textured sienna-colored bricks. The black-and-white horizontal bands of granite on the tower and ground-floor columns con-trast nicely with the brick. The interior is a mix of granite, birch wood, and vast expanses of smooth white plaster.

45. St. Patrick's Church,
1872, 1914
756 Mission Street

Gordon Cummings, architect (1872)

Shea and Lofquist, architects (1914)

The original Gothic Revival church was damaged in 1906 but repaired. In 1914, the church was rebuilt with a steel frame, new upper walls, steeple, and interior. The central Gothic-arched entry has leafy capitals carved from sandstone, a rare example of Victorian stone carving. The interior has a high nave with a vaulted ribbed ceil-ing, side aisles are defined by columns of green marble, win-dows are stained glass with Gothic tracery, and the altar is intricately carved.

East of St. Patrick's, the Contemporary Jewish Museum, by architect Daniel Libeskind, is scheduled to open in 2008.

46. Yerba Buena Center,
1978–2003
Bounded by Mission, Folsom, Third, and Fourth Streets

As part of the South of Market Redevelopment Plan begun in the early 1950s, which stretched from the Embarcadero to Twentieth Street, the Yerba Buena Center project began in the late 1970s with low-income housing and Phase I of the Moscone Convention Center, completed in 1981 (Hellmuth, Obata + Kassabaum, architects; Y. T. Lin, engineer).

Towers to the west, some exceeding 400 feet, which were not imagined in the original redevelopment plan, now obscure views and even crowd and diminish the Museum of Modern Art.

The buildings of Moscone South and North, on either side of Howard Street between Third and Fourth Streets and mostly underground, have a variety of attractions perched on top of them. On the south block is a colorful 1906 carousel that once stood at Playland-at-the-Beach.

The third phase, Moscone West (2003; Gensler Architec-ture & Planning), is a curved glass wall of a building at the corner of Howard and Fourth Streets. The thirty-two-story InterContinental Hotel at 888 Howard opened in 2007 (Patri Merker Architects; Hornberger + Worstell, architects).

On the roof of the north block is Yerba Buena Center Theater (1993; James Stewart Polshek & Partners, architects), Yerba Buena Center for the Arts (1993; Fumihiko Maki & Associates, architects), and the Esplanade Gardens (1993; MGA Partners, with Romaldo

Giurgola, architects) facing Mission Street, St. Patrick's Church, and the soon-to-be-completed Contemporary Jewish Museum. On the park's west side is Metreon (1996; Gary Handel & Associates/ SMWM, architects), a chaotic jumble of movie theaters, shops, and restaurants clad in sheet metal.

The Esplanade is a great urban amenity, a respite of greenery with an expansive, gently rolling lawn, granite-paved paths, trees, boulders, floral plantings, and a granite waterfall.

47. Southern Police Station, 1925
360 Fourth Street

John Reid Jr., city architect

Of Spanish Renaissance design with a great Baroque entrance, the police station has been incorporated into a Salvation Army housing complex.

48. U.S. Branch Mint, 1869–1874
Northwest corner of Fifth and Mission Streets

Alfred B. Mullett, U.S. Supervising Architect

Greek Revival in style, the build-ing is constructed of British Columbia sandstone resting on a base of Penryn granite. The sym-metrical façade features a central, projecting temple front with a pediment resting on six fluted Doric columns, approached by a grand central stairway. Flanking wings have square pilasters and slightly peaked parapets. The building served as the mint until 1937; it will soon become the Museum of San Francisco.

3 · Civic Center

When the earthquake of 1868 damaged the City Hall on Portsmouth Square, it provided the opportunity to build a new city hall in a different district. The city chose the area where the new San Francisco Main Library and Asian Art Museum now stand, which was the former location of Yerba Buena Cemetery. Construction began in 1871, but the New City Hall was not completed until 1896 due to graft by contractors.

Plans to create a civic center in the aesthetic of the City Beautiful Movement were made by architect B. J. S. Cahill in 1899, 1904, and 1912. The Burnham Plan of 1905 also envisioned a similar civic center for San Francisco. After the 1906 earthquake destroyed City Hall, Mayor James Rolph appointed a team of architects that included John Galen Howard, Frederick H. Meyer, and John Reid Jr. to develop a new plan that was used to create the core of the Beaux-Arts Civic Center that stands today.

1. City Hall, 1913–1915
*Block bounded by
Van Ness Avenue, and
Polk, Grove, and
McAllister Streets*

*Bakewell and Brown,
architects*

City Hall [1] projects a feeling of grandeur and elegance; its gilded-ribbed dome and lantern rise proudly. Over the central entrance [1a], heroic figures support balconies; Doric colonnades support entablatures; and iron doorframes and balconies, painted blue and gold, add a dash of color to the white granite. The interior is dominated by the rotunda, from which a grand staircase of pink marble and foliated iron railings ascends to the second floor. In the upper floors are many vantage points from which to view sculptural work by Jean Louis Bourgeois.

**2. War Memorial Opera
House and Veterans'
Building,** 1931–1932
301, 401 Van Ness Avenue

Arthur Brown Jr., architect

*G. Albert Lansburgh,
architect (theater spaces)*

This building was built by the city as a joint project of veterans' organizations, which needed office space, and the San Francisco Opera, which wanted a permanent home. The monumental classical exteriors, designed by Brown, are a matched pair, except the Opera House is clad in granite,

and the Veterans' Building
is a first-rate imitation.

3. Louis M. Davies Symphony Hall, 1980

*Southwest corner of
Grove Street and
Van Ness Avenue*

*Skidmore, Owings &
Merrill, architects*

A widely curved, glazed
corner looks out toward
City Hall.

4. Commercial High School, 1910

*Northeast corner of
Fell and Franklin Streets*

*Newton J. Tharp, City
Architect*

Completed after the architect's death in 1909, the
school was named in his
memory; "Newton Tharp
Commercial School" is
inscribed in the frieze. This large
building was moved from the
Civic Center in 1913 to its present site after the Civic Center
plan was adopted. It is tan brick
on a steel frame with beautiful
classical ornament at the entrance
and a graceful window arcade
across the first story. The former
High School of Commerce at
135 Van Ness Avenue (1927;
John Reid Jr., architect) has a
Churrigueresque entrance bay,
almost Art Deco in style.

5. Masonic Temple, 1911

25 Van Ness Avenue

Bliss and Faville, architects

Here is a fraternal hall in the
form and style of a Florentine
Romanesque palazzo. The many-
layered entrance contains a sculptural group within the arch, and
a sculpture of Solomon juts from
the corner.

3 • Civic Center

6. Civic Auditorium, 1913–1915

*Grove Street between
Polk and Larkin Streets*

*John Galen Howard, Frederick
H. Meyer, and John Reid Jr.,
architects*

The bold Beaux-Arts Classic
façade exhibits considerable
imagination and flair; curved
brackets support balconies, and
there are deeply molded arches in
the monumental upper-story
windows. The auditorium was
built to host conventions, and
was home to the San Francisco
Opera from 1923 to 1932.

7. State Building, 1926

350 McAllister Street

Bliss and Faville, architects

A Classic Revival–style building
is faced with expertly carved

granite but is less sculptural than
the earlier Civic Center buildings. A granite-clad addition to
the north at **455 Golden Gate
Avenue** (1999; Skidmore,
Owings & Merrill, architects)
fortunately hides most of
the Federal Building at **450
Golden Gate.**

8. Old Main Library, 1916–1917

200 Larkin Street

George W. Kelham, architect

*Gae Aulenti, architect
(conversion to Asian Art
Museum, 1999–2003)*

The Beaux-Arts façade of the former Main Library is a classic
three-part composition of granite
set on a rusticated base. Tall
arched windows covered with
grilles and separated by pilasters

span the block-long north and south sides; a recessed second-story bay with four paired Doric columns graces the narrower ends. When the building was unfortunately converted to the Asian Art Museum, most of the library rooms and hallways were replaced with modern spaces to house the ancient artwork. However, the grand staircase and former card catalog room remain as the lobby entrance.

9. New Main Library, 1993–1996
100 Larkin Street

Pei Cobb Freed & Partners, architects

There are faint references to Beaux-Arts classicism in the north and west façade, while the south and east façades are starkly modern. The interior layout is confusing, and there is no more room for books in the new building than there was in the old one.

10. Federal Building, 1936
Northeast corner of Fulton and Hyde Streets

Arthur Brown Jr., architect

A concave entrance bay, Doric colonnades, and sculpted heads of gods distinguish this classically styled building, the last one built in the Civic Center.

11. Orpheum Theater, 1925
1192 Market Street

B. Marcus Priteca, architect

The exterior is a confection of heavily textured spiral columns, with plenty of Baroque ornament. The new marquee and blade sign convey the spirit of the 1920s.

12. Trinity Center, 1989
1145 Market Street

Backen Arrigoni and Ross, architects

The lower five stories are clad in white marble, relieved by diamond panels, cappings of green marble, and faceted bay windows of ornamental bronze. The setback upper stories are all glass.

South of Market

South of Market Street between Sixth and Twelfth Streets is an eclectic social and economic

mix of industrial/warehouses, a bit of skid-row grittiness, affordable new housing, and gentrification. Among the hundreds of vernacular buildings are scattered examples of noteworthy ones designed by major San Francisco architects, both historic and contemporary.

13. Mangrum and Otter Building, 1928
1235 Mission Street

Bliss and Fairweather, architects

A riot of Spanish ornament in orange and green terra-cotta has spiky finials across the top. The building advertised architectural tiles, one of Mangrum and Otter's products.

14. St. Joseph's Catholic Church, 1913
1401 Howard Street, at Eleventh Street

John J. Foley, architect

Although constructed of reinforced concrete, the Romanesque cross-transept church is richly articulated. A gabled entry bay is flanked by slightly projecting square towers capped by cupolas with ribbed domes. The transepts and entry bay contain layered recessed arches with rose windows. The parish is closed, but several buildings on the grounds are still used for social services.

15. Harrison School, 1920, 1929
1440 Harrison Street

John Reid Jr., architect

A redbrick school building has a beautiful terra-cotta swan's neck pediment and urn in the entrance pavilion. The older part of the school has multipaned wood-frame windows; the 1929

14

addition has industrial steel sash windows.

16. Jackson Brewery,
1906–1912
1475–1489 Folsom Street, at Eleventh Street

James T. Ludlow, engineer

The six-building complex is red brick, with the base, corbels, and parts of the entrance arch made of Colusa sandstone. The style is early-twentieth-century industrial with Romanesque elements—corbelling, arched windows, and a six-story tower—that impart a medieval feeling.

17. New loft buildings
1100 Block of Folsom Street

Several buildings in this vicinity illustrate how new buildings are being mixed with the old. **1150** and **1168 Folsom Street,** and **7 Hallam Street** are typical residential "loft" buildings. Large expanses of windows, rectangular bays, and sheet-metal cladding are the dominant motif. At **33–67 Hallam Street** (1991;

Donald McDonald and Associates) [17] are rather more imaginative townhouses with irregularly shaped gabled roofs and split-level arched windows; the fronts are clad in plywood.

18. Eng-Skell Company Building, 1930
1035 Howard Street

A. C. Griewank, engineer

Great expanses of industrial-steel sash windows are topped off by Art Deco cresting. **1130 Howard** is another fine Art Deco industrial building designed the same year by the same architect. **1028 Howard** (1994) is a low-cost housing project by Simon Martin–Vegue Winkelstein Moris. Its five bays are each clad in different materials and colors.

19. U. S. Post Office and Court of Appeals, 1902–1905
95 Seventh Street

James Knox Taylor, U. S. Supervising Architect

Three stories of monumental Classicism are carved from

Raymond granite. The lower stories are rusticated and convey strength; hammered granite creates texture. In contrast, the stone on the top story is cut smoothly. The pedimented entrances on both Seventh and Mission Streets are showcases of fine carving. Windows are arched in the lower stories and pedimented in the third. The doors on Mission Street, lanterns, and streetlights are masterpieces of cast bronze. The interior is even finer.

20. Federal Building Complex, 2005–2006
Seventh and Mission Streets

Thom Mayne, architect

This radically modern 234-foot-tall building is designed to consume half the energy of a conventional building; its glassy upper stories are quite visible from the Civic Center.

The Tenderloin

Between the Civic Center and the Retail District, Market Street and blocks to the north have been known as the Tenderloin since the 1880s. After 1906, the Tenderloin was rebuilt with a denser mix of residential apartments, tourist hotels, commercial establishments, theaters, and churches. After World War II, a long period of decline began that has started to turn around with the rehabilitation of hotels such as the Cadillac at **380 Eddy Street** (1909; Meyer and O'Brien, architects) and the Herald at **308 Eddy Street** (1910; Alfred Henry Jacobs, architect). It is advisable to be "streetwise" when walking through this neighborhood.

17

20

21. Odd Fellows Hall, 1909
26 Seventh Street,
at Market Street

G. A. Dodge, architect

Still occupied by several Odd Fellows lodges, the building is rich in texture and ornament; a large panel on the Seventh Street side displays imagery associated with the Odd Fellows.

22. Eastern Outfitting Co. Building, 1909
1017–1021 Market Street

MacDonald and Applegarth, architects

Giant fluted Corinthian columns support an entablature with the words "FURNITURE AND CARPETS" proudly emblazoned across the frieze. Between the columns is a vast expanse of glass, held in place by copper framing, which admits light to the interior lofts, once used for manufacturing.

23. Wilson Building, 1900
973 Market Street

Percy and Polk, architects

This earthquake and fire survivor is important as a collaboration of George W. Percy (at the end of his career) and Willis Polk (early in his career). The fenestration is Chicago School, and the splendid ornament is Sullivanesque.

24. Golden Gate Theater, 1922
1 Taylor Street

G. Albert Lansburgh, architect

Stylistically, this theater is a blend of Spanish Colonial and Classical Revival styles. The arcaded base and top story are clad in terra-cotta; the middle stories are brick. The chamfered corner of the building is topped

by an ornate dome. Lansburgh's **Warfield Theater** at 982–998 Market (1921) is clad in mono-chrome terra-cotta, with simple Classical Revival ornament.

25. St. Boniface Roman Catholic Church,
1900–1902, 1907
133 Golden Gate Avenue

Brother Adrian Wewer and Brother Ildefonse Lethert, designers

Designed by two Franciscan brothers, this church was partially destroyed in 1906, and was rebuilt in 1907 using the original design and retaining much of its original fabric. It is a restrained vertical example of the Romanesque style. The central domed tower is closely flanked by subordinate towers; columns of Penryn granite support the paired entrance arches. The dramatic interior is richly embellished with paintings of biblical figures, saints, and floral and abstract patterns, while stained-glass windows impart colorful hues.

26. Hibernia Bank,
1889–1892
1 Jones Street

Pissis and Moore, architects

The Classic Revival banking temple was designed as a result of an architectural competition. It is white Rocklin granite above a base of dark Penryn granite, and the stone is finely carved. Both façades feature high arched windows alternating with Corinthian columns that support an entablature and a balustraded parapet; a colon-naded entrance pavilion supports a copper dome topped by a finial. The interior is as rich as the exterior, and features two marvelous art-glass domes. The building survived in 1906 but is now a prisoner of the run-down neighborhood surrounding it; it is currently unused.

27. YMCA, 1920
351 Turk Street

Frederick H. Meyer, architect

This former YMCA is a twelve-story building covered with Romanesque ornament. Its monumental entrance arch is beautifully detailed, and a handsome arcade stretches across the second story. There are beautifully painted ceiling beams in the lobby and common room.

28. Deutsches Haus, 1912
601–625 Polk Street

Frederick H. Meyer, architect

Built to house several German social organizations, the building is German Baroque in style. The center of the main façade rises to an immense stepped dormer that stands in front of the mansard roof. The quality of detailing is superb. The **Tenderloin Community School** at 627 Turk (1998) was designed by EHDD.

Van Ness Corridor

29. Stadtmuller House, 1880
819 Eddy Street

Peter R. Schmidt, architect

This late Italianate is richly textured with a profusion of ornament. The portico and window bay are amazing. This house, and the Englander House at **807 Franklin** (1880; Wildrich A. Winterhalter, architect) that is

more restrained, not only survived 1906 but also subsequent development pressures.

30. Family Service Agency, 1928
1010 Gough Street

Bernard Maybeck, architect

This wide-gable, tile-roofed, three- to four-story Mediterranean is a vertical version of Maybeck's Berkeley houses from this period, and, although altered, retains industrial sash windows, stucco siding, picturesque massing, and his signature massive chimney.

31. St. Mark's Lutheran Church, 1895
1111 O'Farrell Street

Henry Geilfuss, architect

The High Victorian, redbrick church is trimmed with buff-colored brick, and the entrance columns are made of polished granite. The triple-arched entry is especially appealing, and the five-story tower serves as an exclamation point.

32. First Unitarian Church, 1888
1187 Franklin Street

Percy and Hamilton, architects

This Gothic Revival church is built of rugged stone masonry and features an entrance with paired pointed arches, a square tower with lancet windows and gargoyles, a giant rose window, and a rounded bay. During the 1960s, the south and west walls and adjacent buildings (with pyramidal roofs) were constructed of textured concrete (1967–1979; Callister, Payne and Rosse, architects).

33. St. Mary's Cathedral, 1971
Southwest corner of Geary and Gough Streets

Pietro Belluschi, architect

Pier Luigi Nervi, architect

McSweeney, Ryan and Lee, associated architects

The cathedral sits on a large open plaza designed to accommodate large crowds and to provide unimpeded views of the building. The square travertine-clad base supports an immense, tapering, cruciform-shaped, reinforced-concrete cupola. The interior has the warmth the exterior generally lacks. Narrow strips of stained glass by Gyory Kepes fill the seams between the quadrants of the cupola; the baldachinos, by Richard Lippold, is a glistening effervescent sculpture that hangs from the soffit.

34. Don Lee Cadillac, 1921
1000 Van Ness Avenue

Weeks and Day, architects

The automobile sales showroom is on the ground floor; repair shops and accessory sales are on the upper three floors. The arched entry is flanked by paired columns with incised decoration. Above the entry is a sculptural work by Jo Mora of two men on either side of a heraldic shield, holding automobile wheels. Between flanking showroom windows are columns with bears on top. There are two other grand auto showrooms, one in Art Deco style at **999 Van Ness** (1938; John Dinwiddie, architect), and the Classically inspired Earle C. Anthony Packard showroom at **901 Van Ness** (1926; Bernard Maybeck, with Powers and Ahnden, architects).

4 · Nob Hill

Nob Hill is shown on some early maps as "Knob Hill." When Central Pacific Railroad executives and others of wealth built their wooden mansions along California and Taylor Streets in the 1870s, the name became Nob Hill, "Nob" being the abbreviation for "nabob," a high-class swell. The Fairmont, begun before the earthquake, was the first of four major hotels to be built at the top of California Street. Grace Cathedral and Masonic Auditorium add to the feeling that the hill is one of the "destination spots" in the city. As before the earthquake and fire, Nob Hill is mainly residential.

Lower Nob Hill is the neighborhood south of Pine Street. It is primarily filled with residential apartment buildings, many that are architecturally interesting. Built up after the devastation of 1906, variations of the Classical Revival style predominate.

1. Ritz-Carlton Hotel, 1909–1953
600 Stockton Street

Napoleon LeBrun and Sons (New York), architects (1909)

Built in five stages over forty-four years for the Metropolitan Life Insurance Company, the final result is so harmonious that it looks like it was built all at once to a unified design. The style is monumental Roman classicism in gleaming white terra-cotta, with Chicago School windows and a colorful frieze of foliated ornament. The oldest portion is the south wing on Stockton Street. In 1990–1991, the grand entry staircase was removed and a compatible porte cochere was added when the building was converted into the present hotel.

2. University Club, 1912
800 Powell Street

Bliss and Faville, architects

A men's club, which achieves its texture through delicate brick-work, includes a pattern created by recessing alternate bricks around the arched windows. The entrance and broad cornice are made of terra-cotta. **830 Powell** (1910; Crim and Scott, architects) and the Francesca Apartments at **850 Powell** (1923; MacDonald and Couchot, architects) were inspired by late-nineteenth-century French designs.

3. Fairmont Hotel, 1905–1907
950 Mason Street

Reid Brothers, architects

This is the most palatial of San Francisco's hotels and one of the city's great landmarks. Just weeks before its opening in 1906, it was gutted by fire after the earthquake but was quickly rebuilt. Built of white granite, the first story is deeply rusticated and imparts a feeling of massive strength. Panels flanking the columned entry display some of the finest stone carving in the state. The upper stories are clad in glazed white terra-cotta and are elaborately decorated with Classical motifs. The sumptuous lobby has faux-marble columns, a grand staircase, and rich ceiling ornament. The twenty-nine-story tower was added in 1962.

4. Mark Hopkins Hotel, 1925
Southeast corner of California and Mason Streets

Weeks and Day, architects

This hotel is in buff-colored brick, with an elaborate Baroque entrance, cornices, belt courses, and gateposts of terra-cotta. The flanking wings are at an angle to the central tower where the Top of the Mark bar is located. On Mason and Pine Streets, the high basalt retaining walls, with pinnacles at the corners, survive from the 1878 Mark Hopkins mansion destroyed in 1906. The same architects designed the Huntington Hotel (entry #7), the **Brocklebank Apartments** (1926), 1000 Mason, and the **Cathedral Apartments** (1927) at 1201 California.

5. Morsehead Apartments, 1915
1001 California Street

Houghton Sawyer, architect

Here is a six-story apartment building with a Renaissance base, cornice and frieze, and gently curved end bays defined by quoins. The first story is clad in glazed terra-cotta that is delicately streaked and spotted to resemble unpolished pink Tennessee marble. The original iron marquee is supported by elaborate brackets.

6. Pacific Union Club, 1884–1886, 1908–1911
1000 California Street

Augustus Laver, architect (1884–1886)

Willis Polk, architect (1908–1911)

Built as the city residence of Comstock Lode silver king James C. Flood, the style is Italianate, with square porch columns, arched first-story windows, and pedimented second-story windows. The brass gates and fence, made by W. T. Garratt's South-of-Market foundry, are splendid. They have oxidized to a green color that contrasts nicely with the red stone. The red sandstone from Connecticut has a delicate banding that imparts a subtle beauty, and is exquisitely carved. The interior was destroyed by fire in 1906. The Pacific Union Club sponsored a competition to build a white granite building on the site, but Willis Polk proposed that the club build within the surviving exterior walls. Polk lopped off Laver's central tower, added the curved wings (using matching sandstone), and created a lavish interior.

7. Huntington Hotel, 1924
1075 California Street

Weeks and Day, architects

This tall hotel building is clad in orange bricks and fills the lot lines, without setbacks, in contrast to the architects' Mark Hopkins Hotel. Slightly differentiated end bays relieve the mass. Renaissance-style trim in the entrance and upper stories is terra-cotta.

8

8a

8. Grace Cathedral (Episcopal), 1928–1964
Northwest corner of Taylor and California Streets

Lewis Hobart, architect (1928–1941)

Weihe, Frick, and Kruse, architects (1961–1964)

The complex occupies an entire city block and contains elements built over nearly a century. Of historical interest are the fence and posts of Penryn granite, basalt, and cast iron that survive from the Charles Crocker mansion, which stood here from 1877 to 1906. The most beautiful element is the set of gilded bronze doors [8a] that are replicas of Lorenzo Ghiberti's fifteenth-century Gates of Paradise at the Baptistry in Florence, Italy. Within the cathedral are tapestries and altars from the fifteenth and sixteenth centuries, excellent stained glass, and other works of art (brochures are available inside the main entrance). The monumental church is Gothic, based on French prototypes; and true to medieval tradition, it took decades to build. For seismic and financial reasons, the building was made of reinforced concrete mixed with gravel for texture.

9. Chambord Apartments, 1921
1298 Sacramento Street

James Francis Dunn, architect

This building is Classic in its detailing and Art Nouveau in its flowing forms. Balconies and bay windows bulge outward from the wall. Apartments at **961 Pine Street** (1912) and **1250 Pine** (1919) are of a similar style by the same architect. **1242 Sacramento Street** (circa 1916; Arthur J. Laib, architect) is yet another Parisian-style apartment, with ornamental cast-iron balconies and bowed windows.

10. La Granja Apartments, 1913
1255 Taylor Street

Falch and Knoll, architects

A great Mannerist apartment building with overscaled Classic elements, its corner balconies are framed by Corinthian columns that rise two stories, and large ornate supporting brackets dominate the composition.

11. Apartments, 1909, 1914
1224–1232 Washington Street

Charles and Austin Whittlesey, architects

The Pueblo-style building climbs up the hill, with low arched passageways leading to various apartments. It has a pebble-dash stucco surface and wooden balconies with cutout patterns.

12. United Railroads Cable Car Powerhouse and Barn, 1907
1201 Mason Street

H. K. Stevens, URR house architect

United Railroads rebuilt this car barn and powerhouse (preserving the old smokestack) after the 1887 original was destroyed in 1906. It still powers all three of MUNI's cable car lines. When the cable car system was rebuilt in 1984, the brick exterior walls and metal window sash were preserved. There is a cable car museum inside.

13. Craftsman Apartments, 1908
1380 Washington Street

Ralph Warner Hart, architect

The first story is clinker brick; the second story is half-timbered with gable-roofed rectangular bays.

14. Keystone Apartments, 1908
1369 Hyde Street

Oliver and Foulkes, architects

A massive redbrick apartment building is divided into three wings by light bays and is notable for a rusticated first story, original iron and wood marquee, and the many keystones in the flat arches over most of the windows.

15. Third Baptist Church, 1908
1255 Hyde Street

Henry Starbuck, architect

This church building is a blend of Craftsman and Gothic Revival styles built for an African American congregation that was founded in 1852.

16. Tudor apartments, 1909
1433 Clay Street

MacDonald and Applegarth, architects

A richly textured building is clad in wood shingles and decorated with patterned panels.

5 · Chinatown

Chinatown began in 1849 as a Chinese tent settlement on the south side of Sacramento Street between Kearny Street and Grant Avenue, and by 1853, it had grown into a Chinatown covering several blocks. When Chinese laborers moved to San Francisco after the completion of the transcontinental railroad in 1869, it expanded further; by the 1880s, it encompassed most of today's Chinatown. The neighborhood became notorious for its tongs, brothels, gambling dens, opium dens, overcrowded conditions, and health problems. At the same time, Chinatown had well-known restaurants, colorful emporiums, and famed herbalists. The neighborhood was sensationalized in the mainstream press, and professional guides took tourists into the more exotic spots. When Chinatown was destroyed in 1906, it was quickly rebuilt with brick buildings, many with corner bays topped with pagoda-style roofs, ornamental balconies, and other Chinese ornament. Zoning protects the neighborhood from Financial District encroachment.

Tourist restaurants and shops are concentrated along Grant Avenue; meat, fish, and produce shops line Stockton Street. Throughout Chinatown the upper floors are occupied by benevolent and family association offices, lodging rooms, and apartments. Although Chinese now live in many San Francisco neighborhoods, Chinatown remains their "downtown," the place to shop and socialize.

1. Old Saint Mary's Church,
1853–1854
Northeast corner of California Street and Grant Avenue

William Craine and John England, architects

The Gothic Revival redbrick, former Roman Catholic cathedral served the San Francisco Archdiocese until 1894, when a new cathedral was built on Van Ness Avenue; this became "Old St. Mary's," a parish church. Although the interior was destroyed in 1906, it was rebuilt in 1909 to resemble the original; the façade remains close to how it looked in the 1850s. It has a symmetrical façade with a central square bell tower, and arched windows on the west side are flanked by buttresses. The granite foundation and granite belt courses are probably imported from China. A wing on the north side is a 1929 addition by architect Edward A. Eames.

2. Sing Chong and Sing Fat Buildings, 1908
Northwest and southwest corners of California Street and Grant Avenue

Ross & Burgren, architects

The pagoda-roofed towers on these buildings have sweeping, upturned eaves, and give a visual focus to this prominent intersection. The Sing Chong building on the northwest corner is buff-colored brick, with pagoda roofs across the tops of both façades and at various places below. The Sing Fat Building on the southwest corner is tan brick with green terra-cotta panels and an elaborate four-tier pagoda crowning the corner.

3. 700 Block of Commercial Street, circa 1906–1907

This block is largely intact and has a very old feeling to it. The most interesting buildings are 728–732 (1929), with attractive brickwork and multi-light windows; 731–747 (1906; Salfield and Kohlberg, architects) has several storefronts; 736 (1907; Lansburgh and Joseph, architects; upper stories added 1928) has a bold second-story cornice; 740–742 (1907) has a Mission Revival parapet and arched entry; 748 (1907; Righetti and Kuhl, architects) has stone window trim; 755–757 (1907; Lansburgh and Joseph, architects) has buff-colored brick trim and a rusticated ground floor; and 761 has a mansard roof over a first story clad in white glazed brick.

4. Soo Yuen Benevolent Association Building, 1922
801–807 Grant Avenue
Albert Schröpfer, architect

This is a remodel of a 1906 brick building. It has a coating of lightly scored cement, an elaborate roofline, a fourth-story balcony, and rounded parapets.

5. Chinese Congregational Church, 1908
21 Walter U. Lum Place
Francis W. Reid, architect

This is Gothic Revival with pointed-arch windows molded in receding layers, with a crenellated parapet at the top. It replaced the congregation's 1876 church destroyed in 1906.

6. Portsmouth Square, 1835
Walter U. Lum Place, and Kearny, Washington, and Clay Streets

This is the site of Yerba Buena plaza where Captain John B. Montgomery raised the American flag in 1846. The city grew from this location, originally one block above the shoreline. Today the former plaza is the heart of Chinatown, a heavily used park set above a parking garage. Several historical plaques and sculptures adorn the space; the most noteworthy is the Robert Louis Stevenson Monument (1897; Willis J. Polk, architect; Bruce Porter and George Piper, sculptors), which depicts the galleon *Hispaniola* from Stevenson's *Treasure Island*.

7. PT&T Chinatown Exchange, 1908–1909
743 Washington Street

Many neighborhoods had distinctive telephone exchanges, but none were quite as wonderful as Chinatown's. The ground floor has been partially remodeled, but the dramatic three-tiered pagoda roof survives.

8. 900 Block of Grant Avenue

This entire block is amazing, with ten brick buildings sporting balconies and various levels of ornamentation. 911–915 Grant has three balconies topped by a swan's neck pediment; 919–925 Grant's top story is like a temple.

9. 1116–1120 and 1115–1121 Stockton Street, 1910, 1920
Luigi Mastropasqua, architect

Both buildings have façades of white glazed brick; 1115–1121 has Art Nouveau ornament

topped with a Chinese pent roof; 1116–1120 has Italianate window hoods on the upper stories.

10. 900 Block of Washington Street
Between Stockton and Powell Streets

A cluster of institutional buildings are located on this block. On the northwest corner of Washington and Stockton is the **Chinese United Methodist Church** (1911; Henry Meyers, architect). Next door to the west, at **940 Washington,** is the former Methodist Chinese Women's School (1907–1910; Julia Morgan, architect); it has an arched entry with colorful floral panels in the keystone and soffit. At 954 Washington is **Commodore Stockton School Annex,** with a Chinese entry and wooden balcony. Across the street is the finest of this group, Commodore Stockton School, recently renamed **Gordon J. Lau School** (1914; Albert Pissis, architect). Built of buff-colored brick, with a monumental arched terra-cotta entry and a beautiful terra-cotta panel in the third story.

11. Chinese Free Masons, 1907
36–38 Spoffard Alley
Charles M. Rousseau, architect

The Chinese Free Masons, also known as the Chee Kung Tong, was founded during the Gold Rush as one of several powerful secret societies. This narrow brick building was home-in-exile to Dr. Sun Yat-sen while he organized the Chinese revolution against the Manchu dynasty until its overthrow in 1911.

12. Goong Quon Cheong Building, 1909, 1920
834–840 Washington Street
A. A. Cantin, architect (1920)

This is a prominent balconied and pagoda-roofed building. All three balconies and roof are highly ornamental. The building is clad in white glazed brick. The top story was added in 1920.

13. Waverly Place
Between Sacramento and Washington Streets

Waverly Place is a narrow, picturesque, two-block-long street; many buildings have pagoda pent roofs, ornamental balconies, recessed top stories that indicate the presence of temples or meeting rooms, and colorful materials. All buildings date from 1907 to around 1911; earlier buildings were destroyed in 1906. Several were built to house benevolent or family associations and still serve that function.

13a. 1–15 Waverly Place, 1908

First Chinese Baptist Church is red clinker brick with trim of contrasting buff-colored brick; the matching third story was added in 1931. Tripartite windows on both the Sacramento and Waverly sides employ Gothic arches.

13b. 125–129 Waverly Place, 1911
O'Brien Brothers, builders

On the top floor is the Tin How Temple, organized during the Gold Rush and dedicated to T'ien Hou, a goddess who protected seafarers and immigrants. Parts of the altar are said to have been saved from the pre-earthquake temple built on this site in the 1870s. The temple is open to visitors.

14. Chinese Six Companies, 1909
843 Stockton Street
Cuthbertson and Mahoney, architects

This is an extremely colorful version of Chinatown's pagoda roof and balcony building type. The façade is blue glazed bricks, yellow-orange tiles, and green roof tiles; the staircase is white terrazzo. The Chinese Six Companies (officially the Chinese Consolidated Benevolent Association) was founded during the Gold Rush as a collection of district associations. Among its many functions, it adjudicated disputes among Chinese and served as a liaison between the Chinese community and City Hall.

15. Chinese YWCA, 1930
965 Clay Street
Julia Morgan, architect

This low-slung brick building, asymmetrical in its composition, has a central arched entry decorated with Chinese patterns and a minimalist pagoda roof. It is now the Chinese Historical Society of America.

16. Donaldina Cameron House, 1907
920 Sacramento Street
McDougall Brothers, architects

The Occidental Board Presbyterian Mission House was founded in 1876 to rescue Chinese girls from slave prostitution and other abuses. This clinker brick building has red-brick trim and a first-story stepped window arrangement that lights an interior staircase. It replaced an 1893 mission house on this site that was destroyed in 1906. From 1897 to the 1930s, its director, Donaldina Cameron, accompanied police officers to rescue the girls; they were then housed and educated in this building.

6 · North of Downtown: Northern Waterfront, Telegraph Hill, North Beach, Russian Hill, Fisherman's Wharf

Northern Waterfront

The first improvements to San Francisco's waterfront were small piers built in 1847 from the foot of Clay Street and Broadway. Beginning in 1849, with the Gold Rush in full swing, Yerba Buena Cove was filled in, and Long Wharf was extended from Leidesdorff Street far into the bay. During the 1860s–1870s, substantial improvements in the form of a stepped pattern of piers and wharfs were made along the entire waterfront. Also in the 1860s, the east side of Telegraph Hill was cut away to create Sansome and Battery Streets, where warehouses and boardinghouses for sailors were built.

Because of silting and the necessity to dredge, a new curved seawall along today's Embarcadero was begun in 1878. The new finger piers on timber piles were quickly eaten away by bay worms called teredos. From 1908 through the 1930s, the finger piers were replaced by piers of reinforced concrete. During the 1890s, the Belt Line Railroad was built along the Embarcadero, with spur tracks efficiently connecting the piers with warehouses; some tracks remain on Green Street.

The advent of containerization in the 1960s relegated San Francisco's waterfront to near obsolescence. A variety of new uses have been found for the historic piers, which are now largely protected.

1. Piers 1–35, 1912–1938
A. A. Pyle, H. B. Fisher, and others, draftsmen (bulkhead buildings)

A. C. Griewank, G. A. Wood, and others, engineers (substructures and transit sheds)

North of the Ferry Building, most of the piers have Classical Revival–style bulkheads, built after 1908 in accordance with the principles of the City Beautiful Movement. Generally the floor and pilings of each pier are reinforced concrete; the aprons are wood to absorb the shock of docking ships. The enormous warehouse-like buildings, called transit sheds, are mostly precast concrete; the roofs are wood with metal or wood supports. With the exception of Pier 7, their Classic Revival façades are nearly uniform.

2. American Biscuit Company, 1906–1908
825–875 Battery Street

Ralph Warner Hart, architect

While the reinforced-concrete building was structurally advanced for its day (the architect was a pioneer in reinforced-concrete construction), traditional design motifs relieve its great bulk. Cornices and rusticated piers divide the building into horizontal and vertical zones, while arched entrances and pedimented parapets give it a classical style. None of the windows and doors is original.

3. Gibbs Warehouses, circa 1855
855 and 915 Front Street

These brick warehouses, the oldest in San Francisco, are not pristine, but an air of antiquity clings to them. Several original iron doors, used for fire protection, remain. Granite windowsills and foundation stones may have been imported from China before local quarries were developed. The handsome rusticated entrances might be sandstone with a protective coating of cement. In 1899, an addition to #915 by architects

Wright and Sanders doubled its size. They were repaired after being damaged in 1906.

4. W. P. Fuller and Company, 1905–1906
1001 Front, 50 Green, and 1010 Battery Streets

Wright and Polk, architects

This was the glass warehouse and mirror factory for Fuller and Co., which also manufactured paints, oils, and varnishes. The firm was founded in Sacramento during the Gold Rush and moved to San Francisco in 1862. Giant arched windows and entrances impart a powerful rhythm to all four façades, enhanced by delicately layered cornices and shallow quoins. Most of the original window sash survives, but entrances have been altered.

5. Union Street buildings

5a. Cudahy Meat Packing Plant, 1907, 1918
55 Union Street

This handsome building of buff-colored brick has dramatic cornices. It was built in two phases: the first two stories in 1907 by architects Henry Geilfuss and Son; the upper two in 1918 by Ward and Blohme. **1050 Battery Street** is another brick meatpacking plant designed in 1907 by Geilfuss and Son, this one for Armour. It has a rusticated base, rounded window heads, and nine-over-nine window sash.

5b. National Ice and Cold Storage, 1914, 1967
151 Union Street

Wurster, Bernardi and Emmons, architects (1967)

Here is an early adaptive reuse of two large brick industrial buildings for design showrooms.

6. Levi Plaza, 1977–1982
Filbert and Battery Streets

HOK, architects

Howard Friedman, consulting architect

Lawrence Halprin, landscape architect

This is a complex of new office buildings and some former warehouses adaptively reused. Built as administrative offices for the blue jeans maker, it was a sensation when it was completed because of the generous open space, the new rounded and stepped-back building forms, and the landscape plan and fountain by Halprin. The complex extends across Battery Street to the Embarcadero, where a park-like open space includes a second fountain and an artificial creek.

7. Italian Swiss Colony, 1903
Southwest corner of Greenwich and Battery Streets

Hemenway and Miller, architects

Built as the office building and bottling plant for Andrea Sbarbaro's Italian Swiss Colony winery in Sonoma County, this is a superior example of Classical Revival styling applied to a red-brick industrial building. Its original window sash has been replaced.

8. City Warehouse Company, 1900
1333 Battery Street

Percy and Polk, architects

A dramatic brick warehouse, it has arched windows of several layers and short "towers" rising from the corners. Two of the

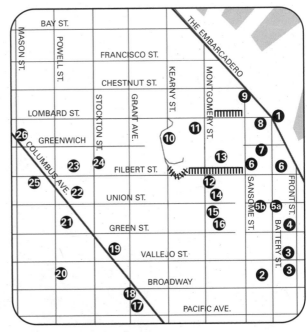

6 • North of Downtown:
Northern Waterfront, Telegraph Hill, North Beach

delivery bays are lined with protective granite. Here, too, window sash is new.

9. Belt Line Railroad Roundhouse, circa 1913
Sansome Street at The Embarcadero

Built as a railroad switching facility, it was used for this purpose until 1982, when it was adapted for commercial use. New door enclosures echo its steel sash windows. **Pier 29 Annex** is the former Belt Line office building, an attractive Mediterranean-style building built in 1909 near Pier 3 and moved here in 1918.

Telegraph Hill

Telegraph Hill derives its name from the semaphore, or telegraph, that was erected on its summit during the Gold Rush to inform downtown merchants of incoming ships. In the decade or so after the Gold Rush, the hill was covered with modest houses built mainly for European emigrants, with Italian, Spanish, and Portuguese predominating as the nineteenth century drew to a close. In 1876, public-spirited citizens purchased the top of the hill to save it from development and donated it to the city as Pioneer Park. Many houses at the top of the hill were saved in 1906, and those that remain form a historic district. The hill is picturesque, with great views and narrow alleys; it is best to walk.

10. Coit Tower, 1933
Telegraph Hill Boulevard, end of Lombard Street
Arthur Brown Jr., architect

The tower was built in Pioneer Park with funds donated by Lillie Hitchcock Coit (1842–1929), who appointed herself mascot to one of the city's volunteer fire companies. Moderne in style, it is notable for its wide shallow flutings that impart a graceful elegance. On interior walls are fresco murals with social, sometimes socialist, themes that were once controversial but are now highly regarded. They have a gritty realism and portray, with restraint, the difficulty of life in the Depression.

11. Julius' Castle, 1923, 1928
302–304 Greenwich Street
Luigi Mastropasqua, architect

This wood-shingled "castle" was built as a restaurant by Julius Roz, who came to San Francisco from Italy in 1898. He operated the restaurant until his death in 1943. Two turrets and several balconies are edged with wood pieces that impart the impression of being crenellated like a castle.

12. Malloch Apartments, 1937
1360 Montgomery Street
Irvin W. Goldstine, architect

An outstanding Streamlined Moderne building, it has silver scrafitto murals by Alfred du Pont on exterior walls, a large and impressive etched-glass transom, a glass-brick elevator column, and an ocean liner staircase in the open vestibule.

13. Workingmen's cottages, circa 1857–1882
200 Block of Filbert Street and Napier Lane

The 200 block of Filbert is a street of steps that terminate more than 200 feet below on Sansome Street. **218–220 Filbert Street** was built in 1882 for quarryman and laborer Patrick McDermott. **222 Filbert** (1879) is an Italianate, now covered with shingles; the ground floor was originally a grocery store. In 1949, Grace Marchant moved here and voluntarily began cleaning up debris; she planted the "street," turning it into an exotic garden of more than 100 species that she maintained until her death in 1982. The cottages at **224, 226, 228,** and **230 Filbert** date from the late 1850s and 1860s and vary in

style. Most are very simple, but 228 (circa 1869) has wavy bargeboard in the gable and Gothic drip molds over the windows. **Napier Lane,** a boardwalk, contains several cottages built between the 1850s and the 1870s.

14. Andrews House,
circa 1858
31 Alta Street

This simple, three-story gabled-roof house with double balconies over a brick first story has had little alteration. Its immediate neighbors, also very old, have been extensively remodeled.

15. John J. Cooney House,
early 1850s
291 Union Street

Originally a two-story house that was later raised a story, its false front and Italianate detailing were added around 1880.

16. David G. Robinson House, 1854
9 Calhoun Terrace

The gable has a cutout bargeboard that gives this house its Gothic Revival style. The first owner was a pharmacist, a city alderman, and owner-manager of a drama theater called the American. **66 Calhoun Terrace** (1940) was designed by Richard Neutra.

North Beach

North Beach refers to the shoreline originally located along Francisco Street before the cove was filled in 1881, creating Fisherman's Wharf. Columbus Avenue, the wide diagonal boulevard that cuts through the grid, was graded in 1873–1874 to make a convenient connection between downtown and the North Beach wharfs.

During its first century, the area was decidedly an immigrant and blue-collar neighborhood in character. Italians arrived in significant numbers beginning in the 1860s, and by the 1890s North Beach, along with Telegraph Hill, was considered to be the city's Latin Quarter. The neighborhood burned in 1906, and was quickly rebuilt with Classical Revival flats by Italian contractors and architects.

North Beach still retains an Italian flavor, especially evident in the number of Italian restaurants, cafes, and bakeries. During the 1950s, Grant Avenue became the center of the Beat Generation (called Beatniks by columnist Herb Caen). North Beach became "cool," and a plethora of establishments along Grant Avenue, Broadway, and Columbus Avenue opened to serve this clientele; Caffe Trieste, Vesuvio's, City Lights, Enrico's, and a revived Purple Onion still remain in business.

17. Vesuvio's, 1918
253–255 Columbus Avenue
Italo Zanolini, architect

The second story of this building has an elegant Classical composition; deeply set arched windows are framed by columns and balconettes; a curved Palladian window is set behind a curved balcony where the façade turns the corner to Jack Kerouac Alley. The plate-glass storefront was painted for Vesuvio's, the Beat-era saloon founded in 1949 by Henri Lenoir that is still in business. The interior is a trip back to the 1950s. The first tenant was A. Cavalli bookstore, which moved here from the City Lights building.

18. City Lights, 1907
261 Columbus Avenue
Oliver Everett, architect

This stucco-clad brick building on a wedge-shaped lot resembles a small Parisian commercial building, and indeed was built for a French owner. In 1953, Beat poet Lawrence Ferlinghetti and Peter Martin opened City Lights, the first bookstore in the United States devoted to paperbacks. The transom has recently been restored.

19. St. Francis of Assisi Catholic Church,
1859–1860
610 Vallejo Street

Thomas England, architect

This twin-towered Gothic Revival church was gutted by fire in 1906 but was rebuilt in 1913 within the old walls by architect Charles J. Devlin. Clustered columns support the rib-vaulted ceiling and divide the nave from the side aisles. There is Gothic tracery in the wainscoting, the front and side altars, the vestibule transom, and even the pews; the stained-glass windows are very nice. The parish closed in 1994, but the church remains open as a shrine to St. Francis.

20. John J. Delucchi Sheet Metal Works, 1921
1526 Powell Street

An amazing display of sheet metal wizardry covers the front of this building; imprints of bricks, Spanish tiles, and classical moldings advertise the business within.

21. Fugazi Hall, 1912
678 Green Street
Italo Zanolini, architect

This grand building has a rusticated first story and intense classical ornament above. A bust of banker and travel agent John F. Fugazi, who donated this building to the Italian community, is in the parapet. This has long been the home of *Beach Blanket Babylon,* the longest-running hit musical revue in theater history, founded by Steve Silver in 1974.

22. Washington Square Park, 1958
Bounded by Union, Filbert, and Stockton Streets, and Columbus Avenue
Douglas Baylis and Lawrence Halprin, landscape architects

Incorporating ideas from ten North Beach clubs, Halprin created a master plan that Baylis's design followed. The park is remarkably uncluttered: a great expanse of lawns bordered by curvilinear paths, with trees and benches along the periphery. The few monuments include a bronze statue of Benjamin Franklin (1879); a monument to San Francisco's fire department (1933), sculpted by Haig Patigian and donated by Lillie Hitchcock Coit; and a concrete bench (dedicated in 1997) that honors Juana Briones, North Beach's first resident from 1836 to 1847.

23. Sts. Peter and Paul Church, 1922–1939
666 Filbert Street
Charles Fantoni, architect

This great North Beach landmark is located opposite Washington Square. Although the rich ornamentation is Romanesque, the church has soaring twin towers profuse with thin pointed pinnacles that give it a distinctly vertical feeling. The building was completed by architect John Porporato.

24. Telegraph Hill Neighborhood House, 1907–1909
1734 Stockton Street
Bernard Maybeck, architect

This picturesque wood-sided building is an important example of Maybeck's rustic architecture and is also significant for its history as a settlement house. The Telegraph Hill Neighborhood Association (Tel-Hi) still exists but at a different location in North Beach. Additions in 1913 and 1928 are also by Maybeck.

25. Hildebrand Stables, 1906
721 Filbert Street
Moses J. Lyon, architect

The former horse stables are clinker brick with redbrick trim; it has a Mission Revival parapet, pent roof, and arched openings. Wood roof trusses allow for an expansive interior. Only the window sash has been changed.

26. North Beach Branch Library, 1958
2000 Mason Street
Appleton and Wolford, architects

This building is notable for its zigzag window treatment along Columbus Avenue.

Russian Hill

Due to its steep slopes, Russian Hill developed gradually between the 1850s and 1880s; parts of the western slope were not built up until the 1930s. In 1906, several areas were saved by residents who defied military orders to leave their homes. These are places where there are scattered nineteenth-century buildings that survived the earthquake. Most of the hill was rebuilt between 1906 and the 1910s in Classical Revival and Mediterranean styles. On the east slope and along Union Street, many houses and flats were designed by Italian architects. Neighborhood commercial districts grew up along streetcar lines at the intersection of Union and Hyde Streets, and along Polk Street. During the 1910s and 1920s, numerous eight- to fourteen-story apartment buildings were erected. A wave of much taller high-rises followed during the 1950s and 1960s; protests led to a height limit of forty feet.

27. The Summit of Russian Hill
Blocks bounded by Broadway, Green, Taylor, and Jones Streets

This cul-de-sac is one of San Francisco's special places. Approached off Jones Street up an elevated ramp, the summit contains a group of significant pre-1906 houses and magnificent views of downtown and the bay.

27a. The Vallejo Street Steps and Ramps, 1914
Willis Polk, architect

This is a three-part project, with ramps at Jones Street, steps at Taylor, and a turnaround in the middle. The balusters have become emblematic of the summit area. Built at the instigation of Horatio P. Livermore, the project was paid for by adjacent property owners.

27b. Mediterranean townhouses, 1916

Willis Polk, architect

These four Mediterranean Revival–style townhouses overlooking the Vallejo Street ramp have arched corner windows, wrought-iron balconies, and dark wood window trim. On Russian Hill Place they are one story and create an intimate streetscape.

27c. Polk-Williams House, 1892–1893

1015–1019 Vallejo Street

Willis Polk, architect

This duplex is one of the landmarks of the Bay Area Shingle style. The eastern half was the home of architect Willis Polk and his family, and the western half housed artist Dora Williams. Wood shingles wrap around corners to provide a uniform textured coating. Bands of casement windows stretch across the main stories, and gables with flared eaves surmount each half of the building. The west gable is filled with a Gothic window divided into many lights.

27d. Livermore House

40 Florence Street

Robert A. M. Stern, architect (1988)

A one-story Gold Rush cottage (1854) was enlarged to its present state by a series of additions (1870s, 1898, 1903, 1988). Willis Polk lived here between 1891 and 1892 when he remod-

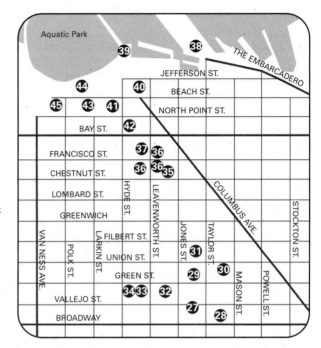

6 • North of Downtown: Russian Hill, Fisherman's Wharf

eled the interior of the first story. From 1897 to 1986, this was home to members of the Livermore family. The latest alterations are by noted eastern architect Robert A. M. Stern.

27e. Marshall Houses, 1888–1889

1034 and 1036 Vallejo Street

Joseph Worcester, designer

These are the oldest shingle-style houses in the city. Worcester was the pastor of the Swedenborgian Church, an amateur architect, and a close friend of Willis Polk's. He rejected the Victorian styles then current and advocated design that was closer to nature. A third house in this series and Worcester's own house to the east are no longer standing.

27f. The Hermitage, 1982

1020 Vallejo Street

Esherick Homsey Dodge and Davis, architects

This shingled condominium project is modern in its massing but was designed to be compatible with the older houses. The wood balusters relate to those on the Vallejo Street Steps and Ramps.

27g. 1000 Vallejo Street, 1957–1958

Anshen + Allen, architects

This L-shaped house with a broad cantilevered corner and repetitive perpendicular window treatment aggressively breaks with the general aesthetic of the neighborhood. It replaced a great house (1905–1906) by the Los Angeles architect Myron Hunt.

27h. The Summit, 1963–1965
999 Green Street

Claude Oakland, architect

This reinforced-concrete high-rise was one of the last projects of developer Joseph Eichler. Structurally daring, it combines International and Corporate Brutalist styles and overwhelms the neighborhood. It replaced a shingled house (1909) by Julia Morgan.

27i. Atkinson House, 1853
1053 Broadway

William H. Ranlett, architect

This is the oldest Italianate-style house in the city. It was modeled after an earlier design by Ranlett, published when he still practiced in New York City. Ranlett's own home at **1637 Taylor** (1854) still stands around the corner but is greatly altered. In 1893, Kate Atkinson, daughter of the first owner, hired Willis Polk to remodel the interior in beautifully carved woodwork and paneling. The home then became a gathering place for artists that included Gelett Burgess, Bruce Porter, and the Polks. After 1906, the exterior wooden siding was replaced by a coat of stucco.

28. Nuestra Sonora de Guadalupe Church, 1911–1912
908 Broadway

Shea and Lofquist, architects

This quietly elegant Baroque church was built for North Beach's Spanish and Portuguese population.

29. Luigi Demartini House, 1895–1896
1809 Taylor Street, at the corner of Macondray Lane

William Mooser and Son, architects

This Queen Anne with a two-story rounded corner window bay is topped by a conical roof.

Macondray Lane is a picturesque two-block-long pathway/staircase between Taylor, Jones and Leavenworth Streets. **15–17 Macondray Lane** (1850s, 1905) was home to artist Giuseppe Cadenasso, who added the view tower and the plaster ornament in 1905.

30. Flats, 1912–1917
869–897 Union Street

A group of five flats, by three of the city's leading Italian architects, all feature patterned brick first stories and wooden upper stories, with plenty of ornament. The bay windows march up the hill in a pleasing rhythm. **869–871** and **873–877 Union** (1912) were designed by John A. Porporato; **881–885 Union** (1913) by Charles Fantoni; and **887–889** and **893–897 Union** (1916–1917) by Paul F. Demartini.

31. 924–926 Union, 1917
Luigi Mastropasqua, architect

This set of flats is typical of Mastropasqua's appeal. The pendant ornament on the bay windows is Art Nouveau in style, and the parapet with an arched cutout is Classical.

32. Houses, pre-1909
1033–1067 Green Street

This group of houses was saved in 1906 when the residents persuaded soldiers to preserve them instead of sacrificing them to create a fire break. **1033 Green** (1868) is an early Italianate, moved here in 1891 from Nob Hill. **1039–1043 Green** (1885;

Newsom Brothers, architects) was raised, and the current first story and lovely staircase were added in 1893. **1045 Green** (1867) was built as a very simple cottage; the bay window was added in the 1880s, and the tower and shingles after 1906. **1055 Green** (1866) was remodeled by Julia Morgan in 1915; only the roof and cornice are original.

32a. Octagon House, 1859
1067 Green Street

As recommended by Orson Fowler in a book about octagons, it was built of concrete. The lower stories are original, while the mansard roof and cupola were added about 1898.

32b. 1088 Green, 1908
Newton J. Tharp, designer

It is the former SFFD Engine No. 31, a charming blend of Tudor and Craftsman styles.

33. Bellaire Apartments, 1930
1101 Green Street

H. C. Baumann, architect

This was Baumann's signature high-rise apartment building loaded with modeled decoration.

34. Shingle-Tudor houses, 1909
1135–1139 Green Street

Maxwell G. Bugbee, architect

These three houses sit dramatically upon a high retaining wall (1877).

35. San Francisco Art Institute, 1926
800 Chestnut Street

Bakewell and Brown, architects

This picturesque Mediterranean Revival has rustic beige textured-concrete cladding, an overscaled Baroque entry, a medieval Italian tower, tile roofs, and a cloister-like entry courtyard. A mural by Diego Rivera (1931) graces the art gallery. The dreary Brutalist-style addition on the north is by Paffard Keatinge-Clay (1968–1970).

36. Group of 1906 survivors
800–900 Block of Chestnut and Leavenworth Streets

A group of earthquake and fire survivors dot these blocks, including **930 Chestnut** (1866) and **944 Chestnut** (1864), which are early Italianates; **2500 Leavenworth Street** (1884; William H. Wharf, architect), a Stick-Eastlake cottage; and **2434 Leavenworth** (1890; T. J. Welsh, architect), a Stick-Eastlake house.

37. Bertram Alanson Residence, 1929–1930
828 Francisco Street

Hyman and Appleton, architects

This massive Tudor house is one of the neighborhood landmarks. It was visited frequently by W. Somerset Maugham, a close friend of Alanson's.

Fisherman's Wharf

In 1900, the state moved the wharf, devoted to the fishing industry, from the foot of Union Street to the foot of Taylor Street. The Del Monte warehouse and cannery as well as Ghirardelli Square are the principal survivors from the industrial period. The first restaurants consisted mainly of open-air stalls where vendors sold a quick lunch to the workers. By the 1920s, restaurants were built, some by former fishermen, and the rest is history. Tourists have greatly outnumbered the fishermen for decades.

38. Pier 45, 1926–1929
At the foot of Taylor Street

Pier 45 is a truly massive pier, with four Art Deco transit sheds. It was designed by Harbor Commission draftsman H. B. Fisher and engineer H. Baldwin.

Immediately south of the pier is a cluster of restaurants that form the heart of Fisherman's Wharf. The most architecturally distinguished is Fisherman's Grotto #9, built in stages for Mike Geraldi, a former fisherman. The Venetian dining room

downstairs was his original restaurant (1935), while the Mediterranean-style second floor is a 1953 addition. Next door is Alioto #8. The numbers refer to the old stall numbers used before the restaurant buildings were constructed.

39. Hyde Street Pier, 1922
Foot of Hyde Street

The pier was built by the Golden Gate Ferry Company for its car ferry service to Sausalito and later to Berkeley. It had a fleet of twenty-six ferryboats with a capacity of eighty-five to ninety cars each. Golden Gate Ferry merged with the Southern Pacific Railroad in 1929, and service was discontinued in 1938. Today it houses the San Francisco Maritime National Historical Park with a great collection of historic ships and boats.

40. Del Monte Warehouse and Cannery, 1907–1909
Block bounded by Beach, Jefferson, Leavenworth, and Hyde Streets

Philip L. Bush, company engineer

Joseph Esherick (adaptive reuse, 1963)

These two buildings were once part of the Del Monte Company's cannery. At the northeast corner of Beach and Hyde, the exterior of the Haslett Warehouse (now a hotel) has been carefully preserved; the National Maritime Park Visitors Center is on the first floor. The Cannery is located at the northwest corner of Beach and Leavenworth, and was altered in 1963, with many new openings added when it was converted into shops.

35

41. Buena Vista Café, 1912
2765 Hyde Street

August Nordin, architect

The Buena Vista was founded across the street about 1890 as a workingman's saloon and restaurant. Irish coffee made its American debut here in 1952. The three-story Classical Revival design is a typical post-earthquake apartment-over-shops building.

42. John W. Sinclair House, 1865
2626 Hyde Street

This lovely Gothic Revival cottage was almost certainly built by the first owner, Sinclair, who was a carpenter. Landscape architect Thomas Church moved here in 1933 and added the north wing in 1938.

43. Ghirardelli Chocolate Factory, 1900–1922
Block bounded by North Point, Beach, Larkin, and Polk Streets

William Mooser II, architect

This excellent collection of red-brick industrial buildings has contrasting beige lintels, quoins, base, cornice, and ornament. The clock tower building is Italian Renaissance in style, while the other buildings are medieval in feeling. In the middle of the block is the 1866 factory building of the Pioneer Woolen Mill, which the Ghirardellis incorporated into their complex. The complex was converted into shopping around 1964 by architects Wurster, Bernardi and Emmons. The North Point façades are immaculately preserved.

44. National Maritime Museum, 1936–1939
At the foot of Polk Street

William Mooser III, architect

Built as the Aquatic Park Casino, this building is a must for those interested in seafaring history as well as for those who love Streamlined Moderne architecture. The exterior etchings are by artist Sargent Johnson, and the interior murals are by Hilaire Hiler.

45. Fontana Apartments, 1960–1965
1000, 1050 North Point

Hammerberg and Herman, architects

These high-rise apartments, which block and privatize views, so outraged the neighbors on Russian Hill that they successfully pushed to have the district's height limit lowered to forty feet.

7 • Fort Mason • Marina District and Cow Hollow

Fort Mason

1. Fort Mason

Bay Street, between Van Ness Avenue and Marina Boulevard

The former U.S. Army base, declared surplus property in 1964, has been part of the Golden Gate National Recreation Area since 1972. It was a Spanish fort as early as the 1790s, and the United States reserved it for military use in 1851 but did not occupy it until 1862. During the interim, several people, including John C. Frémont, built their homes here as squatters. With the exception of a few older buildings, the former base has a Mediterranean look with white stucco walls and red-tile roofs.

1a. McDowell Hall, 1877

East side of Franklin Street

This was built as the residence of the Commanding General of the Department of the Pacific, and during the second half of the twentieth century, it was an officers' club. A Stick-style porte cochere fronts a plain clapboard building with a hipped roof, whose broad eaves are supported by brackets. North of McDowell Hall are three remaining but much altered "squatters" houses from the mid-1850s. At the very end of Franklin Street is an 1863 brick battery.

1b. Early Fort Mason buildings

West side of Franklin Street

The former Post Headquarters, flanked by two small Greek Revival buildings, were built between 1862 and 1864, just after the army took control of the site. There are also two simple Queen Anne houses dating from 1891 that served as Hospital Stewards' Quarters; a parade ground, just to the west, is now the location of a community garden. The Golden Gate National Recreation Area Headquarters, Building 201, was built in 1902 as the Post Hospital.

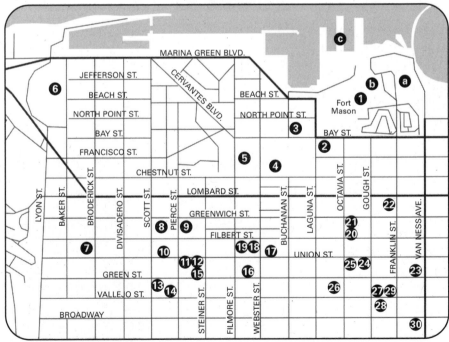

1c. Port of Embarkation, 1910–1912
Lower Fort Mason, east of Laguna Street

Rankin, Kellogg, and Crane, architects

Lower Fort Mason has three piers and five warehouses, all made of reinforced concrete with industrial steel sash windows. The piers have military insignia in each gable end, and the warehouses have hipped clay-tile roofs. This was the U.S. Port of Embarkation for military activities in the Pacific. Arriving wounded were transported to Letterman Hospital in the Presidio via a rail line along Marina Boulevard. The buildings are leased and managed by the Fort Mason Association for use by nonprofit arts groups and as exhibition halls.

Marina District and Cow Hollow

During the 1850s, the sparsely settled district known as Spring Valley was dotted with farms and dairies as well as tanneries and roadhouses. As it became more settled, industries such as the Fulton Iron Works, a gas plant, distilleries, and a pork packing plant all located here, but dairy farms proliferated, and by the 1880s, it was known as "Cow Hollow." The last dairy closed in 1911.

In 1912, nearly all land north of Chestnut Street was condemned for the 1915 Panama-Pacific International Exposition. After the fair closed, all of the buildings except the Palace of Fine

Arts were either demolished or moved. The site was soon filled with residential buildings that have a homogeneous look of Mediterranean stucco and tile. South of Chestnut Street, there is a more varied mix of buildings— a hodge-podge but an interesting one. Lombard Street, widened in 1937 to accommodate Golden Gate Bridge traffic, became lined with motels.

2. The Heritage, 1924–1925
3400 Laguna Street

Julia Morgan, architect

The redbrick building with terra-cotta trim is restrained English Tudor. It was built for the Ladies' Protection and Relief Society, founded in 1853 to serve destitute women and orphans. It is now a home for the elderly.

3. San Francisco Gaslight Company, 1893
3640 Buchanan Street

Joseph B. Crockett, designer

This picturesque brick building with pressed clay trim and round tower is the last industrial building in this neighborhood. It served as the meter room and offices for the San Francisco Gaslight Co., which made gas for heating and lighting from coal and petroleum that were delivered to its nearby wharf. Crockett, the company president, designed the complex and supervised its construction. PG&E closed the plant in the 1950s.

4. Marina Branch Library, 1953
1890 Chestnut Street

Appleton and Wolford, architects

Here is another of these architects' angular libraries of brick, wood, and glass.

5. Marina Middle School, 1935
3500 Fillmore Street

George W. Kelham and Will P. Day, architects

A Moderne school with Art Deco details is typical of the Depression era.

6. Palace of Fine Arts, 1913–1914; rebuilt, 1960s–1970s
Baker Street, south of Marina Green Boulevard

Bernard Maybeck, architect

This is San Francisco's most popular building, which is unsurprising, because Bernard Maybeck is the city's favorite architect, and the Palace was Maybeck at his most inspired. Built for the 1915 Panama-Pacific International Exposition, this was the fair's art gallery—"Palace of Fine Arts."

The Palace consists of a rotunda half-surrounded by a colonnade and fronting on a lagoon. It was built of a durable plaster that imitated travertine and was colorfully tinted—burnt orange for the dome, a turquoise-green

3

6

border around the dome, and columns of pale green and ochre.

Maybeck wrote that his motifs were sadness, beauty, and the ruins of antiquity. These qualities are easily seen in the expressions of the god-like figures adorning the various planters, and the classical imagery. The colonnade seems to recede into infinity. The atmosphere is intimate and monumental at the same time. The Palace is a place to linger.

After the fair closed and the land cleared for development, a groundswell for preserving the Palace emerged. It helped that it was located on land belonging to the Presidio and not the city. By the 1950s, it had deteriorated badly, but again the public demanded that it be restored and saved. Casts were taken of the original structures, and it was rebuilt in reinforced concrete. The rotunda was rebuilt between 1964 and 1967, and the colonnade between 1973 and 1975. The major donor was businessman Walter Johnson. Today, parts of the Palace are again suffering from decay; a nonprofit

group, the Maybeck Foundation, is raising funds for its next restoration.

7. Shingle houses, 1901
2715–2727 Filbert Street

John A. Hoots, builder

These four houses illustrate how deftly local builders absorbed the latest styles, often without benefit of architects. Each is slightly different, but all have steeply pitched gable roofs, sawtooth shingle patterns, and eyebrow projections in the gables.

8. North End Police Station, 1912
2475 Greenwich Street

Alfred I. Coffey, architect

Meyer and Reid, architects

Generally Spanish Revival in style, the former police station has a central arched entry outlined in buff-colored brick, and a Spanish tile roof; spiky lanterns flank the entry.

9. John Glynn Fourplex, 1877
2371–2379 Greenwich Street

This one-story four-unit Italianate is a rare example of its type. It has a symmetrical façade, with triangular pediments over each

entrance and a segmental arch pediment in the middle of the cornice; door brackets and window trim end in acanthus leaves.

10. House, 1892
2460 Union Street

Mooser and Cuthbertson, architects

An extensively remodeled older house has a mansard roof pierced by a gambrel-roofed dormer containing a pair of arched windows. An elaborate projecting roof held by carved brackets shelters the entry.

11. Apartments, 1930–1931
2383 Union Street and 2860 Pierce Street

Albert Schröpfer, architect

The picturesque massing of this Mediterranean Revival apartment building sets it apart from its neighbors. A rounded tower and a gable-roofed wing define an entry courtyard. It is clad in stucco, has a balcony and bay windows of carved wood, and has plaster ornament.

12. St. Mary the Virgin Episcopal Church, 1891
2325 Union Street

This modest neighborhood church was enhanced by improvements made between 1934 and 1952 by architects William Wurster, Ellsworth Johnson, and Warren C. Perry. Mosaics are by Ruth Cravath, and the courtyard fresco is by Lucienne Bloch and Stephen Dimitroff. The shingled church is quiet, rustic, unassuming, and artistic.

13. Houses, 1891–1893
2421, 2423 Green Street

Ernest Coxhead, architect

The McGauley House (1892) at **2423** is a traditional English cottage dominated by a tapering brick chimney that pierces the eave. Coxhead's own residence (1893) at **2421** is a spare Shingle-style house, almost modern in its massing and composition.

14. Casebolt House, 1868
2727 Pierce Street

Hoagland and Newsom, architects

The neighborhood was almost rural when this mansion was built for Henry Casebolt, a prominent manufacturer of carriages and wagons, and the owner of a horse-car line, for which he made the cars. A columned entrance porch fronts a projecting central bay with paired arched windows and a crowning pediment.

15. St. Vincent de Paul Church, 1916
2320 Green Street

Shea and Lofquist, architects

This is one of the picturesque churches that Frank Shea designed for the Catholic Church, variously with his brother Will and John Lofquist. The sanctuary is covered by a large gambrel roof. Its square tower is the neighborhood landmark. The exterior texture is imparted by wood and brick. The interior is bathed in a warm glow of colors from the stained-glass windows.

16. Leander Sherman House, 1876–1877
2160 Green Street

This Italianate house with a mansard roof is one of the cultural landmarks of San Francisco.

It was built as the home of Leander Sherman, founder of the Sherman, Clay and Co. music store. As a promoter of the musical arts, he helped establish the local symphony and opera companies, and held recitals in this house.

17. James Cudworth Residence, 1874
2040 Union Street

S. C. Bugbee and Son, architects

Although altered to provide retail space, this Italianate retains its basic character, and is important as one of the last surviving houses by S. C. Bugbee, an important early San Francisco architect who designed four Nob Hill mansions in the 1870s. Cudworth, one of Cow Hollow's first dairy ranchers, became a bank director and real estate speculator.

18. Vedanta Society, 1905, 1907
2961–2963 Webster Street

Joseph Leonard, architect-builder

The Vedanta Society is a branch of Hinduism that emphasizes the universality of all religions. This one-of-a-kind building sports five different roof towers, said to represent the world's different religious traditions. The first two stories, typical San Francisco flat design, were built in 1905. The third floor and the multi-domed roof were added in 1907. The third floor is surrounded by an open arcade with scalloped ogee arches. Similar ogee arches have been added above the first-story windows, second-story cornice, and Filbert Street entrance. Although the society built a new temple in 1953 at 2323 Vallejo, this one continues to be used.

19. Triplex, 1882
1978–1982 Filbert

James G. Behrens, architect

A rare Stick-style triplex of three cottages, each has a gabled roof with decorative bargeboard, and gabled roofs over each entrance.

20. Bareilles Farm House, 1870
2940 Octavia Street

This is one of the last dairy farm houses standing in Cow Hollow. The crisp, finely detailed window and door trim and the cornice also make this an important early example of the Italianate style.

21. Italianate house, 1872; moved to this site in 1900
1753–1755 Greenwich

Cow Hollow became the destination for many houses that were considered obsolete. Built in Pacific Heights in 1872 and moved here in 1900, this house is the most elegant of such. Note the generously wide trim around the paired second-story windows.

22. Blackstone Court
Off Franklin Street, between Lombard and Greenwich Streets

This cul-de-sac is a remnant of the informal street system that served the district in the 1850s before the current street grid was surveyed. At **9–11 Blackstone** is a simple balconied house that was probably built in the 1850s and was moved to this site between 1889 and 1893. The house was raised a story in 1906.

23. Holy Trinity Russian Orthodox Cathedral, 1909
1520 Green Street

C. B. Ripley, architect

The congregation relocated to this property after its church in North Beach burned in 1906. This small church has blue onion domes and classical ornament.

24. Octagon house, 1861
2645 Gough Street

One of five octagonal houses built in San Francisco in the 1850s–1860s is also one of two that survive. When threatened with demolition in 1952, the Colonial Dames of America moved it across Gough Street to its current location. Although the interior is altered and the siding is not original, its shape and style convey its early date.

25. The James S. Dyer House, 1860s or 1870s
1757 Union Street

This is another rare survivor of Cow Hollow's early history; the first owner began farming here in 1860. The flat and false-fronted Italianate is notable for its window hoods and quoins.

26. Golden Gate Valley Branch Library, 1917
1801 Green Street

Ernest Coxhead, architect

A curved façade and classical ornament executed in terra-cotta contribute to this very inspired library design.

27. Burr House, 1878
1772 Vallejo Street

T. J. Welsh, architect

This impressive Italianate has a pair of three-story angled bays gracing its façade. The third story of these bays extends to become dormers in the mansard roof.

28. Digby Brooks Studio, 1921
1737–1757 Vallejo Street

Henry Gutterson, architect

Built for an art-metal artisan as his home and studio, the picturesque medieval complex is constructed of reddish, reinforced, hollow clay-tile blocks and wood. Additions have been made to accommodate condominiums.

29. Art Nouveau flats, 1902
2413–2417 Franklin Street

James Francis Dunn, architect

Swirling plaster ornament falls from the second-floor balconies to embrace the arch of each first-story opening. Lush classical ornament frames the second- and third-story windows, and male figures peer dramatically from beneath the cornice.

30. St. Brigid Catholic Church, 1902, 1930
Southwest corner of Broadway and Van Ness Avenue

Shea & Shea, architects (1902)

Henry A. Minton, architect (1930)

This granite church was originally constructed in 1902–1904, but the façade was remodeled in 1930. The granite blocks were reused; the rose window and its general character were retained. A new compound-arched entrance of carved terra-cotta using some Celtic motifs was added, and the height of the tower was raised in 1965. The parish founded on this site in 1864 was closed by the archdiocese in the 1990s; former parishioners are attempting to save the church from demolition.

8 · Pacific Heights · Presidio Heights

Pacific Heights

The area between Van Ness Avenue and Fillmore Street, and California Street and Broadway was named Pacific Heights in 1868. Today, Pacific Heights extends north and west of these early boundaries. By the 1880s, it was the city's premier residential district, even surpassing Nob Hill in esteem. While most of the truly grand Victorian houses have been replaced by apartment buildings, there remain wonderful houses from the late nineteenth and early twentieth centuries.

1. Haas-Lilienthal House, 1886
2007 Franklin Street

Peter R. Schmidt, architect

The impressive Queen Anne has complex massing, numerous gabled bays, a round corner tower with a conical roof, and projecting and receding elements. All gable ends and the top of the conical roof have finials providing an upward thrust. Since the

1970s, it has been home to the Foundation for San Francisco's Architectural Heritage and is open for weekly tours.

2. Italianate houses, 1871–1875
1911, 1913, 1915 Sacramento Street

Three flat-fronted Italianates have elegant window surrounds typical of the period.

3. First Church of Christ, Scientist, 1911
1700 Franklin Street

Edgar Mathews, architect

The windows and corbelling are Romanesque, while the form is late medieval or Renaissance. The polychrome terra-cotta is brightly hued, while the variegated brick is more subtle.

4. Victorian houses
Northwest corner of California and Franklin Streets

Here are three prominent Victorians with spacious yards.

1834 California (1876) was built in the Italianate style with a gabled roof. In 1895, architects Percy and Hamilton added the conical tower. **1818 California** (1876) is a typical, but large, bay-windowed Italianate with a second-story pedimented window. **1701 Franklin** (1895; William H. Lillie, architect) is a sprawling Queen Anne with corner towers and a band of classical rinceaux (plant motifs).

5. Atherton House, 1881–1882
1990 California Street

Horizontal lines, clipped gable, and short tower place this Queen Anne close to those on the East Coast. It was built for Dominga Atherton, widow of merchant Faxon Dean Atherton, and mother-in-law of novelist Gertrude Atherton, who wrote of Dominga and this house in her memoirs. The architect was likely John Marquis, who did other work for the family.

6

High-quality Beaux-Arts classicism is applied in miniature to this narrow two-story building, the home and medical office of Dr. Albert Abrams.

8c. Queen Anne houses, 1885, 1889
2000, 2004 Gough Street

2000 Gough (1885; William F. Smith, architect) is a blend of Stick and Queen Anne. **2004 Gough** (1889; J. C. Mathews and Son, architects) is a full-fledged Queen Anne, complete with corner tower, fishscale shingles, sunbursts, and delicate plaster ornament.

8d. Community Apartments, 1925
2006 Washington Street

C. A. Meussdorffer, architect

The ten-story cooperative apartment block overlooks a garden to the west. The composition has a rusticated base with arched windows and port cochere; the top floor is defined by a balcony and arched windows. **2000 Washington** (1922) and **1925 Gough** (circa 1908) are apartments also by Meussdorffer.

8e. Spreckels Mansion, 1912
2080 Washington Street

MacDonald and Applegarth, architects

Built for Adolph Spreckels (son of Claus Spreckels, the sugar manufacturer) and his wife, Alma, the mansion is an essay in formal French classicism and occupies half a square block. The carved white stone and the sugary source of the family's wealth have spurred many references to the confectioner's art.

6. Victorian houses
2018–2026 California Street

These Victorians drip with milled ornament, most of it Eastlake: **2018** (1886), **2020** (1882; Kenitzer and Raun, architects), **2022** (1882; Charles Geddes, architect), and **2026** (1878).

7. Sherith Israel, 1905
Northeast corner of California and Webster Streets

Albert Pissis, architect

This great Romanesque synagogue built of Colusa sandstone has been painted rose ocher. Giant arched windows with deep reveals face both streets and a dome rises from the center; interior paintings are by Attilio Moretti.

8. Lafayette Square
Laguna, Gough, Washington, and Sacramento Streets

In 1867, the city acquired this block and gave it its name. It was landscaped with curvilinear paths and concrete coping by John McLaren after 1900.

8a. Lafayette Apartments, 1905
2135 Sacramento Street

C. A. Meussdorffer, architect

Massive classical brackets flank the entry and support the second-floor balcony. There is a flowing quality to the ornament in the upper stories.

8b. Abrams House, 1921
2151 Sacramento Street

Mel I. Schwartz, architect

8f. Senator James Phelan House, 1915
2150 Washington Street

Charles Peter Weeks, architect

Here is a U-shaped brick-clad Mediterranean.

9. Glenlee Terrace, 1912
1925–1955 Jackson Street

Arthur J. Laib, architect

• A picturesque terraced apartment complex steps up the hillside; it has arched porticos, tapering porch posts, clay-tile roofs, and a central courtyard, a blend of Mission Revival and Craftsman styles.

10. Tuckerville House, 1870
2209 Jackson Street

David Farquharson, architect

"Tuckerville," as it became known, was a project of architect David Farquharson and jeweler J. W. Tucker. On this square block they built twenty-six one-story duplexes; this is the last survivor. The modest dimensions and restrained Italianate ornament indicate that Pacific Heights had not yet become the destination of moneyed society in 1870.

11. Montellano Apartments, circa 1914
2411 Webster Street

James Francis Dunn, architect

Note the fine sculptural lions' heads and garlands below the balcony and the first-story window trim on one of Dunn's French-inspired apartment buildings.

12. Bourne House, 1896
2550 Webster Street

Willis Polk, architect

The Bourne House is built of red clinker brick with sandstone trim. Polk has blended English Tudor with Italian Renaissance that has resulted in something quite unique. The chimney stacks are stunning.

13. Flood Mansion I, 1901
2120 Broadway

Julius Krafft, architect

The first of two Pacific Heights mansions built for James Leary Flood (son of the Silver King, James C. Flood) is a wood-frame three-story house loaded with columns, pilasters, and pediments, which achieves its intended formal effect. It became Sarah Dix Hamlin School for girls in 1928.

14. Flood Mansion II, 1914
2222 Broadway

Bliss and Faville, architects

This second Flood mansion is faced with marble. The formal, three-story Italian Renaissance mansion has a central arched entry framed by Corinthian columns with spiral fluting, supporting an academically correct entablature flanked by arched windows. The central interior hall has marble floors and a grand marble staircase. In 1940, the house was donated to the Convent of the Sacred Heart.

Next door, the brick-and-stone **J. D. Grant Mansion** (1897; Weekes and Hiss of New York, architects) [14a] looks like a Manhattan mansion. Purchased by the convent in 1948, it is part of the Sacred Heart School complex.

15. Tudor and Georgian–style house, 1919
2090 Vallejo Street

Clarence Tantau, architect

A tall oriel window trimmed in white dominates the west side of the two-and-a-half-story brick house with steeply pitched gabled roofs punctuated by arched dormers.

16. Hillside Apartments, 1909
2263–2265 Jackson Street

Stone & Smith, architects

Architect Henry C. Smith became known for his multifamily hillside complexes. This one is Arts and Crafts in style with a clinker brick base and side-facing gable roofs. Stone and Smith also designed hillside apartments at **3834–3842** (1908) and **3848** (1906) **Sacramento Street.**

17. Calvary Presbyterian Church, circa 1902
2515 Fillmore Street
McDougall Brothers, architects

When this congregation moved from its old site at Geary and Powell to make way for the St. Francis Hotel, they reused the bricks, pews, and iron balcony supports from the old church. This church looks much like the old one of 1869. The central pavilion features three arched openings with Corinthian columns above, with a frieze reading "CALVARY," topped by a classical pediment. Recessed side pavilions finish the symmetrical façade.

South of the church, along Fillmore, is the neighborhood shopping district, where several shop buildings date from the late 1870s and 1880s, as evidenced by their remarkably intact second and third floors.

18. Alta Plaza
Bounded by Scott, Steiner, Clay, and Jackson Streets
John McLaren, designer (after 1900)

18a. Gibbs House, 1895
2622 Jackson Street
Willis Polk, architect

This Tuscan villa in ochre-colored sandstone has a projecting portico inspired by the Temple of Vesta at Tivoli.

18b. Italianate row houses, 1875
2637–2673 Clay Street
The Real Estate Associates, builders

These alternating flat-front and bay-windowed Italianates create a notable rhythm, nicely articulated by the shelf moldings over windows and doors.

19. 2800 Block of Pacific Avenue

A number of grand houses are located on the crest of Pacific Heights, between Divisadero and Broderick Streets.

19a. Spooner House, 1899
2800 Pacific Avenue
Ernest Coxhead, architect

Here is a redbrick Georgian with some dramatic variations on the theme. The central projecting entrance bay and the side bay on the east have slanted sides. Quoins and bay fronts are rusticated, adding texture to the brick walls. A rounded broken pediment with scroll ends graces the entry. The roofline has been altered.

19b. 2810 Pacific Avenue, circa 1910

Another impressive brick, white-trimmed, Classic Revival Georgian has a side-facing gable roof inset with three arched roofed dormers.

19c. Raycliff Court, off Pacific Avenue

Stripped of applied decoration, a group of mid-twentieth-century Moderns (dated between 1951 and 1959), located in this cul-de-sac, display a subtle and unpre-

tentious quality: **1** (1951; Gardner Dailey, architect), **25** (1959; Wurster, Bernardi and Emmons, architects), **55** (1957; Germano Milano, architect), **75** (1951; Joseph Esherick, architect), all on Raycliff Court, and **2870 Pacific** (1937; Wurster, Bernardi and Emmons).

20. House, 1938
2660 Divisadero Street
John E. Dinwiddie, architect

Dating from the first decade of modernism in the Bay Area, this house is notable for its board-and-batten wood siding, band of grouped windows, and distinctive canted window bay.

21. Bliss Residence, 1899
2898 Broadway
Bliss and Faville, architects

This was Bliss and Faville's first commission, built for Walter Bliss's parents. The stepped gable is faintly Dutch in style, but the classical entry, flat-arched windows, cornices, and dormers are Georgian.

22. 3095 Pacific, 1959
Wurster, Bernardi and Emmons, architects

This two-story rectangular box has grouped corner windows and vertical board siding.

23. Shingle house, 1891
3198 Pacific Avenue
J. Cather Newsom, architect

With its smoothly flowing, gently curving surfaces, this house is true to the spirit of the Shingle style.

Presidio Heights

As a westward extension of Pacific Heights, this area developed somewhat later, being farther from downtown. While houses are generally Period Revival—Classic, Tudor, Georgian, French—there are also some Shingle style and mid-twentieth-century Moderns.

24. 3200 and 3300 Blocks of Pacific Avenue

This is the finest, most cohesive group of Shingle-style houses in the city.

24a. 1 Presidio Avenue, 1902
corner of Pacific Avenue,
Julius Krafft, architect

This house, by an architect best known for his Victorian work, is among the oldest in the group.

24b. 3232 Pacific Avenue, 1902
Ernest Coxhead,
architect

It has a flat shingled surface with boldly scaled classical ornament at the entrance and above.

24c. 3234 Pacific Avenue, 1904
Ernest Coxhead,
architect

This house also has a flat shingled surface, and here the focal point is the overscaled Corinthian pilasters flanking the second-story balcony.

24d. 3233 Pacific Avenue, 1909
Bernard Maybeck,
architect

This house has an irregular form and unconventional roofline; be sure to notice the bronze downspout and the flanking Gothic tracery windows.

24e. 3240 Pacific Avenue, 1908
William Knowles,
architect

Here, shallow pilasters "support" corbelled brackets from which rises a wooden arch, with a gabled roof above. The other half of the duplex at **3236** seems to be a slightly later addition.

24f. 3333 and 3343 Pacific Avenue, 1903
Albert Farr, architect

These two tall shingled houses have a touch of classical ornament. The house at **3377 Pacific** (1908; Julia Morgan, architect) is also shingled.

25. Shingle apartments, 1903
100–114 Walnut Street
Edgar Mathews,
architect

Setbacks and recesses divide this apartment block into vertical sections. The roofline is picturesque, with front-facing and side-facing gables, gabled dormers, and flared eaves with carved supports.

24d

26. 3300 Block of Jackson Street

This block contains a nice display of Period Revival styles popular between 1898 and 1910. **3349–3351** and **3353–3355** (1910), and **3320** (1909) are by C. A. Meussdorffer, architect. **3356–3362 Jackson Street** (1898; Tharp and Holmes,

architects) is a Tudor-style duplex with woodcarving that has many chamfered edges and incised ornament. Most windows are elaborately leaded. **50 Laurel** (1917; Bliss and Faville, architects) is Georgian Revival, and **55 Laurel** (1910; Carter and Foley, architects) is also brick but with bolder trim.

27. Roos House, 1909
3500 Jackson Street
Bernard Maybeck, architect

A tour-de-force, one of Maybeck's best houses, takes after medieval half-timbered houses, and it is elaborated with hammer-beam eave supports and Gothic ornamentation. Most first-story windows are leaded, with diamond-shaped panes. Balcony and porch projections create irregular massing.

28. Tudor House, 1929
3828 Jackson Street
Willis Polk and Co., architects

This grand Tudor mansion with brick walls, cement window trim, and a slate roof has multiple gables, dormers, and chimneys to enliven the roofline.

29. 3778 Washington, 1952
Eric Mendelsohn, architect

A dramatic cantilevered round window bay juts out from the northwest corner of the large but minimalist three-story house.

30. Wagner House, 1928
3701 Washington Street
Bakewell and Weihe, architects

This French chateau has elaborate stone carving in the pedimented entrance composition. **3690 Washington** is another French chateau built in the same year by Arthur Brown Jr.

31. House, 1951
3700 Washington Street
Joseph Esherick, architect

With its flush vertical wood siding, grouped windows, and

full-height, three-part window doors with iron balconies, this house has a sleek and spare yet warm feeling to it.

32. Swedenborgian Church, 1894
Northwest corner of Washington and Lyon Streets

A. Page Brown, architect

The understated façade is textured cement with brick trim around the arched window and door openings. From the street, steps lead up to a garden courtyard supported by the tall retaining walls at the corner of the steeply sloping lot. The church and its office wing form an L around the garden and are approached by pathways. The campanile was made from a drawing of a small Italian church by artist Bruce Porter. The interior, with its wood wainscoted walls, brick fireplace, and maple chairs, is like a rustic living room; services have the feeling

of a family gathering. Madrone logs support the roof. Historians debate whether Brown (the architect of record), his draftsman Albert Schweinfurth, or church pastor Joseph Worcester should receive credit for its design, but it was certainly a collaborative effort.

33. Shingled flats, 1905
2100 Lyon Street, at Washington Street

Edgar Mathews, architect

A row of shingled flats with steeply pitched roofs steps up the hillside. Mathews designed a number of shingled apartment houses in Pacific Heights.

34. 3000 Block of Washington Street

The north side of this block has a long intact row of Victorians. Notable are the Queen Anne house with tower at **3020** (1886) and a former firehouse at **3022**

(1893; Henriksen and Mahoney, builders). A pair of Italianates at **3024–3026** was built by one of the Hinkel brothers in 1886. **2201 Broderick** (1889), at the corner of Washington, is a Queen Anne by Percy and Hamilton.

35. Italianate row houses, 1882
1800, 1900 Blocks of Baker and Lyon Streets

Hinkel Brothers, builders

Italianate houses built by the Hinkel brothers—Henry, George, and William—occupy these blocks. Most are one story and nearly identical. The bay windows and porticos are filled with carved and incised ornament; the one-story houses are topped with "French caps," or miniature mansard roofs. At Sacramento and Lyon Streets is a relatively intact group of commercial buildings from the same period.

9 • Western Addition

For a few years after the Gold Rush, the city limit was Larkin Street, and all land to the west was claimed under often-conflicting preemption claims. In order to sort out the land titles, the city passed the Van Ness Ordinance in 1855 and conducted surveys for streets. The new tract was referred to as the "Western Addition" and included Pacific Heights and Marina Districts.

The area that is known as the Western Addition today (California to·Market Streets) was sparsely populated until the 1870s, when housing development boomed. It was soon filled with intensely ornamented Victorian architecture. Fillmore became the main shopping street and, for a few years after 1906, the city's main shopping center.

As outlying areas west of Twin Peaks were built up with new houses between the 1920s and 1950s, this older neighborhood and its out-of-fashion housing stock became less desirable; large Victorians were divided into small flats during World War II; after the war, near-slum conditions prevailed. Postwar redevelopment projects resulted in several dozen blocks condemned by the Redevelopment Agency. Surrounding the redevelopment housing projects and Japantown are blocks of remaining Victorians, most lovingly restored over the past four decades.

1. Fallon Building, 1894
1800 Market Street
Edward D. Goodrich,
architect

The style is Queen Anne, moving toward Classical Revival. The building has a rare, largely intact Victorian storefront. This building was incorporated in the new Lesbian, Gay, Bisexual and Transgender Community Center (2001; Cee/Pfau Architects) with a glassy wall incompatible with the old building.

This complex and the First Baptist Church at **21 Octavia Street** (1910; Wright, Rushforth, and Cahill, architects) serve as a gateway to a new Octavia Boulevard that opened in 2005, replacing the Central Freeway.

2. Former San Francisco State College, 1921
55 Laguna Street
George B. McDougall,
State Architect

This Spanish Colonial Revival–style complex with industrial steel sash windows was an early campus for San Francisco State College and, until 2005, the campus for UC Extension.

3. Nightingale House, 1883
201 Buchanan Street
John Marquis, architect

This rambling Stick-Eastlake chalet sprouts wings with gabled roofs and a square tower; hammer beams decorate two of the gables, adding to the extravagant effect.

4. San Francisco Zen Center, 1922
300 Page Street
Julia Morgan, architect

The redbrick building has a restrained formality; a second-story arched loggia is flanked by four-story wings. Built for the Emanu-El Sisterhood as a residence, school, guidance center, and home for single or orphaned Jewish women, it has been the San Francisco Zen Center since 1969.

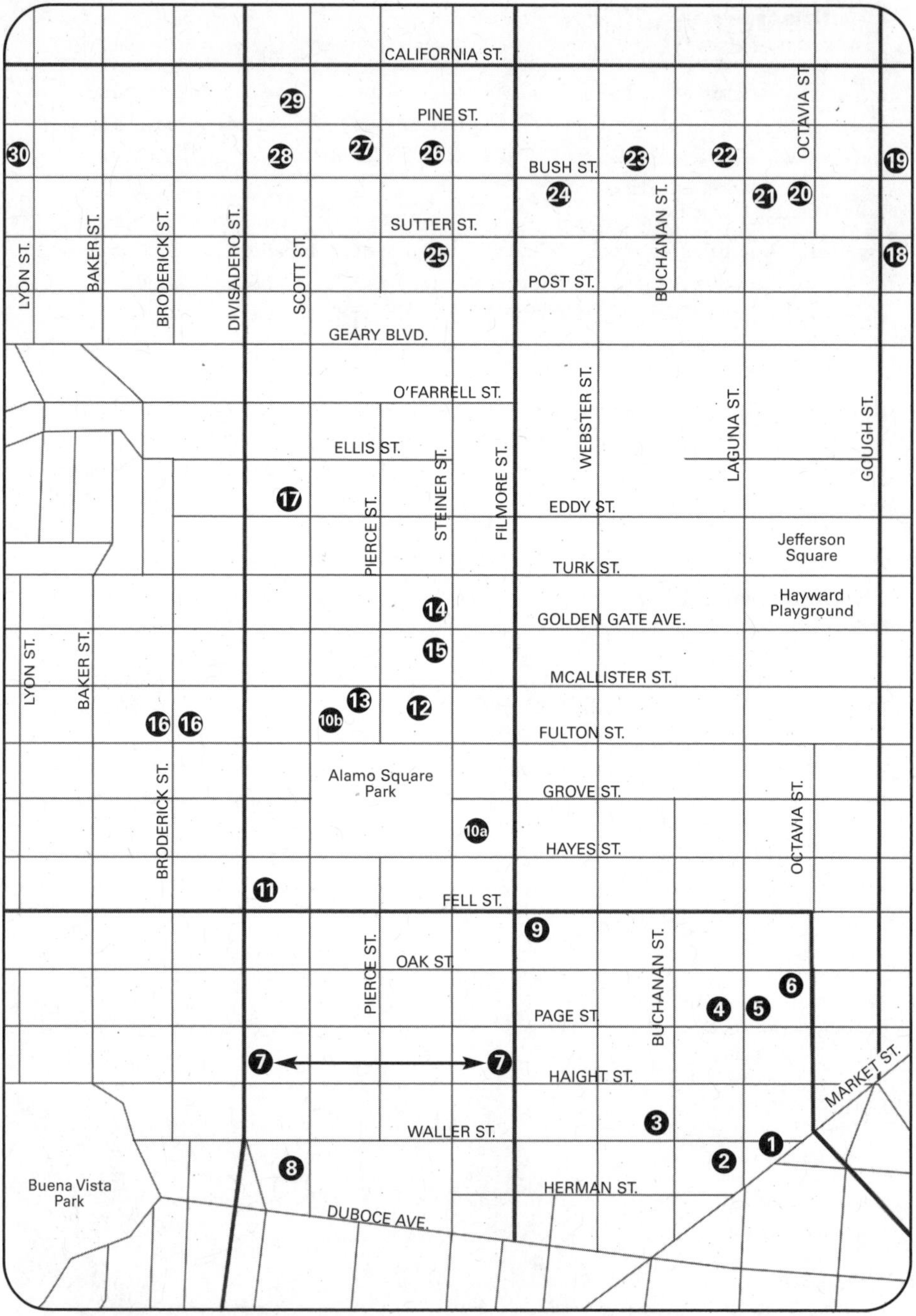

9 • Western Addition

5. Victorian houses
200 Block of Page Street

Here are three Victorians by three prominent nineteenth-century architects: **273 Page** (1878; Edward Swain, architect) is an Italianate with bay windows and lacy decoration. **284 Page** (1878; John Marquis, architect) is a transition to the Stick-Eastlake style. **294 Page** (1888; Henry Geilfuss, architect) is one of the architect's Stick-Eastlake confections.

6. Italianate house, 1866
361 Oak Street

This is one of the city's early Italianates. It has a recessed wing with a porch, broad eaves, and Baroque window trim.

7. Victorian sampler,
1881–1893
*Haight Street,
between Fillmore and
Divisadero Streets*

A nice concentration of Victorians by known architects or builders is located here: **588–592** (1884; Newsom Brothers, architects), **598** (1889; William Mooser I, architect), **610–612** (1886; William Mooser I, architect), **618** (1886; John Marquis, architect), **626–628** (1885; John Marquis, architect), and **803–847** (1884; John Hinkel, builder) are all Eastlake. The oldest building along this stretch is an Italianate store and flat at **800** (1881; Henry Geilfuss, architect). **751** (1893) is Queen Anne. **307 Steiner** (1881; John Marquis, architect) and **311 Steiner** (1891; Prosper Huerne, designer) are on side streets.

8. Duboce Park
*Scott, Waller, and
Carmelita Streets*

Along the northern edge of this small park, set aside in the 1850s for public purposes, is a splendid collection of Victorian houses, many by Fernando Nelson. Overlooking the west end of the park is a nice row that includes **79 Scott Street** (1888; Henry Geilfuss, architect) with cross-braces, decorated porch columns, and incised ornament. At **93 Scott Street** (1891; John Foster, builder) is a Queen Anne with a narrow tower.

9. Sacred Heart Church, 1898
*Southeast corner of
Fillmore and Fell Streets
T. J. Welsh, architect*

The church is built in the form of medieval Lombard churches, with a Romanesque tower and Classical Revival detailing; the materials are pressed yellow brick and matching terra-cotta trim. Its situation at the top of the Fell Street hill reinforces the aspect of an Italian hill-town church.

10. Alamo Square Park
*Hayes, Fulton, Scott, and
Steiner Streets*

Another of John McLaren's post-1900 park designs, this one is the centerpiece of a historic district.

10a. "Post Card Row,"
1894–1895
*710–720 Steiner Street
Matthew Kavanaugh, builder*

With Alamo Square in the foreground and downtown as a backdrop, this attractive unaltered row of Queen Anne houses is the most photographed in the city.

10b. Westerfeld House, 1889
*1198 Fulton Street
Henry Geilfuss, architect*

Pediments and delicate Eastlake ornament enliven the bay windows, which are topped by clipped gables. A square tower with finials adds a romantic note.

11. Theodore Green Apothecary, 1889
*500–502 Divisadero Street
Samuel Newsom, architect*

Rounded oriels, oval windows, arched windows, and circular windows make this building a study in curves, but sharp gables over the oriels add an angular motif.

12. Art Nouveau flats, 1901
*1345–1349 McAllister Street
James Francis Dunn, architect*

Classical Revival and Art Nouveau ornament is on every level, second-story windows are topped by male heads enframed by flowing plasterwork, and the oversized ocular dormers are notable.

13. Stick-Eastlake row,
1889–1891
1400 Block of McAllister Street

A spirited display of Eastlake ornament, these homes are crowded together in row-house fashion. Notable are **1443–1445** (1889), **1447–1453** (1889; William Mooser I, architect), **1463–1465** (1889; Charles Havens, builder), **1469–1489** (1889; John and Zimmerman, designers), and **1493–1499** (1891; Charles J. Devlin, architect).

14. Sharon Flats, 1884
*1400–1412 Golden Gate Avenue
John P. Gaynor, architect*

This row of flats is a transition between the Italianate and Stick-Eastlake styles. Faceted pyramidal roofs over projecting bays are unusual. The flats were built

for William Sharon, who also built the Palace Hotel; both are designed by the same architect.

15. Seattle Block, 1893
1057 Steiner and
1403–1425 Golden Gate

William H. Armitage, architect

This stunning complex consists of a large residence and twelve flats displaying a wide range of Queen Anne–style imagery, which includes gables, several towers, arched entrances, clustered columns with Romanesque capitals, and classical rinceaux. A faithful restoration shows iron cresting on the roof and an authentically Victorian paint scheme.

16. 700–711 Broderick Street, 1891–1892
Cranston and Keenan, builders

Here are two rows of highly decorated, two- and three-story Queen Annes, some with rounded window bays.

17. Holy Cross Catholic Church and Parish Hall, 1899
1822 Eddy Street

Shea and Shea, architects

This Classical Revival former church is built of Colusa sandstone and features a porch in the form of a Roman temple, a rusticated base, and twin Baroque towers rising to cupolas.

The former parish hall (to the east) is Greek Revival. It is the city's oldest wood-frame church. It was built as St. Patrick's (1854) on the site of the Palace Hotel located on Market Street. Before ending up in this location in 1891, it had been moved in 1872 to Eddy Street near Octavia Boulevard.

18. Payne House, 1882
1409 Sutter Street

Curlett and Cuthbertson, architects

This large house is a transition between Stick-Eastlake and Queen Anne, but it is closer to the latter. The belvedere adds a romantic touch.

19. Trinity Episcopal Church, 1892–1894
Northeast corner of Bush and Gough Streets

A. Page Brown, architect

This is a massive composition built of Colusa sandstone, with Gothic arches and spires, and medieval castellated imagery such as towers and battlements.

20. Green's Eye Hospital, 1928
1801 Bush Street

Frederick H. Meyer, architect

The Mediterranean-style tile-roofed wings of this L-shaped building flank a courtyard. The highly ornamented Romanesque entry is at the junction of the wings.

21. Temple Ohabai Shalome, 1894
1881 Bush Street

M. J. Lyon, architect

Here is a building of wood designed to look like stone. Above a receding arched entry, a Florentine-style open loggia is flanked by Romanesque-style end bays. The unusual edifice has recently been restored. It was built originally as a synagogue; in 1959, the San Francisco Zen Center was founded here.

22. Stick-Eastlake row, 1890
1801–1855 Laguna Street

William Hinkel, builder

Each house is a variation of exuberant Eastlake ornament, and these are colorfully painted.

23. Stanyan House,
circa 1857–1864
2006 Bush Street

This simple gabled house with a full-width porch and shelf moldings over the windows resembles houses from the early 1850s. For a long time, it was home to the family of Supervisor Charles Stanyan, for whom Stanyan Street was named. On either side are flats the family built in 1885.

24. Flat-front Italianates, 1875
2115–2125 Bush Street

The Real Estate Associates (TREA), builders

This row of six flat-front houses by TREA stands immaculately intact. Triangular pediments top the second-story windows, while rounded pediments top those in the first story. Broad shelf moldings cover the porches. **2101–2107 Bush** is a row of bay-window Italianates built in 1874. In the adjacent alley, **Cottage Row,** is a group of tiny Eastlake houses built in 1882.

25. Macedonia Missionary Baptist Church, 1907
2135 Sutter Street

O'Brien and Werner, architects

Constructed of red brick with copious amounts of terra-cotta trim, the style is an unusual blend of Tudor and Baroque revivals. Originally the Golden Gate Commandery No. 16 of the Knights Templar, a Masonic

order, the present church moved here in 1950.

26. St. Dominic's Catholic Church, 1923–1928
Northwest corner of Bush and Steiner Streets

Beezer Brothers, architects

The soaring quality of this granite Gothic Revival church was diminished somewhat because of the 1989 Loma Prieta Earthquake, which resulted in the removal of the upper tier of the tower and the addition of simple concrete flying buttresses. Nonetheless, this is an impressive church.

27. Crocker Old People's Home, 1889–1890
Southwest corner of Pine and Pierce Streets

A. Page Brown, architect

This building and a mausoleum in Oakland were A. Page Brown's first commissions after he arrived in San Francisco from the East Coast. He soon became one of the city's leading society architects. This is one of the Bay Area's earliest East Coast Shingle-style buildings. The original third story and dormered attic have long vanished, but the first two stories of brick and wood shingles survive intact with their rounded bays and textured surface. The building has been painted and most original windows have been replaced.

28. Philadelphia Seventh Day Adventist Church, 1904
2570 Bush Street

T. Patterson Ross, architect

Built of red brick, this church building has a base and Romanesque-style arched

entrance of roughly chiseled Colusa sandstone. A square tower and an octagonal tower flank the entrance pavilion.

29. Ortmann-Shumate House, 1870
1901 Scott Street

This fine Italianate house was modernized a little in 1889, when the front bay window was increased from one to two stories in height, and the cornice was made to wrap around the raised bay. Three generations of the Ortmann-Shumate family lived here for 128 years. Dr. Thomas Shumate owned a chain of thirty-two pharmacies; his son, Dr. Albert Shumate, was a San Francisco historian.

30. Hoadley House, mid-1850s
2908–2910 Bush Street

A squarish Italianate with a porch that spans the width of the first story is among the city's oldest houses. The first owner, Milo Hoadley, proposed a plan to remove Telegraph Hill when he was the city engineer.

10 · Lone Mountain to the Haight

Lone Mountain

Lone Mountain is one of the more prominent geographical features west of Van Ness Avenue, a distinction that led to a tall wooden cross being placed upon it in 1862. Beginning in 1853, several cemeteries were established around it. In the late nineteenth century, modest Victorian houses were built on the blocks between the cemeteries.

New burials were forbidden in 1901; in 1937, the cemeteries were condemned and removed to make room for development. Laurel Heights, Anza Vista, Francisco Heights, and University Terrace replaced the old cemeteries.

1. Odd Fellows' Columbarium, 1897
1 Loraine Court, off Anza Street

B. J. S. Cahill, architect

When the city removed the cemeteries, it retained this exercise in Beaux-Arts classicism. It is a drum rising to a copper dome, with rectangular projections at the four compass points. Acanthus leaves and swags are the dominant ornamental motifs.

2. John W. Geary School, 1930
20 Cook Street

Ashley, Evers and Hays, architects

Though the school is restrained, it has a very beautiful Spanish Baroque entrance pavilion. An Art Deco influence can be found in the column capitals and in the scrolls and drips over the windows.

3. Lone Mountain College for Women, 1932
2600–2800 Turk Street

Henry A. Minton, architect

Situated on the top of Lone Mountain is this former Catholic college for women (now part of the Jesuit Community at the University of San Francisco). The pedestrian entry, off Turk Street, is elegant; it has a Classic double staircase amid formal landscaping with a Baroque fountain located halfway up. The main U-shaped symmetrical building has an ornate Gothic tower in the center of its composition. On the interior, the Del Santo Reading Room is beautifully finished.

4. Montgomery Husted House, 1884
2694 McAllister Street

Its saltbox form gives the impression that this house is even older than it is; the Eastlake window trim dates it to the 1880s. **2508–2548 McAllister** is an intact row of Eastlake cottages built by Joseph M. Comerford that date from 1890 to 1891.

5. Carmelite Monastery of Cristo Rey, 1956–1958
721 Parker Avenue

Ryan and Lee, architects

Architect Paul Ryan, who trained at the École des Beaux-Arts in Paris, created one of the last Spanish Baroque buildings in San Francisco. The entrance pavilion is faced with cast stone, and features columns that are

lavishly decorated with images of leaves and grapes; a curvilinear pediment is bisected by a sculpture of a Madonna and Child.

6. St. Ignatius Church, 1911–1914
Northeast corner of Fulton Street and Parker Avenue

Charles J. Devlin, architect

Soaring twin towers, visible from many locations, establish this huge Italian Renaissance–inspired church as a San Francisco landmark and icon. A center bay is flanked by the tall, four-story twin towers embellished by copious Classic ornament and detail and by many arched openings. The entrance pavilion is lavishly ornamented. It is constructed of buff-colored brick, with columns and pilasters of ochre terra-cotta. The interior is as splendid as the exterior.

North Panhandle

The North Panhandle is, as its name implies, north of the eastward extension of Golden Gate Park. It consists mostly of Victorian- and Edwardian-era houses and flats.

7. Baker Street houses

7a. Queen Anne house, 1891
401 Baker Street

Wyneken and Townsend, architects

This is a big, extravagant Queen Anne, complete with two dissimilar towers, clustered porch columns, and plenty of plaster ornament.

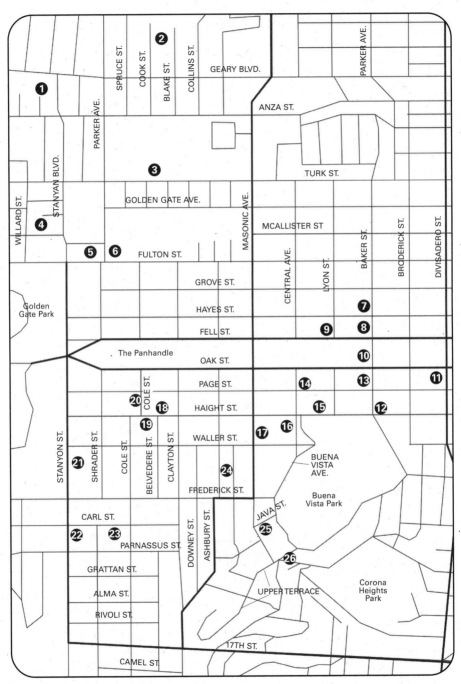

10 • Lone Mountain to the Haight

7b. Spanish Colonial Revival house, 1902
405 Baker Street

James Francis Dunn, architect

This narrow four-story house, with a recessed fourth-floor porch, is quite eclectic, exhibiting stylistic images that include Italian Villa, Craftsman, and Spanish Baroque.

8. Southern Pacific Hospital, 1908
333 Baker Street

D. J. Patterson, architect

The Southern Pacific Railroad Company was so vast that it built this Classic Revival–style hospital for its employees on an entire city block. Facing Fell Street, the original main entrance is a three-story Classic temple front held by Corinthian columns supporting an entablature and pediment. Ornamental ironwork frames the windows between the wings. When the building was remodeled during the 1980s for housing, original details such as wood sash windows, outbuildings, and iron fencing were retained.

9. Clunie House, 1897
301 Lyon Street

William Curlett, architect

Half-timbering in the gable and an arched entry faintly suggest Tudor. Plaster floral ornament frames the second-story windows. An open belvedere faces Fell Street.

10. McKinley Monument, 1904
East end of Golden Gate Park Panhandle

Robert I. Aitken, sculptor

B. J. S. Cahill, architect

Aitken's solemn robed female is made of bronze and stands on a granite base, holding out a palm leaf for McKinley.

Haight-Ashbury

The Haight-Ashbury grew into a suburban middle-class neighborhood during the 1890s. The Queen Anne houses built during that decade constitute one of the best collections in the city. The neighborhood became more urban in character as it filled with flats and apartments in the 1910s. In the 1960s, hippies found the area, and the Haight became a world-famous haven for the counterculture.

Buena Vista Park was reserved as a park in 1870. To the south, Corona Heights was the site of one of the Gray Brothers' quarries and brick factories from 1900 until the 1920s. Its summit, approached from Roosevelt Way, has great views of the city.

11. Oak Street houses

11a. Abner Phelps House, circa 1851
1111 Oak Street

This is generally acknowledged to be the oldest house in San Francisco, though one or two on Telegraph Hill may match it. The broad verandah gives it a southern feeling, while the wavy bargeboard in the gables is Gothic Revival. For many years the house sat in the middle of the block and was surrounded by other buildings; in the 1970s, it was reoriented to face Oak Street.

11b. Sarah Mish House, 1885
1153 Oak Street

Barnett McDougall and Sons, architects

This is a large and intensely ornamented Stick-Eastlake.

12. Spencer House, 1896
1080 Haight Street

Fred P. Rabin, architect

This house is exotic even for a Queen Anne. It incorporates a Romanesque porch, a Moorish first-story window, and an almost Palladian treatment in the first story of the tower.

13. Rountree Block, 1891
110–124 Lyon Street and 1387 Oak Street

William H. Lillie, architect

These seven Queen Anne houses are "of a piece," yet each is a variation.

14. Shingle and Craftsman apartments, 1903
1390–1392 Page Street and 200 Central Avenue

Edgar Mathews, architect

These apartments feature ski-slope shed roofs over the entrances, grouped ogee arched windows in projecting bays, and carved brackets.

15. Third Church of Christ, Scientist, 1915
1250 Haight Street

Edgar Mathews, architect

This is an outstanding Romanesque-style church. There are terra-cotta columns, voussoirs, window trim, and delicate decorative panels The variegated buff and tan brick façade forms a suitable backdrop for the ornament. The former church is now senior housing.

16. Classical Revival flats, 1904
91 Central Avenue

James Francis Dunn, architect

The façade is entirely but wonderfully overscaled. A rusticated base with giant consoles supports Corinthian columns that flank the projecting window bays.

17. Queen Anne houses, 1895–1896
1226–1238, 1250–1256 Masonic Avenue

Cranston and Keenan, builders

Cranston and Keenan always put a little more verve into their Queen Annes. This row illustrates their ornamental palette.

18. Sunset Theater, 1911
1660 Haight Street

Bernard J. Joseph, architect

Built as a nickelodeon, it operated until 1924, first as the Sunset Theater and then as the Superba. The arch spanning the transom is impressively decorated with classical ornament and drama-related imagery.

19. Art Nouveau flats and storefront, 1904
1677–1681 Haight Street

James Francis Dunn, architect

The flowing surface of the Art Nouveau ornament is typical of Dunn early in his career.

20. Queen Anne flats, 1894
500–506 Cole Street

Cranston and Keenan, builders

Four flats, with gables separated by a central tower, have a double staircase leading to a four-arched porch. **508–516 Cole** (1898–1899) has delicate classical ornament. **1777 Page** (1894) is one of their finest Queen Annes; note the owls' heads and other plaster ornament. **1550 Page** (1891) has sunbursts in the west gable.

21. Stanyan Park Hotel, 1905
750 Stanyan Street

Martens and Coffey, architects

Here is a very fine Classical Revival hotel building that has been completely restored based on a historic photograph.

22. Lange House, 1912
199 Carl Street

August Nordin, architect

The ornament is Classical Revival; its corner tower is reminiscent of Queen Anne. The Lange family came to the Haight-Ashbury as dairy farmers in 1870.

23. Shingle cottages, 1905
55–63 Carl Street

Maxwell G. Bugbee, architect

Three Shingle-style cottages are arranged around a common yard, with gambrel roofs, Baroque ornament, and diamond-shaped window lights.

24. Residential buildings
800 and 900 Blocks of Ashbury

These two blocks contain an especially fine collection of residential buildings in a wide range of styles from the first decade of the twentieth century: **852–854** (1910; Albert Schröpfer, architect) are Classical Revival flats; **858–864** (1903; Eugene Fritz, builder) are Spanish-inspired apartments; **880** (1908; A. A. Cantin, architect) is a Mission Revival house with a sculpted parapet and quatrefoil window; and **979** (1905, Eugene Fritz, builder) is a shingled house with an interesting roofline.

25. E. B. Power House, 1910
1526 Masonic Avenue

Bernard Maybeck, architect

This Shingle-style house has a dramatic side-gabled roof with a second-story porch and dormer. The roof slopes down to shelter the entrance porch.

26. Dettner House, 1917
45 Upper Terrace

Ida McCain, architect

Here is Romantic revival in clinker brick with a steeply pitched tile roof with clipped gables and flared eaves, small paned windows, and a projecting triple-arched entry. Ida McCain also designed numerous bungalows in Westwood Park and the Richmond district; this may be her largest and most prominent.

11 · Duboce Triangle · Eureka Valley · Noe Valley

Like the Mission District, Duboce Triangle, Eureka Valley, and Noe Valley developed during the nineteenth century. Although they had their own identities, they were also considered part of the Mission District to the east. Churches, built by different immigrant congregations, provide clues to the neighborhood's early population.

In the late 1960s, Eureka Valley and Duboce Triangle attracted numerous gay men, who called the neighborhood simply "the Castro." The Gay Freedom Day Parade brings visitors from around the country, while the Castro Street Fair and Halloween night on Castro Street are major local events.

Duboce Triangle

This is a small triangle north of Market bounded by Market, Duboce and Castro Streets. Within this triangle, tree-lined Noe has good examples of post-1906 Classic Revival flats; side streets (Fourteenth, Fifteenth, Henry, and Beaver Streets) are scattered with houses that date as early as the 1870s, such as **22 Beaver** (1876).

1. St. Francis Lutheran Church, 1906
152 Church Street

This redbrick Gothic Revival church has a tower and steeple of wood, and very fine stained glass. It was built as Ansgar Evangelical Lutheran for a Danish congregation.

2. Swedish-American Hall, 1907
2174 Market Street

August Nordin, architect

The hall was picturesquely designed to evoke northern European architectural themes. The dominant element is a giant gable with wavy bargeboard, split at the top to create two peaks.

3. St. Nicholas Russian Orthodox Church, 1902
2005 Fifteenth Street

Built as St. Luke's German Evangelical Church, it has Gothic windows, Classical ornament, and Victorian fishscale shingles in the tower, which is now topped by an onion dome.

Eureka Valley

4. 400–500 Block of Castro Street

Castro Street is the main commercial street for the Eureka Valley–Duboce Triangle area, and was such an important commercial street that it has two Classic bank buildings, including Bank of Italy's first branch at 400 Castro Street (1922; Edward T. Foulkes, architect), outside the downtown area.

4a. Castro Theater, 1922
429 Castro Street

Miller and Pflueger, architects

The most prominent building on Castro Street, it is the most renowned movie theater in San Francisco for its architecture and its programming. It is Spanish Renaissance/Baroque, with a richly decorated central bay rising to a shaped Baroque parapet. The

4a

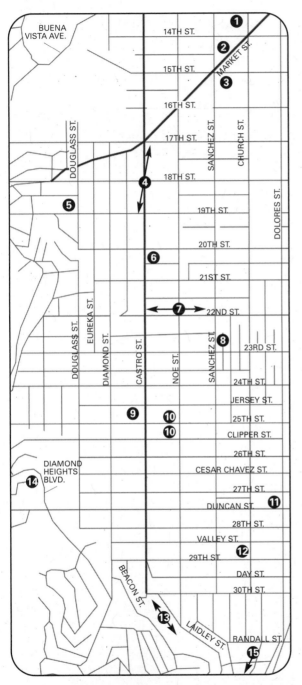

open vestibule contains an original freestanding, six-sided ticket booth with a base of polychrome tile; multipaned double doors are framed by an arch of polychrome tile work; the sumptuous interior contains gold-leaf sculpture and bas relief. The marquee and blade sign date from the 1930s.

4b. Castro Camera, 1894
573–575 Castro Street

Fernando Nelson, builder

An Eastlake flat over a 1940s-remodeled storefront, the store was Harvey Milk's camera shop from 1973 to 1978. It also doubled as his campaign headquarters in four election campaigns, culminating in his election as City and County Supervisor in 1977. Although he served only eleven months in office before being assassinated, he lifted gay politics in the city to a level of effectiveness unprecedented in American history.

5. Nobby Clarke's Folly, 1890
250 Douglass Street

Charles J. Colley, architect

Eureka Valley's lone mansion, by the same architect who designed Adolph Sutro's Cliff House several years later, is Queen Anne in its form, with rounded towers capped by domes. The entrance porch, facing Caselli Street, is Classical Revival.

6. Fernando Nelson House and Flats, 1897
701–733 Castro Street

Fernando Nelson, builder

The Queen Anne cottage at 701 was Nelson's own residence. The Eastlake flats at **711–733** are among the dozens he built in Eureka and Noe Valleys in the 1890s. Four more can be found directly across the street at **704–710** (1893).

Noe Valley

7. Queen Anne row houses
3733–3777, 3817–3871 Twenty-Second Street

Of the twenty-four houses on these two blocks, twenty-two are close to original, except for the usual addition of garages inserted into the raised basements. **3733–3745 Twenty-Second Street** (1897; Hans Peterson, builder) have exquisite plaster ornament under the gable. **3749–3777 and 3817–3871 Twenty-Second Street** (1906; John Anderson, builder) have varied attic treatments but are recognizable as a group, with plaster bands of leaves bound by ribbons across the width of each house.

8. Noe Valley Ministry, 1888, 1891
1021 Sanchez Street

Charles Geddes, architect

The Eastlake-style main story, by Geddes, is the oldest part; in 1891, architect William Curlett raised the building and added a new Gothic-style first story. Originally known as Lebanon Church, it has always been Presbyterian.

9. Noe Valley Branch Library, 1916
451 Jersey Street

John Reid Jr., architect

The two-story Renaissance Revival library of tan textured

brick is copiously trimmed with polychrome terra-cotta, each piece made by hand in plaster molds.

10. William Axford House, 1877, 1885
1190 Noe Street

This 1877 house was remodeled into a Stick-Eastlake in 1885. There is a barn on the west, and an impressive iron fence most likely made by Axford, an iron founder.

James Lick Middle School, 1220 Noe (1932; William H. Crim Jr., architect) [10a], is a large Art Deco school.

11. Italianate houses, 1879
225, 227 Twenty-Seventh Street

Joseph Comerford, builder

Comerford built so many houses in this part of Noe Valley in the 1870s and 1880s that the area was known as Comerfordville. Most were simple one-story, flat-front Italianates with central entrances flanked by windows. These are two of the now-rare survivors.

12. St. Paul's Church, circa 1900–1902
Southwest corner of Church and Valley Streets

Shea and Shea, architects

This is a very nice Gothic Revival church and the major Noe Valley landmark. The exterior is light granite, with darker granite in the base, columns, belt courses, and alternating blocks around the rose window. The porch has three Gothic arches, with rugged voussoirs bordered by smooth-cut trim. The towers of granite and wood rise to copper-clad steeples of slightly uneven height. Inside, the nave and side aisles are defined by wooden columns that rise to support rib-vaulted ceilings. The stained glass is as richly hued as any in the city.

The Central Hills

This hilly land was part of Jose de Jesus Noe's Mexican-era San Miguel Rancho, and known in the nineteenth century as the San Miguel Hills, or the Mission Hills, because they rise above the Mission District. Land on the northeast side of Twin Peaks was subdivided in the 1860s when a few scattered houses were built, but most of the hill was not built up until the twentieth century. The twin peaks are unbuilt and somewhat bleak, but they offer magnificent views of the city. North of Twin Peaks is Mt. Sutro, where Mt. Sutro Tower,

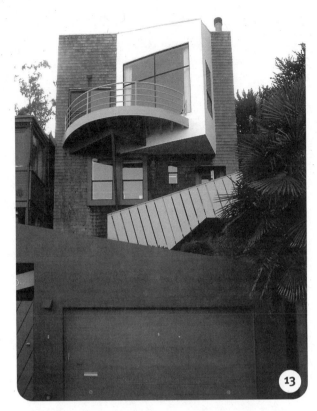

this plan are townhouses and apartments that constitute a fairly intact mid-twentieth-century Modernist neighborhood. Development began with the **Red Rock Hill Townhouses** at Diamond Heights Boulevard and Duncan Street near Clipper Street (1962; Cohen and Leverson, architects).

Prominent architects are represented by **Diamond Heights Village** (1972; Gensler and Associates, Joseph Esherick and Associates) on Red Rock Way at Duncan. There are a group of houses by Joseph Eichler on the 1000 block of Duncan Street and on both sides of Cameo (1962–1964).

Most inspiring is the natural feature, Glen Canyon, a deep rift in the land with a creek and rocky outcroppings. It is accessible at its south end via Bosworth Street.

15. Sunnyside (unmapped)

The Sunnyside neighborhood was created by real estate speculator and industrialist Behrend Joost and his partners in 1891. To bring people out here, he built the city's first electric streetcar line. Sunnyside developed gradually from the 1890s to the 1960s, and a smattering of houses from its first two decades can still be found. **236 Monterey** is the Sunnyside Conservatory (1916), an octagonal frame (once glazed) whose pyramidal roof, supported by wooden trusses, shelters palm trees and ferns; it is the most unusual structure on the street. Built as part of the property to the west, it is now a city park.

a 977-foot TV tower erected in 1972, dominates the skyline from many places.

13. Glen Park

The south end of Noe Valley, where the hills begin, was subdivided in 1862 as the Fairmount Tract; the western half was laid out in stages around the turn of the nineteenth century. A modest commercial district is located at the intersection of Chenery and Diamond Streets. The Stick-Eastlake-style Poole-Bell mansion at **192–196 Laidley** (1889) is the most imposing. Architect Jeremy Kotas and his partners are the architects of **140 Laidley** (1990; Kotas and Shaffer, architects), a

shingled house with a giant central window topped by an eyebrow parapet; **134 Laidley** (1994; Shaffer and Kotas, architects) is Neo-Art Nouveau in feeling, with hints of Pueblo and Medieval; **102 Laidley** (1987; Kotas/Pantaleoni Architects) [13] is a house of angles and bold primary colors. Holding its own against this modern virtuosity is a century-old Queen Anne cottage with classical detailing at **125**.

14. Diamond Heights

This range of hills was sparsely developed until 1953, when the Redevelopment Agency implemented a development plan. The buildings resulting from

12 · Mission District

The Mission District and the Presidio were the first places settled by the Spanish in 1776. The Mission church, known as Mission Dolores, is the city's oldest building.

This is a large district, laid out in a grid that is not impacted by freeways. Except for the blocks between South Van Ness and Dolores, north of Twentieth Street, it escaped the devastation of 1906. It also escaped the huge redevelopment projects found in the Western Addition. It is a district of many distinct small neighborhoods that overlap and merge. Ethnically, socially, economically, it is diverse and there is a distinct Latino flavor in some areas. The main shopping streets—Mission, Valencia, Sixteenth, and Twenty-Fourth Streets—change as they pass through the different neighborhoods. Numerous narrow streets and alleyways are located between South Van Ness and Dolores. An industrial district fills the northeast corner of the Mission.

1. Independent Order of Foresters, 1930
170 Valencia Street

Harold G. Stoner, architect

This benevolent association hall, long used as a Baha'i Temple, has a splendid Art Deco front made of concrete imbedded with crushed stone. Foliated imagery is found throughout the entrance pavilion and across the top.

2. 102 Guerrero Street, 1883

Henry Geilfuss, architect

This handsome example of an Italianate Victorian has a two-story three-sided window bay, and tall sash windows partially framed by small freestanding columns. To the south at **120–126 Guerrero Street** and **226–235 Clinton Park** are six Italianate houses (1878–1879) built by The Real Estate Associates.

3. California Volunteers Monument, 1906
Dolores Street at Market Street

Douglas Tilden, sculptor

William Curlett, architect

One can certainly read the spirit of the times in monuments such

as these. The bronze statue consists of a female warrior astride a winged stallion, alongside two soldiers, one standing and the other fallen. It honors California soldiers who served in the Spanish-American War. As craftsmanship, it is truly splendid. Of course, there is no homage to the Filipinos who resisted American conquest.

4. Italianate house, 1869
1876 Fifteenth Street

James E. Wolfe, architect

This house was moved here from Haight Street after the 1906 fire. The elegant window moldings and sparsity of other ornament was typical of 1860s domestic architecture.

5. Tanforan cottages, 1850s
214, 220 Dolores Street

These remarkably intact, nearly identical one-story cottages are reputed to date to the 1850s; their false fronts, full-width porches with square posts, four-over-four window sash, and shallow depth of each house are common features of that decade.

6. Mission San Francisco de Asis (Mission Dolores) 1782–1791
Southwest corner of Dolores and Sixteenth Streets

Except for a single wall in the Presidio, this is the only building in the city that survives from the Spanish and Mexican periods. Built with Indian labor, this chapel represents the founding of San Francisco.

Mission Dolores is about 30 feet wide by 114 feet deep. The material is adobe coated with a smooth plaster that reveals the irregularity of the bricks. In the front, four squat columns rest upon a high base and support a wooden balcony. Above the balcony, four smaller columns rise nearly to a gabled roof with broadly overhanging eaves. The interior consists of a long rectangular space, with the meeting of nave and sanctuary defined by square columns spanned by an arch. The main and side altars are hand-carved wood, Baroque in style, imported from Mexico by 1810. Indians painted the ceiling beams with vegetable dyes. The Mission was saved in

6

11. Churches, 1910, 1917
*600 Block of Dolores Street,
facing Dolores Park*

These are two churches of similar
size but contrasting styles and
color. The Gothic Revival church
at **601 Dolores** (1910; George
C. Meeker, architect) is red brick
with red terra-cotta trim around
its many arched windows. The
**Second Church of Christ,
Scientist** (1917; William H.
Crim Jr., architect) has the form
of a domed Roman temple with
Tuscan columns.

**12. Harris Garcelon
House,** 1865
3747 Twentieth Street

This simple flat-fronted
Italianate is one of the oldest in
the neighborhood; houses built
later were more decorated.

13. Guerrero Street houses

**13a. John McMullen
House,** 1890
827 Guerrero Street

*Samuel and J. Cather Newsom,
architects*

The Newsoms completely
remodeled an 1881 residence,
now notable for its moon-gate
entry, clipped gable, corner
tower, and picturesque form.

**13b. Marsden Kershaw
House,** 1871
845 Guerrero Street

Here is a flat-fronted Italianate
whose simplicity belies its
careful composition. The shelf
molding above the arched entry
is supported by elegant curved
brackets.

14. Italianate houses,
1860s–1870s
*Liberty Street between
Valencia and Dolores Streets*

1906 when the fire was stopped
at Dolores Street. It was restored,
and seismically reinforced with
steel beams, by Willis Polk in
1920, and restored again in
1988–1992. To the south is a
cemetery with graves of notable
and notorious San Franciscans.

7. Mission Dolores Basilica,
1914, 1926

*Henry A. Minton,
architect (1926)*

The basilica was built in 1914
but was entirely remodeled in
the Spanish Baroque style, with
towers of different heights and
a central bay rich in bas-relief
decoration. A complex of additional buildings includes an
International-style building
at **445 Church Street** (1955;
Blanchard and Maher, architects)
that served until recently as the
archdiocese offices.

8. Notre Dame College,
1906–1907
347 Dolores Street

Theodore Lenzen, architect

This replaced a school built in
1866 and destroyed in 1906. Set

behind a wall and an iron gate,
it has a high rusticated basement,
a stucco-clad main story with
Italianate windows, and a curved
Mansard roof with dormers; a
short tower is topped by a cupola.
It is now a home for the elderly.

**9. St. Mathews Lutheran
Church,** 1907
3281 Sixteenth Street

Herman Barth, architect

This is a Gothic Revival church
clad in wood shingles and generously festooned with Gothic
arches, pinnacles, a large rose
window, and a soaring tower.

**10. Mission High
School,** 1926
*Northwest corner of
Eighteenth and
Dolores Streets*

John Reid Jr., architect

This large school is Spanish
Baroque in style, with complex
Churrigueresque ornament. The
lobby has glazed tilework and a
carved wooden ceiling. To the
south is **Mission Dolores Park,**
with a good view from its
southern end.

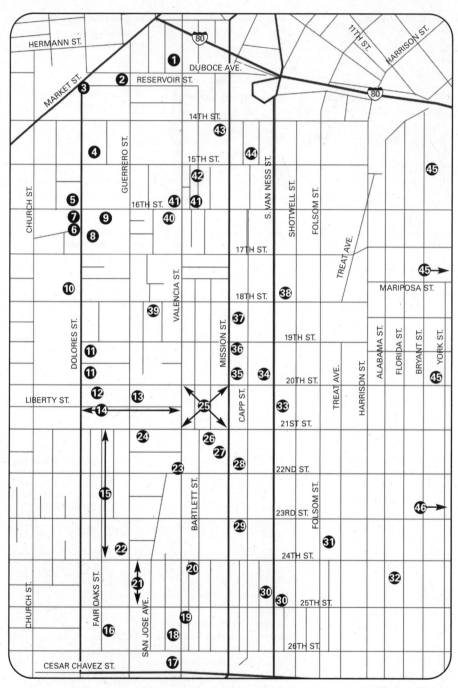

These two blocks of Liberty Street contain a remarkable collection of Italianates: **19–21** and **23–25** (1878; The Real Estate Associates, developers) are in practically perfect condition; **58** (1877; S. C. Bugbee and Son, architects) was designed by the same architects who designed the vanished Colton, Stanford, and Croker Mansions on Nob Hill; **109** (1869) has arches or pediments over each window; and the Judge Daniel J. and Mary E. Murphy house at **159** (1878; Hoffman and Clinch, designers) was the site of a visit by Susan B. Anthony in 1896.

15. Fair Oaks Street
Between Twenty-First and Twenty-Fourth Streets

Like Liberty Street, Fair Oaks is another street that retains much of its Victorian feeling. Numbers **8** (1892; Percy and Hamilton, architects) and **31** (1888; George Bordwell, architect) are a blend of Shingle and Queen Anne styles. **68** (1888; August R. Denke, architect) is a splendid Stick-Eastlake with a lacy porch roof. **St. James School** at 180 (1906, 1911; Martens and Coffey, architects) is red brick and has slightly projecting end pavilions flanking an entrance bay. **200–202** (1886; Wyneken and Townsend, architects) is an Eastlake duplex, and **212** (1873) is an intact Italianate.

16. Holy Innocents' Episcopal Church, 1890
455 Fair Oaks Street

Ernest Coxhead, architect

This small early-Shingle-style church has shingle patterning over the arched entry and the rounded corners. The front

wing is an addition so compatible that it appears original.

17. Buckingham and Hecht Shoe Factory, 1888
1500 Valencia Street

Macy and Jordan, architects

This is the best example of a nineteenth-century factory building in the city. The pedimented entrance pavilion, brick pilasters, and cornice give the building a Greek Revival feeling, but there is a Gothic arch supported by Romanesque columns in the entry. An arm-and-hammer motif in each capital represents the workers. Most windows have original nine-over-nine wood sash. The building is occupied by the Salvation Army.

18. SFFD Steamer #13, 1883
1458 Valencia Street

This former firehouse is the oldest in San Francisco. It is Italianate in style, with cast-iron ornament on the first story and sheet metal ornament on the second.

19. Victorian storefronts and flats, 1889
1413–1419 Valencia Street

Henry Geilfuss, architect

Unaltered Victorian storefronts such as these are rare. These and a nearby set at **1035–1041 Guerrero Street** (1893) evoke nineteenth-century window-shopping.

20. Mission Branch Library, 1915
300 Bartlett Street

G. Albert Lansburgh, architect

Mediterranean in style, this is clad entirely in terra-cotta, with carvings of books and leaves

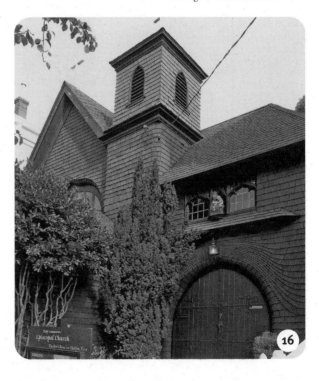

around the tall arched windows. A wide overhanging cornice has carved wood brackets; the roof is tile. Great harm was done when the grand staircase was removed and the Twenty-Fourth Street entrance was blocked, making a demeaning side stairwell the only access down to the reading room.

21. Stick-Eastlake houses, 1880s
1200 Block of Guerrero Street

At **1201 Guerrero** (1880; George Bordwell, architect) is an intensely decorated flat over a storefront; **1233–1235** (1889; Absalom J. Barnett, architect) and **1241** (1887) each use floral ornament; **1253** (1887) features an interesting entrance porch and plenty of Eastlake millwork; and **1259–1261** and **1263** (1889) are a matching pair.

22. Italianate duplex, 1884
1180–1182 Guerrero Street

William Mooser I, architect

This typical bay window Italianate duplex is in sparkling condition.

23. Hibernia Bank, 1924
1098 Valencia Street

Bakewell and Brown, architects

A somewhat severe Classic Revival banking temple is made of carved granite, with new windows.

24. Stick-Eastlake houses, late 1880s
3300 Block of Twenty-First Street

Numbers **3333–3337** (1889; Charles Havens, architect) have curved elements; **3343–3345** (1889) are more highly ornamented; **3367–3375** (1885;

Pissis and Moore, architects) are three identical houses.

25. TREA houses, 1875–1878
Block bounded by Valencia, Mission, Twentieth, and Twenty-First Streets

The Real Estate Associates, builders

This is the largest cluster of houses built by The Real Estate Association (TREA), which was the city's largest house builder during the 1870s. Of the ninety-nine Italianate houses built by TREA on this square block, thirty-seven are still standing and largely intact. The largest concentration is on Lexington Street, where all of the TREA houses have flat fronts and some still have original iron fences and gates. The houses on San Carlos are a mix of bay-windowed and flat-front houses; those on Twentieth and Valencia Streets all have bay windows.

26. 3243–3245 Twenty-First Street, 1884
Samuel and J. Cather Newsom, architects

This ornate Eastlake house is typical Newsom Brothers.

27. New Mission Theater, 1916, 1932
2550 Mission Street

The narrow front is little more than a marquee from which rises the most dramatic blade sign in the city. It was designed by Miller and Pflueger in 1932 to add pizzazz to the Reid Brothers' great classical interior of 1916. The building is now a furniture store, the subject of a recent preservation struggle.

28. St. Johannes German Evangelical Lutheran Church, 1900
3126 Twenty-Second Street

Martens and Coffey, architects

This Gothic Revival church has towers of unequal height and an elaborate central entrance.

29. Mission Presbyterian Church, 1892
3261 Twenty-Third Street, at Capp Street

Percy and Hamilton, architects

This is a magnificent blend of Romanesque and Shingle styles, with a touch of Gothic in the soaring corner tower. The base is made of buff-colored brick, beautifully finished with rounded corners and moldings.

30. South Van Ness Avenue houses

30a. Frank M. Stone House, 1886
1348 South Van Ness Avenue

Seth Babson, architect

This is a beautifully intact Queen Anne with a semi-detached corner tower. Both this house and the Havens house (below) still have iron fences and gates around their front yards.

30b. Charles Havens House, 1884
1381 South Van Ness Avenue

Charles Havens, architect

The elaborate details are mostly Italianate but the spirit is closer to Eastlake. The architect was a prolific designer of houses, but he also designed downtown office buildings.

31. Mannerist Classical flats, 1899
2731–2735 Folsom Street
James Francis Dunn, architect

This is the oldest surviving work by the architect, and dates from the first year of his practice. It exhibits the French-inspired massing and ornament he developed more fully later in his career. The rusticated base supports a bowed window bay with Corinthian columns rising to a leafy frieze and cornice.

32. St. Peter's Catholic Church, 1886
East side of Alabama, south of Twenty-Fourth Street
Bryan J. Clinch, architect

Although the exterior of this Gothic Revival church was stuccoed, the portals and window moldings are intact. The interior is resplendent. The nave and side aisles are defined by rows of clustered columns that rise to support rib-vaulted ceilings. Tracery fills the stained-glass windows in both the lower level and clerestory. Intricate tracery is painted on the ceilings.

30b

33. John Coop House, 1889
959 South Van Ness Avenue
Henry Geilfuss, architect

John Coop, owner of a South-of-Market planning mill, clearly used his residence as an advertisement for his products: studs, buttons, sunbursts, overlapping rings, curvilinear brackets, turned posts, molded dentils, decorative shingles, and plaster ornament jostle for space on this façade. A corner tower rises to a steep witch's cap.

34. Claus Mangels House, 1883
822 South Van Ness Avenue
Henry Geilfuss, architect

This Italianate is enlivened by full-arched windows, scroll ornament, and other elaborations. The third story is an early addition.

35. El Capitan Theater, 1928
2351–2361 Mission Street
William H. Crim Jr., architect

Spanish Baroque in style, it has a great entrance pavilion that rises to a curvilinear parapet.

36. Emanuel Church of the Evangelical Association, 1915
Southwest corner of Capp and Nineteenth Streets
Falch and Knoll, architects

Through the architects' skillful manipulation of scale, this Classic Revival–style church has an imposing, if not monumental, feeling to it. Paired arched windows supported by spiral columns range across both façades of the main/upper story.

37. Girls Recreation Club, 1911–1913
362 Capp Street
Ward and Blohme, architects

The Shingle-style two-story, side-gable-roofed building has small-paned sash windows, a two-story angled window bay, and a base of clinker brick. It is now the Mission Neighborhood Center.

38. St. Charles Borromeo Roman Catholic Church, 1887
3250 Eighteenth Street
Charles J. Devlin, architect

This Italianate church has an arched entry flanked by engaged columns and topped by a pediment; above the cornice is a broken pediment. In 1916, this building became a school for the new **St. Charles Church,** located at the southeast corner of Eighteenth Street and South Van Ness Avenue.

39. Mission Turn Verin, 1910
3543 Eighteenth Street
August R. Denke, architect

The four-story building is notable for rows of arched windows across the second and fourth stories, a pent roof that spans the top, and huge murals portraying goddesses and women. It was built as the Mission Turn Verin, a German athletic club; around 1940, it became Dovre Hall, home to the Sons of Norway; and in 1979, it became the Women's Building.

40. Roxie Theater, 1913
3117–3125 Sixteenth Street
Alfred I. Coffey, architect

Built as two storefronts, each is delineated by a curved parapet arching across the top. The eastern half has always been a movie theater; the blade sign and marquee date to the 1930s. It is the last "storefront" movie theater, once a common type, that still functions as such in the city.

41. Neighborhood banks, 1907, 1910
Sixteenth and Valencia Streets

Two banks founded in the Mission District attest to the neighborhood's importance in the early twentieth century. The former Mission Bank, at **3060 Sixteenth Street** (1907; S. H. Woodruff, architect) has a Roman temple composition. **3100–3116 Sixteenth Street** is the former Mission Savings Bank (1910; Crim and Scott, architects), which has a Mediterranean feeling.

42. St. John's Episcopal Church, 1909
1661 Fifteenth and 120 Julian Streets

Herbert B. Maggs, architect

A Gothic Revival church sheathed with shingles, its windows are filled with fine Gothic tracery, Gothic spires rise from the corners, and the buttresses are flared. Inside, the central aisle rises to a high gabled ceiling supported by hammer beams. Inside and out, this is one of the great small churches in the city.

43. National Guard Armory, 1913
1800 Mission Street

John W. Woollett, state architect

This armory, faced with clinker brick, takes the form of a massive fortress, with corner towers that broaden at the base to give added support. Narrow slit windows beneath a wide arch add to the "defensive" style of the building. Entrances and belt courses are made of granite. It is an amazing edifice.

44. Capp Street Project, 1981
65 Capp Street, at Adair Street

David Ireland, designer

This house was built for a residency program in conceptual art. Its corrugated metal siding and irregular massing of rectangular forms were an early use of industrial materials.

45. Industrial buildings
North of Twentieth Street and east of Harrison Street

Industrial buildings dating from Victorian times to the mid-twentieth century dominate the northeast quadrant of the Mission District. A sampling includes the Golden Gate Woolen Mills at **2800 Twentieth Street** (1880; Augustus Laver, architect); the Potrero Block, a brick and granite warehouse at **100 Potrero Avenue** (1910; Nathaniel Blaisdell, architect); and the Continental Baking Company at **1550–1590 Bryant Street** (1928–1929; Bliss and Fairweather, architects).

46. San Francisco General Hospital, 1909 ongoing (unmapped)
Northeast corner of Twenty-Third Street and Potrero Avenue

Newton J. Tharp, city architect (1909)

Martin Rist, architect (1932–1935)

The six oldest buildings in this complex display some of the finest brick-pattern work in San Francisco. These were designed by Newton J. Tharp and erected from 1909 to 1914. They are mainly Romanesque, with wonderful glazed terra-cotta window bays (with corner gargoyles) facing Potrero Avenue. The psychopathic ward, with a sculptural grouping in its main entrance (1932–1935; Martin Rist, architect) is Art Deco, but sympathetic. Early pieces of the complex include nicely detailed perimeter walls, gatehouse, bus shelter, and light standards. The complex now includes modern connecting wings between the wards and a Brutalist main hospital building (1973) that replaced Tharp's administration building.

46

13 • Potrero Hill

During the Mexican era, the Potrero (Spanish for "grazing lands") was the rancho of Francisco DeHaro. In the early 1860s, development occurred next to the bay where major industries—including Pacific Rolling Mills, San Francisco Gas Light Company, California Sugar Refinery, Union Iron Works, and American Can Company—needed a waterfront location. Workers' houses and hotels were built along and near Third Street. During the 1880s and through the 1940s, the rest of the hill was gradually developed.

1. Union Iron Works, 1883–1917
Twentieth Street, east of Illinois Street

Union Iron Works, founded in 1849 as a blacksmith shop by Peter Donahue, quickly grew into one of the city's leading iron foundries. It moved to this site as a shipbuilding firm in 1883. The company merged with Bethlehem Steel in 1905. From 1888 through World War II, it built and repaired ships for the U.S. government. The most substantial buildings are located along Twentieth Street. They are now unoccupied and have an air of sad neglect.

Administration Building #2 (1a) at the northeast corner of Twentieth and Illinois Streets (1917; Frederick H. Meyer, architect) and the **Powerhouse** (1912; Charles Peter Weeks, architect) next door are both constructed of reinforced concrete in a Classical Revival style. **Administration Building #1** (1897; Percy and Hamilton, architects) is a handsome red-brick three-story building with a textured concrete base, sandstone entry and trim, terra-cotta window corners, copper cornice, and classical detailing. On the south side of Twentieth are two brick manufacturing buildings (1b): a machine shop and foundry (circa 1883; D. E. Melliss, engineer) and an erecting shop.

2. American Can Company, 1915–1929
2325–2495 Third Street
C. G. Preis, architect

The American Can Company of New York had maintained a business office in San Francisco before building this factory. Several buildings make up the architecturally harmonious complex that fills an entire block. Designed by the company's architect, each has a reinforced-concrete frame with brick infill walls and industrial steel sash windows, with the exception of the redbrick office building.

3. Potrero Hill Police Station, 1914
2300 Third Street
Alfred I. Coffey, city architect

The two-story Mission Revival building has a tile hipped roof pierced with a central shaped parapet with a quatrefoil medallion.

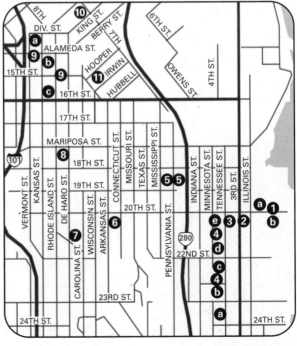

4. Dogpatch

900–1100 Blocks of Tennessee Street and adjacent blocks

This is a neighborhood of worker housing built for employees of nearby industries. With the decline of industry and loss of jobs, the neighborhood became a rough place, and by the 1970s, it was called "Dogpatch," after the town where Li'l Abner lived in Al Capp's comic strip. It has since rebounded and is now a historic district.

4a. 1102–1116 Tennessee Street, 1885–1886

T. J. Welsh, designer-builder

These four sets of Eastlake flats have elaborate window trim.

4b. Former Irving Scott School, 1895

1060 Tennessee Street

T. J. Welsh, architect

This simple wood-frame Classic Revival school is the city's oldest school building.

4c. 1002–1012 Tennessee Street and 903–915 Minnesota Street, 1890–1891

John C. Pelton, designer

Approximately twelve small houses from Pelton's "Cheap Cottage" series are located on these two blocks. Only fifteen feet wide, they have Eastlake trim.

4d. William J. Thompson House, 1872

720 Twenty-Second Street

This simple front-gable house is the oldest in Dogpatch. Thompson was a boat-builder.

4e. SFFD Engine Co. #16, 1925

909 Tennessee Street

Meyer and Johnson, architects

The Romanesque-style brick-sided building has its original truck doors.

5. Charles Adams houses, 1865, 1873

301, 300 Pennsylvania Street

These large houses, across the street from one another, illustrate the changes the Italianate style went through during this period. 301 (1865) is foursquare and restrained, with a one-story bay window relegated to the side façade; the house has lost its porch and cupola. Eight years

later in 1873, 300 [5] was built with two-story window bays (one dominating the main façade), a cornice that wraps around the bays, and a higher level of ornament.

6. Stick-Eastlake houses, 1890

512–524 Connecticut Street

William Hollis, developer

This lively row of seven houses was built by the same man who presided over The Real Estate Associates (TREA) in the 1870s.

7. Potrero Hill Neighborhood House, 1921

953 DeHaro Street

Julia Morgan, architect

This is a modest clubhouse clad in wood shingles and clapboards, with gabled roofs. The paneled main hall is cluttered with an amazing array of electrical conduits for modern lighting fixtures.

Here and there are a few recently built or remodeled single-family houses such as the simple, geometrically massed house at **1127 DeHaro** (2005; Joshua Aidlin, architect) that fits nicely onto a small lot.

8. St. Gregory of Nyssa Episcopal Church, 1995

500 DeHaro Street

John Goodman, architect

Mark Dukes, artist (dancing saints)

The uplifting feeling is unmistakable in this modern rendition of the Craftsman style. The towers, roofline of exposed rafters and purlins, battered foundation walls, tile mosaic over the entry, and textured wooden doors combine to give visual delight.

9. Showplace Square
Henry Adams, Division, and Eleventh Streets

A group of early-twentieth-century brick factories were converted into designer show-places beginning in 1971. The first two blocks of Kansas Street have been renamed Henry Adams, after the developer who began adaptively reusing the former factories. Since the 1970s, many modern buildings have also been built in the area as infill.

9a. Dunham, Carrigan and Hayden, 1915
Southwest corner of Division and Kansas Streets

Leo J. Devlin, architect

The four-story brick, former wholesale hardware plant was the first building to be converted by Adams in 1971.

9b. The Galleria
101 Kansas Street

Two three-story brick buildings are connected by a glazed entry bay.

9c. Schlesinger and Bender, 1911
299 Kansas Street, at the corner of Sixteenth Street

G. Albert Lansburgh, architect

The former wine cellar and cooperage has an angled corner.

10. Pacific Hardware and Steel, 1905
700 Seventh Street

Sutton and Weeks, architects

Here is a large, handsome, three-story brick store and factory building with a rusticated base, end and center pavilions defined by quoins, and a sandstone entrance. Pacific Hardware and Steel was founded in the 1850s by Mark Hopkins and Collis Huntington, of later Southern Pacific Railroad fame. In 1918, the firm merged with Baker and Hamilton.

11. Greyhound Bus Repair Facility, 1951
1111 Eighth Street

Skidmore, Owings & Merrill, architects

Bands of steel sash windows stretch the full length of three long façades and along most of the fourth, making this a transition between early-twentieth-century Industrial and International styles. This was the project that brought Skidmore, Owings & Merrill to San Francisco, the most prolific firm in reshaping the city's downtown over the past half-century. The building is now occupied by the **California College of the Arts,** Graduate Center (2003; adaptive reuse by Jensen & Macy Architects), though Greyhound still occupies the yard along Seventh Street.

14 · Southeast Neighborhoods: Bayview, Hunter's Point, McLaren Park, Portola, Excelsior, Outer Mission, Bernal Heights

Bayview, Hunter's Point

During the Gold Rush, Robert and Philip Hunter, for whom Hunter's Point is named, farmed near Oakdale and Griffith Streets. Industry arrived in 1867 when a granite dry dock was built at the end of Hunter's Point. In the 1870s, the city's slaughterhouses were moved from South-of-Market to "Butchertown," where the India Basin post office facility now stands. The meat industry, along with associated tanneries and glue works, became the economic mainstay of the neighborhood.

When World War II brought thousands of jobs to Hunter's Point shipyards, housing projects were constructed on the hill for the workers. The collapse of shipbuilding jobs after the war and the gradual decline of the slaughterhouses left an economic vacuum from which the neighborhood is still recovering. For this reason, visitors are urged to be "streetwise." The recent opening of a light-rail line along Third Street will help connect the area with other parts of the city.

1. South San Francisco Opera House, 1888
South side of Newcomb Avenue, just east of Third Street

This is the oldest theater building in the city; it doubled as a Masonic hall in the early years and later became a community hall. The style is exuberant Eastlake.

2. Gothic Revival cottage, circa 1860s
1547 Oakdale Avenue

A one-story Gothic Revival cottage with a symmetrical façade has a front door with a transom flanked by two tall, four-over-four sash windows, a full-width front porch, and cutout patterns on the side gables and suspended from the shed roof of the porch.

3. Sylvester House, circa 1870
1556 Revere Avenue

This stately Italianate has a symmetrical façade with elaborate rounded pediments over the second-story windows and a full-width front porch with fluted columns. Located originally on Quesada Avenue, it was owned by a family of wholesale meat dealers during the 1880s–1900 and was moved here in 1913.

4. All Hallows Catholic Church, 1888
Newhall Street at Palou Avenue

John J. Clark, architect

14 • Southeast Neighborhoods: Bayview, Hunter's Point

This impressive wood-frame Gothic Revival church has a particularly fine central tower and steeple, wood tracery, and buttresses.

5. Pearl Gate Tabernacle Baptist Church, circa 1871
Bay View Street at Latona Street

This is Gothic Revival in style, featuring pointed-arch windows with hood moldings that end with pendant drops.

McLaren Park, Portola

McLaren Park, the second-largest park in the city, is relatively undeveloped and underused. It is named for John McLaren, superintendent of Golden Gate Park from 1887 to 1943. The park is surrounded by several distinct neighborhoods including the Portola District, the Excelsior, and the Outer Mission. Because of its remote location, the area developed late in the city's history, mostly during the 1920s and 1940s. The optimism of the real estate speculator knew no bounds, however, and some tracts were laid out in a standard grid pattern as early as the 1860s. A number of Victorian- and Edwardian-era buildings are indeed scattered throughout these neighborhoods. Though not the most picturesque in San Francisco, there are some treasures to be discovered in these neighborhoods.

6. Portola Shopping District, 1890s–1920s
San Bruno Avenue, south of Silver Avenue

Few of these small commercial buildings are especially distinguished, but some are rather old, and together they form a lively streetscape. The **Avenue Theater** (1927; Reid Brothers, architects) at 2650 San Bruno Avenue, now used as a church, is the most prominent building. Most of the exterior ornament is Spanish Colonial Revival in style; the interior has been remodeled.

7. Reservoir Keeper's House, circa 1880s
401 University Street

This is the last surviving reservoir keeper's house of the several the Spring Valley Water Company built in the nineteenth century. It is Stick-Eastlake in style, with carved brackets supporting the eaves and incised ornament in the gable.

8. University Mound Old Ladies' Home, 1931–1932
350 University Street
Coffey, Rist, and Gottschalk, architects

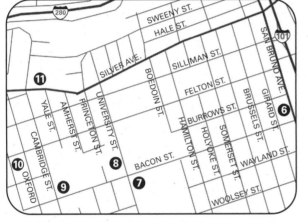

14 • Southeast Neighborhoods: McLaren Park, Portola

The large brick and white-trimmed Georgian-style building, set back from the street on a large parcel, replaced one built in 1863 for University Mound College.

9. Home of the Good Shepherd, 1933
501 Cambridge Street, at Bacon Street

Henry A. Minton, architect

The south wings and the bell tower of this Spanish Colonial Revival complex are especially fine. It was built as a Catholic convent and girls' school and is now a Baptist school.

10. 1539 Felton Street, 1991

Kotas/Pantaleoni Architects

The distorted angles, curved bay window, and vivid colors are in keeping with this firm's quirky houses on Laidley Street.

11. Salvation Army Training School, 1927–1928
801 Silver Avenue

R. F. Inwood, architect

At one time Salvation Army workers wore spiffy uniforms and underwent extensive training. Here is where they received that training. The brick building features a central pavilion with triple-arched windows trimmed in terra-cotta. Side wings have arcaded entries flanked by towers with pyramidal roofs. The building is now a private school.

Excelsior, Outer Mission

12. Chemical Engine Company #43, 1911
724 Brazil Avenue

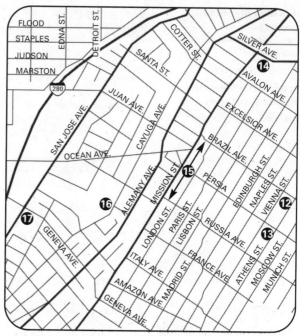

14 • Southeast Neighborhoods: Excelsior, Outer Mission

This former firehouse has a large arched entry; three arched windows are shaded by a shed roof.

13. Franklin R. Smith House, circa 1880
750 Persia Avenue

Built as dairy ranch house, the narrow raised-basement Italianate once stood quite alone here. There are decorated pediments over the windows and front door, and carved eave brackets under the false-front cornice.

14. Jewish Old People's Home, 1921–1922
302 Silver Avenue

Samuel Hyman, architect

This major institution retains its original use. The original building of the complex is Classic Revival and Georgian, with a two-story pedimented entrance portico. The institution has expanded, and there are buildings from many periods.

15. 4600–4700 Blocks of Mission Street

This is the heart of the Excelsior neighborhood commercial district, lined mostly with one- and two-story buildings that display a sometimes-amusing array of styles and decoration ranging from architect Arthur Brown Jr.'s small, sober granite Hibernia Bank (1928) at **4600 Mission Street** to the fun, one-of-a-kind Art Deco Royal Baking Co. (1932) [15] at **4773 Mission,** with a green-tile storefront and a parapet like a loaf of bread rising into Art Deco spikes.

16. Balboa High School, 1927–1931
1000 Cayuga Avenue, at Onondaga

John Reid Jr., architect
Hyman and Appleton, architects
Bakewell and Weihe, architects

The main wing facing Cayuga, by Reid, was built first, but the best part is the section along Onondaga, by Bakewell and Weihe (1931). The blend of Romanesque, Byzantine, and Spanish Colonial Revival styles is monumental in feeling.

17. Geneva Office Building and Power House, 1901
2301 San Jose Avenue, at Geneva

Reid Brothers, architects

A rare early-mass-transit-related building built for the city's first electric streetcar company, the San Francisco and San Mateo Railroad; it is now owned by MUNI. Damage suffered in the Loma Prieta Earthquake of 1989 has been partially repaired. The building badly needs a new use.

Bernal Heights

The hill is named for Jose Cornelio de Bernal, who received Rancho de las Salinas y Potrero Nuevo as a Mexican land grant in 1839. In 1859, Harvey S. Brown purchased Bernal's rancho and subdivided it into small narrow blocks that are not part of the Mission District grid. He reserved two areas for parks: today's Precita Park on the north and Holly Park on the south.

Because of Bernal Heights' distance from downtown and its hilly topography, development was gradual. Several dozen houses were built in the 1860s, but the hill was not fully developed until the 1950s. Houses around Precita Park are older and generally larger than on the south side of the hill. But mostly these were modest working-class houses.

18. Precita Street houses

18a. Peterson House, 1866
124 Precita Street

Simple, gabled houses such as this were extremely common in the 1850s and 1860s; this is a now-rare example. The first owner, Sivert Peterson, worked as an expressman.

18b. Hyde House, 1870
147 Precita Street

By 1870, the Italianate style had become the style of choice. This house, a fine early example, was built for Michael Hyde, a tailor.

19. Brookes Residence, 1866
34 Prospect Street

Samuel Marsden Brookes (1816–1892) was one of the finest still-life painters in the city's history. For twenty-four years the bearded Bohemian artist commuted from this house to his fourth-floor studio at 611 Clay Street. He and his wife raised six children in this Gothic Revival house. It is uncertain whether the elegant swan's-neck pediment over the entry is original.

20. Bernal Branch Library, 1936
500 Cortland Avenue

Frederick H. Meyer, architect

Located on the main shopping street of Bernal Heights, the

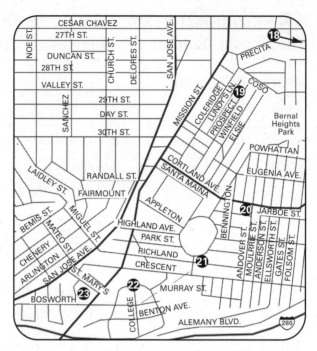

14 • Southeast Neighborhoods: Bernal Heights

library is restrained and similar to Meyer's West Portal Library of the same year. Across the street, **433** is the neighborhood Bank of America (1928).

21. Kawalkowski House, 1887
450 Murray Street

All three major Victorian house styles are incorporated here: Italianate (first-story quoins), Eastlake (window trim), and Queen Anne (gables). The square corner tower imparts a villa quality. Frank Kawalkowski, a cabinetmaker and mill hand, probably built the house in stages beginning in 1887.

22. St. Mary's Park, 1924
Mission, Justin, and Crescent Streets

Punnett and Parez, surveyors

This is a pleasant subdivision of detached stucco-clad houses placed along gently curving streets with occasional greenswards. It was built on the site of St. Mary's College (1862). In the 1880s, the college moved to Oakland before moving to Moraga in 1928. In 1924, the Roman Catholic archdiocese created the housing tract.

23. Church of St. John the Evangelist, 1902
19 St. Mary's Avenue

Shea and Shea, architects

This is a small wood-framed church made quite grand by its Corinthian-columned porch, with pediment and frieze, and flanking Baroque towers that are beautifully sculpted. The adjacent Classical Revival parish hall complements the church building.

15 · Southwest Neighborhoods: West-of-Twin-Peaks, The Sunset District, Lake Merced

West-of-Twin-Peaks

"West-of-Twin-Peaks" is a collection of neighborhoods surveyed between 1912 and 1931. The land was originally part of Jose Noe's Mexican-era Rancho San Miguel. It was purchased in the early 1880s by Adolph Sutro, and became available for subdivision after his estate was settled in 1910. At that time two transportation projects were begun: the Twin Peaks Tunnel for electric streetcars and Portola Drive for automobiles, both linking the district with downtown.

The first neighborhoods surveyed were Forest Hill, St. Francis Wood, and Ingleside Terrace in 1912. West Portal and parts of Edgehill followed later in the decade, while Balboa Terrace, Monterey Heights, Mt. Davidson Manor, Westwood Highlands, and Westwood Park were created in the 1920s. Miraloma Park and Sherwood Forest on Mt. Davidson's upper slopes were laid out by 1931 but were not fully developed until the 1950s.

To promote these neighborhoods, developers often included entrance gates or pillars, fountains, hillside staircases, and public lawns, which fostered a sense of exclusive graciousness. Covenants prohibited apartments and commercial establishments as well as selling lots to people of color (now illegal). Two subdivisions have clubhouses.

Nearly all the streets are curvilinear; the predominant architectural style is Period Revival in all its variations and sizes.

1. Laguna Honda Hospital, 1926–1939
375 Laguna Honda
John Reid Jr.,
architect

This complex is situated on a northwest flank of Twin Peaks, with views of Forest Hill, Edgehill, and Mount Davidson. The main entrance is set within a monumental arch filled with terra-cotta ornament and flanked by huge urns. Behind, a Romanesque tower rises to a considerable height. To the left is a service wing, and to the right is the first of a long series of wards that step up the hillside in a nice rhythm. Colorful Spanish tiles are used to wainscot the lobby on each floor, and wooden hopper windows bring natural ventilation and light to each bed. This complex replaced an almshouse built in the 1860s.

There are plans to replace most of the wards.

At the northeast corner of Laguna Honda Boulevard and Clarendon Avenue is a natural lake converted to a reservoir by the Spring Valley Water Company. Laguna Honda Reservoir was built between 1927 and 1930 by city engineer Michael M. O'Shaughnessy.

2. Forest Hill

Forest Hill was surveyed in 1912–1913 by architect/engineer Mark Daniels, who included the triangular lawn at Magellan Avenue and Pacheco Street and the grand staircase that marches up to Castenada Avenue as amenities. The neighborhood developed gradually—houses can be found from each decade between 1910 and 1950.

2a. Forest Hill Station, 1915
Laguna Honda and Dewey Boulevard

Michael M. O'Shaughnessy, city engineer

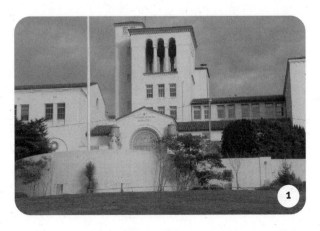

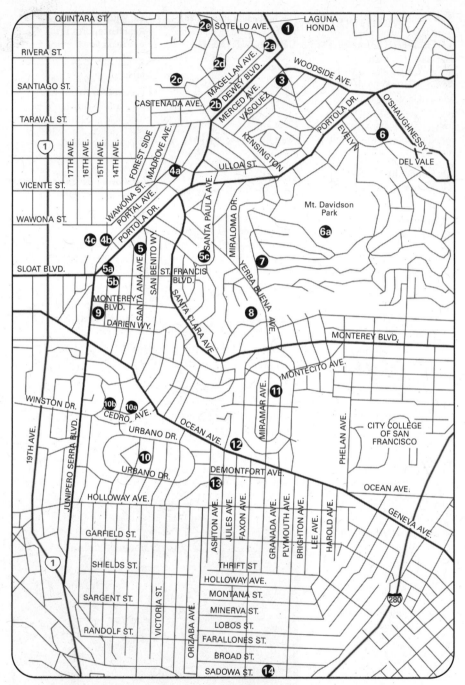

15 Southwest Neighborhoods • West-of-Twin-Peaks

This was built as part of the Twin Peaks Tunnel project to serve residents of Forest Hill and Forest Hill Extension. It is a restrained Classical Revival station notable for its carefully proportioned composition and the fine interior moldings. Behind the building is the lawn with paths up to the residential streets.

2b. Forest Hill Clubhouse, 1919
381 Magellan Avenue

Bernard Maybeck, architect

This takes the form of a rambling medieval tavern. The walls are half-timbered in the second story, and scalloped bargeboards are in the gables. The wood and brick interior is open to the rafters.

2c. English cottage, 1925
400 Castenada Avenue

Harold G. Stoner, architect

This English medieval cottage is made of rubble limestone. The front wing has a pointed arch window beneath a cross-braced gable; the main body of the house steps up the hill and has a modified hipped roof. The massing is very effective.

2d. Erlinger House, 1916
270 Castenada Avenue

Maybeck and White, architects

Made of red brick and wood shingle, this house has a faintly Tudor air.

2e. E. C. Young House, 1913
51 Sotello Avenue

Bernard Maybeck, architect

Here is one of the first houses built in Forest Hill—not a bad way to start a neighborhood!

This medieval half-timbered house has a corner pulpit with Gothic quatrefoil patterns.

3. Edgehill

Edgehill consists of four small subdivisions created between 1912 and 1931. The oldest, Forest Hill Extension, is the only one still widely known by its original name. The neighborhood consists mostly of modest, detached stucco houses. The most prominent building is **St. Brendan Catholic Church** at 29 Rockaway Avenue (1929–1930; Edward A. Eames, architect). It is Mediterranean with stucco cladding, clay-tile roof, and irregular massing. Its bell tower gently tapers to a belfry topped by a blue tile dome.

4. West Portal

West Portal formed as a series of small real estate subdivisions between 1914 and 1925. The largest, West Portal Park, was developed by Fernando Nelson and Sons and was named for the massive classical arch that framed the western portal of the Twin Peaks Tunnel, completed in 1917. Alas, the arch was demolished in the 1970s when the MUNI streetcar station was rebuilt.

4a. William A. Nelson Residence, circa 1919
935 Ulloa Street

Fernando Nelson and Sons, builders

This Mission Revival villa is notable for its parapet, pent roofs, and arcaded porch. Its first owner, William Nelson, worked with his father, Fernando, as a builder.

4b. Row of five houses, 1925
420–470 West Portal Avenue

Fernando Nelson and Sons, builders

Of the rows of houses built by the Nelsons in this neighborhood, this is the best. The styles are Mediterranean, Colonial, and Tudor.

4c. Arden Wood (Christian Science Sanatorium), 1929–1930
445 Wawona Street, at Fifteenth Avenue

Henry H. Gutterson, architect

Though tucked away in a valley, this building is prominently visible because of its very high, steep, slate-covered roof. In form, the building follows French Norman prototypes; it is medieval in feeling while the ornament is Classical.

2d

5. St. Francis Wood

At its groundbreaking ceremony in 1912, the developers (the Mason-McDuffie Company of Berkeley) announced they "shall spare neither effort nor money to make St. Francis Wood the finest residence park . . . ." The first phase of the garden-city-style sub-division was completed in 1914.

Frederick Law Olmsted Jr. designed the landscape plan; architect John Galen Howard designed the entrance gates, street monuments, St. Francis Fountain, and tract office; Henry Higby Gutterson designed the upper fountain and became supervising architect in 1914, a post he held until his death in 1954.

Architecturally there is quite a variety of Period Revival styles even though the Italianate villa was favored initially. The residential development has retained its cachet for nearly a hundred years. Excellent planning combined with control over what was constructed solved some of the problems the developers experienced in their earlier work in Berkeley.

5a. Spanish Colonial Revival house, 1922
45 St. Francis Boulevard
John Reid Jr., architect

A column in the first story rises and flares outward to become a beautiful oriel window. The iron entrance gate is great.

5b. Monterey Revival house, 1930
98 St. Francis Boulevard
Masten and Hurd, architects

This house has hints of the Mediterranean, old Mexico, and colonial Monterey, effectively accented by palm trees and other plantings. The architects designed about 100 houses in St. Francis Wood, several in a style similar to this house.

5c. Gutterson houses, 1922–1925
200 Block of Santa Paula
Henry H. Gutterson, architect

These three houses with very different aesthetics were designed by the same architect. 240 (1925) is Norman or English in style, with a steep roof, a purposefully uneven stucco surface, and wood casement windows. 262 (1922) is Colonial Revival and formal in feeling. The entry has a pedimented porch roof and a spider-web transom over the door and six-over-six windows with shutters. 200 (1922) was featured in the International Exposition of Architecture and Allied Arts,

New York, in 1925 as a "Cotswold Cottage" [5c].

6. Miraloma Park

Miraloma Park covers most of Mount Davidson's upper slopes. The Meyer Brothers surveyed the tract during 1926–1931 and spent the next twenty-plus years developing it with 2,400 houses built to the lot lines, in contrast with other West-of-Twin-Peaks neighborhoods. The woodsy neighborhood clubhouse, built and donated by Meyer Brothers in 1940, is on Del Vale Avenue near O'Shaughnessy Boulevard.

6a. Mt. Davidson Cross, 1934
George W. Kelham, architect
Henry Brunnier, engineer

The top of Mount Davidson has been surmounted by five different crosses. The current 103-foot cross is reinforced concrete, plain but durable. It is the focal point for Easter sunrise services, a tradition that began in 1923. The remnant of Adolph Sutro's eucalyptus forest is a city park. The east side of the hill has magnificent views.

7. Sherwood Forest

Located on the southwest slope of Mount Davidson, Sherwood Forest was surveyed in two

sections, once in 1930 and again in 1950. For the most part it consists of bland boxy houses from the 1940s and later. Older houses, such as **101 Lansdale** (1937), **235 Lansdale** (1936), and **33 Robin Hood** (1939), all designed by architect Martin J. Rist, lend charm to these streets.

8. Monterey Heights and Westwood Highlands

Located on gently rolling hills, these neighborhoods of detached stucco houses were surveyed in the mid-1920s. Many houses have irregular footprints, with wings and/or pavilions. **55 Elmo Way** (1926; Charles F. Strothoff, architect) is an example; this one is Renaissance Revival.

9. Balboa Terrace and Mt. Davidson Manor

These subdivisions, on lower and flatter land, were also surveyed in the mid-1920s. The latter was a project of Fernando Nelson and Sons. The modest houses are almost uniformly clad in stucco with restrained ornament.

9a. Craftsman-Tudor house, 1935
141 Junipero Serra Boulevard
Harold G. Stoner, architect

The first story is clad in chert and serpentine rubble, with bits of brickwork inserted to engender a feeling of vernacular primitivism. The second story is half-timbered.

9b. Ninth Church of Christ, Scientist, 1941
175 Junipero Serra Boulevard
Henry H. Gutterson, architect

Here is Romanesque style in reinforced concrete. While the detailing is minimal, the composition and form are

well-conceived. This is a replacement or remodeling of an earlier church (1921) on this site.

10. Ingleside Terrace

Joseph Leonard built many houses in Alameda before moving to San Francisco. He had Ingleside Terrace surveyed in 1912 and built most of the larger houses himself. Very impressive sandstone pillars mark the perimeter of the tract. Curiously, Leonard preserved the memory of the old Ingleside racetrack by laying out Urbano Drive along its oval route. Even more unusual, a giant concrete sundial (1913) can be found in a circle at the apex of Entrada Court, within Urbano Drive.

10a. Craftsman-style house, 1912
70 Cedro Avenue
Joseph Leonard, architect and builder

This very dramatic Craftsman-style house is clad in wood shingles and has a base of rugged sandstone. The several setbacks follow the curve of the street and result in a staggered footprint and complex roofline.

Next door, at **90 Cedro** (1911), is a similar Craftsman house that Leonard built as his own home. In 1957, after racial covenants were set aside by the courts, it became the home of Cecil F. Poole, an assistant district attorney, later federal judge, and the first African American owner and resident in Ingleside Terrace.

10b. Sandstone house, 1914
140 Cedro Avenue
William Curlett, architect

The first story is brilliant red sandstone, cut smooth except for nar-

row courses that were left rough. The second story is stucco with Spanish molding in the cornice.

11. Westwood Park

Westwood Park was surveyed in 1917 and was marketed to homebuyers of average means. Architect Charles F. Strothoff was hired to design over 70 percent of the tract's 650 modest bungalows, and Ida McCain, a prolific San Francisco female architect, designed most of the rest; examples of her work include **676 Miramar** and **796 Faxon** (both 1918). The entrance portal (1916) at Monterey Boulevard and Miramar Avenue, by Louis Christian Mullgardt, is made of textured concrete, with decorative iron grilles and lanterns.

Ocean View, Merced Heights, Ingleside

Ocean View, Merced Heights, and Ingleside (also known under the acronym OMI) were surveyed in 1867, 1870, and 1890, respectively, and, given their distance from downtown, developed very slowly. Small farms dotted the district in its early years. After the Twin Peaks Tunnel brought the K and M streetcar lines in the 1920s, the area began to urbanize.

12. Ocean Avenue Commercial District
Ocean Avenue, between Plymouth Avenue and Victoria Street

This is the main commercial area. Its most distinctive building is **1700–1716 Ocean Avenue**

(1921; Adolph Morbio, engineer and builder) in Olde English style, with an imitation thatched roof and half-timbered gable. The neighborhood's Bank of Italy (1927; Henry A. Minton, architect) at **1649 Ocean Avenue** is a blend of Classical, Spanish, and Art Deco; it is now the Ingleside Branch Library. The Ingleside Presbyterian Church, **1345 Ocean Avenue** (1922; Joseph Leonard, architect and builder) was donated to the community by Joseph Leonard, the developer of nearby Ingleside Terrace.

13. St. Emydius Catholic Church, 1928
301 DeMontfort Avenue

John J. Foley,
architect

This monumental Spanish Colonial Revival church is the landmark of the Ingleside neighborhood. Twin towers rise to domed cupolas and flank a slightly recessed pavilion with arched entrances. This replaced the parish's 1914 wood-frame church.

14. Engine Company #33, 1896
117 Broad Street,
off Plymouth Avenue

Charles R. Wilson,
architect

The Classical Revival former firehouse is the most prominent of the nineteenth-century buildings along Broad Street, once Ocean View's downtown. This neighborhood developed initially as a stop on the road to San Jose and then as a train switching station and stop on the 1864 railroad. Highway 280 now cuts through the old community.

The Sunset District

The Sunset District, located south of Golden Gate Park and generally west of Mt. Sutro, Twin Peaks, and Mt. Davidson, is a sloping plain extending to the Pacific Ocean. On early maps, the Sunset and Richmond Districts were identified as the "Outside Lands." After the city gained title to the property from the U.S. government in 1866, the land was sold to speculators, but development did not begin until the 1880s.

The first residents were dairy farmers and employees of gunpowder works, who settled here in the 1860s. Their modest ranks grew in the 1870s with workers who planted trees in Golden Gate Park and graded H Street (now Lincoln Way). Public transit arrived in 1883 when a steam railroad opened along Lincoln Way from Stanyan Street to Ocean Beach. In the late 1880s, realtors coined the name "Sunset" as a way of advertising their property.

The district is laid out in a grid, with numbered avenues running north to south and named streets running east to west. Although known for seemingly unending treeless blocks of attached, two-story, stucco-sided homes built between the late 1920s through the 1950s, there is quite a bit of variety scattered throughout.

During the 1920s–1940s, developers such as Henry Doelger and the Gellert Brothers built up the blocks in the Outer Sunset with thousands of stucco-front houses. A few are distinctive, but a feeling of sameness pervades.

Inner Sunset District

The Inner Sunset (from Arguello Boulevard to Funston Avenue) saw an explosion of development between 1900 and 1918, mainly in the Classical Revival and Craftsman styles.

15. University of California Medical Center,
various dates
Parnassus Avenue

Overlooking the Inner Sunset, on the north slope of Mt. Sutro, is the University of California Medical Center (UCSF), a complex of approximately twelve large-scaled buildings. It is located on land donated by Adolph Sutro in 1898. The oldest building is a seven-story hospital (1917–1918) by Lewis Parsons Hobart. Behind, is a forest of eucalyptus trees (owned by the university) that Sutro planted in the 1880s and 1890s as a hobby.

16. Sunset Heights Subdivision
Willard Street, and Woodland and Edgewood Avenues

This small enclave is predominately Arts and Crafts in style, especially on Edgewood, which borders on forest. **1403 Willard** (1904) is Shingle style whose receding gables create a dramatic roofline. **1423–1425 Willard** (1900; Charles Paff, architect) have whimsical shingle patterns on the second and third stories. **1456 Willard** (1919; William Terry, carpenter) is Craftsman with some Tudor half-timbering and carved brackets. **1460–1462 Willard** (1909; Fred B. Wood, architect) have a Mission Revival parapet. **1506 Willard** (1905; Denke Brothers, architects) has a curvilinear parapet pierced by a quatrefoil window. **123 Edgewood** (1906; William Knowles, architect) is Craftsman with texture and a complex roofline. **109 Edgewood** (1906) is a shingled house built as the home of architect T. Patterson Ross. Farnsworth steps connect Edgewood and Willard.

17. Craftsman houses,
1909, 1911
1214 Third Avenue and
325–327 Hugo Street

Here are two beautifully detailed Craftsman-style houses. **1214 Third Avenue** (1909; Cox Brothers, builder)

has a stuccoed second story over a base of clinker brick; **325–327 Hugo** (1911; Harvey E. Harris, builder) are shingled and half-timbered flats.

18. St. John of God Church, 1919
1290 Fifth Avenue
Ward and Blohme, architects

The simple stucco-sided church with a gable roof and a projecting gable entry has a splendid wood-paneled interior and scissors-truss roof supports. The former Lutheran church now serves the Catholic community of UCSF.

19. Craftsman houses,
1910–1911
100 Block of
Judah Street
Cox Brothers,
builders

The largest cluster of Craftsman houses in the Inner Sunset faces Judah and wraps around both corners to include **1365–1391 Sixth** and **1366–1390 Seventh Avenues.** Each house is notable for having a distinctive design that always includes grouped window bays.

20. Commercial District
Irving Street between
Seventh and Tenth Avenues

The Classic Revival Bank of Italy at **701 Irving** (1922; William D. Shea, architect) anchors the main retail district. The Little Shamrock saloon, **807 Lincoln Way** (1893, 1924), is the neighborhood's oldest business; it received a Mission Revival parapet in 1924. Chemical Engine Co. #2, **1348 Tenth Avenue** (1899; Charles R. Wilson, builder), is a former firehouse with a shingled upper story and a distinctive tower. **1049 Irving** (1894) is a Queen Anne house. **1230 Tenth Avenue** (1897; William H. Lillie, architect) is a blend of Colonial Revival and Shingle styles. A particularly inventive Mission Revival–style storefront with flats above is **1797–1799 Tenth Avenue** (1911; L. M. Weismann and Son, builder), which has an unusual corner tower.

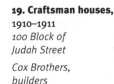

15 • Southwest Neighborhoods: Inner Sunset District

21. St. Anne of the Sunset Roman Catholic Church, 1929–1932
Northwest corner of Funston Avenue and Judah Street

William D. Shea, architect

William Adrian, engineer

This monumental twin-towered edifice is beautifully decorated with molded concrete ornament. The style is Romanesque with strong Spanish and Classical influences. A frieze of eighty religious figures marches across the main façade, created by Sister Justina Niemierski of Mission San Jose. The parish was founded in 1903.

Outer Sunset District

Although a Lincoln Way streetcar line opened in 1883, only the blocks between Lincoln Way and Irving Street were partially developed by 1918. Until the Sunset Tunnel opened and the Judah streetcar began operating in 1928, most streets had not been graded and sand dunes were more numerous than houses.

22. Sunset Branch Library, 1917
1305 Eighteenth Avenue

G. Albert Lansburgh, architect

This handsome Renaissance Revival–style library has a deeply recessed triple-arched entry, tall arched windows, and hipped tile roof.

23. Earthquake shack house, 1906
1227 Twenty-Fourth Avenue

More than 5,000 wood-frame cabins were constructed for refugees after the 1906 earthquake and fire. Few remain; this tiny cottage is made of several shacks and is a designated city landmark.

24. Doelger row houses, 1933
1301–1383 Twenty-Ninth Avenue

Henry Doelger, builder

Middle Sunset contains about three hundred blocks filled with thousands of stucco-fronted houses dating between 1920 and 1950. Many large-scale builders such as the Gellert Brothers, the Stoneson Brothers, Chris McKeon, and Ray Galli were active, but none more so than Henry Doelger. Set on twenty-five-foot lots, they were stucco-sided, two-bedroom, one-bath houses set above a one-car garage. The 1300 Block of Twenty-Ninth Avenue is composed of alternating Mediterranean, French Renaissance, and Tudor houses with lively ornament.

25. Rousseau row houses, 1932–1933
*1500 Block of
Thirty-Sixth Avenue*

Oliver Rousseau was another major builder. This row is distinctive for exaggerated chimneystacks, picturesque massing, and inventive variations on the romantic Period Revival mode. They face the greensward of Sunset Boulevard, San Francisco's longest divided parkway.

26. Harrington houses, 1911–1913
*1200 Block of
Forty-Second Avenue*

Alonzo Harrington, builder

Here is an interesting row of fifteen Craftsman-style houses. Two blocks southwest is Francis Scott Key School, at **1530 Forty-Third Avenue** (1935; Mooser, Eames, and Stone, architects), with a fine Art Deco entrance pavilion.

27. Oceanside

The blocks closest to the ocean were developed earlier than middle Sunset, becoming a beach community known as Oceanside around 1903. It began in 1895 as "Carville," a group of houses composed of surplus streetcars hauled out to the beach. The last survivor stands at **1632 Great Highway** (1908). A rustic aesthetic prevailed; many houses were shingled and have Craftsman features, including **1468 Forty-Seventh Avenue** (circa 1901) and **1984 Great Highway** (1905); the modest redwood home of architect Ernest Born at **2020 Great Highway** (1951) is a continuation of the neighborhood's early aesthetic.

28. Shriners' Hospital for Crippled Children, 1922–1923, 1929
*Southwest corner of
Nineteenth Avenue and
Lawton Street*

Weeks and Day, architects

This Italian Renaissance–style former hospital is extremely rich in white glazed terra-cotta ornament that contrasts with patterned, reddish orange brick walls and a Spanish tile roof. Broad lawns and mature cypress trees create an oasis of greenery. This was the third of ten hospitals for children built by the Shriners offering free treatment. In the 1990s, this building was converted into an assisted living center.

29. Infant Shelter, 1928–1929
1201 Ortega Street

*Louis Christian Mullgardt,
architect*

The building is Mission Revival with Baroque elements. The main entrance is framed by glazed terra-cotta, with floral ornament and panels of infants' heads by sculptor Carlo Taliabue.

Secondary entrances on Nineteenth and Twentieth Avenues are framed by alternating bands of orange and green terra-cotta beneath sheet copper canopies. Between the 1950s and 2005, it housed the Conservatory of Music.

South Sunset District

30. St. Cecilia's Roman Catholic Church, 1956
*Northwest corner of
Seventeenth Avenue and
Vicente Street*

Martin J. Rist, architect

This large Spanish Colonial Revival church for a parish founded in 1917 is uncompromised by modern design trends; it looks like it had been built thirty years earlier.

31. Parkside Branch Library, 1951
1200 Taraval Street

*Appleton and Wolford,
architects*

The first of several attractive modern libraries by these architects is marred by replacement aluminum doors and windows.

32. Taraval Police Station, circa 1931
2345 Twenty-Fourth Avenue

Coffey and Rist, architects

This beautifully detailed Romanesque-style building is clad in brick with terra-cotta ornament.

33. Edgewood Children's Center, 1924
1801 Vicente Street

Bliss and Faville, architects

The San Francisco Protestant Orphanage Asylum, founded in the Western Addition in the 1850s, built this complex as its new home. It consists of a central administration building surrounded by six "cottages" for the children. The Italian Renaissance buildings are clad in stucco, with terra-cotta ornament.

34. Junior League House, 1928
2685 Thirtieth Avenue
Ashley, Evers and Hays, architects

Set on spacious grounds, this rectangular two-story brick building with hipped tile roof is a simplified version

of Renaissance Revival. Until 1946, it served as a home for children from broken families.

35. Trocadero Inn, 1892
In Stern Grove,
at Nineteenth Avenue and
Sloat Boulevard

This small valley was part of the 1847 homestead of George Greene, who planted the groves of eucalyptus. His son George Jr. built the Trocadero Inn in 1892. The inn is San Francisco's best example of a nineteenth-century roadhouse. It is a Queen Anne with sunburst ornament in the roof and porch gables. In 1931, Greene sold the property to Mrs. Sigmund Stern, who, in memory of her husband, donated it to the city for use as a park.

Stern Grove is a natural amphitheater, located to the west of the inn and surrounded by eucalyptus trees. In 2005, Lawrence Halprin added board-and-batten performance-related structures and stone benches. These support the musical events that long have been held in this amphitheater.

Lake Merced

At one time, the area was entirely owned by the Spring Valley Water Company, which used Lake Merced for a water supply. The land was gradually sold off and developed during the 1930s–1950s. The first residential subdivision, **Merced Manor** (1931), lies between Nineteenth and Twenty-Sixth Avenues and consists of attractive, detached Spanish-style houses. Henry and Ellis Stoneson's Lakeside subdivision (1937–1940) lies between Junipero Serra Boulevard and Nineteenth Avenue, and consists mainly of Streamlined Moderne and Colonial Revival–style houses designed by architect Harold G. Stoner. **Lakeshore Park** (1940–1948) and **Country Club Acres** (1952) are other tracts of detached houses.

Park Merced is a large complex consisting of low- and high-rise apartments, built between 1943 and 1952 to designs by architect Leonard Schultze of New York and landscape architect Thomas Church of San Francisco. The complex is ordered, manicured, and devoid of whimsy. **Stonestown** shopping center (1952) was named after its

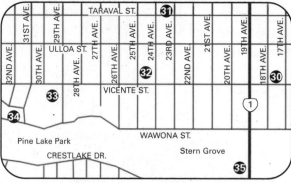

15 • Southwest Neighborhoods: South Sunset District

developers, the Stoneson brothers, and was designed by Los Angeles architect Welton Beckett. Only Macy's and the medical building at 595 Buckingham survive from the original complex. **San Francisco State University** was begun in the late 1940s; construction has been more-or-less ongoing since then. The Brutalist-style architecture is saved only by a sloping greensward in the middle of the campus.

Brief mention should be made of the **San Francisco Zoo.** Begun in the 1930s, it has generally been rebuilt since then. Military bunkers at **Fort Funston** (1917), three public and private golf courses, and modern-era churches along Brotherhood Way, of which **Holy Trinity Greek Orthodox Church** (1964; Reid, Rockwell, Banwell & Tarics, architects) at 999 Brotherhood Way is the most outstanding.

36. Merced Manor Reservoir, 1912
Sloat Boulevard between Twenty-Second and Twenty-Third Avenues

Willis Polk, architect

There is a sculptural group over the entry and fountains at the corners. The fish-and-trident motif is the same as that on the entrance gate to Polk's Sunol Water Temple.

37. Mediterranean houses, 1933
2900 Block of Twenty-Sixth Avenue

James A. Arnott, builder

These lively Spanish Baroque and Mediterranean houses feature arched windows,

spiral columns, wooden and iron balconies, and colorful tile steps.

38. Lakeside Village, 1940s
2500 and 2600 Blocks of Ocean Avenue

Holy Trinity Greek Orthodox Church, Lake Merced

This is the neighborhood shopping strip, primarily one- and two-story Moderne versions of Colonial Revival. The most prominent building

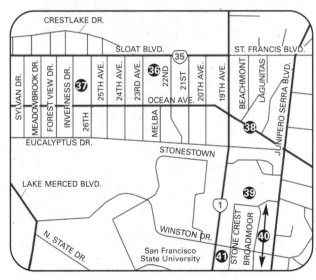

15 • Southwest Neighborhoods: Lake Merced

is the Streamlined Moderne–style **Lakeside Medical Center** (1941; Harold G. Stoner, architect) [38] at **2105–2115 Ocean Avenue,** which features an Art Deco tower.

39. Ellis and Henry Stoneson houses, 1938, 1941
30 and 100 Stonecrest Drive

Harold G. Stoner, architect

30 Stonecrest (1938) has a swan's-neck pediment and fluted

pilasters at the entry, while 100 Stonecrest (1941) features tall pipe posts supporting a semi-circular porch roof. Restrained elegance is the keynote to both houses.

40. Stoneson speculative houses, 1939–1941
Broadmoor Drive between Stonecrest and Winston Drives

Harold G. Stoner, architect

This is a pleasing block of stucco- and wood-clad houses with front yards, some with white picket fences. Most are Moderne versions of Period and Classic Revival.

41. Merced Branch Library, 1957
155 Winston Drive

Appleton and Wolford, architects

This was the third library these architects designed in San Francisco. The redbrick walls and wooden window frames impart a warm feeling, and the plate-glass windows admit a flood of natural light. The slanted roof gives the building a distinctly modern look.

16 · Golden Gate Park

Golden Gate Park was 1,017 acres of sand dunes and scrub brush in 1870 when it was reserved as a park. Civil engineer William Hammond Hall was the park's first superintendent; before he left in 1876, he laid out the grounds and planted vegetation to keep the drifting dunes at bay. Hall returned in 1886 for just one year, and then John McLaren succeeded him as superintendent in 1887. McLaren retained this post until his death in 1943 lat age ninety-six. Both men favored a natural look and small-scale charm, and contended against commercial establishments, statues, and large-scale projects such as the Midwinter Fair of 1894.

One of the fair's attractions was a Fine Arts Museum, which was retained as the de Young Museum. The Academy of Science (currently being rebuilt) moved to the south side of the concourse in 1916. The western half of the park is more notable for lakes and meadows than for structures and formal landscapes.

1. McLaren Lodge, 1896
John F. Kennedy Drive at Stanyan Street

Edward Swain, architect

Built to house the Park Commissioners' offices, it was also the home of John McLaren. It is constructed of blue-black stone from the Gray Brothers' quarry at Twenty-Sixth and Douglass Streets, and gray Colusa sandstone. The heavy stonework and arched openings lend a Romanesque feeling, while the clay-tile roof adds a Mediterranean touch.

2. Alvord Bridge, 1889
Kezar Drive, north of Waller Street

Ernest Ransome, engineer

This is the first reinforced-concrete bridge built in the United States, designed by the engineer who did more to advance concrete technology than anyone else in this country. The concrete is rusticated and textured to resemble stone masonry. Stalactites hang from the ceiling to impart a cave-like atmosphere. Like many bridges in parks, its purpose was to separate a footpath from a road for horses and carriages; it now carries auto traffic.

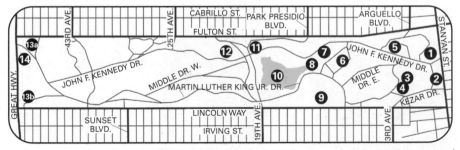

3. Sharon Art Studio, 1888
*Bowling Green Drive between
John F. Kennedy and
Martin Luther King Jr. Drives*
Percy and Hamilton, architects

Originally built as a children's
playhouse, the Romanesque-style
building of San Jose sandstone
features a wealth of fine ornamental carving, and rewards
leisurely study.

4. Carousel Pavilion, 1892
*Kezar and
Martin Luther King Jr. Drives*
*A. Page Brown,
architect*

The carousel enclosure is sixteen
Doric columns supporting a
domed roof. The carousel, made
in Buffalo, New York, in 1912,
was purchased by the city and
placed within the enclosure in
1941. It was restored in 1984.

5. Conservatory of Flowers, 1878
*John F. Kennedy and
Conservatory Drives*

This huge High Victorian
greenhouse has a central domed
entrance pavilion flanked by
wings and end pavilions.
Apparently the greenhouse was
built for James Lick to a design by
architect John P. Gaynor, and was
donated to the city after Lick's
death. An 1883 fire destroyed the
dome, which was rebuilt to a
slightly different design by John

Gash. A vast lawn and floral car-
pet bedding front the structure.
Opposite, on JFK Drive, is a
handsome reinforced-concrete
pedestrian tunnel (1890) by
architects Percy and Hamilton,
and engineer Ernest Ransome.

6. Music Concourse
*Between John F. Kennedy and
Martin Luther King Jr. Drives*

The concourse bowl was
created by engineer Michael M.
O'Shaughnessy for the Midwinter
Fair. After the fair closed, the
concourse area was reshaped
as the Music Concourse. The
Spreckels Temple of Music
(1899; Reid Brothers, architects;
Robert I. Aitken, sculptor), a classically styled band shell of Colusa
sandstone, was built as a stage for
the park band. Pedestrian tunnels
were built beneath roadways to
facilitate traffic; of these, the
finest is the one under JFK Drive,
north of the de Young Museum
(1896; Ernest Coxhead, architect;
Douglas Tilden, sculptor). This
area also contains numerous
pieces of sculpture, some that
date back to the fair.

7. de Young Museum, 2005
Hagiwara Tea Garden Drive
*Herzog and de Meuron,
architects*

After the old de Young Museum
was damaged by the Loma Prieta
Earthquake in 1989, this new
museum building, which opened

in October 2005, replaced it. It
is a long, horizontal building
clad in sheets of copper that are
variously perforated and dim-
pled; there is a ten-story office
and classroom tower on its north
side. This tower is sculpture
achieved through geometry and
engineering. It tapers down
rather than up; each side and
edge has a different quality and
shape; the floors pivot slightly,
giving the tower a "twist" and
the impression of having sloping
floors, which they are not; and,
depending on the light and one's
distance, it gives contrasting
impressions, from dark and
somber to light and transparent.
The tower's observation deck
provides new views of the city
that are undeniably inspiring.
On the west side, an exaggerated
projecting overhang extends
beyond the building over an outdoor patio space with huge skylit
"cutouts" where wings of the
building meet at angles.

While the building does not
relate well to the classically
detailed monuments and fountains in the concourse area, it
may blend better with its general
surroundings because the copper
skin oxidizes to green.

The museum's interior finish is
generally flat; the lobby, which
should be the most welcoming
part of the building, is perhaps
the least so. Galleries on the
first floor have white walls and
ceilings, and they lack warmth.
By contrast, the second-story
galleries, home to nineteenth-
century American art, and artifacts from Africa, New Guinea,
and Oceania, are more richly
hued, and half have wood floors
and ceilings. Here the museum
is at its best.

8. Japanese Tea Garden
Hagiwara Tea Garden Drive

The Japanese Tea Garden also dates from the Midwinter Fair and has grown to five times its original one-acre size. It is reputed to be the oldest Japanese-style garden in the United States. For almost fifty years it was designed and attended to by Makoto Hagiwara and his descendants, until the family, like other Japanese-Americans, was sent to an internment camp during World War II. Between the 1940s and 1970s, many changes were made but the various parts hold together well, and the garden is well worth the price of admission. The elaborate wooden entrance gates [8] were reconstructed in 1985, replacing originals that had rotted.

9. Strybing Arboretum,
1930s–1960s
Bounded by Martin Luther King Jr. Drive and Lincoln Way

A modest arboretum was begun here in the 1890s by John McLaren, but development began in earnest in the 1930s with a bequest by Helene Strybing in memory of her husband. New master plans, beginning in the 1960s, brought the arboretum to its present appearance. A vast central lawn is ringed by pocket gardens showcasing plants from a wide variety of climates, with special emphasis on native California plants.

10. Stow Lake and Strawberry Hill
Between John F. Kennedy and Martin Luther King Jr. Drives, east of Nineteenth Avenue

The hill is natural, but the lake around it was created in 1893, as were the two bridges that lead to the hill. The Rustic Bridge on the south side is built of rugged chert boulders, Colusa sandstone, and brick, while the smoothly curved Roman Bridge on the north side is reinforced concrete (A. Page Brown, architect). Huntington Falls (1894) on the east side, long unused, was the idea of John McLaren, and features fake rocks.

11. Prayer Book Cross, 1893
North side of John F. Kennedy Drive, east of Crossover Drive
Ernest Coxhead, architect

This Celtic cross made of Colusa sandstone rises sixty-four feet from the top of a hillock some distance from the road.

12. Portals of the Past
North side of John F. Kennedy Drive, west of Transverse Drive

After the fire of 1906, only the Colonial Revival portico of the Alban Towne House (1891; A. Page Brown, architect) on Nob Hill remained. It was salvaged and moved to this site in 1909.

13. Dutch and Murphy Windmills, 1900s
Northwest and southwest corners of the park

These shingle-clad windmills were built in 1903 and 1908, respectively, to pump fresh water for the park's plants. The Dutch Windmill (13a) was restored in 1981, minus its pumping works. The superstructure of the Murphy Windmill (13b) will be rehabilitated; next door is the millwright's cottage, a brick Colonial Revival (1909; Reid Brothers, architects).

14. Beach Chalet, 1925
West end of the park
Willis Polk, architect

The Beach Chalet is austerely detailed and has a well-proportioned, nicely sculpted massing appropriate for the western end of the park. The second-floor dining room takes the form of a wide glassed-in porch supported by eight pairs of columns. The lobby is decorated with fresco murals (1936–1937) by Lucian Labaudt, and tile murals and carved staircase railings of nautical themes.

17 · Richmond District

As in other outlying areas of the city, early residents were dairy ranchers and farmers. Tourists came in 1863, when the first Cliff House opened, and later to visit Sutro's Garden, roadhouses, horse-racing tracks, and Golden Gate Park. The original thoroughfare was the Point Lobos Toll Road, today's Geary Boulevard. Scattered residential development occurred in the 1870s, and by the 1890s, a small community had formed in the area bounded by Anza Street, Lake Street, Arguello Boulevard, and Funston Avenue. Improvement clubs lobbied successfully for streetlights, paved roads, and cable-car lines.

1. Presidio Terrace, opened 1905
Presidio Terrace, west of Arguello Boulevard

Baldwin and Howell, developers

This suburban-style subdivision consists of thirty-five large houses arranged on an oval street. The stone entrance gates are by Albert Pissis, and most of the houses were designed by top San Francisco architects.

The most unusual is **30** (1909; MacDonald and Applegarth, architects), a quintessential "English cottage" of brick, textured stucco, wooden half-timbering, and faux thatched roof; **16** (1910; Bakewell and Brown, architects) is Colonial

Revival; **15** (1905; Havens and Toepke, architects) has a Mission Revival porch flanked by a square tower; **10** (1909; Charles Whittlesey, architect) [1] is a Shingle-style featuring a giant, brick arched entry; and **34** (1910; MacDonald and Applegarth, architects) is a formal Classical Revival.

2. Temple Emanu-El, 1924–1926
Northwest corner of Lake Street and Arguello Boulevard

Bakewell and Brown, and Sylvain Schnaittacher, architects

The main domed structure is Byzantine with ornament verging on Art Deco, while the surrounding wings are Romanesque. Past

the entry gates, one enters a courtyard with a small but beautiful fountain. The main lobby has a barrel-vaulted ceiling with painted patterns on a brilliant blue background. The austerity of the domed sanctuary is relieved by cast-stone ornament, green marble columns, and a travertine altar. There are numerous gargoyle figures in the column capitals. Two large, modern stained-glass windows impart brilliantly colored hues to the interior. Architects Bernard Maybeck and G. Albert Lansburgh served as consulting architects.

3. St. John's Presbyterian Church, 1905
Southwest corner of Arguello Boulevard and Lake Street

Dodge and Dolliver, architects

The style is Gothic Revival clad in wood shingles. Two entrances, each with many-layered drip moldings, are located in the square corner tower. Steeply pitched cross-gable roofs, gabled dormers, and gothic arched windows contribute to its complex massing. The stained-glass windows are beautiful.

4. Campfire Girls' Headquarters, 1929
325 Arguello Boulevard

Henry H. Gutterson, architect

1

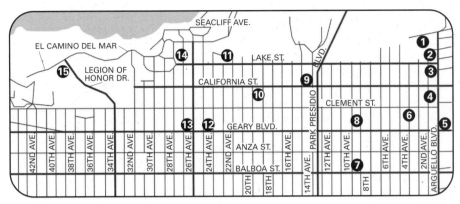

17 • Richmond District

This L-shaped stucco-clad building, with unpainted wood trim, an open covered porch, and steep roofs pierced by dormers, combines the picturesque qualities of English cottage with Craftsman details.

5. Roosevelt Middle School, 1930
460 Arguello Boulevard
Miller and Pflueger, architects

This block-long redbrick school is Art Deco with extensive zigzag brickwork across the top; on the tower there is an overlapping brick diamond pattern; and bays are defined by piers with end bricks that protrude at an angle. The gymnasium wing has original windows with ornamental bronze framing. At the northwest corner of Geary and Arguello is the **Geary, Park and Ocean Railroad Carbarn** (1893), a plain, white, industrial-type building, one of the last cable-car-related buildings in the city.

6. Victorian cottages, 1890s
Second to Fourth Avenues, near Clement Street

Relatively few nineteenth-century houses remain in the Richmond District, but scattered clusters survive at its eastern end. There are lively Stick-Eastlake cottages from the early 1890s in the 300 block of Second Avenue, and a row of eleven Queen Anne and Stick-Eastlake cottages (1893–1895) in the 200 block of Third Avenue.

7. Richmond Heights, circa 1910
Bounded by Anza and Balboa Streets, Ninth and Eleventh Avenues
Joseph Leonard, builder-architect

This is one of three residential tracts developed by Joseph Leonard in San Francisco (the others are Jordan Park and Ingleside Terrace). Most of the two-story, single-family detached houses are Craftsman in style, and clad variously in wood shingles or stucco. Some are quite picturesque, and all are different. Roofs are generally side-facing gables with front-facing gabled dormers, exposed rafter ends, projecting window bays, and grouped windows, often with transoms. The 500 block of Tenth Avenue is especially pleasant because both

sides of the street are lined with Leonard's houses.

8. Richmond Branch Library, 1914
351 Ninth Avenue
Bliss and Faville, architects

The library is a severe, somewhat monumental classical design made of closely fitted blocks of Colusa sandstone. Polychrome terra-cotta ornament trims the arched entry.

9. Row houses, 1911–1912
107–163 Fourteenth Avenue,
106–162 Fifteenth Avenue,
1301–1347 Lake Street
Ludwig Heilmann, builder

This cluster of Craftsman-, Mission Revival–, and Baroque-style houses has overscaled features and a picturesque feeling.

10. Our Lady of Kazan Russian Orthodox Church, 1967
5725 California Street
W. W. Granitow, architect

Sublimely graceful and perfect in its proportions, this was a complete remodeling of an older Orthodox church on the site.

11. Lake Street houses
Lake Street between
Twenty-First and
Twenty-Third Avenues

Along the north side of Lake, there is a pleasant row of two-story, detached, single-family dwellings, with enough space to have front gardens. They generally date from the 1910s through the 1920s, and several are brick.

12. Santa Monica Roman Catholic Church, 1916
Northwest corner of
Twenty-Fourth Avenue and
Geary Boulevard
Shea and Lofquist, architects

This nicely composed church is rich in moldings but spare in ornament. It is predominantly Spanish Baroque in style, though the recurring use of arched open-ings hints at the Romanesque.

13. Holy Virgin Russian Cathedral, 1962
6210 Geary Boulevard
Oleg Ivanitsky, architect

Golden onion domes make this building an imposing landmark. The otherwise spare exterior gives little hint of the rich inte-rior, painted by Father Cyprian of New York.

14. Sea Cliff, 1907–1930s
From Twenty-Fifth Avenue
to Thirty-Second Avenue,
north of California Street
William B. Hoag,
survey engineer
MacRorie-McLaren Co.,
landscaping

Sea Cliff was subdivided in stages between 1907 and 1929, and was largely developed after 1916 by Harry B. Allen. His

architects—Earle B. Bertz, Farr and Ward, and Hyman and Appleton—set the tone with mostly stucco houses in predom-inately Spanish, Mediterranean, Tudor, and Classical styles.

The wide, curving, and divided 2900 block of Lake Street is a good place to view a group of gracious Sea Cliff houses. In Renaissance and Colonial Revival styles, **2900** and **2910 Lake** (1926; Earl B. Bertz, architect) are brick sided; **2940** (1928; Farr and Ward, architects) has a bit of Tudor half-timbering; **2950** and **2970** (1930, 1931; Hyman and Appleton) are Spanish. Other Period Revivals are **9, 25,** and **45 Scenic Way** (1915–1917), a row by Willis Polk; **130** and **140 Sea Cliff Avenue** (1927; Sylvain Schnaittacher, architect) have Classic moldings. There are a few mid-century Moderns such as **100 Thirty-Second Avenue** (1950; Joseph Esherick, archi-tect) that are sheathed with unpainted shingles.

15. Palace of the Legion of Honor, 1920–1924
In Lincoln Park via
Thirty-Fourth Avenue and
Clement Street
George Applegarth, architect

Lincoln Park was the city ceme-tery from 1870 to 1910, when the city acquired it for a park. The trail around its perimeter, from Sea Cliff to the Cliff House, overlooking the pounding Pacific Ocean, is the most dramatic in the city. South of the trail is a golf course developed during the 1910s by John McLaren.

The Palace of the Legion of Honor was built as a World War I memorial and donated to the city by Adolph B. and Alma de Bretteville Spreckels. During visits to the Panama-Pacific International Exposition of 1915, Alma had admired the French Pavilion, which was a copy of the eighteenth-century Palais de la Legion d'Honneur in Paris. She instructed Applegarth to use it as a model for her museum. The perfectly symmetrical exterior features Ionic colonnades and a central Roman arch leading to an entry courtyard. It is home to a large collection of Rodin sculp-tures (also donated by Alma), among other European artworks. In the 1990s, the building was retrofitted for seismic strengthen-ing, new underground galleries were added, and a pyramid-shaped skylight now graces the courtyard.

18 • The Presidio

The Presidio was a military reservation since the arrival of the Spanish in 1776. On the site of the parade ground, the Spanish built a compound of adobe buildings. Later, a battery was built on a bluff above where Fort Point is now located. Although the Spanish imported six bronze seventeenth-century Peruvian cannons for the fort (on display at the Officers' Club, Wright Hospital, and Fort Point), the facility was not strongly fortified. The Mexicans essentially abandoned the post in 1834 for Sonoma. When the United States occupied it in 1846, they did so without a skirmish; President Millard Fillmore directed that an American post be established here in 1850, as well as Fort Mason, Fort Baker, Alcatraz, Angel Island, Mare Island, and Benicia. Over the next century, the Presidio grew and expanded as world events dictated.

Legislation that created the Golden Gate National Recreation Area (GGNRA) in 1972 included the Presidio, if it should ever be closed. Although the army announced it would close the Presidio in 1989, it was not officially added to the GGNRA until September 30, 1994. After the Presidio was transferred to the GGNRA, its administration was handed over to the Presidio Trust.

The Presidio is a unique urban park of 1,480 acres, with beaches, marshlands, and forests; 850 buildings (more than half designated historic), an eighteen-hole golf course, a cemetery, and more than 1,000 residential units that include large, detached single-family houses on Simonds Loop as well as apartments overlooking Baker Beach. The Presidio is also notable as designed landscape, planned by Major W. A. Jones in 1883. Eucalyptus, pine, Monterey cypress, and redwood were planted between 1889 and 1900, and make up its forested areas. The Presidio has several distinct areas, each with its own character and history.

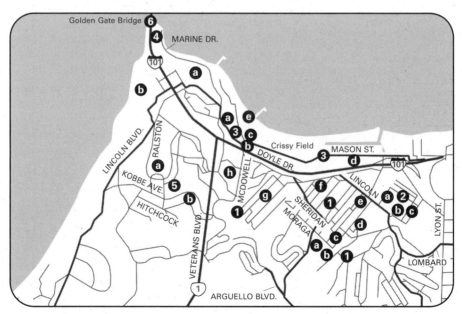

1. Main Post
Lincoln Boulevard, Funston and Moraga Avenues, and Montgomery Street

The Main Post has been the heart of the Presidio since Spanish days, and contains the most important collection of historic buildings.

1a. Comandancia (Officer's Club)
Moraga Avenue, south side

After numerous remodels and additions and a none-too-faithful restoration in 1934, little remains of the original Spanish- or Mexican-era fabric save for the front wall, which is adobe. Two seventeenth-century Peruvian cannon stand in front.

1b. Pershing Hall, 1903
Moraga and Funston Avenues

The three-story redbrick building was originally bachelor officers' quarters. With its central pavilion, flanking two-story

wings with balconies, and stylistic references to the Colonial Revival and Georgian styles, it is an imposing building in the Main Post area.

1c. Officer houses, 1862, 1878
Funston Avenue, west side

A row of twelve Greek Revival houses originally faced the parade ground. In 1878, they were remodeled; their backs became fronts so they would face the street. It is probable that original porches were reused, so they still retain a Civil War–era appearance.

1d. Officer houses, 1885–1893
Funston Avenue, east side

Seven houses in Greek Revival, Stick, and Second Empire styles are restrained, with fine details but little ornament.

1e. Wright Hospital, 1864
Funston Avenue, near Lincoln Boulevard

Like the houses of 1862, it originally faced the parade ground but was reoriented in 1878 to face Funston. It has been substantially enlarged but retains its original character, with three stories of verandahs now partially enclosed. One Peruvian cannon is nearby. To the rear are two 1906 earthquake refugee shacks, recently rescued.

1f. Enlisted men's barracks, 1895–1897
Montgomery Street, west side

Five redbrick Colonial Revival–style buildings with hipped roofs, hipped dormers, and broad verandahs form a stately row facing the parade ground; as a group they make a strong and memorable architectural statement.

1g. San Francisco National Cemetery, 1854

Designated a National Cemetery by the War Department in 1884, post burials have occurred here since 1854. It is enclosed by a decorative cast-iron fence made by the Phoenix Iron Works in 1885.

1h. Horse stables, 1913–1924
Cowles Street and McDowell Avenue

Five very large redbrick stables have gabled roofs rising to clerestories.

2. Letterman Hospital
Lincoln Boulevard, and Torney, Kennedy, O'Reilly Avenues

Letterman was founded in 1899 for soldiers returning from duty in the Philippines; it was used through the 1980s.

2a. Administration building, 1899
Lincoln Boulevard at Torney Avenue

W. H. Wilcox, architect

The sole surviving building from the original hospital complex has recessed second-floor balconies with Ionic columns. The **Clinic** (1924–1933) is a concrete building located next door, to the east. Around the corner on Kennedy is the **Ward Building** (1930). The backs of these buildings are linked by enclosed galleries.

2b. Officers' houses, 1902–1908
O'Reilly Avenue

Here is a nice neat row of gable-roofed houses.

2c. Letterman Digital Arts Center, 2005
Gensler and HKS Inc., architects

Lawrence Halprin, landscape architect

George Lucas's twenty-three-acre complex of large brick, stucco, and glass-sided buildings are remarkably unassuming from

all perspectives. The mass of more than one-million square feet is broken up into four separate buildings, with projecting wings linked by glass-sided corridor-galleries, much like the galleries linking the former ward buildings. Well-tended lawns and pathways enhance the landscape.

3. Crissy Field
North of Doyle Drive

In 1912, the tidal marsh that is now Crissy Field was filled for the Panama-Pacific International Exposition. After the fair, the west half was used as an army airfield. By the mid-1920s, a row of support buildings was constructed in a curvilinear alignment along the south and west sides of Crissy Field, and most of these still stand. They include a cluster of gambrel-roofed hangars and shop buildings (3a), a Mediterranean Revival–style administration building (3b), and a Mission Revival–style enlisted men's barracks (3b).

Larger aircraft requiring longer airstrips for takeoff and landing, and the hazards posed by the towers of the new Golden Gate Bridge, rendered Crissy Field obsolete in the 1930s. As part of the GGNRA, some changes have been made: the western end of the field was restored as an airstrip (3c), and an eighteen-acre salt marsh was re-created near the east end (3d).

At the northwest corner of Crissy Field is the former Fort Point Life Saving Station (3e), consisting of a shingled, gambrel-roofed, Colonial Revival–style residence plus a boathouse, each built in 1889–1890 [3e].

4. Fort Point
Long Avenue and Marine Drive

In 1853, the bluff where the Spanish battery—Castillo de San Joaquin—was located was carved away, and over the next eight years the brick-and-granite Fort Point was built in its place on a shelf of land ten feet above high tide. The seven-foot-thick brick

walls are pierced on all three levels with numerous embrasures for cannon, which were also placed in the barbette tier on the roof. A seawall made of Penryn granite runs along the coastline around the fort.

4a. Battery East, 1873–1876
Overlooking the Golden Gate Bridge

Fort Point became obsolete when rifled cannons were invented. A low-tech alternative was then developed, which consists of vaulted brick magazines and a tunnel buried under the earth. Such earthworks were effective because shells would explode harmlessly in the earthen berms.

4b. Battery West
Overlooking the Pacific Ocean

Battery West was replaced from 1891 to 1900 by partially buried reinforced-concrete Endicott batteries.

5. Fort Winfield Scott
Ralston Avenue and adjacent streets

Fort Winfield Scott was developed between 1910 and 1912 as headquarters for the army's Coast Artillery district. The main buildings are Mission Revival, which are arranged in a J formation around a parade ground. The **Headquarters** is at the south end of the J (5a). The other buildings in this row were **Enlisted Men's Barracks.** To the south along Kobbe Avenue is a curvilinear row of houses for officers, built variously in Colonial Revival style of brick and stucco (5b).

6. Golden Gate Bridge, 1933–1937
Highway 101

Joseph B. Strauss, chief engineer

This was the longest suspension span in the world at the time it was built. The bridge approach is supported by a tremendous steel arch over the western end of Fort Point and dominates the landscape. The Art Deco cladding of the bridge towers, the distinctive burnt orange coloring, and the magnificent setting have made this bridge one of the best-known structures in the world. Other major designers were Charles Ellis, design engineer, and Irving Morrow, architect of the tower cladding.

II
San Mateo County

Mitch Postal (historian) and Ward Hill (architectural historian), co-authors
Ward Hill, photographer (unless otherwise noted)

When California became a state in 1850, most of what is now San Mateo County was part of San Francisco County. In 1856, through political compromise, the separate counties of San Francisco and San Mateo were created. At that time San Mateo County had a population of only about 2,500 residents.

It was from today's Sweeney Ridge, which separates the cities of Pacifica and San Bruno, that Gaspar de Portola saw San Francisco Bay in 1769. After the Spanish padres had built their mission and presidio at the northern end of the peninsula in what would become San Francisco, they discovered that the sun never seemed to shine, the soil in most places was sandy, the little fresh water available was brackish, and no stands of trees were available for lumber.

They found it necessary to build agricultural outposts at San Pedro Creek (at Linda Mar Boulevard in Pacifica) and San Mateo Creek (in the downtown San Mateo area). The establishment of these outposts was essential to the success of the mission community and presidio at San Francisco.

After the San Francisco mission lands were secularized in 1835, seventeen land grants were carved out of what would become San Mateo County. Before the California Gold Rush began, a number of Americans and other foreigners inhabited the southern hill country between Woodside and Redwood City. They began logging operations that became significant after gold was discovered in 1848 and San Francisco became the most important city on the West Coast.

The early San Mateo industries focused on providing San Francisco with resources: agriculture, lumbering, oyster cultivation, shrimp fishing, whaling, and waterworks.

After the completion of the San Francisco/San Jose Railroad in 1864, San Mateo County became the first railroad suburb west of the Mississippi where the elite of San Francisco's industrial and commercial circles established country estates. Families like the Mills, Floods, Haywards, and Parrotts called the peninsula home but controlled economic resources from offices in the city. Large suburban estates, not subdivided until the first third of the twentieth century, retarded growth and gave San Mateo County a distinctive character.

Although San Francisco was largely known as a "wide open" city for most of its

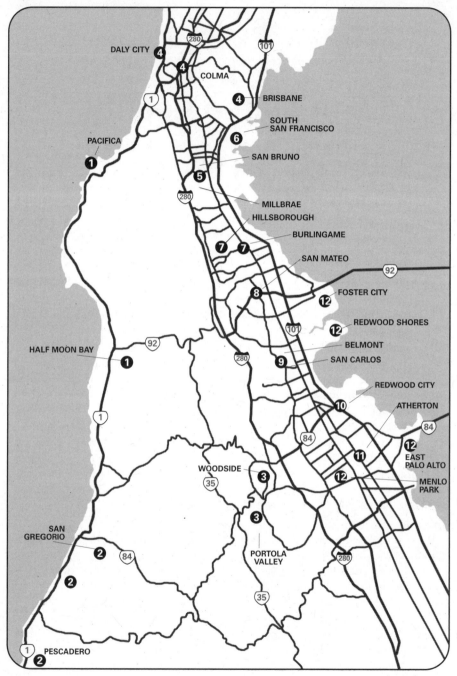

II • San Mateo County

history, it was also known that if you couldn't get away with some activity in the city, you could do it by crossing the county line into San Mateo County.

Dueling, for example, outlawed everywhere in California, was practiced here. Gambling, prostitution, and other activities were only slightly regulated by the county's weak local law enforcement agencies. By 1900, activities that were illegal in San Francisco but legal in San Mateo County (notably prizefighting and horse racing) enhanced this legacy. During Prohibition, the county became famous for its rum running and speakeasies, and in the 1930s, flagrant illegal gambling operations prompted one gangster to declare the county the most corrupt in California.

The twentieth century brought considerable growth to San Mateo County. After the 1906 earthquake, there was a large migration to the peninsula. A newly constructed streetcar system from San Francisco all the way to San Mateo allowed the hamlets along the line to become home to a new middle-class suburbanite. The affordability and popularity of the automobile through the 1920s added to this growth.

However, it was World War II that had the greatest impact on the built environment. The airport east of Millbrae, termed a "mud hole" before the war by San Francisco newspapers, was improved to such an extent by the U.S. Army that it was handling one-tenth of all air traffic in the United States by 1946. Supporting businesses sprang up nearby. Partially because of the growth of the airport, a wartime electronics industry exploded onto the scene. Firms such as EIMAC, Varian, Dalmo Victor, and, after the war, Ampex became huge employers.

Home building for the growing population attracted a new breed of housing developers. Schooled in mass building techniques during the war, Henry Doelger, Fred and Carl Gellert, David Bohannon, Jack Foster, and others constructed thousands of tract homes through loans made possible by the federal government.

The original electronics companies are mostly history today, but they gave rise to the computer software and biotech industries that make international headlines daily and call San Mateo County home. Today the population of San Mateo County is well over 700,000.

II • SAN MATEO COUNTY

1 · North Coast: Pacifica to Half Moon Bay

Pacifica

It was from Sweeney Ridge in present-day Pacifica that Gaspar de Portola saw San Francisco Bay in 1769. Within seven years the Spanish established Mission San Francisco de Asis (also known as Mission Dolores) at the northern end of the peninsula. Between 1785 and 1786, the padres also built an agricultural outpost in the San Pedro Valley (today's Linda Mar district in Pacifica), where they planted wheat, corn, grapes, and pear and peach orchards.

After secularization of the mission lands, Francisco Sanchez was granted Rancho San Pedro, now part of the city of Pacifica. Between 1842 and 1846, he constructed a grand adobe home (see below) on the ruins of the old mission outpost. The building still stands at 1000 Linda Mar Boulevard and is a museum run by the San Mateo County Historical Association as part of the San Mateo County Parks System.

Like his father, Jose Sanchez, who lived on the other side of the hill facing the bay, Francisco was chosen captain of the regional civic militia and, in 1842 at the age of thirty-seven, was made *alcalde* of Yerba Buena (San Francisco). Francisco led the Californios against American marines and volunteers at the Battle of Santa Clara in 1847. After the Mexican-American War (1846–1848), while all his rancho neighbors gradually lost their properties to lawyers and bankers, Francisco managed to keep his land until the day he died in 1862, after falling from a horse. For the rest of the nineteenth century, the north coast remained a rather quiet place, isolated by coastal hills on the east and the Pacific Ocean on the west.

In 1908, the Ocean Shore Railroad Company began construction of a railroad that would link San Francisco with Santa Cruz and open the entire coast to real estate development. Good progress had been made when the earthquake and fire on April 18, 1906, caused significant damage. Nevertheless, building continued. Five future communities were laid out at today's Pacifica—Edgemar,

Salada Beach, Brighton Beach, Vellemar, and San Pedro Terrace. A tunnel was punched through at Devil's Slide, and the railroad began serving the coast while planning the communities of Montara, Moss Beach, Princeton, El Granada, and Miramar.

It was at El Granada that the Ocean Shore Railroad held its greatest hopes; it hired nationally renowned architect D. H. Burnham to lay out a town and hotel resort, which they pronounced the future "Coney Island of the West." Sadly for the railroad and its promoters, real estate investment went primarily to rebuilding San Francisco. While construction of the railroad along the San Mateo Coast made it all the way down to Tunitas Creek, a crucial twenty-six-mile gap between there and Swanton in Santa Cruz County was never completed. The railroad stopped service in 1920, and the coast remained largely agrarian until after World War II, the beginning of the California postwar real estate boom. Pacifica was incorporated in 1957 and now has a population of about 39,000.

Sanchez Adobe, Pacifica

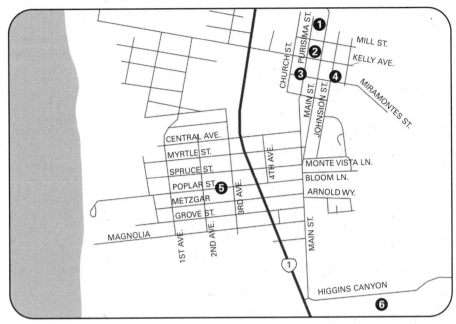

1 • North Coast: Half Moon Bay

Half Moon Bay

When hostilities began between the Americans and the Californios during the Bear Flag Revolt (1846), two San Francisco land grant families decided to move to their coast-side ranchos to avoid the violence. The Vasquez family built a few adobe structures north of the creek that separated their lands from the Miramontes family, who also constructed some buildings on the south side of the creek. Other Californios moved to this remote place too. They called their community San Benito; over the hill, the Americans called it Spanishtown; and later, it became know as Half Moon Bay. After a century of slow growth, the community was incorporated in 1959 and today has a population of more than 12,000. Half Moon

Bay has been separated from the north coast area by mountains and a dangerously winding road over ever-sliding and shifting cliffs, which will soon be replaced by a tunnel.

1. Estanislao Zaballa House, 1863
326 Main Street

The large Greek Revival–style building is one of the earliest houses in central Half Moon Bay, but a retail center that now surrounds it has destroyed any sense of its original setting. Zaballa, who married the daughter of the original land grant owner, Candelario Miramontes, plotted the original "Spanishtown" in 1863. The quoins and siding resemble stone. The front gabled section appears to be an early addition.

2. Dutra Funeral Home, 1928
645 Kelly Avenue

The severe, cubistic symmetrical forms of this unusual Art Deco building contrast with the intricate ornament between the pylons over the front entrance. The building somewhat resembles a Tibetan mosque.

3. Dr. Albert Milliken House, 1872
546 Purisima Street

This is one of the few Gothic Revival houses in San Mateo County, a simple straightforward example of the style. The lacey bargeboards and the lancet window under the gable are Gothicizing details dressing up the otherwise boxy form. At 340 Purisima Street is a simple early farmhouse.

4. Methodist Episcopal Church, 1872
Corner of Johnston and Miramontes Streets

Charles Geddes, architect

This charming little Gothic Revival village church has unusual round arched windows with a heavy hood molding and an open bell tower.

5. Ocean Shore Railway's Concrete Model Home, 1908
460 Poplar Street

Paul Harte Bosworth, architect

Bay Area architects experimented with a variety of fireproof materials, particularly reinforced concrete, after the 1906 conflagration in San Francisco. Bosworth designed this reinforced-concrete Mission Revival–style house as a model house for the projected Arleta Park subdivision. The Ocean Shore Railway serving the development went bankrupt in 1909, so the subdivision was never built.

6. James Johnston House, circa 1855
Higgins Canyon Road, east of Highway 1 (Cabrillo Highway South)

This may be the oldest wood-frame house in San Mateo County, and its New England saltbox form is quite unusual in the Bay Area. The wood for the house was milled in Santa Cruz and shipped to this site. The house is built with braced frame mortise-and-tenon construction. Viewed from Highway 1, the house luckily retains its historic setting, a dramatic white abstract form set on a bare grassy knoll facing the ocean. The William Johnston House in the Italianate style with original barns is located across the road.

2 · South Coast: Pescadero, San Gregorio

Just south of Half Moon Bay, Gold Rush forty-niner James Johnston of Ohio purchased 1,162 acres from Candelario Miramontes to create a dairy farm. Following Johnston's lead, other dairymen established farms all the way to Ano Nuevo.

By the 1860s, the village of Purisima, located south of Johnston's farm, consisted of a saloon, hotel, school, store, livery stable, and post office. Founded by American, Irish, and German emigrants, many thought that Purisima would become the leading community of the coast, but Half Moon Bay's better location on the road to San Mateo gave it the advantage, and Purisima slowly disappeared. Only a cemetery marks this place today.

In the 1850s, two other towns grew up south of Half Moon Bay: San Gregorio and Pescadero. Both supported nearby agricultural communities. While San Gregorio at one point even boasted a little Chinatown, it was Pescadero that rivaled Half Moon Bay, and had become the fourth largest town in the county by the late 1860s.

Throughout its history, the South Coast has maintained its agrarian character. A number of early Greek Revival–style houses still survive in Pescadero, but the original downtown burned in the 1920s.

The coastline is dangerous to sailors, and early on, Ano Nuevo Island, Franklin Point, and Pigeon Point all witnessed maritime disasters. A major shipwreck occurred in 1853 when the *Carrier Pigeon,* a new clipper ship, ran aground at La Punta de la Ballena. While no one was killed, the entire 1,300 tons of cargo was lost. So memorable was the incident that the point was renamed for the wreck—Pigeon Point. Twelve years later, a little north of Pigeon Point, the *Sir John Franklin* went down with the loss of twelve seamen—and Franklin Point got its name.

To protect sailors from danger, two lighthouses—one on Ano Nuevo Island and the other at Pigeon Point—began operating in 1872. At that time Pigeon Point was already serving as a station for Portuguese whalers. Ano Nuevo Island became famous for its marine animals, becoming part of an important wildlife reserve in 1976.

Pescadero

1. Thomas W. Moore House, 1863
80 Stage Road

Pescadero probably has the largest, not to mention the finest, group of Greek Revival–style houses in the Bay Area, and the Moore house is one of the earliest. A number of 1860s houses in this style are visible along Pescadero Road. Thomas Moore was the younger brother of Alexander Moore, the town's first settler. The pierced porch columns, louvered shutters, and simple gabled form seen here are

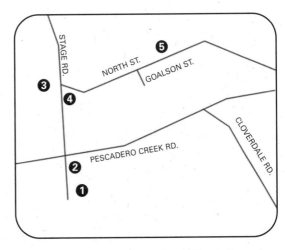

2 • South Coast: Pescadero

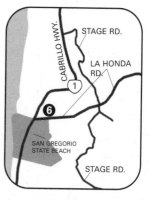

Pescadero. Set on a generous lot, the spacious front porch wraps around to the south side of the house. The unusual wide porch columns have inset panels and the front façade has large floor-to-ceiling windows. The front door has octagonal-shaped panels.

5. St. Anthony's Catholic Church, 1869
696 North Street

This charming little church combines Classical and Gothic Revival details, like the rose window over the entrance and the pointed arch dormers on the octagonal spire.

San Gregorio

6. San Gregorio House, 1850s
Cabrillo Highway

This is an impressive two-story, wood-frame building with a side-gable roof and shallow closed eaves. Across the front, a second-story balcony covers a full-width porch. According to local lore, it was originally built to serve as an inn for hunters and fishermen.

signature details of the vernacular Greek Revival house. A nice 1890s Queen Anne house is located at 94 Stage Road.

2. Methodist Episcopal Church (Native Sons Hall), 1890
112 Stage Road

The cruciform interior of this small Gothic Revival church has soaring truss vaults constructed of redwood. After the church became a Native Sons Hall in 1942, the seventy-foot-high bell tower was removed.

3. Pescadero Community Church, 1867
363 Stage Road

The Greek Revival–style church has an entablature and front pediment. The horizontal wood siding and the quoins are scored to simulate stone. The steeple was added to the square bell tower in 1889. The 1920s Baroque ceiling rosettes contrast with the church's original strikingly spare interior space. This is the earliest church in San Mateo County remaining on its original site.

4. James McCormick House, late 1860s
358 Stage Road

The McCormick House is the largest and most impressive Greek Revival house in

3 • Hill Country: Woodside, Portola Valley

The hills of San Mateo County divide the coastal area from the bay side and are dominated by a variety of forest vegetation, including gigantic redwood trees. Beginning in the 1830s, Americans and other foreigners lived in the hills and worked in sawmills and as hunters. Most had jumped ship at Yerba Buena or Monterey. They found themselves continually at odds with Mexican officials for dodging taxes and building illegal stills. The numerous grizzly bears may have been a greater concern.

This relatively quiet world changed dramatically in 1849. Although no gold was found in the hills, San Francisco needed lumber to build wharves, hotels, warehouses, and saloons. By 1853, there were fourteen sawmills active in just the Kings Mountain area alone.

The Woodside Store, which still stands today as a museum, was the center of the hill-country community. Dr. R. O. Tripp and his partner, M. A. Parkhurst, who established the store, were also pioneers of the logging industry.

A reliable source of fresh water for San Francisco, a concern since mission times, was exacerbated by the Gold Rush population boom. During certain times of the year, water was barged to the city from Marin County.

In 1858, the Spring Valley Water Company was incorporated. The company built reservoirs in San Mateo County and piped water to San Francisco. By 1900, it owned 20,000 acres of land from San Bruno to Woodside. Today the watershed and man-made lakes give the hills of San Mateo County a lush appearance.

The system of lakes and dams was mostly designed by Herman Schussler, a German-born Swiss-trained engineer. Crystal Springs Dam, located just under Doran Bridge on Highway 280 and completed in 1890, is his greatest achievement: a 150-foot-high engineering marvel constructed with interlocking concrete blocks.

While Crystal Springs Dam was undamaged by the 1906 and 1989 earthquakes, the 1906 earthquake crippled the water delivery system. Broken pipes meant no water to put out the fires in San Francisco, and the Spring Valley Water Company was blamed for the losses. But even before the 1906 earthquake, San Francisco had adopted a new charter allowing it to purchase its own water system and saw the Hetch Hetchy Valley as a site for a dam.

Recognizing that the city would one day purchase the Spring Valley Water Company's holdings as part of the huge Hetch Hetchy system, entrepreneur William Bourne bought the company in 1908. The water system was not completed until 1930.

Woodside

At the turn of the nineteenth century, San Francisco business leaders August Schilling and James Folger built country estates in Woodside, inspiring others to do the same. In the 1950s, the elite Woodsiders watched the Redwood City housing tracts began crowding up the hill. To prevent being gobbled up, they incorporated in 1956.

In 1964, when Atomic Energy Commission and Pacific Gas and Electric threatened to bulldoze a lane through Woodside to create power lines for the Stanford Linear Accelerator, an environmental movement emerged to stop the project. Organizers enlisted the legal assistance of Portola Valley attorney Pete McCloskey, who faced down the giants in federal court. The power lines were placed underground, and McCloskey became a local legend. In 1967, he achieved a stunning political victory over former film star Shirley Temple Black of Woodside in a

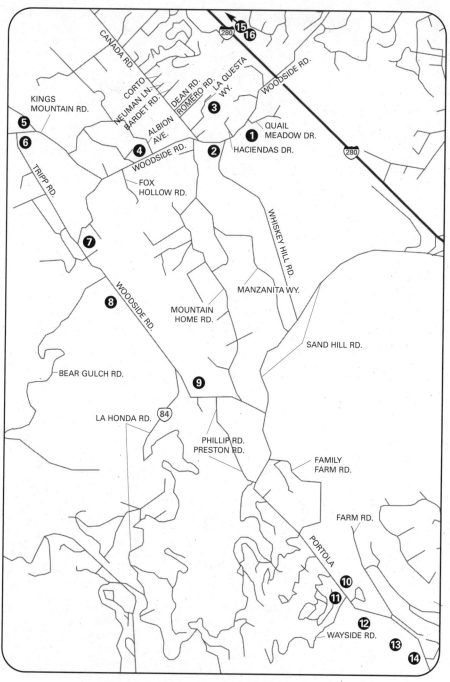

3 • Hill Country: Woodside, Portola Valley

Republican primary election for the United States Congress. He later became known as one of the few Republican congressmen to speak out against the Vietnam War and later to support Palestinian claims against Israel.

Today, Woodside has elevated its status to one of the most desirable places in the country to reside with a population of around 5,400. The cream of the "high tech" business community owns homes here, including Lawrence Ellison, Steven Jobs, and Gordon Moore.

The town of Woodside has an impressive number of the Bay Area's great historic estates, virtually none of which are visible from the public right-of-way. The 1911 Mortimer Fleishhacker Estate, "Green Gables," at 329 Albion Avenue is a major Northern California design by noted Pasadena architects Charles and Henry Greene. The 1927 Roman water garden at Green Gables, designed by Charles Greene, is occasionally open to the public for charity events. The 1925 Jackling House (Robles Road at Mountain Home Road) is a significant Northern California work by another Southern California architect, Santa Barbara's George Washington Smith; it was slated for demolition or moving in 2005. The James Folger House at 3860 Woodside Road is also not visible, although the Folger Stable is now in a public park. Like the older estates, modern estates like tech tycoon Larry Ellison's sprawling, $100 million Japanese villa are usually hidden from public view.

1. House, 1933
2887 Woodside Road
William Wurster, architect

A large, early Wurster house on a hillside exhibits his pleasing signature proportions and crisp window detailing.

2. Pioneer Hotel, 1878; later additions, 1880s
Woodside Road at Whiskey Hill Road

An early commercial building in Woodside, the Pioneer Inn originally functioned as not only a hotel but also a grocery store and barn. The building has been remodeled as offices.

3. La Questa Wine Cellar, 1902; renovated, 1949
240 La Questa Way

Emmett Rixford developed La Questa Winery in the nineteenth century. The picturesque old wine cellar, constructed with stone on the property, has walls eighteen inches thick. The building was converted into a private residence in 1949 with remarkably few changes.

4. Woodside Village Church, 1893; church/offices, 1963
3154 Woodside Road
Wurster, Bernardi and Emmons, architects

The Woodside Village Church is a handsome, simply detailed Gothic Revival–style building with a particularly spare interior. The village church was moved to this location in 1963 and incorporated as a chapel into a new church complex designed by Wurster, Bernardi and Emmons.

5 . Charles Josselyn House, "Vinegrove," 1906
400 Kings Mountain Road
Maybeck, Howard & White, architects

Projecting pavilions flank an impressive central entrance with Ionic columns in this eclectic single-story Italian villa with French Baroque and Craftsman details. The magnificent over-scaled redwood brackets in the very wide eaves are signature Maybeck.

6. Woodside Store, 1854
3300 Tripp Road

6

Dr. Robert Tripp and Mathias Parkhurst developed the Woodside Store as a general store supplying local lumbermen. The building became a multifunction community center used variously as a bank, a post office, a stage stop, a lending library, and a meeting space. Dr. Tripp's house remains across from the store. The earliest surviving commercial building in San Mateo County, the county government purchased the store in 1940, which is operated today as a museum by the San Mateo County Historical Association.

7. William Matson House, "Why Worry Farm," 1900; expanded, 1917
3763 Woodside Road

Here is a large, handsome Tudor Revival–style house built for William Matson, the famous shipping line magnate. Matson's daughter Lurline and her husband, William Roth, moved from this house in 1937 when they purchased "Filoli" (see #15).

8. Folger Stables, 1905
4040 Woodside Road

Arthur Brown Jr., architect

Arthur Brown Jr., architect of the San Francisco City Hall and the

Opera House, designed the stables and an exceptional home for James Folger, founder of the Folger Coffee Company. The house is not visible, but the Folger Stables are in Wunderlich Park, owned by the county; the interior is not open to the public. As a stable, it is a luxurious building for its type. Its architectural style could be described as a rather eclectic conflation of the Craftsman style with the French Baroque. The tall hipped roof and the beautifully detailed second-floor balcony give the building a definite aristocratic air. The complementary carriage house is across from the stables.

9. Charles Brown Adobe, circa 1842
3000 Portola Road

Along with the Sanchez Adobe in Half Moon Bay, the Brown Adobe is the only surviving Mexican Period adobe in San Mateo County and is thought to be the oldest building in San Mateo County. Brown, who had purchased part of Rancho Canada de Raymundo from John Copinger in the early 1840s, later built the first sawmill in the county here in 1849. The adobe is privately owned, but is visible through the trees.

Portola Valley

South of Woodside in the Portola Valley, farming and stock ranching predominated until well after the turn of the century. Englishman Andrew Hallidie, the inventor of San Francisco's cable car railroad in the late 1860s, was the valley's most famous early resident. After he bought property in Portola Valley in 1883, he donated land for a school and post office that became the nucleus of a small community. He also continued to experiment with cable transportation here, constructing a model tramway that ran from the Portola Valley floor to the surrounding hillside.

Portola Valley was incorporated in 1964 after a failed attempt to become part of Woodside in 1956. Like Woodside, Portola Valley is an extremely desirable place to live today. Its population is about 4,500.

10. Our Lady of the Wayside Catholic Church, 1912
930 Portola Road

Timothy Pflueger, architect

Our Lady of the Wayside Church is believed to be the first building designed by Timothy Pflueger; he later became famous for Art Deco–style office and theater buildings such as the Paramount in Oakland and the Castro Theater in San Francisco. The church is a curious combination of Mission Revival (Mission Dolores in particular) with a prominent Georgian Revival entrance portico that includes a theatrically overscaled swan's neck pediment.

8

11. Valley United Presbyterian Church, 1965
945 Portola Road

Inwood & Hoover, architects

The church, with striking natural imagery, has poured concrete walls embedded with large boulders; a high gabled interior space is faced with natural wood, and

behind the altar is a completely glazed wall that looks out on a beautiful redwood forest.

12. Christ Episcopal Church, 1957
815 Portola Road

Clark & Beuttler, architects

Another woodsy Portola Valley church is notable for the beautiful laminated natural wood beams in the finely detailed, steeply gabled main sanctuary.

13. The Sequoias, 1961
501 Portola Road

Skidmore, Owings & Merrill, architects

Garrett Eckbo, landscape architect

An award-winning retirement community, the large Sequoias development is especially notable for its skillful site planning, beautifully sensitive to its wooded hillside setting. The serene Japanesque main building complex around the main courtyard suggests a group of Buddhist temples set in a Zen garden.

14. Willowbrook Gate House, 1912
451 Portola Road

Dr. Herbert Law, owner of the Fairmont Hotel in San Francisco, purchased ninety acres in Portola Valley in 1912 to grow herbs and plants for Viavi, his company that produced various remedies for a wide range of "female complaints." Law built the unusual and picturesque Willowbrook Gate House, a Romanesque-style natural stone mini-castle, as the residence for his horticulturist Henry Schoelhamer and the company offices. Law closed the herb farm and sold the land in 1920; he then built a grand Italian villa, "Lauriston," in 1925 on another property in Portola Valley; this house still survives off Alpine Road but is not visible to the public.

15. William Bourne House, "Filoli," 1917 (unmapped)
86 Canada Road

Willis Polk, architect

Bruce Porter, landscape architect

15

Photo by Barbara Braun

"Filoli" was the third, and by far the largest, of three houses Polk designed for his patron William Bourne, owner of the Empire Mine in Grass Valley and the Spring Valley Water Company. This eclectic, Neoclassical Georgian Revival redbrick mansion includes French windows and a Spanish tile roof. The cavernous mansion has forty-three rooms and seventeen fireplaces laid out in a symmetrical U-shaped plan. The main staircase is black marble and the seventy-foot-long ballroom has twenty-two-foot-high ceilings. The magnificent sixteen-acre formal garden, laid out on a north/south axis to the main hall, complements the design of the mansion; it was originally part of a 650-acre estate. The garden house was designed by Arthur Brown Jr. William Roth and Mrs. Lurline Matson-Roth purchased the house in 1937.

In 1975, the Roths donated "Filoli" to the National Trust, which operates it as a museum. The property is the only surviving great estate on the peninsula open for public tours. Tour information is available at www.filoli.org.

16. Pulgas Water Temple, 1934 (unmapped)
*Canada Road
(one mile north of
Edgewood Road exit
off Interstate 280)*

*William Merchant,
architect*

*Albert Bernasconi,
stone carver*

The San Francisco Water Department built this fine Roman temple in an appropriately sylvan setting as a monument to the Hetch Hetchy aqueduct's terminus at Crystal Springs Lake. Located at the

16

end of a reflecting pool lined with cypresses, the temple and its setting possess a magical sense of classical calm and repose. Aqueduct water that originally rushed in torrents into the temple's basin has been diverted to a nearby treatment facility.

4 • Daly City • Colma • Brisbane

During the nineteenth century, much of north San Mateo County was called Colma. Businesses, mainly gambling and drinking houses, were clustered near Mission Street. By the turn of the nineteenth century, a variety of activities, such as dog tracks and boxing arenas that San Francisco had either outlawed or had no room for, drew thousands of San Franciscans across the county line, although fields of crops and dairy ranching actually dominated the landscape.

Beginning with the consecration of Holy Cross Cemetery (Roman Catholic) in 1887, cemeteries serving San Francisco came to be located in the area, due to the shortage of land around Lone Mountain, where the city's cemeteries were then located. In 1888, Home of Peace Cemetery (Jewish) was established; in 1892, Cypress Lawn Cemetery (nonsectarian) opened and was immediately recognized as one of the most beautiful burial grounds in the country.

For years this cemetery section of the county was known as Lawndale; it was incorporated as Colma in 1924. Today this "City of the Dead" has a living population of about 1,200.

Dairy rancher John Daly provided shelter for refugees fleeing across the county line after the 1906 earthquake and fire. Later, he subdivided his property for suburban development, and the town was incorporated in 1911.

After World War II, the city's population grew from 15,000 to 60,000 between 1950 and 1960; the population today is more than 104,000, the largest city in the county.

In 1945, builder Henry Doelger purchased 1,300 acres west of Daly City and began creating Westlake. Over a twenty-year period, homes for 20,000 people were constructed, and Westlake was annexed to Daly City in stages. Similarly, Fred and Carl Gellert purchased 1,000 acres after the war and created the Serramonte subdivision.

Brisbane and the north side of San Bruno Mountain were originally part of Rancho Guadalupe la Visitacio y Rodeo Viejo. The 9,000-acre land grant was owned by Jacob Leese, an American who married into the California family of General Mariano G. Vallejo.

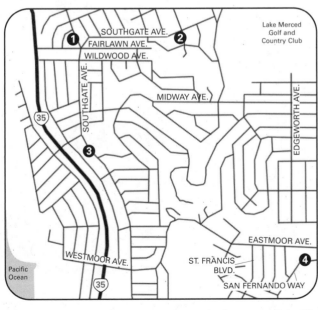

4 • Daly City

It was not until the 1930s that Brisbane as a town began to take shape. Many of the original settlers were poor Depression-era families who created a rather dilapidated community. After World War II, there was considerable suburban growth.

In 1961, Brisbane was incorporated to defend themselves from such threats as the expansion of the San Francisco dump. Citizen's action committee "Garbage A-Go-Go" was victorious. The creation of the San Francisco Bay Conservation and Development Commission in the mid-1960s was partly due to such groups. Today the city numbers about 3,600 people.

Daly City

1. Westlake, begun 1945; completed 1970

Henry Doelger Company

Chester Dolphin, principal architect

Ed Hageman, designer

Henry Doelger created a complete "city within a city": Westlake. It was planned to include more than 10,000 housing units in both detached single-family houses and apartments, along with schools, churches, shopping centers, and offices.

A number of Modern cubistic-style tract houses were built by Doelger, and the façades were designed by Ed Hageman. The bold massing, contrasting roof angles, and odd window shapes and sizes certainly make these houses wonderful artifacts of the "fabulous fifties." The Modern exuberance the houses exude is a stark contrast to the pallid historicism of tract houses today. A group of these houses (1949–1954) can be seen at **125, 145,** and **166 [1] Ashland Drive.** The house at **115 Fairlawn Avenue** resembles the quirky formal geometry of Southern California Modernist Rudolf Schindler.

2. Daly City Library, Westlake Branch, 1998

275 Southgate Avenue

Group 4 Architecture

This splendid small library, a virtual glass box, is reminiscent of the early Modernist interest in glass architecture seen in the work of Walter Gropius or Bruno Taut. The cylindrical glazed entrance

foyer and the fishbowl-like reading room are luminous spaces.

3. Mario Ciampi Schools, Various locations

Architect Mario Ciampi designed a series of widely admired Modernist schools and many of the public buildings for the Doelger Company in Westlake in the 1950s. Landscape archi-

tect Lawrence Halprin collaborated on a number of these projects. Donut-shaped with an
accordion roof, the **Vista Mar
Elementary School** (1959) at
Southgate Avenue and Bradley
Drive, now the Marjorie Tobias
Elementary School [3], is a
particularly imaginative design
(school as a merry-go-round?)
that won a number of awards in
its day. The more-sober 1958
International Style **Westmoor
High School** at 131 Westmoor
Avenue, now appearing a bit
threadbare, is an essay in abstract
geometry rendered in white stucco and glass. Other Ciampi-
designed schools in Daly City
include the **Fernando Riviera
Intermediate School** at 1255
Southgate Avenue, **Garden
Village Elementary School**
(1956) at 208 Garden Lane, and
the **Pauline Margaret Brown
Elementary School** (1957) at
305 Eastmoor Avenue.

4. Hope Lutheran Church, 1955
55 San Fernando Way

*Mario Corbett,
architect*

An inventive church design,
all roof—steep and gabled—
no walls. The geometrically

patterned wood and willful
asymmetry of the front façade
add further visual panache.

Colma

5. Cypress Lawn Cemetery, founded 1892
1370 El Camino Real

*Hamden Noble,
landscape architect*

Cypress Lawn has the
finest collection of funerary art and architecture in
Northern California, and
it is an excellent example
of the picturesque land-
scaping principles of the
rural cemetery movement.
Also, no cemetery in
Northern California has
as many graves and related
monuments for significant
figures related to the state's
economic, political, and
intellectual history.
Hamden Noble, a San
Francisco financier,
designed the cemetery
after a study tour of the
great rural cemeteries
designed by Frederick
Olmsted and others in the

eastern United States. He spared
no expense on landscaping.

The major early cemetery monuments at Cypress Lawn reflect the
City Beautiful movement predilec-
tion for Neoclassical architecture.
Significant architects designed
many of the mausoleums, such as
the one for the Crocker family by

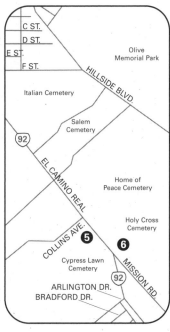

4 • Colma

A. Page Brown, the Hearst family
by Albert C. Schweinfurth, and
the Tevis Monument by John
Galen Howard [5a]. The Claus
Spreckels Monument is an
imposing Classical temple [5b].
A significant departure from the
Neoclassical monuments is the
Gustave Niebaum (founder of the
Inglenook Winery) Mausoleum, a
variation on the Getty Tomb
designed by the great Chicago
architect Louis Sullivan. B. J. S.
Cahill designed many of the
major cemetery buildings, including the Office Building, the
Lakeside Columbarium, and the
Catacombs. The interior of the
Catacombs (1915–1924) has a
very large and significant installa-
tion of stained glass, including a
spectacular stained-glass dome
designed by artists such as Harold
Cummings, Walter Judson, and
Joseph and Richard Lamb.

6. Holy Cross Cemetery, founded 1887
1500 Mission Road

Holy Cross Cemetery is a combination of the picturesque rural
cemetery style and the traditional
rectilinear style. A number of the
early mausoleums are designed
in a rustic Richardsonian
Romanesque style, unlike the
predominately Neoclassical
temples found at Cypress Lawn.
The James Phelan Mausoleum
(he was a San Francisco mayor
and U.S. senator) is a notable
Richardsonian monument [6].
Shea and Shea designed the
imposing stone Richardsonian
Romanesque Old Lodge/Office
building for the cemetery and
the cemetery entrance gates. The
equally imposing Classical-style
Holy Cross Mausoleum, designed
by sculptor John MacQuarrie,
covers more than four acres.

5 • San Bruno • Millbrae

San Bruno, Millbrae, South San Francisco, the southern portion of Mount San Bruno, and the northern part of Burlingame were all part of Jose Sanchez's Rancho Buri Buri. Within fifteen years after the American takeover of California, the Sanchez family was forced to give up 95 percent of this land to bankers, attorneys, and the taxman.

During the late nineteenth century, San Bruno consisted of farms, a couple of well-known roadhouses, and a railroad stop. In 1899, Polish Prince Andre Poniatowski financed a 120-acre horse-racing track and named it "Tanforan." The California Jockey Club bought the track in 1902. Only a year later, the California Auto Club, who sponsored car racing, leased the track from the club; in 1908, when California outlawed gambling at such tracks, the site was used for air shows.

Tanforan served as a military training field during World War I, but in 1923, the track again returned to horse racing. When pari-mutuel betting was legalized in 1933, the track became quite successful. With the outbreak of World War II, Tanforan was used as a center for assembling San Francisco Bay Area Japanese Americans before they were transferred to internment camps in the interior of the country. Today Tanforan is a major regional shopping center.

After the 1906 earthquake, San Bruno began growing into a suburban community. The railroad and an electric streetcar provided good transportation to San Francisco. San Bruno incorporated in 1914 and today has a population exceeding 40,000.

Millbrae, south of San Bruno, developed more slowly. Until the end of World War I, most of Millbrae was owned by descendants of Darius Ogden Mills, who had purchased a

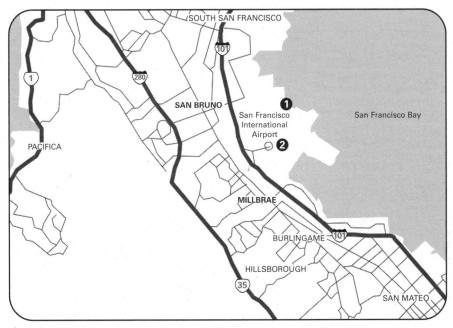

1,500-acre tract of land in 1860. Mills created one of the great private estates on the Peninsula; he built a lavish three-story mansion he named "Mill's brae," a dairy, reservoir, a huge glass-covered greenhouse, and an expansive garden with a forest of eucalyptus.

   Although the Millbrae area experienced some suburban development after World War I, it was not until after World War II that the town experienced the large spurt in population that led to its incorporation in 1948. Today, Millbrae's population is about 21,000.

1. San Francisco International Airport

The San Francisco International Airport had its origins as Mills Field, 150 acres of grazing land, purchased by the city of San Francisco in 1926. The first terminal was a simple single-story wood-frame structure, and the airport's first commercial flights began in October 1927. As air traffic increased, the city financed, through the Public Works Administration, the construction of an attractive Spanish Colonial Revival terminal and administration building in 1936. Passenger volume reached one million by 1945, and then doubled in the early 1950s with the postwar boom. A $10 million bond issue financed a new airport terminal, built in 1954. Additions to the Central Terminal included the South Terminal in 1963 and the North Terminal in 1979. In 1983, the Central Terminal was extensively modernized. Today the San Francisco International Airport has 2,383 acres, some of it bay fill, serving forty million passengers annually.

2. International Terminal, 2000

Skidmore, Owings & Merrill Architects, Michael Willis Architects, Del Campo & Maru Architects, other architects (boarding areas and BART station)

Photo courtesy of San Francisco International Airport

Given its rather modest earlier buildings, San Francisco Airport sought to make a grand architectural statement in the design of its new International Terminal. The $2.4 billion project included not only the vast multistory terminal but also a new surface-road infrastructure for twelve lanes of automobile traffic in the basement, and an Airport BART station.

The International Terminal, the largest international terminal in North America, contains 1.8 million square feet. Although constructed of the latest modern materials and structural innovations, the terminal's symmetrical front façade communicates a traditional formal civic authority and decorum. The building's great visual coup de theatre is the enormous free-span public space that recalls the great transportation terminals of the world. The complex double-cantilever-form

roof (100 feet above the terminal's floor) and the exposed football-shaped roof trusses (suggesting a kind of metaphor of flight in their backward sweep, based on the wing structure of a Boeing 747) enhance the interior's visual drama. The monumental open greenhouse interiors of the past are suggested in the variety of interior plants in the main public space, including twenty-six planters with Japanese bamboo, reaching heights of sixty-five feet. The terminal was built over 250 base isolators, the largest building in the world using this structural system for seismic stability. As homage to the airport's history, the Spanish Colonial Revival lobby area of the original 1936 terminal has been reconstructed inside the International Terminal as part of the San Francisco Airport Commission Aviation Library and the Louis A. Turpen Aviation Museum.

6 • South San Francisco

South San Francisco is perhaps the most unique community of all the Peninsula's incorporated areas because it began as a company town. By the time it incorporated in 1908, the city of nearly 2,000 people had ten industries—including a meatpacking plant, Fuller Paint Company, two steel mills, a tannery, brickyards, and a lumber company.

Before the arrival of these industrial companies, much of what would become South San Francisco was the ranch of Charles Lux, who had purchased the land in 1856. In 1858, he and Central Valley cattle rancher Henry Miller formed the partnership of Miller and Lux, creating the West Coast's largest livestock company of its day. For more than thirty years, cowboys drove thousands of cattle from massive Central Valley ranches up El Camino Real to Lux's spread. The cattle were kept there before being butchered in San Francisco.

After Lux died in 1887, Gustavus Swift, a Chicago meatpacking giant, joined forces with other meatpackers and bought some 3,500 acres, including Lux's ranch. The group created the South San Francisco Land and Improvement Company. During the 1890s, additional companies opened and a residential area for employees was built.

During both World War I and II, shipbuilding took place at South San Francisco. After the Second World War, the old smokestack industries went into decline. Their place has been taken by other endeavors, most notably Genentech, Inc. This firm, organized in 1976, moved into a South San Francisco warehouse in 1978. Since that time it has become one of the world's most important biotech firms, making international headlines for its work in fighting cancer and other advances.

South San Francisco still has a diverse economy with a population of more than 61,000.

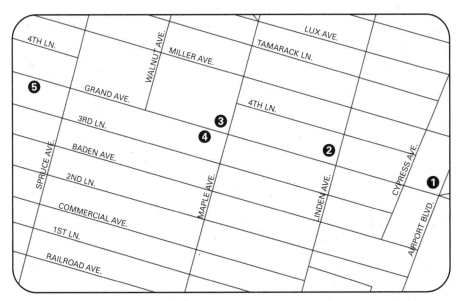

3. City Hall, 1920
400 Grand Avenue

Coffey & Werner, architects

South San Francisco has the only "historic" city hall in San Mateo County—and what a city hall it is! The dignified Georgian Revival building, modeled on Independence Hall in Philadelphia, is set on a hill in a small civic park with the City Library. A formal stair leads up to the imposing two-story building (with cupola), literally towering above the Grand Avenue commercial area. The 1916 City Library acts as a nice Neoclassical bookend to City Hall, balancing this fine civic complex [3a].

4. Commercial Building, 1931
411 Grand Avenue

An Art Deco gem across from City Hall has an unusual façade of patterned blue glazed brick.

5. Coombes House, 1893
527 Grand Avenue

The Coombes House is one of the largest and most impressive Queen Anne's in South San Francisco.

Grand Avenue Commercial District

South San Francisco has a wonderfully un-gentrified commercial district with buildings displaying an unparalleled variety of architectural periods and styles from the nineteenth and twentieth centuries. The streets parallel to Grand Avenue (like Commercial and Baden Avenues) still have a number of early houses, primarily Queen Anne–style cottages from the 1890s.

1. Merrian Block, 1891
100 Grand Avenue

An early downtown commercial building, the Merrian Block retains its second-floor ornamental exuberance although the ground floor has been mercilessly modernized. A rooming house was on the second floor; a first-floor saloon stood on the corner.

2. Bank of South San Francisco, 1918
300 Grand Avenue

A monumental Classical banking temple, this large building anchors an important corner in the commercial district. The red-brick 1912 Metropolitan Hotel is situated on the opposite corner.

7 • Burlingame • Hillsborough

After W. D. M. Howard died in 1856, his Rancho San Mateo was divided between his wife, Agnes, and her father, Dr. Joseph Henry Poett, who in turn gave the western portion of his holdings to his other daughter, Julia (Mrs. John Redington). For decades the Howard, Poett, and Redington families controlled much of Rancho San Mateo and established some of the Peninsula's great estates.

In 1860, Poett sold diplomat-adventurer Anson Burlingame approximately 1,000 acres of the rancho lands in today's Burlingame and Hillsborough. Burlingame planned an English-style residential park, but it wasn't realized when he died in 1870.

William C. Ralston then bought the property from Burlingame's widow. Ralston, California's most famous capitalist of the time, believed in Burlingame's dream and planned his own country community that he wanted to call Ralstonville, but he died in 1875 in debt.

William Sharon, Ralston's largest creditor, received much of Ralston's estate, including his San Mateo County properties. Sharon also believed in Burlingame's country residential park idea, and although he had the area surveyed, published a map, and called it Burlingame, he did not finally develop the area. He sold a portion of it and created a dairy on the remaining acres to supply his Palace Hotel in San Francisco.

After Sharon died in 1885, his son-in-law Francis G. Newlands became the manager of Sharon's huge estate that encompassed holdings in San Mateo County, San Francisco's financial district, and silver mines in Nevada. Earlier, Newlands had created Chevy Chase, Maryland, and its Chevy Chase Country Club.

Newlands was a founder of the Burlingame Country Club in 1893, which attracted men from San Francisco's elite business community. A year later, club members built the

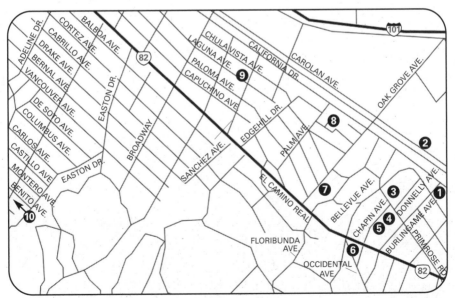

7 • Burlingame

Burlingame train station, and a small business district grew around it. As a result of the 1906 earthquake, Burlingame's population grew from 200 in 1906 to 1,000 in 1907. The town incorporated in 1909; Hillsborough followed in 1910.

Today Burlingame and Hillsborough are attractive communities. Burlingame (population 28,000) has a pleasant pedestrian atmosphere, especially along downtown's Burlingame Avenue. Hillsborough (population about 11,000) has a more exclusive, country feeling.

Burlingame

1. Burlingame Railroad Depot, 1893–1894
Burlingame Avenue at California Drive

George Howard and Joachim B. Mathison, architects

The Burlingame Railroad Depot is considered to be one of the earliest examples of the Mission Revival style in the Bay Area; it is a significant architectural landmark on the peninsula. Architect Mathison had submitted a Mission Revival–style building to the competition for the California Building at the Columbian Exposition in Chicago, but A. Page Brown was the winner. This depot is a variation on Mathison's competition drawings. Howard was one of the founding members of the Burlingame Country Club and his family owned much of what is Hillsborough today.

2. Burlingame High School, 1923
400 Carolan Avenue

William H. Weeks, architect

This is one of the most impressive school designs by the prolific architect William Weeks. The building's formal Palladian Classical façade seems even more monumental in its verdant landscape of sweeping lawns and large trees (the site was an earlier Burlingame estate).

3. Burlingame Public Library, 1930
480 Primrose Road

Ernest Norberg, architect
Group 4 Architecture (renovation, 1997)

The original 1930 library was extensively rebuilt in 1997. The new design incorporated the best features of the original, including the main reading room (with its magnificent wood truss ceiling), the children's room, and much of the Spanish Colonial Revival front façade. The open, light-filled airy spaces of the main floor are quite lovely.

4. Retail Buildings, 1930s
300 Block of Primrose Road (west side)

A charming row of Period Revival retail buildings is located on this side street in Burlingame's upscale downtown commercial area.

5. George Farrell House, 1905
1421 Chapin Avenue

George Farrell, brick mason

English Master Brick Mason George Farrell built this mini-English manor using a variety of brick types and patterns. The house is a virtuoso exhibition of the brick mason's art. The building is now occupied by the Burlingame Garden Center.

6. St. Paul's Episcopal Church, 1927
1415 El Camino Real
George Gilliam, architect

St. Paul's is an attractive Gothic Revival church that would be at home in an English village. The architect was a Burlingame resident. The interior has wonderful stained-glass windows and ornate dark-stained hardwood.

7. First Church of Christ Scientist, 1930
1449 Oak Grove Avenue
Henry H. Gutterson, architect

The eclectic sources for this church include the Spanish Colonial Revival with a dash of Italian Renaissance (Alberti primarily).

8. Willborough Place, 1928
Willborough Road
George Gilliam, architect

The small English Medieval Cottage houses and narrow winding streets make Willborough Place one of the most charming residential enclaves in Burlingame. The original development included fifteen houses, and its name is a conflation of builder-developers George Williams and Frank Burrow.

9. Rognier House, 1910
1120 Sanchez Avenue

A petite version of the Grand Trianon is an essay in how to fit architectural grandeur onto a small lot. Start with a large projecting porch with Ionic columns, add to each side of the entrance large French windows with balconies, and voila! Owner Gaston Rognier was an artist/entrepreneur who designed ornamental garden statuary that he sold from his store in San Mateo.

10. Kohl Mansion, 1914
2750 Adeline Drive
Howard & White, architects

The Kohl Mansion is certainly one of the grandest Tudor Revival buildings on the Peninsula. With 44,000 square feet and thirty-eight rooms, it is also huge. The detailing of the brick is particularly fine and the large multi-light bay windows are fit for a king. The interior finishes are also sumptuous; the architects described the dining room as "a dream in Nile green and pale ivory." The mansion became Mercy High School in 1931. Today the mansion is often used for weddings, and chamber music concerts are held in the grand hall (www.musicatkohl.org).

In the neighborhood of the Kohl Mansion are many Period Revival Houses of interest: 2811 Hillside is a splendid Tudor Revival.

Hillsborough

11. "Villa Roma," 1922
1904 Forest View Avenue
Arthur Brown Jr., architect

This grand and formal Renaissance-style house by the architect of San Francisco City Hall is set back a good distance from the street behind beautiful lush landscaping.

12. George Newhall House, "La Dolphine," 1914
1761 Manor Drive
Lewis Hobart, architect

Hobart's elegant variation of the Petite Trianon at Versailles is one of the best known of the Hillsborough early estates. The house is on a lovely street lined with cypresses.

13. House, 1895
1615 Floribunda Avenue
A. Page Brown, architect

This magnificent Tudor-style house is one of the original five "cottages" designed by A. Page Brown for developer Francis Newlands. Three of Brown's original Tudor-style houses survive, including the equally large house next door at 50 Kammerer Court and a smaller one at 141 Pepper Avenue. The A. Page Brown houses established Hillsborough as an upscale community of large houses on lavishly landscaped lots, and Tudor Revival as the town's signature style. Today, Neo-Tudor-style houses are still built in Hillsborough.

14. House, 1939
1800 Floribunda Avenue
William W. Wurster, architect

A handsome Wurster house with finely detailed brick walls, originally painted pale gray, is now red since the paint was removed. The original created a more seamless surface; the red brick walls make the house now look rather Neo-Georgian.

15. Henderson House, 1933
711 Bromfield Road
William W. Wurster, architect

Wurster's elegant and modern interpretation of the French Norman fits comfortably in this upscale Hillsborough neighborhood. Another Wurster house nearby at 735 Bromfield Road has a Thomas Church garden.

16. Houses
200 Block of West Santa Inez Avenue

The 200 block of West Santa Inez Avenue, near El Camino Real, captures the gracious rural

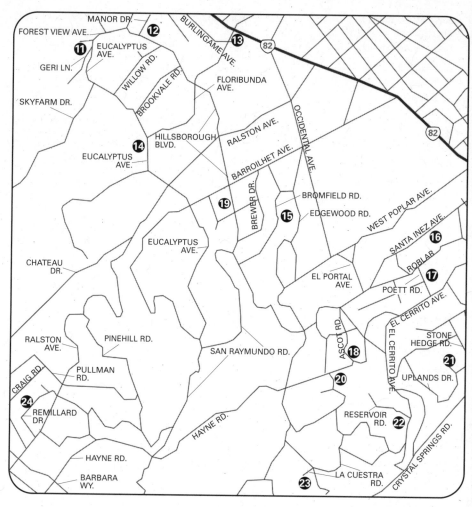

ambience of early Hillsborough. The substantial but understated houses are in a variety of revival styles popular in the early twentieth century and are set in rich mature landscaping. The house at 234 is a Craftsman-style house built in 1902. The two houses at 200 and 255 are attractive Tudor-style houses, while 259 and 263 are good local variations on the houses of Spanish Andalusia. An early modernist design at 217 (1937) is by Gardner Dailey, and George Howard did a Shingle-style house at 120 (1903).

17. Richard Tobin House, 1906
360 Poett Road

George Howard, architect

This charming English-medieval-style house, one of Howard's seven early houses, has a garden to match. Across the street at 337 Poett Road is an impressive Tudor-style mansion from 1910. An early Gardner Dailey house is next door at 417 Roehampton Road.

18. Dinkelspiel House, 1940
301 Ascot Road

William W. Wurster, architect

A classic example from this period of Wurster's career

displays his signature fine window details and seamless flush horizontal wood siding.

19. Dean Arnold House, 1932
635 Hillsborough Boulevard
Gardner Dailey, architect

An early Gardner Dailey design in Spanish Colonial Revival is reminiscent of the work of Santa Barbara architect George Washington Smith. The flat stucco façade has a sophisticated asymmetrical sequencing of various window sizes and shapes.

20. Houses, 1920S
South side of Hayne Road, from Ascot Road to Chiltern Road

The fine row of Tudor-style houses set in a verdant landscape on this section of Hayne Road makes you feel like you are driving through the English countryside. The house at 730 Chiltern has a front yard the size of a small park with magnificent landscaping.

21. The Uplands, 1913–1917
400 Uplands Drive
Willis Polk, architect

"Rosecliff"—the Newport, Rhode Island, "cottage" designed by McKim, Mead and White—was the inspiration for this large Neoclassical Italian palazzo

designed by Willis Polk for Templeton Crocker of the railroad and banking family. The garden façade is a richly layered composition with a pair of Ionic columns framing the large window bays on the first floor, balustrades on the second floor, and a set-back attic floor with classical pilasters framing the windows. The eclectic interior is primarily Italian Renaissance classicism but includes a Gothic Tudor smoking room. The house, originally set in a 160-acre estate, is now part of the private Crystal Springs School.

22. Bazett House, 1940
101 Reservoir Road
Frank Lloyd Wright, architect

This house is a smaller, less expensive version of the famous Hanna House on the Stanford University campus; the clients were friends of the Hanna family. Joseph Eichler lived in this great house during the late 1940s, and was inspired to market moderately priced well-designed modern houses to the middle class, thus becoming one of the most innovative homebuilders in California. The low-slung design, strongly horizontal with wildly overscaled roof eaves, hugs the brow of the hill above the street below.

23. Hofmann House, 1937
1048 La Cuesta Road
Richard Neutra, architect

Neutra designed this house as a version of his acclaimed 1929 Lovell House in Los Angeles, considered one of the first modern houses in the United States. Although constructed of a conventional wood frame rather than the more avant-garde light steel frame, the Hofmann House stands out as an exceptional Modern design in the conservative residential environment of Hillsborough. Given the rarity of International Style Modernist designs in Hillsborough, the town's upscale 1930s and 1940s clientele found William Wurster's "soft modernism" more to its taste than Neutra's more hardcore version. Interestingly, a later 1952 Neutra house nearby at 1430 Carlton Road is rather less severe, recalling Wright's Usonian houses in its horizontal wood siding and clerestory window. The Hofmann House is listed on the National Register of Historic Places.

24. The Carolands, 1914–1916
565 Remillard Drive
Ernest Sanson and
Willis Polk, architects

This grand French chateau looks like it should be set in the Bordeaux countryside. The French Neoclassical-style house was originally part of a 500-acre estate, now subdivided with post–World War II Ranch-style houses. One of the largest houses in Hillsborough, it was the residence of Francis Carolan and his wife, Harriett, who was the daughter of George Pullman of the Pullman railroad car fame.

21

144

8 · City of San Mateo

The San Mateo area along San Mateo Creek was also an agricultural outpost for the San Francisco mission where thousands of sheep were grazed.

During the Mexican period the 14,639-acre Rancho Buri Buri was granted to Jose Sanchez in 1835; the Arguello family received the southern portion of Rancho San Mateo in 1836; the northern section was awarded to Cayentano Arenas of Los Angeles in 1846.

With the uncertainties of the Bear Flag Revolt and then the Mexican-American War, Cayentano's father, Luis, sold Rancho San Mateo to the American mercantile firm of Mellus and Howard. Eventually, W. D. M. Howard bought out his partner, Henry Mellus.

Nicolas de Peyster built the first roadhouse between San Francisco and San Jose in 1849 in the abandoned mission outpost building at Rancho San Mateo.

After the San Francisco/San Jose Railroad reached San Mateo in 1863, Charles B. Polhemus, one of the railroad's organizers, laid out a town on both sides of San Mateo Creek. The town slowly took shape and grew; in 1894, the city was incorporated.

San Mateo became the terminus of the San Francisco streetcar line in 1902. Following the 1906 earthquake, the town grew and became the focus of a variety of projects that contributed to making San Mateo an important center of the county: San Mateo Junior College (1922), San Mateo County Community Hospital (1923), San Mateo Hayward Bridge (1929), Bay Meadows Race Track (1934), San Mateo County Fair (1935), and the San Mateo County Historical Museum (1941).

After World War II, developers such as David D. Bohannon, who built the Hillsdale shopping center and constructed apartment houses and single-family homes from El Camino Real to the western hills, contributed to the growth of San Mateo. It is now the second-largest city on the Peninsula, with a population of more than 94,000.

1. Woodland Residential Community, 1965
Southwest corner of Peninsula Avenue and North Humboldt Street

Wurster, Bernardi and Emmons, architects

Lawrence Halprin, landscape architect

Halprin's innovative landscape design is considered the major contribution of this influential multiunit residential development.

2. San Mateo High School, 2005
East Poplar at Delaware Street

The Steinberg Group, architect

This is a convincing updated version of a Tudor Revival–style school, beautifully detailed and constructed in quality materials, a welcome departure from pallid recent efforts at designing in historic styles in the Bay Area. The new school replaces the original, a beloved 1920s Tudor-style school considered to be seismically unsound.

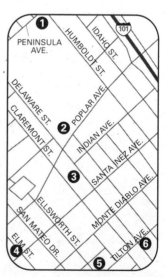

3. House, 1895
51 North Claremont Street

This small Queen Anne–style cottage has unusually exuberant architectural details.

4. Ernest Coxhead House, 1891
37 East Santa Inez Avenue

Ernest Coxhead, architect

This is a charming interpretation of an English Medieval country cottage: the exterior half-timbering exhibits an idiosyncratic modern abstract quality. The dining room with its large window looking out to the garden is a tour de force. The house is now a bed-and-breakfast known as "The Coxhead House." Another Coxhead-designed house is nearby at 134 West Poplar Avenue.

5. Masonic Temple, 1910
100 North Ellsworth Street

This monumental, Neo-Renaissance-style building

has very odd proportions: a wide arched opening flanked by pairs of two-story-tall pilasters below a squished-down top floor and pediment.

6. North and South Delaware Street Victorians, 1890s

The intersection of Delaware Street at Tilton has a nice group of houses representing a variety of nineteenth-century architectural styles: **5 North Delaware Street** is a Queen Anne–style house from 1891; the 1892 William Brown house is at **2 South Delaware Street [6]**; and **8 South Delaware** dates from 1880. The Gothic Revival-style William Sands House at **45 South Delaware,** probably the oldest house in San Mateo, dates from 1866. The 1878 Lawrence Maynard house, in the Italianate style, is a few blocks away at **809 South Delaware Street.**

7. Church of St. Matthew, 1908
El Camino Real at Baldwin Avenue

Willis Polk, architect
Milton Pflueger (addition, 1957)

A rare Willis Polk church design, the Gothic Revival style of St. Matthew's, a somber stone structure surrounded by lawns and mature trees, would fit comfortably in the English countryside. Milton Pflueger inserted a seamless addition, retaining the original west façade while expanding seating by 160. By contrast, the ever-versatile Polk designed "The Uplands," a huge Italian palazzo for the Crocker family in nearby Hillsborough (see entry #21, page 143).

8. San Mateo Railroad Depot, 2000
2 North B Street

ROMA Design Group, architect

Roma Design Group has designed a wonderful modern railroad depot incorporating the traditional forms and Craftsman-style details of an early-twentieth-century depot.

9. Downtown Commercial District
B Street and East Third Avenue

Downtown San Mateo has an impressive collection of commercial buildings, primarily Period Revival but also notable examples of Art Deco. They are located on B Street, from Baldwin Avenue to East Third Avenue, and west on East Third Avenue to El Camino Real. A few highlights are described on the next page:

6

9a. 22 South B Street, 1931
Edwards & Schary, architects

A major Spanish Baroque building on a corner anchors the south end of the B Street commercial area. In the next block are 100 South B Street (1907); the Odd Fellows Building (1891) at 113 South B Street; and the Wisnom Company Building (1925) at 164 South B Street, which was designed by William Weeks.

9b. House of Merkel, 1931
201 South B Street

Edward & Schary, architects

This building has probably the most elaborate Art Deco terracotta ornament on the San Francisco Peninsula. At 240 South B Street (1937) is another Art Deco retail building, and the Medical Arts Building (1929) at 205–221 East 3rd Street was designed by Edward L. Norberg.

9c. Levy Brothers Store, 1931
55 East Third Avenue

Hyman & Appleton, architects

A particularly handsome Tudor Revival–style retail building forms a strong visual anchor on this block with adjacent Tudor Revival–style buildings at 71 and 77 East Third Avenue, also from the early 1930s. At 72 East Third Avenue is a Spanish Colonial Revival building from 1936.

9d. Ben Franklin Hotel, 1926
36 East Third Avenue

William Weeks, architect

This building is a fine example of the Spanish Colonial Revival style translated into a major downtown high-rise, the first in San Mateo. William Weeks was also the architect of Burlingame High School.

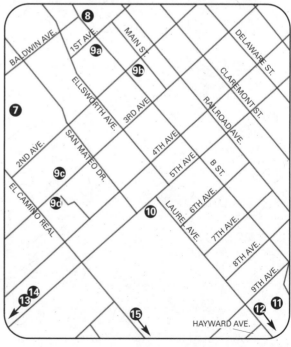

10. San Mateo Park Japanese Tea Garden, 1966
Fifth Avenue at El Camino Real

Nagao Sakurai, landscape architect

The city of San Mateo purchased the nineteenth-century William Kohl estate in 1922 for a city park. The Kohl estate house, later razed, was at first used as a junior college. The surviving features of the estate include some original trees, paths, and the handsome stone-and-iron fence on El Camino Real. Designed by Nagao Sakurai, a former landscape architect of the Imperial Palace in Tokyo, the one-acre Japanese Tea Garden opened in 1966. Members of the San Mateo Gardener's Association contributed their labor in creating the garden.

11. Glazenwood, 1920
Residential Subdivision

S. A. Born Building Company

The Glazenwood residential development was originally marketed as a "restricted residential park," characterized by open landscaped areas between the houses and unencumbered by fences and other obstructions. The charming Spanish Colonial Revival houses in the development are best viewed on Rosewood Drive and Hayward Avenue.

12. Gas Station, 1932
(unmapped)
1641 Palm Avenue

A rare survivor, this beautifully intact Spanish Colonial Revival gas station fits comfortably in a neighborhood of handsome Period Revival–style 1930s houses along Palm Avenue.

13

13. Parrott Family Tomb, St. John's Cemetery, 1885
(unmapped)
End of Oregon Avenue, off Alameda de las Pulgas

Early San Francisco financier John Parrott built a San Mateo summer home in 1868. The Parrott family donated the land to the Catholic Church for St. John's Cemetery, where they constructed the family mausoleum, an impressive central-plan Renaissance-style stone building that looks like it was designed by one of Palladio's students.

14. Aragon High School, 1960
(unmapped)
900 Alameda de las Pulgas

Reid, Rockwell, Banwell & Tarics, architects .

From the mid-1950s to the early 1960s, John Reid and his various partners designed Aragon High School in addition to three similar minimalist Miesian-style high schools in San Mateo County. Engineer Alexander Tarics played an important role in developing the firm's industrial vocabulary. Also in San Mateo, Hillsdale High School was the earliest, opening in 1955, and was a winner of an AIA award; in San Bruno, Crestmoor High School, built in 1962, was the last (it closed in 1980); Mills High School in Millbrae dates from 1958. Within the four schools, the geometric rigor of the Vierendal I-beam frames with large gray panels perfectly reflects American thought regarding postwar techno-optimism— technology could solve the world's problems, society would be totally rationalized, and schools would become factories mass-producing educated citizens—ideas many now find strangely quaint in this post-modern age. Not surprisingly, a bond issue passed in 2000 is financing an extensive remodeling (designed by The Steinberg Group) of the three remaining schools.

15. Apartments, 1937
(unmapped)
2454 South El Camino Real

E. A. Neumarket, architect

A muscular Art Deco building (now offices) anchors an important corner on El Camino Real.

9 · Belmont · San Carlos

Belmont and San Carlos were once part of Rancho de las Pulgas that was granted to the Arguello family. During the California Gold Rush, the Arguellos engaged the services of Simon Mezes to help them retain their land. In exchange for Mezes' services, the Arguellos gave him about one-quarter of their rancho.

In 1854, Mezes sold some of his land to an Italian named Leonetto Cipriani, who in turn sold to capitalist William Ralston. Adding to the Cipriani house, Ralston created the huge fifty-bedroom mansion that stands today as part of the Notre Dame de Namur University campus.

After the San Francisco/San Jose Railroad began operating in 1863, Carl Janke built a German-style biergarten east of Ralston's estate and named it Belmont Park. It attracted crowds of up to 10,000 for a single organized picnic. Eventually Belmont Park developed a reputation for drunkenness and brawling; the Southern Pacific stopped excursions, and by the late 1890s Belmont Park closed.

Nevertheless, a small community had developed at the railroad tracks. Fearing annexation by burgeoning San Carlos to the south, Belmont residents incorporated in 1927. Today the city has a population of more than 25,000 people.

San Carlos originated as the dream of successful merchant and politician Timothy Guy Phelps, who bought 3,500 acres of property along the railroad tracks. In 1887, he had formal plans drawn up for a town. A railroad station was built in 1888.

San Carlos grew slowly until after World War I, when skilled promoter Fred Drake came on the scene. During the 1920s, under Drake, San Carlos was said to be growing faster than any other community in California. Incorporated in 1925, its population is approximately 28,000.

Belmont

1. St. Michael's Hall (Church of the Immaculate Heart of Mary), 1920
1060 Alameda de las Pulgas

St. Michael's Hall is a curious ecclesiastical combination of the Mission Revival and Craftsman styles. The unusual steep gable façade projects out below the church's prominent main gable roof. The nearby Church of the Holy Cross at 900 Alameda de las Pulgas is a 1964 design by Reid, Rockwell, Banwell & Tarics, best known for their school designs.

2. Ralston Hall, 1853; 1865–1875
1500 Ralston Avenue

John P. Gaynor, architect

Ralston Hall has probably the greatest nineteenth-century interior in the Bay Area. The house is also the only major Peninsula estate surviving from the 1870s. William Ralston was founder of the Bank of California and developer of the Palace Hotel. He had investments in the silver mines of Nevada's Comstock Lode and real estate, and became one of the most powerful and wealthy men of his time. The remodeling of the 1855 Leonetto Cipriani villa resulted in a lavish freewheeling combination of French and Italian architecture and the Peninsula's most splendid mansion. The 55,360-square-foot mansion has eighty rooms on four floors. The exterior retains some original details, but there have been additions and a covering of exterior stucco. The multilevel foyer with its many arched openings, the formal dining room, and the large

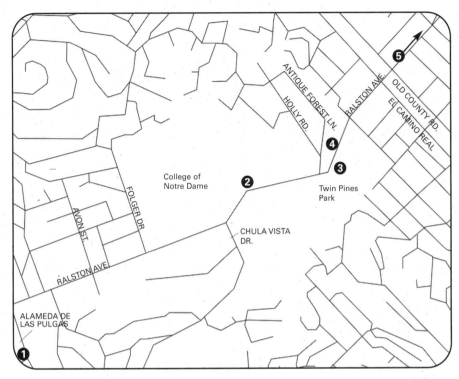

9 • Belmont

Neoclassical mirrored Grand Ballroom are truly magnificent spaces that retain their original finishes. Today, concerts are held regularly in the Grand Ballroom, and the interior is available for receptions and weddings.

3. George Center House, 1907
1085 Ralston Avenue

A major Mission Revival–style house with a formal symmetry, prominent end pylons, and a huge porch with paired columns leads one to expect a public building—a school or a railroad station? Not surprisingly, the house has been primarily in public use, beginning as a sanitarium in the 1920s, and is now the Peninsula Museum of Art.

4. Woodmont Apartments, 1967
1050 Ralston Avenue

Backen Arrigoni and Ross, architects

This unusual apartment design is characterized by the expressionistic vertiginous forms of its long, steep downward-pitched roofs and crisply incised white walls. The nearby Belmont Vista Senior Housing, 900 Sixth Street, is a pleasant Neo-Craftsman design in the prominent location.

5. Autobahn Motors, 1995
700 Island Parkway, off Hwy 101

Esherick Homsey Dodge & Davis, architects

An elegant modern auto dealership building, its sleek-bowed tapering form clad in steel plates also functions as a freeway billboard. The reflective materials have a gold glow at sunset. How appropriate for the Mercedes-Benz dealer!

San Carlos

6. San Carlos Railroad Depot, 1888
599 El Camino Real

Charles Coolidge, architect (attributed)

The San Carlos Depot is a rare Richardsonian Romanesque

sleek green Vitrolite cladding and stainless-steel streamlining, and the towering marquee "Carlos Club" sign in elegant neon.

9. Union 76 Gas Station, 1946
888 El Camino Real

One of few surviving "Streamline Moderne" gas stations in the Bay Area has been managed by the Nielsen family (now the third generation) since it opened in 1946. The angled glazed building with its stepped roof and connecting service bays are striking features.

railroad depot in the Bay Area. Through his friendship with Leland Stanford, early San Carlos resident Nathaniel Brittan reportedly hired architect Charles Coolidge to design the depot. Coolidge's Boston firm—Shepley, Rutan, and Coolidge (H. H. Richardson's successor firm) were the architects of Stanford University, and the same quarry used for the Stanford buildings (Greystone Quarry in the Almaden Valley near San Jose) was the source for the depot's brown sandstone. The building has a distinctive conical tower, and a large porte cochere that was originally on the west was removed in the 1920s. Recently the tracks have been elevated above the depot, regrettably ruining the setting.

7. Fred Drake Building, 1929
1101 San Carlos Avenue, at El Camino Real

An intricately detailed Moorish Alhambra knockoff anchoring a major downtown corner is a perfect foil for the brownstone San Carlos Railroad Depot across El Camino. Built for the first successful San Carlos real estate mogul, the building exudes the exuberance of America in the go-go twenties just before the Wall Street crash, which resulted in the Great Depression.

8. The Carlos Club, 1949
612 El Camino Real

The Carlos Club is a wonderful small Art Moderne building that packs a lot of visual punch: giant circular ocean liner window,

10. St. Charles Catholic Church, 1929
737 Walnut Street

The very prominent entrance to this substantial Mission-style church has a deeply recessed opening with a sensuous curved arch. After the Civic Garden Club of San Carlos moved here in 1956, the church became known as "Casa de Flores."

11. Hacienda Garden Apartments, 1931
San Carlos Avenue at Elm Street

These Spanish Colonial Revival garden apartment buildings are each unique, exhibiting an inventive variety of forms, window shapes, and entrance doors, all set among a series of courtyards. Sadly, the large apartment building next door replaced two of the original five buildings.

12. Adolph Paulsen House, 1912
408 Elm Street

A veritable encyclopedia of classical ornament, the formal symmetry of the house contrasts with the exuberant intricacy of its details. Paulsen, who had a successful business as a well borer, built one of the most impressive houses in San Carlos. A few blocks away, the 1000 block of Elm Street includes a number of Period Revival houses from the 1920s.

13. Nathaniel Brittan House, "The Manor," 1888
40 Pine Avenue

Nathaniel Brittan, one-time Bohemian Club president, built this large country house on land inherited from his father, John, who owned a successful San Francisco hardware store. The picturesque asymmetrical house resembles a German Bavarian chalet. The Brittan "Lodge" around the corner from "The Manor" at 125 Dale Avenue, also known as the "party house," is an octagon-shaped house with a curious octagonal cupola.

14. Brittan Acres Elementary School, 1952
Belle Avenue at Tamarack Avenue

John Reid & Partners, architect

Low slung with a wide prominent gable, this early finger-plan, wood-frame school by John Reid blends seamlessly in its Ranch House neighborhood.

15. George Hein Building, 1936
1660 Laurel Street

Among the many fine Art Moderne–style buildings in San Carlos, this one would fit comfortably in Miami Beach. The horizontal ocean liner windows wrap around the corners of the clean sleek geometry of the front façade. The side stair has a sensual sculptural quality. George Hein was an inventor of dental tools.

9 • San Carlos

10 · Redwood City

Redwood City is located on a portion of Rancho de las Pulgas, which was given to Simon Mezes by the Arguello family in the mid-1850s. When Mezes acquired the property, there was already a small community squatting at a waterfront landing. In response, he surveyed the land, divided it into lots, and sold them to the squatters. He called his town "Mezesville," but the name was changed to Redwood City when the post office opened in 1856. It is remarkable that the town plan—the streets and blocks that Mezes laid out—exists today in downtown Redwood City.

In 1856, Redwood City was the only town on the Bay Shore and became the San Mateo County seat of government. Business activity centered on and around Broadway, and resembled a typical western community with dirt streets and planked sidewalks. The town incorporated in 1867. After the 1880s, due to the decline of logging and the rise of agriculture, the town's character changed to a law-abiding, family-oriented community.

Redwood City differed from some other San Mateo County towns because it was controlled by businessmen rather than by wealthy country estate owners. By the 1940s, it had a modern port, tanneries, and cement and salt works. Today, the population is more than 76,000.

Downtown

1. Diller-Chamberlain Store, 1859
726 Main Street

This very early brick building, which has a simple classical design, is probably the oldest commercial building in town; originally it housed a grocery and dry goods.

2. Bank of San Mateo County, 1900
2000 Broadway

Alfred Coffey, architect

The richly ornamented French Baroque bank building with its prominent domed corner tower is part of a particularly strong ensemble of early-twentieth-century commercial buildings in downtown Redwood City. Architect Coffey joined the adjacent building on Main Street, including a new façade design, to the corner building in 1910. The Neoclassical Fitzgerald Building at 2020

Broadway retains its original stained-glass storefront. The Bank of San Mateo County building and the 1912 Neoclassical Sequoia Hotel, 800 Main Street, with its rounded corner entrance across Broadway, provide a distinguished entry portal to the historic downtown district.

3. San Mateo County Courthouse, 1904, 1910
2200 Broadway

Dodge & Dolliver Architects (dome, 1904)

Glenn Allen, architect (main building, 1910)

A free interpretation of Roman Renaissance architecture, the

2

dark sandstone San Mateo County Courthouse has colossal pilasters with American eagle capitals flanking the main entrance. Severely damaged by the 1906 earthquake, this building was largely rebuilt in 1906–10, although amazingly the original kaleidoscopic stained-glass dome survived. An equally colorful stained-glass skylight is in the main courtroom. The old courthouse building now houses the San Mateo County Historical Association's museum, offices, and research library.

Between Main Street and Jefferson Avenue, the 1997 Redwood City Hall (Fisher-Friedman Associates) has received several awards for its stunning use of exposed structural elements, walls of curved glass, and its design program that will be integrated with future mixed-use development.

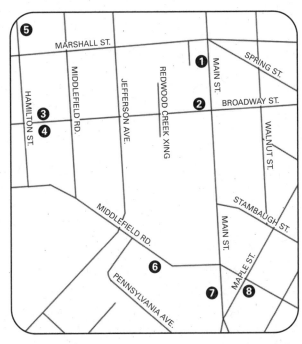

10 • Redwood City

4. Fox Theater (now New Sequoia Theater), 1928
2211–2225 Broadway

Reid & Reid, architects

The imposing façade of the former Fox Theater now combines eclectic elements of the Gothic Revival, Spanish Colonial Revival, and Art Deco styles. Originally built as a vaudeville house, the Fox Theater chain turned it into a movie palace soon after it opened. In recent years, the Fox returned to its original use as a venue for live performances.

5. Lathrop House, 1860
627 Hamilton Street

One of the largest Gothic Revival houses in San Mateo County, the house (moved to this site) has seven gables with

particularly lacey bargeboards. B. G. Lathrop was the first county assessor/recorder, a member of the San Mateo County Supervisors, and a director of the Southern Pacific Railroad.

6. Fire Station No. 1, 1921; remodeled, 1988
1044 Middlefield Road

Ripley and Associates, architects

A stately, richly detailed Italian Renaissance–style fire station is the frontispiece for a new main Redwood City Library. Patrons enter through the large round-arched central openings (originally used for the fire engines) into the large library building.

7. Hancock House, 1857
1018 Main Street

The Hancock House, originally a single-story Greek Revival, is the earliest house in Redwood City; the second story was added in 1889. An attractive Stick-Eastlake cottage is next door at 1020 Main Street.

8. Foresters of America Lodge Hall, 1913
1204 Middlefield Road

Like the nearby Redwood City Fire Station, the Foresters of America Lodge is an accomplished free interpretation of the Italian Renaissance palazzo.

Stambaugh-Heller Residential District

South of the downtown area, the Stambaugh-Heller area is

the earliest surviving residential district in Redwood City, boasting the county's largest collection of nineteenth-century houses dating from the late 1850s to the 1890s.

9. Albert Hanson House, circa 1860
743 Elm Street

This large Greek Revival–style house was moved to this location from Main Street in 1924.

10. Thompson House, 1867
418 Stambaugh Street

This early Greek Revival–style house appears to retain its original porch. The house at 406 Stambaugh dates from 1865.

11. Hartley House, early 1890s
1503 Middlefield Road

Here is an elaborate Queen Anne.

12. Hynding House, 1891
446 Heller Street

Another elaborate Queen Anne was moved from its original location next to 1018 Main Street.

13. Baptist Church, 1874
402 Heller Street

Originally built for a Baptist congregation, this charming Gothic Revival style is probably the oldest church in Redwood City.

14. Sequoia High School, 1923
1201 Brewster Avenue

Coffey & Werner, architects

The first union high school in the county, Sequoia High School was developed on land that had been a lavishly landscaped, forty-acre private estate owned initially by Horace Hawes, later by Moses Hopkins (Mark Hopkins' brother), and then by architect

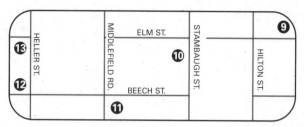

10 • Redwood City: Residential

Albert Pissis. A Japanese garden and various exotic trees survive today on the campus. The main Spanish Colonial Revival school building has a picturesque campanile tower and Spanish Baroque ornament around the main entrance. Carrington Hall, the school auditorium, has a richly ornamented entrance portico that recalls Spain's Alhambra.

15. First Church of Christ, Scientist, 1929
1504 Brewster Avenue

Henry Gutterson, architect

A charming English Medieval village church on a prominent corner, the building has a particularly steep gabled roof covered with ceramic tiles cut to look like wood shingles. Gutterson designed several churches for the Christian Scientists in the Bay Area.

Hopkins Avenue–Edgewood Road Residential District

The residential area north of Brewster Avenue has an impressive concentration of substantial early-twentieth-century houses on large landscaped lots.

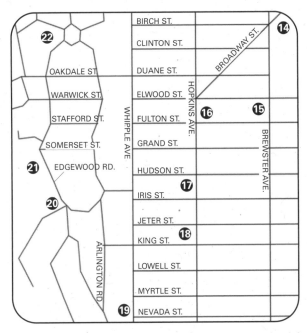

10 • Redwood City: Residential

16. Mary Beeger House, 1923
1533 Hopkins Avenue

A rather plain but stately Colonial Revival house provides a strong anchor to this large corner lot.

17. Richard Schmidt House, 1908
1816 Hopkins Avenue

A richly detailed and unusual Craftsman-style house has a large gable roof, wide sheltering eaves, grouped casement windows that open into what must be a lovely sunroom, and four bull's-eye circular windows with diamond panes.

18. Clarence Hayward House, 1910
2004 Hopkins Avenue

A large Craftsman bungalow mixed with Tudor Revival details sits on a corner lot.

19. Sam Winklebeck House, 1927
2414 Whipple Avenue

The dollhouse scale and details of the English Medieval Cottage style are perfectly displayed in this charming house: a steep hipped roof covered with wood shingles laid in a wavy pattern resembling a thatched roof, a tall

natural stone chimney, and handsome brick window surrounds.

20. John Grey House, 1924
802 Edgewood Road

This large Spanish Colonial Revival–style house would be at home in Beverly Hills. The lush landscaping combined with the house's complex play of forms (varying roof levels, shapes, window sizes, etc.) make it one of the most impressive and imaginative examples of this style on the Peninsula.

21. John Britton House, 1912
650 Edgewood Road
Frederick Meyer, architect
John McLaren,
landscape (attributed)

Set in a magnificent grove of redwoods, the Britton House is one the finest examples of the Craftsman style on the Peninsula. It perfectly reflects the rustic ideals of the Craftsman style with a woodsy mountain resort appearance, sheltering low-pitched roofs, natural materials, and the unusual length of the front porch.

22. Henry Martens House, 1909
226 Edgewood Road

This large Queen Anne–Colonial Revival house has a substantial corner tower with a conical roof.

11 · Atherton

South of Redwood City and north of Menlo Park, the estates of the elite dominated the landscape during the late nineteenth century. In 1880, Chilean hide-and-tallow businessman Faxon Atherton bought six hundred acres of Rancho de las Pulgas for his spectacular summer home, "Valparaiso." Soon after, prominent capitalists such as James C. Flood joined the Athertons, and until the creation of the Burlingame Country Club in 1893, this was the most popular section of the county for the upper classes. Atherton incorporated in 1923 to avoid becoming part of Menlo Park; the population today is about 7,300.

1. Fred McNear House, 1909
60 Parkwood Drive

Bliss & Faville, architects

A stately Neoclassical house has a back porch with a long classical colonnade reminiscent of a Greek Revival southern plantation house. In 1904, Bliss & Faville also designed the Neoclassic Augustus Taylor House at 3 Altree Court, and the grand Neo-Georgian Edna Hopkins Lowery House at 41 Lowery Drive.

2. Arthur Mathews House, 1950
83 Wisteria Way

Frank Lloyd Wright, architect

Built on a diamond module, Wright's low-slung redbrick house has a U-shaped plan with a large central courtyard, perfectly illustrating his work from the 1950s. The beautiful large flat lot has a number of sprawling oak trees. This and the Bazett House in Hillsborough are the only two houses designed by Wright in San Mateo County.

3. House, 1953
19 Irving Avenue

Anshen + Allen, architects

The nicely preserved early Anshen & Allen is an angled low-slung house constructed in red brick, reflecting the influence of Wright's work of the same period.

4. Aron Dowd House, 1895
36 Middlefield Road

This is a grand richly ornamented Queen Anne with a large corner tower. The prominent entrance porch opens out to a splendid semitropical landscape of palms and various exotic plants.

5. George A. Davis House, 1940
49 Rittenhouse Avenue

Mark Daniels, architect

This is one of the best Streamline Moderne houses on the Peninsula; architect Daniels adroitly composes its cubistic massing complemented by streamline trim detail (here painted in perfect pastel colors). The varying levels of the house step south to a fabulous glazed

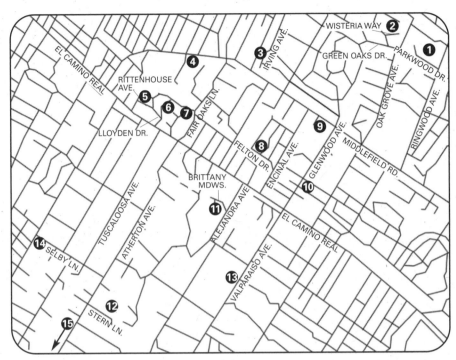

11 • Atherton

sunroom opening to the surrounding garden.

6. Joseph Coryell Carriage House, 1902
45 Lloyden Drive

Willis Polk, architect

An early promoter of the Mission Revival style, Polk led the early efforts to restore Mission Dolores in the 1890s. A fascinating composition of varying forms and openings, suggesting a structure constructed in many phases over many years, this is one of Polk's most sophisticated Mission Revival designs. The carriage house was to be part of an ambitious estate, including a larger main house in the same style, that was never realized.

6

7. Colonial Perry Eyre House, 1895
175 Fair Oaks

Mathison & Howard, architects

The gigantic paired Corinthian columns on the entrance porch create an impressive entry to this large Colonial Revival–style house in what appears to be a richly detailed version of Mount Vernon. Another major Colonial Revival–style house is nearby at 85 Edwards Lane.

8. William Corbus House, 1939
239 Felton Drive

William W. Wurster, architect

The contrast of dark-stained wood siding and large windows creates a deceptively simple composition for this nicely reposed Wurster house.

9. Charles Felton House, 1870s
4 Surry Lane

An early Stick-style house is in beautiful condition.

10. William Downey House, 1915
124 Glenwood Avenue

Early-twentieth-century Atherton residents clearly preferred the more formal baronial Neoclassical or Colonial Revival styles to the rustic Craftsman style. The Downey House and the nearby Albert Schwabacher House (1915) at 168 Isabella Avenue are particularly good local examples of Craftsman houses.

11. Commodore James Watkins House, 1866
Alejandra Avenue at Brittany Meadows

This Gothic Revival house, probably the oldest house in Atherton, was built by shipwrights in New London, Connecticut, and shipped around the Horn. The house was moved twice: once in 1903 and then again in 1998, when it was cut in half and moved in sections to this location.

12. Abraham Stern House, "Oak Meadows," 1907
47 Stern Lane

Houghton Sawyer, architect

"Oak Meadows" is one of the largest (thirty rooms) and most impressive Tudor-style mansions in Atherton. The rounded front bay windows and half-timber details are especially fine. Subsequent owner Emanuel Helle hired John McLaren to design the property's formal landscaping.

13. Sacred Heart Convent, 1898
150 Valparaiso Avenue

John J. Devlin, architect

A monumental French Second Empire design, the Sacred Heart Convent has particularly fine brick- and stonework. The man-

nerist rusticated columns on the porte cochere are pretty wild.

14. House, 1942
254 Selby Lane

Wurster & Bernardi, architects

A compact house exhibits classic clean details of this firm. The influence of the work of Wurster and Bernardi on the Eichler Company houses from the early fifties is evident.

15. Philip Fitzgerald House, 1937
10 Sargent Lane

Gardner Dailey, architect

A fine early, classic modernist design by Dailey, the house spreads out over the crest of a hill, its extensive windows opening to the surrounding landscape and views.

12 • Menlo Park • East Palo Alto • Foster City • Redwood Shores

Menlo Park

After the Menlo Park train station opened in 1867, a dozen businesses sprang up nearby. Although the community incorporated as a town in 1874, political pressure forced the town to reverse the action in 1876. Menlo Park had a rough reputation in its younger years, and it is said to be the reason Leland and Jane Stanford established their college south of the county line in 1891.

During World War I, twenty-five acres in Menlo Park were leased by the U.S. government as a training center and was named Camp Fremont. Menlo Park was incorporated in 1927 after an aborted attempt to include the community of Fair Oak (present-day Atherton). After World War II, Menlo Park developed into an attractive suburban community. Since 1951, it has been the location of *Sunset Magazine's* head offices. Its population exceeds 31,000.

1. James Coleman House, 1882
Peninsula Way at Berkeley Avenue

Augustus Laver, architect

Among the early surviving large estate houses, the twenty-two-room Coleman House is also one of the finest Italianate-style buildings on the Peninsula. James Coleman, nephew of Comstock Lode silver baron William O'Brien (a partner of James Flood), built and owned the house for thirty years but never lived in it. The huge entrance porch of the richly ornamented front façade of the Coleman House displays a complex array of angles and curves. Architect Augustus Laver also designed the James Flood Mansion (now the Pacific Union Club) on Nob Hill in San Francisco. The house became part of the Peninsula School for Creative Education in 1925, and the interior has been extensively altered.

2. Sunset Magazine Headquarters, 1962–1963
Middlefield Road at Willow Road

Higgins & Root/Cliff May Architects, Clark & Stromquist/ Cliff May, architects

Known as the "magazine of Western Living," *Sunset Magazine* played a critical role in promoting the postwar California Ranch House style by publishing architect Cliff May's house designs in the popular 1946 book *Western Ranch Houses*. Not surprisingly, *Sunset's* headquarters is a sprawling super-sized "ranch house" designed by none other than Cliff May. Like one of May's houses, the building wraps around a series of gardens representing plants and landscapes of California's different regions. The original garden design was by Thomas Church, the icon of California landscape architecture.

3. St. Patrick's Seminary, 1898, 1908
340 Middlefield Road

Charles J. Devlin, architect (1898)

McLaughlin & Walsh, architects (rebuilt, 1908)

This is monumental architecture unparalleled for its period on the Peninsula. Located at the terminus of a beautifully landscaped entrance driveway, the building combines elements of the Neoclassical and Romanesque with a mansard roof and is considered an example of the French Second Empire style. Its formal Classic Palladian façade has a richly detailed central pavilion flanked by large projecting end pavilions. The interior of the

Seminary chapel has a richly ornamented barrel vault. Devlin's Second Empire Sacred Heart Convent in Atherton dates from the same year.

4. Aaron Gale House, 1892
417 Glenwood Avenue

Here is a good example of a Queen Anne house in the Menlo Park area.

5. Church of the Nativity, 1872
210 Oak Grove Avenue

With its 120-foot-tall spire, the Church of the Nativity (the first Catholic Church in Menlo Park) is one of the Peninsula's largest nineteenth-century churches and is a particularly fine, well-preserved example of the Gothic Revival style. The pointed arch interior has magnificent exposed ribbed vaults. The church has been moved twice: once in 1877, and then to this pastoral site in 1887.

6. Edgar Mills Mansion, 1870
1040 Noel Drive

Edgar Mills, brother of Darius Ogden Mills (the multimillionaire namesake of Millbrae), purchased this large Italianate house in 1880. After Mills' death, the house had many lives over the

years, serving as a hotel, a military academy, a restaurant, an antiques shop, and now as offices.

7. Stanford Research Institute, 1971
333 Ravenswood Avenue
Skidmore, Owings & Merrill, architects

An imposing brick structure is built around an attractive courtyard.

8. Latham-Hopkins Gatehouse, 1870
Laurel Street at Ravenswood Avenue

The Second Empire–style gatehouse is the sole survivor of the

lavish Menlo Park estate of U.S. Senator and railroad/banking magnate Milton Latham. The estate included vast landscaped grounds, a richly ornamented fifty-room mansion, and a stable for thirty-two carriages. Mary Hopkins, widow of railroad magnate Mark Hopkins, acquired the property in the 1880s. The Hopkins' adopted son, Timothy, developed a large nursery operation on the property (now known as "Sherwood Hall") in the 1890s. The Hopkins family donated much of the land to Stanford University in the 1940s. The city of Menlo Park owns the gatehouse.

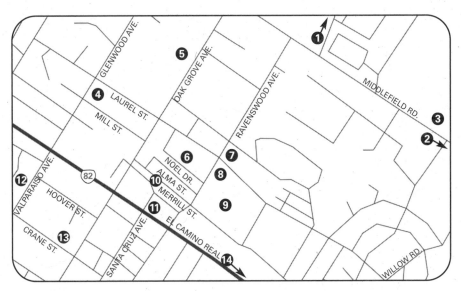

12 • Menlo Park

10. Menlo Park Railroad Depot, 1867; expanded in the 1890s
1100 Merrill Street, at Santa Cruz Avenue

The oldest railroad depot on the Peninsula and a locally revered historic landmark, the quaint Menlo Park station has a large Queen Anne–style addition on the south that included a "Ladies Parlor" with its own angled bay window. The variety of gingerbread ornament on the south façade includes fish-scale shingles and a "saw tooth and donuts" stringcourse.

9. Menlo Park Civic Center, 1963–1970
Ravenswood Avenue at Laurel Street

Kingsford Jones, architect

Arthur Cobbledick, landscape architect

By far the most successful design for a postwar city government complex on the Peninsula, the handsome residential scale buildings are joined by an equally strong informal landscape design, incorporating preexisting oak, redwood, elm, and ginkgo trees augmented with cherry and chestnut trees. Footpaths over sloping and sunken areas surround the centerpiece of the landscape design—a small lake with rapids, a waterfall, and a rustic wooden bridge.

11. Palo Alto National Bank, 1910
1090 El Camino Real

This impressive Neoclassical brick banking temple anchors a major corner in the downtown and once served as the Menlo Park City Hall.

12. Pauline & Theodore Payne House (Menlo School), 1910
50 Valparaiso Avenue

William Curlett, architect

The immense Neoclassical mansion has fifty-six rooms, including eight master bedroom suites; fireplaces, mantels, and a grand staircase constructed of Italian marble; and elaborate parquet floors. Unusual for this date, the massive exterior walls are made of reinforced concrete. In 1921, inventor Leon Douglas, a pioneer in developing audio recording and motion picture technology, purchased the house. Now part of Menlo School, the house has a series of extensive rear additions.

13. Holy Trinity Church, 1886
1220 Crane Street

An attractive village church with geometric Eastlake ornament, the building was moved here in 1947. Originally Episcopalian, the church is now Russian Orthodox.

14. Allied Arts Guild, 1927
75 Arbor Road,
at Cambridge Avenue

Gardner Dailey, architect

One of the most charming Spanish Colonial Revival designs in the Bay Area, the four-acre Allied Arts Guild complex is reminiscent of Santa Barbara's El Paseo retail district. The buildings represent a significant early design by Dailey before he became a noted Modernist. The buildings, including an earlier 1880s barn, are designed around several courtyards and extensive gardens inspired by Classic Spanish gardens. A variety of colorful tiles used on buildings and fountains came from Spain,

Tunis, and Morocco. Maxine Albro, Pedro de Lemos, and members of his family executed the mosaics and frescoes. Original owners were Garfield and Delight Merner, who built the Allied Arts Guild as a center for the appreciation of regional handicrafts. The Woodside-Atherton Auxiliary has managed the Guild complex since the 1950s, and the buildings continue to provide exhibit space for various artists and craftspeople. The center was restored in 2004 by Cody, Anderson & Wasney, architects.

East Palo Alto

East Palo Alto had its beginnings in 1849 when Isaiah C. Woods built an embarcadero that he named Ravenswood. The embarcadero venture was not successful, and the area remained a rural place of wheat fields until around 1900, when berry farming and Japanese flower growing replaced the wheat fields.

In 1916, William Smythe, an ardent socialist, acquired 600 acres from poultry rancher Charles Weeks. Smythe established a Little Landers Colony, one of five communal communities he founded in California, and called it Runnymede. The utopian commune had a population of nearly 900 by 1925. Its main economic activity was poultry ranching. During the Depression the community failed; only a few structures, including some chicken coops, remain.

Although suburban neighbohoods were built in the 1930s and 1940s, the Bayshore Freeway, completed in the 1950s, physically isolated East Palo Alto from the other Peninsula communities; it became one of the few residential areas on the Peninsula that allowed African Americans to purchase property, and soon became a suburban ghetto. Jobs were scarce, business investors were few, poverty increased, neighborhoods deteriorated, and crime worsened. During the 1960s, trouble erupted at Ravenswood High School, and East Palo Alto went through a period when it was known as one of the most lawless communities in America.

The city (incorporated in 1983) has overcome many of its problems. With a population of more than 31,000, big-box retailers and chain hotels have found a place in East Palo Alto along Highway 101. Investment dollars have come back to the community, improving its outlook for the future.

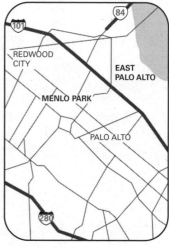

12 • Menlo Park • East Palo Alto

Foster City

Until the 1930s when the bay became polluted, San Mateo County had a substantial maritime fishing industry. The Morgan Oyster Company began operations in 1874 and eventually owned tens of thousands of tidal acres, including today's communities of Foster City and Redwood Shores. So successful was the Morgan Company that by the late 1800s, its facilities had become the sole supplier of market oysters for the Pacific Slope.

About the same time, the Chinese set up shrimp-fishing operations. Utilizing equipment and techniques similar to what they used in China, they soon dominated shrimp-fishing in California. By the late nineteenth century, San Mateo County "China Camps" were providing about 25 percent of the shrimp for the California and international markets.

As the oyster and shrimp industries declined, the underwater

properties were bought by Leslie Salt and the Pacific Portland Cement Company. Both were unique industries. The Bay offers one of the few places in the world where salt can be economically produced through solar evaporation, and vast fossilized shell deposits make it one of the few places where the lime from shells can be used to create cement.

Among the Leslie Salt Company properties was an island diked by dairy rancher Frank M. Brewer in 1900. Developer T. Jack Foster Sr. purchased Brewer's Island from Leslie Salt in 1958 to create a "planned community," which he called Foster City. Foster's plans were considered so innovative that in 1963 they were displayed at the San Francisco Museum of Modern Art.

Foster's vision of a comprehensively planned "new town" led to the construction of Foster City on eight square miles of tidal mud flats east of Highway 101 and south of Highway 92. In 1961, engineers and land plan-

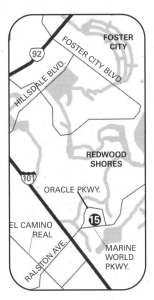

12 • Foster City
• Redwood Shores

ners Wilsey & Ham developed the complex hydrology and design of Foster City's system of roads, canals, and lagoons. The town plan included extensive office, retail, civic, and residential areas. T. Y. Lin, engineers, and Lawrence Lackey, consulting

Foster City

architect, designed the high arch bridges over the canals. Edward Durell Stone designed a number of the major early Foster City developments in his signature "modern" Neoclassicism, such as the still extant Admiralty Apartments (1962) at Foster City Boulevard and East Hillsdale. The first homes in Foster City were completed in 1964 and were an instant commercial success, but many of the early 1960s buildings have largely been replaced.

From its inception, Foster City had a commitment to quality modern residential design, and hired Eichler Homes to build the first single-family residences. The 1000 block of Egret Street includes a good enclave designed by architect Claude Oakland for Eichler in 1965. In the 1970s, the Islands and Whaler's Cove residential developments won AIA and *Sunset Magazine* awards.

DES Architects & Engineering have designed a new complex of Foster City civic buildings (city hall, police department, and fire station) in the vicinity of East Hillsdale Boulevard and Shell Boulevard. Although constructed of modern steel and glass, the City Hall's formal symmetry alludes to traditional concepts of civic dignity and order. The Library/Community Center (1997), with wonderfully quirky battered brick walls, was designed by the Miami-based firm of Arquitectonica.

Initially governed by the Foster family and other investors, residents decided to control their own destiny by incorporating in 1971. The population today is nearly 30,000.

Redwood Shores

In 1959, south of Foster City, a similar project called Redwood Shores took shape on land owned by Leslie Salt. The property was annexed to Redwood City and a planned community was proposed. However, this project became mired in environmental concerns such as bay fill, water quality, and protection of wildlife.

The convoluted drawn-out planning process began with a 1959 plan by the Architect's Collaborative, Walter Gropius, senior partner. In 1964, landscape architects Dean, Austin, Williams developed a second plan. In 1968, Daniel, Mann, Johnson & Mendenhall made a third plan that included the 1969 town house development, highly lauded in its time, by Stanley Schwartz. Also in 1968, part of the property became the site of Marine World (later Marine World/Africa USA). In the early 1970s, the Redwood Shores project went into foreclosure for a period. The fourth (and final) plan—by EDAW and Royston, Hanamoto & Beck in

1973 for Mobil Land Development Company—has a system of waterways and lagoons.

15. Oracle World Headquarters, 1989–1995
500 Oracle Parkway
Gensler & Associates

The almost three-million-square-foot World Headquarters for Oracle Corporation, the world's second-largest software company, is a major modern landmark on the Peninsula, visible for miles. The six steel-frame office structures, eight to sixteen stories tall, in oval-shaped curved sapphire blue glass with precast concrete bands would be considerably less striking if not for their stunning setting on the edge of a large reflective blue lagoon. The Wizard of Oz–Emerald City quality of the whole ensemble has a monumental but rather surrealistic quality. The Oracle buildings were the futuristic headquarters of the fictional company NorthAm Robotics in the 1999 movie *Bicentennial Man*. In addition to the office structures, the complex includes four parking structures, fitness and conference centers, and a substation.

Photo courtesy of Oracle Corp.

III
Santa Clara County

Charlene Duval, author & photographer
with Leslie Dill, Franklin Maggi, Bonnie Montgomery

Santa Clara County is primarily a broad urban metropolitan area of thirteen cities spread out across the northern portion of Santa Clara Valley. San Jose, the largest city and the county seat, was the site of California's first civilian settlement in 1777 and the location of California's first state capital in 1849. The county was created by the state in 1850.

After California's admission to the United States, Santa Clara County gained a worldwide reputation as an important agricultural region known as the "Valley of Heart's Delight." During the 1950s, the county became a desirable destination for America's westward migration, losing its rural and pastoral ambience as its economy grew. The aerospace, computer, and other nonagricultural industries attracted a rapid influx of population, creating an explosion of urban growth; Santa Clara Valley became known as "Silicon Valley."

In 1777, Lt. José Joaquin Moraga and Franciscan Fray Tomás de la Peña established the Mission Santa Clara de Asís on the west bank of the Guadalupe River. Later that year, Moraga returned to found El Pueblo de San José de Guadalupe on the Guadalupe's east bank for the Spanish Crown.

For seventy-five years the mission, pueblo, and an evolving rancho system developed under Spanish and then Mexican rule, transforming the fertile valley into a frontier agricultural region that exported beef and hides to world markets. The rural agricultural character of the valley continued after the American takeover of California in 1848, as the American pioneers continued to exploit the fertile rangeland of the valley.

During the Gold Rush, San Jose served as one of the supply centers for hopeful miners. Many of them returned to the valley to take up dryland grain farming, which dominated the valley until about 1880. Throughout today's broad modern urban areas are examples of both the adobe buildings of the first Hispanic settlers as well as many old wood and brick buildings of early farmers and businesses. Sawmills established in the Santa Cruz Mountains utilized an abundance of old-growth redwood that fueled construction in the valley until the beginning of the twentieth century. Combined with local brick manufacturing, San Jose grew quickly during the latter part of the nineteenth century as the valley's economic center.

III • Santa Clara County

A railroad was completed from San Francisco to San Jose in 1864, and distribution of Santa Clara County's agricultural products was further facilitated with a regional connection to the transcontinental railroad in 1869. By the late 1880s, fruit orchards supplanted grain as land was subdivided into smaller parcels. During the early twentieth century, large canneries and packing plants were built to process the abundant production of fruit.

The rich diversity of historic buildings from the late nineteenth and early twentieth centuries is a result of the economic vitality of the area as a horticultural region. Architectural styles represent the popular styles of each period—a mix of Victorian, Neoclassical, Arts and Crafts, and Period Revival—and were consistent with what was happening throughout the United States but were adapted to the South Bay area's relaxed and agricultural-based society.

World War II, like the Gold Rush a century before, had a major effect on Santa Clara County. The large naval air station at Moffett Field became a gateway to military activity in the Pacific, with thousands of personnel brought to the area for training and processing. Soon after the war, the local business community launched an active campaign to attract new nonagricultural-related industries. International giant FMC (now National Defense) led the way, followed by the Accent plant and GE's nuclear division. Cold War industries began to locate near Moffett Field in the Sunnyvale and Mountain View areas. When IBM settled in downtown San Jose in the early 1940s, the invention of the Winchester Disk Drive set the stage for the eventual creation of the place we now know as Silicon Valley. William Shockley's Transistor Lab and spin-off innovators like Fairchild and then Intel, as well as equipment manufacturers such as Hewlett-Packard and Varian, provided breeding grounds for innovative engineers. The 1970s saw the development of the personal computer industry stimulated by Apple, Atari, IBM, and others.

Between 1945 and 1964, orchards were subdivided further into residential tracts, industrial parks, shopping centers, and schools at an average rate of 17,000 acres per year. By the 1990s, the northern valley's agricultural land was nearly all developed. Architecturally, this unique American experience in economic development is still little understood. The first high-tech buildings were but windowless warehouses, quickly subdivided into offices and assembly lines. Later, a new breed of young fast-paced architects and speculative designer/builders looked to high-tech building techniques to connect architectural design with the creative culture of engineers and software designers who were to occupy them. A drive through the industrial parks of the South Bay area is a must for those interested in the architectural character of modern industrial development, a genre of styles yet to be dissected in a critical way by architectural historians.

The present urban and rural landscape of Santa Clara County is diverse, a complex social and economic setting that overlays a rich historic, multicultural, and natural environment. Within the cities and their environs that constitute the urban topology of the county, some of the rural character that was once the "Valley of Heart's Delight" continues to exist today, side by side with the modern constructions that house high-tech factories and think tanks. The explosive growth of new software giants like eBay will continue to transform the physical environment as companies respond to technological advancements in information, biotech, and electronics.

1 · Stanford

Stanford University was founded by Leland Stanford and his wife, Jane Lathrop Stanford, as a memorial to their son, Leland Stanford Jr., who died while the family was touring Europe in 1884.

Stanford had begun acquiring property in the Santa Clara Valley in 1876 and, by 1882, had assembled 8,000 acres. An experimental horse farm was among his endeavors.

Frederick Law Olmsted, the nation's eminent landscape architect, was engaged to design the plan and the Boston architectural firm of Henry Hobson Richardson was selected to design the buildings. The plans that Charles Coolidge (successor to Richardson, who died in 1886) and Olmsted presented to Stanford in 1887 embodies the best qualities of campus planning and architectural design. Its spatial composition, location, and Romanesque/Mission Revival–style buildings have become the enduring image of Stanford University.

The campus, of course, has become larger than its historic core, and is a showplace of architectural design from all subsequent eras, of which only a sample can be presented here.

1. Stanford Quadrangle and Memorial Chapel, 1887–1903
450 Serra Mall
Shepley, Rutan and Coolidge, architects
Frederick Law Olmsted, landscape architect

The Stanford Quadrangle is the original campus and continues to serve as the architectural symbol of the university. The inner quad was nearly complete when the university opened in 1891. A masterpiece of design, the

Stanford Quad represents the largest complex of Romanesque/Mission Revival–style buildings constructed of stone in California and was the first major campus design in the

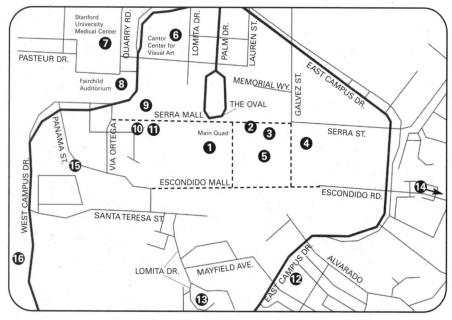

West. It integrates a superb mix of imported and local materials and exemplary architectural detailing with visionary overall master planning and landscaping.

The complex consists of two main central quadrangles enclosed by arcades and punctuated by towers; clusters of outer quadrangles, also linked by arcades, surround these major spaces. There are two ceremonial courtyards: Memorial Court and the Inner Quad. The Richardsonian Romanesque idiom also echoes California's mission architecture. The buff-colored sandstone was quarried in the Almaden Valley and carved by Italian stonecutters brought from Italy specifically to do this work. Architect Clinton Day supervised the building of Memorial Chapel beginning in 1899, using 1887 sketches by Charles Coolidge. The mosaic murals on the exterior and interior are exquisite. The Outer Quad, actually two wings with inner courtyards flanking Memorial Arch, was completed in 1906. This complex sustained significant damage in the 1906 and 1989 earthquakes, but 1992 repairs have been in keeping with the original architectural design by Hardy Holzman Pfeiffer Associates.

2. Thomas Welton Stanford Art Gallery, 1917
419 Lasuen Mall

Bakewell & Brown, architects

Leland Stanford's younger brother was Thomas Welton Stanford. The gallery building replaced an art gallery damaged during the 1906 earthquake, and was intended to be the cornerstone of a new quadrangle that was never completed. It is sheathed with rough-cut stone over concrete and has a richly carved entry arch, in keeping with the original quad. The nearby Green Library, designed by the same architects only two years later, comes close to being a Moderne version of Romanesque.

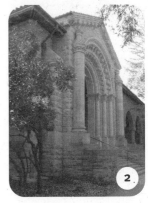

3. Hoover Tower, 1941
550 Serra Mall

Bakewell and Brown, architects

The prominent 285-foot-high Classic Moderne tower, with its distinctive red-tiled dome topped by a diminutive carillon cupola, serves as the second architectural symbol of the university. At the base is a tiled roof entry out of which the nearly windowless shaft rises. Below the stepped-back, polygonal observation pavilion are three pairs of small arched windows; pinnacles rise at the corners. The building is named for U.S. President Herbert Hoover, a Stanford alumnus whose archive and research institution are housed in the tower.

4. Encina Hall/ Institute for International Studies, 1891
616 Serra Street

Shepley, Rutan, and Coolidge, architects

Hardy Holzman Pfeiffer Associates, architects (restoration, 1998)

Encina Hall, the first men's dormitory, was inspired by a Swiss resort the Stanfords visited in 1888. The Romanesque-style building exhibits subtle differences of window detailing at the various levels. It was last used as a dorm in 1950.

5. Cecil H. Green Library, West, 1919
459 Lasuen Mall

Bakewell and Brown, architects

The Green Library is a fascinating blend of Richardsonian Romanesque, Mission Revival, and classically inspired Beaux-Arts design bordering on Classic Moderne. It features a sandstone façade, a columned arcade, and a red-tile roof. A sprawling concrete-and-glass wing was added in 1980 by architects Helmuth, Obata + Kassabaum. This new wing is Brutalist but has a red-tile roof and detailing that is compatible with the early Romanesque wing.

6. Leland Stanford Junior Museum/Iris and B. Gerald Cantor Center for the Visual Arts, 1891
328 Lomita Drive

Percy and Hamilton, with Ernest Ransome, architects

This formal Classical Revival museum was a step away from the original campus plan in both location and design. The mosaics

and proportions of the original building are exquisite, and the new rear additions (1999; Polshek Partnership Architects) create exterior spaces that are welcoming and elegant. Earthquake damage repair was completed in 1999.

7. Lane Medical Center, 1959
300 Pasteur Drive

Edward Durell Stone, architect

Decorative concrete blocks, uncompromisingly stacked and repeated, create a monumental edifice with bold oversized forms. Concrete-block screens embellish the bold poured-concrete structure that is so thoroughly characteristic of Stone's work throughout the United States. The smaller units are arranged in a no-nonsense rhythm of three-story pillars and pilasters; the pattern is heightened with a succession of bronze, oversized, saucer-shaped light fixtures the size of balconies. The building's courtyards, contrastingly cozy with smaller-scale custom light fixtures, have been exquisitely landscaped. Nearby is the Medical School Lab (1992) by Stone Marraccini Patterson.

8. James H. Clark Center for Biomedical Engineering and Sciences, 2003
318 Campus Drive

Foster and Partners/MBT, architects

Three sides of the building are rectilinear; the north side, in the center of the building block, is a hollowed-out serpentine curved court; horizontal balconies and bands of color accentuate the linearity of its walls. Exposed staircases, glazed walls, a pedestrian bridge, flowing landscape design, and a wing-shaped roof screen emphasize the curvature of the interior courtyard. The functionality of the building is expressed by exposed mechanical systems and flexible interior access panels.

10

9

9. William Gates Computer Science Building, 1996

353 Serra Mall

Robert A. M. Stern, architect

Fong and Chan Architects

The first three stories emulate the proportions and textured stone of the original Romanesque buildings on campus; three additional smooth-concrete stories emerge above the rough-finished stone and create a dense Neo-Romanesque design. The building has a red-tile hipped roof and a Roman arched entrance, but also sports a modern convex wall that looks toward the original quad.

10. Paul Allen Center for Integrated Systems, 1984, 1996

330 Serra Mall

Ehrlich-Rominger, architects

Antoine Predock, architect (addition, 1996)

The 1984 portion has long, low proportions with an oversized galleria entrance to the east; a copper barrel vault is punctuated with a grid pattern. The remainder of the one-story metal-roofed building has a glazed façade recessed behind round concrete pillars, and it works as a colonnade background for both the large galleria and the newer two-story north wing. The north wing is strong, distinctive, and beautifully detailed and proportioned. It has a solid feeling, with little fenestration and broad wall surface; and the wide variation of color and texture of the sandstone veneer lend a stunning grain and color to the exterior of the hall. The northeast corner emulates the northeast corner of Encina Hall with its arch and staircase.

11. W. R. Hewlett and D. Packard Science and Engineering Quad, 2000

Pei Cobb Freed, architects

Olin Partnership, landscape architects

The complex of recent buildings that surrounds and creates the W. R. Hewlett and D. Packard Science and Engineering Quad (SEQ) demonstrates a variety of approaches to campus design and a variety of responses to the original Main Quadrangle to the east. A pair of grand architectural gestures flanks the primary north opening to the quad at Serra Mall. These two buildings have some reference to the stone, copper, and tile of the rest of the campus, but also provide avant-garde angled and curved elements and modern finish materials. The remaining buildings are moderate in their form and massing, acting more as a background for the landscaped space. These buildings share a special vocabulary of segmental-arched windows at the main floor with copper accents at the "attic" level and eaves, and simple, red-tile hipped roofs that pay homage to, but are distinct from, the original quad. The SEQ is not surrounded by heavy arcades as in the original quad, but by more delicate, fabric-roofed colonnades that are separate landscape structures. The SEQ includes an assortment of spatial qualities: pathways, nodes, and edges; however, the design is united with sculptures, fountains, and plantings.

11a. David Packard Electrical Engineering Building, 1999

350 Serra Mall

Pei Cobb Freed, architects

Maya Lin, artwork: Timetable

11d

11a

11d. Varian Physics Building, 1957
382 Via Pueblo Mall

Gardner A. Dailey, architect

Pei Cobb Freed, architects (renovation, 2004)

A typical mid-twentieth-century utilitarian structure, this solid rectangular building is decorated with smooth formed-concrete panels in a V pattern and exposed-aggregate wall panels. This building and nearby McCullough Hall were incorporated into the new quad. Sequoia and Moore Halls, similar in size and massing, were placed between and adjacent to this preexisting pair, creating garden corridors.

11e. Gordon & Betty Moore Materials Research Building, 2000
466 Lomita Mall

Pei Cobb Freed, architects

Although lower in height than the Varian and McCullough Buildings, the Moore Building repeats their size and vocabulary. It has a modest recessed colonnade linking the main quad with the engineering quad, and provides an indoor-outdoor boundary with the garden space to the south.

11f. Jack A. McCullough Building, 1957
476 Lomita Mall

Gardner A. Dailey, architect

Pei Cobb Freed, architects (renovation, 2004)

Similar to the Varian Physics Building, a segmented arched bridge was added to link it to the newer adjacent Moore Building. The bridge highlights the connection of the buildings and produces small-scale landscaped spaces.

This building has an archetypical Pei Cobb Freed angular space-frame glass-and-steel wedge that juts out from the rectilinear stone mass; it is one side of the quad's main entry portal and acts as counterpoint to the curved mass of the Hewlett Center across the quad. Jointed stone veneering on its large wall surfaces interacts with stone-veneered corner wings that are part of the SEQ vocabulary.

11b. William R. Hewlett Teaching Center, 1999
370 Serra Mall

Pei Cobb Freed, architects

The round crown-like Hewlett Teaching Center, with its outward-leaning, silver-painted

aluminum walls, rises to a quasi-crenellated roofline; the building serves as the second anchor at the entrance of the quad. Vertical windows project from the walls and exaggerate the form of this fascinating building.

11c. Sequoia Hall, 1998
390 Serra Mall

Pei Cobb Freed, architects

Four buildings on the east side of the SEQ form a series of peaceful garden corridors that lead between the Main Quad and the Engineering Quad; Sequoia Hall is one of them, with curved balconies and metal stair elements that face the quad and harmonize with the metal finishes of Hewlett Center and Packard Hall.

12. San Juan Hill Residential Neighborhood

Off East Campus Drive, on either side of curving Mayfield Avenue, is Stanford's hillside residential neighborhood. The streets closest to the central campus were the first developed in 1891. Although many of the early large residences have been converted to other uses, enlarged, or altered over time, enough remains to get a sense of the late-nineteenth- and early-twentieth-century neighborhood.

As the university expanded, additional lots were made available for housing, where the homeowners lease the land from the university. The neighborhood of winding streets and large gardens has many beautiful homes; following is a list of just a few.

Houses located at **623 Cabrillo** (1904); **553 Mayfield** (1894) and **565 Mayfield** (1899); **767, 774,** and **775 Santa Inez** (1909–1910) were designed by Arthur B. Clark, an architect who joined the Stanford faculty in 1892 as Assistant Professor of Drawing and became head of the Art Department.

Architect John K. Branner, son of Stanford president John Casper Branner, designed the Hesperides/Mosher-Hilton House at **766 Santa Inez** in 1926. He also designed **635 Gerona** and **692 Mirada** in 1926 and **716 Salvatierra** in 1935.

Between 1929 and 1930, architect Charles Kaiser Sumner designed a group of houses that include **635, 707, 708, 711, 712,** and **715 Salvatierra.**

Mid-twentieth-century Modernism is represented by the work of A. Quincy Jones and Frederick Emmons at **715** and **724 Frenchman's Road** (1961, 1965) and **820** and **823 Pine Hill Road** (1958, 1959). Wurster, Bernardi and Emmons designed houses at **796 Cedro Way** in 1962, and **844 Pine Hill Road** in 1958; Geraldine Knight Scott was the landscape architect for these two houses.

12a. Hoover House, 1919
623 Miranda Avenue

Arthur B. Clark and Birge Clark, architects

The Modernist abstract composition of pale stucco-sided rectangles and cubes, flat roofs, stacked elements, and deeply recessed windows was built by U.S. President Herbert Hoover and his wife, Lou Henry Hoover, the first woman to receive a degree in geology from Stanford. The design, said to be a close collaboration between architect and owner, provides for a gracious relationship to its outdoor spaces. When Hoover was elected President, this remained his legal residence; they retired here from 1933 to 1944.

12b. Hanna House, 1937
737 Frenchman's Road

Frank Lloyd Wright, architect

Architect Frank Lloyd Wright created spectacular spatial effects by designing outside the confines of traditionalism. In this house, he first used the hexagon to organize the arrangement of rooms and circulation. Wright intended the Hanna House to be a prototypical Usonian house with a flexible modular wall system. Angled roofs, soaring walls of multipaned glass, redwood siding, and garden walls and chimneys of red brick are combined for dramatic effect. The Hanna family resided here until 1975, when they donated it to the university. After its restoration in 1999 (Architectural Resources Group, architects), the house is used for receptions. It is a National Landmark.

13. The Knoll/ Wilbur House, 1918
660 Lomita Court

Louis Christian Mullgardt, architect

The three-story, Beaux-Arts- and Baroque–style mansion has ornate detailing and the purity of formal symmetry. It was designed to be the university president's house. In 1946, it was used by the Music Department. After renovations are complete (Simon Martin-Vegue Winkelstein Moris, architects), it will house the Center for Computer Research, Music and Acoustics, and the Center for Computer Assisted Research in the Humanities.

14. Escondite Cottage, before 1875
Escondido Village
857 Escondido Road

The Escondite Cottage was constructed sometime before 1875 when Peter Coutts acquired this property. Coutts enlarged the Carpenter Gothic–style cottage and created a large L-shaped nine-room house with a sixty-five-foot hall. It is one of three buildings that remain from Coutts's Ayrshire Farm. The Stanfords purchased Coutts's farm in 1882. The cottage serves as the office for Escondido Village, the graduate-student housing complex.

Escondido Village is a large complex of student housing built between 1959 and 1971. There are five "villages" in the complex. In 1959, Wurster, Bernardi and Emmons designed the first village with landscape architect Thomas Church.

14a. Tower House/ Frenchman's Library, 1876
860 Escondido Road

Coutts built the Tower House of brick to house his library. The design is Italianate with wide eaves and lattice used as crown molding. Damaged in 1989, it is currently unused.

14b. Frenchman's Tower, circa 1881 (unmapped)
East side of Old Page Mill Road

The mysterious cylindrical red-brick tower with a crenellated top, lancet window openings, but no door, was built by Coutts and is called "Frenchman's Tower." The purpose of the tower has eluded historians. One Stanford University publication refers to the tower as a "crenellated boundary tower"; others believe it is pure folly.

15. Carnegie Institution, 2004
260 Panama Street

Esherick Homsey Dodge and Davis, architects

A group of "green" buildings that look somewhat like vernacular barns were designed to recall Stanford's agricultural past. Low gabled roofs with pop-up dormers and towers, decorative roof trusses, grouped window units, and a variety of interesting recycled materials are used to create energy efficiency. They are located in a somewhat open and natural landscaped corner of the campus.

16. Palo Alto Stock Farm/ Red Barn, 1878–1879
119 Fremont Road

Esherick Homsey Dodge and Davis, architects (restoration, 1986)

The Red Barn was one of a cluster of nine buildings that were part of Stanford's experimental horse farm, one of the largest in the world. There was once a blacksmith's shop, a feed mill, housing for 150 workers, and a school. The Red Barn is one of the few surviving examples of a Victorian-era barn with elegant but practical materials. It is still used as an equestrian facility. In 1878 and 1879, this is where photographer Eadweard Muybridge proved Stanford's claim that when a horse is running, all four feet are off the ground simultaneously.

2 • Palo Alto

Downtown

Palo Alto was created in 1887 at the same time as Stanford University, and incorporated in 1894; the town was established to serve the university community. The city has beautiful tree-lined streets and good examples of pre–World War II homes. Its population is 58,000.

1. Hostess House, 1918
25–27 University Avenue
Julia Morgan, architect

During World War I, the YWCA built a number of "hostess houses" at military camps as meeting places for soldiers and their families; Julia

Morgan was their architect. Only two survive, and this one was moved from its original location at Camp Fremont in Menlo Park in 1919. The Craftsman-style board-and-batten building has an unassuming profile with out-stretched side wings, shallow gable roofs with deep eaves, exposed rafter ends, a central arbor, and multipaned windows. On the interior, a large main meeting room has open trusses, a fireplace, and an open balcony at either end.

When the building was moved to Palo Alto, it became the city's first community center and was renamed Community House. When the Lucie Stern Center opened in 1935, it was used by veterans' organizations; since the 1980s, it has been a restaurant.

2. Southern Pacific Railroad Depot, 1940–1941
95 University Avenue
J. H. Christie, chief of the Southern Pacific Design Office, architect

This Streamline Moderne station is the third station on this site. It has a lean, horizontal brick-and-stucco profile, extensive reed-glass block, and Art Deco signage. Inside, a mural by John MacQuarrie depicts Leland Stanford's dream of a university and events important to the development of transportation in California.

3. Fraternal Hall, 1898
140 University Avenue
Samuel Newsom, architect

Originally constructed as a meeting place for various fraternal organizations, the two-story brick building, now stuccoed, stands on a prominent corner. A band of six arched, fanlight windows with turned balustrades are flanked by shallow window bays with arched windows extravagantly framed with plaster decoration. The heavy cornice is richly articulated.

4. Stanford Theater, 1914
223 University Avenue
Weeks and Day, architects
Barrett and Hilp, builders (remodel, 1924)

The Stanford Theater (originally the Marquee Theater) has a fanciful and eclectic façade, with tall, thin, fluted corner towers topped with ornate flowery parapets above the roofline. The center of the façade includes additional fluted pilasters with Ionic capitals and its own parapet with a floral oculus and volutes. The remaining wall surface is an open screen, created from stacked barrel tiles. The glorious interiors

have been meticulously restored with stenciling and plaster embellishments.

5. Bank of America, 1906, 1928
251 University Avenue

William H. Weeks, architect

H. A. Minton, architect (1928)

The Renaissance Revival building has colossal two-story pilasters crowned by composite capitals, expanses of recessed glazing with recessed spandrel panels at the floor level, and a robust classical cornice with a patterned frieze band and acanthus brackets under the hipped red-tile roof.

6. 436–452, 460–476 University Avenue, 1927
Birge Clark, architect

These ten fanciful storefronts, which read as separate buildings, flank the Varsity Theater. Elements of Spanish eclecticism, such as applied bas-relief on the stucco façades, a variety of lancet, ribbon, and arched windows, and red-tile roofs of different heights make them distinctive. They were built by dentist/developer Charles H. Strub.

7. Varsity Theatre, 1927
456 University Avenue

Reid Brothers, architects

The façade of this former movie palace is Mission Revival and includes a grand castellated gateway that opens into a unique and splendid colonnaded forecourt that led to the original main lobby. Iron chandeliers and Churrigueresque detailing accent the overall scheme. The theater closed in 1994; although adapted for retail use, it retains much of its architectural character.

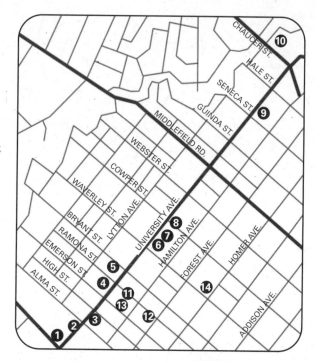

2 • Palo Alto: Downtown

8. Hotel President,
1929–1930
480–498 University Avenue
Birge Clark, architect

This six-story former hotel exhibits some Monterey-style inspiration. Its smooth stucco walls are accented by a high, cantilevered, heavy-timber balcony and spindled transoms at the scalloped storefronts, as well as a red-tile coping at the rooftop; its more urban aspirations are delicately ornamented, bronze entry canopies and art-tile patterns in the storefront bulkheads.

9. Squire House, 1904
900 University Avenue
T. Patterson Ross, architect

This mansion has a stately and elegant presence with its two-story Ionic portico, classically symmetrical façade, Palladian window groupings, oval window with lead tracery, widow's walk, and a profusion of cornice modillions. The fight to preserve Squire House during the 1970s led to the enactment of Palo Alto's Preservation Ordinance in 1979.

10. J. G. Kennedy House, 1922
423 Chaucer Street
Julia Morgan, architect

One of Morgan's straightforward Mediterranean Revival designs has stucco siding, a tile roof, deeply recessed casement windows with no trim, and an undecorated arched, recessed entry over which there is a wrought-iron balcony with a fleur-de-lys.

11. Ramona Street National Register District

Placed on the National Register as a district in 1985, the 500 block of Ramona Street, between University and Hamilton Avenues, is a showcase of Spanish Colonial Revival featuring archways, wrought-iron work, tile roofs, and picturesque courtyards. The development of Ramona Street expanded the city center south from the University Avenue commercial core. Pedro de Lemos, an artist and curator of the Stanford Museum, built the Gotham Shop at **520 Ramona** in 1925. Architects Birge Clark and William H. Weeks continued the theme.

11a. 532–536 Ramona Street, 1926
Birge Clark, architect

This Monterey-style building, with its setback and arches, provides a subtle picturesque quality to the street.

11b. 535 Ramona Street, 1938
Pedro de Lemos, architect-builder

This is a complex of nicely detailed Spanish eclectic buildings with a tripartite form, full-width arcade, and deep tiled eaves, featuring inlaid tiles, pebble finishes, and studded wrought iron.

11c. 538–542 Ramona Street, 1927
Birge Clark, architect

The interior of 538 Ramona is noteworthy for its ceiling, which features a pattern of heavy beam rafters. The rear room has an original fireplace.

12. Winsor's Cabinet Shop, 1926
668 Ramona Street
Wells Goodenough, builder

A square central tower rises between two gable-roofed wings of this intriguing two-story stucco-sided building, which is an eclectic combination of elements that include wrought-iron balconies and a variety of fenestration.

13. John B. Daley Flats, 1902
625–631 Emerson Street
Mr. Cooke, builder

The notable wood-framed four-unit residence in the Colonial Revival style has multiple front gables with scroll-cut bargeboards, an assortment of bay windows, stoops and porches, and both board-and-batten and tri-bevel siding.

14. Saint Thomas Aquinas Church, 1901
745 Waverley Street
Shea and Shea, architects

The highly decorated Gothic Revival church has a triple pointed-arched entry porch, with three stained-glass lancet windows above, a square corner tower topped by a spire, extended shaped gable ends of steeply pitched intersecting roofs, buttresses and small spires, and shiplap siding. It is said to be the oldest church in Palo Alto.

Professorville Historic District

Bounded by Kingsley and Addison Avenues and crossed by Ramona, Bryant, and Waverley Streets, this area was subdivided in 1889 to make lots available to professors at Stanford University. The neighborhood has excellent examples of late-nineteenth to early-twentieth-century architecture.

15. Theophilus Allen House, 1905
601–603 Melville Avenue

W. Smith, architect

The shingled chalet has a wide front-facing gable and a recessed entry behind an extended shed roof. A second-story porch has been glassed in. Architect W. Smith also designed **430 Kingsley, 1201 Waverley,** and **301 Addison.**

16. Norris House, 1929
1247 Cowper Street

Birge Clark, architect

The T-shaped Spanish Colonial Revival house was carefully sited on a large lot with ancient oaks, the most important feature in determining the design of the house; several courtyards integrate indoor and outdoor spaces. It was built for authors Charles and Kathleen Norris; Kathleen Norris was the most popular romance novelist during the 1920s–1940s.

17. Pettigrew House, 1925
1336 Cowper Street

George Washington Smith, architect

The epitome of a walled Mediterranean residence, the house has a long, low

exterior wall with tiled side-gabled roofs. The house turns its back to the street, and there are only a very few, widely spaced and ornately grilled openings on its façade.

18. John O. Snyder House, 1909
1357 Cowper Street

Surrounded by other excellent examples of Craftsman-style residences, this particular example exhibits ziggurat brackets as part of its unusual detailing, along with proportions and materials that are archetypal of its era.

19. Lucie Stern Community Center, 1932–1940
1305 Middlefield Road

Birge Clark, architect

This community center, funded by Mrs. Lucie Stern, is both a social and visual focal point for the community. The low, rambling, Mission Revival–style buildings, built of brick, stucco, and heavy timber framing, create an extensive sequence of covered and open walkways that work in harmony with gardens and courtyards.

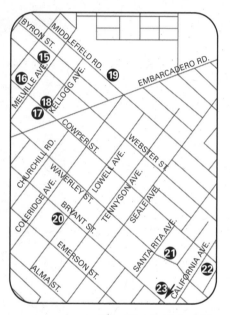

2 • Palo Alto: Professorville Historic District and Vicinity

South of Embarcadero Road

Palo Alto's early-twentieth-century residential district continues south of Embarcadero Road. Not officially part of Professorville, the tree-lined streets share similar qualities of graciousness. The **Elizabeth F. Gamble Garden,** part of an estate built in 1902, is located at 1431 Waverley Street at Embarcadero; it is open to the public.

20. 1680 Bryant Street, circa 1910

John Hudson Thomas, architect

This is one of Thomas's Secessionist designs featuring roughly textured stucco siding, casement windows, geometric detailing, and angled bays.

21. 2102 Waverley Street, 1934

Carr Jones, designer

Berkeley designer-builder Carr Jones created the ultimate in romantic picturesque buildings, and this is among his best. A multitude of slate roofs, casually laid brick siding, half-timbering, and multipaned steel-frame windows are surrounded by a picture-perfect country-style garden.

22. 2240 Cowper Street, 1939

William Wurster, architect

This is Ranch style but way more elegant and sophisticated than found in later post–World War II housing tracts. The wide one-story front section is asymmetrical with windows grouped in different ways.

23. Walter Miller House, 1893 (unmapped)
2275 Amherst Street

J. Fairley Wieland, architect

This is a large twelve-room Queen Anne with some quintessential Queen Anne elements, including a two-and-one-half-story square bay, a corner tower with a steeply pitched hip roof, and an unusual clerestory above the second-story windows.

3 · Mountain View

Mountain View has a compact downtown and several residential neighborhoods. Along the shore of San Francisco Bay is Shoreline at Mountain View Park that includes a lake; Shoreline Golf Links is just south of the park; industrial, research and development blocks are located on either side of Highway 101.

The center of Mountain View was first located on El Camino Real, the main road between San Francisco and San Jose. After the train arrived in 1864, a new commercial district grew up along the tracks; it was called Mountain View Station, serving as a shipping point for agricultural products, and remains Mountain View's downtown center where the Valley Transportation Authority's (VTA) light-rail line begins.

Incorporated in 1902, the city of twelve square miles has more than 70,000 residents. It is a major part of Silicon Valley, revitalized with high-tech money after the 1980s.

1. Rengstorff House, 1867
(unmapped)
*3070 North Shoreline
Boulevard, off Highway 101*

*Page & Turnbull, architects
(restoration, 1991)*

The grand two-story Italianate house has a symmetrical façade, carved brackets, quoins, bay windows, and a hip roof crowned by a widow's walk. After the house was purchased by the city of Mountain View in 1979, it was moved to its present location and restored.

**2. Community School of
Music and Arts/
Finn Center,** 2004
(unmapped)
*230 San Antonio Circle,
off San Antonio Avenue, south
of Central Expressway*

*Mark Cavagero Associates,
architects*

Rudolph and Sletten, builders

The Finn Center has clean forthright lines, created by its expressed structure of scored concrete that frames alternating square panels of horizontal wood siding and dark-mullioned curtain walls with a slight reveal that marks the seam between the con-

crete and wood. The building won a California AIA Award in 2004.

Downtown

A cluster of restored and well-maintained early-twentieth-century, two-story commercial buildings are located near the intersection of Castro and Villa Streets. The Mission Revival **Ames Building** (1903) at 171–175 Castro has a shaped Mission-style parapet with contrasting colored coping; the **Mockbee Building** (circa 1906) at 191 Castro is a two-story Neoclassic building that anchors the corner of Villa and Castro Streets. The **Jurian Building** (1913; Frank Delos Wolfe, architect) at 194–198 Castro has shaped parapets, a decorative fluted band, and geometric panels with a coved underside from which stylized tassels hang. The Romanesque Revival former **Farmers &**

Merchants State Bank (1905; Wolfe & McKenzie, architects), at 201 Castro, is constructed of buff-colored sandstone blocks, and has an angled, recessed corner entrance with a pair of columns supporting a slice of Doric entablature. On the

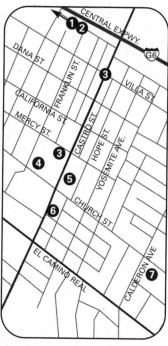

3 • Mountain View: Downtown

5. Saint Joseph's Church, 1928
582 Hope Street

Creston H. Jensen, architect

The Italian Palazzo–style church is the oldest religious building in Mountain View. It has arched corbelling on its exterior gabled walls, rose windows, a large bell tower, and a pair of Romanesque columns that support statuary at the front entry, as well as decorated arched panels recessed over the three front doors. Jensen, who died in 1931, specialized in ecclesiastical work for the Roman Catholic Archbishop of San Francisco, including Sacred Heart Church in San Jose.

6. Spangler Mortuary, 1931
799 Castro Street

Erwin Reichel, architect

The one-story building has a gable-roofed entry wing, and an arched entry, surrounded by a decorative relief made of a "ribbon" of thick plaster. Above the entry is a deeply recessed oval window, and flanking the entry are narrow arched windows. In the chapel is a 10-by-15-foot mural by Carlo Marchiori. The building was renovated in 1997 under the direction of Annette Fagundes.

second story are paired arched windows, pilasters, cornices, and frieze bands. A cumbersome hipped metal roof covers the recently added third story.

3. Mountain View Civic Center/Center for the Performing Arts, 1991
500 Castro Street

William Turnbull Associates, architects

The complex includes City Hall offices, two indoor theaters, an outdoor theater, and an art gallery, all facing a public plaza. It is multifaceted, with a variety of setbacks, angled footprints, exposed stairways, and octagonal towers at various levels, all in terra-cotta-colored stucco.

The rhythm of the exterior is enhanced with piers and rectangular openings that screen the main wall surfaces.

4. Masonic Temple, 1931
890 Church Street

Alexander A. Cantin, architect

This Mission Revival–style building with Romanesque accents has a wide double-arched main entry, with a fleur-de-lys tile border that dominates the center of the tall stucco façade; the red-tile hipped roof is flanked by a pair of stucco towers. Architect Cantin is best known for his theaters, which include **Mountain View Theatre** (1926), the Studio in San Jose, and the Orinda Theater.

7. Houses, early 1900s
711, 725 Calderon Avenue

On either side of Castro Street are early-twentieth-century residential neighborhoods. Representative examples include **725 Calderon,** a front-gabled, one-and-one-half-story Craftsman home with knee braces, a porch recessed behind heavy porch posts, and multi-paned upper sash in the windows. **711 Calderon** is also Craftsman style.

4 · Los Altos · Los Altos Hills

Los Altos

The small business center of Los Altos was established in 1907 as an agricultural shipping center after a train station was built. About the same time, Paul Shoup, a real estate developer under the name of the Altos Land Company, subdivided and promoted the sale of building lots. The community remained small and rural until after World War II. The seven-square-mile city incorporated in 1952 and now has a population of about 28,000.

1. Altos Land Company Office, circa 1909
388–398 Main Street

This modest one-story, Mission Revival retail building with two storefronts is one of the oldest in Los Altos. Both storefronts retain the shallow red-tile shed roof below a shaped Mission Revival parapet, but only #388 has its glass transom exposed.

2. Copeland Building, 1911
397 Main Street

Charles S. McKenzie, architect

The Altos Land Company built this two-story Mission Revival–style building with apartments over ground-floor retail spaces. The second story appears original, with decorative parapet walls and an almost full-width red-tile shed roof.

3. Marini House, 1926
220 University Avenue

Perseus Rhigetti, architect

Here is an impressive two-story Mediterranean-style house with arched fanlight windows and doors, a simple red-tile hipped roof, a cupola, bay windows, and small balconies.

4. Chamber of Commerce, 1961
321 University Avenue

Goodwin Steinberg, architect

Set in an open park, the unassuming one-story, pavilion-type building has mostly glass walls covered by a shingled gable-on-hipped roof with flared eaves and projecting rafter ends. It is an example of Bay Area mid-twentieth-century Modernism. The building was built by the community; the architect donated his services.

5. Christ Episcopal Church, 1914
461 Orange Avenue

Ernest Coxhead, architect

The church is distinctive for its huge, steeply pitched, one-and-one-half-story gable roofs that rise above long, horizontal, one-story walls. It is a redwood timber-frame structure covered with white stucco; many windows contain panes of diamond-shaped leaded glass. The church is now part of a complex of buildings that create a quadrangle. It was the first church constructed in Los Altos.

6. St. Nicholas Church, 1942
473 Lincoln Avenue

Andrew H. Knoll, architect

The simple façade of this Mission Revival–style church has an arched entry flanked by small windows with an arched window above; at the corners, the walls are gently curved under the gable ends. A bell tower has arched openings, wrought-iron balcony rails, and some nice decorative stuccowork such as a pattern of embossed "tiles."

7. Paul Shoup House, 1909
500 University Avenue

Wolfe & McKenzie, architects

This is a large and unusual, two-and-one-half-story Craftsman Shingle-style house. It has a wide entry porch sheltered under an enclosed gable roof held by slightly battered shingled porch posts. In its gable end are two recessed windows.

8. Merriman House, 1860s, 1888
762 Edgewood Lane

J. O. McKee, architect (1888)

A rambling shingled Queen Anne with angled window bays and some delicate ornamentation may have begun as a squatter's cabin in the 1850s and enlarged in the 1860s. After Sarah Pardee Winchester purchased the house for her sister in 1888, it was extensively remodeled.

Los Altos Hills

Los Altos Hills is primarily a residential city of single-family houses on generous lots; streets follow the contours of the hilly terrain and the area has a rural character. Los Altos Hills is the location of Foothill Junior

College in a designed park-like setting. The city, incorporated in 1956, has a population of around 8,000.

9. Foothill College, 1961
12345 El Monte Road

Ernest J. Kump Jr.; Masten and Hurd, architects

This is Earnest J. Kump's most notable work, and it became a prototype for the community college movement in the United States in the 1960s. Kump created a spread-out site plan of classroom pods connected by covered breezeways, a plan often referred to as a "Pacific-style" facility. His use of natural wood, brick, and concrete has an unpretentious quality. Recognized by *Progressive Architecture Magazine* in 1960, the design won subsequent awards from the American Institute of Architects, including a Special Commendation in 1980.

10. Hidden Villa Ranch, circa 1865
26870 Moody Road

A small white vernacular cottage, a large stock barn, and a black-

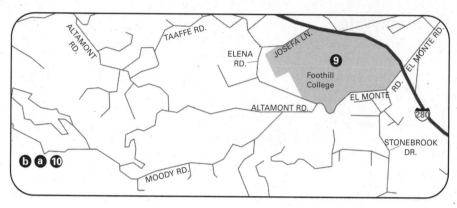

4 • Los Altos Hills

smith shop, which were once owned by G. W. Moody and date from about the mid-1860s, are evidence of Hidden Valley Ranch's long history. Josephine and Frank Duveneck purchased the 1,600-acre Hidden Villa Ranch in 1923 and moved to the property in 1929. In 1937, the Duvenecks opened the first American Youth Hostel here on the West Coast; in 1945, they established the multiracial Hidden Villa Summer Camp.

10a. Duveneck Home, 1931

Charles Kaiser Sumner, architect

Steve Aced, architect (restoration, 1997)

The large Mediterranean-style house has stucco siding reminiscent of adobe; stucco patio walls extend out into the landscape.

10b. Hidden Villa Youth Hostel & Summer Camp Facility, 2002

Arkin Tilt Architects

This environmentally friendly building is a subtle composition of materials and forms that blend harmoniously with its rural set-

ting. A deep porch has a shallow-sloped roof that rises into a steeper main gable with a large distinctive shed dormer. The walls are rammed earth, formed

by volunteers. Passive energy features, such as shade provided by the deep porches and earthen walls providing thermal mass, make this a "green" structure.

5 • Sunnyvale

The Martin Murphy Jr. family, one of the earliest pioneer families to reach California overland by wagon, arrived in Santa Clara County in 1841, acquired land, and developed a ranch in the center of the Santa Clara Valley. In 1897, a Murphy heir sold a portion of land around the train station to real estate developer Walter Everett Crossman, who subdivided the property and promoted it for homes, businesses, and industry. He named the community Sunnyvale in 1901. At first Crossman was only partially successful in attracting industry; but after the 1906 earthquake, he enticed Hendy Iron Works, with the offer of free land, to relocate from San Francisco. Today, companies such as Lockheed-Martin and Westinghouse are important Sunnyvale industries. The city, incorporated in 1912, has a population of almost 132,000.

1. Dirigible Hangar No. 1 Moffett Field, 1933
Moffett Boulevard, off Highway 101

Moffett Field's mammoth oval-shaped and curved Hangar No. 1 was built in 1933 to house the dirigible USS *Macon*. This hangar and nearby World War II blimp hangars are among the largest unsupported structures in the country. A plan to convert the landmark into a space and science center has local and national support, but due to hazardous materials leaching

from its walls, the future of the building remains unknown.

2. Onizuka Air Force Station, 1969
1080 Innovation Way

The windowless, sky-blue concrete, box-like structure, known locally as the "Blue Cube," was built to operate the world's first "spy satellite system," and is striking for its functional straightforwardness. The surrounding Onizuka Air Force Station, scheduled for closure, was the command center of the Air Force Satellite Control

Network. The intriguing complex, with its parabolic dish antennas, occupies the southern corner of Moffett Field.

3. Hendy Iron Works Office Building, 1907
501 Hendy Avenue

Founded in San Francisco in 1856, Joshua Hendy Iron Works produced mining equipment used all over the world, as well as a wide variety of heavy machinery and metal castings. The company moved to Sunnyvale after the 1906 earthquake. The long, one-story Mission Revival–style

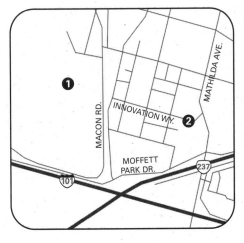

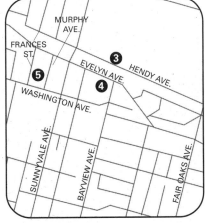

building, now a museum, has regularly spaced, domed entrance towers. Dashed stucco walls have a series of shallow relief arches and stepped parapet copings that add élan to the façades. Their products played critical roles in both World War I and World War II.

4. Ryan Hotel, 1907
394 East Evelyn Avenue

Wolfe & McKenzie, architects

This two-story stucco-sided building, located on a corner, has a square cornice, a belt-course of trim between the first and second stories, and regularly spaced, angled window bays.

5. Murphy Heritage Landmark District
100 block of Murphy Avenue, between Washington and Evelyn Avenues

This is all that remains of what was once downtown Sunnyvale. The largest building is the **Madison and Bonner/Del Monte Building** (1904) [5] at 100 South Murphy Avenue, a former fruit packing and drying

barn that was moved here in 1993. Three other corner commercial buildings are modest two-story structures that date from 1897 to 1907.

6. Sunnymount Gardens, 1949–1950
593 and 599 Dawn Drive

Joseph Eichler's early housing developments in Sunnyvale are important in the evolution of the thousands of Modernist homes he built in hundreds of subdivisions until the early 1970s. Inspired by living in a house designed by Frank Lloyd

Wright, Eichler began building Modernist-style tract homes in 1947. Sunnymount Gardens (1949–1950) was his second housing development in Sunnyvale, where thirty-six houses, using stock plans, were built on a horseshoe cul-de-sac. The houses have flat or angled roofs covered with tar and gravel or with foam. Construction was often post-and-beam, with floor-to-ceiling windows and radiant heating in the slab floors. The homes located at **593** and **599 Dawn Drive** are unaltered examples.

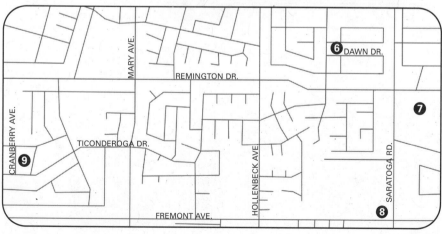

7. Sunnyvale Community Center
550 Remington Drive

7a. Sunnyvale Senior Center, 2003
Steinberg Group, architects

Set in an open park, the long, one-story building is a composition of contrasts; the walls are brick, and multi-shaped roofs are brown standing-seam metal; three steep mansard-like dormers rise above exaggerated asymmetrical hipped roofs on one side of the building. The entrance pathway is covered by a tall, slightly sloping roofed portico structure supported by two silver posts.

7b. Bianchi Barn, circa 1918

In Orchard Heritage Park (behind the Senior Center) is an example of a typical, vernacular Northern California barn built of vertical boards, with a central gable and shed-roofed side wings. The barn was moved to this site from San Jose, and houses the equipment for Sunnyvale's ten-acre apricot orchard.

8. Fremont Union High School, 1925
1279 Sunnyvale-Saratoga Road

William H. Weeks, architect

After two renovations (1969, 2004) the Mediterranean-style school retains much of its original design. The main building is one story with a small arched front portico, gable roof, and cupola bell tower. One- and two-story wings have red-tile gable roofs, stucco siding, floral plaster motifs, archways, tile, and ironwork.

9. William Wright House, circa 1865, 1918
1234 Cranberry Avenue

An 1860s Gothic Revival ranch house was transformed into a Colonial Revival in 1918. Mature landscaping and a water tower remain on the property.

6 · City of Santa Clara

The City of Santa Clara grew up around Mission Santa Clara, established in 1777. Large industrial parks are located on the north side of the city, including Sun Microsystems, situated on the former site of Agnews State Hospital, where many Mediterranean Revival–style former hospital buildings remain on a landscaped site with extensive lawns, old palms, and pepper trees. The city, incorporated in 1857, has a population of more than 102,000, and covers approximately nineteen square miles.

1. James Lick Mill Complex, 1857–1882 (unmapped)
4101 Lick Mill Boulevard and 554 Mansion Park Drive (east off Montague Expressway)

James Lick (1796–1876) was born in Pennsylvania; he came to California in 1848 from Peru, where he made money by building pianos. As a pioneer California entrepreneur, he immediately began accumulating wealth through dealings in real estate and other ventures. In April 1848, he bought an established flourmill on the Guadalupe River, north of the town of Santa Clara.

The Lick Mill complex, located on the grounds of the Mansion Grove Apartment complex, consists of four buildings, of which the centerpiece is Lick's two-story, twenty-four-room, 1860s Italianate villa (open by appointment). The house, which has arched windows, a variety of carved brackets, turned balusters, and paneled pilasters, was never furnished; it is said that he and his son

preferred smaller quarters on the property. There is also an immense round brick granary (1857), a Victorian mill office (1860s), a post-1882 office/recreation hall, and a millpond.

When Lick died, he was among the wealthiest men in the state; his land holdings were extensive. He was the benefactor to various charities, but the bulk of his estate created Lick Observatory.

1a. Lick Observatory (unmapped)
Mt. Hamilton

In 1874, James Lick created a trust to construct "a powerful telescope, superior to and more powerful than any telescope ever yet made . . . and a suitable observatory." The top of Mt. Hamilton was chosen for the observatory in 1875, and the federal and state governments granted 2,500 acres toward the

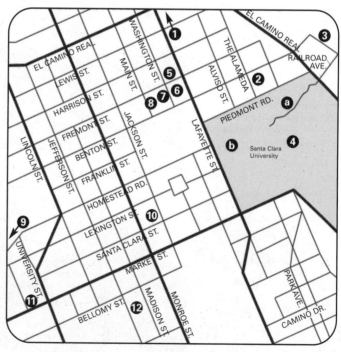

6 · City of Santa Clara: Downtown

endeavor in 1876. Construction began in 1880 for the Italian Renaissance–style two-domed observatory, designed by architect S. E. Todd of Washington, D.C., and built of brick made on the site. By 1881, the smaller of the two domes was complete and a twelve-inch telescope installed. Lick was buried under the building in 1887, a year before its completion.

Lick Observatory was the first permanent mountaintop observatory in the world; it contains the original Lick thirty-six-inch refractor, which is operational. It is part of the University of California–Santa Cruz, and open to the public.

Downtown

2. Santa Clara Women's Club, circa 1790, 1913
3260 The Alameda

William E. Higgins, architect
(adaptive reuse, 1913)

The simple one-story adobe has a tile roof and full-width front porch supported by heavy timber posts. It is the only surviving structure of the third mission complex, and was one of thirty housing units, laid out in five parallel rows, built for married neophyte Indian couples. It is also one of the oldest adobes in California. The Santa Clara Women's Club purchased the building in 1913 and remodeled it for their headquarters.

3. Santa Clara Railroad Station 1863, 1877
1005 Railroad Avenue

This board-and-batten depot, with its deep eaves and Stick-style knee braces, was built on

the east side of the tracks by the San Francisco & San Jose Railroad Co. It was moved to its present location in 1877. The South Bay Historical Railroad Society completed a restoration in 1993.

4. Santa Clara University
500 El Camino Real

The university was founded in 1851 as an outgrowth of the Mission Santa Clara de Asís.

4a. Arts and Science Building, 2001
Saitta Architects

The building has a vaguely Mission Revival feel but with sweeping proportions that rely on modern structural materials. The façade is a complex series of built-up and carved-away

layers that include angled walls visually supporting extended arches, arched colonnades—some with engaged columns and some with freestanding columns—and wide cantilevered rooflines and balconies.

4b. Mission Santa Clara de Asís, 1926

Charles S. McKenzie, architect

This mission church is an elaborate version of the fifth mission church (1825), which was destroyed by fire in 1926. The façade is ornamented with Mission-style plaster relief and statuary niches. The bell tower has a pair of arched openings on each side and the roof is octagonal. St. Francis Chapel, located at the rear, is a remnant of the original church.

5. C. C. Morse House, 1892
981 Fremont Street

This impressively decorated Queen Anne Victorian was built by Charles Copeland Morse, "the American Seed King" of Santa Clara Valley. It is a profusion of multiple gables, angled bays, a rounded window bay with a steep conical roof, spindled porch railings, turned posts, textured wall shingles, scroll-cut bargeboards, dormers with elaborate carved trim, and lacy roof cresting.

6. Fred Franck House, 1905
1179 Washington Street
Louis Theodore Lenzen, architect

This is an eclectic variation of a Colonial Revival–Classic box with a side-porch entry portico. The symmetrical façade has a half-round window bay flanked by small leaded windows in a floral pattern. At the corners of the second-story, square corner bays with hipped roofs are supported on narrowly spaced brackets. Narrow clapboard siding, a hipped roof with hipped roof dormers, and closed eaves were typical.

7. Russell-Robinson House, 1850s–1862
1184 Washington Street

The front portion of this typical Carpenter Gothic–style house was constructed in 1862. A small wing at the rear is a prefabricated house that may date from the early 1850s.

8. Samuel Johnson House, circa 1851
1159 Main Street

This is believed to be one of twenty-three prefabricated houses brought to Santa Clara from Boston by Peleg Rush in 1850. It has the simplicity of an early Italianate showing a pyramidal roof with a flat central section.

9. Central Park Library, 2004 (unmapped)
2635 Homestead Road
Group 4 Architectural, Research and Planning, architects

The 80,000-square-foot library is an environmentally "green" building with deep eaves for shade and clerestory windows for ventilation and light.

10. Andrew J. Landrum House, circa 1867
1217 Santa Clara Street
A. J. Landrum, builder

This pristine Gothic Revival cottage was inspired by Andrew Jackson Downing.

11. Harris-Lass House, 1865
1889 Market Street

The Harris-Lass House and farm complex includes a barn, tank house, summer kitchen, and chicken coop. It was purchased by the city in 1987 as the last farm site in Santa Clara, and now houses one of the city's historic museums. The house is a two-story Italianate with an asymmetrical façade, an off-centered entry porch, arched windows, and a pyramidal roof.

12. Berryessa Adobe, late 1840s
373 Jefferson Street
Gil Sanchez, architect (restoration)

Reflecting a Greek Revival–inspired design, the one-story adobe has a symmetrical façade with the front door in the center and a single window on either side, simple small pediments over the windows and door (called Territorial pediments on adobes), and scored plaster that resembles ashlar blocks. The Berryessa family purchased it in 1861. Recently restored, it is a city museum.

7 · Cupertino

In the late 1840s, Elisha Stephens settled in the western foothills above present-day Cupertino and established a vineyard. A post office opened in 1882 at "West Side," the intersection of today's Stevens Creek and De Anza Boulevards. The city incorporated in 1955 when its economy was still primarily agricultural and equestrian. After Apple Computer established its headquarters in Cupertino in the 1970s, development dramatically increased.

1. Maryknoll Seminary, 1926
23000 Cristo Rey Drive

McGinnis & Walsh (Boston) and Henry A. Minton, architects

The seminary complex, set in lush landscaped grounds, combines a traditional Mission Revival composition with an Oriental flare. The stucco-sided buildings have green-tile roofs with extended "curved false-front" gable parapets, curled eave ends, and wide multi-band coping. The church incorporates traditional parti such as a clerestoried nave; the adjoining bell tower (rebuilt after the Loma Prieta Earthquake) has a decorative top, with miniature pagodas at each corner, above a tall

arched bell opening framed by pilasters and scrolled keystones.

It serves as a home for retired priests and brothers.

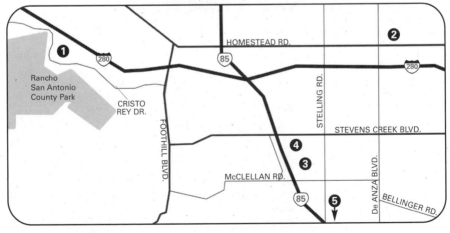

2. Collins School/Cupertino de Oro Club, 1889, 1908
20441 Homestead Road

Wolfe & McKenzie, architects (1908)

In 1908, a one-room 1889 schoolhouse designed by Joseph McKee was remodeled and expanded with a new wing on the west side, and the earlier bell tower was replaced with one in the Craftsman style; a hipped roof and decorative shingles connect the old and the new. The first schoolhouse on this site was constructed in 1869. The building has been owned by the Cupertino de Oro Club since 1921.

3. De Anza College, 1968
21250 Stevens Creek Boulevard

Ernest J. Kump Jr., with Masten & Hurd, architects

Royston, Hanamoto, Beck & Abey, landscape architects

The beautiful multilayered campus included the preservation of several elements of the preexisting Beaulieu Estate. The campus design has a motif of arches and arcades, rose-pigmented concrete, and red-tile roofs, as well as exposed and unpainted wood accents; it is a Modernist interpretation of Mission-style architecture, with a low profile and a mannerist use of traditional elements using modern materials.

4. Beaulieu/ Le Petit Trianon/ California History Center, 1895
21250 Stevens Creek Boulevard

Willis Polk, architect

The one-story Neoclassic pavilion was designed for millionaire Charles Baldwin as the center of his grand estate "Beaulieu." The house, also called "Le Petit Trianon," is now the archive and gallery of the California History Center.

5. Fremont Older Ranch, "Woodhills," 1913
22800 Prospect Road

Frank Delos Wolfe, architect

"Woodhills" is a shingled, flat-roofed Prairie-style house located on property now owned by Mid-peninsula Open Space District. Although it is only open on special occasions, it is visible from a nearby public park. The grounds include gardens, garden structures, and an unusual Prairie-style pool house (1927) constructed of fired adobe bricks salvaged from the Amesquita Adobe in San Jose, and paneled with salvaged interiors. The original owners were Fremont Older, the reformist editor of the *San Francisco Call Bulletin*, and Cora Baggerly Older, an author and local historian.

8 • Campbell

In 1888, about a decade after the railroad was laid between San Jose and Los Gatos, Benjamin Campbell established the roots of the city of Campbell when he subdivided a portion of his property to build a new community around the local train stop, where agriculture was the basis of the economy. A small business district sprang up and Campbell became known as "The Orchard City." Incorporated in 1952, the city has a population of more than 38,000.

West of Highway 17

1. Campbell High School, 1936, 1938
1 West Campbell Avenue

William H. Weeks, architect (1936)

Harold H. Weeks, architect (1938)

The campus has a mix of Mission Revival–style buildings, but the auditorium (1938) is a wonderful example of Mission Revival folded into Classic Moderne, with a tile roof, stucco siding, and bands of colored tile. Both the 1936 and the 1938 wings are decorated with tiles by Solon & Larkin and other tile makers. The school closed in 1980 and is now a community center.

2. Campbell Elementary School, 1923, 1926, 1929
11 East Campbell Avenue

William H. Weeks, architect

The Renaissance Revival–style school has graceful Neoclassic details and arcaded wings. Additions were constructed in 1926 and 1929. The school closed in 1964 and is now offices.

3. Country Women's Club, 1923
274 East Campbell Avenue

Howard W. Higbee, architect

An L-shaped Mediterranean-style, former library building has a three-sided entry portico at the turn of the L, and arched fanlight windows.

4. Bank of Campbell, 1911
360 East Campbell Avenue

William Binder, architect

This Italian Renaissance–style former bank has boldly arched windows, pale brick siding, and a deep overhanging cornice with curved brackets.

5. Bank of Campbell/ Farley Building, 1895
365 East Campbell Avenue

Built of brick, it has segmented arches over the doors and windows, a corbelled cornice, and an angled corner entrance.

6. Grower's National Bank/ Gaslighter Theatre, 1920
400 East Campbell Avenue

Wolfe & Higgins, architects

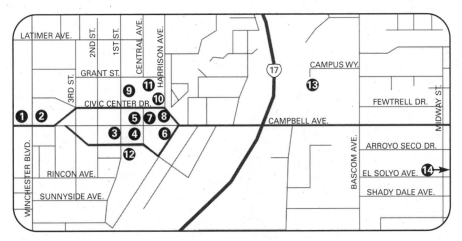

The quintessential bank building (now a theater) sports a colossal pair of recessed fluted Doric columns, tall side windows, and a classical entablature that includes triglyphs and a parapet screen, all in terra-cotta.

7. B. O. Curry Building, 1913
409–415 East Campbell Avenue

Frank Delos Wolfe, architect

The Mission Revival–style building has a square corner tower, broadly hipped roof, arched openings, and a shaped stucco parapet with brick accents. It is clearly visible when approaching historic downtown Campbell from the east.

8. Ainsley Corporation Headquarters, 1938
43 North Harrison Avenue

Binder & Curtis, architects

A small one-story, redbrick commercial building has steel casement windows and white trim, with a rounded broken pediment over the portico—a conservative, mildly Georgian, mid-twentieth-century design.

9. Campbell City Hall, 1971
70 North First Street

William C. Hedley Jr., architect

This Modernist complex incorporates hallmarks of the early 1970s: reinforced concrete, oblong window surrounds, partially below-grade ground floors, a sunken atrium, curving brick borders, and heavy horizontal roof planes that extend into broad steel-edged eaves supported by slender steel columns. Some of the columns have flared tops that mimic the curved window shapes.

10. Campbell Library, 1975
77 Harrison Avenue

William C. Hedley Jr., architect

Together with City Hall, the library shelters a landscaped plaza with curving walks, performance areas, and a large lawn. The cruciform sugar-cube massing of the clock tower is thrust into the air on thin steel posts.

11. J. C. Ainsley House, 1925
300 Grant Street

Addison M. Whiteside, builder

The English Tudor–style home, with a faux-thatched roof, was moved to the Campbell Civic Center in 1990 from the property at the northeast corner of Hamilton and Bascom Avenues,

which subsequently became eBay's world headquarters. Now a historic house museum, the fifteen-room mansion has many of its original furnishings; it showcases domestic life in the 1920s.

12. Campbell Water Company Tower and Pump House Building, 1928
94 South First Street

Andrew Johnson, builder

The 130-foot-high water tower has become a symbol for Campbell's historic downtown. Its Mission-style pump house is also noteworthy.

East of Highway 17

13. PruneYard Shopping Center and Towers, 1968–1970
South Bascom Avenue at Campbell Avenue

Bruce Moody, Walter & Moody, architect (shopping center)

The town-and-country-style office and specialty-goods shopping complex opened in 1971 and, although remodeled, retains much of its original timber and tile character. As counterpoint to the shopping center, there are three towers rising above it in bronzed steel and smoked glass. The eighteen-story Tower #1 was designed to be in San Francisco but ended up in suburban Campbell. The more recent six-story tower is by Hornberger & Worstell, Inc.

14. Guerraz/Leigh House. 1850s, 1890s
140 Peter Drive

The earliest part of this house was constructed in the early 1850s. The Queen Anne–style wing was added in the 1890s.

9 • Saratoga

The main village of Saratoga is nestled in the western foothills of the Santa Clara Valley along Saratoga Creek, where a water-powered sawmill was operating by late 1847. When the town was established in 1850, it was called McCartysville. A mineral spa and resort, Congress Springs, opened in the late nineteenth century and became a popular vacation destination. The twelve-square-mile city, incorporated in 1956, has a population of 30,000.

1. St. Andrews Episcopal Church, 1963
13601 Saratoga Avenue

Warren B. Heid, architect

Large, steeply pitched, intersecting hipped roofs, Scandinavian in their proportions, dominate the stucco-sided church. **Mark Adams** designed both the interior and the stained-glass windows.

2. Saratoga Library, 2003
13650 Saratoga Avenue

Mark Schatz, architect

Recalling rural buildings, the library has vertical board-and-batten siding and horizontal V-groove siding, as well as clerestory dormers that recall the monitor roofs of barns. The simple shapes of the wings and bays are arranged in a complex and sophisticated composition.

3. Odd Fellows Home, 1912
14500 Fruitvale Avenue

Ralph Warner Hart, architect

The immense Mission Revival–style building has domed twin bell towers flanking a shaped Mission Revival parapet; the rest of the building is more utilitarian.

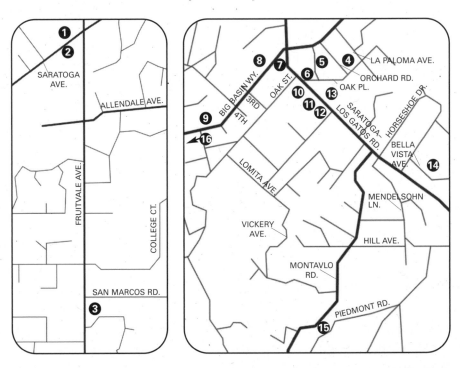

10

10. Sheldon P. Patterson Memorial Library, Saratoga Community Library, 1927
14410 Oak Street
Eldridge Spencer, architect

The Mediterranean Revival one-story building, constructed of rough-finish Thermotite concrete blocks, has a side-facing, red-tile gabled roof with an extended section over a recessed entry. Windows are multipaned steel casements. With an emphasis on form rather than decoration, the elegant small building foreshadows the work Spencer did at Stanford University.

4. Fontaine House, 1924
20250 La Paloma
A. P. Hill Jr., architect

This Tudor-Revival cottage was the family home of actresses Olivia De Havilland and Joan Fontaine. Built in a streetcar suburb, the picturesque house, with half-timbering, multipane windows, and multiple rooflines, is set in mature landscaping.

5. Saratoga Foothill Clubhouse, 1916
20399 Park Place
Julia Morgan, architect

Under a wide gable roof, a high oversized circular window dominates the façade of the one-story building. Clad in natural shingles with an alternating reveal, the clubhouse contains a large meeting hall with half-timbered finishes and first-growth unpainted redwood paneling.

6. Chapel of the Saratoga Federated Church, 1923
20390 Park Place
Julia Morgan, architect

Although enlarged over the years, this Mission Revival–style chapel and hall remain largely as Julia Morgan designed them. The church has a multitude of one-

and two-story stucco-sided wings; different-sized arched windows and openings; and red-tile gable, hipped, and shed roofs. A large square bell tower with hipped roof extends through the east gable of the sanctuary.

7. Saratoga Memorial Arch, 1919
Big Basin Way and Saratoga–Los Gatos Road
Bruce Porter, architect

Saratoga's Memorial Arch was built to honor those who died in World War I. The arched opening, with engaged columns, is covered by a gable-roofed pediment. In 2004, it was moved to this plaza, its original location, after being located on two other sites.

8. Saratoga State Bank, 1913
14421 Big Basin Way
Charles S. McKenzie, architect

As its Neoclassic style might suggest, this one-story brick commercial building was originally a bank.

9. John Chisolm House, circa 1875
14605 Big Basin Way

The two-story cube-shaped house has a pyramidal roof, six-over-six-light windows, and simple trim.

11. McWilliams House, 1850s
20460 Saratoga– Los Gatos Road

One of the oldest remaining structures in Saratoga, the hall-and-parlor-style house, with a side-facing gable and front porch covered by a shed-roof, was moved to Saratoga Historical Park in 1973.

12. Saratoga Historical Museum, circa 1905
20450 Saratoga– Los Gatos Road

A typical one-story, pioneer-style, false-front commercial building was moved to Saratoga Historical Park in 1976.

13. Woodleigh/ G. A. Wood House, 1911
20375 Saratoga– Los Gatos Road

Set behind a sweeping lawn, the Neoclassic house has a distinctive semicircular portico held by two-story Ionic columns. There are Ionic corner pilasters and a fan-light above the front door flanked by decorative sidelights. A dormer with a Palladian window is set into a truncated hipped roof.

14. Rancho Bella Vista/ Blaney Villa, 1917
20021 Bella Vista Avenue

Willis Polk, architect

Although partially obscured by vegetation, "Bella Vista" is breathtaking. The stucco and red-tile roofed villa has a tall bell tower and a collection of chimney tops, including one that soars above the tower. The house, best viewed from Horseshoe Court, has been noted as Polk's "greatest contribution to American architecture."

15. Villa Montalvo, 1914
15400 Montalvo Road

William Curlett, architect

George Doeltz, landscape designer

Banker, politician, arts patron, and U.S. Senator, James D. Phelan purchased 160 acres in the Saratoga foothills in 1911. He retained William Curlett to design the nineteen-room Mediterranean-style villa, and construction began in 1912. When Curlett died in 1914, his son Alex Curlett and his partner Charles E. Gottschalk replaced him and completed the project

in 1914, the year Phelan was elected a U.S. Senator.

The house is a two-story, symmetrically arranged, Classical three-part composition with a wide central section containing a triple-arched, recessed entry portico below a recessed balcony. Flanking the entrance are hipped roof wings, with an arched window on the ground floor and double casement window on the second. The roofs are red tile and the siding is buff-colored stucco. The house is noteworthy for its interior paneling, and there are art tiles both inside and out. Colonnades, arbors, and distinctive outdoor features and spaces, including a secluded sunken "Spanish Courtyard" with small fountains, surround the house. The estate, donated to the state of California in 1930, is an arts center.

15a. Orchard of Artists, 2004
15400 Montalvo Road

StastnyBrun Architects, Inc.; Daniel Solomon (cottage); Hodgetts and Fung Design Associates; MACK Architects; Jim Jennings Architecture; and Santos Prescott and Associates, architects

Marta Fry Landscape Associates, landscaping

Scattered on a steep hillside near the main entrance to Montalvo is the "Orchard of Artists," which contains ten small cottages and a common meeting space and dining hall at the base of the hill, for Montalvo's artists-in-residence program. The buildings are a collaboration between authors, musicians, painters, sculptors, and architects. The designs are sculptural and innovative, adhering to "green" design principles. Landscaping is in keeping with the natural surroundings.

16. Paul Masson Winery, circa 1906, 1941 (unmapped)
14831 Pierce Road, off Big Basin Way

Martin Ray, designer (renovations, 1941)

Established in 1896 as the Paul Masson Champagne Company, the post-1906 winery building with its distinctive Romanesque-style stone portal presents a backdrop for a popular Mountain Winery concert series. The vineyards and Masson's La Cresta residence, a Mission Revival stone-faced chateau, was the site of actress Anna Held's notorious champagne bath, promoting California's most renowned champagne of the first half of the twentieth century.

15

10 · Los Gatos

Los Gatos was established in 1850 at the foot of the rugged area between Santa Clara and Santa Cruz Counties. It served as a center for logging and later for orchards. The community grew substantially after a toll road opened in the late 1850s, and expanded when a narrow-gauge railroad to San Jose opened in 1878. The town incorporated in 1887 and has almost 29,000 residents today.

Architect Francis W. Reid, raised in the Willow Glen neighborhood of San Jose in the 1880s, set up an architectural office in Los Gatos in 1890 after graduating from the local University of the Pacific. In 1892, he and architect George C. Meeker formed the firm of Reid and Meeker. Before moving to Alameda in 1896, Reid and the firm of Reid and Meeker designed a number of significant houses. Other notable residents included writer and social reformer Charles Erskine Scott Wood and violinist Yehudi Menuhin.

Monte Sereno

1. Mitchell/Hamsher House, 1891
17940 Saratoga Road

Francis W. Reid, architect

A high-style Queen Anne has ball-and-spindle fretwork in circular arches on the front porch, Palladian windows, and stained glass. This house is located in the small town of Monte Sereno. With less than 3,500 residents, it has a rural character with winding tree-lined roads, and is entirely residential except for the City Hall and Post Office complex.

Los Gatos

2. Harry Perrin Building, 1894–1895
315 University Avenue

A distinctive redbrick Romanesque-style house with sandstone trim, it was built by brick mason Harry Perrin.

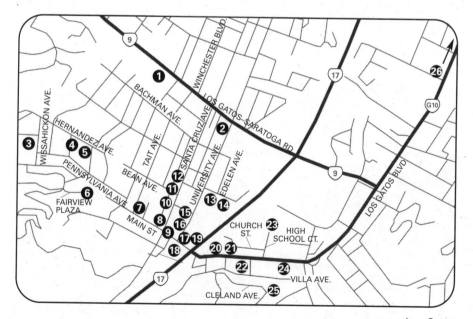

3. La Estancia/ McCullagh-Jones House, circa 1880, 1901
18000 Overlook Road

Willis Polk, architect (1901)

A former farmhouse was substantially remodeled into a gracious Mission Revival. It was featured in the magazine *House and Garden* in 1902.

4. Malpas House, 1892
55 Hernandez Avenue

Reid and Meeker, architects

An exuberant Queen Anne, with some Shingle-style influences, has a large oculus window, curvaceous columns, domed turret, and stonework. The house fell into its basement during the 1989 Loma Prieta Earthquake but was raised and restored (1991–1993) by builder Tim Lantz.

5. Franklin House, 1914
25 Hernandez Avenue

Frank Delos Wolfe, architect

This is an excellent example of Wolfe's Prairie style. The enormous bowl-shaped capitals on the front porch pillars are unusual, but they are also used on 45 Hawthorne, San Jose.

6. Fairview Plaza, 1880s–1925
Fairview Avenue (Terminus)

A wonderful cluster of about twenty homes built during the 1880s, when Frank McCullagh subdivided the property, and about 1925. The homes (interspersed with a few modern apartment buildings) surround a neighborhood park. A narrow pedestrian path, Turnstile Walk, connects this historic district to downtown.

7. Los Gatos Museum, 1927
4 Tait Avenue, at West Main

A Mediterranean-style one-story former firehouse is home to the art and nature collections of the Los Gatos Museum. The history collection is located at 75 Church Street off East Main in an 1880 stone structure.

Historic Commercial District

The intersection of Main Street and Santa Cruz Avenue is the center of a National Register Historic District comprised mainly of commercial buildings from around the turn of the nineteenth century.

8. Hofstra Block/La Cañada Building, circa 1875, 1894
1 North Santa Cruz Avenue, at Main Street

This brick commercial block, with its tall corner turret, anchors the main intersection of downtown Los Gatos. The unreinforced masonry buildings suffered severe damage in 1989; restoration was completed in 1991.

9. Bank of America, 1931
2 North Santa Cruz Avenue

Henry A. Minton, architect

The Art Deco bank building, with an atypical hipped tile roof, includes heroic female figures at the upper corner panels, deeply fluted two-story pilasters, Art Deco capitals and cornice, and subtle spandrel trim.

10. Los Gatos Theater, 1915, 1930
41 North Santa Cruz Avenue

Roland S. Tuttle, architect (1930)

With its tall neon marquis, the Los Gatos Theater (originally The Strand) is the epitome of an early local movie house. Constructed in 1915 by developer

J. A. Marshall, it was remodeled in 1930 after a fire. After the Loma Prieta Earthquake, the building was rehabilitated and reopened. When the large theater was divided, painted fantasy figures from the 1930s were retained in one of the theaters.

11. Coggeshall House, 1891
115 North Santa Cruz Avenue

Francis W. Reid, Reid and Meeker, architect

This impressive Queen Anne has a round tower above a recessed porch and an open arched entry with corner spindle work and patterned shingles. It is the last of the great houses that once lined the street when it was almost entirely residential.

12. Peerless Stage Depot, 1938
133–145 North Santa Cruz Avenue

Edward T. Foulkes, architect

A tiled Art Deco former bus station has strong colors that enliven the façade; it inspired the newer building to the south.

13. Reid-Skinkle House, 1893
129 Edelen Avenue

Reid and Meeker, architects

Reid designed this Queen Anne with turret for himself in 1893, but only lived here for a year.

14. Miles House, 1892–1893
130 Edelen Avenue

Also a large Queen Anne, but with less ornate decoration, it is attributed to Reid.

15. Wagner Cobblestone House, 1906
15 University Avenue

An unusual bungalow entirely faced with cobblestones is still a residence in the core of downtown.

16. Libante French Laundry, 1930
11 University Avenue

Herman Baumann, architect

Although the Art Deco façade exhibits a spare minimalism, the shaped transom has a marvelous abstract leaded-glass pattern; pilasters and a decorative band below the parapet have abstract angular motifs.

17. First National Bank, 1920
160 West Main Street

MG West Company, architects

A Renaissance Revival–style bank has an ornate terra-cotta entrance surround and bas-relief mission images in the top of the two tall arches.

18. Rankin Block, 1901
145 West Main Street

Attributed to Wolfe & McKenzie, architects

This Mission Revival business block has a shaped parapet edged with exuberant coping, flanked by square window bays with hipped tile roofs. After the Loma Prieta Earthquake, the exterior was restored and retrofitted by architect John Lien.

19. Fretwell Building, 1906
98 West Main Street

The Romanesque one-story building is concrete scored to resemble carved sandstone. The corner storefront, different in character, has high multipaned transoms and slender corner columns.

East of Highway 17

20. Beckwith Building, 1893, 1992
27–35 East Main Street

Frank Lobdell, architect

The extraordinary highly decorated brick building with sandstone moldings suffered severe damage in 1989. Architect John Lien reconstructed its façade in 1992.

21. 37–45 East Main Street, various dates

These three buildings replaced buildings destroyed during the 1989 earthquake. Three different owners and their architects created a composition that echoes design elements of the Beckwith Building. Built over a period of several years, the three buildings successfully blend with one another and the textual quality of downtown.

22. Los Gatos Civic Center, 1967
110 East Main Street

Stickney and Hull, architects

Sasaki, Walker and Associates, landscape architects

This award-winning Modern civic complex features brick-and-concrete buildings set on three corners of a plaza that functions as the roof of the Council Chambers. The clean forms, low massing, and use of hard-edged materials provide a good example of mid-sixties design. The raised clerestory window boxes add some verticality to the otherwise horizontal composition. Across East Main at 75 Church Street is the **Forbes Mill** building where the city's history collection is located.

23. Los Gatos High School, 1925
East Main Street at High School Court

William H. Weeks, architect

The large formal and imposing Greek Revival school, set on an oak knoll above a broad front lawn, is integrated with expansive landscaped grounds.

24. First Church of Christ, Scientist, Los Gatos, 1929
238 East Main Street

William H. Crim Jr., architect

A temple front adorns this two-story Classic Revival church.

25. Stanfield House, 1891
126 Cleland Avenue

Francis W. Reid, architect

Although remarkably similar to many of Reid's Queen Anne designs, this house has lovely upper-porch lattice in a complete moon design and beautiful window trim. At **#3 Kimble** is another 1891 Queen Anne by Reid for J. J. Fretwell.

26. Magneson Cottage, 1928 (unmapped)
16751 Magneson Loop

W. A. Roberts, builder

Located in a neighborhood with a dominant storybook character, this house has a steep faux-thatched roof and complex picturesque massing.

11 · San Jose: Central, West, and East

San Jose is the largest city in Santa Clara County and the Bay Area. When San Jose was established in 1777, it was the first Spanish *pueblo* (town) in California Alta (just earlier than Los Angeles); most Spanish settlements were either missions or presidios rather than towns. The pueblo was located close to where Guadalupe and Los Gatos Creeks merge, three miles south of Mission Santa Clara. Incorporated in 1850, San Jose served as the first capital of the state of California for a short time. Once noted for its agriculture and later for its aerospace industries, San Jose is now the center of Silicon Valley.

The city is redeveloping its historic central core. Valley Transportation Authority—light-rail service from Mountain View to Alum Rock in east San Jose and through central San Jose and the downtown along First Street—extends south to Santa Teresa and west to Almaden. A linear pedestrian parkway along the Guadalupe River is partially complete.

San Jose encompasses 174 square miles, and more than 900,000 people call the city home. Its boundaries stretch throughout the Santa Clara Valley and surrounding foothills. The city, located between the Peninsula and the East Bay, is crossed by numerous freeways and expressways that divide the sprawling congested metropolis.

Central San Jose

Downtown

1. Peralta-Fallon Historic Park

1a. Peralta Adobe–Fallon House Historic Site, circa 1800
184 East St. John Street

The Peralta Adobe is the only adobe still standing in San Jose from the Spanish/Mexican period. It is believed to have been built by Manuel Gonzalez, an Apache Indian who came to California with the De Anza Expedition of 1776, and who was San Jose's second *alcalde* (mayor). By 1808, it was owned by Luís María Peralta, who had also come with the expedition as a child. He was a longtime *comisionado* of the pueblo, handling government affairs for both Spain and Mexico. The Peralta family lived at this location until the mid-1860s. Long used for storage, it was restored by architect Gil Sanchez for the city of San Jose in 1977.

1b. Fallon House, circa 1854
175 West St. John Street
Levi Goodrich, architect (attributed)

The two-story Italianate villa is one of the oldest frame houses in San Jose. Thomas Fallon, a participant in the Bear Flag Revolt, is credited with raising the American flag in San Jose, now memorialized in a larger-than-life-size bronze equestrian statue located at the intersection of West Julian and St. James Streets. Fallon's wife was Carmelita Castro.

2. St. James Park, 1848
North First, East St. James, North Third, and East St. John Streets

The nearly eight-acre St. James Square appeared on Chester Lyman's 1848 survey of the "Town of St. Joseph" as two undivided blocks. The blocks remained undeveloped until the late 1860s when William O'Donnell was hired to design the park. In 1887, Rudolph Ulrich's redesign transformed it into a Victorian-style park, a center of civic life where memorials and monuments still stand.

The park today contains a **Senior Center** (1967; Higgins and Root, architects), a light-rail track (1988) along North Second Street, a Victorian-style replacement fountain (1985), and a children's playground.

Beginning with the construction of Trinity Episcopal Church in 1863, many of the city's most distinguished public and commercial buildings were built on the blocks surrounding the park. The St. James Park Historic District was placed on the National Register of Historic Places in 1979. Information plaques are located in front of historic buildings.

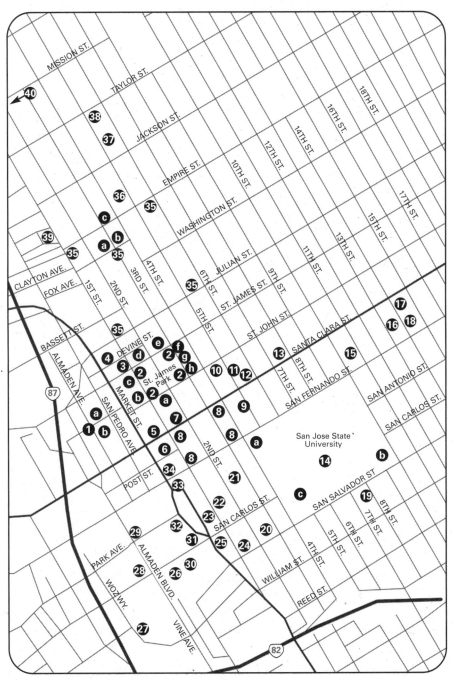

2a

2a. Trinity Episcopal Church, 1863

81 North Second Street

John W. Hammond, builder

An excellent example of Carpenter Gothic, the church has redwood board-and-batten siding, a steep hipped roof, lancet windows, and a rose window over the apse. The stained-glass windows, crafted by the New York firm of Doremus, were shipped around the Horn.

2b. San Jose Post Office, 1933

105 North First Street

Ralph Wyckoff, architect

This Spanish Revival–style post office, part of a WPA project, is clad with terra-cotta and a mix of Churrigueresque ornamentation and Classical detailing. The interior has marble floors, terra-cotta wainscoting, and painted exposed-beam ceilings. Wyckoff, a Watsonville-born

protégé of architect William H. Weeks, attended the École des Beaux-Arts. By the end of the 1930s, Wyckoff had become a noted Modernist.

2c. Santa Clara County Court House, 1868, 1931–1932

Corner of North First and St. James Streets

Levi Goodrich, architect

Binder & Curtis (1931–1932)

The Neoclassic building has been remodeled and rehabilitated several times, most recently by the Steinberg Group in 1994 after the 1989 Loma Prieta Earthquake.

2d. First Church of Christ, Scientist, San Jose, 1905

43 East St. James Street

George A. Wright and Willis Polk, architects

Inspired by the Temple of Ilysus near Athens, the façade has four large Ionic columns and a dome

centered over a Greek-cross floor plan.

2e. Sainte Claire Club, 1893

65 East St. James Street

A. Page Brown, architect

The Mission Revival–style building was built by James D. Phelan, later mayor of San Francisco and a U.S. Senator. Phelan was an important supporter of arts and culture and eventually gave the building to the Sainte Claire Club.

2f. Scottish Rite Temple, 1925

196 North Third Street

Carl Werner, architect (1925)

Iyama Partnership, architects (restoration, 1981)

This Beaux-Arts temple has Neoclassic- and Egyptian-style ornamentation by Carmel sculptor Jo Mora. In 1981, the building was restored and enlarged to house the San Jose Athletic Club.

2g. Unitarian Church, 1891

160 North Third Street

George W. Page, architect

The Romanesque Revival–style church has a wide, cylindrical central chapel topped by a dome and bell-cast lantern. There is a large, triple-arched, stained-glass window on the front façade, a one-story bell-shaped tower on the north, and a tall square tower with an octagonal cupola on the south.

2h. Scottish Rite Temple/ Eagles Hall, 1909

152 North Third Street

George W. Page and Henry F. Starbuck, architects

Only the 1909 entrance portico with its Doric columns remains, preserved on the face of a nine-story brick office building constructed in 1985. The façadism was a compromise in lieu of total demolition.

3. Tognazzi Building, 1892
261–264 North First Street
W. D. Van Siclen, architect
The two-story brick, Romanesque-style building trimmed with rusticated sandstone, floral terra-cotta capitals, and low-relief garlands is one of three commercial buildings that give this block a late-nineteenth-century flavor. This building and the **Moir Building** (1893) to the south are examples of the commercial designs of architect W. D. Van Siclen.

4. Sherward Apartments, 1915
79 Devine Street
Frank Delos Wolfe, architect
The multifamily residential building built by the Ward family is in the Prairie style. Next door at **93 Devine Street** is the Neoclassic former Ward Funeral Home.

5. San Jose Building and Loan, 1926
81 West Santa Clara Street
Roller-West Co., architects
Here is a small treasure of a classic Beaux-Arts building.

6. Glein-Fenerin Building, 1875
69 Post Street
This Italianate-style brick building with a Wild West image is one of downtown's oldest-remaining commercial structures. Used as a saloon for most of its early history, it stands in what was once the middle of San Jose's red-light district.

7. Realty Building, 1925
19 North Second Street
Wolfe & Higgins, architects
This retail building has a highly articulated façade: beaded pilasters have leafed capitals rising to a multilayered cornice with a leaf frieze, egg-and-dart molding, and vertical fluting.

8. National Register Downtown Commercial Historic District
East Santa Clara and East San Fernando Streets, between South First and South Fourth Streets
The historic district, designated in 1983, covers three blocks and contains the most intact group of San Jose's early commercial buildings.

8a. Bank of Italy Building, 1926, 1927
814 South First Street, at East Santa Clara Street
H. A. Minton, architect
The thirteen-story Renaissance Revival–style bank was the city's first skyscraper; it anchors the northwest corner of the historic district and has long been the visual focal point for downtown San Jose.

8b. Crydenwise Building, 1889
27–29 Fountain Alley
J. O. McKee, architect
A three-story brick Italianate structure features an exceptional pair of Victorian two-story bay windows. The **Newhall Building** (33 Fountain Alley), which dates from about the same year, is a narrow, three-story Neoclassic building with fluted pilasters, decorative swags, and corbelled cornices.

8c. Knox-Goodrich Building, 1889
34–36 South First Street
George W. Page, Page & Goodrich, architect
An elegant Richardsonian Romanesque–style building is sheathed in sandstone from the Goodrich Quarry in the Almaden Valley. Sarah Knox-Goodrich was active in the suffrage movement.

8d. El Paseo Court Building, 1932
40–44 South First Street
Charles S. McKenzie, architect
A charming Spanish Colonial Revival complex surrounds a picturesque courtyard featuring red-tile roofs, small wrought-iron balconies, terra-cotta cartouches, tiled fountains, and flower boxes.

8e. Letitia Building, 1889
66–72 South First Street
Jacob Lenzen, architect
The four-story Romanesque-style building with a skylit atrium was built above stores and used as a rooming house. Letitia Burnett Ryland was the daughter of California's first American governor, Peter H. Burnett. Next door at 74–98, the **Ryland Block/Security Building** (1892; Jacob Lenzen & Son, designers) is a three-story Romanesque/Renaissance Revival masonry building. Both were renovated by architect John C. Howland in 2000.

8f. Toccoa Block/Lawrence Hotel, 1893
67–89 East San Fernando Street
Frank Lobdell, architect

The two-story building has exposed brick piers and broad glazed storefronts, corbel arches, and regularly placed double-hung windows.

8g. Knights of Pythias/ Hewlett Building, 1893
86–90 South Second Street

J. Fairley Wieland, architect

This building is Mission Revival. At #83–85, the **Dougherty Building** (1908; Louis T. Lenzen & Son, designers) is a two-story building with tall, second-story arched windows and decorative brickwork.

8h. Wenger, Knapp & Clark Building, 1904
40–50 South Second Street

Wolfe & McKenzie, architects

The large, three-story commercial/residential building has a prominent cornice with terra-cotta medallions and dentils. A 1990s renovation retained most of the upper façade. At #62–64, the **Theater Jose** (1904; William Binder, architect) is Spanish Revival with brick arches and pilasters.

8i. Kirk Block/Medical Arts Building, 1870, 1946
42–48 East Santa Clara Street

Ralph Wyckoff, architect (1946; remodel, 1952)

A radically remodeled Victorian façade resulted in a flamboyant Art Deco design featuring fluted pilasters and zigzag detailing. The adjacent building, also constructed in the 1870s, was remodeled to match in 1952.

8j. New Century Block, 1868, circa 1902
52–78 East Santa Clara Street

A gilded Renaissance dome marks the corner of this long, Renaissance Revival–style business block, which is embellished with scrolled keystones above arched windows, heavy quoins, and a dentilled cornice.

8k. Odd Fellows Building, 1885
84–96 East Santa Clara Street

Jacob Lenzen & Son, architects

This three-story Italianate defines the character of late-nineteenth-century downtown San Jose. Although modified over time, the overall appearance is distinctly mid-1880s, featuring a round corner window bay, street-level cast-iron pilasters, and both Romanesque and Gothic arched windows on the upper stories. The **Hagan Block** at #82 is Italianate, dating from the 1870s.

8l. YMCA Building, 1913
100–104 East Santa Clara Street

William Binder, architect

The five-story Prairie-style building, with some Neoclassic elements, has unique first-floor wall ornament giving the appearance of fine Art Deco jewelry. The attic level has square quoin-like designs in rectangular patterns.

9. San Jose Civic Center, 2006
East Santa Clara Street, between Fourth and Sixth Streets

Richard Meier & Partners, architects

The Steinberg Group, associate architects

San Jose's latest monument to local government is an eighteen-story Postmodern City Hall tower, which rises above a three-story domed rotunda that brings a Classical elegance to the largely monochrome skyline surrounding it. It is located in the center of the city's newest public plaza. The Civic Center complex conforms to sustainable design principles.

10. Donner-Houghton House, 1881
156 East St. John Street
John T. Burkett, architect

The original owners of this imposing two-story Italianate Villa were Sherman Otis Houghton, a prominent early California attorney and senator, and his wife, Eliza Donner, one of the survivors of the Donner Party. It is an example of the large homes that once stood on the perimeter of central San Jose in the 1860s–1880s. The architect, John Burkett, was active in San Jose during the 1880s, and this is the only known remaining example of his work. The house was moved three times before becoming an apartment house at this location in 1909. The Roberts House, a Craftsman bungalow at **99 North Fifth Street,** was designed by George W. Page in 1910.

11. Home of Truth/Christian Assembly Church, 1923
72 North Fifth Street
William Binder, architect

This is a Neoclassic design based on the Petite Trianon in Versailles. The symmetrical façade has a recessed front porch with Corinthian columns supporting a classical entablature and decorative parapet.

12. Medico-Dental Building, 1928
235 East Santa Clara Street
William H. Weeks, architect

The eleven-story Art Deco building was one of two sky-scrapers designed by Weeks during the 1920s in San Jose. Decorative spandrel panels emphasize its verticality. The upper floor is set back for roof gardens. In the late 1980s, the building was converted into apartments.

13. Horace Mann School, 2003
55 North Seventh Street
Moore Ruble Yudell Architects and Planners

A Postmodern multistory grammar school was built on a small site at the edge of the central business district. It has a variety of courtyards, turf play areas, terraces, and gathering spaces. A stair tower, exterior stairways, and corridors covered by translucent canopies link rooftop play areas and open galleries with classrooms. It is designed to be flexible for a variety of daytime and seasonal uses. The public art is by Seyed Alavi.

14. San Jose State University
Bounded by San Fernando, San Salvador, Fourth, and Tenth Streets

Founded in 1857 in San Francisco as a teacher's training school, the legislature redefined and renamed it in 1862 as the California Normal School. When it was proposed the school be moved to San Jose, the city donated the Washington Square block for the campus; the first building was completed in 1871. Today, San Jose State University

has more than 26,000 students and offers degrees in more than 130 subjects.

During the tenure of university president and architect J. Handel Evans (1991–1994), the disparate old and new campus buildings were unified by the use of compatible color schemes and new internal circulation patterns, and by defining the perimeter of the campus with paving and entry pillars of similar design and color.

In the center of the Washington Square block is **Tower Hall** (1910), a picturesque ivy-covered building with multiple tile roofs and a tall gable-roofed tower; it is the symbol of the university. In 1963, when other buildings in the quadrangle were demolished, Tower Hall was saved.

14a. Dr. Martin Luther King Jr. Library, 2003
150 San Fernando Street
Carrier Johnson, architect
Gunnar Birkerts Architects
Anderson Brule Architects

The eight-story library is unusual because it serves as both the university and the city's main branch library. The building's entrance, at an angle to its corner location, links the city and university. There are numerous works of art throughout the building.

14b. Campus Village, 2005
Tenth and San Salvador Streets
Niles Bolton Associates, Inc., architect

This is a large residential complex located near downtown with the hope that students will enliven the area. The building

16

complex brackets the campus, and the towers lend an urbane historicism.

14c. Martin/Scheller House, 1904
San Carlos and Fifth Street

Theodore Lenzen & Son, architects

The asymmetrical façade, with its off-center entrance and its wide, two-story bow window, represents a less-common variation of the Colonial Revival style. In 2000, the house was moved slightly to face the San Carlos pedestrian corridor and was restored by the university.

Naglee Park

15. San Jose Women's Club, 1928
75 South Eleventh Street

Wolfe & Higgins, architects

This is a Mediterranean-style two-story building with a symmetrical hierarchy of arched openings and recesses. Decorative details include rope trim, small balconies, and light fixtures.

16. Gates House, 1904
62 South Thirteenth Street

Bernard Maybeck & Mark White, architects

The imposing and unusual stucco-sided house, with a broad gable roof, has an oversized, arched, second-story front balcony resting on brackets shaped like volutes; the balustrades are turned. A second balcony of the same design is located under the gable end on the other side, with a larger veranda below it.

17. Arthur M. Free House, 1905
66 South Fourteenth Street

Emily Williams, architect

This brown shingle has a recessed entry under a central gable. Between 1919 and his death in 1953, it was the home of six-term congressman Arthur M. Free. The house was placed on the National Register in 2002 in recognition of Free's role in the establishment of Moffett Field in Mountain View.

18. George Herbert House, 1905
96 South Fourteenth Street

Wolfe & McKenzie, architects

The largest house in Naglee Park, it is an exuberant variation of the Colonial Revival.

South and West of San Jose State University

19. Farley House, 1895
405 South Eighth Street

J. Fairley Wieland and William Binder, architects

This crisp, angular Queen Anne is one of the few by Wieland & Binder to survive.

20. Rucker House, 1891
418 South Third Street

J. O. McKee, architect

With its circular turret, this is one of the most outstanding Queen Anne houses in San Jose. The sandstone foundation is from the Greystone Quarry.

21. San Jose Repertory Theatre, 1997
101 Paseo de San Antonio

Holt Hinshaw Architects

The exterior is a combination of profiled metal panels, louvers, and stucco finishes, with deeply colored walls and bold forms. The theater is one of San Jose's recent civic buildings that form a collection of delightful, colorful architecture that brightens the center of downtown.

22. Twohy Building, 1917
210 South First Street

Binder & Curtis, architects

The Renaissance Revival–style building is one of three remaining historic buildings in downtown San Jose's eight-block urban-renewal project known as San Antonio Plaza. Its delicate

Classic details are a counterpoint to the Postmodern structures that surround it. It was renovated in 2002 by Monighan & Associates.

23. Montgomery Hotel, 1911
211 South First Street

William Binder, architect

Page & Turnbull, architects (restoration, 2004)

Once a fashionable place, the Renaissance Revival–style hotel had become derelict and was nearly demolished. After being moved 180 feet south, it was restored as a boutique hotel, and is an excellent example of preservation work.

24. Fox California Theatre, 1927
345 South First Street

Weeks and Day, architects

ELS Architects (restoration, 2004)

Constructed during the heyday of the movie palace, this is a swirling mix of Mission and Spanish eclectic details, sometimes referred to as California Churrigueresque. Unused for more than thirty years, it was brought back to life in 2004 by the Redevelopment Agency and philanthropist David Packard as the home for the Opera San Jose.

25. St. Claire Hotel, 1926
302 South Market Street

Weeks and Day, architects

BAR Architects (renovation, 1992)

The six-story Renaissance Revival–style hotel is one of several buildings designed by the architects for developer T. S. Montgomery. It has a diagonal-cut corner, rusticated base, brick walls, and Neoclassic detailing.

26. San Jose McEnery Convention Center Complex, 1989
150 West San Carlos Street

Mitchell-Giurgola Associates, architects

The center is a large open pavilion under a series of barrel vaults, best seen from the air while approaching San Jose–Mineta International Airport. The neo-Brutalist complex frames a vibrant 125-foot abstract tile mural by Danish artist Lin Utzon. Two hotels complement the convention center area: **San Jose Hilton & Towers** (1989; Mitchell-Giurgola Associates, architects), an eighteen-story tower at 300 Almaden Avenue, and the **San Jose Marriott** on the opposite corner (2002–2003; Hornberger + Worstell, Inc., architects).

27. Children's Discovery Museum, 1990
180 Woz Way

Ricardo Legorreta, architect

This is a striking, 52,000-square-foot, ultramodern purple-colored building. The interaction of wall planes and rooflines, as well as the bold use of color, are typical of Mexican architect Legoretta's distinctive approach to design.

28. Center for the Performing Arts, 1972
241–271 Park Avenue

William Wesley Peters (Taliesin Fellowship/Aaron Green), architect

This is one of a number of community centers designed by Frank Lloyd Wright's atelier

Taliesin West after his death. Following the stylistic direction of the Marin County Civic Center, the first of these theaters was built in Tempe, Arizona. This building exhibits a recurring and uncompromising use of circular forms in plan, elevation, finish, and landscaping. The original design incorporated a moveable ceiling, which was removed after it collapsed.

29. Sumitomo Bank/ Family Court, 1979
170 Park Center Plaza

Cesar Pelli & Associates, architects

This spare sculptural building is an outstanding example of the expressionist approach to modern architecture. Stark materials evoke dramatic forms and contrasts.

30. Former San Jose Public Library, 1970
180 West San Carlos Street

Norton Curtis and Associates, architects

A five-story concrete bunker of a building is a modern echo of Greek Revival. The floating pavilion is embellished by colonnades with curved capitals. The lower two floors are walls of glass; the upper two walls, which contained the stacks, are solid concrete.

31. Civic Auditorium, 1934
145 West San Carlos Street

Binder & Curtis, architects

A Moderne interpretation of Spanish Revival, with a Romanesque arcade, octagonal tower, and a variety of sculptures on the exterior and interior depicting the county's history, the auditorium was built on land donated by T. S. Montgomery.

32. Tech Museum of Innovation, 1998
201 South Market Street

Ricardo Legorreta, architect

A glass form within a colorful, planar, stucco frame is set within a plaza. Each face of the three-level building has its own distinctive color, and the building features an "audio-kinetic" art installation by George Rhoads.

33. U.S. Post Office/San Jose Museum of Art, 1892
110 South Market Street

Willoughby Edbrooke, architect

The Romanesque-style former post office building is buff-colored sandstone from the Greystone (Goodrich) Quarry. The building has been remodeled and reused several times: in 1906, after being damaged in the earthquake; in 1933, for use as the public library (Ralph Wyckoff, architect); in 1970, when it became the San Jose Museum of Art; and in 1991, when a 5,000-square-foot wing was added (Skidmore, Owings & Merrill, architects).

34. St. Joseph's Cathedral, 1877
90 South Market Street

Hoffman & Clinch, architects

The Neoclassic church is a visual and culture monument in downtown, located on the site of a Catholic parish founded in 1849. The restoration in the 1980s by architects K + CZL included interior alterations.

North of Downtown San Jose

35. Hensley Historic District
Bounded by North First, Sixth, East Julian, and Empire Streets

This is San Jose's largest and most impressive Victorian-era residential neighborhood; it contains more than two hundred examples of late-nineteenth-century domestic architecture that contribute to the National Register district. North Third Street is lined with wonderful Victorians.

The Hensley District is named for Major Samuel J. and Mary Helen Hensley, whose lives are interwoven with the early days of California. Samuel was a leader of the Bear Flag Revolt, and, with her blue silk umbrella, Mary Ellen carried the documents that announced California as part of the Union when she came to California in 1850 by way of Panama. The umbrella is in the California State Museum.

35a. Luis L. Arguello House, 1891
456 North Third Street

This prominent Queen Anne is unusually eclectic and sports a square bay window and turret, a multifaceted façade, a multitude of roofs, and decorative shingled siding. The house at 460 North Street (1892; W. D. Van Siclen, architect) is a classic Queen Anne with turret.

35b. C. W. Gerichs House, 1891
467 North Third Street

J. O. McKee, architect

A three-story, highly decorated Stick-style Victorian has a square corner tower topped by a steeply pitched hipped roof punctuated with gable-roofed dormers. A multitude of fishscale shingles and millwork adorn its façade. Just up the street at 499 North Third (1891; George W. Page, architect) is the Knowles House, a large Shingle-style house with spindle work and curved window surrounds.

35c. Louis Auzerais House, 1889
155 East Empire Street

Theodore Lenzen, architect

This is a substantial two-story Queen Anne with a large rounded window bay topped by a conical roof and arched eyebrow dormer.

36. Kuwabara Hospital, 1910
565 North Fifth Street

Nishiura Brothers, builders

Financed by the Kumamoto Kenjin-Kai, this Neoclassic-style hospital was constructed to serve Japanese emigrants. After restoration in the 1980s, it now houses Japanese American community organizations, including the Japanese American Museum, and is known as the Issei Memorial Building.

The Nishiura Bros. designed and/or built many other buildings, including **Okita Hall** (circa 1915) at 587 North Sixth Street, the **Japanese Pavilion** at the 1915 Panama-Pacific International Exposition, cottages at Gilroy Hot Springs (1935), and the **San Jose Buddhist Church Betsuin** (1937) designed by architect George Gentoku Shimamoto. They also built the Japanese Pavilion at the 1939 Golden Gate International Exposition, also designed by Shimamoto, which was later reassembled on the ranch of Kiyoshi Hirasaki in Gilroy.

37. San Jose Buddhist Church Betsuin, 1937
640 North Fifth Street

George G. Shimamoto, architect

Nishiura Brothers, builders

The traditional Japanese, gable-on-hipped roof with wide flaring eaves dominates the silhouette of this wonderful temple, which is surrounded by an equally beautiful, traditional Japanese garden. It is the center of San Jose's Japantown, which began in the late nineteenth century as a home for Japanese and Chinese emigrant bachelors who had come to the Santa Clara Valley for agricultural work.

38. Fuji Towers, 1976
690 North Fifth Street

Yuzuro Kawahara, architect

Carl Swenson, builder

Builder Carl Swenson, who constructed hundreds of buildings in San Jose, was also innovative in the use of concrete. Beginning in the 1930s, Swenson's firm built design/build projects using an in-house architect named Yuzuru Kawahara. Although not well known, Kawahara designed more than 200 buildings in San Jose for Swenson. The six-story residential tower is constructed of prefabricated concrete panels; it is part of a senior housing complex serving the Japanese American community and is adjacent to Nihonmachi, San Jose's Japantown.

39. Vendome Neighborhood
North First Street at Ayer Street

This residential neighborhood got its start during the Depression when the Vendome Hotel (immortalized in a multitude of historic postcards) was demolished in 1930 and its grounds subdivided. The area contains a sizeable collection of homes in a variety of Period Revival styles. Among the Spanish/Mediterranean–style houses, **150 Ayer Street** is a picturesque one-story house (1938; Charles S. McKenzie, architect); **45 Hawthorne** is a one-story Prairie-style house, with square porch posts topped by bowl-shaped capitals like those by Wolfe & McKenzie at 25 Hernandez in Los Gatos.

40. San Jose City Hall, 1958
801 North First Street, at Mission Street

Donald F. Haines (Norton Curtis & Associates), architect

The former Civic Center, located north of downtown, illustrates the suburban movement of the 1950s away from old central downtowns. New City Hall and Civic Center (entry #9) reverses this mid-century trend. The four-story partial circle of curved glass makes Old City Hall offices easily accessible along quiet sunny corridors. The building symbolizes public openness and involvement in all aspects of municipal government.

West San Jose

Stockton and The Alameda

1. Julian Street Inn, Shelter (for the Homeless), 1990
546 West Julian Street

Christopher Alexander, architect

Christopher Alexander's 1984 book, *A Pattern Language,* presented a vision and framework for owner/architect collaboration; that vision was used during the design process of this building. The resulting complexity of forms and picturesque massing, vaguely Mediterranean in feeling, along with many handmade details and ornamental design accents, has a great deal of personality and appeal.

2. HP Pavilion (San Jose Sports Arena), 1993
525 West Santa Clara Street

Sink Combs Dethlefs, architects

HP Pavilion, with its broad expanse of roof, accented by clipped corners, full-width cantilevered bow windows, and a massive glass entry, is constructed of concrete with space-frame steel trusses and ribbed stainless steel siding; it is prominent in an uncluttered site. The massive 450,000-square-foot arena seats 17,000.

3. Southern Pacific Passenger Station, Diridon Station, 1935
65 Cahill Street

J. H. Christie, architect

The Italian Renaissance–style station has a tile roof and restrained ornamenta-tion. On the waiting room wall is a large mural by John MacQuarrie, depicting the history of Santa Clara Valley.

4. Avalon at Cahill Park
754 The Alameda

Steinberg Group, architect

A high-density urban experiment in mixed-use housing, the complex lies adjacent to Cahill Park. The buildings, which use vernacular materials and a varied design idiom, are related, and they complement the neighborhood around them. Living space, work-space lofts, and retail along The Alameda are combined to create a complex that provides a strong identity for its residents. Also planned is converting the old Del Monte Plant 51, a historic dried-fruit packing factory east of Bush Street, into residential units that use design elements of the valley's agricultural/industrial period in a new high-tech way.

5. Tiny's Drive-In, 1941
1205 The Alameda, at the corner of Martin Avenue

Nielsen & Erbentraut, builders

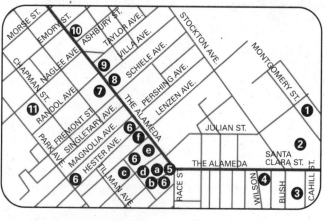

A typical semicircular drive-in plan with a neon-outlined Art Deco clock tower has a cantilevered roof under which cars were able to park.

6. Hanchett and Hester Park Conservation Area
Bounded by
The Alameda and Mariposa, Park, and Magnolia Avenues

This area was laid out in 1907 by John McLaren, superintendent of Golden Gate Park from 1887 to 1943. Wide tree-lined streets and large lots lend an air of relaxation to the Period Revival neighborhood.

6a. Blair House, 1911
1145–1147 Martin Avenue
Louis T. Lenzen, architect

A shingled Craftsman bungalow with a symmetrical façade, this house has a full-width covered entry porch held by square posts set on brick pedestals, a gabled dormer in the center, and two projecting gabled roofs over the porch; brackets and bargeboards enliven the composition. There are also bungalows on the 1200 block of Martin.

6b. Peter & Blanche Col House, 1913
1163 Martin Avenue
Frank Delos Wolfe, architect

This is one of Wolfe's best-known Prairie-style homes. It features strong horizontal lines carried through the stepped rooflines and ribbon window patterns. Details include decorative bas-relief on the eaves, stained glass in the upper transoms, and single tiles set at the end of perpendicular "ribbons" of stucco between windows and on columns.

6c. Ralph and Myrtle Wyckoff House, 1922
310 Sequoia Avenue
Ralph Wyckoff, architect

This Mediterranean stucco-sided, one- and two-story house was designed by the architect for his family.

6d. Hiller House, 1922
1186 Hanchett Avenue
Wolfe & Higgins, architects

This Mediterranean Revival, with its broad Romanesque entry arch, was designed for Stanley Hiller Sr., inventor and aviation pioneer who built his first plane in 1910. After World War I, he came to San Jose and formed the Pacific By-Products Co. for the manufacture of oil and charcoal from nutshells. His son Stanley Hiller Jr. was an extraordinary inventor of things aeronautical and is the namesake of the Hiller Aviation Museum in San Carlos.

6e. Westminster Presbyterian Church, 1926
1100 Shasta Avenue and 1429 The Alameda
Carl Werner, architect

The neo-Gothic church has an arcaded entrance with an upper balcony accented by a smaller-scale arcade, a rose window, and a tile roof.

6f. Bank of Italy Branch, 1927
1445 The Alameda
Henry A. Minton, architect

The Classic Revival building was the first branch bank constructed outside San Jose's central business district.

7. Bocks House, 1923
1645 The Alameda
Herman B. Krause, architect

This formal but eclectic Mediterranean-style house, with a wall relief and hipped tile roof, is among the gracious homes built on The Alameda during the 1920s. Charles O. Bocks was the first to grow cherries on a large scale in the valley.

8. James H. & Marion Pierce House, 1908
1650 The Alameda
Julia Morgan, architect

This L-shaped two-story, simplified Tudor Revival has an arched entry in the corner of the L, intersecting hipped roofs, stucco walls, and grouped windows of delicate leaded glass. This is the only known work by Julia Morgan in San Jose.

6b

9. Grace Spencer Hall House, 1922

1694 The Alameda

William E. Higgins (Wolfe & Higgins), architect

The architect described this stucco-sided house as "Spanish design in every detail." In the center of its otherwise plain symmetrical façade, the entrance bay has an arched front door framed by a rich Churrigueresque design, and an arched window and balcony above. The flat roof is edged with tile.

10. Bogen-Bonetti House, 1907

1794 The Alameda

Wolfe & McKenzie, architects

This is a one-and-one-half story, stucco-sided Bungalow with a side-facing gable roof punctuated by a large gable-roofed dormer. The symmetrical façade has a wide recessed entry flanked by bowed window bays containing distinctive four-over-one sash windows.

11. Rosicrucian Park and Egyptian Museum, 1929–1970s

1342 Naglee Avenue

Nine unique, if not eccentric, Art Deco–style buildings with stylized Egyptian decorative motifs. They surround a five-acre Peace Garden, with wandering pathways, fountains, and statues of pharaohs, animals, gods, and more. The museum building contains a large private collection of Egyptian artifacts, and the planetarium presents public astronomy shows. The complex is owned by the Rosicrucian Order, AMORC, Inc.

Willow Glen

During the late nineteenth century, this area was known as "The Willows" and consisted of small farms. By 1900, a few businesses and a school had been built at Lincoln and Minnesota Avenues. The small community was incorporated in 1927 but was annexed nine years later to the City of San Jose. **Palm Haven,** a subdivision nearby, was laid out in 1913; it was annexed to the city of San Jose in 1922 and is a preservation conservation area.

12. Roberto-Sunol Adobe, "Laura Ville," 1830s, 1847, 1854

770 Lincoln Avenue

This Monterey Colonial has a small adobe on its north side that is thought to have been constructed sometime between 1836 and 1847 by a Mission Indian named Roberto, who received title to Rancho Los Coches in 1844. Antonio Sunol purchased the property in 1847

and built a one-story three-room addition of field-fired brick. In 1853, Augustus Spivalo became the owner; he added three additional ground-floor rooms and a wood-frame second story; in 1854, he sheathed it with clapboard. Around 1900, the home was named "Laura Ville." It narrowly escaped demolition during the construction of Interstate 280. It was restored in the 1970s.

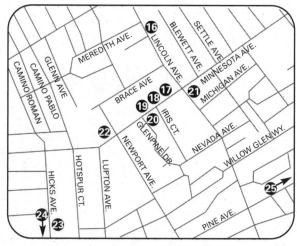

12

13

13. Charles S. Allen House, 1916
901 Plaza Drive

This is a wonderful example of the Prairie style attributed to architect Frank D. Wolfe. It has deep eaves, extremely low-sloped roofs, geometric ribbon windows, and inventive ornamentation.

14. Thomas H. Manning House, 1921
725 Palm Haven Avenue

Henry A. Bridges, designer-builder

Here is a gem of a Craftsman bungalow.

15. Herman B. Krause House, 1919
600 Palm Haven Avenue

Herman B. Krause, designer

Krause, a former sign illustrator and store decorator, launched his career into residential design with his own house. It is Spanish eclectic with a central two-story bay flanked by one-story wings. It has simple stucco finishes, decorative ironwork, and a wrought-iron-and-glass marquis at the front door, recalling the Art Nouveau awnings of the Paris Metro. Krause went on to design houses in the San Jose area throughout the 1920s.

16. Jopson/Buffington House, 1904
1224 Lincoln Avenue

Wolfe & McKenzie, architects

This painted shingle-and-clapboard house is a variation of Queen Anne and Colonial Revival; it has a second-story polygonal bay that looks like a modified tower. The deeply recessed front porch has widely arched beams between round columns with simple Doric-like capitals.

17. Miles Hill House, 1880s
1115 Minnesota Avenue

Miles Hill, who subdivided ninety-six acres here into smaller lots, built this Queen Anne as his home. It has been used commercially since 1921.

18. Paul Clark House, 1912
1147 Minnesota Avenue

Frank D. Wolfe, architect

The superbly horizontal and ornamented Prairie-style house was once home to Paul Clark, first mayor of Willow Glen, and

This commanding Neoclassical house has a two-story temple-front entry portico supported by paired Tuscan columns; the pediment features a Palladian window.

24. Kirk-Farrington House, 1878 (unmapped)
1615 Dry Creek Road

This is an excellent example of a rural 1870s Italianate. Its original owner, Theophilus Kirk, came to Santa Clara County in 1858, owned a large grain farm, and became a successful orchardist. Dorothy Bogen Farrington, a descendent of Kirk, donated the house to the Junior League of San Jose in 1978; it is used for offices and meetings.

25. Ernesto Galarza Elementary School, 2001 (unmapped)
1619 Bird Avenue

Bill Gould Design, architect

A sophisticated elementary school design with an intense color scheme and sculptural complexity also features arched rooflines, a clock tower, and artwork by the students.

his wife, May, an archaeologist and well-known local poet.

19. Edward Maynard House, 1892
1151 Minnesota Avenue

This is an impressive and unusual two-and-one-half-story Victorian-era house with elements of Stick, Queen Anne, and Colonial Revival. A rear four-story corner tower is octagonal-shaped on the third story and is capped by a small rounded fourth story with a conical roof. The elaborate design is said to have come from a pattern book by architect George F. Barber & Co. of Knoxville, Tennessee.

20. Foote House, 1880s
1146 Minnesota Avenue

The simple front-gabled farmhouse was once the home of Horace S. Foote, author of an 1888 history of Santa Clara County titled *Pen Pictures of the Garden of the World.*

21. Home Savings and Loan Association/Washington Mutual Bank, 1971
1402 Lincoln Avenue

Millard Sheets, mural artist

This modernist building and its colorful corner mural represent a 1960s–1970s approach to bank architecture. The clean form and tall proportions of the building are a modernist interpretation of the monumentality and permanence required of bank design, while the mural adds a level of public art and sense of community to the composition.

22. William W. Cozzens House, 1880s
1195 Minnesota Avenue

Adding to the variety of styles that dot this area, this Stick-style house has a wealth of detail.

23. Richards House, circa 1915
1550 Hicks Avenue

Winchester and Stevens Creek Boulevards

26. Santana Row, 2002
Stevens Creek and Winchester Boulevards

StreetWorks, master planner

Backen Arrigoni and Ross, architects

Sandy & Babcock International, architects

SWA and April Phillips, landscape architects

Santana Row is a synthetic traditional downtown in Nuevo Mediterranean Revival. The buildings are set along a simple street and sidewalk grid (parking garages are hidden in the periphery). Outdoor music and games in small public squares provide instant community life, be it anonymous. While the real downtown San Jose, three miles to the east, struggles to thrive, Santana Row is surrounded by gridlock seven days a week as shoppers jockey to find a nearby parking space. This mixed-use shopping center is a must-see for the architectural aficionado.

27. Sarah L. Winchester House, 1886–1922
525 South Winchester Boulevard

Various architects and builders

In 1886, Sarah L. Winchester bought forty-five acres on what is now Winchester Boulevard; the property at that time included an eight- or nine-room house. It is thought that a good portion of construction on the property, which ultimately resulted in a rambling, elegantly detailed, 160-room Queen Anne–style mansion, was done after 1898 when she inherited a reported $20 million dollars worth of shares in the Winchester Repeating Arms Company. Prior to that, carpenter J. E. Perkins was employed by Winchester for ten years in the 1890s to do carpentry work. Sarah was known to have used both J. O. McKee and Jacob Lenzen as architects for a variety of projects on her various properties in the 1880s and 1890s. After her death in 1922, the house became a

tourist destination: the Winchester Mystery House.

28. Allison Pontiac, 1966 (unmapped)
4202 Stevens Creek Boulevard

Paul R. Williams, architect

A grand curved wall of glass showcased new Pontiacs and now features Toyotas. It was described in a contemporary article as a "dream dealership" and hailed as ". . . the most beautiful and efficient automobile dealership in the world." It is one of the few buildings in Northern California designed by Los Angeles–based architect Paul R. Williams (1894–1980). He had a prolific career from 1921 to 1973 and is now considered one of the nation's greatest African American architects. This building remains largely unaltered.

29. Sylvester Graves House, 1868 (unmapped)
4146 Mitzi Drive

This substantial Italianate and its grounds were illustrated in the 1876 Thompson & West Atlas of Santa Clara County.

11 • West San Jose: Winchester and Stevens Creek Boulevards

East San Jose

1. East San Jose Carnegie Library, 1907
1102 East Santa Clara Street

Jacob Lenzen & Son (Theodore Lenzen), architects

This Classical Revival–style library building is the older of the remaining two (of five) original buildings in Santa Clara County (the other one is in Gilroy) and the only one that has been used continuously as a library. In the early 1980s, it was expanded by city architect Omar Baltan.

2. Church of the Five Wounds, 1918
1375 East Santa Clara Street

John Foley, architect

The striking Manueline-style building replaced a small 1914 chapel, and incorporates portions of Portugal's exhibit at the 1915 Panama-Pacific International Exposition. The church was once the centerpiece of San Jose's Portuguese community.

3. Mexican American Heritage Plaza, 1999
1700 Alum Rock Avenue

Martin Del Campo, Del Campo & Maru, architects

Mark Knoerr, project architect

The simplicity of colorful wall surfaces creates a backdrop for the marvelous open plaza that is the heart of this complex. Rhythmic forms include square-post colonnades, long balconies with wide rectangular openings (unabashedly simple), broad red-tile roofs, long wall planes, and the distinctive parade of flagpoles.

4. Mark's Hot Dogs, 1936
48 South Capitol Avenue

This hot dog stand in the shape of a giant orange is similar to the roadside stands once numerous along Highway 99. Architectural historian Alan Hess calls the style "Googie." It was moved to this location in 2003.

5. History Park at Kelley Park
1650 Senter Road, at Phelan Avenue

Located at the southern end of Kelley Park is a collection of twenty-seven structures that tells the story of Santa Clara Valley's past. Some of the buildings are original, others reconstructed. Buildings in the park include an authentic fruit barn, a relocated 1870 one-room schoolhouse, a scale model of the city's Light Tower, reproductions of a local livery, a historic hotel, a Bank of Italy branch, and a large number of relocated Victorian residences. Among the historic houses is one that belonged to photographer, artist, and environmentalist Andrew P. Hill, and one that was home to the poet Edwin Markham.

Of particular interest is the **Ng Shing Gung** [5], originally built in San Jose's Heinlenville Chinatown in 1888 and replicated with original façade components as a museum of local Chinese history.

6. Oak Hill Memorial Cemetery, established 1850s
Monterey Road at Curtner Avenue

Oak Hill Memorial Park is an early American cemetery where many pioneers important to the region's history are buried. Headstones and mausoleums offer a wide range of funerary architecture and sculpture, from Classic, Romanesque, Gothic, and Egyptian to Modern, with a variety of ethnic influences. Two buildings of particular architectural interest include the following:

6a. Chapel of Roses, 1933

Francis H. Slocombe, architect

This is one of the most elaborate and uniquely detailed examples of the English Tudor style in San Jose. The building has a prominent complex gable and a hip faux-thatch roof of wood shingles, with multiple small dormers and an unusual colonnaded corner tower that is rather Romanesque in form. Picturesque stonework is scattered across the stucco wall surface, along with hewn half-timbering. The chapel has a large rose window.

6b. Great Mausoleum, 1928

Albert Roller, architect

From its hilltop site overlooking San Jose, this large imposing edifice has a central two-story, triple-arched entrance bay topped by a large circular drum-like cupola, punctuated by a continuous open arched arcade, and a domed red-tile roof. Symmetrical wings, with double arched windows set within arched surrounds, flank the entrance.

7. Dolce Hayes Mansion/Hotel, 1904 (unmapped)

200 Edenvale Avenue

George W. Page, architect

Dennis Meidinger, architect (additions and restoration, 1994)

Rising from the center of the symmetrical composition, and behind a porte cochere with arched openings, is a four-story square tower with a hipped tile roof. The house is substantial, multi-winged, and an eclectic mass of Mission, Italian Renaissance, and Colonial Revival. It was built for the Chynoweth family, who operated the local newspaper. Owned by the city of San Jose since 1983, it was the Hayes Renaissance Conference Center before becoming a hotel.

8. St. Francis of Assisi Catholic Church, 1999

5111 San Felipe Road

Goodwin Steinberg, Steinberg Group, architect

This modern church complex has strong Gothic references. Tall and steeply pointed arched metal roofs form a cross between one-story glazed corner bays, with hipped roofs and wide eaves. The tall arched sections are glazed with elongated Gothic-like tracery.

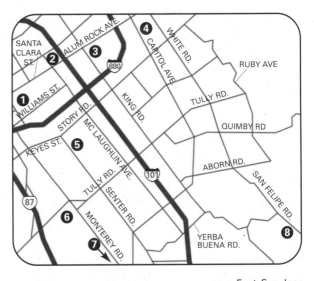

11 • East San Jose

12 · Alviso · Milpitas

Alviso

Before the railroad bypassed Alviso in the mid-1860s, the town had served as the port and point of transportation for Santa Clara Mission and the pueblo of San Jose. The small community is located on a navigable slough at the very south end of San Francisco Bay. It is named for Ignacio Alviso, who received a land grant for Rincon de Los Esteros in 1838.

The town was laid out in 1849, incorporated in 1852, and a post office opened in 1862. Although quite separate from central San Jose, it was annexed to the city in 1968. For decades it has been a backwater type of place, but the city is fast encroaching. The center of town is listed on the National Register as a Historic District and the marshland to the north is a wildlife refuge.

1. Tilden-Laine House, 1887
970 Elizabeth Street
Theodore Lenzen, architect

The elegant classic Italianate home is the most prominent building in town. It has a side entry porch and a two-story angled window bay. Next door, Tilden operated a grocery store in the now-crumbling commercial building thought to have been built in 1865.

2. Martin/Vahl House, 1860s
1080 Catherine Street

This is a two-story, vernacular clapboard-sided cottage with a covered porch on two sides.

3. South Bay Yacht Club, 1903
Northeast corner of Hope and Taylor Streets

Founded in 1888, the clubhouse was constructed with volunteer labor and donated materials. It is an informal frame building with board-and-batten siding, a distinctive cupola with windows on four sides, and a second-story sunroom dormer overlooking the slough. The design is attributed to member and architect J. O. McKee.

4. Wade Warehouse, 1860s
1657 El Dorado Street

This is among the earliest brick buildings still standing in the county and is a reminder of the era when Alviso was the main shipping port for Santa Clara County. The Wade house, built in the 1850s and now unused, is located east of the warehouse.

Milpitas

Founded around 1850 and incorporated in 1954, Milpitas (meaning "little cornfield") was a small agricultural community for much of its existence. After Ford Motor Company built an assembly plant here in 1955, the population more than quadrupled by the 1960s. Today the population is approximately 63,000.

5. Jose Maria Alviso Adobe, 1837, 1853 (unmapped)
Terminus of
Alviso Adobe Court
(off Piedmont Road,
south of East
Calaveras Boulevard)

Jose Maria Alviso, grantee of Rancho Milpitas, originally constructed this building as a one-story adobe in 1837. The wood-frame second story was added in 1853 and includes a wraparound *corredore* (porch), making the building an excellent example of the Monterey style. It is now owned by the city of Milpitas and is under restoration. It is listed on the National Register of Historic Places.

6. Milpitas City Hall, 2002
455 East Calaveras Boulevard
STUDIOS Architecture

Curves of stone and ribbons of windows intersect in this deconstructivist building that is a prominent civic presence. Within a vocabulary of lines and arcs, a rotunda is expressed on the interior and exterior; the variety of materials is united by articulated grids of differing sizes that consist of expansion joints, stone seams, and window mullions.

7. Milpitas Grammar School, 1916
160 North Main Street

Frank Delos Wolfe, architect

The stucco-sided building has a three-part Classic composition with a temple-front entry portico. At each side is a projecting wing with richly framed grouped window bays. After the school closed in 1954, the building served as the first city hall, the library, and a community center; it is currently part of a plan to become the centerpiece of the new 60,000-square-foot Milpitas Library.

8. Renselaer J. Smith House, 1915
163 North Main Street
Frank Delos Wolfe,
architect

A Prairie-style house, which served as both home and doctor's office, has heavily textured stucco siding and a huge projecting, covered front porch with large square openings; it is quite geometric and simple in its detailing. The Mid-Peninsula Housing Coalition relocated the house to the corner of the site in 2006 to become a part of the DeVries Place senior-housing complex.

12 • Milpitas

5

13 · Santa Teresa Park · New Almaden

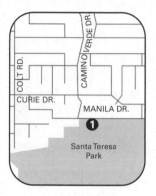

13 • Santa Teresa Park

Santa Teresa Park

1. Bernal-Gulnac-Joice House, circa 1860
372 Manila Drive

The compact, vernacular-style house was the home of the Bernal family and their descendants for 120 years. Rufina Bernal (granddaughter of Rancho Santa Teresa founder José Joaquín Bernal) and Carlos Gulnac raised their family here.

Their daughter Susan married Patrick F. Joice in 1894, and the Joices continued to operate their family cattle business on the ranch until 1980. The ranch compound is now part of the Santa Clara County Park system and is open to the public.

New Almaden

Historic District

The quicksilver mine at New Almaden, located in the hills at the southern end of the Almaden Valley, was California's earliest and largest mercury mining operation. Mining began in 1845, and the mines produced quicksilver of greater total value than any other in California. The Hacienda at New Almaden is the only one of three residential settlements that remains. It was during the Barron, Forbes

Company ownership between 1846 and 1863 that most of the structures in the historic district were constructed. The Quicksilver Mining Company operated the mines between 1863 and 1912.

2. Casa Grande (Mine Manager's House), 1855
21350 Almaden Road
Francis Meyers, builder

In most company towns, including the Hacienda at New Almaden, the home of the company manager was usually the most imposing and prominently located structure. New Almaden was no different, and Casa Grande, the home of the general manager, is a massive two- and three-story Gothic Revival residence built of brick and originally stuccoed with a faux-stone texture. In 1997, the county purchased Casa Grande, and it now houses the New Almaden Quicksilver Mining Museum.

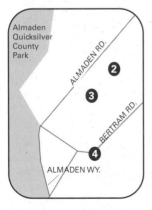

Almaden Quicksilver County Park

ALMADEN RD.

BERTRAM RD.

ALMADEN WY.

2
3
4

13 • New Almaden

3. Hacienda Cottages, 1847–1858
21472–21700 Almaden Road

The company-owned cottages built along Almaden Road represent several vernacular architectural styles. The earliest are constructed of adobe (21570, 21590, and 21600 Almaden Road), which date from the late 1840s. Between circa 1855 and 1858, numerous frame cottages were built on Almaden Road; these were mostly simple gable-roofed, board-and-batten struc-

tures with six-over-six-light windows. House #1 at 21472 Almaden Road was used by upper management and is more high style than most; it has clapboard siding and Greek Revival details. House #24–26 at 21744 Almaden Road was constructed as a triplex. The cottage known as Bulmore House at 21560 Almaden Road [3] is brick construction, often mistaken as adobe. The Hacienda had its own brick-yard where the bricks were made for Casa Grande, Bulmore House, and those used for furnaces and other mining buildings.

4. St. Anthony's Church, circa 1899
21800 Bertram Road

This Shingle-style church, with a gable roof and battered walls, has small lancet, multi-paned windows. It is a smaller version of a traditional cruciform church.

14 · South Santa Clara County: Morgan Hill, San Martin, Gilroy

Morgan Hill

Morgan Hill began as a rail-road stop (originally named Huntington) in 1898, near the 4,500-acre ranch of Hiram Morgan and Diana (Murphy) Hill. She had inherited a portion of the 9,000-acre Rancho Ojo de Aqua de la Coche from her father, Daniel Murphy, the youngest son of early pioneer Martin Murphy Sr. Incorporated in 1906, the town continues to serve as an agricultural center, even though its population is more than 33,000.

1. Morgan Hill Grammar School, 1924
410 Llagas Road

William H. Weeks, architect

The school served the Morgan Hill community until 1987. Faced with demolition, it was cut into fourteen sections and moved to its present location, where it reopened in 2002 as the Carden Academy. Although some original building material was lost, the one-story, stucco-sided, tile-roofed building, with its symmetrical façade, row of arched windows, and flanking gable-faced wings, evokes the feeling of the original school.

2. Villa Mira Monte/ Morgan Hill House, 1886
17860 North Monterey Road

Jacob Lenzen & Son, architects

The symmetrical Stick-style cottage has a broad three-sided veranda, tall hipped roof with two gabled dormers on each side and a small gable dormer in the center, and a bit of half-timbering. It was constructed on Rancho Ojo de Aqua de la Coche. Restoration was completed by the Morgan Hill Historical Society in 1998; the house is open to the public.

3. Britton Middle School Auditorium, 1931
80 West Central Avenue

John J. Donovan, architect

Here is a symmetrical Classic Moderne–style auditorium with glass-block windows set into a curved corner.

4. Votaw Block, 1905
17400 Monterey Road

Frank L. Merrill, builder

Faced with concrete, which was scored and rusticated to look like stone, the two-story commercial building is Classic Revival but without specific Classic details.

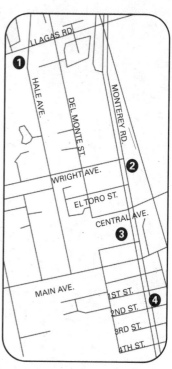

14 • South Santa Clara County: Morgan Hill

San Martin

When the unincorporated town of San Martin was established in 1895, it consisted of eight blocks adjacent to the Southern Pacific Railroad. A year later, it had a post office and a telephone, telegraph, and express office. With a population of 4,200, San Martin has a rural atmosphere. The streets are broad, there are no sidewalks or other street improvements, there are many mature trees, and the buildings are generously spaced.

5. Machado School, 1895
15130 Sycamore Drive

Charles Smith, builder

The Neoclassic-style school was constructed on land donated by Barney and Mary Frances (Murphy) Machado. In 1910, the school was enlarged so that it could accommodate eight grades. The school served the community until 1967, when it fell into disrepair. In the early 1980s, it was restored and members of the community added the bell tower. It is now Paradise Valley/ Machado Elementary.

6. San Martin Presbyterian Church, 1904
13200 Lincoln Avenue

William Binder, architect

The church has a large oculus window under a wide gable roof, curved knee braces at the front entry portico, heavy exposed rafter tails, and an elegantly proportioned low steeple. The pews are from a church in San Luis Obispo, and are said to have "come around the horn."

Gilroy

Gilroy, the most southern city in Santa Clara County, was incorporated in 1870. Located at the foot of the valley where the foothills of the Diablo Range and the Santa Cruz Mountains converge, the city was established at the crossroads of El Camino Real and the road to the Central Valley over Pacheco Pass. With more than 41,000 residents, the city is surrounded by rural agricultural land. Gilroy is known for the production of food products, especially garlic. Many of Gilroy's finest buildings were designed by William H. Weeks, who began his career in Watsonville, just over Hecker Pass in Santa Cruz County. Plaques on many downtown buildings give their history.

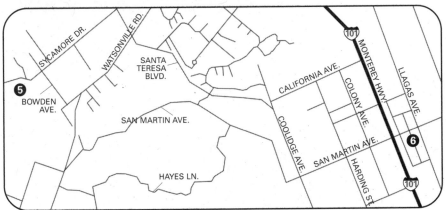

14 • South Santa Clara County: San Martin

7

Historic District

7. Paul H. Cordes House, 1912 (unmapped)
10550 Watsonville Road

Frank Delos Wolfe, architect

The house is an exceptional example of a high-style, one- and one-half-story Craftsman bungalow, with a grand wrap-around porch and river-stone porch posts. Photos of the house appeared in *Architect and Engineer* in February 1914. Some outbuildings on the property date from the nineteenth century.

8. Strand Theater, 1921
7588 Monterey Street

Reid Bros., architects

Although the theater has lost its elegant interior and front mar-quee, the Neoclassic building is of architec-tural interest on Gilroy's main street.

9. Gilroy Bowl, 1958
7554 Monterey Street

This stripped-down industrial Moderne

with an unadorned façade and angled storefront is accented by the cursive lettering of the neon sign.

10. First National Bank of Gilroy, 1912
7488–7490 Monterey Street, at Martin Street

William Binder, architect

This two-story bank building features a pair of recessed, fluted,

two-story columns and Neoclassical design motifs, including a triglyph cornice, a classical pediment over the front door, and transoms above the main windows.

11. Gilroy City Hall, 1905
7400 Monterey Street

Wolfe & McKenzie, architects

The former City Hall is Gilroy's most famous landmark, a unique blend of finials, complex curved red-tile roofs, projecting bays, a bell tower with an open octagonal cupola, and round-, oval-, and arch-shaped windows. It has a ground floor of rusticated stonework. It has been described as "Flemish" or "Baroque" but perhaps could best be labeled "exuberant eclectic." The unusual and prominent building served as Gilroy's City Hall for more than half a century. Damaged in the Loma Prieta Earthquake, the building was restored, and it now serves as the New Renaissance Center. It is listed on the National Register of Historic Places.

12. Southern Pacific Depot, 1918
7250 Monterey Street

Southern Pacific House Architects

The Mission Revival, former Southern Pacific Railroad depot now serves as Gilroy's transit center. The two-story building has a symmetrical façade, with projecting corner bays that rise above the side-facing tiled roof somewhat like towers. Across the central section on the second story is a band of windows. The station is a reminder of the importance the railroad had in the founding of the city of Gilroy.

13. Barshinger & Son Mortuary, 1928
129 Fourth Street

William H. Weeks, architect

This Spanish Eclectic–style building is just one of many in the area that were designed by William H. Weeks.

14. Fifth Street

Fifth Street has an excellent variety of different architectural styles from the 1850s to the 1930s. A self-guided walking-tour brochure for this area is available at the Gilroy Historical Museum, 195 Fifth Street. Highlights of this area include the following structures:

14a. Gilroy Fire Station, 1916
55 Fifth Street

William Binder, architect

This boldly detailed brick building, with its arched ribbon of second-floor windows, served as the fire station until 1978.

14b. Clarence Weaver House, 1900
60 Fifth Street

William H. Weeks, architect

A classically detailed Queen Anne house near the main street served as both the family residence and Weaver's dental office.

In 1978, the house was restored by the Mussallem Development Corporation under the direction of Bruce Nyberg, a Watsonville architect.

14c. Christian Church, 1857
160 Fifth Street

This is the oldest church in Gilroy. Originally located at the corner of Church and Third Streets, it was moved to its present location in 1886. At that time, some Victorian elements, new façade siding, a small rear addition, and a bell tower were added to the simple Greek Revival.

14d. Carnegie Library/Gilroy Historical Museum, 1910
195 Fifth Street

William H. Weeks, architect

This Neoclassical jewel box served as Gilroy's library until 1975. Now the Gilroy Historical Museum, it is an excellent small-town museum.

14e. Eustice House, circa 1869
213 Fifth Street

The Gothic Revival cottage, with its symmetrical façade and covered front porch (partially enclosed), is similar to other older buildings in the neighborhood.

14f. United Presbyterian Church, 1869
214 Fifth Street

William Furlong, builder

Although modifications have been made over time, this remains a fine example of Carpenter Gothic architecture.

The first Presbyterian church in the area was constructed in

1859 in the community of San Ysidro; it is still standing at 6780 Holsclaw Road but is now used as a residence.

14g. Wheeler Hospital, 1929
650 Fifth Street

William H. Weeks, architect

The Mediterranean Revival–style hospital, with tiles produced by S&S Tile of San Jose, was designed to have the very latest in health-care technology and design innovations. The twelve-inch-diameter roundel tile portraying a stylized flowering plant in a pot is a rare tile, according to tile historian Riley Doty, and was previously seen only in S&S Tile catalogues.

15. Edgar Holloway House, 1903
7539 Eigleberry Street

William H. Weeks, architect

Listed on the National Register of Historic Places, this is a beautifully restored Queen Anne, and is an example of the early residential work of William H. Weeks. The house has a prominent and unusual Dutch gambrel front dormer over a rounded window bay, in addition to its more typically Victorian octagonal corner turret.

IV
Alameda County

Beth Armstrong, author & photographer (1, 2)
Betty Marvin, author & photographer (3, unless otherwise noted)
Gail Lombardi, author & photographer (3, where noted; 4)
Susan Dinkelspiel Cerny, author & photographer (3, where noted; 7)
Woodruff Minor, author & co-photographer (5)
Anthony Bruce, co-author & co-photographer (6)
Susan Dinkelspiel Cerny, co-photographer (5); co-author & co-photographer (6)

Stretching from San Francisco Bay to the Livermore Valley east of the Coast Range, Alameda County was created from portions of Santa Clara and Contra Costa Counties in 1853. The county seat of government was first located in Alvarado followed by San Leandro in 1856, and was relocated to Oakland in 1873.

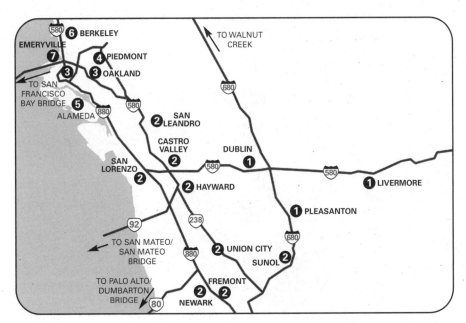

IV • ALAMEDA COUNTY

Sproul Plaza, University of California–Berkeley

1 • Southeast Alameda County: Dublin, Pleasanton, Livermore

The eastern inland area of Alameda County contains almost half of the county's land area, but its high ridges and rolling foothills surrounding the valleys were considered unsuitable for agriculture when the county was formed in 1853.

During the Mission era, thousands of head of cattle from Mission San Jose roamed the area, which contained few human occupants, until the Mexican government created five ranchos that brought permanent residents; with them, small communities developed near the ranch houses.

During the Gold Rush, the roads between Martinez and San Jose, through the Livermore Valley, and east to the gold fields, brought passing travelers. Grain was the main crop until the Martinez–San Ramon railroad was completed in 1891, when more perishable crops could be transported easily to market.

Highway 50, the Lincoln Highway (now 580), from Hayward to Tracy was completed in the 1930s. However, East Alameda County remained rather sparsely populated and rural.

During World War II, the Naval Air Station (now Lawrence Livermore National Laboratory) and Seabee Base (now Camp Parks) were established. After the war, there was not a large influx of postwar residents because it was far from business centers, manufacturing, and jobs. Beginning in the 1960s with the completion of Highway 680, the population

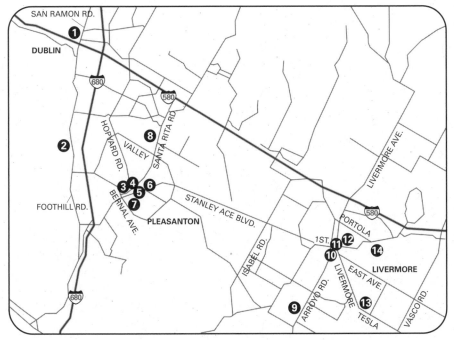

1 • Southeast Alameda County: Dublin, Pleasanton, Livermore

began to increase. In the past twenty years, the area between Dublin and Livermore—the Tri Valley area: San Ramon, Amador, and Livermore—has become fully suburbanized along the freeway corridor with business parks, large retail malls, and all types of housing. However, pockets of agriculture, particularly vineyards, do remain.

Dublin

The community that became Dublin (in San Ramon Valley) began near the headquarters of Rancho San Ramon where Jose Maria Amador manufactured farm tools and wagon parts; this was located approximately where Highways 680 and 580 cross today. The present city, with a population of 30,000, incorporated in 1982. It is a modern one with very little remaining from its past.

1. Murray School–Dublin Heritage Center, 1856
6600 Donlon Way

The Greek Revival wood-frame building with some Gothic touches is one of the oldest remaining schoolhouses in the Bay Area. Classes were held here until 1952. It was moved across the freeway, becoming part of historic Dublin, with Old Street, Raymond's Church, Dublin Pioneer Cemetery, and the Green Store. The bell tower was reconstructed (2003) from photos.

Pleasanton

Pleasanton, incorporated in 1894, began as the community of Alisal near the Bernal family home on Rancho Valle de San Jose. By the 1860s, a racetrack (now part of Alameda County Fairgrounds) was operating. When the transcontinental railroad opened in 1869, the center of commerce shifted

from Dublin to Pleasanton, where grain, hay, hops, and grapes were grown, gravel was mined, and, later, movies were made. Today Pleasanton has a population of 67,000.

2. Alviso Adobe, circa 1854
3461 Old Foothill Road

The exact date of this vernacular one-story adobe building is unknown, but legends linking John C. Frémont to it appear unfounded. By 1860, Francisco Alviso was raising milk cows. In 1919, the Meadowlark Dairy was established, becoming the first certified diary in Alameda County. Today the building is unused, and the surrounding land will be developed.

3. Veteran's Memorial Building, 1932
301 Main Street

Henry H. Meyers & Mildred S. Meyers, architects

Here is a Spanish Revival–style building with a decorated spandrel under its entrance arch that includes the bust of a World War I doughboy. There are colorful tiles under some windows.

4. White Corner–Kolln Hardware Store, 1896
600 Main Street

Charles Bruce, architect-builder

With its corner tower, this two-story Queen Anne–style commercial building is a focal point of Pleasanton's historic business district that also

includes Pleasanton's 1932 signature sign.

5. John W. Kottinger Barn, 1852
200 Ray Street

This adobe brick barn, rare in the Bay Area, also served as a jail after its builder, John Kottinger, was appointed justice of the peace in 1853.

6. Southern Pacific Railroad Depot, 1894
30 West Neal Street

This is a Southern Pacific standard "Two Story Combination Depot #22," where the upper floor served as a residence for the station agent. Used until 1965, it was remodeled for an office and restaurant in 1988.

7. Charles Bruce House, 1896
4636 Second Street

Charles Bruce, architect-builder

Charles Bruce, who designed and built this Queen Anne cottage as his own residence, was a local builder. He also built the house next door at **4672 Second Street** (1910) and the Mission-style bank at **700 Main Street** (1911). Other turn-of-the-nineteenth-century houses are nearby.

8. Century House, 1870s
2401 Santa Rita Road

This Gothic Revival–style cottage was built as a duck-hunting retreat and then used as a farmhouse. Now part of Bicentennial Park, it is located on a site once used by Native Americans.

Livermore

Robert Livermore, for whom the valley and city are named, settled here around 1835. In 1839, he and Jose Noriega were granted the 8,000-acre Rancho de las Positas. Livermore later bought out Noriega's interest. Livermore planted the first grapes in the valley, and wineries continue to flourish. Nearby, Alphonso Ladd built a hotel in 1855, and that area became known as Laddsville. After the Central Pacific Railroad opened in 1869, the town of Livermore was platted next to the tracks. When Livermore was incorporated in 1876, it included the community of Laddsville. With a current population of nearly 73,000, the city is dealing with the effects of rapid growth.

9. Ravenswood, Main House, 1885, 1891
2647 Arroyo Road

Until 1920, Ravenswood was the summer country estate of San Francisco political boss Christopher A. Buckley. A Queen Anne–style cottage built in 1885, it was the family living quarters; the kitchen was located in the tank house behind. A stately Queen Anne "Main House" was built only for entertaining, and contained just two parlors that could be combined for large groups. The grounds had vineyards, a winery, and a carriage house. Restored by the Recreation and Parks Department, it is now a house museum and is listed on the National Register.

10. Carnegie Library, 1911
2155 Third Street
William H. Weeks, architect

This Greek Neoclassical library has paired Ionic columns, pilasters, and lion heads on the pediment. A formal garden surrounds the building. Weeks used the same design for libraries in San Leandro (demolished) and Gilroy (still standing). It served as a library until 1966, and now houses the Livermore History Guild's History Center and Art Association's Art Gallery.

11. L. Schenone Building, 1914
2211 First Street
Italio Zanolini, architect

One of Livermore's first reinforced-concrete structures, the building is somewhat Mission Revival in style with a decorated arched parapet in the central bay. Other early-twentieth-century buildings line First Street.

12. Southern Pacific Railroad Depot, 1892
20 South L Street

Used as a train station until 1962, this is the Southern Pacific "Two Story Combination Depot #18" design.

13. Gordon House, 1894
4520 Tesla Road
C. H. Rasmussen, builder

This large Queen Anne, with a square tower, a wraparound porch, and a balcony, was moved from Fourth and K Streets in the 1970s. It sits amicably next to the historic Concannon Winery, the entrance to the historic Livermore wine region.

14. Albert H. Merritt House, 1913
273 Trevarno Road
C. H. Rasmussen, builder

Trevarno Road was the company town of Coast Manufacturing Company, with the homes of the president and vice president at one end, the factory (now an office building) at the other end, and bungalows for the workers in between. The Mission Revival–style house at 273 Trevarno Road has a large enclosed front porch with a shaped parapet and coping; it was the home of the president, Albert H. Merritt. Chinese employees lived on the other side of the factory.

2 · Southwest Alameda County: Fremont, Union City, Newark, Sunol, Hayward, Castro Valley, San Lorenzo, San Leandro

Southwest Alameda County (south of Oakland to Mission San Jose) remained largely rural until after World War II. With the exception of San Leandro and Hayward, incorporated in the 1870s, Fremont, Union City, and Newark were incorporated during the late 1950s by assembling unincorporated towns and communities that grew up near landings, crossroads, and, later, railroad stops; their names still appear on maps. Castro Valley and Sunol remain unincorporated.

Small groups of Ohlone Native Americans once lived in the area. **Coyote Hills Regional Park** (A) and the **Ohlone Cemetery** (B) at Mission San Jose are places where glimpses of Ohlone life may still be seen.

The struggle to balance growth with conservation and preservation is a major concern as the population spreads onto former farm and ranchland.

Fremont

The sprawling city, with a population of 210,000, was incorporated in 1956. It was created by assembling the unincorporated towns of Mission San Jose, Centerville, Irvington, Warm Springs, Niles, and the boundaries of the Alviso School District.

Mission San Jose

Founded in 1797, the town grew up as a rest stop for travelers at the terminus of the Mission/Stockton Pass. The Franciscans grew crops and grazed cattle for the hide and tallow trade with Spain.

1. Mission San Jose, 1809, 1985
43300 Mission Boulevard

Gil Sanchez, architect (reconstruction, 1985)

Founded in 1797 by Father Fermin Francisco de Lasuen, this was the fourteenth Alta California mission. Constructed by Native Americans, its design was based on those by Father Felipe de la Cuesta of San Juan Baptista. The only portion of the old mission that dates from the Spanish era is the priests' living quarters, built in 1809; it is the oldest building in Alameda County. The mission church collapsed in the 1868 earthquake. It was replaced by a smaller wood-frame Gothic church that was moved in 1982 so that the original mission church could be replicated on its original site. The nearby cemetery was used throughout the nineteenth century.

2. Palmdale Estate, circa 1927
159 Washington Boulevard

The Palmdale Estate was begun in the 1850s by agricultural pioneer E. L. Beard and was further developed in the 1880s by Juan Gallegos. This lushly landscaped estate contains two impressive Period Revival houses: the Tudor Revival Starr House, and the Norman Revival Best House. It has been Sisters of the Holy Family convent since 1947.

3. Costa-Faria Farm, 1895–1905
41252 Mission Boulevard

This Queen Anne–style farmhouse, with its barn, tank house, orchard, and pasture, is representative of the area's small farms. It is still owned by the Faria family, who purchased it in 1915.

Centerville

In 1846, a group of Mormons led by Sam Brannan arrived on the ship *Brooklyn;* some settled in this area, where they grew grain and vegetables. The town was established in the early 1850s.

4. Cloverdale Creamery, 1938
37085 Fremont Boulevard

This Moderne-style building housed the production and commercial aspects of the Cloverdale Creamery. The delightful milk-bottle-shaped opening above the door is infilled with glass block and outlined in neon.

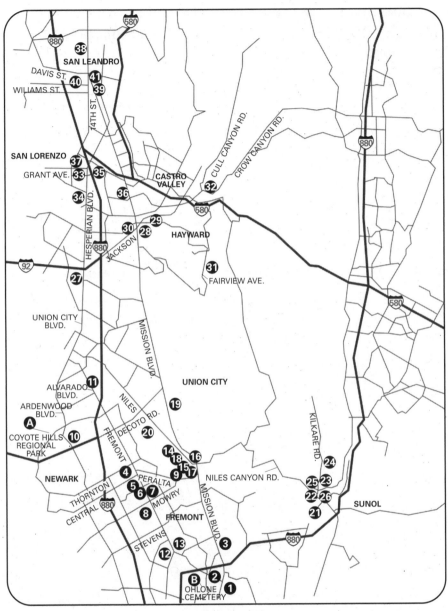

2 • Southwest Alameda County: Fremont, Union City, Newark,
Sunol, Hayward, Castro Valley, San Lorenzo, San Leandro

5. Centerville Garage and Associated Service Station, 1935, 1939
37247 Fremont Boulevard
Miller & Warnecke, architects (1935)

The former service station and automobile showroom was erected in 1935 and the utilitarian machine shop in 1939. Although the gas pumps have been removed and the doors altered, it is a charming example of Spanish Colonial Revival style with an angled bay topped by a faceted tile roof.

6. Bank of Centerville, circa 1906
37251 Fremont Boulevard

The small Italianate-style bank has Classical Revival details.

7. Historic Centerville Train Depot, 1910, 1995
37200 Block of Fremont Boulevard

In 1909, Southern Pacific passenger service arrived in Centerville. The "One Story Combination Depot #23" was built in 1910. Passenger service ended in 1940, and in 1961, the depot was no longer in use. In 1995, it was moved across the tracks and renovated; it is now serving the Amtrak Capital Corridor and ACE lines.

8. Chadbourne Carriage House, circa 1880–1890
39100 Block of Fremont Boulevard

This exceptionally ornate Stick-style carriage house is almost all that is left of the historic Chadbourne farm complex. When a shopping center was built there in 1964, the building was moved closer to the street.

9. James and Lucy Shinn House, 1876
1251 Peralta Boulevard

Shinn Historical Park includes an 1876 Italianate- and Stick-style Victorian villa home (open for tours), a ranch office with attached tank house, several outbuildings, the 1850s Sims Cottage moved from elsewhere on the property, and exotic plants from the family business. James Shinn was an early nurseryman, and the property was given to the city of Fremont by the Shinn family in 1962. Relocated to 1113 Mowry Avenue is the **Millicent Shinn House,** designed by architect Lillian Bridgman and built around 1916. Millicent Shinn was the first woman to earn a PhD from the University of California–Berkeley and was a noted child psychologist.

10. Ardenwood/ George W. Patterson House, 1857, 1889
34600 Ardenwood Boulevard
Samuel Newsom, architect (1889)

After George W. Patterson abandoned gold mining, he made a fortune in farming. At the time of his death in 1895, he owned more than 6,000 acres. Ardenwood, now a City and East Bay Regional Park, consists of Patterson's house, farm buildings, and a horse-car railroad. The house, originally a simple farmhouse built in 1857, became a large Queen Anne in 1889, with an addition designed by Samuel Newsom; there are Romanesque influences, including an arched entry and floral motifs. The porch and kitchen wings were added between 1910 and 1914. Tours are available.

11. Sylvester P. Harvey House, 1854, 1868
3590 Grand Lake Drive

The Gothic Revival–style farmhouse sits in the center of a city park. It features a one-story porch with a balustrade, shallow arches between the supports, quoins, and finials at the gable peaks, as well as an attached 1854 cabin. The 100-acre Harvey family farm operated until 1975.

Irvington

This area had its beginnings when a saloon was built at a five-corner crossroad that was once known as Washington Corners, or simply "The Corners." The **Irvington Community Center** (1995; ELS Architects) is a glass, stucco, and vertical-wood-sided building with crisp utilitarian lines.

12. Clark's Hall, 1876
4002 Bay Street

This two-story Italianate-style commercial building, originally a public hall and store, is the oldest commercial building standing in Fremont; it is located on one of the corners of the historic "five corners" intersection. The building has undergone changes over the years but retains windows and doors with segmental arches, and some iron shutters from 1889.

13. Hiram Davis House,
circa 1854; restored, 1974
40846 High Street

This is a small one-story, side-gabled vernacular farmhouse with a front porch covered by a shed roof held by curved brackets that may have been added. The surrounding land was recently developed with faux farmhouses; the barn and tank house are not original.

Warm Springs

This was the name of the Central Pacific Railroad station near the warm springs used by the Ohlone. A resort was established here prior to 1869. The community of Harrisburg/Peacock was nearby. Very little remains of the historic community.

Niles

This area was platted by the Central Pacific Railroad in 1869 and was named after a railroad attorney. It was adjacent to . Vallejo's Mills—the settlement that grew near the flourmill of José de Jesús Vallejo, the older brother of General Mariano Vallejo—and the entrance to Niles Canyon. Gravel quarrying was an early industry; movies were made here in the 1910s.

14. Vallejo Adobe, circa 1842
36501 Niles Boulevard

The Vallejo Adobe was built soon after José Vallejo was granted Rancho Arroyo de la Alameda in 1842. The simple one-story, whitewashed gable-roofed building is located in the California Nursery Historic Park.

15. Essanay Studio Bungalow, 1912
37374 Second Street

Ten rustic Craftsman bungalows were built by the Essanay Film Manufacturing Company for actors and technicians in 1912. The least altered is 37374 Second Street, which has diamond-shaped transom windows in the middle bay and above the side windows. Among the films the Essanay Film Manufacturing Company produced was *Bronco Billy* with Charlie Chaplin and Wallace Beery.

16. Niles Railroad Depot, 1901
36995 Mission Boulevard
J. D. Isaacs, draftsman

The Southern Pacific depot is notable for its open waiting platform covered by a hipped roof held by round columns, and for its classic details. Originally, a

garden of ferns and palm trees surrounded the building. Closed in 1974, it was moved from downtown Niles in 1984 to this location, and houses the Tri City Society of Model Engineers.

17. Butt House, 1889
37899 Third Street

The richly ornamented Victorian-era farmhouse has both Stick and Queen Anne features. Second and Third Streets have the largest concentration of nineteenth- and early-twentieth-century houses in Fremont.

18. Niles School, 1939, 1947
37141 Second Street
John J. Donovan, architect

The Colonial Revival–style Niles School is the most intact of the three remaining pre–World War II school buildings in Fremont. The quatrefoil window in the front gable lends interest and gives it a Mission flavor. The setting is enhanced by mature landscaping. John J. Donovan also designed the **Clough Library** at 150 "I" Street.

Union City

Created by combining the towns of Alvarado and Decoto, Union City was incorporated in 1959 and has a population of 67,000.

Alvarado was settled in the early 1850s, and it was the location of Alameda County's first seat of government between 1853 and 1856. Alvarado was also the location of the first sugar beet industry in California, established in 1870, which continued off and on until the 1960s. Salt making was also an important industry. There are many late-nineteenth- and early-twentieth-century houses in the old district.

Decoto was surveyed in 1870 by the Decoto Land Company for the Central Pacific Railroad. Though numerous trees were set out, the town was slow to develop. The major industry was shipping agricultural products. Despite its early settlement, few early structures remain.

19. The Masonic Home for Adults, founded 1898
34400 Mission Boulevard

William Mooser II, architect

The Masonic Home was founded in 1898 by the Grand Lodge of Free and Accepted Masons of the State of California. The Mediterranean-style administration building with its north wing (1922) and south wing (1928) replaced the original 1898 building; it can be seen above Mission Boulevard. The building and the 200-acre complex is approached along a tree-lined road. Renovations and retrofitting were completed by the Ratcliff Architects in 2001.

20. John H. Peterson Farm, 1884
35261 Alvarado-Niles Road, on Quarry Lakes Drive

One of the last farm complexes remaining in the area is owned by the state of California. The property includes a large Queen Anne farmhouse with an ornate two-story main section and a utilitarian one-story kitchen wing, a tank house, and a barn set among mature trees, a large patch of prickly pear cactus, and surrounding unused fields.

Newark

In 1876, the Pacific Land Investment Company, land agent for the Pacific Coast Railroad, acquired a town site from a developer; the railroad built maintenance shops and soon a town grew nearby. Early industries included railroad car manufacturing, a foundry, and salt production. While the old industrial buildings are gone, a fringe of older structures remains downtown. A housing development spreading north of downtown, residential tracts, and their decade-by-decade progress can be observed as the style of houses changes. Newark was incorporated in 1955 and has a population of 43,000.

Sunol

Sunol is an unincorporated community at the eastern end of Niles Canyon. It is still small, with a population of only 1,500. The area was first settled by Antonio Maria Sunol, who built an adobe for his cattle operation. The Central Pacific Railroad's transcontinental line initially came through Niles Canyon and Sunol in 1869 (to avoid the watery Delta) on its way to its terminus in Oakland.

21. Sunol Water Temple, 1910, 2000
505 Paloma Way

Willis Polk, architect

The Spring Valley Water Company (now San Francisco Municipal Water Company) built this elegant temple structure to mark the joining of water

from various local sources. The structure was inspired by the Temple of Vesta at Tivoli, Italy. The open, classically inspired, raised temple form is thirty-six feet in diameter, with twelve fluted columns that support a domed roof, topped with a bronze finial against which four bronze dolphins rest. The temple is open from 9 a.m. to 3 p.m. weekdays.

22. Sunol Railroad Depot, circa 1884, 1998
6 Kilkare Road, at Main Street

This Southern Pacific "One Story Combination Depot #7" was moved in 1941. It was then used as a restaurant and, later, a residence. In 1998, it was returned to the railroad tracks and is now the depot for the Pacific Locomotive Association's Niles Canyon Railway, which runs a volunteer-operated excursion train through Niles Canyon.

23. Elliston, 1890
463 Kilkare Road

Henry Hiram Ellis, designer

Built of stone quarried in Niles Canyon, this grand Richardsonian Romanesque–style house is a rarity in this area. Ellis, a California pioneer, built it as his retirement home, where he planted vineyards and olive orchards. Other houses on the grounds were built for his children.

24. Thomas Foxwell Bachelder Barn, 1888
1011 Kilkare Road

This substantial vernacular stone barn is built of sandstone from the creek across the road. It is a "bank barn," set against the hillside where hay can be carted to the second floor for storage; it is an unusual type of barn for the Bay Area as it was mostly used for wineries in Napa Valley. The façade appears original, and includes a sliding wood door; in the gable is a medallion that states "T. F. Bachelder 1888."

25. Welch-Apperson House, 1880
86 Kilkare Road

This large Queen Anne has a three-story tower with a conical roof. It was purchased in 1889 by Elbert Apperson, brother of Phoebe Apperson Hearst.

Kilkare Road continues along Sinbad Creek and ends at Pleasanton Regional Park. The rural setting that attracted early settlers and, later, summer visitors can still be enjoyed. **Kilkare Woods,** an enclave of summer log cottages built during the 1920s, still survives.

26. Sunol Glen School, 1926
11601 Main Street

William H. Weeks, architect

Although additional buildings have been added to the campus, the original Mediterranean-style school remains, with three original classrooms and their cloakrooms, transoms, and multipaned windows. The old gymnasium/auditorium, with stage, projection booth, and original chandeliers, is used by a community theater group.

Hayward

In 1851, William Hayward settled on land that was part of Guillermo Castro's Rancho San Lorenzo, close to Castro's adobe home. After Castro laid out a town site in 1854, Hayward built a hotel and store. The city of Hayward was incorporated in 1876; the unincorporated communities of Mt. Eden and Russellville were annexed in the 1950s. Today, its population is 140,000.

27. Oliver House/Mt. Eden Mansion, circa 1918
2451 West Tennyson Road

Wolfe and Higgins, architects

This is an unusually grand, two-story Prairie-style house with a symmetrical façade, a yellow-brick foundation, and strong horizontal lines accented by deep eaves and a parapet. Adjacent to the house is a cubistic stepped water-tank structure.

28. Old City Hall, 1930
22738 Mission Boulevard

E. P. Whitman, architect

This is a truly unique Art Deco–style building with a grand, central two-story arched entry flanked by a pair of over-scaled pilasters, with large protruding abacuses and topped by snakes winding around torches. Between these are enormous rams' heads. Above the entrance door is a frieze panel featuring toga-clad figures with farm implements.

29. Bank Building, 1927
1004 B Street

The Hermann Safe Company, designer

Here is a Greek Revival–style bank building that has Doric columns, Greek key designs, and details highlighted in blue.

30. Hayward Emporium, 1899
808 B Street

This is a nicely preserved, vernacular, two-story commercial building with rustic siding, a recessed entry, transoms, and a pediment that bisects the parapet. The interior is largely intact, including a creaking wood floor. Nearby are several late-nineteenth-century houses.

31. C. W. Tarkington House–Butterfly House, 1964
26800 Fairview Avenue

N. Kent Linn, designer

This mid-century Modern two-story house of glass and cedar siding has curving concrete steps up to the deck, and stands out in the neighborhood because of its flared paraboloid roof made of corrugated metal covered by a waterproof membrane.

Castro Valley

This valley was also part of Guillermo Castro's Rancho San Lorenzo. The fertile soil drew farmers in the 1850s and, later, chicken farming became popular. The community initially grew up next to the Hayward-Dublin road. The town has a population of 57,000, but remains unincorporated.

32. Greenridge, 1960
Greenridge and Highwood Roads

Eichler Homes, Inc., builder

Joseph Eichler used mass production to bring architect-designed contemporary modern homes to the middle class. Influenced by Frank Lloyd Wright, he used walls of glass to bring the outdoors inside, made possible by post-and-beam construction methods. This largely intact 200-home development is the only Eichler project in southern Alameda County.

San Lorenzo

San Lorenzo is located north of San Lorenzo Creek and was known as Squattersville in the 1850s because of the numerous squatters. San Lorenzo includes the former unincorporated areas of Four Corners (Hesperian and Lewelling Boulevards), Ashland,

Cherryland, and San Lorenzo Village. The area was once known for its fertile soil and proximity to transportation at Robert's Landing. Today San Lorenzo is noted as a planned community of moderately priced housing, built just after World War II.

33. San Lorenzo Community Church, 1946
945 Paseo Grande

Bruce Goff, architect

Built during World War II at Camp Parks Seabee Base, McGann Chapel was purchased when the base closed in 1947, and was moved to this location. Constructed of Quonset huts and brick with protruding mortar, this is a rare nonutilitarian use of an almost vanished building type.

34. Neal McConaghy House, 1886
18701 Hesperian Boulevard, Hayward

John Haas Sr., builder

The Stick-style Victorian-era home and its carriage and tank house are located in a park and operated as a museum. A member of the McConaghy family lived here until 1972.

Cherryland

South of San Lorenzo Creek, Cherryland roughly approximates the land holdings of William Meek, whose nearly 3,000-acre estate was subdivided over several decades beginning in 1911.

35. William Meek Mansion, 1868; with addition, circa 1907
Hampto and Boston Roads, Hayward

This is truly a grand Italianate-style villa with asymmetrical massing, a three-story square tower glazed on all sides, and a mansard roof with flared eaves; there are quoins, brackets, and etched window glass framing the front door. William Meek, along with partner Lewelling, helped establish the horticulture industry in the area. The mansion, fountain, carriage house (1900), and caretaker's house are located in a ten-acre public park.

36. The Burr House, 1911
636 Grove Way, Hayward
Frank Delos Wolfe, architect

This large two-story stucco-sided house is truly eclectic, containing elements of Craftsman, Prairie, and Mission styles. It is located in the first subdivision of the Meek Estate, which featured cement sidewalks, macadam streets, and family orchards on large plots.

Ashland

This area grew during the 1870s into a community along Ashland and Kent Avenues. A number of Portuguese settled here; their social IDES Hall is located on Kent Avenue. The area is mostly post–World War II housing developments.

San Leandro

San Leandro comprises land that was part of both Rancho San Leandro and Rancho San Antonio. During the Gold Rush, squatters planted grain and vege-tables here. In 1856, the county seat was moved from Alvarado to San Leandro, where it remained until 1873 when it was moved to Oakland. Along with crops, bay-shore oyster beds were an economic mainstay. Many Portuguese settled in the area and San Leandro became a center for their religious, frater-nal, and beneficial organizations. The town was incorporated in 1872 and today has a population of 79,000.

37. Capt. William Roberts House, before 1878
526 Lewelling Boulevard

Capt. Roberts, an early resident of Squattersville, built one of the first American-era landings in the East Bay. The site of Roberts' Landing is at the end of Lewelling Boulevard. The his-toric Roberts house was built before 1878 and can be seen from the freeway.

38. Peralta House, 1860, 1875, 1909
561 Lafayette Avenue

A pair of old magnolia trees stand in front of the brick Italianate built by W. P. Toler for his father-in-law, Ignacio Peralta, the grantee of Rancho San Antonio. It is reportedly the first brick house in southern Alameda County. A porch and a wood-frame addition were added in 1875; the brick received a coat of stucco in 1909. The house became the Alta Mira Club in 1926.

39. Best Building, 1911
1300 East Fourteenth Street
William H. Weeks, architect

One of the few intact early-twentieth-century buildings in San Leandro, this Beaux-Arts building is decorated with swags and cow skulls, pilasters with Ionic capitals, and a working clock; the letter "B" appears in numerous cartouches.

40. Southern Pacific Railroad Depot, 1898, 1924
801 Davis Street and 1302 Orchard Avenue

San Leandro's second train depot is similar to a "One Story Combination Depot #23." Passenger service was discontinued after World War II. In 1988, it was moved to this location, and now houses the San Leandro Historical Railroad Society.

41. Medical offices, 1953, 1960
333 Estudillo Avenue
Hechiro Yuasa, architect (1960)

The exuberant Moderne-style medical/office building has a tall stepped spire with rectan-gular and round sections, and a rounded glazed corner. It provides a bit of Space Age whimsy to the neighborhood.

3 · Oakland

Central Oakland

Oakland's first town plat was oriented around the foot of Broadway; water transportation and waterfront industry have always been vital to the city's economy. Since the mid-twentieth century, the waterfront has been evolving to more recreational and residential uses.

"Old Oakland" refers to the six blocks bounded by Broadway, Jefferson, Seventh, and Tenth Streets. This 1870s commercial district grew up along the Seventh Street railroad line. For most of the twentieth century, it survived by neglect as new development moved north up Broadway. The shopping district of the late nineteenth and early twentieth centuries, centered at Twelfth and Washington Streets, underwent decades of "misguided improvements" and was cleared with barely a whimper in the 1970s.

The adjoining residential area, once continuous with West Oakland, was disrupted in the 1970s by freeway construction; Preservation Park is a result of that project.

Waterfront

1. Heinold's First and Last Chance Saloon, circa 1880
Foot of Webster Street

One of Oakland's most loved landmarks is a world-renowned shrine to Jack London. Reportedly constructed from an old ship and/or bunkhouse, it originally hung over the water; the land

has grown up around its sunken sloping floor. Nearby is London's 1890s Yukon gold rush cabin, part relocated and part replicated.

2. Jack London Square, 1951 and after
Foot of Broadway

A Port of Oakland redevelopment begun in 1951 to compete with San Francisco's Fisherman's Wharf, the square was largely redone in the late 1980s. A few of the original 1950s–1960s "waterfront contemporary" buildings by Harry Bruno remain, considerably updated: the Grotto, now Kincaid's; the Sea Wolf, now Scott's; and the Boatel, now the Waterfront Plaza Hotel.

3. C. L. Dellums Amtrak Station, 1993–1995
245 Second Street, at Alice Street
VBN Architects

This vaulted glass-and-metal structure is described as "evocative of the grand, turn-of-the-century, wrought iron railroad stations." A statue by Carol Tarzier of labor and civil rights leader C. L. Dellums stands in front.

4. Waterfront Warehouse District, 1914–1932
Third to Fifth Streets, Jackson to Webster Streets

Now mostly converted to apartments and work/live studios, and surrounded by dense new

3 • Central Oakland: Waterfront, Old Oakland, Preservation Park

residential buildings, this area developed from the 1910s along the Third Street Western Pacific and First Street Southern Pacific tracks for processing and shipping foods and building materials. This district was listed on the National Register in 2000. Plaques in the district identify all the buildings.

5. American Bag Company, 1917
228 Harrison Street, at Third Street

Leonard H. Thomas, architect

This mill-type industrial building with outstanding polychrome and three-dimensional brickwork was occupied by the original business for more than seventy years.

6. The Leviathan (Ace Architects office), 1991
330–332 Second Street

Lucia Howard and David Weingarten, Ace Architects

The architects characterize this building as "a maritime assemblage that explodes and recombines parts of ships, sea creatures, and the Alameda Naval Air Station."

7. Wholesale Produce Market, 1916–1917
145–327 Franklin Street, 370–423 Second Street

Charles McCall, architect

The matching canopied and screen-fronted Fruit and Produce Realty Company buildings were developed along the Third Street Western Pacific tracks by a consortium of Old Oakland produce merchants. Neighboring structures were also built or remodeled for produce businesses.

8. Western Pacific Depot, 1909–1910
470–496 Third Street, at Washington Street

W. H. Mohr, architect

Ransome Concrete Co., builder

The arrival of Western Pacific and the opening of a new rail line along Third Street ended Southern Pacific's monopoly along the Oakland waterfront and prompted a burst of industrial and warehouse development. The Neoclassical station became Oakland's first city landmark in 1974 when it was threatened with demolition.

9. Mme. de St. Germain's Oenophile Store, circa 1857
301 Broadway

Except for the cutaway corner, Oakland's oldest brick building is virtually unchanged from an 1860 drawing. Its two neighbors to the north (311–313 and 315–319 Broadway) are only

slightly newer (1861) though camouflaged, as is 131 Broadway (1860).

10. Buswell Block, 1861–1869, 1884
318–334 Broadway

Three 1860s buildings were joined and modernized in the 1880s to revitalize lower Broadway after business was drawn north to the new railroad line on Seventh Street. Together with the four buildings in the previous entry, this is a remarkable survival of Oakland's earliest business district.

11. Police Administration Building, 1959–1962
620 Washington Street, Broadway, and Sixth to Seventh Streets

Confer & Willis, architects

Sleek black granite pilotis (piers) and green amoeba-patterned terra-cotta identify this as a vintage 1960s government building, part of a boom in civic construction in Oakland at that time. The early-1960s Alameda County Probation and Social Service buildings at **400** and **401 Broadway**, by Reynolds & Chamberlain, are two other products of that boom.

Old Oakland

12. Oriental Block, 1885–1886
718–726 Washington Street

*John Marquis,
architect*

This elaborate Stick-Eastlake type is unusual in Oakland. The Peniel Mission has occupied the building since the 1960s, a pre-redevelopment establishment in the area.

13. Dunn Block, 1878–1879
721–725 Washington Street

*Haskell & Smilie,
builders*

This building and its partly reconstructed neighbors at **715–719** have rare nineteenth-century-type storefronts.

14. Gooch Block, Ratto's Building, 1876
*817–829 Washington Street,
at Ninth Street*

*John S. Tibbals,
architect*

The architect's name is known from a rare inscription on the doorstep. Ratto's Grocery, founded in 1897, has owned and occupied the building since the 1930s.

15. Victorian Row, 1868–1884
*450–497 Ninth Street,
Broadway to
Washington Street,
821–933 Broadway*

The magnificent Italianate block of Ninth Street known as Victorian Row is the centerpiece of the Old Oakland project, a pioneering redevelopment through restoration begun in the early 1980s by Storek and Storek. The Victorian Row buildings are the following:

15a. Arlington Hotel, Nicoll Block, 1876
*484–494 Ninth Street,
at Washington Street*

Clinton Day, architect

15b. Ashmun C. Henry House, Portland Hotel, 1877
468–482 Ninth Street

*William Stokes,
architect (attributed)*

15c. LaSalle Hotel, A. J. Snyder Block #1, 1876
*491–497 Ninth Street,
at Washington Street*

Clinton Day, architect

15d. Ross House, A. J. Snyder Block #2, 1879
477–587 Ninth Street

*Clinton Day,
architect (attributed)*

15e. Delger Block, 1880, 1884
*901–933 Broadway,
Ninth to Tenth Streets*

Kenitzer & Raun, architects

15f. Wilcox Block, 1868
*821–835 Broadway,
at Ninth Street*

16. Swan's Market, 1917–1940, 1997
901 Washington Street

This white glazed brick, tile, and terra-cotta sanitary free market was begun in 1917 by architects Oliver & Thomas and expanded in stages until 1940, when it filled the entire block bounded by Ninth, Tenth, Washington, and Clay Streets. The building was reworked to a mixed-use complex by Pyatok Architects for East Bay Asian Local Development Corporation (EBALDC) and partners.

17

17. Pardee House, 1868
672 Eleventh Street

*Hoagland & Newsom,
architects*

This Italianate villa was home to three generations of the Pardee family, among them Oakland mayors, a California governor, the founder and namesake of Pardee Reservoir, and art and ethnography collectors. A private foundation maintains the Pardee Home Museum just as the last family member left it in 1981.

Preservation Park

18. Preservation Park, 1976–1991
*Twelfth to Fourteenth Streets,
Martin Luther King Jr. Way to
Castro Street*

*Preservation Ventures,
Oakland Redevelopment
Agency, Bramalea Pacific,
developers*

*Architectural Resources
Group*

*CHNMB and Blair Prentice,
landscape design*

246

This office park and conference center of sixteen buildings includes eleven moved from the 980 Freeway and other development sites, selected to provide a museum of Oakland architecture of the 1870s to 1890s. The five on the north side of Thirteenth Street are on their original sites, part of a ring of Victorian residential neighborhood fragments at the fringe of downtown. Plaques in the park give dates, styles, and historic names.

19. First Unitarian Church, 1890–1891
685 Fourteenth Street

Walter J. Mathews, architect

One of Oakland's rare 1890s Romanesque structures, First Unitarian is still occupied by its original congregation.

20. Oakland Public Library, 1900–1904
African American Museum and Library at Oakland (AAMLO)
659 Fourteenth Street

Bliss & Faville, architects

The earliest and most classical of Oakland's six Carnegie libraries, this was Oakland's main public library until the new library at 125 Fourteenth Street opened in 1951.

Above Twelfth Street

21. Fifteenth Street house group, 1876–1879
619, 627 Fifteenth Street, 1430–1432 Martin Luther King Jr. Way

These three well-kept 1870s houses have survived surprisingly close to the core of downtown. Several other fine clusters of nineteenth-century houses remain in the area around Eighteenth, Nineteenth, and Castro Streets.

22. Evangeline Home, The Claridge, 1930–1931
634 Fifteenth Street

Douglas Dacre Stone, architect

This substantial and elegant Spanish Colonial residence was originally a Salvation Army home for girls.

23. Elihu M. Harris State Office Building, completed 1998
1515 Clay Street, Fourteenth to Sixteenth Streets, Clay to Jefferson Streets

DMJM Keating, Hansen Murakami Eshima et al., architects

This sleek building occupies parts of two city blocks. It wraps around the historic 1913–1914 Oaks and Touraine Hotels, and its vast indoor-outdoor atrium is part of a pedestrian Segment of Fifteenth Street through Frank Ogawa Plaza and Kahn's Alley.

24. Ronald V. Dellums Federal Building, completed 1993
1301 Clay Street, Twelfth to Fourteenth Streets, Clay to Jefferson Streets

Kaplan McLaughlin Diaz, David Hobstetter, architects

This complex is distinguished by high-quality materials, pyramid-roofed towers alluding to Oakland's signature County Courthouse and Tribune Tower, a stonework map of the Bay Area in the atrium floor, and plentiful outdoor art.

Broadway Corridor

The location where Broadway, Telegraph Avenue, and San Pablo Avenue converged at Fourteenth and Broadway became Oakland's main intersection, seat of government, and site of several handsome flatiron buildings. In front of City Hall, the streets have been absorbed into Frank H. Ogawa Plaza (named for Oakland's first Asian American City Council member). Two new city administration buildings flank the plaza. Around the plaza are several Beaux-Arts commercial buildings built at the same time as City Hall, part of the northward spread of the central business district.

German city planner Werner Hegemann wrote admiringly in 1915 of the "ideally spaced" southwest-facing skyscrapers along Broadway from Eleventh to Seventeenth Streets. These eight- to thirteen-story buildings were outgrown in later years, but the distinctive skyline of well-spaced towers remains. Many of these early-twentieth-century office buildings have opulent and intact lobbies. West of Broadway, Washington Street was historically the street of department stores, mostly demolished in the 1970s. In the 1920s, a row of building-and-loan and title companies developed along Franklin Street to the east.

The Uptown district, along Broadway and Telegraph north of Seventeenth Street, was the luxury shopping and entertainment district of the Art Deco era. The district has two movie palaces among its wealth of 1920s–1930s commercial architecture.

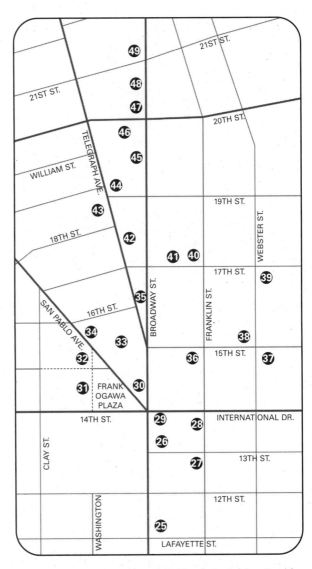

3 • Central Oakland: Broadway Corridor

25. Security Bank and Trust Building, Key System Building, 1911
1100 Broadway

Frederick H. Meyer, architect

The southernmost of the corner skyscrapers is elegantly clad in pressed brick and terra-cotta.

31

26. Union Savings Bank Building, 1903
*1300 Broadway,
at Thirteenth Street*

Walter J. Mathews, architect

Oakland's first steel-frame sky-scraper was built in a year of major East Bay transportation advances.

27. Oakland Tribune Building, 1906; tower, 1922
401–417 Thirteenth Street

D. Franklin Oliver, Edward T. Foulkes, architects

The Tribune occupied the former Breuner furniture building at the corner, then raced Bank of America to add a tower in 1922–1923, and later established its presses in the former **Pantages Theater** (1912; O'Brien & Werner, architects) on Twelfth Street.

28. Financial Center Building, 1928
401–415 Fourteenth Street

Reed & Corlett, architects

Art Deco was applied to the brown brick skyscraper and its ornate lobby. Ground-floor terra-cotta was sandblasted and has been stabilized with a protective coating.

29. First Interstate Bank Building, Smith's Building, 1956–1959
1330 Broadway

Stone Mulloy Marraccini & Patterson (SMMP), architects

Oakland's miniature Lever House replica was the first International-style high-rise office building in the East Bay. It has an innovative second-floor banking hall, reserving the ground-floor retail space for Smith's clothing store.

30. Broadway Building, First National Bank Building, 1907
*1401–1419 Broadway,
150 Frank Ogawa Plaza*

Llewellyn B. Dutton, architect

This is a miniature of the Flatiron Building in New York;

Dutton had worked for Burnham before coming west during the 1906 building boom. After a vigorous post-1989 earth-quake campaign to Save the Broadway Building, it is now part of the city administration complex, joined to Fentress Bradburn and Hensel Phelps's new Lionel Wilson Building (1995–1997).

31. City Hall, 1911–1914
1 Frank Ogawa Plaza (histori-cally 1421 Washington Street)

Palmer, Hornbostel & Jones, architects

The winning design in a 1909 national competition, this Beaux-Arts skyscraper helped anchor Oakland's 100 percent corner at Fourteenth and Broadway. John Donovan, Palmer and Hornbostel's on-site representa-tive, stayed to become the archi-tect of many Oakland libraries and schools. The design some-what echoes New York's Municipal Building. The repair and retrofit after the 1989 earth-quake was an early use of base isolation in a historic building.

32. Plaza Building, DeDomenico Building, 1913
200 Frank Ogawa Plaza

O'Brien & Werner, architects

This attractive small speculative office building was developed by local clothier Charles Heeseman.

33. Kahn's Department Store, The Rotunda, 1912, 1923
*350 Frank Ogawa Plaza,
1501–1539 Broadway*

Charles W. Dickey, architect

*E. W. Cannon, architect
(addition, 1923)*

Here is a Parisian-influenced department store whose great

35

elliptical dome gives it its current name. Elaborate adaptive reuse for offices, stores, and restaurants took advantage of the historic preservation tax credits.

34. First Trust and Savings Bank, Westlake Building, 1913
300 Frank Ogawa Plaza, at Sixteenth Street

Llewellyn B. Dutton, architect

This building marked one end of the Sixteenth Street Canyon, celebrated by the *Oakland Tribune* in 1914; Oakland had achieved a dark and narrow, windy big-city streetscape of its own.

35. Federal Realty Building, Cathedral Building, 1913–1914
1605–1615 Broadway, 1606–1616 Telegraph Avenue

Benjamin Geer McDougall, architect

This unusual Gothic-Chateauesque flatiron sky-scraper is clad in terra-cotta over a concrete structure.

36. Oakland Title Guaranty Company Building, Lincoln University, 1921
1447–1459 Franklin Street

Maury Diggs, architect

This elaborate polychrome terra-cotta temple was one of the first buildings to bring Oakland's financial and real estate center east to Franklin Street from Broadway.

37. White Building, 1924
327–349 Fifteenth Street, at Webster Street

Clay Burrell, architect

This glass-fronted Chicago-style building is only twenty feet deep, built on a sliver-sized lot after Fifteenth Street was opened east of Franklin.

38. YWCA of Oakland, 1914
1515 Webster Street

Julia Morgan, architect

This lovely buff brick and terra-cotta palazzo with a splendid interior court is one of a score of YWCA clubs and residences designed by Morgan.

39. Howden Building, 1925
325–343 Seventeenth Street, 1628–1630 Webster Street

McWethy & Greenleaf, designer-builders

This is a showpiece for the Howden Tile Company, both outside and in.

40. First Church of Christ, Scientist, 1900–1902
1701 Franklin Street

Henry A. Schulze, architect

This rare stone church building is still occupied by its original congregation.

41. Wakefield Building, 1924
426 Seventeenth Street

McCall & Davis, architects

This handsome brown brick office building has a deep arcade and T-shaped plan that maximize window space.

42. Mary Bowles Building, 1931
1713–1721 Broadway, 1712–1720 Telegraph Avenue

Douglas Dacre Stone, architect

The south half of this dazzling Art Deco terra-cotta commercial building was restored in 2004 after fifty years in a white stucco box.

43. Fox Oakland Theater, 1927
1807–1829 Telegraph Avenue

Maury Diggs and Weeks and Day, architects

Wraparound commercial wings nest this 3,000-seat Exotic Revival theater into its low-rise surroundings. Since it closed as a theater in the early 1970s, its preservation has been an ongoing drama.

44. Oakland Floral Depot, 1931
1900–1932 Telegraph Avenue

Albert J. Evers, architect

This midnight blue and silver terra-cotta gem was developed as rental property by the 20th and Broadway Realty Company, a placeholder until Capwell's might expand.

45. Sweet's Ballroom, 1923
1921–1933 Broadway

Schirmer-Bugbee Co., architect

Inside the Beaux-Arts terra-cotta-clad upper story is an intact period ballroom that flourished in the big band era.

46. H. C. Capwell Co. Department Store, 1928
1935–1975 Broadway, Twentieth Street, Telegraph Avenue

Starrett & Van Vleck, Ashley & Evers, architects

Capwell's was the store that established Uptown as a fashionable shopping district, and remained here until 1995. After the 1989 earthquake, the brown brick walls were covered over and most of the Beaux-Arts terra-cotta removed, but the cornice, display windows, and overall scale are still impressive.

47. I. Magnin, 1930
2001 Broadway

Weeks and Day, architects

This building features gorgeous variegated-green terra-cotta, period lettering, and a 1963 black marble and plate-glass ground floor. Operated as I. Magnin department store until 1994, it was later converted into offices.

48. Paramount Theater, 1930
2025 Broadway

Timothy Pflueger, architect

This unique Art Deco masterpiece is a pioneering restoration of a movie palace now used as a performing arts theater.

49. Security Pacific Bank, 1974
2101 Broadway

ORS Corporation, Los Angeles

With three tiers of cantilevered glass boxes, this is one of a cluster of stylish late-twentieth-century bank buildings in the Uptown area.

Lakeside, Chinatown

Along the west shore of Lake Merritt are apartments, office towers, and a vast if miscellaneous civic and educational center. The southeast corner of the central business district is Oakland's traditional twentieth-century Chinatown, and an older residential strip extends along Seventh Street.

50. Kaiser Center and Roof Garden, 1958–1960
300 Lakeside Drive

Welton Beckett and Associates, architects

Theodore Osmundson, landscape architect

One of the premier symbols of Oakland is this curved twenty-eight-story office building clad in gold-tone Kaiser aluminum-alloy panels. The low-rise base houses a shopping mall and multistory garage, and it is topped by Osmundson's renowned roof garden. Connected by a bridge to the north is the **Ordway Building**, 1 Kaiser Plaza (1968–1970; Skidmore, Owings & Merrill, architects), a twenty-eight-story tower of silvery aluminum with a tall glass base.

51. The Regillus, 1921–1922
200 Lakeside Drive
(front on Nineteenth Street)

Willis Lowe, architect

By the 1920s, the edge of the lake was established as a luxury apartment district. On the long blocks from Nineteenth to Fourteenth Streets, big houses on big lots were replaced one by one over the next fifty years. These two magnificent complexes replaced the August Schilling home; its carriage house and gardens remain as part of the property at 244.

52. 244 Lakeside Drive, 1924–1925
244 Lakeside Drive

Maury Diggs, architect

This prominent ten-story apartment building has a profile that suggests the Art Deco style, but its sparse decoration is an eclectic combination of historic images, mostly Baroque, including nearly life-sized armored knights standing sentry at the cornice.

53. Madison-Lake Hotel Apartments, Lake Merritt Hotel, 1927
1800 Madison Street

William H. Weeks, architect

This reinforced-concrete Spanish Colonial is a semi-twin of Weeks hotels all over the state, including Oakland's **Hotel Leamington** at 1800 Franklin Street (1925) and **Hotel Jackson** at 1569 Jackson (1927).

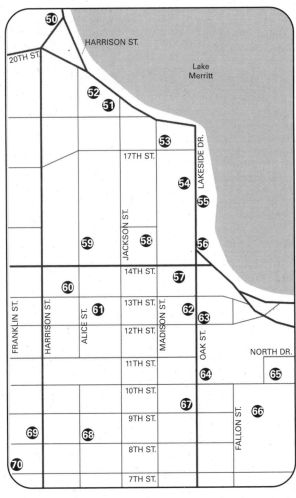

3 • Central Oakland: Lakeside and Chinatown

54. Scottish Rite Temple,
1926; remodeled, 1938
1547 Lakeside Drive

Carl Werner, William Corlett, architects

Werner's 1926 temple façade was remodeled to the present monumental Classic Modern after its high-tech artificial stone surface failed. The opulent 1920s interiors include an enormous domed auditorium.

55. OFD High Pressure Pumping Station and Municipal Boathouse,
1909; addition, 1913
1520 Lakeside Drive

Howard & Galloway, Walter Reed, architects

Mayor Frank Mott's vast program of City Beautiful civic improvements included recreation facilities and fire stations throughout the city: the two were combined in this dual-purpose building.

56. Camron-Stanford House, 1875
1418 Lakeside Drive

Samuel Merritt, developer-designer

This graceful Italianate is the last of a whole neighborhood of mansions near Lake Merritt, many of them developed by Mayor Dr. Samuel Merritt himself. After a series of eminent residents, this became one of the early estates acquired in 1907 in the city's park expansion program, and until 1967, it was the Oakland Public Museum. It is now a house museum.

57. Oakland Main Public Library, 1950
125 Fourteenth Street

Miller & Warnecke, architects

An outstanding postwar Classic Modern civic building, its tall deep-set windows turn the exterior walls into a colonnade; interior finishes still evoke the streamlined era.

58. Madison Street Masonic Temple, Islamic Center of Northern California,
1908–1909
1433 Madison Street, at Fifteenth Street

O'Brien & Werner, architects

These architects designed most of the early-twentieth-century Masonic temples in California, but this spectacular Mission Revival stands out among their mostly classical work. It is an early institutional use in the lakeside area.

59. Women's City Club, Malonga Casquelourd Arts Center, 1927–1928
1426 Alice Street

Miller & Warnecke, architects

One of the most ambitious of the many women's club buildings erected in the 1920s, this Mediterranean palazzo provided meeting rooms, a theater, dining, swimming, and tennis, and seventy-five residential rooms. Since the late 1980s, it has been a city-owned arts center.

60. Hotel Oakland, 1910–1912
250 Thirteenth Street (Thirteenth to Fourteenth Streets, Harrison to Alice Streets)

Bliss & Faville, architects

The grandest of the ring of early-1910s hotels around the downtown core, it was originally promoted as the Bankers' Hotel in the hotel boom attributed to preparation for the 1915 World's Fair. Used as a military hospital during World War II, it was later adapted as senior housing.

61. Main Post Office, 1931
201 Thirteenth Street (Twelfth to Thirteenth Streets, Alice to Jackson Streets)

William Arthur Newman, architect

James A. Wetmore, Supervising Architect of the Treasury

A formal classical Treasury Department post office was designed well into the Art Deco era. Modernity is displayed in the materials of the glass-and-metal interior.

62. Ralph Hoyt County Administration Building,
1961–1964
1221 Oak Street

Ratcliff & Ratcliff, Van Bourg Nakamura, architects

This classic early-1960s government building is an angular grid of glass and precast panels set in a terrazzo and granite plaza. This team also designed the circular county parking structure and heliport a block west.

63. Alameda County Courthouse, 1935
1221 Fallon Street

Corlett, Minton, Plachek, Schirmer, Werner, architects

A major monument of WPA Modern in the Bay Area, the courthouse was designed by a panel of distinguished architects, several of whom continued to work on civic center plans for the lakeside area. The lobby has marble WPA murals by Marian Simpson and Gaetano Duccini, which depict Alameda County history.

64. Oakland Museum, 1964–1968
1000 Oak Street

Kevin Roche, John Dinkeloo & Associates, architects

Dan Kiley, landscape architect

A complex series of terraces and courtyards house the museum's art, history, and science departments on three levels. The landscaping is an integral part of the angular, inward-looking concrete-and-glass building.

65. Oakland Auditorium, Kaiser Convention Center, 1913–1915
10 Tenth Street

John J. Donovan, architect

Henry Hornbostel, consulting architect

This vast building at the end of the lake houses a large theater, arena, ballroom, and accessory spaces under a light truss roof engineered by Maurice Couchot. The allegorical sculptures in the niches facing the lake are by Alexander Stirling Calder.

66. Laney Community College, 1971
Tenth and Fallon Streets

Skidmore, Owings & Merrill, architects

The sharp-edged labyrinthine, brick and concrete campus centers on a signature triangular tower.

67. Madison Park Apartments, 1908
100 Ninth Street, at Oak Street

Charles M. MacGregor, designer-builder

This ninety-eight unit Colonial Revival apartment building

developed in the boom after the 1906 earthquake combines classical cast-plaster cornice ornament with a rugged clinker-brick base.

68. Engine House #11, 1909
817 Alice Street

Frederick Soderberg, architect

One of several similar Beaux-Arts firehouses built throughout the city during the City Beautiful era was converted to a private residence in 1966 after the new station across the street was built.

69. Hebern Electric Code Building, Asian Resource Center, 1922–1923
801–833 Harrison Street (Eighth to Ninth Streets)

Reed & Corlett, architects

P. J. Walker Co., builder

Designed and built by prestigious firms of the day, this sparkling, extravagant, Gothic-inspired terra-cotta-clad building was the factory and office of a short-lived cryptographic technology start-up. By 1925, it passed into a variety of miscellaneous uses, and in 1979–1980, it became an early adaptive reuse by the East Bay Asian Local Development Corporation.

70. Pekin Low Café Building, now Legendary Palace, 1924
710 Franklin Street, at Seventh Street

W. K. Owen, designer

This exuberantly faux-oriental building is comparable to those in San Francisco's Chinatown.

63

West Oakland

West of the Grove-Shafter Freeway (980) and south of the MacArthur Freeway (580) is West Oakland. The westernmost neighborhood, historically known as Oakland Point and now generally called Prescott, grew up around early rail and ferry transit. Oakland Point became the terminus of the transcontinental railroad, whose regional railroad yards and shops were a big employer by 1872. A flourishing commercial district along Seventh Street (Railroad Avenue)—all but obliterated by public works projects, earthquake, and fire—was a legendary African American music, business, and entertainment center in the early to mid-twentieth century.

The neighborhood to the east, now called Oak Center, was somewhat tonier than the Point; its lots are generally larger and its houses a little newer and bigger. When it was declared a redevelopment area in the 1960s, neighborhood activists redefined redevelopment to mean the rehabilitation of houses, parks, and underground utilities.

The Clawson neighborhood, west of San Pablo Avenue and Market Street, has a long history of mixed uses, continuing in the present-day development of live/work lofts.

To the east is the Hoover neighborhood, a streetcar suburb with many stately Colonials, now bounded on the east by the freeway.

1. Central/Southern Pacific Car Paint Shop, 1874; addition, circa 1901
Foot of Wood Street

Central Pacific Railroad

This is the only survivor of the huge complex of nineteenth-century railroad shop buildings that was West Oakland's economic base.

2. Arcadia Hotel, 1906
1632–1642 Seventh Street, at Campbell Street

Thomas D. Newsom, architect

The blocks at the far west end of Seventh Street (beyond the present freeway entrance) were crowded with 1870s railroad hotels. Though newer, this is the last of the type.

3. Stephen Porter Rental Houses, 1877
1509–1523 Third Street

Below the tracks in South Prescott, small houses like these raised-basement Italianate workers' cottages backed up against the marsh and railroad yards. Other distinctive 1870s–1900s groups are found on the 300 blocks of Henry and Chester Streets.

4. Mandela Gateway, 2003
1300–1400 Blocks of Seventh Street, Seventh to Eighth Streets, Union to Center Streets

Michael Willis Associates, architects

This HOPE VI project replaced an earlier housing project with a mixed-use and mixed-income development that aims to reconcile the density dictated by economics with respect for the historic districts to the north and west. The complex takes its name from Mandela Parkway, the route of the Cypress Freeway that fell in the 1989 earthquake.

5. Samm-Dalton-Cooper House, 1877, 1895, 1945
1454 Eighth Street, at Center Street

This Italianate house was built for a flourmill operator and modernized into a Queen Anne by a foundry owner and politician around 1895; it was converted to a rooming house in the 1930s. A storefront was added in West Oakland's postwar building and small-business boom in 1945.

6. Liberty Hall, Western Market Building, 1877
1485 Eighth Street, at Chester Street

Originally Zeiss and Breiling's market and flat, by 1925, this turreted Italianate was headquarters of the local chapter of Marcus Garvey's Universal Negro Improvement Association. Later it was the Oakland branch of Father Divine's Peace Mission. In the 1980s, Jubilee West rescued it from condemnation and housed their community service programs here.

7. Chester Street Methodist Episcopal Church, 1888
835 Chester Street, at Ninth Street

This is the one surviving nineteenth-century church building in Oakland Point out of many denominations and nationalities. By 1920, this was Parks Chapel A.M.E., and, later, True Light C.O.G.I.C. Churches in the area, located in converted houses and storefronts and postwar church buildings, are as numerous as ever.

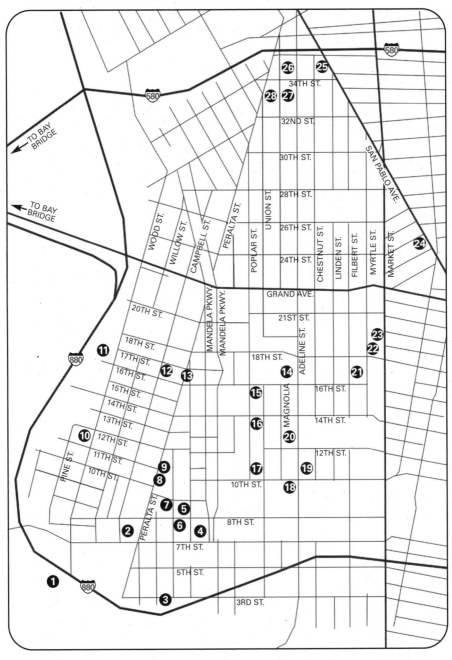

3 • West Oakland

8. St. Patrick's Convent, Prescott-Joseph Center, 1871, 1912
920 Peralta Street

An 1870s house was moved here in 1912 and converted to a convent with exquisitely matched additions to the rear and in the front L. It was part of St. Patrick's Catholic Church complex, a historic spiritual, social, and political center of the Point. The present church was designed in 1945 by architect Martin Rist.

9. John Ziegenbein House, 1870
1004 Peralta Street

John Ziegenbein, developer

John Ziegenbein was a German merchant turned developer. His own house is like the many fine Italianates he developed in the immediate vicinity along Peralta, Center, Chester, Eighth, and Ninth Streets, only larger and on a larger lot. At least 100 of his houses still exist in the Oakland Point district.

10. Urban Meliors Neo-Italianate Duplex, 2002–2004
1103 Wood Street

Jon Havrilesko, Bruce Capron, and Abel Morales, designer-builders

This is a creative response to the city's requirement that infill be compatible with the character of the historic district.

11. Southern Pacific Station, 1910–1912
1798 Sixteenth Street, at Wood Street
Jarvis Hunt, architect

A Beaux-Arts company design with near-twins around the country, Oakland's depot was abandoned by Amtrak in the late 1980s and suffered earthquake and weather damage while awaiting a reuse. Though located on the far west edge of the city, it was well connected with interurban trains and local streetcars. Two small hotels at Sixteenth and Wood are contemporary with the station.

12. Oakland Mazda Lamp Works, 1910–1916
1600–1648 Campbell Street (Sixteenth to Seventeenth Streets)

Samuel Austin and Son, Izant & Frink (Cleveland), designer-builders

Industry grew on the West Oakland Marsh as the bay was filled to the west. This attractive brick Arts and Crafts factory for a General Electric subsidiary was damaged in the 1989 earthquake, just a block from where the Cypress Freeway collapsed.

13. Walsh & O'Brien Center Junction Cash Grocery, 1884
1615 Center Street

Charles Mau, architect

This prominent flatiron is situated on the corner where Center and Peralta Streets met at the edge of the marsh.

14. De Fremery House and Park, circa 1863
1651 Adeline Street

Banker James De Fremery's suburban villa is among the oldest houses in Oakland, as is evident in its Greek Revival form, clapboard siding, and triple-hung windows. In the early 1900s, the estate was bought by the city as a park.

15. Seymour Davison House, 1884
1529–1531 Union Street

Samuel and Joseph Cather Newsom, architects

This elaborate pattern-book house is straight from the Newsoms' *Picturesque California Homes*. It is one of many fine houses on the blocks of Union, Magnolia, and Adeline Streets below the park.

16. Shredded Wheat Company–Nabisco Plant, 1915–1916
1267 Fourteenth Street, Union to Poplar Streets

Lewis P. Hobart & Charles Cheney, architects
H. J. Brunnier, engineer

Advertised as "the factory beautiful," the plant was designed with Gothic detailing and gracious landscaping to be a good neighbor to the residential neighborhood.

17. Cole School, 1936
1001 Union Street

William H. Corlett, architect

This is one of many 1930s Deco makeovers of 1920s and earlier schools after passage of the Field Act.

18. Beth Eden Baptist Church, 1945–1951, 1980
1025 Adeline and 952 Magnolia Streets

J. I. Easterly & Charles McCall, architects
E. Paul Kelly, architect (1980)

The postwar sanctuary (now the education building) reused every scrap of the 1900s home of Oakland's oldest African American church.

19. Albert Church House, 1891
1025 Chestnut Street

A. W. Pattiani, designer-builder

Set on a raised basement, this two-story house has a projecting entrance portico with arched openings, fishscale shingles, and angled corner windows.

20. Walter Morrison House, 1892
1223 Adeline Street

A. W. Pattiani, designer-builder

These two fine Queen Annes were designed by a virtuoso of the style, with a wealth of brackets and gables and bays and textures.

21. Holland-Canning House, 1878
954 Sixteenth Street, at Myrtle Street

Outbuildings record successive generations at this ornate Italianate house, with the original carriage house behind and the 1920s hardware store (largely reconstructed) alongside.

22. Joseph Willcutt House, 1889
918 Eighteenth Street, at Myrtle Street

Robert Smilie, designer-builder

Willcutt was an official of the Southern Pacific and its associated interurban and street railways. The house lost an elaborately patterned brick chimney in the 1989 earthquake but is otherwise remarkably intact.

23. St. John Missionary Baptist Church, 1908
1909 Market Street

Etienne A. Garin, architect

Built as St. Andrew's Catholic Church at Thirty-Sixth and

Adeline Streets, this Mission Revival showpiece was moved here (in two parts) in 1958, when the freeway went through its site. It was carefully restored after a 1993 fire.

24. Willowbrook Creamery, 1930
2515–2521 San Pablo Avenue, at Athens Street

Maury Diggs & Carleton Marshall, architects

Here is an astonishing orange brick and cast-concrete Art Deco industrial building. Diggs was a colorful Oakland and San Francisco architect and developer whose jobs ranged from the Fox Oakland Theater to San Quentin Prison.

25. California Hotel, 1929
3501 San Pablo Avenue

Clay Burrell, architect

A large and impressive redbrick hotel has Spanish Colonial towers oriented to appeal to motorists entering Oakland from the north. It was famed in the 1950s and 1960s as the favored lodging for traveling African American entertainers.

26. Boman Building, 1891
3401 Adeline Street

Edson W. Merwin, designer

This showy Victorian-era commercial building housed the North Oakland Free Reading Room from 1891 to 1909.

27. OFD Engine Co. #22, 1922–1923
3320 Magnolia Street

Ralph A. Beebee, engineer

This fire station had an African American crew for thirty years, a milestone toward integration of Oakland's public services. Later, the Romanesque Revival design adapted well to use as a church.

28. Clawson School, 1915
3240 Union Street

John J. Donovan, architect

This Beaux-Arts school building was abandoned for years before it became a pioneering condo conversion by developers Premises Inc. in 1998. The colorful **Magnolia Row** townhouses (2001–2002; David Baker + Partners, architects) occupy the former Clawson schoolyard.

North Oakland

Upper Broadway and Piedmont Avenue roughly follow the course of Glen Echo (Cemetery) Creek, connecting Mountain View Cemetery and Lake Merritt. Traces of the area's suburban beginnings remain among the layers of Auto Row, Pill Hill, and uptown churches. From the 1860s, Piedmont Avenue has been the well-traveled route to the cemetery and has a lively neighborhood commercial strip.

East of Broadway, Temescal Creek attracted a Native American settlement, a Peralta hacienda, and early industry, and by 1873, the Telegraph Avenue car line ran north to the university in Berkeley. A large and early Italian community included many workers at the Bilger Quarry on upper Broadway. East and north of Temescal, the area now commonly known as Rockridge, was a nineteenth-century suburb whose renowned estates have left ghostly footprints including today's subdivision boundaries.

1. St. Augustine's (originally Trinity) Episcopal Church, 1892
2845 Telegraph Avenue, at Twenty-Ninth Street

William Hamilton, architect

This little Gothic gem has been meticulously maintained inside and out, and still serves its congregation. The rector at the time of construction was Rev. John Bakewell, father of architect John Bakewell of Bakewell and Brown.

2. First Presbyterian Church, 1913–1914
2619 Broadway, at Twenty-Seventh Street

William C. Hays, architect

Cram, Goodhue & Ferguson, consulting architects

This imposing Gothic Revival is executed in steel frame and reinforced concrete with remarkable concrete window tracery. It is one of old Oakland's "First" congregations that moved uptown in the early twentieth century.

3. Temple Sinai, 1913
356 Twenty-Eighth Street, at Webster Street

G. Albert Lansburgh, architect

A stately temple for the First Hebrew Congregation of Oakland is distinguished by cream-colored three-dimensional brickwork, ornate colonnade, elliptical dome, and magnificent stained glass.

4. Biff's II Coffee Shop (later JJ's), 1962–1964
315 Twenty-Seventh Street

Armet & Davis, architect

This flying-saucer coffee shop was designed by leading practitioners of the Googie style. The shingled mansard was added in 1975, and the showy period interior has been mothballed since JJ's closed in 1996.

5. Cuyler Lee Packard and Maxwell Showroom and Garage, 1913–1914
2355 Broadway, at Twenty-Fourth Street

Willis Polk & Co., architect

This monumental showroom helped establish upper Broadway as Oakland's auto row. The auto palaces on Broadway were supported by early garage buildings like the well-preserved collection along Twenty-Fourth and Twenty-Fifth Streets.

6. Connell Oldsmobile, 1946
3093 Broadway

Alben Froberg, architect

This fine Streamlined Moderne showroom has glass walls, terrazzo floors, streamlined tower and canopy, and free-standing neon-edged letters.

7. J. Mora Moss House and Mosswood Park, 1864
3612 Webster Street, at Broadway

S. H. Williams, architect

Unique in Oakland, this fine Gothic Revival country house is in the tradition of A. J. Downing's pattern books. The Moss property was acquired for a city park in 1912 under Mayor Frank Mott's "City Beautiful" administration.

8. King's Daughters Home, 1912 and after
3900 Broadway

Julia Morgan, architect

Morgan designed this gracious brick and terra-cotta palazzo as a nursing home for the King's Daughters, a women's welfare organization of which her mother and sister were board members. The home operated until 1980.

9. Elsie Turner Store and Flat Building, 1916
4001–4029 Piedmont Avenue, at Fortieth Street

Julia Morgan, architect

This exquisite mixed-use building in dark red brick has Della Robbia terra-cotta wreaths and pilasters.

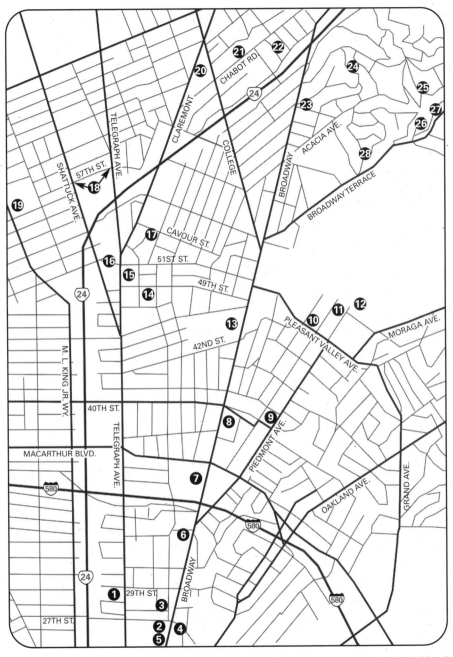

3 • North Oakland

10. Oakland Cremation Association Columbarium, Chapel of Memories, 1902
4401 Howe Street

This domed columbarium, attributed to architect Walter J. Mathews, was a companion to the Oakland Cremation Association's demolished crematorium and chapel designed by Mathews in 1901, when cremation represented "advanced thought." The 1925 addition is by architect Stafford Jory.

11. Chapel of the Chimes, 1910, 1921, and after
4499 Piedmont Avenue

Julia Morgan, architect (1921)

Morgan's twenty-year involvement began with a 1921 remodeling and addition to Cunningham and Politeo's California Crematorium; over the years, Morgan and her successors established the familiar Gothic character. Later additions by Aaron Green and others provide a time trip through funerary architecture.

12. Mountain View Cemetery, 1864
5000 Piedmont Avenue

Frederick Law Olmsted, landscape architect

Olmsted's expansive "rural cemetery" has filled in over the years with architect-designed tombs, fraternal headstones, mausoleums, and the 1929–1930 Gothic Revival chapel-crematorium and office by Weeks and Day.

13. Oakland Technical High School, 1913
4351 Broadway

John J. Donovan and Henry Hornbostel, architects

After coming west to work on City Hall for Palmer & Hornbostel, Donovan settled in Oakland and wrote a classic textbook on school architecture. This magnificent school building was seismically upgraded from 1977 to 1983 when others of the City Beautiful era were demolished.

14. Mouser House, 1892
449 Forty-Ninth Street, at Clarke Street

C. A. Wedgewood, architect

The suburban home of a downtown physician, this is one of Temescal's most elegant and intact nineteenth-century houses, with its bell-shaped tower and wraparound porch.

15. Cattaneo Block, 1871
5006–5010 Telegraph Avenue

One of the oldest masonry commercial buildings in the city was developed as a restaurant and saloon by one of Temescal's early Italian settlers. The right and left bays are perfectly matched additions from 1922 and 1927.

16. Temescal Public Library, 1918
5205 Telegraph Avenue

C. W. Dickey and John Donovan, architects

This is one of four Carnegie branch libraries built in Oakland between 1915 and 1918. They are similar in plan but different in costume; this is the Old English model, still wonderfully intact.

17. Siegriest House, 1900
5185 Miles Avenue, at Cavour Street

A. W. Smith, architect

This fine Shingle house, an expansive suburban version of Smith's steep-roofed houses, was the family home of famed California painter Louis Siegriest.

18. Idora Park, 1931–1932
Carberry Avenue, Fifty-Sixth to Fifty-Eighth Streets, between Shattuck and Telegraph Avenues

Edward Larmer, C. J. Pfrang, and other builders

The original Idora Amusement Park was torn down after the crash of 1929 and replaced with this exquisite development of Period Revival houses, with custom light standards and underground utilities.

19. University High School, 1922
5714 Martin Luther King Jr. Way, Fifty-Eighth Street to Aileen Street

Charles W. Dickey, architect

Dickey's California Mission-inspired school was restored from 1996 to 1998, after years of abandonment, for the Children's Hospital Research Institute and the North Oakland Senior Center.

20. College Avenue Presbyterian Church, 1917
5951 College Avenue

Julia Morgan, architect

Low nested gabled roofs, a clerestory, and an open-beamed interior make this a 1910s Prairie counterpart of Morgan's earlier Craftsman-style St. John's Presbyterian Church in Berkeley.

21. Bivins House, circa 1873
6165 Chabot Road

This Italianate villa retains enough land to convey the early suburban character of this area halfway between Oakland and Berkeley. Across the street, the **College of St. Albert the Great** (1934–1949; Arnold Constable, architect) is an intensely Tudor Revival quadrangle of college and chapel buildings, all reinforced concrete, in a beautifully landscaped creekside setting.

22. Oaklawn Manor Tract, begun 1929
5700–5800 Blocks of Ross Street and Ivanhoe Road

W. W. Dixon, designer-builder

Here is a tract of unabashedly charming Provincial and Tudor Revival cottages, set off by underground utilities and distinctive concrete paving with rolled curbs. These "Modest Mansions" (builder Ernest Urch's trademark) occupy a tract subdivided from the early Roselawn estate in 1928 by Harvey and Maud Sorenson, who also built themselves the magnificent Mediterranean at

5809 Ivanhoe designed by W. E. Schirmer.

23. Rock Ridge Properties Gates, 1910
Broadway at Lawton Avenue

Walter Reed, architect

The Rock Ridge Properties tract was laid out by Laymance Real Estate and Fred Reed, with contoured streets, natural rock outcroppings, and lot sizes that increased with elevation above Broadway. Much of upper Rock Ridge was destroyed in the 1991 fire, but survivors such as the following two entries hint at its early glory.

24. F. E. Allen House, 1911
6075 Manchester Drive

F. E. Allen, architect-builder

This castle was shown in early Rock Ridge promotional literature.

25. C. S. Cherry House, 1915
5950 Romany Road, at Cross Road

John Hudson Thomas, architect

Here is a charming clipped-gable provincial farmhouse that somehow escaped the 1991 fire.

26. Harvey Lindsay House, 1910
5932 Ostrander Road

Another early tract largely destroyed in 1991 was **Claremont Manor**, along Broadway Terrace and the golf course. At the bottom of the hill, some remarkable houses from the early years of the tract still stand. Lindsay was the developer of Claremont Manor, and his tantalizingly anonymous chalet appears to have been the first house in the tract.

27. Horatio Harper House, 1912
5960 Broadway Terrace

Louis Christian Mullgardt, architect

This showy and mannered eclectic house is situated near the more restrained **6000 Broadway Terrace** (1910), also by Mullgardt.

28. Oakland Tribune–Schlesinger Model Home, 1928
2 Westminster Drive, at Country Club Drive

Frederick H. Reimers, architect

This grand Mediterranean was used to promote the Claremont Pines tract, subdivided in 1927 from the Philip Bowles estate ("The Pines"), with large lots, underground utilities, decorative streetlights, and winding streets with British names to attract showplace Period Revival homes.

Lower Hills

Adams Point, the triangle between two creeks flowing into Lake Merritt, was the estate of city cofounder Edson Adams. In the boom following the 1906 earthquake, homes of the upwardly mobile were designed by Julia Morgan, Charles McCall, the Milwain Brothers, Bakewell and Brown, and many other prominent architects of the day. By the mid-1920s, the neighborhood was filling in with apartments as downtown moved north and apartments ringed Lake Merritt.

The neighborhood above the Lakeshore Highlands portals is a Period Revival showplace. Businesses on Lakeshore Avenue were developed in the late 1920s over homeowner objection, with the compromise that the area be included in the fire limits—hence, brick and concrete construction—and that it be subject to architectural review. The result is a commercial strip of unusually high visual quality.

The Glenview neighborhood flanks Park Boulevard, a main route from the hills to Lake Merritt and downtown. Subdivided in 1907 and after, it has a picturesque collection of bungalow, Prairie, and Craftsman homes, and a memorable Period Revival commercial center.

1. First Congregational Church, 1925
2501 Harrison Street

John Galen Howard, architect

This prominently sited Romanesque Revival church has sculptures by the architect's son Robert Boardman Howard.

2. Cox Cadillac Showroom, 1925
216 Bay Place

Clay Burrell, architect

This Gothic-clad façade of a former auto palace was built on the skeleton of the Consolidated Piedmont Cable Car Company carbarn and powerhouse.

3. Seventh Church of Christ, Scientist, 1915
2333 Harrison Street

William Arthur Newman, architect

Here is a fine neighborhood-scale Craftsman church.

4. Veterans Memorial Building, 1926
200 Grand Avenue

Henry H. Meyers, architect

This is one of ten Alameda County veterans' buildings designed by Meyers' office between 1926 and 1935, and is the most Beaux-Arts in character, with a profusely ornamented pavilion on a generous site in Adams Park.

5. St. Paul's Episcopal Church, 1912
114 Montecito Avenue

Benjamin Geer McDougall, architect

This fine Gothic Revival church has a "contemporary compatible" school addition (1964–1965) by Victor Gruen Associates.

6. Pon de Leo Apartments, The Park View, 1929
315 Park View Terrace

Lawrence Flagg Hyde, architect

This theatrical Spanish Colonial apartment building, with its grand entry and two-story brick garage, is one of the highlights of the 1920s boom in apartment construction in Adams Point.

7. McElroy House, 1907
401 Lee Street

Julia Morgan & Ira Hoover, architects

Morgan's distinctive refined details distinguish this shingled and half-timbered house. City attorney John McElroy, the short-lived first resident, is commemorated by the McElroy fountain in Lakeside Park near the foot of Lee Street.

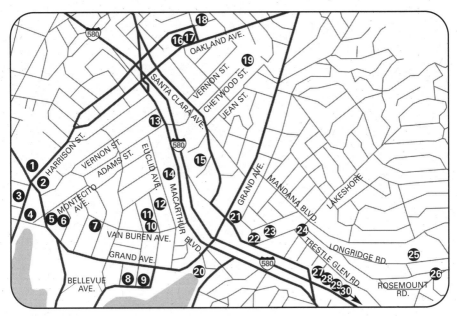

3 • Oakland: Lower Hills

8. Women's Athletic Club, The Bellevue Club, 1928

525 Bellevue Avenue

Charles F. B. Roeth, E. Geoffrey Bangs, Maurice Couchot, architects

This concrete chateau facing the lake is one of the most ambitious of the many women's club buildings constructed in the 1920s.

9. Bellevue-Staten Apartments, 1928

492 Staten Avenue

H. C. Baumann, architect

The astonishing Art Deco–Baroque apartment tower is visible all around the lake.

10. Bates House, 1907

399 Bellevue Avenue

Charles W. Dickey, architect

This large and stately house was constructed for a partner in Bates and Borland, a heavy construction firm that built the University of California stadium and East Bay reservoirs.

11. Joe Shoong House, 1922

385 Bellevue Avenue

Julia Morgan, architect

An understated, finely detailed Beaux-Arts house was built for Joe Shoong, founder of National Dollar Stores and philanthropist in the Chinese community.

12. Ralph Coxhead House, 1908

360 Bellevue Avenue

J. Cather Newsom, architect

This bizarre house carries into the Craftsman era the "picturesque and artistic" aesthetic of the Newsoms' better-known Victorian buildings.

13. Henry C. Morris House, 1911

205 MacArthur Boulevard

Lewis E. Chapin and Henry C. Morris, designer-builders

Chapin and Morris were contractors and developers who seem to have done their own designing—or adapting—as in this near-copy of a Greene and Greene house in Pasadena. Chapin built himself a nearly identical house in Berkeley in 1912.

14. Temple Beth Abraham, 1929

327 MacArthur Boulevard

George Ellinger, architect

Imposing steps and a semicircular entry pavilion distinguish this elegant redbrick temple.

15. El Mirador Apartments, 1928
491 Crescent Street

Douglas Dacre Stone, architect

A large and elaborate Spanish Colonial makes the most of the long street frontage on its angled lot.

16. E. D. Ormsby House, 1891–1892
625 Oakland Avenue

John Conant, architect

This showy Queen Anne has a grotto-like balcony in the gable end. The Linda Vista Terrace area around Oakland Avenue was an architectural showplace of the 1890s but is now largely eroded by apartment and freeway construction.

17. Eugene Braden House, Towne House, 1910
629 Oakland Avenue

Herbert Chivers, architect

Here is an unusual asymmetrical Georgian by an architect who advertised his business location as "New York, St. Louis, San Francisco."

18. Locke House, 1911
3911 Harrison Street

John Hudson Thomas, architect

This magnificent geometric Secessionist house is a grand assembly of wings, tower, parapets, bays, and archways.

19. Morcom Amphitheater of Roses, 1933
Jean Street to Vernon Street

Arthur Cobbledick, landscape architect

A natural amphitheater was transformed into a formal, geometric Italian-style garden with WPA assistance.

20. El Embarcadero Pergola and Colonnade, 1914
Grand and Lakeshore Avenues

Walter Steilberg, architect

This classical feature crowns the spot where Trestle Glen (Indian Gulch) and Wildwood Creeks converge to form the east branch of Lake Merritt. City Beautiful projects in the early 1910s included extensive improvements and embellishments to the lake, transforming it from a slightly tamed slough to an urban feature.

21. Grand Lake Theater, 1925
3200–3222 Grand Avenue

Reid Brothers, architect

This French Baroque movie palace has a unique, animated, bare-bulb roof sign.

22. Hill and Salisbury store buildings, 1936, 1940
3247–3251, 3255–3257 Lakeshore Avenue

Miller & Warnecke, architects

Here are two glowing tile façades by the prominent firm who also designed 3236, 3264, 3276, 3291–3293, and 3306 Lakeshore, as well as many Period Revival homes in the neighboring areas and major civic and commercial buildings downtown. The storefront at 3257 has 1985 enhancements by Ace Architects, who also designed **3201 Lakeshore** (1986) to echo the Grand Lake Theater as a gateway to the commercial district.

23. F. T. Malley store building, 1928
3311–3331 Lakeshore Avenue

A. W. Smith, architect

Malley was a builder and developer who initiated the commercial development along Lakeshore. Between 1927 and 1930, he also developed 3339–3343, 3347–3351, 3401–3411, and 3421–3425 Lakeshore in Smith's endless variations of 1920s store design, with decorated parapets, sparkling transoms, and Kawneer storefronts.

24. Lakeshore Highlands Portals, 1917
Lakeshore at Longridge and Trestle Glen Roads

Bakewell & Brown, architects

Ornate ironwork pylons lead to the "residence park" laid out by the Olmsted Brothers in 1917 for Wickham Havens and the Walter Leimert Company after the city declined to buy the area as parkland.

25. W. H. Eliason House, 1927
894 Longridge Road

William E. Schirmer, architect

This fine Spanish house was designed by probably the most prolific architect in the neighborhood; along this part of Longridge alone, 774, 816, 814, 820, 830, 894, 906, and 986 are all known to be Schirmer's work.

26. J. W. Calkins House, 1921
901 Rosemount Road, at Sunnyhills

Maybeck & White, architects

Maybeck hallmarks include the wide low roofs, the chimney vents, and the tall end window.

The following entries are unmapped:

27. Harry P. Fisher store buildings, 1925–1929
4193–4219, 4206, 4214 Park Boulevard

William E. Schirmer, architect (4206 and 4214 Park Boulevard)

Spanish on the east side, Tudor on the west—the Tudor Revival buildings have no architect credited, but Schirmer was certainly fluent in that style as well.

28. Glenview Branch Library, 1935
4231 Park Boulevard

Archie & Noble Newsom, architects

Glenview's civic organizations lobbied intensely to win this State Emergency Relief Administration project. It was sold for commercial use in 1997.

29. Elston Avenue, 1933–1935
3700 Block of Elston Avenue, East Thirty-Eighth Street to Excelsior

J. C. Scammell, developer

This remarkable tract of Spanish houses with decorative brick and metalwork and cracked-ice paving has a twin nearby on Castello and Cordova Streets in the Fruitvale neighborhood.

30. The Altenheim, 1908; additions, 1914–1938
1720 MacArthur Boulevard to Excelsior

Oscar Haupt, architect

A German retirement home was established on this site in 1893 and operated by the original organization until 2002. Haupt's plan was said to be "patterned after the famous castle Sans Souci in Potsdam."

Brooklyn

East Oakland, from Lake Merritt to approximately Twenty-Third Avenue, was made up of three early settlements: Clinton (First to Fourteenth Avenue, also known as Eastlake), San Antonio (east of Fourteenth Avenue), and Lynn (the hills to the north). San Antonio, whose lumber and hide wharves date back to the Peraltas, was platted as a town in 1854—the only part of Oakland laid out with alleys. In 1870, San Antonio, Clinton, and Lynn incorporated into the town of Brooklyn, but it was annexed to Oakland two years later.

1. C. H. Eastman Building, 1881
657–663 East Twelfth Street

Clinton Park—between Sixth and Seventh Avenues and East Fourteenth (International Boulevard) and East Twelfth Streets—was dedicated as Washington Square in the 1854 subdivision of Clinton; it still retains some of its original geometric paths. This Italianate with multiple bays and mansard-like roofs is the most intact of the nineteenth-century commercial buildings that faced the park on East Twelfth Street.

2. Tubbs-Henshaw House, 1887
544 International Boulevard

This fine Queen Anne was one of several buildings around the park associated with the neighborhood's early business dynasty.

3. Asa White House, 1878
604 East Seventeenth Street

Lumber merchant White's elaborate Italianate villa has tall arched windows, quoins,

a deep columned porch, and a full story of attic windows tucked into the frieze.

4. Tenth Avenue Historic District
1930–2136 Tenth Avenue

In 1988, two blocks of Tenth Avenue were designated as Oakland's first residential historic district, ensuring design review over two lots that had become vacant. These were filled in 1994 by two neo-Victorian duplexes designed by architect Kirk Peterson, at **2042** and **2050**. This district is not a recognizable tract but a cluster of fine individual "specimen" houses. Among them are **2100** (1891; John J. and Thomas D. Newsom, architects), **2020** (1912; Julia Morgan, architect), and **2004** (1907; Albert Farr, architect).

5. James Presho House, 1893
1806 Tenth Avenue
Julius and Edgar Mathews, architects

This intensely decorated Queen Anne on a prominent corner site was built for a San Francisco silk manufacturer. Presho subdivided the lot in 1907 and developed

the two gambrel-roofed houses designed by John Conant.

6. Sunset Telephone Co., 1906
1649 Twelfth Avenue
A. A. Cantin, architect

One of Cantin's early projects for the telephone company, this elegant redbrick Georgian was adapted as a church around 1950.

7. St. James Episcopal Church, 1860, 1886
1540 Twelfth Avenue
Wright & Sanders, architects (1886)

This tall Carpenter Gothic church has multiple lancet windows. The board-and-batten parish hall is the original church (circa 1860).

8. Brooklyn Presbyterian Church/Grace Temple Baptist Church, 1887
1141 East Fifteenth Street
George Bordwell, architect

This magnificent Victorian Romanesque church with its complex steeples, gables, and cupola was built for a congregation founded in 1861 that remained here until 1972.

5

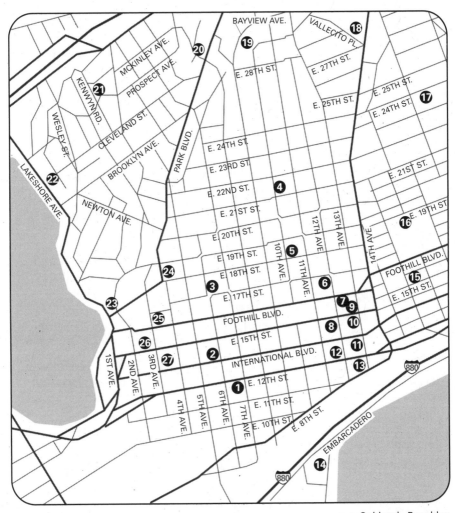

3 • Oakland: Brooklyn

9. David Carrick House, 1890

1212 East Fifteenth Street

John J. Newsom, architect

This big solid Queen Anne with a distinctive attic balcony was designed by one of the elder Newsom brothers.

10. William Bamford House, pre-1870

1235 East Fifteenth Street

Cross-gabled roof, multipane windows, clapboard siding, and split porch columns mark this as a very early house. Reputedly, it was moved from a site near the estuary and could be as old as the 1850s. Bamford was an early physician in Brooklyn, and treated Robert Louis Stevenson in 1880.

11. Fowler Block, 1886

1245–1249 International Boulevard

George W. Flick, builder

Thirteenth Avenue was the main route from the Brooklyn

residential neighborhoods in the hills to rail and water transportation. At its base is still a remarkably intact nineteenth-century commercial district. George Fowler ran the corner drugstore and lived upstairs. He also developed the ornate 1888–1889 Stick-Eastlake row house next door at **1241 International Boulevard.**

12. Williams Block, 1885
1148–1156 East Twelfth Street

This fine Stick structure anchors a small locally designated historic district.

13. Olander's Saloon, 1894
1249 East Twelfth Street
John Conant, architect
A. W. Cornelius, builder

This magnificent building originally had its storefront deeply recessed behind the pointed-arch arcade. Neighboring Vantage Point Park is where steps led down the bluff to the estuary and East Oakland Station.

14. Ninth Avenue Terminal,
1929; addition, 1951
Foot of Ninth Avenue
Arthur Abel, Port of Oakland Chief Engineer

The Port of Oakland's last surviving break-bulk cargo terminal is 1,000 feet from end to end with a grand monumental façade. It was built under a 1925 harbor-improvement bond measure that marked the beginning of the modern Port of Oakland.

15. St. Anthony's Church,
1965–1967
1610 East Fifteenth Street
John Lyon Reid, Alexander Tarics, architects

A concrete-and-redwood modern church is the latest in a line of St. Anthony's Catholic churches built on this corner since the 1860s.

16. San Antonio Park
Sixteenth to
Eighteenth Avenue,
Foothill Boulevard to
East Nineteenth Street

This twelve-acre park overlooking the early embarcadero at the foot of Fourteenth Avenue has been a public plaza since Spanish times. It was dedicated as Independence Square in the 1854 town plat. A 1958 clubhouse by Kolbeck & Peterson wraps gracefully around the base of Walter Reed's 1910 pavilion.

17. Wilkinson-Hogan House, 1884
1807 East Twenty-Fourth Street

An elegant Stick-style tower house was successively owned by proprietors of the Brooklyn Lumber Yard and Humboldt Lumber Company. The neighboring Taylor House (1884) at **1819 East Twenty-fourth** is another rare Stick-Eastlake Victorian.

18. Highland Hospital,
1921–1925
2727 Fourteenth Avenue
Henry H. Meyers, architect
Howard Gilkey, landscape architect

Meyers reportedly modeled the monumental Spanish Colonial administration building and hospital wings after "the old Cathedrals of Mexico" and thereby sought to elevate the image of a county hospital.

19. Austin and Mignonette Hills House, 1892
1047 Bella Vista Avenue
Walter J. Mathews, architect

Bella Vista is a picturesquely sited hilltop neighborhood of large and varied 1890s–1910s houses. The tract was promoted in 1890 "to those who will agree to build Beautiful Residences." This big Queen Anne tower house was built for an original Hills Brother and a vice president of the King's Daughters Home.

20. Mary R. Smith's Trust Cottages:

The Lodge, 1902
2901 Park Boulevard
George W. Flick, builder

Evelyn Cottage, 1905
3001 Park Boulevard
Julia Morgan, architect

The palm trees along East Twenty-Eighth Street and adjoining streets mark the location of Arbor Villa, the estate of real estate and transit magnate Francis Marion "Borax" Smith. On the hill across Park Boulevard, Smith's wife established a complex of ten cottages for girls in need. Several other cottages still exist, more or less altered, behind these two and up the hill.

21. Haddon Hill model home,
1924, 1932–1936
650 Kenwyn Road
Guy L. Brown and Williams and Wastell, architects (1924)
William E. Schirmer, architect (1932–1936)

In 1920, real estate promoter Fred T. Wood had this distinctive tract laid out by Mark Daniels, replacing the nineteenth-century street grid with a picturesque setting for what became a remarkable collection of Period Revival homes. The front part of this house was developed by Wood as a six-room "Southern California bungalow" to market the tract in 1924. It was greatly expanded in the 1930s.

22. Cleveland Cascade, 1923
Cleveland Avenue

Howard Gilkey, landscape architect

Here is a uniquely elaborate pedestrian path linking the hilly streets where water cascaded down the center over colored lights. Community volunteers began a restoration of the neglected and overgrown cascade in 2004.

23. Ida Christensen Apartment Building, 1908
1800 Lakeshore Avenue

William Arthur Newman, architect

Vigorous and prominently sited, this textbook example of Mission Revival set a high standard for later generations of lakeside apartment buildings.

24. Parkway Theater, 1925
1834 Park Boulevard

Mark T. Jorgensen, architect

An exotic neighborhood theater was developed by the Golden State chain. This area also has a number of small, attractive 1920s commercial buildings.

25. Vue du Lac Apartments, 1906
302 Foothill Boulevard

Charles M. MacGregor, builder

This large shingled complex with corner belvedere is an early lake-view apartment building and an early development by MacGregor, who built and sometimes designed hundreds of houses in Albany and throughout the East Bay.

26. First Swedish (Lakeside) Baptist Church, 1926
238 East Fifteenth Street, at Third Avenue

Julia Morgan, architect

Morgan provided a handsome Mediterranean-eclectic design for one of Oakland's many early ethnic churches.

27. Casa Madrona Apartments, 1915
1426–1444 Third Avenue

Rousseau & Rousseau, architects

This group of four Mission–Art Nouveau apartment buildings is distinguished by deep courtyards and overscaled stucco ornament.

East Oakland

In 1909, the established communities of Fruitvale, Melrose, and Elmhurst were annexed to East Oakland.

Fruitvale was the area where the Peralta rancho was settled in 1820; later, farms, orchards, country estates, and resorts were established in the "vale" between Sausal and Peralta Creeks. At the waterfront, industry and a workers' neighborhood known as Jingletown was established by the 1880s. Even before annexation, Fruitvale had a well-developed economic and civic life. By the 1920s, its business district was called Oakland's "second downtown," when it served the rapidly growing industrial suburbs of East Oakland.

1. Antonio Peralta House, 1871
2465 Thirty-Fourth Avenue

When Luis Maria Peralta divided his vast Rancho San Antonio lands among his four sons, the original 1820 Peralta homestead site went to his son Antonio Peralta. Peralta Hacienda Historical Park offers interpretive exhibits about the Peralta family, the present-day neighborhood, and the archaeology of the adobes that preceded the existing Italianate farmhouse.

2. St. Elizabeth's Catholic Church, 1920-1921
1464 Thirty-Fourth Avenue

John J. Foley, architect

The Spanish Colonial church is part of a complex that also includes a high school (1924) and a Franciscan monastery (1937). The high school and monastery were designed by John J. Donovan. Another notable church nearby is the **Third Church of Christ, Scientist,** (1922) by Henry H.

Gutterson at 1642 Fruitvale Avenue, a simplified Romanesque on its way to Moderne.

3. American Bank Building, 1922
3400 International Boulevard

Edward T. Foulkes, architect

A classic banking temple with two-story arches has U.S. coin medallions on its massive corner piers. Fruitvale's vitality is evident in its many substantial branch banks dating from the 1920s to the 1980s, some still banking and some reused.

4. Fruitvale Masonic Temple, 1909, 1926
3353 International Boulevard

Hugo Storch, architect

Howard Schroeder, architect (addition, 1926)

The storefront has recently been refurbished by the Unity Council, a Fruitvale community-development corporation that runs the Main Street program and that also developed the Fruitvale Transit Village. The blind windows on the upper story conceal intact lodge rooms awaiting reuse.

5. Fruitvale Transit Village, 2004
Thirty-Fourth Avenue and East Twelfth Street

McLarand, Vasquez and Partners, architects

Colorful De La Fuente Plaza leads from the historic commercial district on International Boulevard to the Unity Council's multi-block mixed-use development adjoining the BART station (1972; Reynolds & Chamberlain, architects).

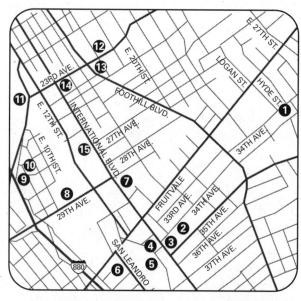

3 • East Oakland

6. Fruitvale Hotel, 1894
3221 San Leandro Street

Snetsinger & Carroll, developers

Fruitvale's oldest extant commercial building was built across from the railroad station at the time Fruitvale was beginning to be promoted as a mass-market residential suburb.

7. Cohen-Bray House, 1884
1440 Twenty-Ninth Avenue

George W. Flick, architect

The last remnant of Fruitvale's country estates, the Stick-Eastlake villa was the dowry house for Emma Bray (whose family home was situated across Twenty-Ninth Avenue) and Alfred Cohen (son of Big Four attorney A. A. Cohen of Alameda). The house has an intact period interior, and is occasionally open for tours.

8. Jingletown homes, 1996–1997
Twenty-Ninth Avenue near East Tenth Street

Michael Pyatok, architect

The townhouse community by Oakland Community Housing Inc. occupies part of the vast Del Monte Cannery site, as does the Industrial-style Fruitvale Station shopping center. The four-story **Lucasey Building** (1922; Maury Diggs, architect) is a surviving fragment of the cannery, once a major local employer.

9. Mary Help of Christians Catholic Church, 1915, 1923
2605 East Ninth Street

Silva & Luvisone, Fantoni & Brown, designer-builders

Founded as a Portuguese-language mission, Mary Help reflects the prominence of the Portuguese in Jingletown from the 1910s to the 1950s, when it began evolving into a Hispanic neighborhood. The Queen Anne cottage next door was enlarged for the rectory in 1927.

10. Stick-Queen Anne triplex, 1888–1890
930–934 Twenty-Sixth Avenue

William S. Wise, builder

Although little "tenements" like these were fairly common in nineteenth-century Oakland, hardly any have survived. This one stands out in a neighborhood of detached Queen Anne and Colonial cottages.

11. California Cotton Mills 1917 Building
1091 Calcot Place

A. C. Griewank, engineer

The California Cotton Mill, founded in 1884, was the first large employer in this area. The four-story heavy timber-and-brick building is the newest and most visible part of the plant that, at one time, extended from here to the estuary; the freeway cuts through the older one-story buildings on the estuary side.

12. 23rd Avenue Baptist Church, 1902
1711 Twenty-Third Avenue

Henry F. Starbuck, architect

A spectacular tower, cupola, and finials distinguish this church, now the Church of Tonga. Twenty-Third Avenue once connected the industrial waterfront to both a commercial district on International Boulevard and a residential neighborhood in the foothills where many Victorians still stand.

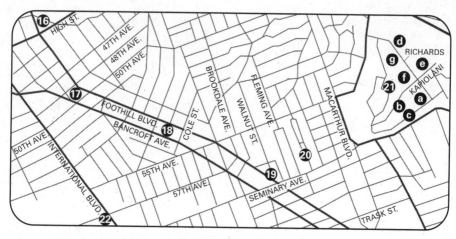

3 • East Oakland

13. Salem German Methodist Episcopal Church, 1891
1650 Twenty-Third Avenue

Axel Wahlstrom, builder

A fine wooden church, now Primera Iglesia Bautista, has large lancet windows and arched bargeboard trim.

14. Twenty-Third Avenue Branch Library, 1917
1449 Miller Avenue

C. W. Dickey and John Donovan, architects

This Spanish colonial library is one of four Oakland Carnegie branch libraries built between 1915 and 1918. Along with a former bank, hotel, and two theater buildings on Twenty-Third Avenue, it marks the location of a major early-twentieth-century commercial district.

15. Little Sisters of the Poor, St. Joseph's Professional Center, 1912
2647 International Boulevard

Leo J. Devlin, architect

Built as a Catholic nursing home, this was a self-contained complex with its own chapel, laundry, maintenance shops, and men's smoking building.

16. High Street Presbyterian Church, 1921
1941 High Street

Julia Morgan, architect

This is a small, gracious Mediterranean-style neighborhood church.

17. Melrose Branch Library, 1915
4805 Foothill Boulevard

William H. Weeks, architect

A classical building with an unusual fan-shaped plan and well-preserved period elements is another of four Carnegie branch libraries built between 1915 and 1918.

18. Fairfax Theater, 1925
5327–5351 Foothill Boulevard

Reid Brothers, architects

This gorgeous Spanish Colonial theater, now a church, is a highlight of the Foothill-Fairfax-Bancroft commercial district, which has other attractive commercial/residential buildings from the 1920s.

19. Bennett Building, 1926
5850–5866 Foothill Boulevard

L. H. Nishkian, engineer

The flagship building of the Foothill-Seminary commercial district is situated on a corner nicknamed "The Hub of East Oakland" in the 1920s. Adjoining at **5846**·**Foothill** is a tiny wedge-shaped structure with a tiled storefront, reportedly featured in *Ripley's Believe It or Not* as the world's narrowest building.

20. Normandy Garden, 1926–1927
5500–5881 Picardy Drive, Fifty-Fifth Avenue to Seminary Avenue

W. W. Dixon, R. C. Hillen, and Ernest W. Urch, designer-builders

This loop street is Oakland's premier Mother Goose neighborhood that is also famed for its Christmas light displays. On the nearby blocks of Morse, Fleming, and Hillen Drives are other picturesque Period Revival homes, most built by Dixon and Hillen or taken from their pattern books.

21. Mills College,
1870s ongoing
5000 MacArthur Boulevard
(gate at Richards Road)

Far out in the country, when Cyrus and Susan Mills's Female Seminary moved here from Benicia, the picturesque 127-acre campus has many distinguished buildings dating from 1870 on. Highlights include:

21a. Mills Hall, 1870
North side of The Oval
S. C. Bugbee and Sons,
architects

This vast timber-framed Second Empire Italianate with a mansard roof originally housed the entire school, dormitories as well as classrooms. It is the last of such huge Victorian-era buildings in the Bay Area.

21b. El Campanil, 1903
South side of The Oval
Julia Morgan, architect

This concrete Mission-style bell tower was donated by Borax Smith and his wife, and established young Julia Morgan's reputation when it stood through the 1906 earthquake. It serves as the symbol of the college.

21c. Margaret Carnegie Library, 1905–1906
East side of The Oval
Julia Morgan, architect

Mills College obtained a grant from Andrew Carnegie by offering to name the library after his daughter. The Beaux-Arts building has a 1954 addition by architect Milton Pfluegar.

21d. Ming Quong Home, Alderwood Hall, 1924
Ming Quong Road
Julia Morgan, architect

Ming Quong Home for Chinese girls was carefully designed to foster their self-esteem and cultural heritage. It was annexed to Mills College as a dormitory in 1936, and was remodeled in 2003 by architect Megan Riera for the Julia Morgan School for Girls, a private middle school.

21e. Music Building, 1928
Richards Road
Walter Ratcliff Jr., architect

The Music Building and the Art Gallery (1925), both by Ratcliff, are two Spanish Colonial designs from Ratcliff's tenure as campus architect.

21f. Chapel, 1967
Richards Road
Callister and Payne, architects

Indoor-outdoor spaces and a soaring round sanctuary distinguish this Japanesque Bay Tradition chapel.

22. Mutual Stores-Safeway Headquarters, 1927
5701 International Boulevard
Reed & Corlett,
architects

Emil Hagstrom's Mutual Stores, absorbed by Safeway by 1931, was a pioneer grocery chain in the Bay Area with 100 branches by the time this remarkable plant was built.

23. Oakland Coliseum and Arena, 1965
7000 Coliseum Way
Skidmore, Owings & Merrill,
architects
Whitney & Amman,
structural engineers

These twin masterpieces of pure and daring structure, now obscured by wraparound entries, skyboxes, and other 1996 appendages, remain among the most important modern symbols of Oakland.

24. Warehouse Union Local 6, ILWU Hall, 1965
99 Hegenberger Road
Herbert T. Johnson,
architect

The roof is suspended on cables from parabolic arches, and the entry has mosaic murals by Beniamino Bufano.

25. North Field, Oakland Municipal Airport,
1927–1929
8601–9501 Earhart Road

Gustavo B. Hegardt and Arthur Abel, Port engineers

These are seven of the original eight buildings of the Oakland Municipal Airport, now used for flight schools and general aviation. A few blocks northwest

at 8260 Boeing Street is the Western Aerospace Museum.

26. Oakland International Airport Terminal 1,
1960–1962
End of Airport Drive

Warnecke & Warnecke, architects

An Oakland icon of the 1960s has cantilevered barrel-vault concrete

canopies over the sidewalk and a glassed-in restaurant and bar suspended from the control tower.

27. Terminal 2, Lionel Wilson Terminal,
1983–1985 (unmapped)
Southeast of Terminal 1

The Ratcliff Architects

A showy space-frame structure was constructed of tinted glass and shiny tubular steel.

28. Brookfield School, 1951
401 Jones Avenue

Ponsford & Price, architects

The wartime Brookfield Village neighborhood has a handsome International-style school distinguished by sleek window walls and a tall auditorium with a wide flat roof, pipe columns, and vertical fins.

29. Elmhurst Presbyterian Church, 1893 (unmapped)
1332 Ninety-Eighth Avenue

Distinctive angular-topped windows echo the gables and steeple of this Carpenter Gothic church.

30. Star-Durant Plant, Durant Square, 1922 (unmapped)
19626–10950 International Boulevard

P.J. Walker Co., builder

Beginning in 1916 with a Chevrolet plant off Seventy-Third Avenue (now the site of Eastmont Mall), Oakland set out to become "The Detroit of the West." Durant Motors was a short-lived offshoot of Chevrolet. In 2001–2003, the plant was converted to commercial and loft space by Flynn, Craig + Grant Architects and the site infilled with neo-Craftsman homes designed by McLarand, Vasquez and Partners for developer Signature Properties.

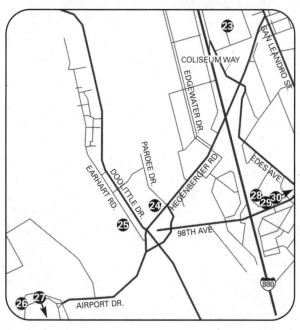

3 • East Oakland

Oakland Hills

Gail Lombardi,
author & photographer

Once a dense redwood forest, the Oakland hills were clear cut by loggers to provide lumber for fast-growing San Francisco following the Gold Rush. Joaquin Miller, "Poet of the Sierras," came to the Oakland hills in 1879, bought seventy acres, planted thousands of trees, and built his Abbey on his "Hights." Farms and country estates dotted the hills: Col. John C. Hays in Fernwood (1852; demolished), Frederick Rhoda in Fruitvale (1900), and Alexander Dunsmuir to the south (1899).

Residential building began in the 1920s when the Realty Syndicate developed the Montclair area. Fernwood, Merriewood, and Piedmont Pines were some of these early tracts, and today they retain the rustic wooded look of an earlier time. The Montclair shopping district began with the 1928 Mission Revival bus terminal.

Residential development in the hills generally spread south from Montclair, and each decade of building is evident by the style of houses found in particular neighborhoods. Walter Leimert's Oakmore has nice Period Revival houses from the 1930s; in the 1940s and 1950s, California Ranch–style houses sprang up near Skyline Boulevard; the Balmoral and Phaeton-Shay neighborhoods exhibit the architecture of the 1960s.

1. Lake Temescal and Beach House, 1938

Broadway at Warren Freeway

Williams and Wastell,
architects

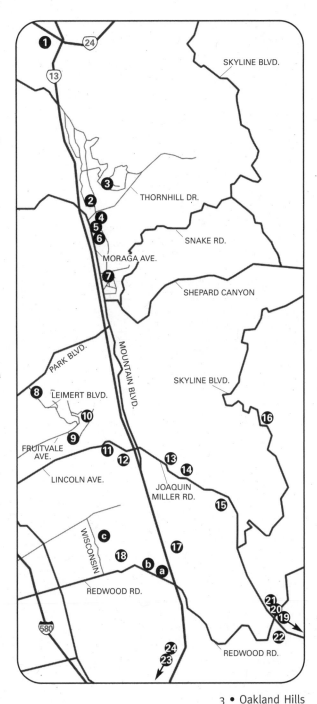

Lake Temescal, developed in 1936, was one of the early East Bay Regional Parks. The stone-faced Craftsman clubhouse was designed to blend with the rustic setting.

2. Fernwood Neighborhood, 1920s
1434–1616 Fernwood Drive

This neighborhood is the former site of Col. John C. Hays's nineteenth-century estate. Developed by the Realty Syndicate in 1925, Period Revival houses line a wooded creek. The William Chryst house at **1600 Fernwood** (1929; Carr Jones, architect) is notable for its Storybook style with brick walls, slate roof, and wrought-iron details.

3. Merriewood Neighborhood, 1920s
5574–6240 Merriewood Drive

Many of the early houses on Merriewood Drive were built as vacation cabins, and several retain their original clapboard siding: 5574 (1924), 5826 (1925), 5844 (1925), 5857 (1925), and 5876 (1926).

4. Montclair Branch Library, 1929
1687 Mountain Boulevard

C. C. Rosenberry, architect

This neighborhood public library looks like an English cottage with a flared slate roof, arched brick entry, and brick chimney.

5. Montclair Firehouse, 1927
6226 Moraga Avenue

Eldred E. Edwards, Oakland Deptartment of Public Works, architect

The Storybook-style former fire-house has a precast concrete roof and flame-shaped finials.

6. Montclair Park and Recreation Center, 1938–1940
6256 Moraga Avenue

The lake in this park was once part of the 1850s Medau family dairy. The Realty Syndicate bought the property in the early 1900s and developed it as a city park in the 1930s. The WPA built the recreation center and stonework.

7. Montclair Business District, 1928 and later
1950–2085 Mountain Boulevard,
6100–6232 LaSalle Avenue

Highlights of this lively and picturesque neighborhood shopping area are the Regency building at **2053–2063 Mountain Boulevard** (1946; F. Harvey Slocombe, architect), the Mission Revival building at **6206 La Salle Avenue** (1928; Hamilton Murdock, architect) and the Provincial building at **616–625 Medau Place** (1946; William E. Schirmer, architect).

8. Sausal Creek Arch Bridge, 1926
Leimert Boulevard between Park Boulevard and Clemens Road

George A. Posey, engineer

Developer Walter Leimert called it "The Bridge that Wrought a Miracle for Oakmore Highlands." Designed as a fixed single-arch bridge, it opened the Oakmore district to development, bringing streetcar, pedestrian, and auto transportation into the area. The residential neighborhood has a fine collection of Mediterranean, Tudor Revival, Spanish, and Monterey Colonial houses, as well as a Streamline Moderne at **1815 Leimert** (1936; F. Harvey Slocombe, architect).

9. Frederick Rhoda Farmhouse, 1900–1901
4300 Fruitvale Avenue

This Queen Anne farmhouse has a wraparound veranda and onion-domed tower. It is a reminder of the days when Fruitvale was the orchard center of the East Bay. Rhoda gave Fruitvale its name after he planted his 400-acre ranch in fruit trees.

10. LeGrand Coleman House, 1946
4381 Arcadia Avenue

Paul R. Williams, architect

Here is a mid-century Modern with wide eave overhangs and pipe posts, with deck and glass walls set at angles. Paul R. Williams, considered one of the nation's great African American architects, was prominent in Los Angeles. He described his style as "conservative modern." He also designed Allison Pontiac showroom in San Jose.

11. Greek Orthodox Cathedral of the Ascension, 1966
4700 Lincoln Avenue

John Lyon Reid & Associates, architects

This Modern Greek cathedral has four arched wings around the copper-covered dome, forming a Greek cross. Three arches in the entry pavilion complement the large dome.

12. Oakland California Temple, The Church of Jesus Christ of Latter-day Saints, 1962–1964
4766 Lincoln Avenue

Harold W. Burton, architect

A landmark in the East Bay hills, the spires of the LDS (Mormon) Temple are covered in gold leaf, reflecting light during the day;

perforated and illuminated at night, they are visible for miles. Temple literature describes this as "modern with an Oriental motif."

13. Joaquin Miller Park and Monuments, 1886–1904
Joaquin Miller Road near Sanborn Drive

California poet Cincinnatus Heine (Joaquin) Miller planted thousands of trees on his formerly barren "Hights," the core of Joaquin Miller Park. Here he built a cabin called "The Abbey" (1886), and a stone tower (1904), dedicated to John C. Frémont, on the site where Fremont named the Golden Gate in 1846.

14. Woodminister Amphitheater, 1938–1940; Cascades, 1937–1940
Joaquin Miller Road

Howard Gilkey, architect (Cascades)

Edward Foulkes and Edgar Sanborn, architects (Amphitheater)

A WPA project "Dedicated to California Writers," this Art Deco concrete outdoor theater steps up the hill with Deco panels and figures on east and west sides. The Cascades flow down a natural spillway of shale and boulders, flanked by alcoves and meandering stairways. Two formal fountains form the base of the Cascades.

15. Thomas H. Boyd Log Cabin, 1923
3551 Joaquin Miller Road
Thomas H. Boyd, builder

This is a five-room cabin with a chinked log exterior and a stone chimney.

16. Chabot Space and Science Center, 1997–2000
10000 Skyline Boulevard
Gerson and Overstreet, architects

This striking new observatory and planetarium has glass, aluminum, and bare concrete walls, and a tinted aluminum dome.

Origins date to the 1883 Oakland Observatory and 1915 Chabot Observatory.

17. Holy Names University, 1955–1958
3500 Mountain Boulevard
Milton Pflueger, architect

A mid-century Modern campus of low-roofed buildings has clean lines and large windows in a modified Spanish style of courts and plazas. The **McCrea House** just outside the campus entrance (1913; George McCrea, designer) incorporates a former Peralta adobe chapel and house.

18. Three modest Period Revival neighborhoods, 1930s

These three residential subdivisions in the south Oakland Hills were developed to provide affordable housing for average workers, but great care was taken to offer the type of amenities found in much more costly homes: varied designs with sometimes wonderfully inventive details, and lots large enough to provide front and back gardens and a garage.

18a. Redwood Gardens, 1939–1941
4314–4363 Atlas Avenue, 4314–4397 Detroit Avenue, off Redwood Road
A. J. Flagg, builder

These Modern split-level houses have hipped and gabled roofs, brick trim, shutters, porthole windows, and glass block.

18b. A Lane in Spain, 1930s
3547–3595 Monterey Avenue, 3390–3457 Guido Street 3426 Guido Street [18b]
J. S. Flagg, builder

The Spanish eclectic houses, developed as "A Lane in Spain," feature arched windows, tile roofs, decorative chimneys, and some turrets.

18c. Laurel Terrace, 1930s
4100–4114 Laurel Avenue,
3200–3220 Wisconsin Street

Fred T. Dooley, builder

A cluster of Spanish houses has unique brick chimneys and arched windows.

19. Fernhoff Road houses, 1950–1977
Fernhoff and Bacon Roads,
off Skyline Boulevard

Various architects

This loop road has Oakland hills houses varying from the builder-designed Ranch-style houses at **5640 Fernhoff** (1956), **5660 Fernhoff** (1960) and **5524 Bacon** (1954), some with stables, to the Modern **5530 Fernhoff** with soaring angled glass bay (1961; Dalton & Dalton, architects) and **5588 Fernhoff** (1977; Aaron G. Green, architect).

20. Eichler houses, 1965
8100 Block of Phaeton Drive
and 8000 Block of Shay Drive,
off Keller Avenue, both sides
of the streets

Claude Oakland, architect

Here is a cluster of Modern Eichler-developed houses designed by Claude Oakland. Most have flat and/or low gabled roofs with exposed beams, clerestory windows, and atrium entrances.

21. Sequoyah Country Club, 1928
4550 Heafey Road,
off Sequoyah Road

Eugene Barton, architect

This Spanish-style clubhouse incorporates the original 1915 building, retaining the original arched arcade, exposed beams, fireplace, and fixtures. The Oakland Open golf tournament was played here in the 1930s and 1940s.

22. Holy Redeemer College, 1925
8945 Golf Links Road

William Mooser III, architect

A complex of Mission-style college buildings surrounds a courtyard with cloistered walkways. The chapel has a three-story tower, an oculus window, and a compound arched entry flanked with columns topped with angels reading. Now operating as a retreat center, the campus includes several outbuildings as well as a newer chapel with stained glass (1962).

23. Dunsmuir House and Gardens, 1899
2900 Peralta Oaks Court,
off 106th Avenue

J. Eugene Freeman, architect

John McLaren, garden landscape designer

This elegant Neoclassical mansion was built by Alexander Dunsmuir for his bride. It became the summer home for San Francisco banker I. W. Hellman Jr. from 1906 until the late 1950s, and is now maintained as a house museum. The estate was a working farm, which included a carriage house, milk barn, Dinkelspiel cottage, and other outbuildings that remain on the forty acres.

24. Sheffield Village, 1939–1941
Covington and Danbury
Streets, Revere Avenue,
and Marlow Drive

Theodore N. Thompson and Irwin Johnson, architects

This is a picturesque tract of small traditional homes, the type of planning promoted by the FHA in the 1930s. Period Revival influences are varied: English, French, Spanish, Monterey, Colonial, and Ranch. The houses on Marlow Drive (1942–1952) are custom built and less repetitive.

Oakland/Berkeley Fire Area

Susan Dinkelspiel Cerny, author & photographer

On October 20, 1991, a raging wildfire devastated an area over a mile in diameter near the Caldecott Tunnel on either side of Highway 24. Within the 1,520 acres that burned, 2,843 single-family homes and more than 300 apartment units were damaged or destroyed. The fire caused twenty-five deaths and 150 injuries.

Most of the area is rebuilt, and the thousands of custom houses and multifamily buildings provide an excellent snapshot of the latest up-to-date styles and popular trends in current domestic architecture. The majority of

the houses are large and neo-traditional, but there are a number that playfully experiment with geometry, angles, materials, textures, and color. Industrial Modernism is the latest trend. Internally, floor plans have become more open; greatly enlarged kitchens have become the focus of family living space. Designers of these hillside homes have generally utilized steep elevations in creative and unusual ways.

Unfortunately, streets were not regraded nor widened after the fire; in the upper hills, the streets remain as narrow, steep, and congested as they were before the fire.

An overview tour of this hilly and often confusing area is best

started on Broadway Terrace at Broadway in Oakland. Wind up to Grizzly Peak or Skyline Boulevards and head north into Berkeley. Come down the hill on Marlborough Terrace, Strathmoor Drive, Alvarado and Vicente Roads to exit onto Tunnel Road behind the Claremont Hotel. Tour the side streets along the way.

Oakland Fire Area

1. 6242 Buena Vista Avenue, 2000

David Pierce Holmann, architect

A vertical Craftsman-inspired three-story house sits above a garage.

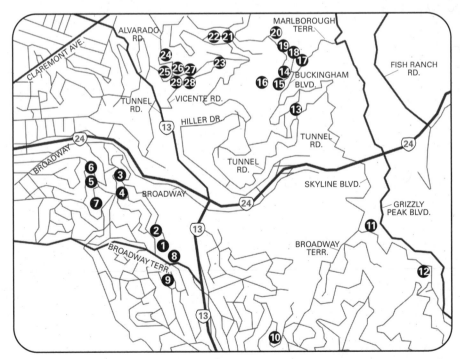

3 • Oakland/Berkeley Fire Area (1991)

2

A neo-traditional but unfussy design has gabled wings flanking a recessed entry.

7. 140 Alpine Terrace, 1995

Mark Horton Architecture

Sheathed in a grid of concrete board, the two-story house has two distinct sections linked by a recessed section with a metal-and-glass awning over the first-floor windows. Angled and rectangular bays punctuate the rectangular volumes. Metal-framed windows and railings are among the materials that define its Industrial Modernism character.

8. Jordan Residence, 1992
6356 Broadway Terrace

Ace Architects

Located in a prominent location on a narrow lot, this residence is said to have been inspired by Bernard Maybeck's Hearst Hall on the University of California–Berkeley campus that burned in 1922. A "gothic" arch sheathed in copper-faced shingles defines the façade and interior of the main room.

9. 5015 Proctor Avenue, 1997
Young & Burton, contractor

This house is intriguingly fortress-like in dark-gray stucco with a steel bridge and layers of rectilinear geometry. Across the street at **5020 Proctor,** and in striking contrast, is architect Glen Jarvis's 1999 white-stucco-sided house with windows everywhere.

10. 11034 Broadway Terrace, 2003

Robert Nebolon Architect

Some houses just stand out as well designed.

2. 6140 Buena Vista Avenue, 1994

Chris Lamen & Associates, architects

Prominent lower and upper window bays with arched roofs give this brightly colored house distinction.

3. 5518 Golden Gate Avenue, 1995

David Stark Wilson, Wilson Associates, designer-builder

Here is a house in two parts: the two-story wing is above the garage and the one-story section is on the north. The house stands out for understated simplicity.

4. Langmaid Residence, 1994
6308 Acacia Avenue

House & House Architects

Located on a corner lot, the large sprawling house looks like many cottages. Its sections are set at different angles and are sheathed in horizontal wood siding, stained light rustic gray, or have burnt-Sienna-colored stucco.

5. Roth House, 1995
6147 Ocean View Drive

Ace Architects

A broken gable end is punctuated by an elongated pyramidal chimneystack flanked by a glazed wall. Deep brick-colored stucco walls, exaggerated triangular brackets, and colorful tile risers and a native stone retaining wall add visual interest. This is only the front of the large multi-faceted U-shaped house.

Also of interest is **6170 Ocean View** (1995) by Swatt Architects.

6. 6139 Ocean View Drive, 1991

Glen Jarvis, architect

11. Aves House, 2004
5895 Grizzly Peak Boulevard
Jim Orjala, Big Dog Construction, architect

Three stories of angled Industrial Modernism are built on a very steep lot. The house can be seen best from below on Skyline Boulevard.

12. 7525, 7535 Skyline Boulevard castles, 2002
Ace Architects

Here are two of the miniature "castles" Ace Architects designed in the Oakland Hills. There is also one at **8047 Skyline** (1993).

13. Henry and Leilani Cotten House, 1994
1985 Tunnel Road
Ace Architects

This fanciful house has two towers that are like the shapes of saxophones. It was well publicized when new.

14. 7027 Devon Way, 2004
Regan Bice Architects

Low horizontal stucco walls spread out from simple rectangular volumes. The one-story street façade is just the first story of a multistory house that descends the hillside.

15. 7000 Devon Way, 1995
David Stark Wilson, Wilson Associates, designer-builder

The house displays clean lines, an angled chimney, pale multi-colored stucco siding, and a gabled tile roof—plus a confident sense of scale and massing.

16. The Felton House, 1996
6889 Devon Way
Glen Jarvis, architect

This is the largest and most prominent house in the Oakland/Berkeley hills. Although its driveway is on Deyon, the house cannot be seen from there, but it is visible from many locations, including the freeway. It has a huge and prominent, rounded window bay looking out toward the views of San Francisco, and sits on its own leveled knoll. Jarvis also designed **7011 Devon** in 1996.

17. Wilson House, 1997
7124 Norfolk Road
David Stark Wilson, Wilson Associates, designer-builder

Located on a level lot, the two-story house has a tall window bay with an arched roof, flanked by different-sized setback wings. **7036** (1994; House & House Architects) and **7133** comprise a nice group of compatible houses.

18. 119 Strathmoor Drive, 1994
Jim Jennings Architecture

Composed of two boxes of unequal size and connected by a recessed section in the middle with a wall of translucent glass, its simplicity is distinctive. The smaller box is sheathed in corrugated metal, and the large one is cement panel.

19. 85 Strathmoor Drive, 1998
David Stark Wilson, Wilson Associates, designer-builder

A gently curved roof, cut back on the end, slopes beyond the window wall. Located on a rather narrow corner lot, the house is placed parallel to the street. The siding is gray stucco.

20. 10 Drury Court, 1994
Mark Horton Architecture

Sheathed in cement board, the connectors in each corner give the wing overlooking the street a polka-dot pattern. A wide curved section sits above a curved concrete retaining wall. In the back, the house has a slate-covered gabled roof.

21. 1060 Amito Drive, 1993
Gary Parsons, architect

A copper angled bay juts out from the house and makes a dramatic statement.

22. 373 Gravatt Drive, 1994
David Baker, architect

A bit of deconstructionism is present here, but the overall effect is modest.

23. 1715 Grandview Drive, 1996
House & House Architects

An interesting massing of curved and angled shapes in contrasting earth tones are the basic components. Windows of various sizes and framing styles, and sloping, gabled, and flat roofs provide a multitude of visual elements.

Berkeley Fire Area

24. 278 Alvarado Road, 1992
Decredico/Sergent Design, architects

This is a strong, bold statement with textured-concrete retaining walls and foundation, pale yellow stucco siding, and bands of natural wood accents. The two-story house is L-shaped around a front garden.

25. 225 Alvarado Road, 1994
Moore Ruble Yudell Architects

The L-shaped multilevel house steps down the hillside and opens at each level to a garden or patio. The stucco siding is soft olive green.

26. 220 Alvarado Road, 1993
Thaddeus Kusmierski, architect

The broad Mediterranean house with tile roof is a reconstruction of a house designed by Bernard Maybeck in 1928. Its owner/architect used original plans found in the archives of the College of Environmental Design at UC–Berkeley.

27. 160 Vicente Road, 2004
Franklin D. Israel Design Associates, architects

When completed, the house stood out because of its copper-sided exterior west wall that wraps around to the front of the house in strong projecting angles. Neighbors and foliage have calmed the shock effect, but it remains a stunning combination of shapes and materials.

28. 95 Vicente Road, 2004
Richard Soenksen & Arken Tilt, architects

David Bass, builder

Steve Rogers, Roger Murray, master carpenters

Many recycled materials, solar electrical and solar heating, and use of a green philosophy make this house ecologically friendly. Trelliswork angles across the façade.

29. 49 Vicente Road, 2003
Charles Warren Callister, architect

This pole house almost replicates the Callister-designed house that was destroyed. It seems considerably larger than the original house, perhaps because its tree-shaded site is gone. A trellis projects over a covered carport.

4 • Piedmont

During the 1860s, most of Piedmont was a dairy ranch owned by Walter Blair. After the discovery of sulfur springs, visitors came to "take the waters" and stayed at the Piedmont Springs Hotel near today's Exedra. Many of the first homes in Piedmont were large estates; Isaac Requa's Highland estate in the 1870s comprised seventeen acres.

Reverend Joseph Worcester came to Piedmont as a tutor and, in 1877, built a shingled cottage. When Bernard Maybeck saw Worcester's Cottage in the 1890s, he called it a "revelation." It and Worcester's three shingled houses on Russian Hill (1889) are considered to be the inspirations for building unpainted wood-frame houses that blended with nature. Today, Worcester's Cottage still stands at 575 Blair Avenue, shingled but greatly altered. Jack London lived in Worcester's Cottage in 1903, part of a bohemian neighborhood on Scenic Avenue that included George Sterling, Xavier Martinez, and Herman Whittaker.

The first building boom began in 1890 when cable cars brought transportation into Piedmont. Prospective homeowners chose Piedmont for its climate, expansive views, and proximity to downtown Oakland and the ferry to San Francisco. In 1907, the city of Piedmont incorporated, narrowly escaping annexation by Oakland.

During the 1910s and 1920s, successful businessmen hired prominent architects to design their homes. The Newsom Brothers, Julia Morgan, John Hudson Thomas, Albert Farr, and others produced some of their finest landmark-quality houses here.

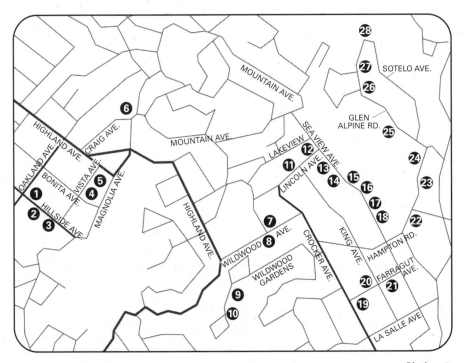

1. Grey Gables, 1908
304 Hillside Avenue

Albert Farr, architect

One of Albert Farr's Jacobethan Tudor Revivals, this one has parapet gables and two-story bays with crenellated parapets. There is curved glass in the gable windows, extensive leaded glass, and flat tiles on the roof.

2. J. T. Barraclough House, 1898
321 Hillside Avenue

D. Franklin Oliver, architect

This Neoclassical design has a dramatic full-height porch with round Ionic columns, dentils, a wide frieze, and arched windows with fanlight and sidelights at the entry.

3. Gorrill House and Wedding Cottage, 1899
337, 345 Hillside Avenue

Cunningham Brothers, architects-builders

Both the Tudor-style Gorrill home and his daughter's wedding cottage to the left exhibit similar high gables, complex half-timbering, and Colusa sandstone chimneys and bases. Lumber merchant R. W. Gorrill's house has a circular dining room, Romanesque stone tower, and stone entry arch.

4. Jesse Wetmore House, 1878
342 Bonita Avenue

Jesse and William Wetmore, builders

This is the oldest unaltered house in Piedmont, the only Piedmont house listed on the National Register. It is a simple square Folk Victorian with spindle-work and jigsaw trim in the veranda. Four farm scenes

painted by L. Blume-Siebert adorn the front door glass.

5. Exedra, 1924
Highland Avenue at Magnolia Avenue

Albert Farr, architect

Part of Albert Farr's 1922 Master Plan for Piedmont's Civic Center, the Exedra was designed as the grand entrance to Piedmont's new municipal park. It shares the same Spanish design with the 1910 Farr-designed city hall and fire station at **120 Vista Avenue.** The "Blue Vase," as it is often called, is a semiofficial symbol of the city of Piedmont. The plaza and fountain were added to the rear in 2002.

6. Hugh Craig House, 1879
55 Craig Avenue

Charles S. Bugbee, architect

Although this Stick Italianate has lost its elaborate stick-work, the house retains its original porch, square bay with tall curved windows, and pull doorbell. Built for the first mayor of Piedmont, the house was moved 200 feet when the six-acre estate was subdivided.

7. Willis Kelly House, 1910
455 Wildwood Avenue

John Hudson Thomas, architect

This is John Hudson Thomas' largest house in Piedmont. It has an entry portico with three massive arches, adding a Mission Revival touch to the asymmetrical Prairie-style house. It also has multiple low-hipped roofs with wide eaves and bands of windows with ornamental sash. The house was featured in early Piedmont publicity promoting real estate development. Willis F. Kelly was vice president of Oakland Traction, and the streetcar line

terminated here. Thomas also designed the house at **431 Wildwood Avenue**

8. Bert Scott House, 1917
456 Wildwood Avenue

Albert Farr, architect

Farr combines parapet gables, tall bay windows, massive chimneys, and extensive leaded glass in another Jacobethan Tudor house. The gardens were designed by Thomas Church.

9. Frank C. Havens Estate, Wildwood, 1908–1913
101 Wildwood Gardens

Bernard Maybeck, architect

This eclectic Oriental mansion was designed in 1908 by Bernard Maybeck for real estate developer Frank C. Havens. Before completion, Mrs. Havens began adding extensive Oriental woodwork, reflecting her interest in Eastern religion. Exterior trim and elaborate interior paneling were carved on-site by Asian craftsmen. Construction continued to 1913. Only the porte cochere with its intricate dragon-like brackets is visible from the street. Maybeck designed two other Piedmont houses, one at **110 Sunnyside Avenue** (1904) and the other at **34 Dormidera Avenue** (1909), both shingled.

10. Harold Huovinen House, 1932
85 Wildwood Gardens

Carr Jones, architect

This Storybook house exhibits Carr Jones signature curved brick exterior, thick walls, tile floors, and recycled timber. Steep swooping roofs suggest the thatch roofs of peasant farmhouses.

11. Walter Leimert–George Q. Chase House, 1910
37 Lincoln Avenue

Arthur Brown Jr., architect

The eclectic French Norman house is built around a tower,

reminiscent of medieval watchtowers; it has tall steeply pitched roofs, half-timbering, and an asymmetrical composition. The sunroom on the left is an addition. It was designed for developer Walter Leimert.

12. Knowland Mansion, 1913–1914
25 Sea View Avenue

Charles Peter Weeks, architect

The Beaux-Arts design exhibits formal symmetry and elaborate ornament with its roofline balustrade, elegant cornice, and

inlaid marble vestibule. Note the unusual fan-shaped glass roof suspended between the paired columns. The first owner was banker and developer Edson F. Adams, son of Oakland pioneer Edson Adams (Adams Point). During the 1940s and into the 1960s, it was the home of Joseph R. Knowland Sr., publisher and editor of the *Oakland Tribune.*

13. Gerald Trayner House, 1930–1931
55 Sea View Avenue

Albert Farr, architect

This Jacobethan Tudor has a striking brick-and-stone exterior with parapet gables, crenellated bays, and numerous large chimney stacks. The driveway goes through the crenellated tower like a tunnel, separating the main part of the house from the garage and servants' quarters.

14. Austin Hills House, 1926
65 Sea View Avenue

Sidney B. and Archie T. Newsom, architects

This large Mediterranean home bears the mark of owners Austin and Mignon Hills of the Hills Brothers coffee business. Two Arabian faces, the same trademark found on Hills Brothers coffee cans, adorn the balcony. Zigzags representing "hills" fill the center shield. There is an unusual green-glazed tile roof and a symmetrical façade with recessed wings that repeat the corbelled arches of the balcony.

15. Annie Moller House, 1922
76 Sea View Avenue

Farr and Ward, architects

This French Chateau has a distinctive through-the-cornice dormer and steep hipped roofs.

The massing is asymmetrical with formal details: a recessed arched entry framed by columns with elaborately carved capitals and a broken curved pediment, keystones above the multipaned windows, and balustrades. Quoins define all corners.

16. James K. Moffitt House, 1911
86 Sea View Avenue

Willis Polk, architect

Designed for banker and paper magnate James Moffitt, the house shows the unconventional aspects of Polk's residential designs after 1900. His interplay between plain and fancy elements is seen in the plain stucco, the bold window surrounds, the flat roof tiles, and the monumental scale of the classical ornament over the columned entry.

17. Samuel Taylor House, 1912
90 Sea View Avenue

William Knowles, architect

This brick-sided Georgian Colonial Revival house has a side-gabled roof and symmetrical two-story façade with a wing on the left. The usual Colonial Revival pediment over a central entry is replaced with an off-center recessed arched entry. The arched dormers were added recently.

18. Mary Alexander House, 1911
92 Sea View Avenue

Charles W. Dickey, architect

The Craftsman design of exposed beams and large-paned windows with ornamental sash is blended with elements that are more for-

mal: stucco exterior, prominent two-story bays, modillions, and classic detailing in the porch. The gardens originally extended more than 300 feet to the right and rear. It was built by Wallace Alexander for his mother. He was the owner of a Hawaiian sugar empire and noted Piedmont philanthropist. A brass plaque in the sidewalk with the word "KAILANI" refers to their Hawaiian roots.

19. Benjamin Reed House, 1925
200 Crocker Avenue

Julia Morgan, architect

This Italian Renaissance home has a central three-story tower, with a projecting entry portico held by four columns with capitals in a floral design; intricate leaded-glass sidelights surround the arched entry. Most windows are glazed with diamond-shaped leaded glass. The house was built for Benjamin Reed and chocolate heiress Carmen Ghirardelli.

20. William Barbour House, 1910
47 Farragut Avenue

This Colonial Revival–style house has Ionic columns at the entry and sunroom, and classical elements in the cornice and windows and around the etched-glass front door.

21. Harrow Manor, 1915–1916
62 Farragut Avenue

Julia Morgan, architect

James Lombard showed Julia Morgan a watercolor of a manor house in Croyden, England, and asked her to build it for him. Designing from a painting was a unique experience for Morgan, and this Tudor mansion is true to the original with its steep roofs, prominent gables, brick base, half-timbering, bays, massive chimneys, and arched brick entry.

22. Clarence Mayhew House, 1941
330 Hampton Road

Clarence Mayhew and Serge Chemayeff, architects

Clarence Mayhew and Serge Chemayeff blended their respective California and International styles in designing Mayhew's own

home. Built in an oak grove, the box-like design seems to float in space, preserving the site's natural beauty. The house has a flexible plan with sliding partitions that unite the indoors with the outdoors. Horizontal redwood boards and simple white trim unify the exterior.

23. Fritz Henshaw House, 1924
360 Hampton Road

Sidney and Noble Newsom, architects

The Newsoms designed only a general plan for this Storybook house, giving craftsmen artistic license to design the details. The house is said to have been inspired by Marie Antoinette's Hamlet at Versailles; the rustic tinted stucco and the rolled eaves suggest the age and thatched roofs of cottages of an earlier time. Stone punctuates the chimneys. Windows are leaded glass, and decorative wrought-iron hinges enhance the front door.

24. Hampton House, 1926
395 Hampton Road

Albert Farr, architect

This grand Mediterranean villa sits on a prominent site. A monumental arched entry is topped with a large shield and finials; there are hoods, shutters, and brackets around the windows, and quoins throughout.

25. Sweetland Estate, 1929
11 Glen Alpine Road

Frederick Reimers, architect

This grand Tudor, designed for a family of nine, is defined by a steep slate roof, smooth stone exterior, elaborate terra-cotta chimney pots, and prominent gables; a Tudor arch and oriel bay enhance the entry.

Sweetland, who invented oil filters for automobiles, gave the house to the Sisters of the Holy Family in 1949. It served as their convent for almost twenty years.

26. Herbert Erskine House, 1926
42 Glen Alpine Road

William Raymond Yelland, architect

This eclectic French Provincial home by the noted master of the Storybook-style has flared roofs

topped with copper fleur-de-lys and copper chimney pots. There are touches here of formality in the entry with an elaborate pilaster and balustrade relief and the Palladian window in the gable.

27. Jean Witter House, 1930
52 Glen Alpine Road

Williams and Wastell, architects

This Tudor mansion built for stockbroker Witter has elaborate bargeboards and a grand two-story leaded-glass bay window with stained-glass shields and bas-relief panels. Steps wind up through a steep garden to an arched brick-and-stone entry.

28. Dawson Estate, 1926
75 Glen Alpine Road

Albert Farr, architect

This French Chateau has a seventy-foot balustraded terrace lined with French doors. The formal entry, with a fountain, is on the far side of the house, approached by a circular driveway. Dormers and finials punctuate the steep slate roof, and there is elaborate ornament in the pediment.

5 · City of Alameda

Alameda is an island six miles in length, linked by bridges and tunnels to Oakland. The low-rise townscape is primarily residential, with a few commercial districts, a dwindling industrial waterfront, and a former military base. It was a farming village in the Gold Rush, and the introduction of rail and ferry service in the 1860s spurred development. By 1902, when a tidal canal turned the former peninsula into an island, the population neared 20,000. In 2005, it was about 75,000.

Alameda remains a remarkably well-preserved city from the late nineteenth and early twentieth centuries, particularly in its residential neighborhoods. Largely intact streetscapes display a rich variety of types, ranging from workers' cottages to substantial upper-middle-class houses. While there are fine examples of most styles, local architecture achieved its amplest expression between the 1880s and 1920s, in a stylistic sequence stretching from Queen Anne and Colonial Revival through Arts and Crafts and its spin-off, the bungalow.

The leading Victorian designer-builders in Alameda were A. R. Denke, Joseph A. Leonard, Marcuse & Remmel, A. W. Pattiani, and Charles S. Shaner. Denke, with offices on Webster Street, did much of his work in the West End. Leonard and Shaner, based on Park Street, and Pattiani, an Alameda resident with offices in Oakland, catered to middle-class clients in the central part of the island. The most prolific local firm, Marcuse & Remmel, was headquartered at Bay Station in the blue-collar Northside district and was known for its moderately priced cottages. The Alameda Land Co., Delanoy & Randlett, George H. Noble, and other firms kept a tradition of "localism" alive into the 1950s.

Alameda houses tend to be small, built on constricted lots. The subdividing of land into ever-smaller parcels, common practice among speculators as far back as the Gold Rush, helps explain why neighborhoods often send mixed signals, both suburban and urban: detached houses with yards, but tightly packed. On some streets, houses have a "toy town" feeling, more caricature than architecture, and even in tonier neighborhoods, the feeling persists of corseted houses straining to be mansions.

In addition to the main island, the city limits take in the west end of Bay Farm Island (actually a peninsula) and Coast Guard Island, a reclaimed island accessible only from Oakland. The main island is connected to the mainland by five bridges—four over the estuary to Oakland and one over the mouth of San Leandro Bay to Bay Farm Island—and two tunnels. The oldest bridges, at Park Street (1935) and High Street (1939), are bascules; the railroad bridge at Fruitvale Avenue (1951) is a vertical-lift span. The Posey Tube (1928), the older of the two tunnels at Webster Street, was one of the longest in the world when it opened. It is named for Alameda County Engineer George A. Posey, who also oversaw the design of the bascule bridges; the tube's portal buildings were designed by county architect Henry H. Meyers.

Downtown

Park Street has been Alameda's commercial and civic center since the advent of the railroad in 1864. The business district grew up around the train station on Lincoln Avenue and later spread north. The district includes a cross section of commercial buildings and storefronts from the 1860s to the 1950s. The architecturally rich civic center dates back to the 1890s. Nearby residential neighborhoods include some of the oldest houses in the city.

The core of downtown, between Encinal and Lincoln Avenues and several side streets, is a five-block area that is listed as a Historic District on the National Register.

1. Encinal Saloon,
circa 1865
2320 Lincoln Avenue

This simple gabled structure is the city's oldest commercial building; it is all that remains of the original business district near the 1864 train station.

2. Early Alameda houses
Everett Street and Eagle Avenue

A residential district also developed near the train station where a number of Alameda's earliest houses are still standing. **1729 Everett Street** (1870; George Severance, builder) and **2412** and **2416 Eagle Avenue** (circa 1868) are two-story Italianates with symmetrical façades, a hallmark of the early phase of the style. The Jenks House at **2500 Eagle Avenue** (circa 1869) is a pristine Italianate cottage, with arched entry and etched-glass fanlight, built for the tract's developer.

3. Fossing Building, 1886
1629 Park Street

Charles H. Foster, designer-builder

This building is a good example of an Italianate with cast-iron storefronts. At 1645 Park is the **Leona Hotel** (1896; Marcuse & Remmel, designer-builders).

4. Masonic Temple,
1890–1891
1327–1331 Park Street

Charles Mau, architect

This is the only major monument of nineteenth-century downtown to escape remodeling or demolition; the eclectic design, by an Oakland architect, has Romanesque Revival elements. **New Masonic Temple** (1926–1927; Edwin J. Symmes, architect) at 2312–2324 Alameda Avenue is a Classic building adjoining the old

temple. **1335–1345 Park** (1925; Alexander A. Cantin, architect) and **1349 Park** (1929; Olin S. Grove, architect) are two distinguished commercial buildings.

5. Alameda Theater,
1931–1932
2315 Central Avenue

Miller & Pfleuger, architects

The last theater by this important firm is notable for its monumental concrete façade with bas-relief floral panels. The interior is largely intact.

6. Old U.S. Post Office,
1912–1914
2417 Central Avenue
William A. Newman, architect

Now used for medical offices, this granite-clad structure with intact lobby attests to the quality of federal architecture of the period.

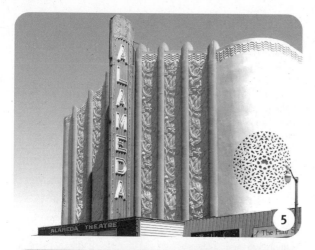

9. Alameda Free Library,
1902–1903
2264 Santa Clara Avenue
Willcox & Curtis, architects

A classicist former Carnegie library has a temple front and light-beige brick walls.

10. Elks Club, 1909–1910
2255 Santa Clara Avenue
J. Eugene Freeman, architect

This is a large Colonial Revival clubhouse of wood construction. At **2233 Santa Clara Avenue** is the city's only intact Second Empire residence (1880; Edward Childs, builder).

11. Alameda Veterans Memorial Building,
1929–1930
2201 Central Avenue
Henry H. Meyers, architect

Here is one of ten veterans memorial buildings in Alameda County designed by Meyers, the county architect. This one mixes Mediterranean and Moderne motifs.

12. Adelphian Club, 1908
2167 Central Avenue
W. H. Wilcox, architect

A picturesque Mission Revival building houses the city's pioneer women's club.

13. First Church of Christ, Scientist, 1920–1921
2164 Central Avenue
Carl Werner, architect

This pristine temple echoes the high school.

14. Alameda High School, 1924–1926
2200 Central Avenue
Carl Werner, architect

7. Alameda Savings Bank Building, 1910
1402–1410 Park Street
Meyers & Ward, architects

A classicist design with arcaded window treatment on the upper story is by a firm that designed numerous buildings in downtown San Francisco.

Civic Center

Extending along Santa Clara and Central Avenues between Oak and Walnut Streets, the civic center was largely developed between 1900 and 1930.

8. Alameda City Hall, 1895–1896
2163 Santa Clara Avenue
Percy & Hamilton, architects

The Richardsonian design, with arcaded portico, is one of the oldest operating city halls in California; it was restored in the 1990s by Ratcliff Architects.

This Classical Revival high school is truly impressive; it stretches the length of a city block, with three wings and a grand portico. The west wing, rebuilt in the 1950s for seismic safety, was designed by Warnecke & Warnecke to complement the original.

15. Twin Towers Methodist Church, 1908–1909
Central Avenue at Oak Street

Meyers & Ward, architects

An Italian Renaissance in beige brick has two *campanili.*

Downtown Residential Neighborhoods

Neighborhoods in the downtown area include a number of early houses, particularly the blocks east of Park Street between Buena Vista and Clement Avenues, along with good examples of later styles.

16. Patterson House, 1883
2253 San Antonio Avenue

Wasson & Pattiani, designer-builders

A small Eastlake villa with a square tower sits across the street from a sumptuous Queen Anne at **2258 San Antonio** (1889; Thomas I. Pyne, builder).

17. Three houses, 1889–1891
2250–2258 San Jose Avenue

Cyrus A. Brown, builder

The most impressive remnant of the work of a lesser-known local builder, this row is a case study in the development of the Queen Anne style, from the transitional design at **2258** (1889) to the turreted residence at **2250** (1891).

18. Alameda Park Tract, 1867
Park Avenue, south of Encinal Avenue

The oval green of this early subdivision, inspired by San Francisco's South Park, became Alameda's first public park in 1895. Renamed Jackson Park in 1909, it contains mature trees and a restored 1890 bandstand. A variety of houses fronts on the park.

East End

In the 1850s, the East End was the site of Alameda's first village, near High Street. When the railroad bypassed the area in 1864, residents relocated to Park Street. Today, little remains of the pioneer settlement. There was no real boom until the Southern Pacific's electric trains began serving the area in 1911. The East End provides an overview of mainstream residential architecture from the early twentieth century, liberally sprinkled with older houses.

19. Webster House, 1854 ·
1238 Versailles Avenue

This Gothic Revival residence, set in a shaded garden, is the oldest documented house in the city.

20. High Street Station commercial buildings, 1891
High Street and Encinal Avenue

Marcuse & Remmel, designer-builders

After the South Pacific Coast Railroad built a station in 1878, a small business district was built where two Queen Anne commercial buildings remain. The **3200 block of Encinal Avenue** is lined with Victorian houses facing a landscaped median on the old railroad right-of-way.

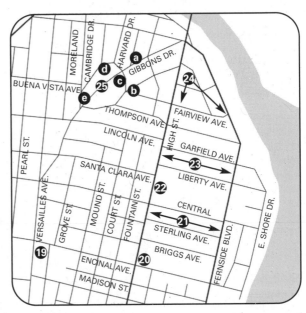

5 • City of Alameda: East End

21. Bungalows, 1916–1918
Sterling Avenue

George Stewart, builder

This narrow street has the feeling of a bungalow court; the lamp-posts are remnants of the city's first streetlight system.

22. Lincoln Park Fence, 1879
High Street at Santa Clara Avenue

This tall cast-iron fence is a relic of an eight-acre estate; the villa is gone, but the grounds became a city park in 1909.

23. Bungalows, 1910–1914
Liberty and Garfield Avenues

W. W. Landgrebe, architect

Robert C. Hillen, builder

These two blocks and adjoining parcels on Fernside Boulevard comprise the city's first large bungalow development, with more than 100 cottages in the Arts and Crafts mode.

24. Waterside Terrace, 1913
3200 Block of Bayo Vista, Fairview, and Monte Vista Avenues

C. C. Adams and Mark T. Cole, builders

Laid out in 1913 with curving streets and concrete pedestals, Waterside Terrace was one of Alameda's first planned subdivisions; it remains a showcase of residential design on the eve of Period Revival, where a number of Prairie-influenced houses were built in 1916 with mannerist eccentricities, of which **3262 Fairview** and **3238 Fairview** are the most outré. **3216** and **3220 Monte Vista** are Secessionist bungalows (1916) by architect Maury Diggs.

25. Fernside

Oakland developer Fred T. Wood laid out this Period Revival subdivision in 1925 on the site of attorney A. A. Cohen's 100-acre estate "Fernside," which had an Italianate mansion as its centerpiece. Gibbons Drive, lined with liquidambar trees, winds diagonally through the tract, adjoined by curving Northwood and Southwood Drives, where the most elaborate houses are found.

25a. Mulvany House, 1928
2927 Gibbons Drive

Fernside Builders

Here is the iconic Fernside house, a picturesque jumble of white stucco and red tile facing two streets and enclosing a courtyard. The original owner, John J. Mulvany, was the tract's sales manager. **2926 Gibbons Drive** (1927; W. W. Dixon, architect) is Spanish Colonial Revival. **2936 Gibbons Drive** (1929; Herbert O. Alden, architect) exudes the feeling of a Norman manor.

25b. Cohen House, 1926
3004 Bayo Vista Avenue

Edwin J. Symmes, architect

Edgar A. Cohen, a son of A. A. Cohen, commissioned this austere house from the subdivision's consulting architect.

25c. Perkins House, 1928
2991 Southwood Drive

Kent & Hass, architects

The house is Spanish Revival by the firm that designed most of Alameda's schools between the 1930s and 1950s.

25d. Hines House, 1928
2986 Northwood Drive

Paul R. Anderson, architect

Anderson, an Oakland architect, designed many houses in Alameda. This Colonial Revival residence is notable for its delicate detailing. **2984 Northwood Drive** (1937; Kent & Hass, architects) is Deco with Ranch dressing.

25e. Cox House, 1935
3101 Gibbons Drive

Francis H. Slocombe, architect

Slocombe, another Oakland architect, produced this stream-lined Moderne design as a demonstration house for electrical appliances.

Gold Coast

The Gold Coast stretches along the old south shore from Grand Street to the vicinity of Ninth Street. This extended neighborhood of tree-lined streets, some retaining globe-top lights, has many impressive houses in the Queen Anne, Colonial Revival, Craftsman, and Period Revival styles. The South Shore Fill in the 1950s replaced the bay shore with landfill and lagoons. Grand Street connects old Alameda with the new developments but more than lives up to its name on the blocks between Palmer Court and Encinal Avenue.

1. Hjul House, 1907 (unmapped)
701 Grand Street

Though altered, this still-impressive Craftsman was the residence of a San Francisco engineer who also may have designed it. A view of the Gold Coast shoreline can be seen from the Grand Street bridge.

2. Jacobi House, 1890
815 Grand Street

Charles S. Shaner, designer-builder

This Queen Anne with corner tower has an arcaded porch.

3. Cornelius House, 1909
824 Grand Street

A. W. Cornelius, architect

This shingled house was the architect's residence.

4. House, 1879
900 Grand Street

Gilbert & Brown, builders

This Italianate with turret addition is one of the oldest houses in the Gold Coast.

5. Stafford House, 1932
912 Grand Street

William E. Schirmer, architect

The architect's creation is Period Revival at its most picturesque. **915** and **917 Grand Street** (1891; A. W. Pattiani, designer-builder) are a pair of Queen Anne residences in the shingled mode.

6. O'Connor House, 1891
1001 Grand Street

Charles S. Shaner, designer-builder

This substantial Queen Anne bears comparison with Pattiani's more advanced designs at **915** and **917 Grand Street** from the same year. **1000 Grand** (1900; C. H. Russell, architect) is a mix of Queen Anne and Colonial Revival by the former head draftsman of the Joseph A. Leonard Co.

7. Jordan House, 1901
1100 Grand Street

J. W. Dolliver, architect

Here is an early Tudor Revival with steeply pitched gables.

8. Dorward and Green Houses, 1910, 1908
1621, 1625 San Antonio Avenue

Wythe & McCall, architects

Two Craftsman houses display the talents of this Oakland firm.

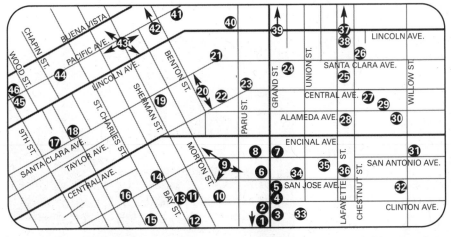

5 • City of Alameda: Gold Coast, Central Alameda, Northside, Waterfront

9. Franklin Park
Paru and Morton Streets,
and San Antonio and
San Jose Avenues

There are a number of distinctive houses in the blocks surrounding this pleasant park.

9a. Davis and Geissler Houses, 1889
1015 and 1023 Morton Street

A. W. Pattiani, architect-builder

Pattiani designed and built nearly two dozen houses in the Gold Coast; these two at **1015 Morton** and **1023 Morton** are flamboyant Queen Annes. Three more Pattiani houses are located in the next block: **1120 Morton** (1889) is a cottage with a turret, **1124 Morton** (1890) displays the designer at the height of his Queen Anne phase, and **1400 San Jose Avenue** (1891) is an elegant Queen Anne with classicized ornament.

9b. 1000 Block of Paru Street
Facing Franklin Park

This is an impressive group: **1000 Paru** (1893; Otto Collischonn, architect) is a looming, muscular Queen Anne; **1004 Paru** (1896; Edmund Kollofrath, architect) was built during the first wave of the Colonial Revival for a San Francisco wine merchant; **1018 Paru** (1889; A. R. Denke, designer-builder) is one of Denke's finest Queen Annes with Moorish overtones; and **1602 San Antonio at Paru** (1889; Charles S. Shaner, designer-builder) is an imposing mix of Eastlake and Queen Anne.

10. Haslett House, 1891
1605 Clinton Avenue

J. C. Mathews & Son, architects

This Queen Anne mansion by a noted Oakland firm retains its original grounds. It was commissioned by the owner of a warehouse company. **1620 Clinton** (1892) is an early Willis Polk in the Shingle style.

11. Palmer House, 1895
1217 Sherman Street

W. H. Lillie, architect

The Palmer House and its neighbor at **1221 Sherman** (1896; J. H. Littlefield, architect) are high-style Colonial Revival in first bloom.

12. Marriott House, 1907
1100 Bay Street

Newsom & Newsom, architects

Perched on a bluff-top site that once looked out over the bay, this low-slung house with stone chimney and curving walk epitomizes Arts and Crafts romanticism.

13. Walker House, 1909
1232 Bay Street

Morgan & Hoover, architects

Richly finished in clinker brick and abstract half-timbering, this large and well-preserved house is Julia Morgan's finest local work.

14. Werner House, 1907
1303 Bay Street

Carl Werner, architect

Werner House was the residence of an MIT-trained architect who served as Alameda's city architect in the 1920s; the roughcast stucco and battered piers show the influence of English Arts and Crafts. **1200 San Antonio Avenue** (1909; O'Brien & Werner, architects) is a robust Tudor Revival.

15. Hooper House, 1901
1234 Hawthorne Street

B. E. Remmel, architect

This "bayshore" mansion of a lumber merchant has a wide gabled entry bay with an arched stone entry.

16. Tilden House, 1896
1031 San Antonio Avenue

Edward H. Denke, architect

A. R. Denke, designer-builder

Modeled after a Nob Hill mansion, this wedding cake was the longtime residence of Charles Lee Tilden, namesake of Tilden Park.

13

Central Alameda

Central Alameda retains impressive Victorian neighborhoods, and Queen Anne is the reigning style. Houses tend to be larger toward the old south shore and on cross-town streets like Central Avenue, with its miles-long canopy of sycamores.

17. Mozart and Verdi Streets

These two tree-lined blocks retain harmonious Queen Anne streetscapes. The row at **1548–1556 Verdi** (1893; Marcuse & Remmel, designer-builders) has ornate gables and porches, **1556** was the home of Felix Marcuse, and **1547 Verdi** (1894; A. R. Denke, designer-builder) is one of the builder's best.

18. House row, 1893–1895
934–940 Santa Clara Avenue

Marcuse & Remmel, designer-builders

A pair of intricate Queen Anne cottages (1893) adjoins a Queen Anne–Colonial Revival cottage (1895).

19. House row, 1885
1402–1410 Santa Clara Avenue

E. W. Lewis, builder

Three ornamented square-bay houses were built for the same owner.

20. House row, 1892–1896
1500 Block of Benton Street

A Queen Anne streetscape bristles with turrets.

21. Stonehenge and Stoneleigh, 1928–1930
1541–1547 Santa Clara Avenue

W. W. Dixon, architect

Developed by contractor C. C. Howard, this complex of Storybook-style cottages is grouped around shared gardens with stone archways.

22. Smith and Tyson Houses, 1889, 1894
1423 and 1501 Central Avenue

A. W. Pattiani, designer-builder

These corner mates are among Pattiani's finest Queen Annes. The Smith House at **1423** was featured in a Newsom brochure; the shingled Tyson House at **1501** has a marvelous tower.

23. Dana House, 1901
1601 Central Avenue

Cunningham & Politeo, architects

An exotic "Venetian villa" has carved griffins and art-glass windows around the arched entry. The upper story and tower were restored in the 1980s. **1630 Central** (1876) is the tastiest Italianate in Alameda!

24. Greenleaf House, 1891
1724 Santa Clara Avenue

Ernest Coxhead, architect

The mannerist masterpiece stands in ironic counterpoint to the naïve eclecticism of the era. The largely intact interior is open to the public.

25. Immanuel Lutheran Church, 1890
1420 Lafayette Street

Julius Krafft, architect

The city's only intact nineteenth-century church is in carpenter Gothic.

26. First Presbyterian Church, 1903–1904
2001 Santa Clara Avenue

Henry H. Meyers, architect

Here is a classicist temple with arcaded stained-glass windows.

27. First Congregational Church, 1904–1905
1912 Central Avenue

D. Franklin Oliver, architect

An unusually bold Gothicized design is shingled and has a rustic stone entry.

28. Von Hagen House, 1885
1900 Alameda Avenue

A. C. Gilbert, builder

This is the best of several Stick Eastlake cottages on this block.

29. Meyers House, 1897
2021 Alameda Avenue

Henry H. Meyers, architect

The architect's Colonial Revival has been a house museum since 1998.

30. Siegfried House, 1885
2044 Alameda Avenue

Charles S. Shaner, designer-builder

Shaner remodeled an Italianate residence to produce these richly detailed square-bay façades.

31. Ghilieri House, 1893
2105 San Antonio Avenue

Charles S. Shaner, designer

This looming Queen Anne has a bell-cap tower and flared bays.

32. Brehaut House, 1893
2070 San Jose Avenue

Charles S. Shaner, designer

David S. Brehaut, builder

The most photographed house in town, this outré Queen Anne with central tower and twin entries was the builder's residence. The design came from a pattern book by a Tennessee architect.

33. Leonard House, 1896
891 Union Street

Joseph A. Leonard, designer-builder

Leonard's brooding shoreline mansion, with shingle veneer and stone base, was Leonardville's largest house. His assistant, C. H. Russell, collaborated on the design. **893** and **899 Union** (1891) are two large and intact Queen Annes also by Leonard.

34. Fink House, 1890
1024 Union Street

A. W. Pattiani, designer-builder

Here is one of Pattiani's richest Queen Anne designs. **1021 Union** (1892; Charles S. Shaner, designer) is Stick Eastlake.

35. House row, 1890
1812–1834 San Antonio Avenue

Joseph A. Leonard, designer-builder

Between 1889 and 1896, Leonard built more than sixty two-story Queen Anne houses in this neighborhood, which was called "Leonardville." This row of eight houses has the image of an early subdivision.

36. St. Joseph Basilica, 1920; St. Joseph Notre Dame High School,
1921, 1928, 1938
1011 Chestnut Street

William D. Shea and Henry A. Minton, architects

This church-school complex is the city's finest example of Spanish Colonial Revival. The basilica replaced an 1894 church that burned. The school was built in phases, with the initial design by Shea and additions by Minton.

Northside, Waterfront

The north waterfront underwent development as a maritime industrial district early in the twentieth century in tandem with federal harbor improvements. Houses in the area tend to be working-class cottages. Relatively little remains of the old waterfront, which is rapidly being reclaimed for new uses.

37. Old waterfront residences (unmapped)

The streets perpendicular to the somewhat obscured waterfront are sprinkled with workers' cottages, many in the Queen Anne style. **1908** and **1912 Schiller** (1896; David S. Brehaut, builder) have Moorish touches, **1918–1928 Lafayette** (1892–1993, Marcuse & Remmel, designer-builders) are full of sunbursts, and **1917** and **1919 Chestnut** (1895; Charles S. Shaner, designer) have curved porches.

38. General Engineering & Drydock Company, 1940–1942 (unmapped)
1815 Clement Avenue
Alben Froberg, architect

A largely intact former–World War II shipyard is now a marina. The centerpiece of the complex is the former machine shop (1941), opposite the entrance gates.

39. Central Substation, 1935–1936 (unmapped)
1828 Grand Street
Andrew T. Hass, architect

In the 1880s, Alameda became one of the first cities in the nation to distribute its own electricity; this Moderne substation, with a dramatic, nearly full-height copper grille above its central entry, was the intake point for power from the regional grid.

40. Gunn Building, 1894
1601 Paru Street and Lincoln Avenue
Hyde & Cox, architect-builder

An intact two-story corner-store building has a projecting second-story polygonal bay. **1607 Paru** (1894; A. W. Smith, architect) is a charming mix of Queen Anne and Colonial.

41. 1500 Block of Pacific Avenue

This stretch of Pacific Avenue retains a number of interesting Victorians. **1525** (1889; Joseph A. Leonard, designer) is Queen Anne with an open footprint and precise detailing. **1548** (1896; Marcuse & Remmel, designer-builders) is Colonial Revival. **1557** (1896; A. W. Smith, architect) [41] is Queen Anne. The two-story Italianate at **1566** (1878) was erected by local builder Robert N. Holt as his own residence.

42. Del Monte Warehouse, 1927 (unmapped)
1315 Buena Vista Avenue
Philip L. Bush, engineer

This warehouse was built by the California Packing Corporation for its Del Monte–brand canned goods shipped from an adjoining terminal; the textured brick walls of this 1,000-foot warehouse curve to follow the street.

43. House group, 1892–1897
1200–1300 Blocks of Pacific Avenue
1600 Block of Sherman Street
Marcuse & Remmel, designer-builders

The firm of Marcuse & Remmel designed and built nearly 400 houses in Alameda, many of them speculative cottages in the Queen Anne style. This group of nearly thirty houses includes a row of ornate cottages at **1615–1627 Sherman** (1894), and an arcaded row that is more Colonial in feeling at **1305–1319 Pacific** (1895).

44. Mastick House, 1889
930 Pacific Avenue

This hulking Queen Anne was built for attorney George H. Mastick, son of E. B. Mastick. The grounds once covered much of the block. **951 Pacific Avenue** (1878; A. Beyer, designer) is a large Italianate on a spacious landscaped parcel.

45. Whidden House, 1878
1630 Ninth Street

Here is a substantial Italianate cottage with rich sculptural detailing.

46. Mastick Park, 1907
Eighth Street to Wood Street

This post-earthquake subdivision north of Pacific Avenue is on the site of the former thirty-five-acre estate of attorney E. B. Mastick. The neighborhood showcases the emergence of the bungalow; cottages such as **911 Pacific Avenue** (1909; Mark T. Cole, builder) merge Colonial and Craftsman elements.

West End

The former village of Woodstock, platted in the 1860s around the railroad terminus as an industrial enclave, grew to include an oil refinery, borax plant, and terra-cotta works. In the 1870s, the Webster Street Bridge provided a streetcar link with Oakland, resulting in new houses and bathing resorts. During World War II, the area boomed with the opening of the naval base and sprawling housing projects next to reactivated shipyards.

1. Naval Air Station Alameda, 1938–1943
West end of Main Street (Main Gate)

U.S. Navy Bureau of Yards and Docks, architect

Commissioned in 1940, closed in 1997, and now being redeveloped as "Alameda Point," this former naval base occupies filled tidelands at the western tip of the island. The streamlined forms of the main building group (by the Main Gate) are

Moderne; they are arranged axially around lawns, with some sculptural ornament. Rows of monumental hangars, based on a prototype design by Albert Kahn, adjoin perimeter roads.

2. Woodstock Homes, 1941
Pacific Avenue at Second Street

Andrew T. Hass and Carl I. Warnecke, associated architects

1

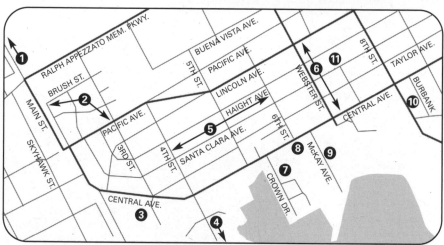

In the 1940s, the Alameda Housing Authority created more than 5,000 units of wartime housing. This 200-unit project (now owner-occupied) was the first built and the only one still standing.

3. Encinal High School, 1951–1952
210 Central Avenue

Ernest J. Kump, architect

Alameda's second public high school is a Modernist period piece.

4. Ballena Bay, 1969–1970
End of Fourth Street

Fisher-Friedman, architect

This Modernist bay-fill development, including dockside townhouses in the Sea Ranch idiom along Tidewater Drive, is best viewed from the bridge.

5. Residential neighborhood

The blocks west of Webster Street between Central and Lincoln Avenues contain a rich sampling of house styles. Ornate Queen Annes by Marcuse & Remmel can be seen at **342 Santa Clara** (1893) and **546–550 Santa Clara** (1893). A striking Queen Anne with mansard-like upper story is at **1529 Sixth Street** (1893). **432 Santa Clara** (1896; Maxwell G. Bugbee, architect) was the residence of a San Francisco architect adept in the Shingle-style mode. **Marion Court** (1920; George H. Noble, designer-builder), off Fourth Street, is a cul-de-sac lined with vaguely Pueblo Revival bungalows. **St. Barnabas Church,** 1427 Sixth Street (1926; John J. Donovan, architect), was designed by a master of Spanish revivalism.

6. Webster Street

Though much altered, Alameda's second-largest commercial district retains notable buildings. The mansard-roofed Italianate Croll Building (1879), **1400 Webster,** once served as a hotel for pugilists who trained at the bathing resorts. Alameda Savings Bank (1917–1918; Edward T. Foulkes, architect), **1442 Webster,** is a classicist jewel of gleaming terra-cotta made locally by N. Clark & Sons. The recently restored Holtz Buildings (1875–1880), **1544–1552 Webster,** are Italianate.

7. Crown Harbor, 1978–1979
500 Block of Central Avenue

Mogens Mogensen, architect

A rustic condominium village by Ponderosa Homes is clustered around landscaped commons and is easily viewed from the shoreline path.

8. Neptune Court, 1925
600 Central Avenue

Willis C. Lowe, architect

This stucco-and-tile, stage-set apartment building with a fountain court is the only surviving structure from Neptune Beach, Alameda's "Coney Island of the West." Opened in 1917, the resort included a Moorish entrance tower and two huge saltwater pools; it closed in 1939.

9. Crab Cove, Crown Memorial State Beach
McKay Avenue

The visitor center includes historic displays. The buildings on the west side of McKay are the remnants of a merchant marine school, which opened in 1943 on the site of Neptune Beach; one simulates a ship's bridge.

10. Bay Park Tract, 1909
Burbank Street and Portola Avenue

Most of the bungalows on palm-lined Burbank Street and Portola Avenue (and portions of Eighth Street and Central Avenue) were designed and built in 1912–1914 by brothers Edward, Frederick, and Verbal Strang in an Arts and Crafts idiom that is mannerist and modernist in feeling. Notable examples include **1356, 1360, 1363,** and **1372 Burbank Street.**

11. Volberg House, 1892
721 Santa Clara Avenue

A. R. Denke, designer-builder

This Queen Anne cottage has rich textures and Moorish exoticism.

6 · Berkeley

Berkeley is located on a sloping plain directly opposite the Golden Gate. Non-Mexicans settled on Domingo Peralta's portion of Rancho San Antonio in 1853 and created a community called Ocean View. In 1860, the College of California (predecessor to the University of California), located in Oakland, selected land on the lower hills for a new campus in a country location. After it was named Berkeley, the site became the first campus of the University of California in 1868. The towns of Berkeley and Ocean View eventually incorporated in 1878. Today, Berkeley is four miles square with a population of 107,000.

The first school of architecture west of the Rockies opened in Berkeley at the University of California in 1903 under University Architect John Galen Howard. He trained a generation of students in the Classical Beaux-Arts tradition, and, later, many studied at the École des Beaux-Arts in Paris. Architects Julia Morgan, Walter H. Ratcliff Jr., John Bakewell, Arthur Brown Jr., Henry Higby Gutterson, John Hudson Thomas, Walter Steilberg, William Yelland, John Reid Jr., and Mark Daniels are among the university's early-twentieth-century students. Mid-twentieth-century architects who later studied at Berkeley include William Wurster, John Funk, Albert Henry Hill, Roger Lee, and Clarence Mayhew.

Berkeley's early-twentieth-century residential neighborhoods contain architectural treasures of the Arts and Crafts movement interspersed with seminal examples of mid-twentieth-century homes.

Residents of Berkeley were instrumental in founding the Sierra Club, Save the Redwoods, the State Park System, and Save the Bay. The Free Speech movement and the Center for Independent Living also had their start in Berkeley.

Berkeley citizens take an active interest in city planning. The city's Neighborhood Preservation Ordinance (1973) was followed by the Landmarks Preservation Ordinance (1974).

Downtown

Berkeley's downtown was established in 1876 when a branch line of the Central Pacific opened along Shattuck Avenue. Beginning in 1900, downtown's wood-frame commercial buildings were replaced with more substantial masonry structures. Enough remains to give the flavor of an early 1900s downtown, even though infill and replacement structures have been built in each subsequent decade. Today, in the twenty-first century, new development challenges preservation as overscaled buildings are squeezed into the remaining spaces.

1. Heywood Building, 1917
2014 Shattuck Avenue
James W. Plachek, architect

This small gem of a building gleams with richly detailed, glazed terra-cotta cladding and Gothic-style window surrounds. The architect's office was on the second floor.

2. S. H. Kress Co. Building, 1932
2036 Shattuck Avenue
Edward F. Sibbert, architect

A Kress store graced almost every "Main Street" in America, and each was a variation on a theme. This buff-colored pressed-brick building, designed by the company architect, features terra-cotta Art Deco ornamentation.

3. Golden Sheaf Bakery, 1905
2071 Addison Street
Clinton Day, architect

This is a classically inspired, two-story redbrick and terra-cotta building with a three-part composition. Four pilasters frame three vertical bays, which contain three sets of paired arched windows on the second story. There is a richly molded terra-cotta sheaf of grain at the top of the parapet.

4. Berkeley Repertory Theater, 1979
2025 Addison Street

Angell, Lockwood & Associates, architects

Complementing the Golden Sheaf Bakery, this two-story building is faced with red brick and has an imaginative parapet wall. Connected by a courtyard to the west at **2015 Addison Street** is the larger proscenium theater (2000; ELS/Elbasani & Logan Architects), which continues the redbrick theme.

5. Francis K. Shattuck Building, 1901, 1998
2100 Shattuck Avenue

Stone & Smith, architects (1901)

The Bay Architects (fourth story, 1998)

This was the first masonry building on Shattuck Avenue. In 1998, a fourth story was added and the missing corner turret was replicated.

6. Shattuck and Berkeley Squares

The train station for the Berkeley Branch Railroad was once located on these two "island" blocks. The Mediterranean-inspired ensemble of three buildings—**48, 64,** and **82 Shattuck Square**—was designed by J. R. Miller and Timothy Pflueger in 1926. The **Kaplan Building** at 150 Berkeley Square (1999; Kava Massih, architect) anchors this "centerpiece" site with its projecting cylindrical tower and crisp lines.

7. Chamber of Commerce Building, 1925
2140 Shattuck Avenue

Walter H. Ratcliff Jr., architect

The 1920s Classic Revival "sky-scraper" was downtown's tallest building until 1969. The impressive interior banking hall remains remarkably intact.

Architect Walter H. Ratcliff Jr. was active in downtown; he also designed **Mason-McDuffie Co. Building** (1928), 2101 Shattuck Avenue; **Armstrong College** (1924), 2220 Harold Way; **Elks Club** (1913), 2013 Allston Way; **Fidelity Building** (1926), 2323 Shattuck Avenue; and **Bancroft Apartments** (1913), 2126 Bancroft Way.

8. Shattuck Hotel, 1909, 1913
2060 Allston Way

Benjamin G. McDougall, architect

Built in stages, the five-story block-long building in the Mission Revival style is another downtown focal point. Square towers, tile roofs, and two-story arches enliven the design.

9. Berkeley Public Library, 1930
2090 Kittredge Street

James W. Plachek, architect

This premiere Art Deco building features sgraffito panels of Egyptian-like figures engaged in book production, by Simeon Pelenc, and bold pylons topped by Mayan-inspired capitals. The library was partially gutted, remodeled, and expanded in 2002 by Ripley/BOORA Architects and Page & Turnbull.

Map labels: OXFORD ST., SHATTUCK, SHATTUCK AVE., UNIVERSITY AVE., ADDISON ST., CENTER ST., HAROLD WY., KITTREDGE ST., BANCROFT, DURANT, CHANNING, HASTE, MILVIA, CIVIC CENTER PARK, ALLSTON, MARTIN LUTHER KING JR. WY.

6 • Berkeley: Downtown

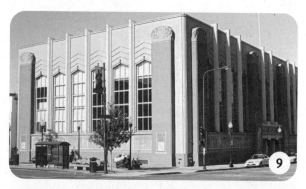

10. Fine Arts Building, 2004
2471 Shattuck Avenue

Daniel Solomon, architect

A successful interpretation of the Streamline Moderne style even captures the spirit of the 1930s in its soft green color, corner windows, and large porthole windows.

11. Manville Apartments, 1995
2100 Channing Way

David Baker Associates, architect

A university residence hall with shops below demonstrates that a "deconstructionist"-style building can be designed to fit and even reinforce the traditional urban streetscape. Its mass is broken by color and design so that it "reads" as three buildings instead of one.

A masterpiece of fanciful Period Revival style, it has sculpted brackets, variegated brick surfaces, wrought iron, and a piper prancing atop a tall chimney.

14. Studio Building, 1905
2045 Shattuck Avenue

Edwin Deakin, designer

Art studios under the tiled mansard roof were once home to the College of Arts and Crafts. Rounded sheet-metal bay windows, a series of ground-floor arches, and an artist's palette in mosaic tile in the entrance floor are noteworthy.

15. Bachenheimer Building, 2003–2004
2119 University Avenue

Kirk E. Peterson & Associates, architects

Complex massing and ornamentation provide appropriate scale, character, definition, and architectural cohesion to this all-important site.

16. Civic Center Historic District

Berkeley's Civic Center was placed on the National Register

12. Masonic Temple, 1905
2105 Bancroft Way

William H. Wharff, architect

This Classically inspired three-part composition is buff pressed brick on a steel frame and has an ornate granite entrance.

13. Tupper & Reed Building, 1925
2275 Shattuck Avenue

W. R. Yelland, architect

of Historic Places in 1998 for its significance as the center of city government and for its architecture and city planning principles. Although envisioned as early as 1901, it was not until World War II that the defining feature—Martin Luther King Jr. Civic Center Park—was finally created and the various civic-related buildings that had slowly emerged around the periphery fell into place.

16a. City Hall, 1907–1909
2134 Martin Luther King Jr. Way

Bakewell & Brown, architects

This is a two-story Beaux-Arts-style building with a symmetrical façade. A taller central section, topped by a cupola with a tall spire, is flanked by lower wings with crested hipped roofs. It sits on a high base that serves as a grand entrance terrace. Huge engaged columns enliven the main façade.

16b. Martin Luther King Jr. Civic Center Park, 1940

Henry Gutterson, Julia Morgan, Bernard Maybeck, architects

John Gregg, Baldwin M. Woods, landscape architects

The park is the physical centerpiece of the Civic Center where the Classic cross-axial composition of civic buildings meets at Civic Center Fountain.

16c. Ronald Tsukamoto Public Safety Building, 1996–2000
2100 Martin Luther King Jr. Way

Holt Hinshaw EKOVA, architects

Robert A. M. Stern, consulting architect

The block-long building has a high rotunda-like entrance bay, with a wide overhang eave supported by heavy brackets, that faces Civic Center Park.

16d. Veterans Memorial Building, 1928
1931 Center Street

Henry H. Meyers, architect

The building is Classic Moderne in form and ornamentation. The Berkeley Historical Society maintains a research library and exhibit space on the first floor.

16e. Federal Land Bank, 1938
2180 Milvia Street

James W. Plachek, architect

The grand entrance façade, with its terraces, elevated courtyard, and imposing Zigzag Moderne stair towers, faces the park and old City Hall to the west. Since 1977, renamed the Martin Luther King Jr. Civic Center Building, it has housed the city government.

16f. YMCA, 1910
2001 Allston Way

Benjamin G. McDougall, architect

A redbrick Georgian-style building has two additions on its Allston Way side; the most eastern respects the original structure (1993; E. Paul Kelly, architect).

16g. United States Post Office, 1914
2000 Allston Way

Oscar Wenderoth, supervising architect

An Italian Renaissance–style post office is a refined version used in several cities. The oak

and marble interior is mostly intact and features a WPA mural (1936) by Suzanne Scheuer and a bas-relief of postal workers (1937) by David Slivka.

16h. Berkeley High School
1980 Allston Way

Berkeley High School moved to this site in 1901, but the oldest remaining structures are the Gymnasium (1921) and Academic Building (1919) designed by William C. Hays.

In 1939, Henry H. Gutterson and William Corlett Sr. designed the Shop (G) Building, Science (H) Building, Florence Schwimley Little Theater, and Berkeley High School Community Theater (completed in 1950). This group is the only planned ensemble of Art Deco–style buildings in the city. On their exteriors are bas-relief murals by sculptors Jacques Schnier and Robert Howard.

On Milvia Street, buildings completed in 2004 (ELS, architects) echo the Moderne/Art Deco–style of the 1939 buildings and enclose the campus courtyard.

South Berkeley (unmapped)

When the Central Pacific branch line opened in 1876 connecting Berkeley with Oakland, several stops were established along the route: Dwight Way Station at Shattuck Avenue and Dwight Way, Newbury Station at Adeline Street and Ashby Avenue, and Lorin Station at Adeline Street and Alcatraz Avenue. Neighborhoods quickly developed

close to these train stops. The streets east of Shattuck between Dwight Way and Ashby Avenue contain very nice groups of nineteenth-century houses. After the electric streetcars began operating in 1891, these "streetcar suburbs" were filled in with blocks of Colonial Revival row houses.

University of California–Berkeley

The University of California was established in 1868 when the private liberal arts College of California merged with the California State College of Agriculture, Mining, and Mechanical Arts, created by the legislature in 1866. The College of California, located in Oakland, had purchased land in Berkeley in 1860 for the "benefits of a country location." Frederick Law Olmsted designed a campus plan for the college in 1864, but those plans were never realized.

The University of California moved to the Berkeley site in 1873. By the 1890s, when new buildings were needed, architect Bernard Maybeck suggested an international competition for a comprehensive master plan. Phoebe Apperson Hearst, widow of Senator George Hearst, financed the competition.

Architect John Galen Howard ultimately became the campus architect and served in that capacity from 1902 to 1924. Howard created a Classically inspired Beaux-Arts plan and ensemble of buildings that are the historic core of the Berkeley campus. Howard also established the first department of architecture west of the Rockies in 1903 and trained a generation of regional architects.

Until the 1950s, new buildings served as backdrops to Howard's buildings. In the ensuing years, new facilities are more representative of their period. Three new buildings under construction or nearly completed, plus plans for the retrofit and expansion of Memorial Stadium and the addition of a sports facility to its west, will further intensify the already densely built campus. Nearly completed are **Stanley Biosciences and Bioengineering Facility** (2007), a seven-story building located between Gayley

Road and Hearst Mining Circle; the **Center for Information Technology Research in the Interest of Society (CITRIS)** (2008), another multistory building near Northgate; and the **Tien Asian Library** (2007) on the Central Campus Glade.

1. South Hall, 1873

David Farquharson, architect

South Hall is the oldest building on the campus. It has a brick and granite façade; a mansard roof enlivened by banks of dormers with ornamental hood moldings, oeil-de-boeuf windows, iron cresting, and numerous chimneys and exhaust flues; and fluted cast-iron pilasters that reinforce the building's corners. The building has been altered and renovated several times, most recently in 1997.

2. The Campanile, 1913–1914

John Galen Howard, architect

The Campanile, also known as Sather Tower, is the center of the campus, a visual symbol of the university, and Berkeley's most prominent landmark. The granite shaft, with Classic details, stands on a raised podium. It was inspired by the campanile in Piazza San Marco in Venice.

3. Doe Memorial Library, 1907–1911, 1914–1917

John Galen Howard, architect

The grand library is a granite-faced, steel-framed, and reinforced-concrete structure embellished with Classic details. Engaged fluted columns, capped with a composite of serpents and open books, separate the

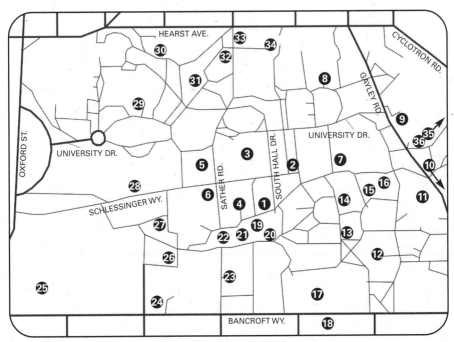

6 • Berkeley: University of California

deeply recessed bronze-framed windows. The main reading room rises two stories, culminating in a barrel-vaulted, richly decorated coffered ceiling. The **Bancroft Library** addition was designed by architect Arthur Brown Jr. in 1949. The **Gardner Stacks** (1994; Esherick Homsey Dodge and Davis, architects) are located on the north side of the library addition; the nearly 500-foot-long building is almost entirely underground.

4. Wheeler Hall, 1917

John Galen Howard, architect

The granite-faced four-story building has a Classic three-part composition, a rusticated base, corner quoins, a colonnaded central section in Ionic order, a hipped tile roof, and six monumental urns over the columns below. It is named for Benjamin Ide Wheeler, the university's eighth president (1899–1919), who was responsible for implementing the grand Beaux-Arts campus plan.

5. California Hall, 1905

John Galen Howard, architect

The two-story Classically styled building has a rusticated raised basement, smooth Raymond granite walls, an entablature containing a frieze of rosettes and a dentil course, and a tile roof culminating in a long raised skylight with an elaborate copper frame along the ridge.

6. Durant Hall, 1911

John Galen Howard, architect

Sheathed in granite, it has a hipped, red-clay tile roof. The interior is original and the library impressive.

7. Gilman Hall, 1917
Le Conte Hall, 1924

John Galen Howard, architect

Gilman and Le Conte Halls form an axis aligned with the Hearst Mining Building. In 1969, Room 307A in Gilman Hall was designated a National Historic Landmark to honor the discovery of Plutonium (Element 94) in February 1941 by Nobel Prize–winners Glenn Seaborg and Edwin McMillan.

8. Hearst Memorial Mining Building, 1902–1907

John Galen Howard, architect

The symmetrical façade has a Classic three-part composition with a triple-arched entry framed in wood. The exterior is faced with Raymond granite. The interior entry hall has delicate cast-iron columns, lattice girders, and dome ribs, which are painted light green; the vault pendentives are filled with Gustavino tile laid in a herringbone pattern. It was financed by Phoebe Apperson Hearst in memory of her husband, Senator George Hearst, who made his fortune in mining. The building was seismically retrofitted and restored in 2002.

9. Hearst Memorial Greek Theatre, 1903

John Galen Howard, architect

This is an open concrete structure with nineteen rows of benches that step up the slope to form a semicircle around the stage. The lowest tiers of benches have twenty-eight carved stone chairs designed by Earle Cummings and based on Greek models. The stage is surrounded on three sides by a high wall with attached Doric columns and a Doric entablature. It opened May 16, 1903, with President Theodore Roosevelt delivering the commencement address.

10. California Memorial Stadium, 1921

John Galen Howard, architect

Inspired by Roman models, the stadium is oval with tall arched openings in a three-and-one pattern encircling the structure. Monumental entrance arches are located on the south, north, and west sides.

11. Haas School of Business, 1995

Moore Ruble Yudell, architects

Cascading down the hillside, the large building has three wings connected by bridges and separated by grand staircases and courtyards. Hipped roofs, small-paned windows, and a rustic green, gray, and beige color pallet give the impression of a mountain retreat.

12. Wurster Hall, 1964

DeMars, Esherick & Olsen, architects

This boldly utilitarian high-rise was built during the period

when "concrete brutalism" was the latest architectural fashion.

13. Hertz Hall and Morrison Hall, 1959

Gardner A. Dailey, architect

The two tile-roofed buildings with rose-colored stucco siding are connected by a covered passageway. They make a gentle backdrop to Faculty Glade.

The **Jean Hargrove Music Library** (Scogin Elam Bray, architects) is a 2004 addition to the Music Department complex. The rectangular building is sheathed with mossy-green slate shingles.

14. Faculty Club, 1902

Bernard Maybeck, architect

The Faculty Club is located in Faculty Glade, a grassy natural amphitheater next to the wooded banks of Strawberry Creek. The Great Hall is the original building, completed in 1902, and the west wing was completed in 1903, both designed by Bernard Maybeck. The interior of the Great Hall is noteworthy for the timber-framing, which carries a system of wood trusses supporting the steeply pitched gable roof.

Beam-ends are carved dragon-heads. The walls are finished in rustic unpainted board-and-batten siding. Compatible additions have doubled its size.

15. Senior Hall, 1906

John Galen Howard, architect

A two-room, rustic redwood log cabin has a band of small-paned windows running the length of the walls under the eaves.

16. Women's Faculty Club, 1923

John Galen Howard, architect

The four-story building with a symmetrical façade is sheathed in unpainted wood shingles and has small-paned casement windows and an entrance portico held by Tuscan columns.

17. Hearst Gymnasium for Women, 1927

Bernard Maybeck and Julia Morgan, architects

Sponsored by William Randolph Hearst as a memorial to his mother, Phoebe, the building is an eclectic interpretation of Classicism. It is constructed of reinforced concrete with a quantity of ornamental detailing that includes Classic balustrades topped by monumental urns.

18. University Art Museum, 1970

Mario Ciampi, architect

The University Art Museum is a hallmark of its period and a most important example of raw concrete used to build a completely sculptural enclosure. It is dramatic and bold: galleries approached by ramps overlook a tall central open space. Seismic concerns threaten this remarkable building.

19. Stephens Hall, 1923

John Galen Howard, architect

Moses Hall, 1931

George W. Kelham, architect

Originally built as the social center of the campus, the two Tudor-style buildings are picturesquely set on either side of the Class of 1925 Courtyard next to Strawberry Creek.

20. Pelican Building/ Anthony Hall, 1956

Joseph Esherick, architect

It was built to house the humor magazine *The California Pelican,* with funds donated by the magazine's founder, Earl B. Anthony. The sophisticated one-story building, next to Strawberry

Creek, is distinctive for its trellis work, post-and-beam construction, gabled tile roof, rose-colored plaster panels, industrial sash windows, and capitals sporting carved pelicans that pay homage to Bernard Maybeck, who had designed several buildings for Anthony.

21. Power House, 1904

John Galen Howard, architect

This utilitarian building has Romanesque elements such as an arched entry and corbels topping the recessed wall panels. It served as the University Art Museum from 1934 until 1970. The mosaics by Florence Alston Swift and Helen Bruton were financed by a 1936 WPA grant.

22. Sather Gate, 1911

John Galen Howard, architect

Sather Gate, the formal entrance to the campus until 1940, is composed of four masonry piers sheathed in granite. Ornamental bronze arches span the space between the piers. Just beyond, a bridge spans Strawberry Creek.

23. Sproul Plaza

Between 1940 and 1960, the commercial and residential buildings on this block of Telegraph Avenue were cleared for **Sproul Hall** (1941; Arthur

Brown Jr., architect) and for the **California Student Center** and **Zellerbach Hall** (1959–1968; Donald Hardison and Vernon DeMars, architects). Sproul Plaza is the location where the Free Speech Movement began in 1964.

24. First Unitarian Church of Berkeley, 1898

2401 Bancroft Way

Albert C. Schweinfurth, architect

The church was built in a residential neighborhood that no longer exists. It is a small brown-shingle building with a wide shallow-gabled roof. In the center of the façade is a large circular window flanked by open, deeply recessed porches supported by sturdy redwood tree trunks, bark and all; original rustic stone garden walls remain. Organized in 1891, the church moved to Kensington in 1961.

25. Edwards Stadium, 1932

Warren C. Perry and George W. Kelham, architects

On the walls surrounding the stadium are huge Art Deco–style pylons consisting of four obelisks surrounding a taller one in the center. On the panels between the pylons are Art Deco zigzags, molded stripes, half-round circular and square reliefs, and open concrete grillwork.

26. Alumni House, 1954

Clarence Mayhew, architect

H. Leland Vaughn, landscape architect

This airy L-shaped pavilion has floor-to-ceiling windows and brick walls. The large reception room opens onto a patio shaded by oak trees, a good example of flowing indoor and outdoor spaces.

27. Dwinelle Annex, 1920

John Galen Howard, architect

Dwinelle Annex is a residentially scaled, two-story, U-shaped brown-shingled building with grouped small-paned casement windows and a gable roof.

28. Valley Life Sciences Building

George W. Kelham, architect (1930)

Robert Howard, sculptor

This huge building is a classically arranged three-part composition decorated with Art Deco–style bas-relief sculpture depicting delightful animals and mythical creatures.

29. The Agricultural Complex

Consisting of **Wellman** (1912), **Hilgard** (1917), and **Giannini** (1929) **Halls**, this complex is an eclectic blending of Neo-classic elements; all have hipped tile roofs and sym-metrical compositions.

30. University House, 1900, 1911

Albert Pissis, architect (1900)

John Galen Howard, architect (1911)

The exterior is a representative example of a Mediterranean/Renaissance villa–style with a wide and deeply recessed veranda behind a triple-arched opening.

31. Haviland Hall, 1924

John Galen Howard, architect

Although concrete substitutes for granite here, the building features elaborately carved quoins with ornament derived from plant forms. The hipped tile roof culminates in a raised copper-framed skylight.

32. North Gate, Class of 1954 Gate, 1990

Gary Demele & Robert Olwell, architects

A pair of Neoclassic pillars won the 1987 competition for a mon-umental north side entrance.

33. North Gate Hall, 1906, 1908, 1912, 1936

John Galen Howard, architect (1906, 1908, 1912)

Walter Steilberg, architect (library addition, 1936)

A simple expression of structure and material, the shingled U-shaped building steps up the hillside, integrating indoor and outdoor spaces around a south-facing courtyard. It was con-structed in stages. The School of Architecture was located here between 1906 and 1964, and was fondly called the "Ark." It now houses the School of Journalism.

34. Drawing Building/ Naval Architecture, 1913

John Galen Howard, architect

The two- and three-story shin-gled building accommodated

an expanded curriculum for the Architecture Department. The two rustic buildings once served as an effective transition in scale, form, and materials between the city and university. Concerned faculty saved this building from demolition in the mid-1970s.

Large university buildings and parking garages spilled across Hearst Avenue beginning in the 1960s. Two major academic buildings are located across Hearst Avenue: **Etcheverry Hall** (1964; Skidmore, Owings & Merrill, architects) and **Soda Hall** (completed in 1994; Edward Larrabe Barnes & Assoc., architects).

35. Botanical Gardens, 1920–1926

Centennial Drive

John W. Gregg, landscape architect

Strawberry Creek cascades through gardens filled with plants from around the world. From moist shady places to dry desert rocky landscapes, these teaching and experimental gardens are a delight.

36. Lawrence Hall of Science, 1968

Centennial Drive

Anshen + Allen, architects

Situated high on the hill, the Lawrence Hall of Science is a museum and learning center. The main exhibition halls are concrete pod-like shapes sitting on a large flat plaza. The plaza and exhibition halls are the roofs of an octagonal-shaped three-story building below.

Northside

In 1889, the area between Hearst Avenue and Cedar Street was subdivided into small lots for homes and grew rapidly after an electric streetcar line began operating on Euclid Avenue in 1903. It was in this area that the concept of "building in harmony with nature" was promoted by the Hillside Club, which was founded in 1898 by a group of neighbors who wanted to keep the hillside as natural as possible. The club incorporated ideas from the English Arts and Crafts movement, which were rooted in an antimaterialism that shunned the ostentatious and sought refuge in nature and handmade objects.

By 1923, the hillside was dotted with unpainted wood or shingle-sided homes. Through the efforts of the Hillside Club, "the north side of the Berkeley Campus became the prime example of enlightened environmental planning," noted cultural geographer Gray Brechin in 1976, "where city and country blended harmoniously."

On September 17, 1923, a raging wildfire emerged over the hills and consumed between 500 and 600 buildings. A contemporary account described the destruction as "a square mile of charred relics spreading from Cragmont to the edge of the University grounds . . . no words could convey the power of the torrent of flame which demolished in a few short hours . . . one of the most beautiful residence tracts of Berkeley."

The fire was not only a personal tragedy for its victims but a significant cultural loss. Most of the homes destroyed represented pioneering efforts in the field of architecture by innovative Bay Area architects, and few remain.

1. Beta Theta Pi House, 1893
2607 Hearst Avenue
Ernest Coxhead, architect

The Tudor Revival–style building, built in the waning years of the Victorian era, was innovative and pioneering. It consists of four distinct sections of contrasting materials with no superficial decoration. Owned by the university since the 1960s, it now houses the School of Public Policy. A new building on the west side of the property (2002; Architectural Resources Group) forms a courtyard with the original building.

2. Cloyne Court Hotel, 1904
2600 Ridge Road
John Galen Howard, architect

This large three-story U-shaped building, timber-framed and shingled, is screened by trees and shrubs. Balconies and large casement windows overlook an interior courtyard. The building exhibits a simplicity that will be identified with the future Modern Movement: trellis square-cut beam-ends and balcony railings. Built as a hotel for university visitors and guests, it is listed on the National Register.

3. Allenoke Manor, 1903
1777 Le Roy Avenue
Ernest Coxhead, architect

The large clinker-brick house features five massive gambrel dormers and is surrounded by formal gardens enclosed by clinker-brick walls.

4. Oscar Maurer Studio, 1907
1772 Le Roy Avenue
Bernard Maybeck, architect

This small, exquisite studio building steps down the hillside along the banks of a creek. It is an eclectic combination of Mission Revival, Classic, Gothic, Japanese, and Modern design forms. Its entrance is recessed behind a heavy, tiled gable roof; a large picture window is bisected by a golden Corinthian column. Photographer Oscar Maurer (1870–1965) lived next door in the 1905 Mission Revival house.

5. Volney Moody House, 1896
1755 Le Roy Avenue
Albert C. Schweinfurth, architect

Originally clad entirely in clinker brick, with stepped gable ends

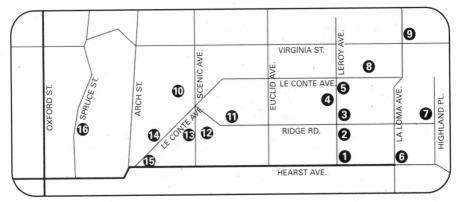

6 • Berkeley: Northside

and an open recessed entry porch, the house was converted to student housing in the 1950s. When a third story was added, the stepped gable ends were removed and the porch was enclosed. Its creek-side setting and clinker-brick bridge still convey a woodsy setting.

6. Foothill Housing, 1991
Hearst and La Loma Avenues

William Turnbull Associates, architects

As a concession to the neighborhood, the massive dormitory complex was sheathed in brown shingles and board-and-batten siding.

7. Charles Keeler House and Studio, 1895, 1905
1770, 1736 Highland Place

Bernard Maybeck, architect

Steeply pitched, flared hipped roofs express the separate sections of this multilevel house that steps down the hillside. Stuccoed after the 1923 fire, the interior remains entirely paneled in unpainted redwood. Today, the house is crowded by apartment houses and dormitories. Keeler

was founder and spokesperson for the Hillside Club. His studio is next door, on the north.

8. Group of pre-1923-fire houses

Rustic houses that survived the 1923 fire include **2683 Le Conte Avenue** (1900; A. H. Broad, designer), a shingled house with a gambrel roof and wide front porch; **2695 Le Conte Avenue** (1908; Julia Morgan, architect), a stucco-sided house that steps up the hillside; **1715 La Loma** (1899; William Knowles & Lilian Bridgman, architects), a shingled chalet; **1705 La Loma Avenue** (1906; A. E. Hargreaves, designer; Bernard Maybeck & John White, architects), a chalet sheathed with half-round logs, creating the illusion of a log cabin; and **1700 La Loma** (1899; William Knowles, architect), a Shingle style.

9. Daley Scenic Park street improvements, 1909
Le Roy, Le Conte, La Loma, Virginia, La Vereda, and Hilgard Avenues

Hillside Club

The steps and retaining walls of thickly textured gray concrete surfaces, as well as the divided road at La Loma, Virginia, and La Vereda, are street improvements promoted by the Hillside Club.

Holy Hill

The hill that rises west of Euclid Avenue is referred to as "Holy Hill" because of the many multi-denominational theological seminaries that are located here. The seminaries are part of the Graduate Theological Union and share a library on Ridge Road.

10. Pacific School of Religion, 1924, 1941
1798 Scenic Avenue

Walter H. Ratcliff Jr., architect

An ensemble of English Tudor–and Gothic-style buildings is set on the edge of a flat open space of lawns, gardens, and pathways. **Holbrook Hall** (1924) on the north side is a U-shaped, stone-clad, Gothic-inspired structure with gabled roofs, deeply recessed multipaned windows, tall pointed arched windows, and pyramidal pinnacles.

11. Church Divinity School of the Pacific (CDSP), All Saints Chapel, Gibbs Hall, 1929
2449 Ridge Road

Walter H. Ratcliff Jr., architect

This is a picturesque grouping of brick and stone-sided buildings connected by an arched passageway.

12. Library of the Graduate Theological Union, 1973–1987
2400 Ridge Road

Louis I. Kahn, architect (initial drawings, 1973)

Esherick Homsey Dodge and Davis, architects (1974–1987)

The bold four-story, reinforced-concrete building softened by wood siding is stepped back, creating wide planted balconies. Louis I. Kahn made the initial drawings, but after his death in 1974, the library was completed by the Esherick Homsey Dodge and Davis firm. Constructed in two phases, it was completed in 1987.

13. Phoebe A. Hearst Reception Hall, 1902
1816 Scenic Avenue

Ernest Coxhead, architect

This house, once shingled, has a classic three-part façade. Behind it, **2368 Le Conte Avenue,** (1900), also designed by Ernest Coxhead for Mrs. Hearst, is a simplified Classic Revival with an exaggerated broken pediment over the entry portico. **1820 Scenic Avenue** (1900; Edgar A. Mathews, architect) is a three-story brown shingle that was home to university president Benjamin Ide Wheeler.

14. Orrin Kip McMurray House, 1924
2357 Le Conte Avenue

Bernard Maybeck, architect

Built at the back of a deep lot after the 1923 fire, the sweeping tile-roofed house has a Mediterranean feeling, gray-brown stucco siding, and a deeply recessed entry.

15. Harris House, 1936
2300 Le Conte Avenue, at Hearst Avenue

John B. Anthony, architect

Built on an odd V-shaped lot, this multileveled Streamline

Moderne house is a symmetrical stacking of cylindrical forms.

16. Normandy Village, 1928–1929
1781–1839 Spruce Street

William Raymond Yelland, architect

Normandy Village is a Romantic Revival–style housing complex consisting of courtyards, gardens, and paths, as well as asymmetrical massing, weathered brick, textured stucco, half-timbering, steep roofs, winding exterior staircases, cupolas, weather vanes, and turrets.

Buena Vista Hill

In 1900, architect Bernard Maybeck and his wife, Annie, purchased four acres in La Loma Park, north of Cedar Street. Maybeck laid out wide irregular-shaped lots on the winding streets and sold them when finances necessitated, often designing the homes as well. Only a handful of houses survived the 1923 fire.

1. Mathewson House, 1916
2704 Buena Vista Way, at the corner of La Loma Avenue

Bernard Maybeck, architect

The wide gabled roofs of the small house evoke the image of a Swiss chalet.

2. Andrew Lawson House, 1907
1515 La Loma Avenue

Bernard Maybeck, architect

Andrew Lawson, the geologist who mapped the San Andreas Fault and traced the Hayward Fault to his own property, built a house of reinforced concrete covered with a surface of color-impregnated stucco enriched with sgraffito designs and patterns of inset colored tiles.

3. Charles Seeger House, 1915
2683 Buena Vista Way

Bernard Maybeck, architect

The original board-and-batten house is at the rear of a new addition.

4. Maybeck Family houses, 1924–1950
Buena Vista Way and La Loma Avenue

Bernard Maybeck, architect

The Maybeck family lost their large shingled 1907 home in the 1923 fire. Rather than rebuild a large house, Maybeck designed a

2

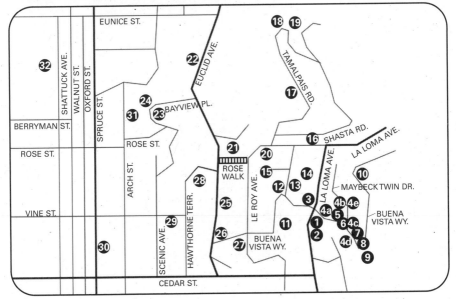

group of five small- to medium-size dwellings between 1924 and 1950 as family needs arose.

4a. The Studio, 1924
2711 Buena Vista Way

This "studio" was partially built on the foundation of the house that burned. Called the "sack" house, its exterior walls are sheathed with gunny sacks dipped in a foamy concrete mixture called Bubblestone. Its main living space has high ceilings, a poured-concrete fireplace, and multipaned industrial sash windows.

4b. The Cottage, 1924
1 Maybeck Twin Drive

This began as a small structure moved to the site and then covered with Bubblestone. Numerous additions have resulted in a rambling cottage with the feeling of being hand-made.

4c. Wallen Maybeck House, 1933
2751 Buena Vista Way, at the corner of Maybeck Twin Drive

Set against a steep hillside lot, the two-story wood-sided house has a second-story "living hall" that combines the living, dining, and kitchen areas under a tall open-gabled roof. The poured-concrete fireplace is huge compared to the size of the room; tall multipaned windows convey spaciousness.

4d. Annie Maybeck House, 1933
2780 Buena Vista Way

The massive poured-concrete chimney, which imitates the alternating pattern of the house's redwood and Douglas fir siding, is a notable feature.

4e. "Arillaga," 1950
2 Maybeck Twin Drive

Constructed of concrete block, the house has floors of naval hatch covers, interior walls of plywood, radiant heat, and other innovative features. This was the last house Maybeck designed on his property.

5. Margaret van Barnveld Cole House, 1968
2717 Buena Vista

Felix Rosenthal, architect

Designed to complement its neighbors, it is sheathed with twelve-inch-long shingles.

6. Tufts House, 1931
2733 Buena Vista Way

Bernard Maybeck, architect

This is an L-shaped, one-and-one-half-story house with a steeply pitched, two-story gabled roof, tall multipaned window facing the bay, and a massive formed-concrete fireplace. The garage doors are decorated with stenciled floral motifs.

7. Rev. John S. Thomas House, 1914
2753 Buena Vista Way

William Charles Hays, architect

A shingled version of an Italianate Villa has an open second-story porch deeply recessed under a side-facing gable roof. A compatible addition is connected by a second-story bridge.

8. 2785 Buena Vista Way, 1948
John Ekin Dinwiddie, architect

Here is an early example of a mid-century Modern with modular bands of windows, an angled entry, and flagstone-faced walls and steps.

9. Temple of Wings, 1911, 1914, 1924
2800 Buena Vista Way

Bernard Maybeck (conceptual drawings, 1911)

Edna Deakin and Clarence Dakin (repairs and remodeling, 1924)

The Temple of Wings was built as a colonnaded open-air residence for Florence Treadwell Boynton. Maybeck did conceptual drawings, but architects William A. Newman and A. Randolph Monroe completed the project in 1914. After the 1923 fire, a two-unit house was

constructed within the framework of the original columns on either side of an open covered courtyard. It served not only as a home but also as a school of dance. It has been extensively restored and updated.

10. Hume Cloister, 1928
2900 Buena Vista Way

John Hudson Thomas, architect

An eclectic composition of Romanesque and early Gothic forms is built on seven terraces of reinforced-and-buttressed concrete-block retaining walls tinted a deep beige. Behind the walls is a cloistered open garden surrounded by arches containing Gothic tracery.

Buena Vista Way, west of La Loma

11. Hillside School, 1925
1581 Le Roy Avenue
(2500 Buena Vista Way)

Walter H. Ratcliff Jr., architect

The Tudor Revival–style school is a wide L shape with stucco siding, half-timbering, and a slate roof. The prominent full-height, multipaned auditorium window overlooks the street. It is listed on the National Register.

Greenwood Terrace, Greenwood Common

12. Francis Gregory House, 1907
1476 Greenwood Terrace

Bernard Maybeck, architect

The Gregory House [12] and the Noyes House next door at 1486 Greenwood Terrace (1912; John Galen Howard, architect) are

fine examples of medium-sized, simple but sophisticated, architect-designed shingled houses for which Berkeley became known.

13. 1471 Greenwood Terrace, 1950
Winfield Scott Wellington, architect

Wellington, a professor of design at the university, produced the archetypical example of Bay Area mid-twentieth-century Modernism.

14. Warren Gregory House, 1903, 1906
1459 Greenwood Terrace

John Galen Howard, architect

The broad two-story shingle house, built as a summer home, was enlarged after the 1906 earthquake when the Gregorys moved here permanently.

15. Greenwood Common, 1952–1957
William Wurster/Lawrence Halprin, landscape architect

Greenwood Common is a small residential subdivision developed by William Wurster, Dean of the College of Environmental Design, after he purchased the Gregory house and property in

1952. The landscape plan is by Lawrence Halprin.

Eight houses are located on the edge of a common green space. They are modest and unobtrusive, with low sloping or flat roofs, modular post-and-beam construction, and stained subdued earth tones. The landscape design emphasizes simple low-maintenance gardens with flowering plum trees, Japanese maples, and juniper; paths are textured concrete comprised of imbedded gravel and small rocks. Greenwood Common serves as a prototype for an integrated fusion of architecture and landscape design; it is a cohesive intact example of mid-twentieth-century Modern design principles:

#1 (1955; Donald Olsen, architect).

#2 (1957; Robert Klemmedson, architect).

#3 (1954; Joseph Esherick, architect).

#4 (1954; Harwell Hamilton Harris, architect).

#7 (1932, with subsequent additions; Rudolph Schindler, architect).

12

#8 (1953; Howard Moise, architect).

#9 (1954; Henry Hill, architect).

#10 (1952; John Funk, architect).

16. 2625 Rose Street, 1958
Charles Warren Callister, architect

Here is an exemplary solution to a very steep lot that uses multiple half-stories around a central staircase. The L-shaped house turns its back to the street and opens up to bay views. On all levels, rooms open onto decks or terraces.

Tamalpais Road

Tamalpais Road is a delightful tree-shaded street that escaped the 1923 fire.

17. Schevill House, 1915
77 Tamalpais Road
David and Jessie Harris, architects
Greene and Greene, architects (addition, 1922)

A U-shaped house, set close to the road and sheathed with long shakes, opens up to a garden on its south side.

21

18. Fairbanks-Rowell House, 1906, 1921
159 Tamalpais Road
John Hudson Thomas, architect (1921)

A rustic picturesque house sits under a grove of redwood trees; it has overscaled shingles and native stonework garden walls.

19. Benner House, 1933
155 Tamalpais Road
William Wurster, architect

The L-shaped, one- and two-story, cream-colored stucco house has a sliding multipaned window wall that opens to the garden. The rounded end of the second-story balcony expresses a strong statement of Modernity.

20. Gregory/Howard House, 1912
1401 Le Roy Avenue
John Galen Howard, architect
Julia Morgan, architect (library addition, 1927)

Reflecting the shape of its corner lot, the two-story L-shaped house has an angled central recessed entry porch flanked by two, two-story polygonal bays. The house is covered with long wooden barn shakes.

21. Rose Walk, 1913
2500 Block of Rose Street
Bernard Maybeck, architect
Henry H. Gutterson, architect

Rose Walk is a public pedestrian pathway linking Euclid and Le Roy Avenues. A Classic double curving staircase rises above Euclid Avenue; retaining walls and paving are stained a rose color.

Cottages and duplexes, 1923–1936

Rose Walk is bordered by four two-story duplexes and two small houses built after the 1923 fire. They were designed to enhance the preexisting walk. Each cottage and duplex is a variation of the same design elements: textured stucco, vertical wood siding, rose-colored window trim, and small-paned windows.

22. Berkeley Municipal Rose Garden, 1933–1937
1300 Block of Euclid Avenue
Vernon M. Dean, landscape architect

Built like an amphitheater with wide stone terraces, the garden faces San Francisco Bay. It was begun in 1933 under the Civil Works Administration. A semicircular redwood pergola stands above the terraces. The roses are arranged to bloom from shades of red at the top to white at the bottom.

23. Senger House, 1907
1321 Bay View Place
Bernard Maybeck, architect

The shingled, half-timbered and stucco house is a complex arrangement of one- and two-story sections that are not set on a continuous plane: each section is treated almost independently. Each part not only varies in scale but also has a variety of different sizes and styles of window, rooflines, and siding materials.

24. 1322 Bay View Place, 1922
Henry H. Gutterson, architect

This stucco and wood-sided house has a stenciled flower design on the ends of perpendicular board siding.

25. George Blood House, 1929
1495 Euclid Avenue

Walter H. Ratcliff Jr., architect

This is the largest house in the neighborhood: an impressive English Tudor with steeply pitched slate roofs, stone foundation, retaining walls, and pathways.

26. Kennedy-Nixon House, 1923
1537 Euclid Avenue

Bernard Maybeck, architect

The U-shaped house, which steps up the hillside, was built to accommodate two separate but small living units (connected by a bridge on the south side) as well as a dramatic music studio with a high ceiling, expressed on the exterior by tall Gothic windows. The combination of Classic, Gothic, Tudor, and Spanish design motifs have resulted in a profound and unique structure.

27. H. E. Jones House, 1928
1500 Le Roy Avenue

Carr Jones, architect

Its picturesque rustic brickwork sets this house apart from its neighbors.

28. Hawthorne Terrace
West of Euclid Avenue

This makes a pleasant walk to the north Shattuck Avenue retail district, also known as Berkeley's "gourmet ghetto," where Alice Water's famous Chez Panisse restaurant is located.

Houses of note along the way include **1404 Hawthorne Terrace** (1911; Julia Morgan, architect), a shingled house with an elaborate leaded front window; **1408 Hawthorne Terrace**

31

(1921; Bernard Maybeck, architect), a stucco-sided tile-roofed Mediterranean with three arched windows behind a balcony; **1441, 1439, 1440,** and **1450 Hawthorne Terrace,** all designed by Henry H. Gutterson between 1924 and 1925; and **3 Vine Lane,** (1924; John White, architect), with gray stucco siding and an angled bay.

29. The Marston Studio, 1930
2330 Vine Street

Eldridge Theodore "Ted" Spencer, architect

A picturesque half-timber cottage has rusticated rose-colored stucco, a large steeply pitched gray slate roof, and small-paned leaded windows. Spencer later became the Stanford University Architect.

30. Second Church of Christ, Scientist, 1926, 1951
1500 Spruce Street

Henry H. Gutterson, architect

Set on a planted berm, the Mediterranean-style church has a triple-arched entry portico flanked by two gabled bays. The materials are unpainted, gray Thermotite concrete blocks that look like stone, leaded windows

set in natural wood frames, and flat red-clay tile roofs.

At **1536 Oxford Street** is Berkeley's largest and most prominent Queen Anne Victorian, the freshly painted Boudrow House (1889; Julius Krafft, architect).

31. Schneider-Kroeber House, 1906
1325 Arch Street

Bernard Maybeck, architect

With wide overhanging eaves and a second-story balcony, the impression is Swiss Chalet but the more complicated massing is Maybeck; **1318 Arch** is Swiss Chalet by architect John White.

32. Isaac Flagg House, 1900
1200 Shattuck Avenue

Bernard Maybeck, architect

There are three Flagg houses in a row on Shattuck Avenue—**1200** (1900), **1208** (1906), and **1210** (1912)—all designed by Maybeck. **1200 Shattuck,** the largest of the three, is a three-story shingled, board-and-batten-sided house, with a low-pitched gabled roof and wide overhanging eaves reminiscent of a Swiss Chalet.

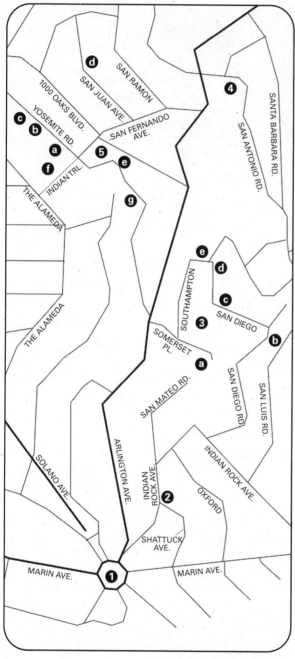

Northbrae

In 1902, the Berkeley Development Company purchased approximately 1,000 acres in what would become the streetcar suburbs of Northbrae (1907), Thousand Oaks (1909), and Cragmont (1910).

Northbrae's broad curving streets and network of pathways and staircases between the streets were designed by landscape architect and university professor R. E. Mansell. The sidewalks are stained a soft rose color. Parks were created around the largest rock outcroppings.

1. The Circle at Marin Avenue, 1910

John Galen Howard, architect

The Circle [1], Fountain Path, and native stone pillars used as street markers were designed by university architect John Galen Howard. The Circle is the center of Northbrae and serves as the transportation hub for Cragmont and Thousand Oaks as well as Kensington. Six streets converge here and it is Berkeley's only "round-about." Beneath it is Berkeley's only tunnel.

Classic balustrades surround the Circle; in the center stands a fountain, a replica of the original 1910 fountain destroyed by a runaway truck. The original bears by Arthur Putnam were replicated by sculptor Sarita Waite.

2. John Hudson Thomas houses, 1910–1911

915, 927, 959, 961 Indian Rock Avenue, and 800 Shattuck Avenue

John Hudson Thomas, architect

These five houses, including **800 Shattuck Avenue** [2], are examples

of Thomas's Secessionist period. They have rusticated stucco siding, with retaining walls and steps made of local stone. They appeared on advertising brochures and postcards for the Northbrae subdivision.

3. John Hinkel Park

John W. Gregg, landscape architect (clubhouse and pathways, 1918)

Vernon Dean, landscape architect (amphitheater, 1934)

John Hinkel Park is six acres of steep hillside with a small creek cascading through it. Paths meander under native oak, bay, and buckeye trees. The park, with its rustic redwood clubhouse, stone fireplace, and network of pathways, was given to the city in 1919 by John Hinkel, a downtown property owner. The outdoor amphitheater was constructed in 1934 under the Civil Works Administration.

The residential neighborhood surrounding the park has some excellent examples of Period Revival–style architecture and several notable mid-twentieth-century houses.

3a. 2 Somerset Place, 1929

Walter H. Ratcliff Jr., architect

This large romantic Tudor has a slate roof and stone fireplace.

3b. 771, 775 San Diego Road, 1954

Donald Olsen, architect

Two International-style houses, including 771 [3b], fit well in their wooded setting.

3c. 754 San Diego, 1926

Roland I. Stringham, architect

The wide shingled house turns its back to the street and has a deep recessed entry.

3d. 743 San Diego Road, 1928

William Wurster, architect

This early work in the Period Revival style was designed by the noted modernist.

3e. 168 Southampton, 1923

Bernard Maybeck & John White, architects

The stucco-sided house and studio has roofs covered with sheets of copper. Its complicated hillside plan is not evident from the street.

Thousand Oaks

4. John Hopkins Spring Estate, 1912

1960 San Antonio Road

John Hudson Thomas, architect

The developer of Thousand Oaks built this huge two-story rectangular concrete mansion overlooking his subdivision and bay. It is a symmetrical Beaux-Arts arrangement, with decorative details that are not classical but,

rather, Austrian Secessionist; corner pilasters are set on tall square bases buttressed by exaggerated volutes; a balustrade, with the pattern of a star within a square, tops the cornice, and this pattern is used on the interior as well.

5. Stone Face Park, 1910

Yosemite Road and Thousand Oaks Boulevard

Mark R. Daniels, architect

The park, with its massive boulders, serves as a backdrop for the earliest houses built in Thousand Oaks. The Period Revival–style houses are located on large wide lots edged with native stone walls.

5a. 1890 Yosemite, 1910

William A. Knowles, architect

This one is Tudor.

5b. 1874 Yosemite, 1911

John Hudson Thomas, architect

Here is another Tudor with massive intersecting gambrel roofs.

5c. 1864 Yosemite, 1910

Mark R. Daniels, architect

This rustic shingle house has rock outcroppings and spreading oak trees gracing the front garden.

5d. 1827 San Juan Avenue, 1915

Bernard Maybeck, architect

Maybeck is responsible for this shingled chalet.

5e. 1900 Yosemite, 1922

Walter T. Steilberg, architect

Here is a house with amber glazed windows, Chinese green tiles, and grouped small-paned windows.

5f. 715 The Alameda, off Indian Trail, 1915

Henry H. Gutterson, architect

This brick and wood-sided U-shaped house steps up the hillside on four levels.

5g. 1962 Yosemite, 1912

Julia Morgan, architect

This wide two-story shingled house has a symmetrical façade with two, two-story gabled bays flanking a recessed entry porch.

Southside

The first subdivisions south of the campus were owned and marketed by the College of California to raise funds. The College Homestead Association Tract (1866) and the Berkeley Property Tract (1868) extend from Bancroft south to Dwight Way, from Shattuck east to Prospect Avenue.

Few buildings remain from the nineteenth century. Pressure from the ever-growing university has created an environment of continual change; some buildings are actually the third on a particular lot. However, historic resources do remain, isolated and vulnerable as they may be, and many of them are among Berkeley's most significant buildings.

1. St. Mark's Episcopal Church, 1901
2300 Bancroft Way

William Curlett, architect

St. Mark's is Mission Revival style with two bell towers, a tile roof, quatrefoil windows, an arcade, and espadaña (gables). The Parish House to the east was designed by Willis Polk in 1912.

2. Berkeley City Club, 1929
2315 Durant Avenue

Julia Morgan, architect

The buff-colored cement-plaster exterior, red-tile roofs, and exquisite ornamentation, together with a composition of varying roof heights, towers, and chimneys, skillfully humanize this very large building.

3. McCreary-Greer House, 1901
2318 Durant Avenue

From the grand sweep of its balustraded porch to the over-scaled pediment on the front dormer, this Colonial Revival style reflects the architectural pretensions of its times; it houses the Berkeley Architectural Heritage Association.

4. Town and Gown Club, 1899
2401 Dwight Way

Bernard Maybeck, architect

In Maybeck's important early work, the architect has used the building's structural members to create visual interest. Particularly compelling are the outrigger-like roof supports. Additions by others have occurred over the years, including the wing with polygonal roof that projects from the front of the building.

5. El Granada Apartments, 1905
2301 Telegraph Avenue

Meyers & Ward, architects

Espadaña (gables) rise from the tower-like corners of this Mission Revival–style building. A recent restoration re-created missing gables, tile roofs, and cast-concrete cornucopias. Between Bancroft and Dwight Ways,

Telegraph Avenue is the main student retail district. The narrow urban street is lined with one- to four-story buildings, mostly dating from 1900 to the 1930s.

6. YWCA, 1958
2600 Bancroft Way

Joseph Esherick, architect

The YWCA is an elegant, understated, mid-twentieth-century building by Joseph Esherick, who was awarded the American Institute of Architects Gold Medal and served as a Professor and Chair of Architecture at the University of California–Berkeley. The YWCA building displays the simplicity and warmth that characterized Esherick's residential buildings.

7. Westminster House, 1926
2700 Bancroft Way

Walter H. Ratcliff Jr., architect

This Presbyterian student center abounds with Elizabethan and English Tudor imagery.

8. Channing Apartments, 1913
2409 College Avenue

Walter H. Ratcliff Jr., architect

2

A distinguished apartment house has a tile roof supported by heavy wooden brackets, walls of a light natural finish, small-paned casement windows, and a recessed arched entry.

9. Samuel Davis House, 1899
2547 Channing Way

William Mooser & Son, architects

This large shingled variation on Colonial Revival rests on a rustic stone base; it is a reminder of what has been lost in this former residential neighborhood.

10. Anna Head School, 1892–1927
2538 Channing Way

Soule Edgar Fisher and others, architects

The former Anna Head School is a remarkable ensemble of shingled buildings constructed over a thirty-five-year period and grouped around a quadrangle. Channing Hall bears a close relationship to the East Coast Shingle style. Three stories high, it is a profusion of gambrel roofs, porches, bays, and various window types. Rough stone is used for the massive chimney and for the supports of the west-facing porch. Designed by Walter H. Ratcliff Jr. in 1927, the Chapel at the southwest corner of the quadrangle on Haste Street was the last of the complex to be constructed. The site has been owned by the university since 1964 and is severely compromised by parking lots.

11. University Student Crossroads Dining Center, 2001
2415 Bowditch Street

Dworsky Associates, architects

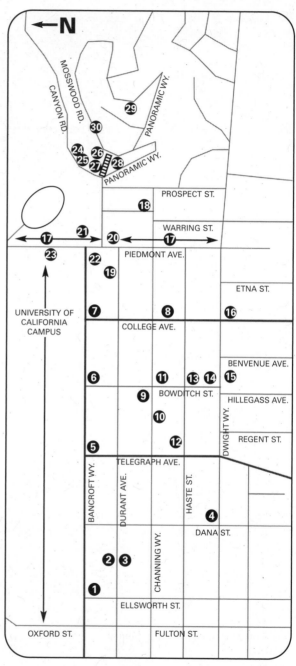

6 • Berkeley: Southside, Panoramic Hill

A stunning contrast to Anna Head School, this building has the sharp lines, complex massing, and glass of Industrial Modernism. The dining center and the Housing and Dining office building behind it are part of a student dormitory building project that began in 2000. The dining pavilions of dormitory block **Units #1** and **#2** (1957; John Carl Warnecke, architect) have been demolished and additional dormitories constructed (2005; EHDD, architect). The **Channing Bowditch Apartments** at 2535 Channing Way and the **Ida Louise Jackson Graduate House** (2002) at 2333 College Avenue are by Pyatok Architects, Inc.

12. John Woolley House, 1876
2509 Haste Street

This raised-basement Italianate cottage is one of the oldest intact structures remaining in the area. Across the street is the infamous **People's Park.** On the north wall of 2455 Telegraph Avenue is the **People's Bicentennial Mural** (1976) that commemorates the Free Speech Movement of 1964 and the People's Park Riot of 1969.

13. Vedanta Society Temple, 1939
2455 Bowditch Street

Henry H. Gutterson, architect

A Romanesque-style archway leads to a recessed entry, and above that, a round lotus window is set within the gable end. Walled gardens enhance the atmosphere of serenity. Gutterson also designed the building for the **Christian Science Society of UC** (1933) at the corner of Durant.

14

14. First Church of Christ, Scientist, 1910
2619 Dwight Way

Bernard Maybeck, architect

Architecturally the most significant building in Berkeley and a National Landmark as well, the First Church of Christ, Scientist, is Maybeck's masterpiece. It is a romantic vision, with wisteria-draped pergolas, column capitals depicting solemn medieval figures, and a complex arrangement of gables supported by heavy wooden brackets. Maybeck also used low-cost industrial materials such as factory sash, transite panels, and exposed concrete. The Sunday School wing, to the east, was designed by Henry H. Gutterson in 1928.

15. American Baptist Seminary of the West, 1919–1963
2606 Dwight Way

Hobart Hall (1919; Julia Morgan, architect) is a Tudor-inspired design. It is the centerpiece of a beautiful small campus, an oasis of tranquility. Later buildings—including the chapel (1949) designed by Walter H.

Ratcliff Jr., and the Academic Building (1963) designed by Ratcliff, Slama, Cadwalader—form a unified ensemble.

16. Newman Hall, 1966
2700 Dwight Way

Mario Ciampi, architect

Newman Hall is a superb and powerful example of the Concrete Brutalist style. Its unpainted, striated concrete surfaces were designed to evoke a cave, an early Christian place of worship. The sanctuary carries out the somber mood, and the rock-hewn cave-like quality is reinforced by the imaginative ceramic altar furniture by sculptor Stephen De Staebler.

17. Piedmont Way, 1865
Between Dwight Way and Gayley Road

Frederick Law Olmsted, landscape architect

When Olmsted prepared a campus plan for the College of California, he also made a plan for a residential neighborhood called the Berkeley Property Tract. Piedmont Way (now Avenue) is the center of this neighborhood; it was designed to be gently curved as it followed the contours of the land, "parked" down the center, and shaded by "overbowering" trees. Once lined with large family homes, the street is now almost exclusively student housing, some of the old residences adapted to a new use.

18. William Colby House, 1905
2901 Channing Way

Julia Morgan, architect

This sophisticated redwood house is one of Julia Morgan's early commissions. Clerestory windows, tucked under a gabled monitor roof, light the attic rooms. Morgan also designed **2311, 2328, 2336,** and **2340 Piedmont Avenue** between 1905 and 1914. All are remodeled for student housing; their façades and profiles retain enough original character and material to give an early-twentieth-century residential character to the street.

19. Percy Atkinson House, 1908
2735 Durant Avenue

Maybeck & White, architects

This is one of Maybeck's Swiss Chalet–inspired redwood houses. The broad overshadowing eaves of the main gable are repeated below in the gable of the enclosed porch.

20. William Thorsen House, 1909
2307 Piedmont Avenue

Greene and Greene, architects

The Thorsen House is a Berkeley treasure and the only example here of the mature bungalow style of Charles and Henry Greene. It exhibits many of the

defining features found in the architects' Pasadena houses: exposed structural members, unpainted exterior, Japanese joinery, and intricate stained glass. The monumental entrance steps and porch of clinker brick are noteworthy. The home of Sigma Phi since 1942, the house is lovingly maintained.

21. International House, 1929
2299 Piedmont Avenue

George W. Kelham, architect

The domed tower of this massive Mediterranean-style building can be seen for miles. Built as a residence hall for both foreign and American students, International House was intended to encourage understanding between cultures. The interior, open to the public, is rich in Mediterranean-style elements: tile floors, wrought-iron fixtures, stenciled and beamed ceilings, and a sheltered rear courtyard.

22. Frank Woodward House, 1909
2302 Piedmont Avenue

Edward B. Seely, architect

This is a large example of the Arts and Crafts style, with broad gables, picturesque massing, plastered surfaces, and lavish use of clinker brick. It has been a fraternity house for more than fifty years.

23. Walter Y. Kellogg House, 1909
2232 Piedmont Avenue

Julia Morgan, architect

Stucco, a touch of half-timbering, and a whimsical roofline distinguish this house, which is part of a group of houses that remain at the northern end of Piedmont Avenue. All are now owned by the university and have been converted to institutional use.

Panoramic Hill

East of Piedmont Avenue is Panoramic Hill, with narrow winding roads, paths, and steps, and closely spaced houses clinging to the hillside. The hill is practically an outdoor museum of Bay Region architecture, predominantly Shingle style; it was placed on the National Register in 2005 as a Historic District. The late architectural historian John Beach wrote: "The quality of this area depends not so much on individual buildings, though there are many fine structures by Berkeley's most important designers, but upon the survival of a complete neighborhood that provides a background for these buildings."

24. Charles H. Rieber House, 1904
15 Canyon Road

Coxhead & Coxhead, architects

This immense, rambling shingled house is one of Ernest Coxhead's masterpieces. Supported by a concrete retaining wall topped by a pergola, the house wraps around the base of the hill with an odd collection of bays, dormers, and stairwells, giving the impression of a house built in stages over a period of time.

25. Frederic Torrey House, 1905
1 Canyon Road

Coxhead & Coxhead, architects

This is a more restrained gable-roofed shingle house designed for a member of the decorative arts firm of Vickery, Atkins, & Torrey.

26. Ferguson-Steilberg House, 1922
1 Orchard Lane

Walter T. Steilberg, architect

Peach-colored stucco, green Chinese tiles, Chinese-inspired window treatment, amber glass, and an octagonal tower impart a flavor of the Orient, while the brown shingles are a reminder that this is a Berkeley house.

27. Orchard Lane, 1910

Henry Atkins, designer

This Classically inspired public stairway, designed by a member of Vickery, Atkins & Torrey, is most romantic, a setting for a Maxfield Parrish–style painting.

28. George Boke House, 1901
23 Panoramic Way

Bernard R. Maybeck, architect

Scroll-sawn porch railings and a shallow gable roof with broad overhanging eaves evoke the

imagery of a Swiss chalet. This small redwood house caught the public's imagination: there is a copy in Oakland and one in Washington State.

29. Weston Havens House, 1939
255 Panoramic Way

Harwell Hamilton Harris, architect

Reached from the road by a bridge, the Havens House is a spectacular early example of mid-century Modernism. Inverted gable roofs protect the two levels with extraordinarily broad eaves, but their upward sweep allows for an unobstructed view. The house can best be seen from below on Arden Road, where there is another Harris design: the Linden Naylor House (1940) at **40 Arden Road.**

30. Joe Feldman House, 1975
13 Mosswood Road

Frank Lloyd Wright, architect

The only Frank Lloyd Wright design in Berkeley was built posthumously for Mrs. Wright's lawyer, using plans from the 1930s for an un-built "Usonian" house.

Elmwood

South of the university campus, extending several blocks east and west of College Avenue, are early streetcar suburbs, laid out in a grid and sometimes referred to as Berkeley's brown-shingle neighborhoods because of the many unpainted, weathered shingled houses that line the streets. On some blocks, overscaled apartment buildings from the 1960s are interspersed with the early-twentieth-century houses. A two-block retail business district on College Avenue between Russell and Woolsey Streets dates from the 1920s.

1. Louise Goddard houses, 1906
2531, 2535, 2539 Etna Street
Julia Morgan, architect

These three houses represent the architect's sophisticated adaptation of the local Craftsman style. They were built as speculative houses for Mrs. Goddard, a repeat client who built another trio, also designed by Julia Morgan, at **2615–2619 Parker Street.**

2. Clark Kerr Campus
Warring Street,
between Dwight Way
and Derby Street
George B. McDougall,
Alfred Eichler, et al., Office
of the State Architect

Now owned by the university and used as a residential enclave for students, this was the home of the **California Schools for the Deaf and Blind** from 1867 until 1980. Red-tile roofs and light-colored plastered walls present a

unifying theme for this sprawling sylvan campus, where buildings evoke the architecture of Spanish California. Most date from the 1920s through the 1950s as earlier brick Victorian structures were gradually replaced. The wall encircling the property, constructed in 1900, is made of stones from the original 1867 building that burned.

3. Julia Morgan houses, 1908
2814, 2816 Derby Street
Morgan & Hoover, architects

Opening onto a shared brick entry walk, these two gable-roofed shingled houses are almost a matching pair, but their individual elements are handled differently. At **2740** and **2742 Derby Street** (1907), Morgan stylistically tied the two-story house and cottage together by using similar roof forms and board-and-batten siding.

4. Julia Morgan Theater, 1908, 1910, 1918
2640 College Avenue
Julia Morgan, architect

Built for the congregation of St. John's Presbyterian Church, this is one of the defining buildings of the Bay Region's Arts and Crafts movement. It is residentially scaled. From the street, it appears as two buildings, each with low-pitched gable roofs, joined by an enclosed one-story gallery-like extension. The former sanctuary is somewhat higher than the Fellowship Hall to the north; the entire structure is sheathed in stained shingles and board siding. The redwood and Douglas fir interior is unadorned, with all structural members exposed; the shadowy upper reaches of the lofty space are filled with elaborate trusswork. The graceful pattern of the clerestory windows and the

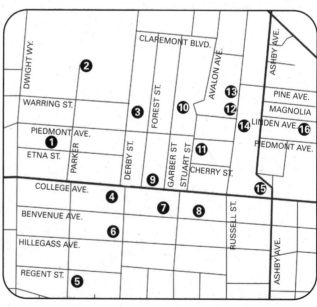

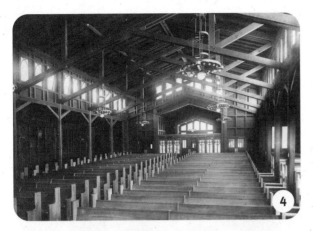

simple hanging light fixtures of wood with bare bulbs add interest. Built in three phases, the Fellowship Hall to the north was built first, followed by the sanctuary, and last by the Sunday School wing in the rear.

5. Annie Edmonds Duplex, 1904
2612–2616 Regent Street

Julia Morgan, architect

The earliest known design in Berkeley by Julia Morgan is a large shingled Craftsman-style duplex built within a month after she obtained her architect's license.

6. Gifford McGrew House, 1900
2601 Derby Street

Bernard Maybeck, architect

Steeply pitched gable roofs with flared ends, sheathed weathered shingles, and small-paned casement windows create a romantic version of the "simple home." The west-facing dormer (1984) carefully matches.

7. Henry Randall House, 1909
2733 Benvenue Avenue

Plowman and Thomas, architects

This large house has a steeply pitched gable roof, small-paned casement windows, and a one-story hipped-roof living room wing with corner buttresses.

8. Charles Westenberg House, 1903
2811 Benvenue Avenue

Dodge Coplin, architect

Large twin gables, a profusion of bays and dormers, and a spacious open garden distinguish this prominent shingled house.

9. St. John's Presbyterian Church No. 2, 1964, 1974
2727 College Avenue

Carlton Steiner and George Hanna, Religious Architecture Association (Fellowship Hall)

John Hans Ostwald, architect (Sanctuary)

The new St. John's was built incrementally on the site of a large nineteenth-century estate. The reinforced-concrete Fellowship Hall, at the rear of the property, was built first; it has broad glass-filled gables and an expansive terrace enclosed by vine-covered pergolas. Ten years later, the church itself was built; it was architect Ostwald's last design. The building is sheathed in unpainted vertical boards and its shed roof rises dramatically to a promontory-like point.

10. Plowman-Thomas houses, 1908
2820, 2826, 2830, 2836, 2844 Garber Street

George T. Plowman and John Hudson Thomas, architects

Between 1908 and 1910, before Plowman left for Los Angeles, the two architects designed many of Berkeley's best Craftsman-style houses. The Garber Street hill is the place to view a number of them en masse.

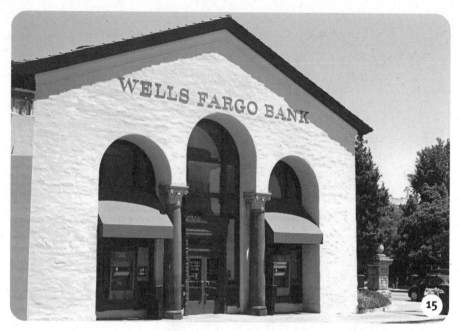

15

11. Leola Hall speculative houses, 1909
Stuart Street between College Avenue and Kelsey Street

Leola Hall, designer

Leola Hall was a designer-builder-developer who built variations on her signature Craftsman-style house, designed for maximum light and privacy in groups of three or four, close together on narrow re-subdivided lots. Three groups of her houses are close together: **2804** and **2806 Stuart Street, 2800 Kelsey Street, 2747 Stuart; 2752, 2754,** and **2758 Piedmont Avenue; 2730** and **2732 Stuart;** and **2800 Piedmont Avenue.**

12. Edward Marquis House, 1910
2827 Russell Street

Henry Lawrence Wilson, architect

A playful and exuberant Mission Revival–style house was built from a plan in *The Wilson Bungalow Book.*

13. Judah Magnes Memorial Museum (Jeremiah Burke House), 1908
2911 Russell Street

D. J. Patterson, architect

John McLaren, landscape architect

The large and rather austere two-story Craftsman-style house is remarkable for its clinker-brick construction and extensive grounds. It has housed the Magnes Museum since 1966, and is now open to the public.

14. Vernon Smith House and Studio, 1927, 1931
2812 Russell Street

William Wurster, architect

An early Wurster that bears the imprint of the 1920s in its Period Revival styling also anticipates his future minimalist approach to architecture.

15. Mercantile Trust Co., 1925
2959 College Avenue

Walter H. Ratcliff Jr., architect

The tile-roofed bank building, with two giant Corinthian columns of polished red granite supporting the triple-arched entry, is the cornerstone of the Elmwood business district.

16. Sarah E. Kellogg House, 1902
2960 Linden Avenue

Maybeck & White, architects

This vine-draped gabled cottage is a most romantic redwood house. It was moved to this site in 1959 to save it from demolition.

Claremont

By the 1880s, Claremont Avenue
and surrounding hillsides were
dotted with country estates.
Although busy Highway 13
(Ashby Avenue) bisects the district today, and one of the broad
boulevards through Claremont
Court is a commuter route to the
university, the Claremont district
remains a desirable residential
neighborhood.

Claremont consists of several
residential subdivisions, created
at different times by the Realty
Syndicate and its associate companies as part of a strategy to
connect outlying areas with its
interurban electric streetcar network known as the Key System.
The Claremont Hotel, at the
line's terminus, is the centerpiece
of the district.

The first subdivision, Claremont
Park, opened in 1905 and was
almost fully built by 1920; it
features shingled and modified
Prairie-style houses. Claremont
Court, from 1907, is an area of
grand formal houses. The streets
are laid out with respect for the
topography and include small
parks, paths, and stairways that
connected to the streetcar lines.
On Tunnel and Roble Roads,
there are a few larger estates
from the 1920s.

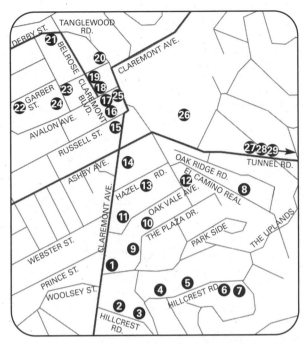

6 • Berkeley: Claremont

1. Claremont Park
Entrance Gateway, 1905
*Claremont Avenue at
The Uplands*

John Galen Howard, architect

The rustic but elegant entrance
gateway to Claremont Park is
constructed of a rough, reddish
local stone, and includes tile-
roofed lodges and pillars topped

by "quaint" wrought-iron
lanterns. Smaller stonework
pillars define the secondary
entrance at Hillcrest Road
and Claremont Avenue.

2. William Duzan
House, 1905
19 Hillcrest Road

W. H. Wheeler, architect

This was the first house built in
Claremont Park, and it is one of
the few in Berkeley designed in
the Mission Revival style.

3. H. L. Johnson houses, 1914
29, 35 Hillcrest Road

John Hudson Thomas, architect

Thomas is well represented
in Claremont, and these are

remarkable hillside examples
of his personal amalgamation
of Arts and Crafts, Viennese
Secession, and Prairie School,
with rough plastered surfaces
and angularity.

4. Richard Lyon House, 1958
125 Hillcrest Road

Joseph Esherick, architect

This is an elegant example of one
of the more formal Bay Region
Modern architects, built on one
of the few remaining empty lots.

5. Lewis Chapin House, 1910
159 Hillcrest Road

This shingled house has broad
eaves and exposed timbers, and
was likely designed by the owner,
a local designer-builder.

6. Claremont Assembly
Club, 1911
214 Hillcrest Road

Charles S. Kaiser, architect

A private neighborhood clubhouse in the Arts and Crafts
style was intended to blend
with its residential neighbors.
The architect's own house at **60
The Uplands** dates from 1907.

7. Austin-Tabancay House,
remodeled 1988
226 Hillcrest Road

Ace Architects, architects

A remodeling of an older home
by an architectural firm is full of
surprises, resulting in this copper-
domed Arabian Nights fantasy.

8. Paul Shobring House
and Studio, 1953
55 El Camino Real

*Julian Taylor and
Robert Benson, architects*

This hillside house and its
adjoining music pavilion are
post-and-beam construction,

and are good examples of mid-
twentieth-century Modern with
a strong Japanese influence.

9. Van Sant and
Brakenridge Houses, 1906
6, 10 Encina Place

Coxhead & Coxhead, architects

These two houses were once
identical except for surface materials. They were designed to overlook their park-like gardens and
Harwood Creek.

10. Walter Wood House, 1909
1 The Plaza Drive

August Peterson, designer

The large shingled house has
a garage (1912) faced with
redwood logs like a log cabin,
and spans Harwood Creek
like a bridge.

11. H. L. Dungan House, 1911
41 Oakvale Avenue

John Hudson Thomas, architect

This steep-gabled, redwood
and half-timbered house is the
ultimate creek-side dwelling:
Harwood Creek flows beneath
the house and emerges through
a large shingled arch under the
two-story living room wing.
Next door are two other creek-
side houses by Thomas: the
Sellander House (1914) at 35
Oakvale and the **Frey House**
(1925) at 39 Oakvale.

12. Thomas Hunt House, 1915
53 Domingo Avenue

Bernard Maybeck, architect

Maybeck used historic styles in
creative ways; in this house, he
designed an overscaled entry
portico for an uncharacteristic
Dutch Colonial–style house.
The house was moved here
in 1964—as was Maybeck's
Chamberlain Studio (1923)

at 8 Hazel Road in 1968—
to escape demolition.

13. T. Slattery House, 1956
56 Hazel Road

Roger Lee, architect

Dramatically perched over
Harwood Creek, this L-shaped
mid-twentieth-century Modern
has an entrance deck suspended
over the water, and the living
room wing at the rear spans
the creek.

14. John Muir School, 1915
2955 Claremont Avenue

James W. Plachek, architect

Although the classroom wings
were reconstructed in 1978, the
Tudor-style auditorium with tall
arched windows is original. The
interior has heavy timber trusswork and is paneled in wood.

15. Claremont Court
Entrance Gates, 1907
*Claremont Boulevard at
Russell Street*

John Galen Howard, architect

Stately brick gateposts mark
the entrances to the Claremont
Court subdivision. Each post is a
cluster of Ionic pilasters, topped
by either a lantern or a terra-
cotta finial, and delicate arched
iron gates. This 1907 subdivision
is noteworthy for its fine collection of Period Revival houses by
noted Bay Area architects.

16. St. Clement's Episcopal
Church, 1909
2837 Claremont Boulevard

*Willis Polk, D. H. Burnham &
Co., architects*

This small shingled church, with
an interior of exposed redwood
construction, is a charming contrast to the large residences surrounding it. **Palache Hall** (1927;

Walter H. Ratcliff Jr., architect) is a brick-sided Tudor-style building.

17. Seldon Williams House, 1928
2821 Claremont Boulevard

Julia Morgan, architect

A quietly elegant two-story Italian villa has stucco siding and a red-tile roof. Decorative fresco work in a floral motif around the entrance, and conservatory windows framed with Gothic tracery are notable.

18. William Campbell House, 1910
2815 Claremont Boulevard

T. Paterson Ross, architect

The distinctive features of this grand brick-sided house are the corbelled and paneled chimney, elaborate belt courses, arched entry porch, and "Dutch" gable.

19. Morse-Palache-Ames House, circa 1878, 1921
2811 Claremont Boulevard

Walter H. Ratcliff Jr., architect (remodel, 1921)

A small-frame ranch house became a sprawling Tudor-style mansion after a major remodel-

ing in 1921. Another of Ratcliff's impressive Tudors (1925) is located at **2721 Belrose Avenue**.

20. John Calkins House, 1926
28 Tanglewood Road

Coxhead & Coxhead, architects

Ernest Coxhead, who helped define the Arts and Crafts movement in the Bay Area in the 1890s, worked almost exclusively in the Spanish Colonial Revival style in the 1920s, of which the Calkins House is a stellar example.

21. Flora B. Randolph School, 1909
2700 Belrose Avenue

Maybeck & White, architects

Bernard Maybeck designed this private school as a cluster of attached shingled pavilions with gable roofs. Residential in character from the start, it has been successfully converted to a single-family home.

22. Gutterson houses, 1912–1924
2904, 2910, 2916, 2922 Garber Street

Henry H. Gutterson, architect

This group of four hillside homes was built over a twelve-

year period, but it exhibits a common idiom of grouped small-paned windows, the combination of stucco and board-and-batten surfaces, and prominent angled bays. Gutterson's own home is at **2922 Garber** (1912).

23. Henry H. Wright House, 1914
2801 Oak Knoll Terrace

Albert Farr, architect

Having first worked in the shingled idiom, Farr later became known for his carefully executed English Tudor–style residences.

24. Benjamin G. McDougall House, 1910
2810 Oak Knoll Terrace

Benjamin G. McDougall, architect

Benjamin McDougall came from a family of architects. He designed six houses in Claremont Court and several downtown buildings. This almost-austere twin-gable house was his own residence.

25. Sophie B. McDuffie House, 1915
3016 Avalon Avenue

Henry H. Gutterson, architect

The U-shaped one- and two-story house wraps around the corner lot to open onto a sheltered rear garden. A canted two-story central section contains a polygonal stair tower sheathed in board-and-batten that provides a pivot point. Cloaked in the safety of the Period Revival style, this is an important early example of a residential design that would evolve into the mid-twentieth-century California Ranch house.

26. Claremont Hotel, 1906
41 Tunnel Road

Charles W. Dickey, architect

Nestled against a backdrop of eucalyptus trees, this sparkling white architectural fantasy can be seen from as far away as the Golden Gate Bridge. One of the last in the nineteenth-century tradition of sprawling resort hotels, the Claremont was designed in half-timbered Elizabethan style and originally painted in contrasting colors. Set on a high stone base, the building follows the contours of the site; its asymmetrical arrangement of gabled wings is punctu-

ated by a square tower with a dome-roofed belvedere.

At **1 Tunnel Road** is the Berkeley Tennis Club (1917; Roland Stringham, architect), sharing the block with the hotel; it is a low, hipped-roof shingled building with a rough stone chimney.

27. Duncan McDuffie House, 1924 (unmapped)
22 Roble Road

Willis Polk, architect

Duncan McDuffie was an officer and shareholder in the various companies that created

Claremont and Northbrae in Berkeley and St. Francis Wood (1912) in San Francisco; he is considered the visionary.

Around 1912, McDuffie began planning a huge country estate with architect John Galen Howard, and the Olmsted Bros. for the landscape plan. McDuffie never built the mansion he envisioned, but he did build this more-modest tile-roofed Mediterranean house that turns its back to the street and overlooks extensive gardens. After McDuffie abandoned the idea of building an estate, he subdivided his land; the large Mediterranean houses along Roble Road are on part of that subdivision.

28. Guy Hyde Chick House, 1914 (unmapped)
7133 Chabot Road

Bernard Maybeck, architect

The grand chalet and magnificent oaks surrounding it miraculously survived the 1991 firestorm. The symmetrical rectangular-shaped house has entrances on both of its long sides that are covered by pergolas, deep overhanging eaves, and colorful yellow, blue, green, and red trim highlighting structural elements; the walls are unpainted shingles.

29. George P. Wintermute House, "The Rocks," 1913 (unmapped)
227 Tunnel Road

John Hudson Thomas, architect

Many of the elements that define the architect's smaller Secessionist-style houses have been translated into the vocabulary of a baronial manor with an Arts and Crafts sensibility.

West Berkeley

What was once Berkeley's industrial district has become an area of research and development interspersed with retail and housing. Industry began in the 1850s, and Berkeley's first real community, **Ocean View,** grew up around Fourth and Delaware Streets. The Central Pacific's transcontinental rail line built a station at Third and Delaware in 1878, the year Berkeley was incorporated.

Today most of the large industrial manufacturing companies are gone, although the German pharmaceutical company Bayer AG has offices and research development labs on approximately forty-five acres, from Dwight Way to Grayson Street and west of Seventh Street, on the former sites of **Cutter Biological Laboratory, Byron Jackson Iron Works, Colgate Palmolive, Peet,** and **Philadelphia Quartz.**

During the Depression, the Works Progress Administration (WPA) built the roadbed for the Eastshore Freeway and created **Aquatic Park** and the **Berkeley Yacht Harbor.** While World War II increased industrial activity in West Berkeley, there was a slow but steady decline in manufacturing after the war.

Berkeley's waterfront was greatly modified by solid-waste landfill between 1923 and 1981. Much of this landfill is now open space and parkland, a yacht harbor, a hotel, and waterside restaurants. The **Berkeley Municipal Pier** (1929) is the remnant of a three-and-one-half-mile-long pier built by the city to accommodate car ferries. It is also the last remaining pier, of many, which once dotted the waterfront, and is a popular fishing spot and promenade.

In the late 1960s, the city created a twenty-block redevelopment district between University Avenue and Cedar Street to stimulate a revival of manufacturing. Citizens protested as historic buildings were taken by eminent domain, and many lower-income people lost their homes. The preservation movement is responsible for the interesting mix of buildings today. Without some controversy, dialogue, and compromise, the land would have been cleared for concrete tilt-up warehouses.

1. Shorebird Park Nature Center, 2004
160 University Avenue, Berkeley Marina

Van Mechelen Architects & Dan Smith and Associates, architects

The one-story strawbale building sports a two-story hipped-roof tower in the center. The "green" building is constructed of recycled materials, and volunteers provided much of the labor.

2. Southern Pacific Railroad Station, 1913
700 University Avenue

J. H. Christie, architect

The Mission Revival–style station is an important feature of the California landscape. This station's arched openings were filled in when converted to a restaurant in 1976.

3. Fourth Street Retail District

Fourth Street between Hearst Avenue and Virginia Street

This is the center of Berkeley's redevelopment project intended to create an industrial park. What it has become is Berkeley's most popular retail and dining area.

Beginning in 1976, the design/ build firm of Abrams, Millikan and Kent converted two old warehouse buildings in the 1800 block of Fourth Street into retail space. The developers' direct hands-on approach brought early success that attracted new developers and businesses to the area.

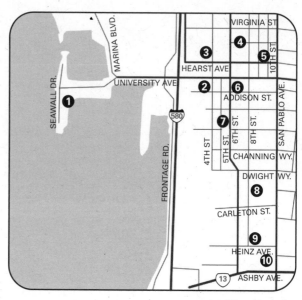

6 • West Berkeley

The district has evolved over three decades, rather than being built in one piece, and includes many reused buildings and some new ones—a streetscape that cannot be replicated. The buildings are vaguely neo-traditional in soft pastel colors. Collectively they are an unassuming backdrop for a lively pedestrian retail district where the whole is more important than its parts.

Spenger's Fish Grotto, 1919 Fourth Street, is Berkeley's oldest business under the same name. In the center of a sprawling complex of dining rooms and bars is a two-story, gable-roofed, pioneer-style building that served as home and market to Johann Spenger beginning about 1890.

4. Delaware Street Historic District, 1854–1910

Rehabilitated and partially reconstructed, 1986

800 Block of Delaware Street

William Coburn, historic architectural consultant

Delaware Street was the center of Ocean View and connected **Jacob's Landing** (1853) with **Bowen's Inn** (1854) on the old Contra Costa Road (now San Pablo Avenue). In 1979, the historic homes were scheduled for demolition but preservationists prevailed. By 1986, houses were reconstructed and rehabilitated. On nearby streets are other nineteenth-century houses.

5. Church of the Good Shepherd, 1878

1001 Hearst Avenue

Charles Bugbee, architect

An excellent example of the Victorian Gothic style, it has an eighty-foot bell tower and is the oldest remaining church in Berkeley. One block to the west at 926 Hearst Avenue is the former **First Presbyterian Church of West Berkeley** (1879; Charles

Geddes, architect), another Gothic Revival with a square corner tower topped by an eighty-foot spire. At 1819 Tenth Street, **Toverii Tuppa/Finnish Hall** (1908; August Trille, designer/builder) has a recessed central entry bay flanked by three-story rectangular "towers" with wide overhangs and scrolled carved-wood brackets.

6. Berkeley Day Nursery, 1927
2031 Sixth Street, at Addison Street

Walter H. Ratcliff Jr., architect

This impressive Tudor-style structure has high gable roofs, hipped-roof dormers, half-timbering, and diamond-shaped leaded windows. The interior has natural redwood walls and beamed ceilings. It was founded in 1908 as a nursery for children of working parents.

7. Berkeley Pump, 1945–1955, 1990
2222, 2233–2239, 2246 Fifth Street

E. H. Buel, designer-builder

Abrams, Milliken & Kent, developers (1990)

David Trachtenberg, architect (1990)

Scattered around West Berkeley is an unusual building type: a prefabricated concrete wall with a latticework of glazed diamond-shaped openings. George A. Scott developed the unit around 1938 with consulting architects Walter Steilberg and Bernard Maybeck. Fred Stadelhofer of Berkeley Pump developed this variation with cement contractor E. H. Buel.

8. Kawneer Window Sash Factory Building, 1912
2547 Eighth Street

Francis John Plym, architect–industrial designer

Chicago architect Francis John Plym patented a design for a metal frame window and named it "Kawneer." The window was in such demand after the 1906 earthquake and fire that he

opened a factory in Berkeley. His former factory building has a row of twenty north-facing, shed-roofed, glass-faced skylights that capture natural light and create the distinctive sawtooth silhouette that was a common feature of early-twentieth-century industrial buildings. The company made window sash here until 1958.

9. 2725 Eighth Street, 2003
Regan Bice, architect

A sophisticated two-story rectangular duplex set back from the sidewalk is shaded and softened by trees. Although there is formality here, the façade is subtly asymmetrical. Two other projects by Bice are at **2720 Eighth** (2004) and **935 Grayson Street** (2004).

10. H. J. Heinz Factory, 1927
2900 San Pablo Avenue

The Austin Co./Albert Kahn, architect

Berkeley's most elegant industrial building is Mediterranean with Romanesque and Moorish details. It is a one- and two-story building that covers the entire block. At the center of its symmetrical San Pablo Avenue façade is an arched entry with loggia above. After the plant closed in 1956, the building was converted to retail, offices, and an education center.

7 · Emeryville

Despite Emeryville's small size (only 1.2 square miles with a population of 6,900), it appears to be a considerably larger place. The former industrial city, known for its card rooms and heavy industry, has been transformed almost entirely during the past ten years into an office, research, residential, and retail center. The changes are happening rapidly; the dynamic feeling of change is palpable. Despite the newness, Emeryville is not a new city; it was incorporated in 1896 and still has a few old residential neighborhoods.

Emeryville is named for Joseph S. Emery, who came west during the Gold Rush and settled in what would later become Emeryville in 1859. Emery established a horse-car trolley line from Oakland to Park Avenue in 1873 and then subdivided his land.

West of the railroad tracks, on either side of the mouth of Temescal Creek, there was once marshland with willow thickets, and a Native American shell mound, the largest on the bay.

Beginning in the 1870s, the area around Bay Street was the location of feedlots, stockyards, and meat-packing plants, and a few continued to operate into the 1980s; the unpleasant area was known as "Butcherville."

The arrival of a railroad in 1879 followed by the Atchison, Topeka and Santa Fe Railroad in 1904 and the opening of the Panama Canal in 1915 stimulated the growth of industry. By 1928, Emeryville claimed to have thirty national companies and hundreds of smaller local ones employing approximately 8,000 workers. The waste from all these manufacturing companies was dumped into the bay.

During the 1930s and 1940s, the bay was filled in on the west side of the new freeway, increasing the size of Emeryville and making possible the Watergate residential development in the 1960s.

Until the 1970s, Emeryville was a thriving industrial, manufacturing, and warehouse center. The first inkling that things were changing was the redevelopment of the Paraffines Companies (PABCO) manufacturing site, established in 1884. Two substantial brick buildings were reused as the Emery Bay Public Market in the early 1970s. The latest renovation of this project was completed in 1988 by Brocchini Architects. The site now occupied by IKEA was the former location of Judson Steel, once one of the East Bay's largest steel foundries, which opened in 1882 and closed in 1991.

Emeryville has the most successful redevelopment project in the Bay Area. It has changed the face of the city in less than ten years and nearly all industrial businesses have closed. Emeryville is booming, but it is a boomtown managed and manipulated with millions of redevelopment dollars. Since many industrial sites were on several acre parcels, and with redevelopment's ability to assemble parcels through eminent domain, some of the new projects are large.

Two older residential neighborhoods in Emeryville have a few houses dating from the 1870s. These neighborhoods, which merge with Oakland, are located between Doyle and Vallejo Streets north of Powell, and between Forty-Eighth and Forty-First Streets between San Pablo Avenue and Adeline Street. The Moderne-style **Veteran's Memorial Building** (1931; Henry Meyers and George Klinkhardt, architects) is located in the second neighborhood at 4321 Salem Street.

1. Old City Hall, 1903
1333 Park Avenue
Frederick Soderberg,
architect

Old City Hall has a rusticated arched entry flanked by Doric columns and topped by a copper dome. It has been restored but modified, and is connected to a new building constructed in 2001 that was designed by Fisher Friedman Architects.

2. Pixar Corporation, 1998
Forty-Fifth Street at Hollis Street and Park Avenue
Peter Bohlin, Bohlin Cywinski Jackson, architects
Peter Walker and Partners, landscape architect

The Pixar Corporation, creators of *Monsters, Inc., A Bug's Life,* and *Toy Story,* is located on a sixteen-acre corporate campus-style complex set behind an eight-foot-high steel fence covered with roses, and a six-foot planted berm. Behind the fence and berm is a large brick-sided, three- to four-story building. Expansion of the complex will cover twenty-one acres. John King, the *San Francisco Chronicle*'s architecture critic, describes the complex "as fragrant but forbidding." There are no tours of this facility.

3. Morehouse Mustard Company, circa 1919
4221 Hollis Street

This block-long, one-story red-brick factory building has been adaptively reused.

4. Bridge Court Apartments, 1998
1221–1331 Fortieth Street
Mclarand, Vasquez & Partners

An articulated massing of volumes and deep-earth-tone colors distinguish this dense 220-unit apartment project, which overlooks the "big-box" retail mall.

5. PG&E Building, 1924
Art in Public Places
4525 Hollis Street
Scott Donahue and Mark Rogero, sculptors (bas-relief, 1993)

Six three-dimensional bas-relief sculptures over roll-up truck doors depict PG&E's work in developing hydroelectric power, its gas service, and the history of the site. They are so well integrated with the building that they appear original.

In 1990, the city passed the Art in Public Places program through a Percent for Art ordinance. Public artworks are now located in public and private developments throughout the city. A guide to the thirty-five works of public art is available at city hall.

6. Emery Bay Village, 1979
Fifty-Third Street
Hansen Murakami Eshima, architects

Secluded in a forested garden setting are 112 condominium units in freestanding two-story buildings, two to four units each, and a community center. This quiet oasis is quite a contrast to the densely packed industrial-style residential units currently being built.

7. Chiron Corp Life Science Center, 1993–1998
Fifty-Third and Hollis Streets
Ricardo Legorreta, architect (with Flad & Associates, architects)

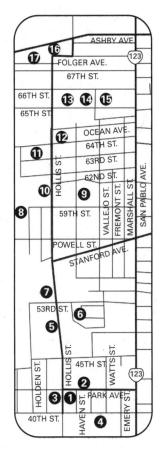

7 • Emeryville

The boldly colored buildings by Mexican architect Ricardo Legorreta are tiered back from the street in a series of rectangular block shapes. Different hues of desert colors on each section, a varied window treatment, and L-shaped spaces for trees humanize the composition of large buildings. The architect also designed the Children's Discovery Museum in San Jose and the Mexican Art Museum in San Francisco. Only a fraction of the fourteen-building, thirty-year master plan has been completed.

8. Amtrak Station, 1993
5885 Landregan Street

Heller Manus, architects

Wareham Development Corporation built this station for the city, which leases it to Amtrak. Between 1999 and 2004, Wareham has developed 330,000 square feet of offices, retail space, and housing on its eleven-acre site across from the station. The three- to five-story buildings are clad in brick.

9. Doyle Street Greenway, 2004
Powell and Hollis Streets, north to Sixty-Seventh Street

ROMA Design Group

Using the former right-of-way of a spur track, this project creates a linear park and multiuse trail. Part of the greenway is located on Doyle Street between Ocean and Sixty-First, passing diagonally between former industrial properties.

10. Westinghouse High Voltage Insulator Co., 1920s
6121 Hollis Street

This reused industrial building with a redbrick façade has an interesting series of false-front projections designed to enhance the end of monitor windows.

11. Hollis Business Center, 2000–2001
1400 Block of Sixty-Third and Sixty-Fourth Streets

Kava Massih Architects

This complex of office buildings, apartments, and garages covers a long block and is quite different on its three sides. The façades of the buildings along Sixty-Third and Sixty-Fourth

Streets, although different, are long and repetitive. The Sixty-Fourth Street building reuses the structure of the **Grove Valve** manufacturing building. The spirit of the old was incorporated into the new.

12. 6400 Hollis Street, 1986
Michael Pyatok, architect

A simple warehouse has been reinvented with fanciful sculpture around its entry doors. Called *Hubcap Façade,* the sculptural elements were funded by the Emeryville Art in Public Places program.

13. Liquid Sugar, 2004
1244–1204 Sixty-Fifth Street

Kava Massih Architects

This is an example of the type of residential loft-style apartments currently being constructed in Emeryville. The units all have separate entries and are narrow and multistoried. Parking is in the inner courtyards. Color and a varied façade liven up the densely packed units. The same architectural firm designed **Elevation 22,** a large housing project on Doyle Street between Hollis and Vallejo Streets, completed in 2005.

14. Oliver Lofts 2003
1266 Sixty-Fifth Street

NPH Architects

This project is built into one of the Oliver Rubber Company buildings. Its symmetrical façade has different-sized windows, materials, colors, and shallow rectangular window bays arranged somewhat like a Mondrian painting. There is a courtyard in the center.

15. 6550 Vallejo and 1150 Sixty-Fifth Streets, 2001
Kava Massih Architects

Once part of Oliver Rubber Company, this building has been altered and expanded several times. A three-story addition at **6550 Vallejo** has a dramatic third story with a circular cutout above a recessed balcony.

16. Studio Buildings, 2002
755 and 757 Folger Avenue

David Wilson, designer-builder

A pair of narrow two-story, corrugated-metal-sided buildings with slanted roofs marks the end of Hollis Street and the beginning of West Berkeley. They are very prominent as one turns the corner onto Seventh Street.

17. The Quonset Hut, circa 1943
741 Folger Avenue

In Emeryville and Berkeley, this may be the last of a once-common building type that could be quickly assembled from prefabricated materials. Shaped like half a cylinder, it was made from corrugated metal. This is a small version of the Quonset hut that was introduced during World War II, and came in several sizes.

V
Contra Costa County

Shelby Sampson, author & photographer (1)
Susan Dinkelspiel Cerny, author & photographer (2, 3)

Contra Costa County consists of three distinct areas:
1. West Contra Costa County on San Francisco Bay extends to the East Bay Hills.
2. Central Contra Costa County sits between the East Bay Hills and Mt. Diablo.
3. East Contra Costa County lies east of Mt. Diablo and runs east to the
   San Joaquin River.

Settlement by non-Native Americans did not begin until after the Mexican government began awarding land grants to prominent Mexican citizens in the late 1820s. Approximately eleven ranchos were created and many place-names date from this era in the county's history. After California became a state in 1850, Contra Costa County was one of the original twenty-seven California counties and included what is now Alameda County until 1852. Martinez has always been the county seat.

Until the 1960s, Contra Costa County's population was greatest along the shorelines of San Francisco and Suisun Bays, with shipping ports, rail lines, and industry. In the valleys of Central Contra Costa, farming and ranching dominated the landscape and economy. Although the Bay Bridge (1936) and Caldecott Tunnel (1937) opened before World War II, it wasn't until after the war that residential commuter suburbs began to expand around communities established in the late nineteenth century. In the past thirty-five years, Walnut Creek, Concord, and San Ramon have become major business and retail centers called "edge cities."

While Californians still refer to the great population boom after World War II as changing the face of the Bay Area, the most dramatic increase in population in Central and East Contra Costa has occurred since 1970, nearly doubling the population that now exceeds one million.

There is still some heavy industry, especially oil refineries, along the bay from Richmond to Antioch, but much is being replaced with new housing, commercial developments, and shoreline parks. Historic industrial sites in Richmond, Hercules, Pittsburg, and Antioch are being redeveloped as new communities.

If critics were appalled at single-family suburban growth before 1970, the ensuing years have not seen abatement to the trend, especially in Central and East Contra Costa. "Farther out" used to mean farther away and a longer commute to employment centers in San Francisco and Oakland. New, edge-city business centers not only create jobs but also support the sprawling new residential subdivisions.

Near business centers and BART stations, there are townhouses and apartment buildings, but single-family houses continue to be constructed in vast numbers isolated from shops and services. The automobile remains essential to suburban life.

Despite Contra Costa County's rapid growth and development, each town and city has a historic center from which the community grew. Even though historic structures may be gone, there is pride in the history of place. There are many historical societies, published histories, and local history museums. It may be surprising that three Mexican-era adobes are still standing that have not been moved or rebuilt.

East Bay Regional Parks

The East Bay Regional Park District manages nearly 100,000 acres of parkland in fifty-nine separate parks in Alameda and Contra Costa Counties. The parks include recreation areas, wilderness, shorelines, preserves, regional trails, and areas being held for future acquisition.

The park district was established in 1933 after the Pardee Dam and Mokelumne River water system was completed in 1930, making some local watershed lands unnecessary. Tilden Park, a 2,000-acre area in the hills east of Berkeley, was the first park established.

The **Brazilian Room** in Tilden Park is one of several structures in the Regional Park District that can be rented for weddings and other events. The Brazilian Room is special in that its interior wood walls, floors, and fixtures were originally part of the Brazilian Pavilion at the 1939 Golden Gate International Exposition on Treasure Island. After the exposition closed, the room was given to the East Bay Regional Park District by Brazil as a gift of friendship. The large gable-roofed building was constructed by the Works Progress Administration (WPA), combining a new exterior of local stone and timber with the original interior.

Below the Brazilian Room's sloping lawn is the park's botanical garden that displays California native plants. Stone pathways meander along Wildcat Creek in this magical spot.

The **Tilden Park Carousel** is also a gem of the East Bay Regional Park system. Built originally in 1911 by Hershell Spielman Company of New York, it was once located in Griffin Park in Los Angeles and moved here in 1948. The fanciful animals are hand carved.

Brazilian Room, Tilden Park

Contra Costa County Trail System

In partnership with various municipalities, government agencies, and the East Bay Regional
Park District, which manages them, a network of multiuse trails has been developed that
provides safe off-road corridors between Central Contra Costa communities. This network
is viewed as an alternative to using private cars. It not only connects residential areas with
schools, shopping areas, and parks, but also with public transportation. Parts of these trails
are wheelchair accessible.

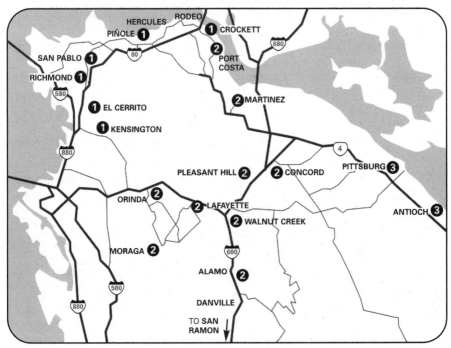

1 · West Contra Costa County: Kensington, El Cerrito, Richmond, San Pablo to Crockett

West Contra Costa County stretches along the shoreline of San Francisco Bay from Cerrito Creek to the Carquinez Strait at Crockett, and east to the ridges of the East Bay Hills. San Pablo Avenue was the main road and highway from the Mexican era until Interstate 80 opened in 1957, and it still remains a commercial corridor. American settlers had moved onto the Mexican land grants by 1850 to farm and set up small businesses. A decade later, industries unwelcome and dangerous in the more populated areas, such as explosives manufacture and smelting plants, were built along the bay shore.

Kensington

The unincorporated community of Kensington, located in the hills just north of Berkeley, developed as a series of residential subdivisions beginning in 1911, just a year before the Oakland Traction Company's streetcar line along Arlington Avenue began operating.

1. First Unitarian Universalist Church of Berkeley, 1961
1 Lawson Road

Wurster, Bernardi and Emmons, architects

The church is a large concrete post-and-beam structure with a gable roof, wide overhanging eaves, and heavy exposed wood rafter ends; some concrete walls are embedded with pebbles. The church moved to Kensington from Berkeley onto land donated by architect Bernard Maybeck, a member of the church.

2. Anson Blake House and Garden, 1922–1924
70 Rincon Road

Bliss and Faville, architects

An Italian Renaissance–style villa has rusticated stucco siding and a tile roof; the arched entry surround is embellished with shal-

low relief patterns molded in stucco. The Blake family donated the house and gardens to the University of California in 1957 for the president's house. The gardens are open to the public.

3. Wallen Maybeck House #2, 1937
135 Purdue Avenue

Bernard Maybeck, architect

Sitting on a grassy knoll, the house was designed to be fireproof. It has corrugated iron roofing and panels of precast concrete, stained beige and separated by insulating rice hulls. The wing on the north, added in 2001, is of the same style and materials. A small subdivision at the end of Purdue, laid out by Maybeck, has several good examples of mid-twentieth-century Modernism.

El Cerrito

On the north bank of Cerrito Creek where El Cerrito Plaza stands today, Victor Castro built his adobe home in the late 1840s. The adobe stood until 1956, when it was destroyed by arson; El Cerrito Plaza was completed two years later. Two settlements, Rust and Stege, incorporated as El Cerrito in 1917.

The town was not always the pleasant, quiet family-oriented place it is today; racetracks, gambling, and associated activities were once common along San Pablo Avenue, and rock quarrying took place in the hills. During the late 1940s and 1950s, El Cerrito was built up with mostly modest Ranch-style houses; in the hills, there are

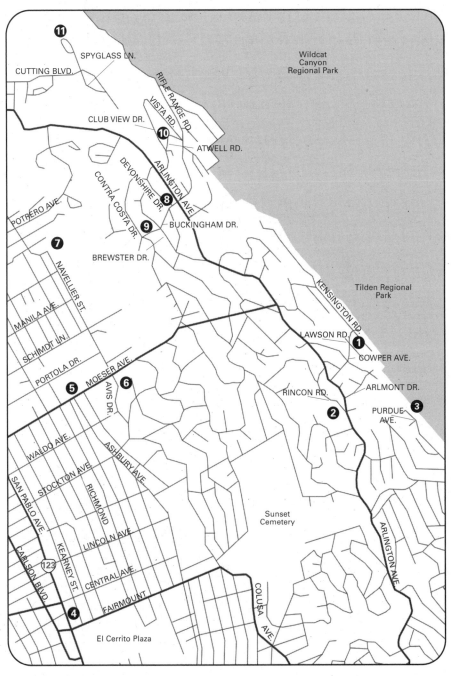

1 • West Contra Costa County: Kensington, El Cerrito

some very good examples of mid-twentieth-century Modernism.

4. Cerrito Theater, 1937
San Pablo Avenue between Central and Fairmount Avenues

William B. David & Associates, architects

Arnie Lerner and Jerri Holan, architects (restoration, 2006)

Within the recently restored building are superb original Art Deco murals, chandeliers and sconces, etched glass and mirrors, all with images of dancing gods and goddesses; it's "an amazing barrel-vaulted space," according to Dave Weinstein, author of the *San Francisco Chronicle*'s "Signature Style" and founder of Friends of the Cerrito Theater. After pressure from citizens, the city bought the building and leased it to a theater concern. Architects Arnie Lerner and Jerri Holan managed its restoration and reconstructed its long-lost marquee.

5. El Cerrito Community Center, 1965
Moeser Avenue at Ashbury Avenue

Wurster, Bernardi and Emmons, architects

Royston, Hanamoto, Mays & Beck, landscape architects

This L-shaped, cross-gable-roofed building with wide overhanging eaves encloses a garden with walls and pebble-imbedded concrete paving. The Community Swim Center was completed in 2004 in a complementary design by MBT architects.

6. Prospect Sierra School, 2003
960 Avis Drive

The Ratcliff Architects

This former public school was remodeled, expanded, and given an attractive new façade.

7. Hillside Swedenborgian Community Church, 1951
1422 Navellier Street

Lloyd Wright, architect

A simple wood-and-glass church with an impressive brick chimney overlooks a lawn and natural hillside park.

8. 1300 Devonshire Drive, circa 1926
John Hudson Thomas, architect

Prominently located on a corner lot, this T-shaped Tudor is exceptional for its tall, steeply pitched layers of intersecting gable roofs and gable roof dormers. **8513 Buckingham** (1964; Wong & Kami, architects) has a dramatic two-story, flared gable roof supported by pole posts.

9. 1366 Brewster Drive, 1955
Donald Olsen, architect

This house is an outstanding example of a wall of glass where the post-and-beam structural elements are clearly expressed.

10. William & Helen Atwell House, 1952
1411 Atwell Road

Richard Neutra, architect

Visible from Arlington Avenue, the horizontal cubist design articulates a post-and-beam structure. The Atwell subdivision is a small enclave of mid-twentieth-century Modernism, where nature dominates. Architect Donald Hardison's home (1958) is at 1415 Vista.

11. Mira Vista Golf and Country Club, 1920
East end of Cutting Boulevard

Walter Ratcliff Jr., architect (clubhouse)

William Watson, landscape architect (golf course)

This elegant clubhouse in English Tudor commands a beautiful hilltop site.

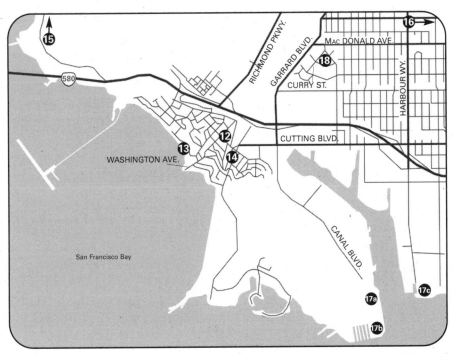

1 • West Contra Costa: Richmond

Richmond

Richmond was established with the arrival of the Santa Fe Railroad (1900) and the Standard Oil Refinery (1902). An industrial town sprang up, spreading from its nucleus in the Point Richmond area east toward the hills.

During World War II, nearly 100,000 people moved to Richmond for jobs in the four massive Kaiser shipyards and war-related industries. Richmond became a 24-hour town with movie theaters and bustling commerce along MacDonald Avenue. Community services were severely stretched: schools ran in shifts, and housing projects filled every inch of available land.

Postwar efforts to meet the demands of the vastly increased, racially diverse new population netted Richmond an "All American City" award in 1952, but, in fact, the city has never fully recovered its WWII prosperity. Several notable public housing developments of the 1950s and 1960s have fallen into disrepair; some, like Easter Hill (Vernon De Mars and Donald Hardison, architects), were razed and replaced with federally funded houses. Major commercial and residential developments are appearing north of town at Hilltop Mall and in neighboring Piñole. Along the bay shore, new housing developments were recently built at Marina Bay and Brickyard Landing. New business

and research "campuses," including the State Public Health Department laboratories, are on sites once occupied by shipyards.

12. Point Richmond

Point Richmond is part of Richmond, but has a distinct character. It nestles in the saddle of a line of hills, once an island. The surrounding marshland was diked and filled for farming in the 1850s.

The business, retail, and residential blocks on the eastern slope of the hill are listed on the National Register of Historic Places as a cohesive, largely intact, early-twentieth-century industrial town. The center of the business district is a two-block area surrounding a triangular-shaped town "square," where the library, community center, and public safety buildings are located.

At **145 Park Place** is Richmond's first firehouse (circa 1902) with two large arched openings. The Hotel Mac (1910) at **50 Washington Avenue** is a three-story brick building that was Richmond's earliest "fine" hotel. The former Bank of Richmond (1902) at **201 West Richmond Avenue** has a rounded corner bay with a newly replaced conical roof.

Four early-twentieth-century churches were built within three years of each other but in different styles. **Our Lady of Mercy Catholic Church** (1903; "William Higgins," architect), 311 West Richmond Avenue, has shingles over its original board siding. The **Methodist Church** (1906), 201 Martina Street, is faced with brick made at the Richmond Pressed Brick Company. **Lissley Chapel** (1903), 235 Washington Avenue, is a former Episcopal Church sheathed in unpainted shingles with two crenellated towers. Although no longer a church, the **First Baptist Church** (1904),

304 Washington Avenue, has retained its distinctive open-porch bell tower.

13. Mid-twentieth-century houses

Washington Avenue goes over the hill to the bay side of Point Richmond. Views are wonderful; the winding streets are worth a tour for the sheer variety of residential styles.

Some notable mid-twentieth-century houses, built just above the water's edge, are mostly obscured by fences and shrubbery. For the record, these include Richard M. Schindler's **Kaun House** (1934–1935) at 125 Western Drive, and two by William Wurster at **215 Western Drive** (1936) and **737 Ocean Avenue** (1937). John Funk designed **111 Western Drive** (1934, 1952) for landscape architects H. Leland and Adele Vaughan. The "tower" of architect Walter Thomas Brooks's own house at **331 Western Drive** (1971) rises above the shrubbery; across the street, at 551 Casey, Brooks remodeled an ordinary 1950s modern in 1993.

14. Richmond Municipal Natatorium, 1925
East Richmond Avenue and South Garrard Boulevard

Housing what was once the largest public indoor swimming pool in the East Bay, this Classic Revival building has a three-part composition with a temple-style central section. The building was closed in 2001 for seismic-safety reasons and has an uncertain future.

15. Winehaven/ Pt. Molate, 1908
2000 Block of Western Drive

This complex of buildings was California's largest winery, a company town, and a tourist attraction from 1906 until closed because of Prohibition in 1920. The largest building is a vast brick structure with a crenellated parapet and corner turrets. Twenty stucco-sided workers' cottages (originally shingled) line the hillside opposite the winery. From 1941 until 1995, it was used by the U.S. Navy as a fuel facility. The property now belongs to the city of Richmond, which hopes its future will be a Native American gambling casino, hotel, and convention center.

East Brother Island Light Station (1874) is the oldest remaining Victorian-era wood-frame lighthouse on the West Coast. Located on an island, it is visible northeast of Winehaven.

Central Richmond and MacDonald Avenues: MacDonald Avenue is Richmond's main east-west road. Once a bustling commercial area, it has declined severely since the 1960s, due to failed redevelopment plans, racial tensions, and relocation of downtown businesses to the Hilltop area. Attempts to revitalize central Richmond are ongoing; **Metro Walk** (2004; William Hezmalhalch Architects, Inc.) is part of a Transit Village adjacent to the BART and Amtrak stations.

16. Civic Center Complex, 1950
*MacDonald Avenue
at Twenty-Fifth Street*

Milton Pfleuger, architect

A complex of four brick-sided buildings is set in a U-shape around a central plaza. Layered rectangular and square elements create a subtle but balanced and elegant composition. The complex received awards and worldwide recognition after its completion in 1950; it is an important example of mid-century Modern civic architecture and planning.

17. Rosie the Riveter
WWII Home Front National Historical Park

As a result of the economic downturn after World War II, many of Richmond's war-related structures remain intact, inadvertently providing a Rosie the

Riveter/World War II Home Front National Historic Park "museum" that is being developed at three locations.

17a. Shipyard #3, 1942
South end of Canal Boulevard

Mory Wortman and A. Larson, architects

An important part of the National Historical Park, this site conveys the spirit of the massive Henry J. Kaiser shipyard complex that covered Richmond's south shore during WWII. The site includes five concrete dry docks, a corrugated metal and glass Machine Shop, the wood-frame First Aid Station and Cafeteria, and the huge, nearly windowless concrete General Warehouse that has a few touches of Moderne.

17b. The SS *Red Oak Victory*, 1944
*1337 Canal Boulevard
Berth 6A*

The SS *Red Oak Victory*, built here, carried ammunition and cargo during WWII and the Korean and Vietnam Wars. It is one of three Victory ships still afloat. Volunteers are restoring it as a museum ship. Visitors are welcome. Nearby is the *Wapama*, a 1914 lumber ship owned by the Maritime Museum. It has been dry-docked here for twenty years while being restored by volunteers.

17c. Ford Plant, 1931
South end of Harbour Way

Albert Kahn, architect

The quarter-mile-long Ford Plant epitomizes Kahn's innovative factory style, providing light and fresh air for the workers. It is planned as the centerpiece of a shoreline redevelopment program.

18. Atchison Village, 1942
*West end of MacDonald
Avenue at Curry Street*

Warnecke and Hass, architects

Richmond's first World War II housing project functions today as an efficient, low-cost, and attractive homeowners' cooperative, with groups of one- and two-story buildings set around grassy open spaces. Retaining much of its original visual integrity, the complex is listed on the National Register of Historic Places.

San Pablo to Crockett

19. San Pablo
The intersection of Church Lane and San Pablo Avenue was the center of Don Francisco Castro's 20,000-acre Rancho San Pablo and a stopping place on the road between Oakland and Martinez. Here, Don Castro's son, Jesus Maria, built an adobe home in 1845. St. Paul's Catholic Church was established in 1853, and a Northern Railroad depot was built in 1868. By the 1880s, at least five manufacturers of explosives had plants along the shoreline, but inland there was much agricultural activity. San Pablo was incorporated in 1948 and has a population of 30,000.

19a. San Pablo Civic Center, Alvarado Square, 1977
*Church Lane and
San Pablo Avenue*

Walter Thomas Brooks, architect

Lawrence Halprin, landscape architect

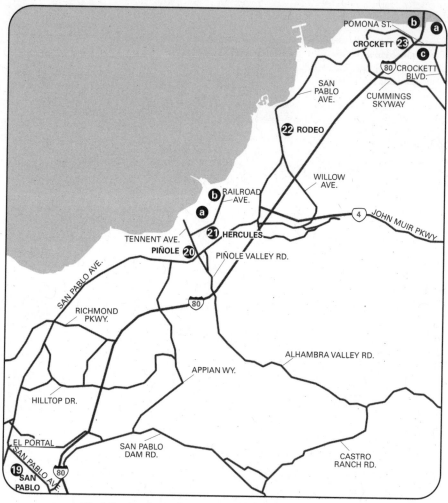

1 • West Contra Costa County: San Pablo, Piñole, Hercules, Rodeo, Crockett

An early California theme was used, with arches, heavy beams, tiles, and a fountain in the central courtyard. The **Castro/ Alvarado Adobe** (1845) was reconstructed on its original site in 1978 during construction of the Civic Center. **The Blume House** (1905) was moved from the Hilltop Mall area in 1979. It is a typical early-twentieth-century wood-frame farmhouse. The San

Pablo Historical Society operates both houses as a museum. At 1845 Church Lane is **St. Paul's Catholic Church** (1931), a parish established in 1853. Across the street, the 1880s Italianate Victorian was moved here to make way for the Civic Center.

20. Piñole

The town takes its name from a 17,000-acre Mexican land grant,

called "El Piñole," made to Don Ignacio Martinez in 1823. Bernardo Fernandez, a Portuguese sailor, built a port in 1854 and ferried local crops to San Francisco. The center of town grew up around San Pablo and Tennent Avenues. Piñole was incorporated in 1903 and has approximately 19,000 residents.

San Pablo Avenue at Tennent Avenue is Piñole's main street. The historic district includes the **Old Bank of Piñole** (1915), the **Antlers Tavern** (1890), and the **Nunes Building** (1920). Queen Anne cottages from the 1890s are located on surrounding streets. **The Bernardo Fernandez House** (1894) at 100 Tennent Avenue is an impressive Italianate with a projecting central bay sporting a mansard roof.

The newest building in this district is the **Piñole Senior & Community Center** (2004; Group 4, architects) [20] at 2500 Valley Avenue; its rough concrete blocks, wood shingles, concrete pillars, and wisteria-covered trellises lend a Craftsman-like air to the complex.

21. Hercules

From 1879 until 1964, Hercules was the company town of the Hercules Powder Company, with offices, production facilities, and company houses on a site surrounded by empty land to buffer the frequent explosions endemic to dynamite production. The plant shifted to fertilizer production in 1964 but closed permanently in 1977.

21a. Hercules Village (1890s)
Santa Fe Avenue,
off Railroad Avenue

Here is a group of two-story Colonial Revival houses built by the Hercules Powder Company. They were restored in the 1980s by the Architectural Resources Group.

21b. Hercules Waterfront District (1999–2006)
North end of Railroad Avenue

The Bixby Company,
developer

This is a mixed-use development on 167 bayside acres that incorporates historic company buildings; a new, neo-traditional residential neighborhood called Victoria by the Bay; a mock-historic town center; and a transit village.

22. Rodeo
Rodeo was named for the cattle, sheep, and hog roundups (rodeos) held by the Union Stock Yard Company, established in 1890. In 1895, the first oil refinery was built and continues to operate. San Pablo Avenue is called Parker Avenue as it runs through Rodeo, and is worth a drive to see its quaint (if slightly shabby) older buildings, like the Windmill Restaurant on the northeast corner of Parker Avenue and Fourth Street.

23. Crockett
Homesteaded by the Edwards family in the 1860s, Crockett attracted early transportation and industry because of its location on the Carquinez Strait. A chain of warehouses and dock facilities once stretched from Martinez to Crockett, shipping agricultural products (mostly wheat) worldwide.

23a. C&H Sugar Company Plant, 1880s
800 Loring Avenue

This impressive brick structure has dominated Crockett since the 1880s when the eastern portion served as the largest flourmill in

the world. In 1906, the C&H Sugar Company moved in and expanded the building; for nearly 100 years, the company has dominated the skyline and the lives of Crockett's 3,200 residents, many of whom have worked here.

23b. Al Zampa Memorial Bridge, 2003
Carquinez Strait

OPAC Consulting Engineers,
design

Cleveland Bridge, construction

The newest suspension bridge in the United States incorporates seismic sensors and an aerodynamically shaped deck to make it the "strongest and safest of its kind in the world." Two reinforced-concrete towers soar 410 feet above the water. It is named for Al Zampa, a local ironworker who worked on the original Carquinez Bridge (1927) and all major local bridges until his retirement in 1970.

23c. Downtown
San Pablo Avenue becomes Pomona Avenue as it passes under the bridge and enters downtown Crockett. For the next few blocks, Crockett's mid-nineteenth- to early-twentieth-century downtown remains very much intact; there are many storefronts, antique stores, and restaurants. Farther east on Pomona, small cottages and picturesque Victorians dot the hillsides.

2 · Central Contra Costa County: Orinda, Moraga, Lafayette, San Ramon Valley, Walnut Creek, Pleasant Hill, Concord, Martinez, Port Costa

Orinda, Moraga, and Lafayette share similar demographics and physically merge in places, yet each has its own distinctive town center, history, and historical society. Major development occurred immediately after World War II when both custom homes and speculative "tract" houses were constructed. The landscape is a combination of valleys, some rather narrow, and moderate to steep hills. Narrow winding roads off major thoroughfares often do not connect with other roads, and many end at a regional park or watershed.

Orinda

The Art Deco marquee of the Orinda movie theater stands on the south side of Highway 24, and it has prominently announced the city since 1941. When threatened with demolition in the mid-1980s, preservationists saved the theater and supported the incorporation of

Orinda so its 17,000 citizens could make their own decisions about future development.

Orinda was created in 1924 as a community when Edward deLaveaga subdivided his family's 1,200-acre parcel; he constructed Lake Cascade, built the Orinda Country Club and an eighteen-hole golf course, established the

town site of Orinda, and built Orinda Village.

Between 1889 and 1901, the California and Nevada Railroad operated a line through Wildcat Canyon to Orinda with three stations: Orinda Park, deLaveaga, and Bryant. Passengers came for picnics and country vacations. The tiny deLaveaga Station,

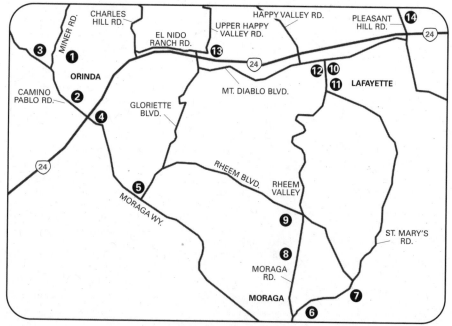

2 • Central Contra Costa County: Orinda, Moraga, Lafayette

the only one that survives, was moved to the corner of Bates Boulevard and Davis Road in 2000.

1. Orinda Country Club & Lake Cascade, 1924
315 Camino Sobrante

Hamilton Murdock, architect

The large Mediterranean-style clubhouse has been altered and enlarged several times, but it remains the center of this part of Orinda. Nearby Lake Cascade was built to provide water to the subdivision and the golf course. Mostly hidden behind lush foliage and at the end of long driveways are good examples of custom-designed mid-twentieth-century homes. Of note is 511 Miner Road, designed by Richard Neutra in 1950.

2. Orinda Library, 2001
24 Orinda Way

Stasny/Brun Architects

The new Orinda Library was dedicated October 7, 2001. Its curved north "corner" overlooks a new town square. The former Orinda Union School, now the Orinda Community Center, is linked to the new library by a walkway covered by a pergola. The school was built in 1924 and renovated in 1997 by Stasny/Brun Architects, Inc., and Architectural Resources Group.

3. East Bay Municipal Utility District (EBMUD) Orinda Filter Plant, 1936
200 Block of Camino Pablo

Mark Daniels, architect

The Mediterranean-style buildings of this attractive utilitarian complex have red-clay tile roofs, soft yellow-ochre stucco walls,

and occasional towers. It is the largest filtration plant in the EBMUD water system.

4. Orinda Theater, 1941
4 Orinda Theater Square

Alexander A. Cantin, architect

Anthony B. Heinsbergen (interior decoration, murals)

This Art Deco theater with its prominent marquee has been beautifully restored, and the interior is alive with vibrant color, murals, and streamlining. On the south side, curving around the corner, is a former bank with streamlined columns; it was designed in 1947 by Cantin's son, A. MacKenzie Cantin.

5. Maynard P. Buehler House, 1948
6 Great Oak Circle

Frank Lloyd Wright, architect

A composition of horizontal and vertical elements in natural gray concrete block with unpainted wood trim is all that is visible from the street. But this Usonian house is full of surprises, with a wide U-shaped floor plan and a soaring roof over the living room.

Moraga

Joaquin Moraga lost most of his land grant in 1859 to infamous Oakland attorney Horace Walpole Carpentier. In 1889, Carpentier sold it to two investors who formed the Moraga Land Company. The **Moraga Land Company Corporation Yard** (circa 1912) at Moraga Way and School Street is a collection of vernacular barns, sheds, former bunkhouses, the base of a water tower, and cottages, all relics from the past. Two huge concrete urns that once lined the road to a company subdivision are stored on the property. Nearby is the Moraga Hotel (1914).

Beginning in the 1950s, the Utah Construction Company and, later, Russell Bruzzone turned nearly 7,000 acres into homesites. Rheem Valley, part of Moraga, bears the name of Donald and Richard Rheem, whose Rheem California Land Co. built the entire community.

6. Moraga Library, 1974
1500 St. Mary's Road

Perata & Sylvester, architects

A very nice refined exterior is based on early Spanish California architecture. One of the Moraga Company's concrete urns was placed in front of the building.

7. Saint Mary's College Chapel, 1928
St. Mary's Road

John J. Donovan, architect

To stimulate land sales, the Moraga Land Company donated 100 acres to Saint Mary's College in 1927; the college moved from Oakland in 1928. The first buildings, designed in the Spanish Colonial Revival style, set the design motif for the campus. The chapel, with an elaborately decorated bell tower, is the centerpiece of the campus. Its interior is elegant and restrained with high ceilings, and the narrow sanctuary is lined with polished red granite columns with carved stone capitals. The chapel is flanked by Dante Hall on the right and Galileo Hall on the left, all connected by recessed arcades. The entire campus complex, including new buildings, forms a cohesive architectural composition that includes courtyards, landscaping, and covered walkways. A "heroic-sized" statue of St. John Baptist De La Salle (1993) by sculptor Bruce Wolfe stands in front of the chapel. The Hearst Art Gallery has a collection of California landscapes by William Keith.

8. Donald Rheem House, 1934
2100 Donald Drive

Clarence Tantau, architect

Hacienda De Las Flores is a U-shaped Spanish-style hacienda with generous lawns and large shade trees. Since 1977, it has served as the Moraga Community Center and Park.

9. Rheem Theater, 1957
350 Park Street

A "space-age" modern movie theater is still showing films; it has a wonderfully intact interior.

Lafayette

After a gristmill was built in 1853, a commercial district grew nearby. By 1914, the Oakland, Antioch & Eastern Railroad line (later the Sacramento Northern) passed through Lafayette to Oakland. Primarily residential, Lafayette was incorporated in 1968.

10. Town Plaza, 1860, 2001
Mt. Diablo Boulevard and Moraga Road

SZFM Design Studio, architects (2001)

Lafayette's town plaza was laid out in 1860 as the center of the town's commercial district. The current landscaping with several new pergolas was dedicated in 2001. South of the plaza is a pleasant older neighborhood of narrow streets and small ranch-style homes.

11. Lafayette Town Hall/ The Barn, 1914
3535 School Street at Moraga Road

The large but simple, two-story, gable-roofed, brown-shingled building was the first Town Hall. Because it resembles a barn, the building is affectionately called "The Barn" and is now used as a community theater.

12. Postino Restaurant Building, 1930s
3565 Mt. Diablo Boulevard

Carr Jones, architect

Carr Jones, the Berkeley architect known for his picturesque

homes, designed this romantic commercial building. The building is L-shaped with a central tower, steeply pitched roofs, and variegated brick walls, all covered with ivy. It originally contained a group of small shops.

13. Bentley School Classroom, Gym, Student Center, 2003–2004
1000 Upper Happy Valley Road

Kava Massih Architects

The classrooms of a former public school have been rehabilitated. New buildings create a visual and acoustical barrier to Highway 24, which is elevated along the school's south boundary.

14. Acalanes Union High School, 1939–1955
1200 Pleasant Hill Road

Franklin and Kump, architects

When the first classrooms were built in 1939, the school was immediately recognized for its innovative concept. The Museum of Modern Art in New York included Acalanes in an exhibit as an outstanding example of American architecture. It's a one-story modular plan of classrooms connected by covered walkways supported by thin, round, metal pipe posts. The concept of classrooms opening onto an open covered hallway became a standard for school architecture between 1946 and 1970. It is remarkable that, despite some alterations, this school retains much of its original fabric. Ernest Kump's **Miramonte High School** (1955) in Orinda (at Moraga Way and Camino Moraga) was exhibited at the World's Fair in Brussels and called a "Space Module School."

San Ramon Valley

The San Ramon Valley extends south from Walnut Creek to the Livermore Valley and includes Alamo, Danville, and San Ramon. All three towns were established in the nineteenth century as business and community centers for farms and ranches.

Growth accelerated after Interstate 680 was completed in the 1960s, but the largest population increases have occurred since 1980. San Ramon in Contra Costa County and Dublin in Alameda County have become major Bay Area business centers, bringing high-paying jobs and fueling housing developments.

Alamo
(unmapped)

By 1860, Alamo was a small town with a post office (opened in 1852), a hotel, several stores, a Presbyterian church, and a school. This is primarily a residential town of about 16,000.

Danville

Danville's main street, Hartz Avenue, retains some of its nineteenth-century charm. The Danville Hotel dates from the 1890s and former nineteenth-century homes have been painted, decorated, and converted into shops.

15. Danville Depot, 1891
Prospect and Railroad Avenues

The Danville Depot is a standard depot design used also at Martinez, Concord, Walnut Creek, and San Ramon. It served both passengers and freight, with

living quarters for the station-master above. It was moved to its present location in 1996 and opened as a museum in 1999.

16. Eugene Gladstone O'Neill House, 1937
Kuss Road, 1/2 mile west of West Danville Boulevard

Frederick Confer, architect

The two-story stucco-sided house, with a wide second-story balcony recessed under an overhanging tile roof, is loosely Monterey Colonial in style. Eugene O'Neill, the country's only Nobel Prize–winning playwright, lived here from 1937 to 1944; he named it Tao House. In

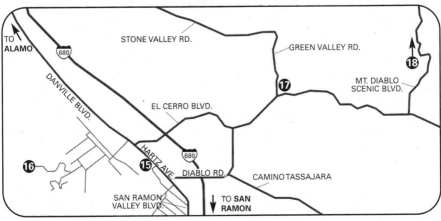

2 • Central Contra Costa County: San Ramon Valley—Alamo, Danville, San Ramon

16

this quiet place, O'Neill wrote *The Iceman Cometh, Long Day's Journey into Night,* and *A Moon for the Misbegotten.* The National Park Service has owned the house since 1980, and it is open to the public by appointment only (925-838-0249).

17. Diablo

Diablo is an unincorporated community, developed in 1912 by Robert Noble Burgess as a summer retreat surrounding a golf course designed by Jack Nevelle, who later designed the course at Pebble Beach. Burgess built a hotel (now condominiums) overlooking the course and created a reservoir for both water and recreation. The Period Revival–style former summer homes date from the first third of the twentieth century. Burgess also built a toll road to the top of Mt. Diablo and, at its entrance, the former Red Horse Tavern hotel (1917).

18. Visitors Center and Museum, 1938, 1993
Mount Diablo State Park
Daniel Quan Design, 1993

There are two roads to the summit of Mt. Diablo: Mt. Diablo Scenic Boulevard, off Blackhawk and Diablo Roads; and from Walnut Creek via North Gate Road on the north.

In 1921, fifteen thousand acres at the summit of Mount Diablo became a public county park; in 1931, it was transferred to the State Park system. The stone walls of a building built in 1938 by the California Conservation Corps (CCC) were incorporated into a museum and visitor's center in 1993. Nearby is a U.S. Geological Survey plaque marking the official Mt. Diablo Meridian and Base Line for most of California, established by surveys in 1851 and 1852.

San Ramon
(unmapped)

Despite its recent population boom and the development of Bishop Ranch Business Park, San Ramon dates to the nineteenth century. A grammar school opened in 1867, the post office was authorized in 1873, and the

David Glass House, San Ramon

train arrived in 1891. Several places carry the names of early settlers such as Crow, Norris, and Bollinger Canyons. The ranch houses of the Boone, Glass, Harlan, and Wiedemann families are still standing. The **David Glass House** (1877) is a two-story Italianate prominently located on the west side of Highway 680. It was saved as mitigation for a residential development, and was moved to this site to be incorporated into **Forest Home Farms Park** (19953 San Ramon Valley Boulevard) as a house museum; the park will also include the twenty-two-room Dutch Colonial Boone House, a barn, and a granary.

Walnut Creek

The commercial center of Walnut Creek began at "The Corners," the intersection of Mt. Diablo Boulevard and North Main Street, where the roads from Martinez and Oakland and the point where four Mexican land grants crossed. In 1855, a hotel (Walnut Creek House) was built at The Corners and soon there was a blacksmith shop and a store. About 1860, a town site was laid out by Hiram Penniman. When a post office was established in 1862, the town was renamed Walnut Creek. The Southern Pacific Railroad's line from Martinez to San Ramon opened in 1891, and direct rail service to Oakland was established in 1914, the year the city was incorporated.

As with other central Contra Costa towns and communities,

growth accelerated after World War II, but the greatest population growth has been since 1970. BART opened in 1973, and by 1985, one million square feet of office space had been constructed. Although the population in 2004 was close to 70,000, Walnut Creek feels like a much larger city; its strategic location serves as the transportation hub and the business and retail center of central Contra Costa County.

The pre–World War II retail and business center was located along Main Street between Mt. Diablo Boulevard and Ygnacio Valley Road. When the Broadway Shopping Center opened in 1951, the retail district shifted south a few blocks. During the 1990s and early 2000s, new retail blocks, such as The Corners (2003) and the Olympus Century Theater complex (2003;

Hans Baldauf of BCV Architects), create a semblance of a traditional main street and connect the two shopping areas together. Unfortunately, the pedestrian will find walks between some blocks long and major intersections dangerous.

19. Golden Triangle
North California Boulevard and Ygnacio Valley Road

The major business center, with more than two million square feet of office space, is located near the BART station. The architectural firm of Kaplan, McLaughlin, Diaz designed Walnut Creek I & II (1982), Tishman Office Center (1985), and California Plaza (1986). The four buildings are set on a podium on the same level as the BART station to create a pedestrian plaza.

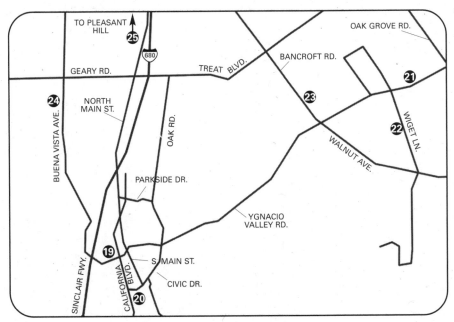

2 • Central Contra Costa County: Walnut Creek

20. Dean Lesher Regional Center for the Arts, 1990
1601 Civic Drive at Locust Street

Boora Architects

The performing arts center wraps around a corner and contains three theaters with seating for 800, 300, and 130, as well as a gallery. Huge, curved, clear-glass bays of different sizes dominate the façade, while gray concrete walls have horizontal bands of textured concrete and a grid of squares with small rose-colored squares at their corners.

21. Hiram Penniman House, 1903
Shadelands Ranch Historical Museum, 1972
2660 Ygnacio Valley Road

This is a large two-story Colonial Revival house with a wraparound front porch and hipped roof punctuated by dormers; it opened as a museum in 1972.

22. Eichler Homes, 1960s
Between Walnut Avenue and Wiget Lane

*Claude Oakland, architect
Anshen + Allen, architects*

This is a nice collection of Eichler's larger models in almost pristine condition. On Bliss Court is a 1920s Mediterranean Revival home built when the area was country estates. A more modest Eichler development, Rancho San Miguel, is located in the vicinity of San Carlos and San Antonio Drives.

23. Hubert Howe Bancroft Farm, 1860s
Ruth Bancroft Garden, 1960
1500 Bancroft Road

In the early 1960s, Ruth Bancroft, a descendent of California histo-

rian Hubert Howe Bancroft, began creating a cacti and succulents garden that includes hundreds of varieties. The large two-story house dates from the 1920s; behind the house are three unpainted wood-sided buildings (Bamboo House, Swiss Chalet, and Log Cabin) that date from the 1870s, when this was Hubert Howe Bancroft's country estate.

24. Lindsay Wildlife Museum, 1993
1931 First Avenue (in Larkey Park)

Carmella Rejwan, architect

This pleasant small museum, wildlife hospital, and rehabilitation center has exhibits of live California wildlife, mostly birds of prey and small animals.

Pleasant Hill (unmapped)

Pleasant Hill was mostly farmland until after World War II. When it incorporated in 1961, the eight-square-mile city had a

population of approximately 30,000. Pleasant Hill is home to Diablo Valley Community College (1951) and Sun Valley Shopping Mall (1967).

25. Pleasant Hill City Hall, 1991
Gregory Lane and Cleveland Road

Charles Moore/Interurban Innovations Group, architects

Fisher Friedman Associates, supervising architects

A double-U-shaped complex of two, two-story buildings, linked and fronted by covered walkways, overlooks an artificial lake; a splashing fountain cascades down a tiled wall and a colorful tiled entry portico greets visitors approaching the building from the west side. The board-and-batten-sided building, originally stained wood but now painted gray and white, was designed to be open and friendly, and it has some interesting spaces. The city's offices were relocated here to enhance a new, neo-traditional "main street" shopping area that is located acres of parking lots away.

Concord

Concord had its beginning in 1834 when Don Salvio Pacheco received the 17,921-acre land grant, "Monte del Diablo." By 1846, the ranch had become a business, social, and cultural center; the town of Pacheco was founded in 1860 near the ranch headquarters. After the 1868 earthquake damaged buildings in the town, the Pacheco family and son-in-law Francisco Galindo created a new town a few miles away. They named it Todos Santos and planned it around a traditional Mexican plaza that remains today. Concord became the town's name when the post office opened in 1869.

At the beginning of World War II, Concord's population was only 1,400; it is now the largest city in Contra Costa County with a population of approximately 122,000. It encompasses nearly thirty-two square miles and will soon expand onto the former Port Chicago Naval weapons base. Concord's official Web site boasts its "dynamic, high-rise business core, regional shopping centers and a vibrant, entertainment-driven downtown . . . balancing Concord's gracious early California heritage with vigorous, thoughtful development."

26. Todos Santos Plaza, 1868
Willow Pass Road,
Salvio and Grant Streets,
and Mt. Diablo Street

A traditional Mexican plaza is the center of the twenty-block town of Todos Santos, laid out in 1868.

27. Bibber House, 1912–1913
2108 Grant Street

Laurence V. Perry, builder

Local designer/builder Laurence V. Perry built this symmetrical "four-square," or Classic Box, that has some unexpected features, such as a hipped-roof dormer that breaks through the front eave of the hipped roof and a rounded center bay. He also built **2156 Grant Street** (1906); **1800 Clayton Road** (circa 1900); **1760 Clayton Road** (1902–1903); L. V. Perry House (1911) at **1990 Concord Avenue**; and the Masonic Lodge (1927) at **1765 Galindo Street.**

28. Foskett & Elworthy Building, 1911
2001 Salvio Street

William H. Weeks, architect

This Spanish Revival, with a rounded corner bay, was the first masonry building in Concord.

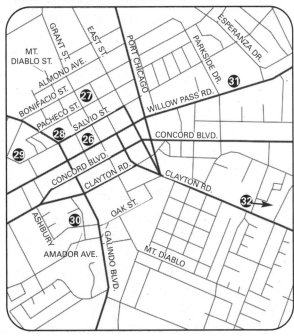

29. Salvio-Pacheco Adobe,
1846, 1853
1870 Adobe Street

The central three bays of this two-story Monterey Colonial–style adobe, with a covered second-story balcony, date from 1853; over time, it was extended to five bays. The building is on its original site and retains features of the original adobe.

30. Francisco Galindo House,
1856, 1880
1721 Amador Avenue

The south side of this two-story ranch house dates from 1856; the north wing was added in 1880, with Victorian-style brackets and window bays. Owned by the city of Concord, it will be restored and used as a cultural center.

31. Concord Civic Center
1950 Parkside Drive

The three-building complex is located between the 2900 block of Salvio Street and Willow Pass Road.

The **Concord Library** (1959; Donald Powers Smith, architect) is a dramatic T-shaped, post-and-beam reinforced-concrete build-ing with a massive shingle roof and board-and-batten siding. On either side of the T are two enclosed gardens, one a Japanese garden (1971) dedicated to Concord's sister city Kitahami, Japan. A mosaic mural in the entry was created by Robert L. Holdeman in 1959.

The **Civic Center** (1966; Ernest Kump & Associates, architects) is a post-and-beam reinforced-concrete structure that uses paired buttressed-concrete piers with glass, concrete, and wood siding. The long, low, single-story building is U-shaped around a square fountain in which the City Council chamber sits like an island in the middle.

The **Recreation Building** was designed in 1963 by Robert W. Ratcliff.

32. Chronicle Pavilion at Concord, **1975**
2000 Kirker Pass Road

Frank O. Gehry & Associates, architects

Formerly named the Concord Pavilion, the structure is a straightforward utilitarian covered amphitheater with three open sides. Its massive steel-truss work is completely exposed and painted black. It is set into a hillside bowl with additional seating on an open lawn with views of Mt. Diablo.

Martinez

In the 1820s, Don Ignacio
Martinez received a 17,000-acre
Mexican land grant that includes
the present city. Ferry service
between Martinez and Benicia,
across the Carquinez Strait,
opened in 1847, and the route
became an important link to the
gold fields. Passenger and then
car ferry service continued,
almost uninterrupted, until 1962
when the George Miller Jr.
Bridge opened.

The town was surveyed in 1849,
and in 1850, it became the
county seat of government and
an important shipping port. Rail
lines to Tracy opened in 1877
and to Stockton in 1890.
Commercial fishing was also an
economic base until prohibited
in 1957; by 1882, there were two
large fish-canning operations.

Beginning in 1904 when the
refinery for Bull's Head Oil
Company was built, and in 1905
when the Mountain Copper
Company's smelter began operating, another economic base was
established. The greatest impact
came in 1912 and 1914 when
Associated Oil and Shell Oil
refineries were built. Shell Oil
and county offices continue to be
economically important.

33. John Muir National
Historic Site, 1849, 1882
Vicente Martinez Adobe, 1849
Strentzel-Muir House, 1882
4202 Alhambra Avenue

Wolfe & Son, architects

The John Muir National Historic
site contains two important
homes: the 1849 Vicente
Martinez Adobe, and the two-
story 1882 Italianate home built

2 • Central Contra Costa County: Martinez

by John Muir's father-in-law, John Strentzel. Vicente J. Martinez, Don Ignacio Martinez's son, built the two-story Monterey Colonial adobe. The Strentzel-Muir House is a two-story plus attic, rectangular Italianate on a raised basement. In the center of its hipped roof is a square tower with arched windows.

Strentzel was a pioneer agronomist who planted orchards and vineyards. After Strentzel's death in 1890, John Muir, his wife, and two daughters lived here. John Muir (1838–1914) was an explorer, naturalist, and author. He is the father of the conservation movement and founder of the Sierra Club. Muir's image, looking at Yosemite's Half Dome, is on the California quarter. The houses and grounds are open to the public.

34. Downtown

Martinez has a real nineteenth-century downtown and an adjoining residential district laid out on a grid. On Main Street, between Alhambra Avenue and Court Street, historical plaques tell the story of historic buildings. The **Contra Costa Historical Society** is located at 610 Main Street in an 1890 residence, and the **Martinez Historic Museum** is located at 1005 Escobar Street. On hillside streets west of downtown are many early houses that also have historical plaques.

34a. Contra Costa County Courthouse, 1901
625 Court Street
William S. Mooser & Son, architects

Now the Finance Building, this imposing Classic Revival has a complete temple-front portico with full entablature. It is faced with gray, rough-cut granite blocks.

34b. Contra Costa County Hall of Records, 1931
725 Court Street
Edward Geoffrey Bangs, architect

A Classic Moderne design has a symmetrical façade and a row of two-story detached columns spanning its central section.

34c. U.S. Post Office, 1937
815 Court Street

Constructed with a WPA grant, the Classic Moderne building has window surrounds of molded plaster. On the interior south wall is a Maynard Dixon mural. Across the street is the simplified Moderne **Martinez Public Library** (1941; Edward Geoffrey Bangs, architect).

35. Amtrak Station, 2001
Foot of Ferry Street
Richard Thompson, architect

A clock tower marks the location of this bright and airy brick-clad station, which replaces the old depot down the street. The interior has a dramatic open-beam ceiling in blond wood.

36. Alhambra and St. Catherine's Cemeteries
Carquinez Scenic Drive

Alhambra Cemetery was set aside in the survey of 1849, but the earliest recorded burials date from 1854. John Muir and early Martinez pioneers are buried here. There are interesting nineteenth-century headstones. St. Catherine's Cemetery dates from the 1870s. The Martinez, Pacheco, and Castro families are buried here.

37. John Swett Ranch House, 1880s
295 Millthwait Drive, off Alhambra Valley Road

John Swett, considered the father of California education, purchased the Altamirano Adobe as a summer home in 1881 and then built a two-story, multi-gabled Gothic Revival home sometime during the late 1880s. The 1840 adobe can be seen to the left of the house. It is a wide, low, one-story building with a tall gable roof and covered porch.

Port Costa (unmapped)

In 1879, the Southern Pacific Railroad opened a ferry connection between Benicia and Port Costa using two enormous ferries, the *Solano* and *Contra Costa*, that could accommodate entire trains. In 1929, the Southern Pacific Railroad bridge between Martinez and Benicia opened, replacing the ferries and bypassing Port Costa.

During Port Costa's heyday, the population was around 3,000; today it is approximately 250; the town feels remote and hidden. Most of its early grain warehouses are gone, but downtown has five impressive buildings, including a large concrete warehouse, a three-story commercial and residential building, and a nice 1897 sandstone building with arched windows. Port Costa's main street, Reservoir Street, is lined with nineteenth-century houses, some dating back to the 1880s. **Port Costa School** (circa 1910) is being restored as a community center by a volunteer group. **St. Patrick's Mission Church** (1898) at 555 Third Street has an impressive bell tower and stained-glass windows.

3 • East Contra Costa County: Pittsburg, Antioch, and Beyond

Driving east on State Route 4 (Highway 4), one reaches the crest of the last hill between central Contra Costa County and the beginning of the San Joaquin Valley. In the distance near the bay, three tall smokestacks dominate one of the last industrial facilities in the area. On the south side of the highway, houses are beginning to cover the hillside.

Coal was discovered in the hills east of Pittsburg and Antioch in 1857. From the early 1860s until approximately 1905, there were five coal-mining towns in the Black Diamond mining district: Nortonville, Somersville, Stewartville, West Hartley, and Judsonville. It was California's largest coal-mining operation.

Between 1922 and 1949, underground mining for silica sand (for glass making) took place near the deserted Nortonville and Somersville town sites. The East Bay Regional Park District's **Black Diamond Mines Regional Preserve's Greathouse Visitor Center** is located in an underground silica sand mining chamber.

Pittsburg

The city is located at the point where the Sacramento and San Joaquin Rivers meet. It was first settled in 1849 by Colonel J. D. Stevenson, a native of New York, who called it New York of the

Pacific. By 1860, the Nortonville mines were shipping coal from New York Landing.

A fishing industry began in the 1870s, and by 1910, there were nearly 1,000 fishermen and several fish-canning operations.

Heavy industry arrived around 1903 when the Redwood Manufacturing Company and Bowen Rubber Company were established, followed by the Columbia–Geneva Steel foundry, Cowells Chemical (later Stauffer and then Dow Chemical), the

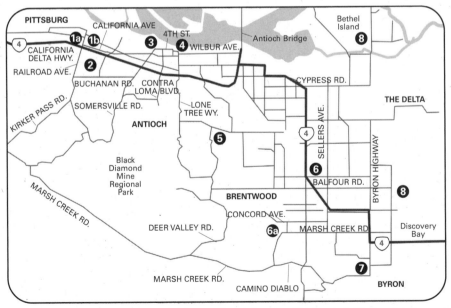

3 • East Contra Costa County: Pittsburg, Antioch, and Beyond

Johns-Manville Company, and Shell Chemical. New York Landing became Pittsburg in 1911.

Pittsburg's Civic Center was moved from downtown in the 1950s, and several civic buildings remain from that period: Unified School District Building (1956), County Court House (1958), and Library (1966), all designed by Beland and Gianelli, architects. The newest addition to the Civic Center is City Hall (1999; Fani Hansen & Associates, architects). It is a wide, slightly curved four-story, aqua-blue glazed building overlooking a park.

1. Downtown

1a. New York Landing Historic District
300–500 Block of Railroad Avenue

Downtown Pittsburg's New York Landing Historic District is a redevelopment area. The old civic center and most residential buildings were demolished, and several vacant blocks remain. Along Railroad Avenue, Pittsburg's historic main street, are the remaining Classic Revival, early-twentieth-century commercial buildings. **St. Peter Martyr Catholic Church** (circa 1930), at 700 Black Diamond Street, has a nice bell tower. The **Post Dispatch Building** (1923) houses the Historical Society. Freshly landscaped streets and medians, pocket parks, civic sculpture such as *The Steel Worker* by Frank Vitale (1993) [1a], a new harbor, and new housing (hiding behind security walls) have recently been completed. On East Third Street are the interesting brick façades of the John Mansfield Company plant that closed in 2004.

1a

1b. The California Theatre, 1920
300 Block of Railroad Avenue

Andrew W. Cornelius, architect

This is a rare surviving example of an extraordinary Beaux-Arts-style vaudeville and silent film theater. It has a symmetrical façade with a second-story arched window flanked by sculpted muses and a row of Corinthian columns.

2. Stoneman Veterans Memorial Monument
Harbor Street, south of Highway 4

The monument marks the location of the World War II military camp built in 1942 that served as the point of departure for thousands of GIs who went to fight in the Asiatic-Pacific operations. The camp closed in 1954. **Camp Stoneman Military Chapel** (1942) is located at 200 East Leland Road.

On Presidio Drive are two large senior housing projects: **Stoneman Housing** (1980s) and **Presidio Senior Housing** (2004). **The Senior Center** was completed in 2004 (Group 4 Architects, Architecture and Planning).

Antioch

Antioch was first settled in 1849, incorporated in 1872, and served the coal-mining districts as a port. The railroad came through in 1878. Antioch's economic base was industrial; industries included the Fulton Shipyards, Hickmott Canning Company, Western California Canners, Fiberboard Products Company, Crown Zellerbach, and Pacific Gas and Electric.

Between 1986 and 2004, Antioch's population grew to more than 100,000. Off Deer Valley Road, south of the freeway, are the latest housing developments, shopping centers, and the new Deer Valley High School.

3. Old Antioch

Old Antioch (A Street to L Street, between First and Tenth Streets) remains an almost undisturbed small town built on a rise above the banks of the San Joaquin River. Laid out in a standard nineteenth-century grid, old Antioch is barely one mile long and a half-mile wide. Within the small area are some good examples of commercial buildings, churches, and houses that date from the 1860s through the 1920s. In 1953, architect William Wurster designed the award-winning Adelia Kimball School, which has since been demolished, but his Antioch High School on West Eighteenth Street (1955) is still standing.

3a. Riverview Union High School, 1910
1500 West Fourth Street and Somersville Road

Cummings & Weymoth, architects

The two-story, Classic Revival brick school building has a symmetrical façade, a parapet, decorated window detail, and quoins at its corners. It is home to the Antioch Historical Society.

3b. Police Station and Animal Services, 1992
West Second and L Streets

George Meiers & Associates, architects

This two-story building has a curved entry bay, brick siding, white trim, translucent glass blocks, and a standing-seam metal roof. The Animal Services building forms an L around a landscaped garden. It is within a block of City Hall (1980; MacKinlay, Winnacker & McNeil, architects), located at Third & H Streets in old downtown. The Antioch Marina, completed in 1988, is located at the end of L Street.

3c. Roswell-Butler Hard House, 1869
815 West First Street

R. B. Hard, builder

This is an imposing brick Italianate owned by the Antioch Historical Society.

3d. Antioch Bank, 1902
640 Second Street

This building is a nicely restored Classic Revival. Other notable structures include El Campanil Theater (1928), decorated in the Spanish-Moorish style, and the Classic Revival Masonic Temple, originally the Belshaw Building (1905), with buff brick and arched windows.

3e. Harkinson House, 1890s
220 Third Street

This picturesque Queen Anne sits prominently on a corner lot in Antioch's historic residential district. Its round covered entry porch with a turret above is distinctive.

The neighborhood was home to well-off business owners as well as their employees.

4. Fulton Shipyard, 1924
Fulton Shipyard Road

Carr Jones, architect

The Period Revival–style buildings of the former shipyard were designed by Berkeley architect Carr Jones. The complex has remarkable wood interiors, including a courtyard covered by a stain-glassed roof that came from the *Delta Queen* ferry. This is the site where Antioch's first landing was located. During World War II, twenty-seven ships were built here.

5. Shannon-Williamson Ranch, 1875
4900 Lone Tree Way

The Shannon-Williamson 4,000-acre ranch was placed on the National Register in 1987 just before it was subdivided for housing tracts and shopping malls. The primary ranch buildings—including a two-story Italianate-style house, three barns, and several outbuildings—have been retained and will become a museum of local agriculture, which no longer exists.

Beyond Antioch: Brentwood, Byron, The Delta

John Marsh was the first non-Mexican to settle in this area, which stretches from Mt. Diablo to the San Joaquin River. In 1837, he purchased the 17,000-acre Rancho Los Meganos from José Noriega. By 1850, farmers began to settle here, and native oak trees were cut to fuel the boilers of steamships traveling on the Sacramento and San Joaquin Rivers.

After the San Pablo and Tulare Railroad opened between Martinez and Banta (north of Tracy) in 1878, Byron was established and Brentwood grew. In 1898, the Santa Fe railroad built an east-west rail line, creating the towns of Oakley and Knightsen.

Until the mid-1980s, fruit orchards and fields of seasonal vegetables dominated the landscape, and the towns were sleepy and quaintly old fashioned; many had seen better days when each town had a main street, a grand hotel or two, commercial buildings on both sides of the street, and proud residential districts.

6. Brentwood

The population here has grown from 7,500 in 1990 to 23,500 in 2000, and it just keeps growing into the agricultural fields that once were its economic mainstay; it is planned to merge physically with Antioch. National and international development companies are transforming the area into a residential and business center.

Brentwood's earliest businesses date back to 1874, and the town was formally established in 1878. Despite its recent growth, the central district retains the feeling of a traditional Central Valley town. It is laid out in a grid with a "four corners" downtown center anchored by a bank building (1913; Hercules Logan, builder), the Art Deco–style Delta Theater (1939) and three churches: the Victorian-era United Methodist Church, St. Albans Episcopal (1927), and a Spanish-style Catholic church (1949). Downtown is surrounded by an older residential neighborhood.

6a. John Marsh House, 1856
Marsh Creek Road

Thomas Boyd, architect

This is the oldest stone building in Contra Costa County and among the oldest in the Bay Area. Visible from Marsh Creek Road, this impressive three-story Gothic Revival house has a steeply pitched gable roof punctuated by three gabled dormers and a four-story tower. The facing stones are rough-cut variegated pieces, while

the quoins and window and door surrounds are finely cut clear sandstone. Marsh lived in the house only a few years (he was murdered in 1856). Since 1960, it has been in public ownership, first by Contra Costa County, and in 1979 by the State Parks Department. As a mitigation to lessen the environmental impact of a massive new development on grazing land north of the Marsh house, the developer will provide funds for its restoration. The house will be restored, but its rural setting will be compromised.

7. Byron

The town was founded in 1878 when the railroad opened, and an inn, post office, and tavern were built. West of town, Byron Hot Springs attracted tourists worldwide from the 1860s until the late 1930s. Nearby was a fuel-oil pumping station and fuel distribution center for crude oil extracted near Bakersfield and pumped through pipes to refineries along the bay. What remains of the town are a few small commercial buildings (three burned in October of 2005) and several bungalow-style houses.

8. The Delta

Once a vast marshland, the San Joaquin River Delta is now a maze of man-made islands, rivers, sloughs, and canals. The islands were originally used for agriculture, but today there are nearly 100 marinas catering to every type of water sport. Although much of the Delta remains rural and peaceful, **Bethel Island** (northeast of Antioch) and **Discovery Bay** (east of Byron, off Highway 4) have become water-oriented communities.

Dozens of ferries once connected the islands, and two car ferries still operate free of charge: the *Ryer Island Ferry* and the *Howard Landing Ferry.* There are more than fifty bridges; many are drawbridges of various types and ages. Two deepwater channels permit freighters to reach Sacramento and Stockton.

The Delta remains an important habitat for migratory birds, and there are hundreds of species of fish. The drinking water for two-thirds of California's population flows through the Delta.

6a

VI
Solano County

Judy Irvin, author & photographer

Solano County is named after Francisco Solano (Sem Yeto), chief of the Suisun and Soscol Native American tribes whose territory extended from Petaluma Creek to the Sacramento River. Padre Altimira, founder of the Sonoma Mission, befriended Sem Yeto and gave him his Spanish name upon his baptism. When General Mariano Guadalupe Vallejo (1808–1890) became commander of Sonoma in 1835, Francisco Solano became his friend as well. Vallejo honored Chief Solano for keeping peace between his people and the Spanish settlers by having the county named for him in 1850.

San Francisco Bay was a formidable barrier to overland travel, and the North Bay remained sparsely populated until General Vallejo was dispatched from the Presidio of San Francisco to secure Californio hegemony, withstand possible Russian incursions, and subdue the less docile Native American tribes. During the Californio period, vast unfenced ranchos covered most of the county. Hides and other agricultural products were shipped from embarcaderos along every navigable waterway.

The Sacramento River was the primary transportation corridor to Sacramento and the San Joaquin Valley until the arrival of the railroad. Along the strategic Carquinez Strait, new settlements and military posts were built at Benicia and Vallejo. In 1867, the first railroad—the California Pacific—was completed from a Vallejo steamship landing to Sacramento; in 1868, it was extended through the Napa Valley. In 1879, the Transcontinental Railroad was rerouted from the Sunol Pass, through Benicia, to its terminus in Oakland via a ferry link to Port Costa; the ferries were replaced by a railroad bridge from Benicia to Martinez in 1929.

In 1927, the first automobile bridge opened across the Carquinez Strait between Crockett and Vallejo. Old Highway 40 (now Interstate 80) was a two-lane road that went through the center of Vallejo, Fairfield, and Vacaville. During the past sixty years, the highway has become a freeway, bypassing the towns, and is now ten lanes wide in some places. The freeway landscape is scarred with suburban development: auto malls, shopping centers, business campuses, and residential subdivisions, all dependent on the automobile. Beyond the freeway are places full of history that are worth a detour.

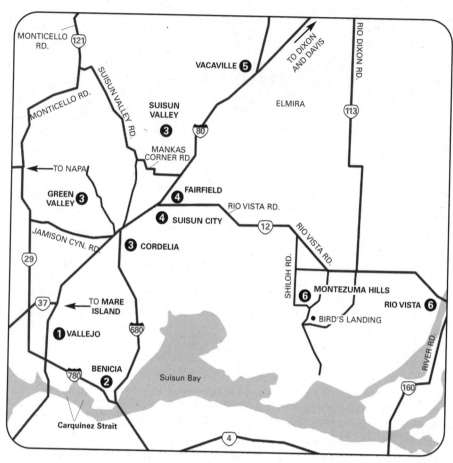

VI • Solano County

1 · Vallejo

General Mariano G. Vallejo dreamed of a great city near the Carquinez Strait on part of his Soscol Rancho. In 1850, he offered 156 acres to the state for a new state capital along with money for the construction of public buildings and gardens. Vallejo suggested the name "Eureka," but the legislature named the new city after its founder. The state capital moved from San Jose to Vallejo in 1852 but left after one week due to inadequate facilities; it returned in 1853 for two months before moving to Benicia and then to Sacramento in 1854.

General Vallejo, disappointed by the legislators' decision, withdrew to his home in Sonoma. He left his son-in-law, General John B. Frisbie, to develop the city of Vallejo.

In 1852, the U.S. Navy purchased Mare Island for its West Coast naval facility. A master plan developed in Washington, D.C., included dry docks, shops, warehouses, military housing, and a hospital. Under Commander David Farragut, construction by civilian workers began in 1854. Housing for the civilian workforce was built across the Napa River in Vallejo, setting the stage for the symbiotic relationship between the shipyard and the city, which continues to this day.

In the early 1850s, Frisbie laid out the city in a grid with wide streets, large lots, and mid-block alleys. By 1860, Vallejo had a downtown, a number of industries along the shoreline, and houses dotting the hillsides. After the California Pacific Railroad began operating in 1867, the economy boomed.

As the U.S. Navy grew in importance, so did Mare Island; its shipyards became Vallejo's largest employer, and the city's pattern of growth reflects the importance of the navy in the history of world events.

Shipbuilding and related heavy industries attracted a large blue-collar population. After the naval shipyard closed in 1996, newcomers, attracted by numerous historic buildings and the proximity to job centers, began changing the city's demographics.

Carquinez Strait

1. Carquinez Strait Heritage Corridor

The Carquinez Strait is the narrow deepwater gap in the coastal mountains, where the waters of the Sacramento and San Joaquin Rivers meet the bay; it had strategic importance as the major transportation route to inland California before the advent of the railroad. The Heritage Corridor includes Mare Island, Benicia, the Benicia Arsenal, Port Costa, Crockett, and Martinez. The first automobile bridge was a cantilever steel-truss span completed in 1927 as a part of historic Highway 40. A second span was added in 1958, and the Zampa Bridge, a graceful suspension span with a pedestrian walkway, opened in 2003.

2. Harbormaster's Office, 1910
Glen Cove Marina at Elliot Cove

The Carquinez Strait Lighthouse and Life Saving Station was moved (without its light and boathouse) to Elliot Cove in 1957, from a pier at the entrance to the deepwater channel leading to Mare Island. The Harbormaster's Office is a 1910 Colonial Revival with twenty-eight rooms.

3. California Maritime Academy, 1929
Morrow Cove in Vallejo

The California Maritime Academy, founded in 1929, moved to this location in 1943. It was incorporated into the California State University system in 1995. Its undergraduate degrees include business, mechanical and marine engineering, and transportation; it has a large training ship, the *Golden Bear*. Buildings on the site date from the 1940s through 2003.

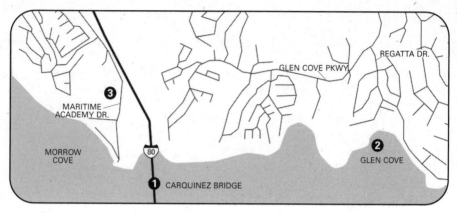

1 • Vallejo: Carquinez Strait

Downtown and Vicinity

4. Starr Mansion, 1878
503 McLane Street

Located on a prominent hill, the finely detailed Second Empire Starr mansion is an imposing two-story Italianate with a bracketed cornice, arched windows with hood moldings, quoins, angled bays, and a mansard roof. The mansion reflects the economic success of the Starr Flour Mill founded in 1869. Now named General Mills, it is the oldest operating industry in Vallejo and the terminus of the railroad. This area is South Vallejo, originally separated from the downtown by a huge tidal marsh that was not filled until after 1914. (See map on p. 372.)

5. Old City Hall, 1889
715 Marin Street

Beginning around 1900, Vallejo's wood-frame downtown commercial buildings were replaced with more substantial masonry and terra-cotta-clad buildings in various Period Revival or Beaux-Arts styles popular from 1910 to 1930. Vallejo's first City Hall is an exception; it is a two-story Italianate, one of the few remaining nineteenth-century downtown buildings.

6. Commercial Building, 1905
337–339 Georgia Street
John Butler, designer

This is a three-story Beaux-Arts-style building, among the few early-twentieth-century buildings remaining in the downtown. Its projecting angled bays, with raised classical swags under the windows, have been beautifully painted during a recent restoration.

7. Empress Theater, 1911
338 Virginia Street
William A. Jones, architect

Vallejo had many theaters, social clubs, and meeting places. The Classical Revival Empress Theater, after several renovations, is again being rehabilitated as the city's Arts and Entertainment Center.

8. City Hall, 1927
734 Marin Street
C. E. Perry, architect

Now the Vallejo Naval and Historical Museum, this tooled, stucco-sided, two-story Spanish Renaissance Revival building is set on a raised plinth. It has a symmetrical façade with a recessed central portico and a decorated surround; it is enhanced by quoins, regularly spaced fenestration, a tile roof, and beautifully detailed bracketed eaves with a decorated frieze band. C. E. Perry worked for thirty-five years in the San Francisco office of Willis Polk; he brought his considerable skills to bear in this imposing composition.

9. Red Men's Hall, 1921
431 Georgia Street
C. E. Perry, architect

Here is a Renaissance Revival–style meeting hall.

10. Masonic Temple, 1917
707 Marin Street
John David Hatch, architect

This imposing four-story Classical Revival building, with beautifully detailed fenestration and cornices, is located on a prominent corner.

11. Casa de Vallejo, 1919
1825 Sonoma Boulevard

This multistory Spanish Colonial Revival building was built as a YMCA structure and completed just after the end of World War I. The eight-story section on the west is an addition designed by architect Francis Slocomb. The building is now low-income senior housing.

12. Civic Center Complex
Santa Clara and Georgia Streets

After World War II, the city of Vallejo suffered the same fate as many other shipyard cities: abandonment and disinvestment. Vallejo responded by implementing a massive Urban Renewal Plan that resulted in the demolition of twenty-four blocks of historic downtown, including a Carnegie Library. The hill where General Vallejo's Capitol building had been located was bulldozed for bay fill. Urban Renewal left some remnants of a once-thriving commercial business center severed by eliminating the traditional grid of

streets from its historic relationship with the waterfront, and became surrounded by a sea of mostly vacant parking lots and subsidized low-income housing complexes. Vallejo is a textbook example of how redevelopment can destroy the life and energy of a historic downtown.

The first of several large-scale redevelopment plans was Marina Vista, a combination business district and low-income housing development. Its fourteen-story Marina Towers (1960) looms over the downtown, dwarfing nearby historic buildings. A waterfront park was designed in 1967 by Royston, Hanamoto, Beck & Abey.

The plan also placed a group of civic buildings (intended as an anchor for a new downtown) at the edge of the waterfront bluff. The firms of Marquis & Stoller and Beland & Gianelli designed the John F. Kennedy Memorial Library and the City Hall in 1970. The two massive, concrete-and-brick buildings range

in height from one to four stories; they have flat roofs, concrete window screens, and vertical pieces dubbed "fins"; façades overlooking the waterfront are windowless. These Concrete Brutalist buildings are not friendly: a foreboding sea of two-story columns and tiny windows creates a no-man's-land along the 200 block of Georgia Street.

In 2001, Vallejo inaugurated a Main Street Program; dedicated citizens, a few enlightened developers, and new building owners are at work to revitalize and restore downtown. In 2004, the downtown was reconnected to the waterfront along Georgia Street. Redevelopment however, remains alive and well in Vallejo, despite the overwhelming evidence that it does not always work as promised.

13. Saint Vincent's Hill Historic District

When the Catholic parish outgrew its 1855 church in the downtown area, John Frisbie donated a city block to the

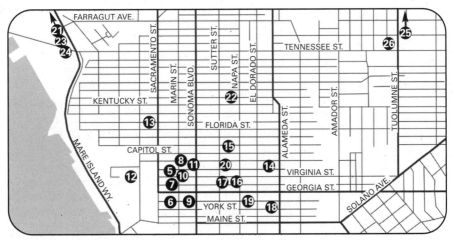

1 • Vallejo: Downtown and Vicinity

parish, located at the top of a prominent hill. Irish Catholic families who wanted to live close to the church and parochial school bought Frisbie's nearby lots and built their homes.

Over time, the proximity of Saint Vincent Hill to Mare Island made it a popular residential area with shipyard workers. During World War II, patriotic owners converted every available space into living quarters; after the war, the substandard dwelling units remained, and the neighborhood fell on hard times with absentee landlords. In 1972, the area was designated a local historic district to protect it from being demolished for redevelopment.

With the closing of the shipyard, this neighborhood has become popular with artists and design professionals; it is close to the Ferry Terminal, and has fabulous views and affordable historic houses. In 2003, the Saint Vincent's Hill Historic District was placed on the National Register of Historic Places. The district includes small, vernacular, single-wall Gold Rush cottages; small Italianate houses located near the church; Queen Anne cottages built during the Spanish American War; groups of Craftsman and Colonial Revival houses built during World War I; alley cottages and barns; and several important buildings by local architect William A. Jones.

13a. Saint Vincent-Ferrar Catholic Church, 1868
434 Florida Street
Patrick O'Conner, architect

This dramatic, redbrick Ecclesiastic Gothic Revival was constructed on a raised plinth to adjust for the sloping site. It is a nave and transept plan, with a symmetrical façade dominated by a three-story bell tower in the center; at the top of the tower, stone crosses and pinnacles stand at the corners. There are few masonry churches from this period in the Bay Area. Adjacent to the church is the Italian Renaissance Revival school building, constructed in 1917; the stucco-sided building is carefully detailed and has a beautiful glazed terra-cotta portico with fluted Doric columns.

14. The Architectural Heritage District

This neighborhood, just east of downtown, was the most stylish place to live; it includes a number of important buildings that have not been substantially altered. The district was listed on the National Register of Historic Places in 1972.

15. Wilson-Hilburg House, 1909
728 Capitol Street
Julia Morgan and William A. Jones, architects

This Shingle-style house is located on the crest of a hill. The Chalet-inspired design has a symmetrical façade and a wide, shallow, sloping gable roof with broad overhanging eaves supported on carved knee braces; the projecting portico has Classical overtones.

Next door is a remarkable Gothic Revival (1860s) with floor to nearly ceiling-high windows, and a central steeply pitched dormer with an arched window.

16. Widemann-Plutchok House, 1868
639 Virginia Street

The commanding two-story Italianate was built for a prominent Vallejo family. It has a

13a

symmetrical composition, a full-width porch supported on square columns, and a pierced rail; its arched upper-story windows have wide, carefully detailed surrounds.

17. Elsa Widemann House, 1921
637 Virginia Street
C. E. Perry, architect

This Classical Revival with a symmetrical façade has a projecting central entry portico supported on classic Tuscan columns. On the alley in the rear are two barns that predate the house.

18. William A. Jones House, 1912
403 Alameda Street
William A. Jones, architect

This Shingle-style house was the architect's home and is currently occupied by his granddaughter. Built on a sloping site, the L-shaped house has intersecting gable roofs with wide eaves; the popular early-twentieth-century sleeping porch has been enclosed. This is a masterfully composed house, typical of Jones's idiosyncratic juxtaposition of stylistic elements; the second floor extends over the first floor and is supported by overscaled cylindrical stucco columns.

19. Harrier-Levee-Riley House, 1890
720 Georgia Street

The symmetrically composed, two- and three-story Shingle-style house is located on a steep uphill site. Flanking a two-story central entry bay are three-story bays with dramatic, steeply pitched gable roofs with flared eaves. The entry portico is held by Ionic columns. **705 Georgia**

Street (1885), a grand Eastlake mansion, is quite a contrast.

20. Tripp House, circa 1865
918 Sutter Street

This is an amusing eccentric example of Carpenter Gothic on a diminutive scale. Its massing is complex, looking a bit pieced together. A tower in the corner, where two wings meet, has a peculiar shallow pyramidal roof with flared eaves and an arched window that projects above the eave line; a double door is set at a strange angle with a rose window above. Bargeboards and eaves are edged with intricately carved lacework.

21. "Arks" (unmapped)
811, 813, 915 Wilson Avenue

Before 1913, the Mare Island Strait was home to more than a hundred houseboats; when the city began landfill operations, they were ordered to depart. These three houseboats remain in their original position but are no longer next to the shore.

22. Washington Park

This residential neighborhood, adjoining both National Register Districts, saw rapid development from the 1890s through the 1920s. Built for skilled craftsmen and their families, it is primarily comprised of single-family houses in the various styles popular at the time.

23. Bay Terrace, 1919 (unmapped)

During World War I, a team of professionals led by architect George W. Kelham designed this rare, almost perfectly intact, community on a hill overlooking the strait. The City Beautiful Movement–inspired community has narrow winding roads and a

variety of Period Revival–style dwellings, most with spectacular views. The remaining 126 buildings represent fifteen variations of six basic plans, including single-family detached houses, flats, and fourplexes.

24. Federal Terrace Elementary School, 1942 (unmapped)
415 Daniels Avenue

This Streamline Moderne elementary school is the only intact survivor of Vallejo's massive World War II emergency housing program. Rows of nearby housing blocks in both Roosevelt and Federal Terrace have been altered significantly, but some maintain their rigid military alignments. During the early part of the war, architects, planners, sociologists, and others were called upon to design thousands of units in planned communities. Among these, William W. Wurster designed twenty-five case-study houses, now demolished, to test new technologies such as stressed-skin plywood panels.

25. Vallejo Highlands and Vista de Vallejo (unmapped)

As Vallejo continued to prosper because of Mare Island, housing development expanded eastward during the 1930s. These included very high-end houses on large lots in the popular Revival styles. Winding streets in Vista de Vallejo follow the contours of the hill and have spectacular water views.

26. 1000 Block of Tuolumne Street

This block includes several well-executed Spanish Colonial and Tudor Revival houses constructed around 1930. The house at **1021 Tuolumne Street** has a fabulous composition of red mission tile roofs on a variety of round and rectilinear stucco shapes.

Mare Island

Mare Island, established in 1852, is the oldest naval installation on the West Coast. Because of its historic importance, it has been designated a National Historic Landmark, the highest level of distinction and honor.

When California joined the Union, a strong naval presence was necessary to protect the state. Mare Island was selected because of its protected site and deepwater harbor. William P. S. Sanger, Bureau of Yards and Docks Engineer, developed a plan for a quay wall along the strait, with a permanent dry dock and two rows of shop buildings aligned with the quay. A third row of

buildings, the officer's mansions, was planned farther inland.

Sanger also identified sites for the Naval Ammunitions Depot, the Hospital, and the Marine Corps. In 1853, a floating dry dock, which had been built in New York and shipped in pieces around Cape Horn, was installed.

During Mare Island's 140-year history, the Pacific Squadron expanded into the greatest naval power in the Pacific region, and Mare Island grew with it. Hills were leveled, marshes filled, and buildings erected; American history between 1852 and 1996 can be read in the layers of buildings and structures.

In 1996, the Naval Shipyard closed, and the island, with its unparalleled collection of historic resources, was transferred to the city of Vallejo and a private

developer. Plans for its reuse include demolishing significant historic buildings and constructing new ones. Mare Island has been placed on the Priority List of Threatened National Historic Landmarks. Tours can be arranged through the Mare Island Park Foundation.

27. Shipyard buildings, 1856–1873
California Avenue (formerly Dock Street)

Building #46 was the first building constructed. It is a large U-shaped, simplified Federal-style building designed by Daniel Turner. Following the Sanger Plan, it was located next to Dry Dock #1. The primarily brick façades have classically organized, arched pilastered walls with tall arched window and door openings. Continuing the rhythm of the historic streetscape are the

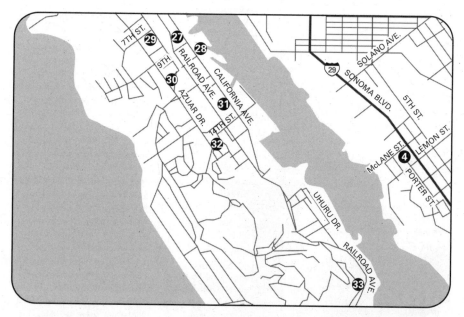

1 • Vallejo: Mare Island

Rubber Shop (1871) and **Platers' Shop** (1873), designed by Calvin Brown, C.E.; both are two-story buildings with brick façades. These three brick buildings and other later brick buildings form a significant grouping with slight variations in style and function but unified by the alignment, size, mass, and use of common red brick. The Mare Island Park Foundation is located in Building #46; the foundation is raising money to bring back the U.S. *Drum*, one of the last submarines built on Mare Island.

28. Dry Dock #1, 1891
California Avenue

Although included in the Sanger Plan and begun in the 1870s, the first dry dock was not completed until 1891. Designed by Calvin Brown, C.E., the stepped structure was excavated to bedrock and then faced with dressed granite blocks; it is 122 feet wide, 508 feet long, and 32 feet deep. To the south are three larger dry docks that were constructed later.

29. Officer's Row, 1900
Walnut Avenue

An impressive row of Colonial Revival mansions was reconstructed in 1900 on the foundations of brick mansions that had

been destroyed by the earthquake of 1896. In accordance with the Sanger Plan, they are located on large lots that include gardens, outbuildings, greenhouses, and servant housing.

30. St. Peter's Chapel, 1901
Walnut Avenue

Albert Sutton, architect

This outstanding interdenominational Shingle-style church is a small cruciform building with steep roofs and a two-part pyramidal roof spire. The interior includes natural wood with heavy timber scissor trusses on knee braces and a large collection of art-glass windows designed and executed by Tiffany in New York. It is located within a large triangular park where the Sanger Plan road alignment breaks to follow the edge of what was once a marsh.

31. Machine Shop (Periscope Shop), 1939
South Shipyard Building #680

This huge International-style, stressed-skin steel building is one of the most recognizable symbols of Mare Island. The central element is a rectangular mass with industrial glazing that soars ten stories, flanked by similar two-story blocks on either side. The

masterful composition of solids and voids is an impressive sight, especially when lit at night.

32. Hospital Complex, begun 1899
Buildings H1, H72, H73, H80

In accordance with the Sanger Plan, the four-story Classical Revival hospital was constructed as a separate mission on the foundations of an earlier building destroyed by the 1896 earthquake. In 1926, two large Spanish Colonial and Mission Revival buildings were added to the complex; in 1941, a three- to five-story Spanish Eclectic building was constructed. The hospital reads as a single unit: building heights, massing, and materials unify the complex within serene landscaped grounds. Nearby support buildings, including the Bachelor Officers' Quarters, are similar. The hospital complex is now home to Touro University.

33. Naval Ammunitions Depot A1, 1857
Daniel Turner, architect

In order to protect the shipyard from the possibility of explosions, munitions were stored at the southern end of the island. The first magazine (A1) was constructed of coursed buff stone ashlar with quoins and a distinctive sculpture of an eagle astride an anchor over one door. Magazines buried in the hillside were built during World War I near the cemetery. During the 1930s and throughout World War II, dozens of reinforced-concrete magazines were constructed. The Naval Ammunitions Depot, its wharfs, and its hillside housing quarters can be seen from the Vallejo ferry, but the depot is off-limits to visitors.

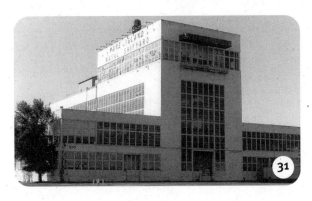

31

2 · Benicia

Benicia was the first city founded in Solano County in 1846. Robert Semple, an American involved in the Bear Flag Revolt and the imprisonment of General Vallejo at Sutter's Fort, convinced Vallejo to deed him a half interest in the town site located on a deepwater port near the Carquinez Strait. In exchange, Semple agreed to name the new town after Vallejo's wife, Doña Francisco Benicia. Within a year, Vallejo was further pressured to deed his half interest to Thomas O. Larkin, the former American consul and wealthy businessman from Monterey.

The town was laid out by Jasper O'Farrell in 1847 on a regular grid plan, with a central commercial street leading directly to the river landing. By 1848, approximately fifteen structures were standing, including Semple's wharf that provided ferry service to Martinez. In 1849, the U.S. Army's arsenal was established on a 345-acre site east of town. The Pacific Mail and Steamship Company built their boat shops and wharfs in 1850. When the Transcontinental Railroad and Ferry began operating in 1879, Benicia became an important transportation hub with canneries, flourmills, wineries, and tanneries.

Benicia has a rich early history: between February of 1853 and 1854, Benicia was the state capital; between 1852 and 1889, it was one of the primary centers for education in the state and called itself "Athens of California." The Young Ladies' Seminary, founded in 1852, was owned between 1865 and 1871 by Mr. & Mrs. C. T. Mills, who went on to establish Mill's College in Oakland. The forerunner of Dominican University in San Rafael was founded in 1870, and there were several private schools for boys. Florida architect Addison Mizner, son of diplomat and judge Lansing Bond Mizner, was born and raised here.

After the train and automobile bridges opened in the late 1920s, bypassing Benicia, the town became a quiet backwater; the lack of development pressure until the 1980s inadvertently preserved much of its historic character.

1. Semple–Von Pfister Store, 1847
End of Von Pfister Street

Sitting under a modern metal shelter, this inconspicuous vernacular adobe building is said to be the place where an employee at Sutter's Mill revealed the discovery of gold.

2. Southern Pacific Train Depot
90 First Street

When the Transcontinental Railroad was rerouted through Benicia to Oakland, train cars were loaded onto "the largest ferries in the world" for a journey across the Carquinez Strait to Port Costa. In 1902, the Southern Pacific Railroad Station at Banta, Contra Costa County, was moved here. Similar to other Southern Pacific stations it was built from standardized company plans. It has horizontal siding on the first floor, staggered shingle siding on the second, decorative timbering, and wide overhanging gable roofs with bracketed eaves.

3. California State Capitol, 1852
115 West G Street
Rider and Houghton, architects

This imposing Greek Revival building served as the California State Capitol from 1853 to 1854. Originally built as City Hall, it was offered to the legislature when the state government decided to abandon the city of Vallejo. The two-story brick building sits on a raised foundation of local sandstone, and has a modified temple-front façade with a recessed portico defined by two fluted two-story Doric columns with sandstone capitals, a header beam, and a grand entry stairway. There are engaged brick pilasters at the corners, also with sandstone capitals and bases. The gable pediment and closed eaves have a heavy cornice with dentils; there is a bull's-eye window in the center of the pediment. The sides are

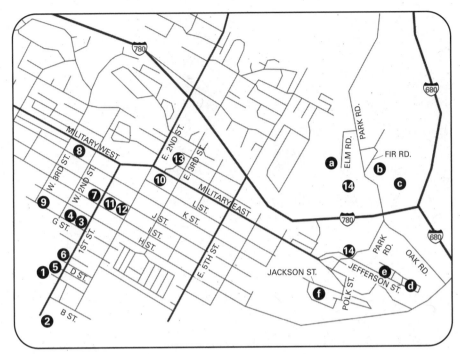

2 • Benicia

simple and have regularly placed four-over-four-light double-hung windows with sandstone header beams. The building is managed by California State Parks and is open Wednesday through Sunday from 10 a.m. to 5 p.m.

4. Fischer-Hanlon House, 1840s, 1856
137 West G Street

Built as a Gold Rush hotel in the late 1840s, the building was moved from First Street to this site and remodeled in 1856. The two-story building is an example of the East Coast Federalist style with clapboard siding, a symmetrical façade, regular fenestration, gable roof, and a front porch. It is a part of the State Capitol Park.

5. "Salt Box" house, 1850
145 West D Street

This little clapboard house overlooking the Carquinez Strait is one of several prefabricated in New England and shipped in sections around the Horn. This particular house was moved to Benicia from Port Costa around 1879.

6. Davis-Merritt House, 1869
123 West D Street

This prefabricated building is from Maine; a simple vernacular building, it was reassembled in its present location around 1869 as a front addition to a two-room structure built prior to 1848.

7. Old Masonic Hall, 1850
110 West J Street

This was the first Masonic Hall in California, built with lumber donated by Robert Semple. The first floor was used as a courtroom and county offices until 1853. The second floor has remarkably intact ornate woodwork. It is a very simple two-story, wood-frame Greek Revival building with clapboard siding, pedimented gable roof with heavy crown molding and frieze, pilasters in the corners, and a small semicircular window in the pediment.

8. Riddell-Fish House, 1890
245 West K Street

This grand three-story Queen Anne with articulated massing and multiple roofs is located on a large site surrounded by a beautifully tended garden. The

10

8

asymmetrical façade has a round corner tower with a conical roof, and a flared gable-roof bay on the other side. The house is covered with patterned surfaces, including fishscale and other patterns of shingles, banding, horizontal siding, and decorated frieze bands. Mrs. Henrietta Riddell Fish was a painter who exhibited a painting at the 1915 Exposition in San Francisco.

9. Crooks Mansion, circa 1880
285 West G Street

Surrounded by extensive gardens, this imposing Stick/Eastlake house on a spectacular site overlooking the strait is two-plus stories with articulated massing,

steeply pitched cross-gable roofs, horizontal channel siding with belt courses, Stick-style decoration, and rectilinear brackets supporting wide eaves.

10. Frisbie-Walsh House, circa 1849
235 East L Street

Built for John Frisbie, son-in-law of General Vallejo, this is one of three identical Gothic Revival houses precut in Boston and shipped around the Horn during the Gold Rush around 1849. Another is the General Vallejo home, "Lachryma Montis," in Sonoma, and the third no longer exists. The two-story building is T-shaped with steeply pitched cross-gable roofs, flush gable dormers, and a one-story porch. This is the oldest building in Benicia on its original site and in original condition. A perfect example of the Gothic Revival style, the residence has highly decorative verge rafters with pendants and finials and pointed arch windows partially in the gable end over an angled bay.

11. St. Paul's Episcopal Church, 1859–1886
120 East J Street

The exceptionally beautiful Gothic Revival Church was completed in 1886 after several stages of development. In 1859, a small rectangular building with a flat roof and entry tower was built, designed by Captain Julian McAllister from the Benicia Arsenal. In 1868, the steeple, transepts, and vaulted ceiling were added, also by McAllister. In 1882, the Gothic Revival Guild Hall was constructed. In 1886, Scandinavian shipwrights from the Pacific Mail and Steamship Company added new paneling, exposed roof rafters, and struts to make the church more in keeping with "High" English parish churches.

12. St. Paul's Rectory
122 East J Street

Captain McAllister purchased a typical New England saltbox house in 1864 that had been built around 1790 in Torrington, Connecticut. It was reassembled after being shipped around the Horn. The one-and-a-half-story balloon-framed building, with a rear saltbox addition, has a side-facing gable roof, a central chimney, and clapboard siding.

13. Bishop Wingfield House
36 Wingfield Way

In 1853, the Episcopal Church decided to establish a pair of schools: St. Augustine's for boys and St. Mary's of the Pacific for girls. This Italianate house, built for Bishop J. H. D. Wingfield, who supervised the two schools, is the only building remaining of the school. The two-story house has a symmetrical façade; steeply pitched gable roofs; heavy cornices, brackets, and frieze; quoins; hooded windows; and a full-width porch supported by slender paired columns.

14. Benicia Arsenal
Army Point and I-680

Like Mare Island, the military presence in Benicia dates to California's entry into the Union. In 1849, The U.S. Army's Pacific Division, under the command of General Persifer F. Smith, chose a site northeast of Benicia for the storage of powder and munitions. The site had a deepwater port and dry climate. (San Francisco's Presidio was too damp for such storage.) Benicia's founders, Semple and Larkin, gave the army 345 acres of land, recognizing this would have an economic benefit for their town. From 1851, when the first wood-frame buildings brought from the East Coast were erected, and throughout the nineteenth and early twentieth centuries, major stone, brick, and wood-frame buildings were constructed. Historian Robert Bruegmann believes that ". . . the buildings of the 1850s at the Benicia Arsenal are the most impressive set of [masonry] structures built before the Civil War in the western United States." Although the Benicia Arsenal closed in 1964, these impressive military buildings are still standing. The 440-acre historic district is listed on the National Register of Historic Places and contains twenty-three contributing buildings.

14a. Hospital, 1856
Arsenal Building #1

Constructed of local sandstone, the utilitarian building appears to have been built from standard army hospital plans.

14b. "Camel Barns,"
1853–1856
Arsenal Buildings #7, #8, #9

Although they are called "Camel Barns," these three stone buildings were actually constructed as storehouses and an engine house. During the 1850s, the U.S. Army experimented with using camels as pack animals in desert regions. The camels proved to be difficult to manage, and during the Civil War, thirty-five were shipped to Benicia to be sold.

The two large storehouses have side-gable roofs with eave returns, and regularly placed, symmetrical arched openings with extended stone keystones and carved embellishments. These flank the smaller engine house. They house the Benicia Historical Museum and the Camel Barn Museum.

14c. Powder Magazines,
1855, 1857
Arsenal Buildings #2, #10

Two nearly identical, massive stone buildings have walls four feet thick, a row of octagonal stone columns down the center, and a vaulted stone ceiling. The exteriors are sheathed with wood to keep moisture away from the powder. The first magazine has little ornamentation. However, the second has elaborate sculptural decoration credited to a French stonecutter.

14d. Main Storehouse and Clock Tower,
1859, 1915
Arsenal Building #29

In 1859, the main munitions storehouse was moved to a more convenient site, closer to where large ships could dock. The three-story fort-like building was constructed of rusticated, carefully fitted local sandstone. Originally, this was a three-story building with two towers. In

1912, after an explosion blew the roof off the building and destroyed the interior, the building was reconstructed as a two-story one-tower building.

14e. Commandant's House, 1860
Arsenal Building #28

During Julian McAllister's tenure as commander from 1860 to 1886, the politically well-connected McAllister made the arsenal the social and cultural center of Benicia. He was also responsible for constructing a large number of important buildings, including this house facing the Main Storehouse. Built in 1860 from standardized plans, the Greek Revival–style building was later modified with Italianate features. The two-story brick building covered with stucco siding has a symmetrical façade with a projecting full-width covered porch supported on cast-iron Corinthian columns, a bifurcated staircase with heavy balusters, and a projecting angled bay over the centered front door.

14f. Shop Buildings,
1876, 1884, 1877
Arsenal Buildings #55, #56, #57

Among the numerous interesting and beautiful buildings is this complex of three brick shop buildings near the waterfront, now used mostly as artists' studios. The one-story blacksmith shop was built first; the two-story carpenter shop and machine shop are similar. The massing, pedimented roofs, pattern of fenestration, and decorative elements suggest East Coast Federal or Adam styles appropriate to this West Coast outpost.

3 · Suisun Valley · Green Valley

Americans settled these two valleys by 1850. Wheat was the main crop, and by 1854, there was a flourmill in Suisun City and one in Green Valley. Fruit replaced wheat as the main crop by 1900.

Notable farmhouses and barns are located in the two valleys, and there are four exceptional early stone buildings constructed of local basalt, marble, sandstone, and tufa, and some stone fences and ruins of other buildings.

1. Green Valley Country Club, 1856
End of Country Club Drive

The 7,000-square-foot Adams-style house is a rectangular two-story stone building with a hipped roof and a central gable supported on stone corbels. Surrounded by elaborate gardens, the ranch grew to include the world's largest cherry orchard. In 1920, local architect William A. Jones added the large projecting porches supported by massive stone columns. The first owner was Granville Swift, who raised the Bear Flag over Sonoma Plaza in 1846. Frederick S. Jones acquired the property through marriage and became the area's largest vintner, producing 50,000 gallons of wine from his extensive vineyards. The Green Valley County Club acquired the property in 1949 and converted the cherry orchards to a golf course.

2. Samuel Martin House, 1861
4015 Suisun Valley Road

Constructed of locally cut stone, the beautifully detailed Gothic Revival two-story house has steep roofs with elaborately cut verge boards. The front is symmetrical with a center gable over a wide recessed front door, and French doors leading to a wrought-iron balcony on the second floor. Windows and French doors are deeply recessed. The house was

remodeled by architect Julia Morgan in the late 1920s when the multipaned French doors were most likely added. Grinding stones are located on the site, indicating that this area was once a Native American settlement.

3. Rockville Stone Chapel, 1856
Suisun Valley Road

Joel Price and George Whitely, masons

The small rectangular stone chapel was built by the Methodist Episcopal Church.

The stone for the chapel, quarried in the nearby hills, contains volcanic ash and magnesium that hardened when it was exposed to air. In 1940, the church was restored as a local pioneer landmark using a WPA grant. Rockville Cemetery, located immediately north of the chapel, began in 1851 with the death of Sarah Alford, who crossed the plains with her family; also buried here is Granville Swift.

4. Baldwin Ranch Barn, 1865
4285 Suisun Valley Road

Built of finely cut local stone, the three-story barn has three graduated arches under the gable roof. There are diamond-shaped windows on the side walls.

5. Davisson House, 1880s
2703 Rockville Road

This two-story Second Empire house was built in Suisun City in the 1880s and moved to this location in 1912 because the owner felt the city taxes were too high.

Cordelia

Cordelia, originally named Bridgeport, lies next to the railroad tracks and just southeast of the intersection of I-80 and I-680. Originally located on the Benicia-Sacramento Road, its importance as a minor transportation hub was augmented in 1867 when the California Pacific Railroad to Vallejo opened. In 1879, the Central Pacific (later Southern) intercontinental railroad was rerouted through Benicia by way of Fairfield/Suisun and Cordelia.

There are a handful of old buildings along the railroad tracts. Thompson's Corner (1902) is a two-story vernacular building that housed a general store and a saloon. 2138 Bridgeport Avenue is one of four Queen Anne houses said to be prefabricated and shipped here by rail.

South of Cordelia, the Suisun Marshes are prime Bay Area duck-hunting grounds; affluent Bay Area men established exclusive clubs in the area; it is said that the Central Pacific rail line was rerouted to provide convenient access to the duck clubs. East of Cordelia, a quarry was established in 1870.

Diking the marshes for agriculture increased the salinity of the water, lowered water tables, and led to flooding, threatening the health of the marsh. Two legislative bills have reversed this: Suisun Resource Conservation District of 1964, and the Suisun Marsh Preservation Act of 1974.

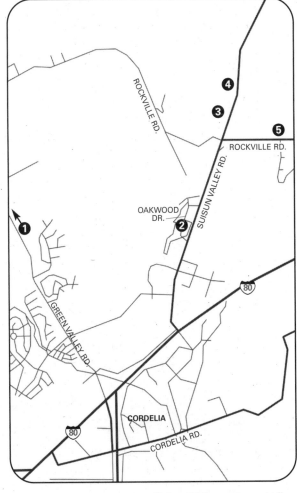

3 • Suisun Valley • Green Valley

4 · Suisun City · Fairfield

Suisun City

Suisun City is two very distinct places: a sprawling residential suburb along Highway 12, and a compact mid-nineteenth-century small town. New Town Hall and old town Suisun are separated by Suisun Slough.

Old Suisun was settled around 1851 by Captain Josiah Wing, who found favorable anchorage at the end of the Suisun Slough next to a small island; he laid out a town with a miniature grid pattern of narrow streets and small blocks. The town became prosperous as a center for shipping and canning agricultural products. In 1868, the California Pacific Railroad depot

and switching station were built in Suisun, and the town became a fashionable metropolis where the most influential citizens in Solano County lived, including State Senator Benjamin F. Rush. Main Street was once lined with commercial buildings on both sides of the street: the three-story block-long Arlington Hotel was the center of social life until it burned in 1930. A large canning company was once located across from the train station next to the slough, and a Chinatown was nearby. A plank boardwalk connected Suisun with Fairfield, the county seat. The historic residential area is located one block west of the historic downtown.

1. Masonic Lodge No. 55, 1888
623 Main Street

The two-story brick lodge building has a distinctive second-story façade that is composed of two Gothic arched windows glazed with stained glass. There is a gabled parapet, and the ground-floor retail spaces have decorated cast-iron piers between the shop windows. Its first retail tenant was the Moses Dinkelspiel & Co. dry goods store.

2. The Lawlor House, 1850s, 1979
718 Main Street

The two-story rectangular-shaped house with hipped roof

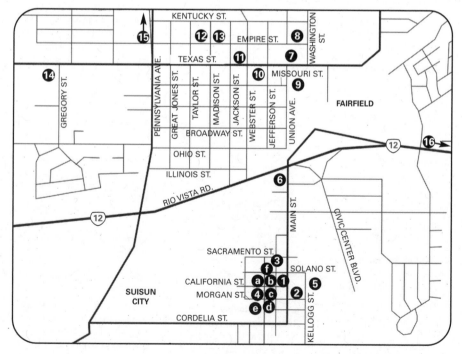

and two-story portico was built on a farm east of town; it was moved to this location in 1979, when the farm was subdivided, and restored for offices.

3. The Wednesday Club, 1926
225 Sacramento Street

William H. Crim Jr., architect

This Mediterranean-style clubhouse for a women's service club was founded in 1911.

4. Historic Residential Suisun

This tiny district, typical of nineteenth-century small towns, is a social and economic mix of houses dating from the 1860s.

4a. Church/ Gregory House, 1901
300 California Street

J. H. Laughlin, architect

A transitional two-story house combines Colonial Revival with a Queen Anne turret.

4b. Wilbur Goodman House, 1915
308 California Street

A two-story Craftsman with a low-pitched roof and wide overhanging eaves that are supported on carved brackets is reminiscent of a Swiss chalet.

4c. 220 Morgan Street, circa 1865

This small, unadorned Gothic Revival and the one next door at 218 Morgan are probably Suisun's oldest houses.

4d. Benjamin Rush House, 1869
301 Morgan Street

An elegant, and early, two-story Italianate has an asymmetrical façade and two-story angled bay. Rush, grandson of Dr. Benjamin Rush of Philadelphia, became a state senator.

4e. 406 Morgan Street, 1880

A two-story Stick/Eastlake with an original cast-iron fence is nearly identical to the house located next door.

4f. Tillman House, 1900
205 Solano Avenue

This three-story transitional-style house has steeply pitched cross-gable roofs, angled bays, and a two-sided wraparound porch.

5. Suisun Slough Redevelopment, 1980s
Main and Kellogg Streets

ROMA, architects

Suisun City began to lose population in the 1930s when fires devastated blocks of Main Street. Beginning in the mid-1970s, a redevelopment plan preserved the old town, cleaned up the slough, and created new marinas. A new City Hall was built in 1989 across the waterway from the historic downtown; it is a modern derivation of a classic civic building with a central dome and oculus—a mini version of the State Capitol dome—a symbol of democracy and prosperity.

6. Suisun City Depot, 1907
177 Main Street

This historic train station was rehabilitated to serve as a multimodal station for Amtrak, Greyhound, and local buses. A Highway 12 overpass looms over a portion of the historic depot, testimony to the importance of the automobile in the developing subdivisions to the east.

Fairfield

Captain Robert Henry Waterman was a successful China Trade clipper ship captain. He arrived in California in 1849, and in 1850, he and Captain A. A. Ritchie purchased an undivided half interest of twelve square miles of Suisun Valley from General Mariano G. Vallejo. Between 1850 and 1853, Waterman planted stands of oak, black walnut, and eucalyptus. His house was completed in 1853 and is still standing at the end of Ten Gable Road off Waterman Boulevard.

In 1856, Waterman platted the town of Fairfield (named after his boyhood town, Fairfield, Connecticut). In 1858, the voters approved his plan to move the county government from Vallejo to Fairfield, deeded approximately sixteen acres to the county for offices, and built a temporary brick office building.

The town is laid out with a main commercial spine along historic Route 40 (Texas Street) with the county buildings anchoring the east end; residential streets are laid out in a grid on either side, where most of the dwellings are modest.

7. Solano County Courthouse, 1911
580 Texas Street

William A. Jones and E. C. Hennings, architects

The two-story granite building has a row of full-height columns with slightly stylized Ionic capitals. The main lobby and grand bifurcated interior staircase is surfaced in white marble with gold accents. Whimsical décor includes the hanging electric

lights in the entry portico that resemble ancient oil lamps, complete with flame-shaped glass. It was designed from schematic plans prepared by County Engineer Frank Steiger.

8. Tank House, 1920
Empire Street, behind the main courthouse

Frank Steiger, county engineer

This interesting water tank tower has a castellated top.

9. Hall of Justice, 1913, 1970
530 Union Avenue

The Beaux-Arts building was designed as the second Armijo Union High School to complement the Courthouse across the street. It was remodeled as the Hall of Justice in 1970.

10. Former Solano County Free Library, 1931
601 Texas Street

Coffman, Sahlberg and Stafford, architects

This two-story Spanish Colonial Revival–style building has

Churrigueresque plaster ornament over the entry, stucco siding, and a tile roof. A 1937 bronze statue of Chief Solano by William Gordon Huff stands in front of the building.

11. Neon Street Sign, 1925
700 Block of Texas Street (Historic Route 40)

In 1925, a beautiful arched neon sign announcing "FAIRFIELD: COUNTY SEAT SOLANO COUNTY" was suspended over the main street in the commercial core.

12. Goosen Mansion, 1905
1010 Empire Street

McCullum, McDougall, Cameron, architects

This Classic Revival mansion, with its grand columned entry portico, is the most impressive of Fairfield's early houses.

13. Church of God, 1893
930 Empire Street

A Gothic Revival shingled church has a three-story corner bell tower.

14. Fairfield Center for the Creative Arts, 1990
West Texas Street
ELS, architects

As part of the revitalization of downtown, this light-filled cultural center has a 400-seat theater, an art gallery, and meeting rooms. A polygonal "campanile" stands on its west side, like a beacon.

15. Edwards Cinemas
Fairfield Westfield Mall

A modern architectural icon, the sixteen-theater multiplex with elaborate neon signs and a vast lobby, is surfaced with a riot of stone and ceramic tile. It is part of Westfield Mall, which also has four anchor stores and is surrounded by smaller strip malls and, of course, vast parking lots.

16. Travis Air Force Base

Following the Japanese attack on Pearl Harbor in 1941, air defense of the Pacific Coast required an inland base of operations. Travis Air Force Base is now home to the world's largest troop transport carriers and cargo planes. Because of security, the base and the Travis Air Museum are closed to non-military visitors.

Along Interstate 80, from Cordelia Junction through Vacaville, tall signs attempt to entice passersby to patronize motels, fast-food restaurants, gas stations, malls, and outlet stores, or to view model homes of subdivisions seductively named for lost or imagined landscapes. Gone are the two popular roadside restaurants: the original Nut Tree and Milk Farm.

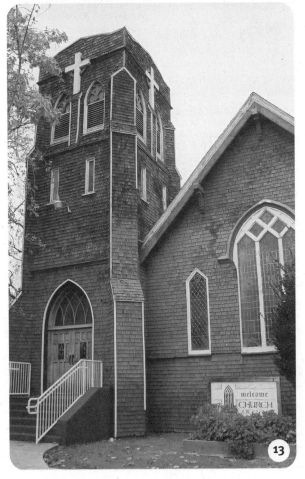

5 · Vacaville and Vicinity

In 1850, William McDaniel, a Kentucky lawyer, rancher, U.S. land agent, and developer, purchased part of Manuel Cabeza Vaca's land grant. In late 1851, McDaniel filed a subdivision map for the town. Surrounded by fertile valleys, Vacaville became a prosperous market town.

Where early pioneers and the Pony Express once traveled, Interstate 80 is lined with ubiquitous freeway-dependent commerce. North of the freeway is old Vacaville, its shady boulevards lined with impressive mansions and remnants of its historic downtown along Ulatis Creek. These are an unexpected treat.

Buck Avenue, an extension of Main Street west of downtown, was settled by Vacaville's most prosperous and influential families. There are impressive homes along Buck Avenue, and the street conveys an intact example of the type of residential districts once found in the larger Central Valley towns. The large level lots, shade trees, and broad lawns are rare in the Bay Area. Walking-tour maps are available at the Vacaville Museum, located at 213 Buck Avenue.

1. Frank H. Buck Mansion, 1890
225 Buck Avenue

George Sharpe, designer-builder

Frank Buck, son of a highly successful fruit rancher, subdivided the area along Buck Avenue for home sites. In addition to farming and ranching, the Buck family had oil and timber interests in central and southern California, and are related to the Bucks of Marin County (Buck Center for Ageing). George Sharpe is responsible for building many Vacaville houses, including this Eastlake mansion on a huge double lot. It has exuberant flourishes that combine elements of the Italianate and Queen Anne

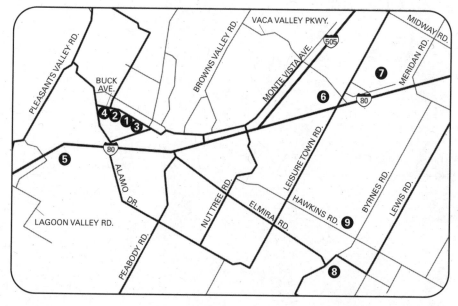

styles. The wood-frame house has a veneer of bricks, added in 1930.

2. William H. Buck House, 1892
301 Buck Avenue

This is a hipped-roof Queen Anne with a three-story gable-roof bay. There is a carriage house in the rear.

3. Hurtley House, 1922
100 Buck Avenue

Reed and Corlett, architects

Facing broad lawns, this grand two-story Mediterranean has a symmetrical façade, decorated entry surround, stucco siding, and hipped tile roofs.

4. Sharp House, 1896
306 Buck Avenue

The elegant Colonial Revival with a symmetrical façade has a Palladian window in its gable-roofed central dormer; the covered entry porch across the front is supported by simple Doric columns.

5. Vaca-Peña Adobe, circa 1841
Lagoon Valley Road, off Interstate 80

The original adobe built by the Vaca family is no longer standing, but the neighboring one-story Peña Adobe, built around 1841, remains just west of Vacaville next to the freeway. The roar of traffic makes it difficult to comprehend how sylvan and peaceful this shady site must have been more than 150 years ago when the only traffic was an occasional rider on horseback.

6. Genentech Research and Development Center
Vaca Valley Parkway

Just east of the junction of Interstates 80 and 505 is the suburban campus of one of the nation's largest research and development labs. The curved roof and carefully massed elements are distinctive in this area of tilt slab, big box warehouses, and manufacturing plants. Because the University of California–Davis is just a few miles east, this area is fast becoming a major center for research and development.

7. Vaca-Dixon Electric Substation, 1922
Interstate 80 at Midway Road

Built by Pacific Gas and Electric Company, this Classical Revival building with a Mediterranean tile roof receives power from a hydroelectric power house on the Pit River more than 200 miles away.

8. Elmira Church
Edwards and B Streets

This small white church is one of the few remaining buildings in the town of Elmira. The California Pacific Railroad built a station here, and it became a major shipping center for produce. Elmira is slowly being absorbed into the Vacaville city limits as development moves eastward.

9. 5381 Hawkins Road, circa 1860

This wonderful, small, two-story Carpenter Gothic house was moved to this site from Elmira. Current owners report that the house, including the elaborate drip molding on the verge boards, is all redwood.

6 · Montezuma Hills · Rio Vista

Montezuma Hills and the Prairie

In sharp contrast to the fertile valleys, prosperous former farm towns, and suburban development to the north, a large area of Solano County is sparsely settled. During the 1850s, landings were built at the head of sloughs that served as transportation points for grain, but the rolling prairie land did not support the agriculture found in the northern valleys. Most of the prairie continues to be grazing lands, and there are scattered ranch buildings.

California's best remaining examples of clay-pan vernal pools and native bunchgrass prairie can be found at the Jepson Prairie Preserve on Highway 113 north of Creed Road. Docents from the Solano Land Trust lead hikes to view the spectacular wildflower displays in the spring.

1. Dixon Methodist Church, 1866
West A Street at Dixon Avenue West

The town of Dixon owes its existence to the California Pacific Railroad and the misspelling of Thomas Dickson's name, a prosperous rancher who donated the town site. When the station was built in 1868, an entire community moved about two miles north to Dixon and the rail line. This small white church (looking like it is missing its spire) was built in Silveyville in 1866 and was moved here in 1870. Dixon's current growth is due to its proximity to Davis and the University of California, a few miles north.

2. Jackson Fay Brown House, circa 1887
6751 Main Prairie Road
N. D. Goodell, of Sacramento, architect

This is a grand two-story Italianate house with twenty rooms and, at the time, was built with every modern convenience. It was surrounded by ornamental trees, orchards, and vineyards. Mr. Brown was in the dairy business.

3. Western Railway Museum
5848 State Highway 12

Until the railroads began operating, wharfs on the sloughs at Denverton, Bird's Landing, Molena, and Collinsville provided access for flat-bottom scows. To experience the picturesque Montezuma Hills, board one of the Museum's authentic electric trains or streetcars for a trip along a segment of the Oakland, Antioch and Eastern Railway (later Sacramento Northern) electric interurban that began operating in 1913. The museum interprets the history of this, many other railways, and their influence on urban growth.

4. Shiloh Church, 1876
Shiloh Road, 3 miles west of Bird's Landing

This simple church has a central bell tower flanked by tall arched windows. It replaced an earlier church destroyed by fire. Early pioneers are buried in the church cemetery.

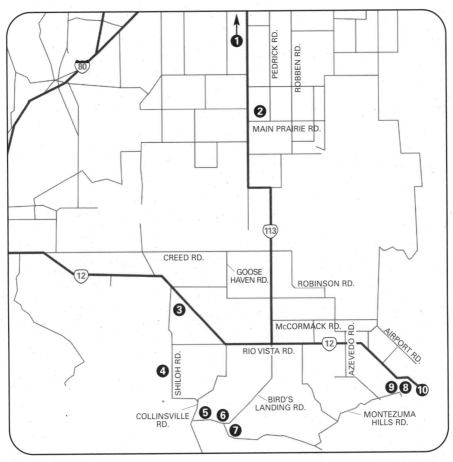

6 • Montezuma Hills • Rio Vista

5. Bird and Dinkelspiel Store, 1876

2145 Collinsville Road, Bird's Landing

About 1869, a small community grew up on high ground north of the wharfs and warehouses on Montezuma Slough. In 1876, Moses Dinkelspiel built this two-story general store with Italianate brackets as a branch of his store in Suisun. He later sold it to John Bird. In 1912, Edward

Dinkelspiel, Moses's son, subdivided a town called Montezuma, a few miles north of Bird's Landing, in expectation of the opening of the electric railroad, but the town was never fully developed.

6. Taylor-Stewart House, 1887
Bird's Landing Road

This two-story Italianate is meticulously maintained by the descendants of the original owner, Frank Taylor. Projecting shed roofs supported by scrolled brackets are located over all the primary windows and doors. A wrought-iron widow's walk and garden fence are all original.

7. Donnell Ranch, 1880s
Bird's Landing and Montezuma Hills Roads

Another meticulously maintained, two-plus-story Italianate ranch house, surrounded by tidy fenced paddocks filled with sheep and goats, is located just east of Bird's Landing in a surreal pastoral landscape dotted with gigantic modern windmills.

Rio Vista

In 1862, the town of Rio Vista moved to its current location overlooking the Sacramento River after an earlier town, established in 1857, washed away in a flood. Rio Vista prospered on river commerce. Historic homes, warehouses, and stores are concentrated within an easy walk from the riverfront. The Rio Vista Museum has a self-guided walking-tour brochure. East of town is a Chinatown.

8. Captain Lars Larsen Family Home, 1897
240 South Second Street

This is a luxurious Queen Anne home on a large site overlooking the river.

9. John McCormack Home, 1900, 1917
Dutra Museum of Dredging
345 Saint Gertrude Avenue

The Dutra Museum is a private collection on the history of dredging in the Sacramento–San Joaquin Delta. Constant dredging and levee maintenance are required to keep waterways open to shipping and reclaimed lands free from flooding.

10. Rio Vista Bridge, 1919
State Highway 12

Joseph Strauss, architect

Designed by Joseph Strauss, architect of the Golden Gate Bridge, this 1919 steel-truss drawbridge provided the first North Bay automobile link from the Bay Area to Sacramento.

VII
Napa County

Susan Dinkelspiel Cerny, co-author & co-photographer
Marianne Rapalus Hurley, co-author & co-photographer

Napa County has a worldwide reputation for premier wines and picturesque vine-yards that extend north from the city of Napa to the base of Mount Saint Helena. The Mayacamas Mountains separate the Napa Valley from Sonoma Valley. East of Howell Mountain there were once mercury mines in the hills north and east of Pope Valley, where remnants are still visible.

George C. Yount is considered the county's first permanent settler; he was awarded the first Mexican land grant in the valley, Rancho Caymus, in 1836. By 1850, the county's population was approximately 400; two years later, it had grown to 2,100. Simpson Thompson established the county's first nursery in 1852 at Soscol (original spelling: Suscol), a few miles south of Napa City; by 1856, Thompson reportedly had 8,000 grapevines comprising thirty varieties.

Most pioneers planted table grapes rather than wine grapes. John Patchett is believed to have planted the earliest wine grapes before 1850. Charles Krug, considered the founder of Napa Valley's wine industry, planted grapes north of St. Helena in 1860, followed by Jacob Schram, south of Calistoga around 1863. After the railroad was extended from Napa to Calistoga in October 1868, the wine industry and the population grew rapidly. Between Calistoga and Oakville, there were thirty wineries by 1876. The St. Helena Viticulture Club, the first in the state, was founded in 1875; Charles Krug was its first president.

Locally available stone was widely used as a building material for wineries, commercial and institutional buildings, a few houses, and dry-stone wall fencing. Napa has the largest number of stone bridges in the state that are still in use, but only 40 of the 326 stone bridges standing in 1914 remain today.

When wealthy San Franciscan Gustave Niebaum, a partner in the Alaska Commercial Company, purchased two farms in 1880, he attracted other wealthy men to do the same. For his "Inglenook" winery, Niebaum hired civil engineer Hamden W. McIntyre, an employee of the Alaska Company, to design the winery building.

Hamden W. McIntyre soon became the primary architect of wineries during the 1880s in the Napa Valley and elsewhere in the state. He made innovations that included using concrete for floors, cast-iron pillars, and roofs that did not condense moisture. His

Depot,
Calistoga

Turnbull Wine Cellars,
Oakville

Community Church,
Yountville

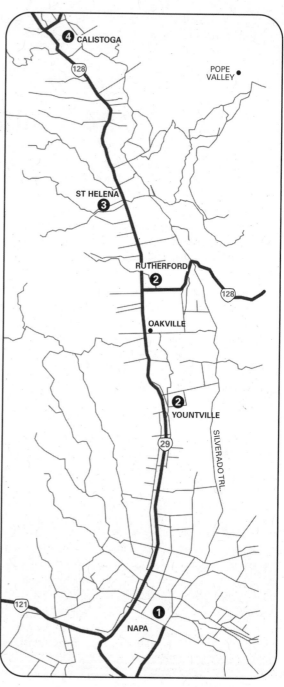

VII • Napa County

wineries were constructed in stone, wood, or a combination of both. Many were designed like a bank barn, with lower floors (usually two) built against a hillside, and the top floor rising above. The grapes were crushed on the upper floor, and the liquid poured into barrels on the floors below.

McIntyre left a lasting stamp on the built environment of the Napa Valley. In addition to Niebaum's Inglenook (now Niebaum-Coppola), his work includes the older buildings at Far Niente (1885), Chateau Montelena (originally Hillcrest, 1886–88), Ewer & Atkinson Winery (1885; now Beaulieu), Estee Winery (1885), Trefethen (1886; originally Eschol), Ehlers Estate (1886) and a large brick winery for Leland Stanford at Vina, Tehama County.

Architect Albert Schröpfer designed remarkable Victorians in the valley, including Thomann House (1874; now Sutter Home Winery), Rosenbaum House (1878; now St. Clement Vineyards), Beringer House (1883), and the Tiburcio Parrott House (1884).

Builder Wilbur A. Harrison, the son of an Oakland and Berkeley builder, became the local expert on winery design after 1900. He built the stone barn at Larkmead Winery for Battista Salimena in 1906, a barn for Anton Forni, the stone bridge to Chateau Chevalier, and several St. Helena buildings.

The wine industry was threatened during the 1890s when the tiny insect Phylloxera began attacking the roots of European grape stock, and again between 1920 and 1933 with the enactment of Prohibition. Beginning in the 1960s, a renewed interest in the wine industry stimulated the founding of new wineries and the restoration of old ones. New modern wineries have been designed by such internationally known architects as Michael Graves, William Turnbull, Cliff May, Herzog & de Meuron, and Domingo Triay. Today, with a population of only 132,000, Napa County has more than 230 wineries.

Darioush Winery, Napa

1 · City of Napa

Since its official beginning in 1847, the city of Napa has been the gateway to the lush agricultural Napa Valley to the north. Located at the headwaters of navigation along the Napa River, the city of 74,000 lies between Highway 29 and the Silverado Trail, with the river winding its way south to Richardson Bay.

Twenty-one-year-old Nathan Coombs formally laid out the town after receiving a large parcel of land in the vicinity of today's downtown. By 1850, the town's population could support a saloon, two stores, and a hotel. The town's early prosperity was linked to the valley's cultivation of grain and other agricultural products that were shipped to San Francisco. Near the present-day Napa Mill, wharfs and warehouses lined a bustling riverfront.

In 1865, the train reached Napa, and extended to Calistoga in 1868, facilitating further development of the town. Early residential neighborhoods are within the boundaries of the thirty-block Napa Abajo and Fuller Park Historic District, listed on the National Register of Historic Places. There are 295 contributing buildings in this district, an astonishing number, and they represent a broad range of domestic architecture from 1870s to World War I.

During the 1880s, as Napa's wealth and prestige increased, San Francisco architect John Marquis designed many of the finer houses in town. The Newsom Brothers also left their mark locally with the Courthouse and Opera House. Later, Napa architects Luther M. Turton (1862–1925) and William H. Corlett (1856–1937) designed a broad range of residences, churches, and commercial buildings well into the twentieth century. Like Brainerd Jones in Petaluma, Turton also apprenticed with McDougall and Sons in San Francisco.

Napa also prospered from a number of factories located along the river; among them were several tanneries, a woolen mill, and a glove factory. During World War II, more than 5,000 Napa residents worked at the Mare Island Naval Shipyard in Vallejo; the population doubled to 13,000 between 1930 and 1950. During the last fifty years, as in much of the Bay Area, the city has spread onto former agricultural and dairy land.

South

1. Former Soscol House, circa 1855
1011 Soscol Ferry Road, off Highway 29

The simple two-story clapboard-sided roadhouse was constructed as a stage stop and transfer point for steamboats in the once thriving community of Soscol (formerly spelled Suscol) on the Napa River. The rear extension was added in 1875. In 1981, the building was moved a short distance to the south for the expansion of Highway 29.

2. Napa State Hospital, founded 1875
Magnolia Drive at Soscol Avenue

Napa State Hospital provided an additional facility to ease the overcrowding at the Stockton Asylum, at that time the only mental hospital in California. Land was purchased from the former Rancho Tulocay for a rambling 500-bed hospital designed by Wright and Sanders that opened in 1875. Although this large Gothic building was demolished in 1949, many other secondary buildings of interest remain at the complex today:

2a. Building 181, 1899
Building 183, 1900
Luther M. Turton, architect

These are both classic designs constructed as residences for the administrators.

2b. Building 178, 1920

The main entrance road for this large English Period Revival Nurses Home is at Magnolia Avenue.

2c. Building 147, 1884

Now the Electric Shop, this building was originally a large stable called the Stone Barn, with a second bay added to the south in 1894. It reputedly was built by patients using stone quarried on the hospital grounds.

3. Former Sawyer Tanning Company Complex
68 Coombs Street, at Spruce Street

F. A. Sawyer built a large and highly successful factory in 1871 to tan sheepskins discarded by butchers. In 1926, the company was the first to produce patent leather west of Chicago, and by the 1930s was the largest tannery west of the Mississippi. After it closed in 1997, the historic complex became studios and offices.

4. Don Cayetano Juarez Adobe, 1840
376 Soscol Avenue, at Adobe Lane

Set on a rise above the street, the one-story adobe was once part of Cayetano's Rancho Tulucay, and is the oldest building in Napa County. For decades it has been a restaurant, but its adobe bricks are exposed at the recessed entry and at the northeast corner. Some ceiling beams and posts appear original on the interior.

5. Ox Bow School, 2000
530 Third Street, off Soscol Avenue

Stanley Saitowitz, architect

1 • City of Napa: South

This arts school complex includes a row of five rectangular two-story buildings along Third Street, whose façades are a composition of multipaned and translucent glass windows, horizontal and perpendicular wood siding, and open porches framed with olive green metal trim. These studios are set on natural gray concrete bases.

6. Copia, 2001
500 First Street, off Silverado Trail

Polshek Partnership, architects

Peter Walker, landscape architect

The American Center for Wine, Food and the Arts is intended to serve as the gateway to the wine

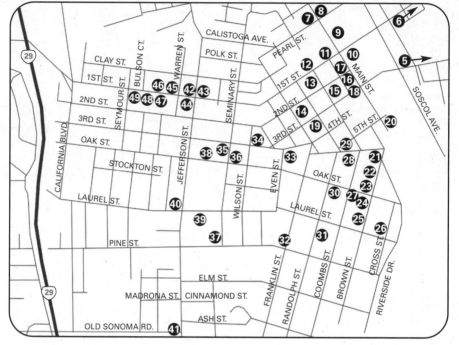

1 • City of Napa: Downtown and Residential

country and to complement the downtown. It boasts a large organic garden, restaurant, exhibit gallery, and theater. Built to attract tourists who come to the Napa Valley, it is still trying to define itself as a cultural institution, museum, and educational organization.

Downtown

The central commercial district begins at the river, with most of the historic downtown along Main and First Streets. The area has been subjected to redevelopment since the mid-1970s with unfortunate consequences that include parking lots, unsightly garages, and a 1970s-style plaza.

7. 1245 Main Street, circa 1875

Thought to be the city's first stone building, it was once a brewery and later a Chinese laundry.

8. Commercial Building, 1886
1124–1142 Main Street
Wright and Sanders, architects

The one-story stone commercial building was designed by leading nineteenth-century San Francisco architects. In 1999, layers of cladding that hid the stone façade were removed. Although the Main Street Bridge over Napa Creek (1860) has been widened at street level, its historic stone structure remains below.

9. Napa Valley Opera House, 1879
1030 Main Street
Samuel and Joseph C. Newsom, architects

The stately Italianate has a colonnaded ground floor, and a grand, three-bay second story; each bay contains three tall windows framed by elaborate moldings; the parapet, surmounted by four pinnacles, is bisected by a pediment. After serving as a vaudeville house and lecture hall until 1914 and then intermittently used as retail space, the building reopened as a theater in 2002 after its façade was conscientiously restored.

10. Semorile Building, 1888
975 First Street

Luther M. Turton, architect

A brick building with buff-colored sandstone trim, the Semorile Building has cast-iron storefront columns fabricated by O'Connell and Lewis in San Francisco. The interior has a pressed copper ceiling. The heavily remodeled Winship Building next door, also designed by Turton the same year, anchors the corner of Main and First. It exhibits similar cast-iron columns.

11. First National Bank, 1916–1917
1026 First Street

The Neoclassic former bank building is faced with pale gray terra-cotta, and has six full-height engaged Corinthian columns, a dentil frieze, and a decorative entry surround.

12. Gordon Building, 1929
1130 First Street

C. Leroy Hunt, architect

The two-and-a-half-story, buff-colored glazed-brick building is richly decorated with polychrome terra-cotta trim. On the second story, triple-arched windows within an arch are trimmed with polychrome terra-cotta. On the next block at 1222 First Street is a companion building of similar design and materials.

13. Goodman Library Building, 1901
1219 First Street

Luther M. Turton, architect

Napa's first library building has a collection of arched openings that are flat, segmented, and round. The quarry-stone-faced building has been headquarters

of the Napa County Historical Society since 1976.

14. Post Office, 1933
1351 Second Street

William H. Corlett, architect

The PWA Moderne post office has a symmetrically arranged façade, with entrances flanked by monumental light standards on either side of a wide central bay, stylized terra-cotta rams' heads along the eaves, and eagles over the doors.

15. Napa County Courthouse, 1879
825 Brown Street

Samuel and Joseph C. Newsom, architects

The Italianate courthouse is the second oldest courthouse in California still in use. The façade is symmetrical, with tall, arched casement windows on the first floor and shallow arches on the second. An onion-shaped dome was removed in 1931 and replaced with a small pediment over the central bay above the word "Justice."

The Hall of Records (1916; William H. Corlett, architect), which is Mediterranean in style, is connected to the courthouse by a building constructed in 1978. The Napa County Criminal Courthouse (1999; Ross and Drulis, architects) across Third Street has a formal modern façade with a projecting entrance bay. It relates well to the older historic courthouse.

16. Alexandria Hotel, 1910
840–844 Brown Street

William H. Corlett, architect

The three-story Mediterranean Revival has corner window bays with groups of arched windows and tiled hipped roofs that extend beyond the roofline, nicely emphasizing its corner location.

17. Bank of Napa, 1923
903 Main Street

H. H. Winner, architect

Here is a Classic banking temple built of reinforced concrete with a granite base and ornamental

cast stone; an Art Deco addition was built behind, on Brown Street.

18. 816 Brown Street, 1904

William H. Corlett, architect

Contrasting colors of native stone enliven the façade of this two-story Classic Revival commercial building.

19. First Presbyterian Church, 1874

1333 Third Street

R. H. Daley and Theodore Eisen, architects

This Gothic Revival church with its tall thin spire is a prominent landmark downtown. Although the buttresses are encased in vinyl siding, the rest of the exterior is painted shiplap redwood. Of particular note are the statues tucked in the niches of the tower.

20. Hatt Warehouses, 1884

550 Main Street

MCA Architecture (adaptive re-use, 2000)

The brick industrial complex is located just south of downtown on the site of the 1862 embarcadero where docks and a collection of early warehouses once stood. In 1912, the Hatt warehouses were converted into a granary and mill, adding a silo building in 1932 and a hay barn in 1959. The buildings were converted into shops and a hotel, the Napa Mill Project, in 2000.

Residential

Three residential districts in the city of Napa—Napa Abajo, Fuller Park, First Street—contain excellent examples of nineteenth-century homes. The

blocks are laid out in an irregular grid pattern that reflects the orientation to the river and the gradual addition of new housing tracts over time.

Napa Abajo

The Napa Abajo (lower Napa), lying just south of downtown and along the river to Franklin Street, is the oldest residential district in town and today illustrates both large mansions and small vernacular cottages. Brown Street near the river was the location of Napa's earliest mansions, but post–World War II apartment houses interrupt the rhythm of the historic streetscape.

21. 549 Brown Street, 1885

The narrow, two-story Italianate was built for Captain Nelson H. Wulff, who operated steamboats from San Francisco to Napa carrying freight and passengers.

22. 529 Brown Street, 1885

John Marquis, architect

This stick-style house was built for Captain George Pinkham, operator of the Steamboat Landing Wharf nearby.

23. 1120 Oak Street, 1872

McDougall and Douglas, architects

Elegant and restrained, this Second Empire design illustrates the river orientation of these upscale houses. Today the front entrance faces an apartment building.

24. 485 Brown Street, 1889

This mansion was once the largest house in Napa when built by Edward S. Churchill, a

wealthy businessman. In 1906, a third story was added within the Mansard roof, and a two-story entry porch with Ionic columns updated the façade.

25. 443 Brown Street, 1886

William H. Corlett, architect

This two-story residence combines elements of Stick and Queen Anne styles, with a Colonial Revival portico added in 1900. It was built for Emanuel Manasse, who improved the tanning process at the nearby Sawyer Tannery, making Napa the leather-tanning center of the United States. Manasse later built a tannery in Berkeley in 1905.

26. 417, 423 Cross Street, circa 1880

These small houses illustrate a type of vernacular cottage dubbed "shotgun," with its one door and one window on the front elevation indicating these are one room wide. Both houses have rear extensions added before 1900.

27. E. Wiler Churchill House, 1892

486 Coombs Street

Ernest Coxhead, architect

This Shingle-style residence exhibits the complex juxtaposition of design elements typical of Coxhead. The entrance is tucked beneath a short colonnaded portico at the base of a projecting rounded bay topped with a conical roof (similar to the Coxhead-designed Greenleaf house in Alameda); two dormers rise above the eye line of the bowed gable roof. The section north of the large leaded window is a 1905 remodeling and upper-story addition. It was built by banker Edward S. Churchill for his son.

28. 1225 Division Street, 1882

John Marquis, architect

This is a two-story Italianate with an 1890s Queen Anne tower. Its original owner was H. Goodman, founder of Napa's first bank and donor of the town's first library, and was later home to Robert Corlett, a state senator and brother of architect William H. Corlett.

29. First United Methodist Church, 1916

601 Randolph Street

Luther M. Turton, architect

This English Gothic Revival–style church, with a square crenellated tower, was constructed of reinforced concrete. It has a wood-paneled sanctuary in a spacious auditorium plan and notable stained-glass windows by San Francisco Art Studio.

Across the street at 608 Randolph (circa 1885–1890) is

a Stick style remodeled into a Queen Anne in 1902. The house at 590 Randolph (circa 1900) is a transitional style covered with shingles. Both were designed by Luther M. Turton.

30. 492 Randolph Street, 1891

John Marquis, architect

Here is an exuberant two-and-one-half-story Queen Anne with a multitude of decorative elements such as window bays of different sizes, leaded-glass windows, patterned shingles, and a hipped roof with intersecting gabled bays.

31. 300 Block of Randolph Street

Italianates mix with Craftsman and Colonial Revivals on this block. Number 306 may be one of the oldest houses on the block; its façade appears to be a typical 1870s frame house.

32. 300 Block of Franklin Street

Although this block of Franklin Street has a number of fine examples of Victorian-era houses, it is the row of mature redwood trees that gives the block its distinctive appearance. 313 Franklin Street (1886) is an elaborately ornamented two-story Italianate.

Fuller Park

Fuller Park was the town's first park, designed by J. H. Chalmers in 1905. The office and restroom buildings were added in 1918. Today the park with its heritage trees anchors the Fuller Park Neighborhood, where excellent examples of late-nineteenth-century and early-twentieth-

century houses and cottages remain. Several highlights are listed:

33. Migliavacca Mansion, 1895

1475 Fourth Street

Luther M. Turton, architect

William H. Corlett, architect

The magnificent and eccentric Queen Anne mansion has a three-story domed tower. It was moved from Coombs Street before 1974 to make space for the city's new library. Migliavacca was successful in the wine industry.

34. 1500 Block of Third Street

There are a few notable houses on this block: 1541 Third (1890) has features of an Italianate and Queen Anne, with prominent two-story gable bays, one at an angle; 1562 Third (1879; Ira Gilchrist, architect) is an Italianate with some Stick-style features.

35. 741 Seminary Street, 1892

Luther M. Turton, architect

This is a particularly lavish Queen Anne with patterned shingles, molded sunbursts, and extensive spindle work.

36. 720 Seminary Street, 1852

The original house was converted into a dormitory for the Napa Ladies Seminary in 1861. In 1888, Luther M. Turton redesigned it into a Shingle-style residence.

37. Yount House, 1884

423 Seminary Street
at Pine Street

John Curtis and A. A. Bennett, architects

The large two-story Stick-style house is set far back from the street with an expansive lawn. It has a front-facing window bay topped by a faceted hipped roof. It was built for the daughter of pioneer George Yount, for whom Yountville is named.

38. 1756 Oak Street, circa 1870

The one-story gable-roofed cottage is located on a block of modest but nicely detailed nineteenth-century homes on smaller lots. The servants who worked in the Migliavacca Mansion once lived here.

39. Luther M. Turton House, 1915
1767 Laurel Street

Luther M. Turton, architect

This stucco-sided Craftsman was Turton's own home. It features a shallow-pitched, front-facing gable roof supported by short piers atop large stone bases, overhanging eaves, and a gable-roofed penthouse.

40. William H. Corlett House, 1908–1910
507 Jefferson Street

William H. Corlett, architect

Located across the street from Fuller Park, architect Corlett designed this Shingle-style house for himself. Striking is the steeply pitched roof that envelops the full-length recessed porch. Corlett was also co-owner of the Enterprise Planing Mills, established by his father.

41. Shopping Center, circa 1940
1805 Old Sonoma Road

This was Napa's first supermarket, Food City, and a good example of Streamline Moderne with steel sash windows and a tower on the corner with an oversized round window. It was built by developer Sam Gordon Sr., who also built several theaters in San Francisco.

First Street

Historically, First Street was the main road leading out of town to the west. Today it is the main one-way thoroughfare to Highway 29 from downtown. The residential neighborhood on First, Second, Jefferson, and Clay, although impacted by

traffic, has a good selection of well-appointed houses.

42. Joseph C. Noyes House, 1892
1005 Jefferson Street

Luther M. Turton, architect

This is one of Napa's imposing Queen Anne houses, located on a prominent corner lot. The interior is finished with redwood burl paneling and extensive stained glass. The palm trees were planted in 1895.

43. Frank Noyes Mansion, 1902
1750 First Street

Luther M. Turton, architect

A huge shingled Colonial Revival, this mansion has pilasters at the corners, a porte cochere, a rounded second-story bay, and a stained-glass skylight. Frank Noyes owned the Noyes Lumber Yard.

44. Residence, 1903
1801 First Street

William H. Corlett, architect

This Shingle-style house has a rounded window bay with a conical roof and Ionic columns inside and out. Strong horizontal lines are emphasized by the windows of the bay and a contrasting stringcourse.

45. 1910 First Street, circa 1905

Luther M. Turton, architect

A shingled Colonial Revival, this house was built for Dr. Adolph Kahn, a prominent physician and surgeon.

46. 1926 First Street, circa 1905

Luther M. Turton, architect

40

Within the shingled triangle formed by the steeply pitched front-facing gable roof is a centrally placed angled window bay of two windows flanked by two narrower windows; above is a balconette, a three-part window group with an interesting draped arrangement of shingles above. The first floor is sheathed with shiplap siding.

47. 1929 First Street, 1875

Set back from the street, two heritage magnolia trees frame this large Second Empire Italianate, which has a rigidly symmetrical façade, two window bays, and a mansard roof.

48. 2021 First Street, 1873

A classic two-story Italianate with a shallow gabled entrance bay is similar in type to 1929 First Street.

49. 2100 Block of First Street

This group includes three designed by Luther M. Turton in the mid-1890s at 2109, 2125, and 2133 First Street.

North

50. Saint John the Baptist Catholic Church, 1967
960 Caymus Street

Germano Milono, architect

Schubart & Friedman, architects

Reflecting the shift accompanying Vatican II, this cruciform-plan church was constructed with a dramatic network of exposed trusses. Designed to be the cathedral for a new diocese, it has a seating capacity of 1,500. Behind the church is the Spanish Colonial Revival Saint John the

Baptist Grammar School (1926; Creston H. Jensen, architect).

51. Former Napa Steam Laundry, circa 1900
1600–1606 Main Street

With remodeled storefronts and elevations stripped of earlier stucco, this stone and brick commercial building presents an array of both round arched and segmented windows at the second floor.

52. Former Lisbon Winery, 1882–1884
1711 Main Street, at Yount Street

Built by Portuguese vintner Joseph A. Mateus, both the native stone winery building and the brick sherry cellar are two survivors of the city's nineteenth-century wineries. Mateus was a skilled stonemason whose work is well illustrated in the dramatic arched openings with prominent keystones. Since 1995, it has been the home of Jarvis Conservatory.

53. Hennessey House, 1889
1727 Main Street

M. E. Johnson, builder

Large residences used to line Main Street north of downtown. This one is a stylish restrained Queen Anne that was built for a local physician.

54. Napa High School, 1922
Jefferson Street at Lincoln Avenue

William H. Weeks, architect

Formal and classically inspired, the school is symmetrically composed with a two-story central entry porch behind a row of two-story columns topped by heraldic shields and classical urns. The flanking two-story and one-story classroom bays have tile roofs and tall 3-by-3-part windows arranged in groups of four.

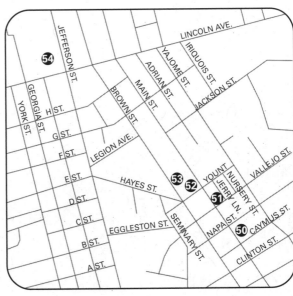

1 • City of Napa: North

2 · Napa to St. Helena

Napa

1. Di Rosa Preserve

*5200 Carneros Highway
(State Highway 121)*

A metal-sided industrial-style gallery building with a round tower, Gatehouse Gallery (1997; Forrest Architects of Sonoma), sets the stage for an unusual art collection. Beyond this gallery, the 217-acre complex also includes a nineteenth-century stone house, an enormous metal-sided gallery building (also designed by Forrest Architects), a large lake, and sculpture scattered on hillsides and valleys. Tours are by appointment and, surprisingly, the fee is worth the price.

Domaine Carneros (1987) at 1240 Duhig Road and Highway 121, a pretentious chateau-style winery (impossible to miss overlooking the highway), is said to have been inspired by a residence in France. The Carneros Inn (4048 Highway 121) is a hotel/restaurant complex that, on a smaller scale, partially mimics industrial/farm-style buildings; guest room cottages were designed to look like workers' housing (2001–2003; Rawn & Associates from Boston, architects).

2. Artesa Vineyards, 1991

*1345 Henry Road,
north off Highway 121*

*Domingo Triay (Spain) and
Earl R. Bouligny (Napa),
architects*

Located on the top of a small hill, the multistoried, stepped-up winery building is covered with native grasses, giving the appearance of being underground. From the parking area, a broad staircase ascends to a flat entrance plaza with reflection pools and great views. On the interior, there is a colorful open courtyard and wedges of angled windows.

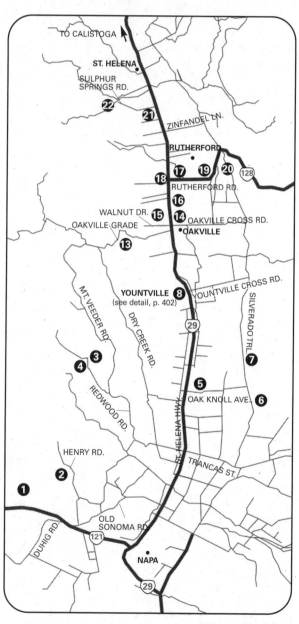

3. Hess Collection, 1903, 1989
4411 Redwood Road

*Beat A. H. Jordi
(Switzerland), architects*

*Richard Macrae,
project architect*

The winery/art gallery is housed in a U-shaped complex of buildings that include a 1903 stone winery built by Col. Theodore Grier. In 1930, during Prohibition, the winery was purchased by the Christian Brothers. In 1985, a portion of the winery was sold to Donald Hess. Two stories of art galleries exhibit important European and American work dating from the 1960s to the present.

4. Mont La Salle, 1932
4401 Redwood Road

*Henry. A. Minton,
architect*

After the Christian Brothers purchased the Grier winery, they built a school, novitiate, retirement home, and conference center between 1932 and 1941. The Mission Revival–style buildings are arranged around two courtyards connected by covered walkways. The chapel's tall domed bell tower is a prominent feature.

5. Trefethen Vineyards (Eschol Winery), 1886
1160 Oak Knoll Avenue

*Hamden W. McIntyre,
architect*

Built for James and George Goodman of Napa, this is an unusual design for McIntyre because it is completely constructed of wood with heavy timber walls. It was purchased by Gene Trefethen in 1968 and restored.

6. Darioush Winery, 2004
4240 Silverado Trail

*Ardeshir Nozari &
Roshan Nozari, architects*

The dramatic Persian-style building of buff-colored sandstone, inspired by the palaces of Persepolis, has an entrance colonnade of freestanding columns topped with double-bull capitals.

7. Regusci Winery, 1878
5584 Silverado Trail

J. R. White, builder

Built by Napa pioneers Terrill and Charles Grigsby, the handsome three-story Grigsby Occidental Building has hand-cut stone walls twenty-four inches thick. The windows are arched, the roof is gabled, and the building is set against a hillside. The Regusci family bought the winery in 1932.

Yountville

Yountville, a few miles north of Napa on Highway 29, is named for pioneer George Yount (1794–1865), a veteran of the War of 1812, a skilled hunter, and a man of many trades who arrived in California in 1831. In payment for his work at the Sonoma Mission, Yount received the first land grant in 1836 in the Napa Valley, Caymus Rancho, consisting of nearly 12,000 acres. Yount laid out Yountville (originally named Sebastopol) sometime in the late 1840s.

Yountville is a small town with a number of historic buildings, vernacular cottages, and several new hotels. Washington Street is Yountville's main street. On the southern end of town, at 6404 Washington, the small Mission Revival–style St. Joan of Arc Catholic Church (1921; William D. Shea and Henry A. Minton, architects) marked the beginning of town before the freeway was built. At the north end of Washington is the Yountville Pioneer Cemetery (1848) on land that Yount set aside for the purpose; his gravesite has the tallest monument. The former Mission Revival Yountville School (circa 1920) at 6550 Yount Street has been City Hall since the 1970s.

8. Downtown

8a. Yountville Railroad Depot, 1888-1889
6505 Washington Street

Decoratively cut shingles and profiled braces support the eaves of this Stick-style former train station, nearly identical to ones in St. Helena and Benicia.

8b. Groezinger Wine Cellars/Vintage 1870
6525 Washington Street

Gottlieb Groezinger, a San Francisco wine merchant, built one of the largest winery-distillery complexes in the county. The large utilitarian brick buildings standing in 1968 were converted to retail shops and restaurants called Vintage 1870. The complex also includes the former Napa Valley Electric Train Station.

8c. French Laundry, circa 1900
6640 Washington Street

Alexander Clark, stonemason

The first floor is double-wall stone construction; the second story is redwood; the balcony replicates one removed in the 1930s. Originally a saloon, it was converted to a steam laundry in 1907 and is now a restaurant.

8d. Charles Rovegno House, circa 1894
6711 Washington Street

Charles Rovegno, builder

Built of locally quarried stone, this simple two-story building was originally a brandy distillery before becoming the home of Charles Rovegno. It has a front-facing gable roof, and its windows and doors have plain-cut stone lintels.

8e. Yountville Community Church, 1876
6617 Yount Street

This simple Gothic Revival, with channel rustic siding, frieze-trim ornament, and double arched windows that flank a central entrance bay topped by a bell tower, was built originally for a Baptist congregation.

9. Veterans' Home of California, founded 1882
California Drive

Built for and by Mexican and Civil War veterans between 1882 and 1884, most of the original frame cottages with broad porches have been replaced by twentieth-century buildings. Today, many of the large buildings, such as the concrete Nelson M. Holderman Hospital (1932; Frederick H. Meyer, architect), with an ornate double-curved entrance staircase, are Mediterranean Revival in style.

Armistice Chapel (1918; George McDougall, architect) is a small Norman Revival church that is now a museum. The two Lincoln Residential buildings, dating from the 1930s, face each other and are connected by a colonnaded walkway.

9a. Lincoln Theater, 1959, 2005
Del Campo & Maru, architects (restoration and additions, 2005)

The Lincoln Theater, which belongs to the Veteran's Home but serves the Napa Valley Community, reopened in 2005 after a three-year project that included adding a new balcony and upper lobby, expanding the lower lobby, and upgrading mechanical and technical equipment. The Moderne-style theater seats 1,200.

10. Napa Valley Museum, 1998
California Drive

Ferneau & Hartman, architects

Located on land leased from the Veteran's Home, this is a private nonprofit art gallery with a multimedia viticulture exhibit in the basement. Predictable materials and design include rusting sheet metal for the elevator tower, wood clapboard, concrete panels, fine mesh and punched sheet metal, concrete block, and corrugated metal.

11. Domain Chandon, 1973
*1 California Drive
off Highway 29*

ROMA, architects

Broad emphatic barrel vaults of laminated wood, terraces that step up the hillside, lawns, and tree-shaded walkways along a brook are a marked contrast to the natural, dry, and rocky hillside setting.

12. Dominus Estate Winery, 1997
2570 Napanook Road

Herzog and de Meuron, architects

Designed by the same architects as the new de Young Museum in Golden Gate Park, Herzog and de Meuron were winners of the Pritzker Prize in 2001. The intriguing winery is not open to the public, but it can be seen from Highway 29 and the end of Napanook Road. The low rectangular building is more than 300 feet long and has two rectangular openings that frame vineyards on the hill behind. The façade is covered with local basalt stones placed in wire boxes and attached to the steel frame, creating a filtered light

pattern in certain places, an effect that would be nice to experience.

Oakville

Oakville is more a crossroads than a town; the settlement is at the intersection of Highway 29 and Oakville Grade, one of the few roads that connects Napa Valley with Sonoma Valley. The Oakville Grocery at 7856 Highway 29, located across from the old railroad depot, was founded in 1881; it has been used as a general store continuously since then, although the building that stands today, with its stepped false front, may date from 1900. Next door at 7862 Highway 29 is a two-story Italianate house that dates from the 1880s.

13. Oakville Winery/ Far Niente Winery, 1885
*Oakville Grade,
west of Highway 29*

Hamden W. McIntyre, architect

The three-story stone winery was built in 1885 by Captain John Benson, a San Francisco real estate man. The stone winery building included concrete floors and a double-roof design that avoided condensation; it is a bank-barn design, where the grapes were brought to the upper level to be crushed. When the winery was purchased in the late 1970s, the stone building was nearly a ruin. The roof, dormers, and windows are new. It is open for tours by appointment.

Across the road, Doak Mansion (1918; John McLaren, landscape

architect), in the Colonial Revival style, is now a Carmelite monastery with a newer chapel.

14. Opus One Winery, 1991
7900 Highway 29

Johnson Fain and Pereira Associates, architects

The limestone winery has a dramatic courtyard entrance; it is a symmetrical arrangement with a central, circular domed pavilion flanked by outstretched sloping walls.

15. Robert Mondavi, 1966
*7801 St. Helena Highway,
on the west side of State 29*

Cliff May, architect

Inspired by Mission architecture, this pretension has an overscaled bell tower, an exaggerated arched entry, and sculptures by Benjamin Bufano.

16. Turnbull Wine Cellars, 1962
8210 Highway 29

William Turnbull, architect

The complex of unassuming barn-like structures has unpainted vertical-wood siding, louvered ventilation cupolas, and few windows. It is such a straightforward design solution that its simplicity is striking and refreshing.

Rutherford

The town of Rutherford has a one-room schoolhouse, facing Highway 29 on the west side, designed by Luther M. Turton in 1888, complete with a bell cupola. The small Holy Family Church (1912), also with a bell cupola, is on Niebaum Lane.

On the west side of the highway is a former train depot with open baggage platforms.

17. Beaulieu Winery, 1880s
1960 Highway 29

Hamden W. McIntyre, architect

The nearly block-long winery is distinctive for its vine-covered two-story walls. In 1880, the two-story gable-roofed section on the north was constructed of stone from Howell Mountain for the Ewer and Atkinson Winery. Behind the winery is the Frederick Ewer House (1913; Luther M. Turton, architect) a Prairie-style mansion considered by some to be Turton's best work. Beaulieu restored the house in 1994 and uses it for private functions.

18. Inglenook Winery/ Niebaum-Coppola Estate, 1883–1887
1991 Highway 29

Hamden W. McIntyre, architect

William Mooser, consulting architect

Gustave Niebaum purchased the Inglenook ranch in 1880. The ranch already had some grapes but was transformed by Niebaum into an important vineyard with a grand stone winery building. The two- and three-story building has a symmetrical three-part composition with a three-story central section flanked by two-story wings. The innovative construction used cross-vaulted concrete ceilings set on cast-iron posts. The elegant oak-paneled tasting room, with frescoes on the ceiling, was completed in 1890. After it was

purchased in 1995 by movie director-producer Francis Ford Coppola, the name "Inglenook" was changed to Niebaum-Coppola Estate.

19. Rutherford Road and Conn Creek Road

There are several large houses and estates on these two roads. At 850 Rutherford Road is a large white Colonial Revival (circa 1905) at the entrance to Honig Winery. 8754 Conn Creek is a Stick-style Victorian-era house from the late 1870s. At 8817 Conn Creek is the stately Italianate Adamson/Cole House, designed by architects Daley and Eisen in 1875.

20. The Winery at Quintessa, 2003
1601 Silverado Trail (Rutherford Road to Silverado Trail)

Walker Warner Architects

Lutsko Associates, landscape architect

The semicircular-shaped building, which includes wine caves and a wide stone-curved façade, is set against a hillside. It functions like many nineteenth-century Napa Valley wineries, where grapes are crushed on the upper level and the liquid is funneled to the fermentation vats below. The architects received awards of merit for the winery from the AIA (2003) and from *Architectural Record* (2004).

21. John Thomann House/ Sutter Home Winery, founded 1874
277 St. Helena Highway South (Highway 29)

Albert Schröpfer, architect

The Victorian house was built in 1874 by John Thomann. Set on the edge of a broad lawn, it has a central gabled bay, a bit of half-timbering, and a wide front porch. The winery was purchased by the Sutter family in 1904 and then by the Trinchero brothers in 1946.

22. Sulphur Springs Road

Just before entering St. Helena, Sulphur Springs Road heads west off St. Helena Highway. The site of the 1852 White Sulphur Springs Resort (3100 Sulphur Springs Road) is marked by stone entry portals; it was the first spa resort in the Napa Valley. A resort still operates here, but none of the original buildings remain standing.

At 2585 Sulphur Springs is a stone and brick building, Distillery #209 (1882), that is part of the historic Edge Hill Winery; it is being restored by Architectural Resources Group. The 1912 former Christian Brothers Retreat House (1912; Luthur M. Turton, architect) at 2233 Sulphur Springs is mostly hidden behind locked gates.

3 · St. Helena

The St. Helena area was part of Dr. Edward Bale's 1841 Mexican land grant, Rancho Carne Humana. Bale built a gristmill in 1846, as well as a sawmill that fabricated clapboards for the early pioneers. After Bale died in 1849, his land was sold in small parcels. Henry Still purchased the future town of St. Helena in 1853 from Bale's estate. He built a house and a general store, donated land for the county road (now Main Street, Highway 29), and offered free lots to anyone willing to start a business.

By the time the Napa Valley Railroad arrived in 1868, St. Helena supported a hotel, saloons, and two churches. As evidenced by the large stone warehouses that are still standing, it soon became the major commercial and shipping center for the upper Napa Valley. A Napa Valley electric train line opened in 1905, but it was replaced with buses in 1938. St. Helena, with a population of 6,000, is the largest town in the upper Napa Valley and is the center of the Napa Valley wine industry.

1. St. Helena High School, 1912
1401 Grayson Avenue
Luther M. Turton, architect
J. B. Newman, stonemason

This is an impressive stone-faced, reinforced-concrete, two-story building with a symmetrical façade; the central bay contains an arched entry portico with a gable dormer above, flanked by gabled bays with grouped windows. The original landscaping was by McRorrie and John McLaren, who also landscaped Golden Gate Park.

2. Ives House, circa 1875
738 Main Street at Charter Oak

The large Gothic Revival house has a projecting central bay with a steeply pitched gable roof, flanked by dormers with smaller steeply pitched gable roofs, each with a pointed arched window and shutters.

3. Saint Helena Sherry House, 1881
1050 Charter Oak
at Main Street

Constructed of native fieldstone with quoins and round-arched

windows, the building was once a distillery for making sherry; it is now a restaurant. A circular plaque on the façade reads "1881."

4. Warehouse, 1889
1216 Church Street

The Special Internal Revenue Bonded Warehouse, First District, No. 13, is a one-story stone building in three repetitive sections, with arched openings, quoins, and a crenellated parapet.

3 • St. Helena: Downtown and Vicinity

5. Pope Street Bridge, 1894
Pope Street and Silverado Trail

R. H. Pithie, stonemason

Of the many stone bridges built in Napa County between 1860 and the 1920s, the three-span, 177-foot Pope Street Bridge is considered the most beautiful. The bridge rises on three arches to a peak in the center; it continues to carry a large amount of traffic. Nearby is the two-span Zinfindel Lane Bridge, constructed in 1913.

Downtown

The center of St. Helena's downtown commercial district, between Spring and Adams Streets, is listed on the National Register of Historic Places. It is a concentrated and cohesive downtown with a number of significant nineteenth-century commercial buildings that are largely intact.

6. Goodman Building, 1890
1201 Main Street

Located on the northwest corner of Main and Spring, the brick building visually announces the beginning of downtown. The building is constructed of stone faced with brick and pressed-brick panels in a floral pattern, and has a bracketed cornice beneath the parapet. Behind the Goodman Building at 228 Spring Street, the refurbished wood-frame William Tell Hotel dates from 1875. The Davis Building at 1231 Main, also constructed in 1875, may be the oldest stone building on Main Street. It is one story with a single storefront, a recessed entry, and a transom window.

7. Noble-Galleron Building, 1903
1200–1204 Main Street

Luther M. Turton, architect

Thick stone columns support a gable-roofed portico, once the porte cochere of a mortuary. The façade walls are covered with painted stamped-metal siding; the side walls are exposed stone.

8. Hunt Building, 1891
1302–1306 Main Street

This is a two-story stone building, two storefronts wide. On the sidewalk in front, the word 'Wonderful' in brass letters recalls the Wonderful Drug Store located here in the 1890s.

9. Hotel St. Helena, 1881
1305–1309 Main Street

This early two-story wood-frame building once had a covered porch with a balcony, which was removed when the exterior was stuccoed in 1925. Original bracketed window hoods remain on the second floor.

10. M. C. Ritchie Block, 1892
1327–1331 Main Street

Corlett Brothers of Napa, architect

Pithie-Birkett, contractors

This is St. Helena's signature Main Street building. The façade is a highly decorated combination of brick and wood that features a central bay topped by a domed roof and a tiny cupola that extends above the parapet; the central bay is flanked by recessed balconies that are framed by paired elliptical openings and latticework wood pieces. Tall sash windows with transoms, a false-front parapet with carved brackets, and a plentitude of carved wood, all painted in contrasting colors, contribute to the decorative composition. M. C. Ritchie, the original owner, arrived in St. Helena from the gold fields in the 1860s.

11. St. Helena Star Building, 1900
1328 Main Street

William H. Corlett, architect

This stately Romanesque Revival building, once the town's post office, is constructed of random-coursed ashlar.

12. Odd Fellows Building, 1886
1352 Main Street

Albert Schröpfer, architect

The elegant brick façade of this two-story building is embellished with pressed-brick rosettes, small lions' heads, molded terra-cotta brackets, and molding. The storefront is framed by cast-iron columns made by McCormick & Bros. of San Francisco. The back of the building, visible from Railroad Avenue, is rough-cut stone with metal window shutters over tall arched windows.

13. St. Helena Post Office, 1940
1461 Main Street

Louis A. Simon, architect

Leo Keller, artist (mural, 1941)

Funded by a WPA grant, the Classic Moderne building has a symmetrical façade, flat pilasters, shallow bas-relief sculptures above the windows and entry, and a powerful mural inside depicting men harvesting grapes.

14. Greenfield House, 1915
1508 Main Street

Located on the corner of Madrona and Main Streets, the large two-story, Craftsman-style house has a distinctive wide covered veranda and many gabled bays.

15. Alexander Court, 1907
1600 Block of Main Street

Alexander Court consists of four shingled bungalows on a U-shaped lane around the larger shingled Alexander House in the center.

16. Public Library/ Silverado Museum, 1979
1490 Library Lane, and Adams Street

L. W. Nieme & Associates

The library building and Silverado Museum form a courtyard entrance. The museum building is a straightforward gable-roofed rectangular building covered with vines. The stucco-sided library building is a strangely curved U-shaped building with a gable roof. The interior is bright and airy with views of vineyards and a good collection of Napa County history.

17. Foundry Building, 1884
1345 Railroad Avenue

Built of native fieldstone with arched windows, the two-story building was originally the Taylor, Duckworth, and Co. Foundry.

18. Pritchard Building, 1906
1102 Adams Street and 1411 Railroad Avenue

Wilbur A. Harrison, designer-builder

Giugni & Bognotti, stonemasons

Anchoring the corner of Adams and Railroad, the rectangular two-story, stone-faced building has been remodeled on the interior, and though every window has been replaced, most of the original openings of varying sizes remain with their rough-hewn stone lintels.

19. Crane-Ramos Sherry Factory, 1877
1468 Railroad Avenue

The narrow two-story, hip-roofed building with a covered second-story porch is rough concrete over stone.

20. Railroad Station, circa 1889
Railroad Avenue at Pine Street

This Stick-style station is nearly identical to Yountville's and is like the ones that still stand in Danville and Benicia. This is a Southern Pacific standard plan but has a longer freight wing. It serves as a station for the Napa Valley Wine Train.

21. Carnegie Library, 1907–1908
1360 Oak Avenue, at the corner of Adams Street

William H. Corlett, architect

The former Carnegie Library (now a community center) is Mission Revival with a large curvilinear parapet, one small parapet, and an arched entry.

22. St. Helena Grammar School, 1932
1401 Adams Street, at Kearney Street

William H. Weeks, architect

The one-story school building has an articulated one-and-one-half-story, Spanish Revival–style entry bay with an arched recessed entry framed by an arch of twisted engaged columns; there is a decorated roundel above the entry and corbels under an extended false-front parapet. West of the entry bay, a square two-story bell tower with stepped buttresses has an open-arched faceted cupola with a tile roof.

23. St. Helena Catholic Church, 1889, 1946
1340 Tainter Street

Father Renatus Becker, architect

Martin Rist, architect (1946)

The Norman Revival stone church has a square bell tower bisecting the front gable end. It was replicated in 1946 after a fire, but the stained-glass windows are original. The Episcopal Church at 1211 Oak Street has a small stone section built in 1883 that is the original sanctuary. A bell tower and larger sanctuary were added in 1971; in 2005, the complex was again remodeled.

24. Native Sons of the Golden West Hall, 1900

1313 Spring Street

The two-story Renaissance Revival lodge hall has square corner towers with hipped roofs, pairs of arched windows, and arched doorways; the stucco siding is original.

25. First Presbyterian Church, 1875

1420 Spring Street

This is a Gothic Revival church with a square tower, an unusual angled entry, and hood moldings over pointed arched windows. Westminster Hall, behind the church, was constructed in 1885. The United Methodist Church (1867; bell tower, 1873) at 1310 Adams Street is also early Gothic Revival.

26. George Schmidt House, 1907

1611 Adams Street

Mr. Dutton of Berkeley, builder

Set on a stone base, the fine Craftsman-style house has a hipped roof, large central dormer with grouped windows, and a deeply recessed porch that wraps around three sides. The 1300 block of Allyn, to the west, has a nice collection of nineteenth-century houses.

27. Frank B. Mackinder House, 1905

1651 Spring Mountain Road

Gus Jursch, builder

The transitional Queen Anne/Colonial Revival has a polygonal second-story corner bay and a covered porch that wraps around two sides. It is one of three large houses in different styles that builder Gus Jursch constructed on this block. Nestled in a lush garden, 1605 Spring Mountain Road (1900) is a shingled Queen Anne with a corner turret and small entry porch. Jursch's own house at 1637 Spring Mountain Road (1907) is a shingled Craftsman with unpeeled redwood porch posts.

North

28. Tiburcio Parrott House, 1884

2805 Spring Mountain Road

Albert Schröpfer, architect

This impressive, picturesque Victorian-era

house (used in the opening shots of the TV series *Falcon Crest*) has a three-story tower topped by a pyramidal roof and cupola, partial stone facade, and elaborate woodwork. It is located on the grounds of Stone Mountain Vineyard. The house,

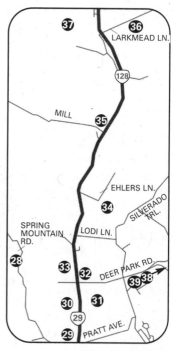

3 • St. Helena: North

30

Napa Valley when he established his winery around 1860. He organized the State Board of Viticulture Commissioners and the St. Helena Viticulture Association. Krug died in 1892.

The oldest building on the site is an 1881 stone winery, a large, rectangular two-story building with stone walls finished in a coat of smooth concrete stucco, exposed stone quoins, an octagonal cupola rising at the center of its hipped and gabled roof, and several hipped-roof dormers.

winery, and grounds are open by appointment.

29. Beringer Brothers Winery, founded 1876

Rhine House, 1883–1884
2000 Main Street

Albert Schröpfer, architect

The opulent seventeen-room Rhine House mansion, designed to recall the Beringer family home on Germany's Rhine River, is currently the winery's visitor's center. It has an elaborate entrance bay with a tall, steeply pitched hipped roof; stone, stucco, and half-timbered siding; fine interior woodwork; and stained-glass windows. Architectural Resources Group supervised its restoration.

Construction of the large three-story winery began in 1876. It is set against a hillside where caves have been tunneled into the rock. The building is stone on the first and second floors, and wood on the third. It features a hipped roof with a tall cupola, arched windows and doors, and quoins at the corners.

30. Greystone/Christian Brothers Winery, 1889
2555 North Main Street

Percy & Hamilton, architect

Hamden W. McIntyre, consultant

This is the most impressive of the nineteenth-century winery buildings in the Napa Valley. The huge 440-by-70-foot, three-story building has a picturesque quality enhanced by its rustic stone walls, gabled bays, grand arches, banks of windows, and tower. It is constructed of locally quarried stone reinforced with iron bars and set with Portland Cement mortar; cathedral-like ceilings are supported by iron columns. It was built as a cooperative winery by William Bourn and Everett Wise. From 1950 until the 1990s, it was the Christian Brothers winery; today it is the Culinary Institute of America.

31. Charles Krug Winery, founded 1858
2800 North Main Street

Charles Krug was a pioneer winemaker credited with bringing the latest techniques to the

32. La Ronde Winery (now Markham Vineyards), 1879
2812 St. Helena Highway North

The façade of this historic two-story stone winery with a gabled parapet is flanked by newer buildings that form a U-shaped composition. The original owner, Jean Laurent, is believed to have designed the 1879 stone building.

33. Fritz Rosenbaum House (now St. Clement Vineyards), 1879
2867 St. Helena Highway North

Albert Schröpfer, architect

The large Victorian, with its prominent square corner tower, stands proudly on the west side of the highway. It was built for a San Francisco glass merchant who began making wine in 1879.

34. Ehlers Estate, 1886
3222 Ehlers Lane

Hamden W. McIntyre, architect

The historic stone winery is a straightforward two-story, gable-roofed rectangular building that commands a prominent site.

35. Old Bale Mill, 1846

3369 St. Helena Highway North

This large wood-frame gristmill still has a functioning overshot wheel. It was built for Dr. Edward Bale in 1846 to grind wheat and barley. It was first restored in 1925 by the Native Sons of the Golden West and again rebuilt by California State Parks. It is still grinding corn for visitors as part of the interpretation at Bale Grist Mill State Park.

36. Larkmead Winery, founded 1884

Stone Building, 1906

1091 Larkmead Lane

Wilbur A. Harrison, designer-builder

The first winery on this site was established by Lillian Hitchcock Coit (see Coit Tower, San Francisco) in 1884. This stone winery building was constructed for Felix Salmina by Wilbur A. Harrison in 1906. Behind the stone building is a Craftsman Bungalow with a wide front porch, now used for offices.

37. Schramsburg Vineyards, founded 1862

Peterson Drive, west off St. Helena Highway North

In 1862, German emigrants Jacob and Annie Schram founded the first winery located on a hillside. The oldest build-

ings on the site are the Schrams' 1862 house, an early cave-entrance structure, and an 1880s board-and-batten-sided winery building; later winery buildings are sheathed in unpainted board-and-batten as well. The winery is open to the public, but an appointment is required to tour its extensive hillside caves, where bottles of sparkling wine are impressively stacked by hand. The narrow, curving, tree-shaded road to the winery is lovely.

Pope Valley

Pope Valley and Pope Creek were named after William Julian Pope, the grantee of the 1841 Locoallomi land grant. Pope was a member of the Sylvester Pattie and James Pattie Party (1828), the second overland party of Americans (by way of the Southwest) to enter California. Pope Valley and the towns of Aetna Springs, Middletown, and the Geyers are in the Mayacamas Mountain District, the mountain chain dividing the Russian River from Clear Lake. From 1863 to 1903, Napa County was California's second-largest producer of mercury; the largest mine was the Phoenix Mine in Pope Valley.

38. Aetna Springs, 1880s–1930s

1600 Aetna Springs Road

Albert Farr and J. Francis Ward, architects

This is one of those intriguing places: an architecturally sophisticated complex of rustic buildings that even today seems very remote. The former resort hotel is a deeply wooded oasis that

consists of approximately thirty-two rustic buildings and structures that were built and/or remodeled between the 1880s and 1930s.

It is documented that San Francisco architects Farr and Ward designed the shingled cottages known as Munro, Locust, Frances Marion, and Carline in 1925, and that the overall quality of the resort is the result of remodeling by the same architects around 1930. An arched entry sign, suspended between boulder-stone pillars and topped with pyramidal shingled roofs, sets the tone for the rustic retreat. Visible behind the entrance is the dining hall, a gable-roofed building constructed in 1905. The stone walls along the road were in place by 1886. After the resort closed in 1972, it served as a religious educational center but has been unused since the mid-1990s. The resort's golf course, built in the early 1890s, remains open to the public. The complex is listed on the National Register of Historic Places.

39. Hubcap Ranch, 1955–1985

6654 Pope Valley Road

Emanuele "Litto" Damonte, designer

What a treat to come across this exuberant and extensive example of roadside folk art. It is constructed from hubcaps and other discarded objects and was assembled over a thirty-year period by Emanuele Damonte (1896–1985) who called himself "Litto, the Pope Valley Hubcap King." It was designated a California Registered Landmark in 1987.

38

4 • Calistoga

Calistoga was also part of Dr. Edward Bale's land grant. By 1845, there were a few settlers, including some members of the Grisby-Ide immigrant party. In 1850, a 500-acre parcel, which included the hot springs, was subdivided; a school was built in 1857.

Pioneer entrepreneur Sam Brannan (1809–1889) purchased the hot springs property in 1857 and began constructing a resort in 1860. Brannan's Hot Springs Resort included numerous cottages, a trotting park, swimming pool, gardens, and a vineyard; the core of the resort was laid out around a small hill called Mt. Lincoln. Buildings that remain from the Brannan era, which ended in 1875, include three resort cottages, several houses, and the 1868 railroad station.

The railroad that Brannan promoted and partially financed was begun in 1864, but it did not reach Calistoga until 1868; it continued to run until 1929 as a Southern Pacific line. The San Francisco, Napa & Calistoga electric train line, completed to Calistoga in 1911, operated until 1938.

Calistoga's commercial/retail district is located between the 1200 and 1400 blocks of Lincoln Avenue. Lined with one- and two-story buildings, these blocks retain the small-scaled rhythm of a late-nineteenth-century main street. Although commercial buildings were constructed as early as the late 1860s, fires in 1888, 1901, and 1907 destroyed most of them; the current buildings generally date from the late 1880s to the 1930s.

1. Calistoga Inn, 1920
1250 Lincoln Avenue

Located next to the Napa River, the two-story, somewhat Mission Revival–style building marks the entrance to downtown.

2. 1300 Block of Lincoln Avenue

The center of downtown Calistoga is the 1300 block of Lincoln. The Odd Fellows Hall (1887) at 1343 Lincoln is constructed of brick; the cornice is decorated with a vine-and-flower motif and there is molded brick above segmental second-floor windows. The former C. A. Stevens Bank (1890) [2] at 1339 Lincoln is exposed rustic gray stone with arched openings and a gabled parapet.

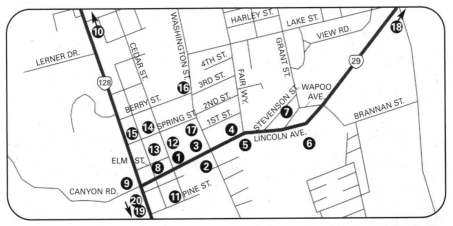

balcony, flanked by bays with gabled parapets and tiled shed-roofed canopies.

5. Napa Valley Railroad, Calistoga Depot, 1868
1458 Lincoln Avenue

This is not only the oldest surviving building on the main street, but one of the oldest train stations in California. It is a tall rectangular building with a gable roof, wide overhanging eaves with simple brackets, horizontal wood siding, and quoins at the corners. The passenger waiting room faces Lincoln Avenue, with a baggage and freight room behind. The interior has been extensively remodeled for retail space.

6. Former Calistoga Hot Springs Resort,
established 1860s
1712 Lincoln Avenue

The present Indian Springs Resort is located on a portion of Sam Brannan's 1860s Calistoga Hot Springs Resort. After Brannan lost his property in 1875, the resort was leased to various managers. The Mission Revival–style main building that stands today probably was built in the 1920s by Jacques Pacheteau. The small hill, where the swimming pool is located, is Mt. Lincoln, the center of Brannan's resort. The palm trees date from Brannan's time, but none of the original Brannan buildings remain on this site.

7. Sam Brannan Cottage,
circa 1866
109 Wapoo Avenue

Wapoo Avenue is one section of the octagon-shaped plan of Sam Brannan's Calistoga Hot Springs Resort. Once there were approximately twenty-five cottages, and of

The Masonic Hall (1902) at 1334 Lincoln has been covered with stucco. 1350 and 1360 Lincoln (1908–1910) are wood-frame buildings covered with stucco siding and distinctive curved parapets. The stone building at 1363 Lincoln was constructed in 1888.

The former Bank of Calistoga (1922; James A. Narbett, architect) at 1373 Lincoln is a Classic bank building of reinforced concrete, notable for tall pilasters separating its double-height windows.

The Armstrong Building (1902) at 1403–1407 Lincoln is a brick-sided building with a double façade and two false-fronts, which have an engaged brick pattern under the cornice, and a small central pediment.

Calistoga's City Hall (1902) at 1232 Washington Street is a modest two-story frame building with a false-front parapet and open bell tower. Along with the public-safety building and the Sharpsteen Museum across the street, this is an informal civic center.

3. Sharpsteen Museum
1311 Washington Street

One of Sam Brannan's Calistoga Hot Springs Cottages was moved to this location, and a new building was added to house the Sharpsteen Museum, which displays the history of the area in several dioramas and historic photos. The cottage has a hipped roof and recessed full-width porch with arched openings edged with scallops; the same scallop design is used for cresting on the roof and above the eave line.

4. Mount View Hotel, 1919
1457 Lincoln Avenue

Perseo Righetti, architect

The two-story Mission Revival–style hotel is a prominent feature of Lincoln Avenue. The building has a central entrance bay with a recessed entry and second-story

the three that remain, this is the only one on its original site; it is one of the larger cottages that has a covered porch with arched openings and a decorated gable end.

At the corner of Wapoo Avenue and Grant Street (203 Wapoo) is the Sam Brannan Store that dates from the early 1860s. The small one-story frame structure has its original false-front parapet with central pediment and brackets; some windows appear original but a number of small additions and alterations over time have given the building a handmade patchwork quality.

Residential

Located primarily to the west of downtown, the majority of houses are small nineteenth- and early-twentieth-century vernacular cottages with a few notable exceptions. Scattered throughout the district are the town's churches.

8. Ayer House, circa 1873
1139 Lincoln Avenue

Just before entering downtown, a few historic houses remain on Lincoln. This two-story Italianate

was moved from across the street in 1978 to avoid demolition.

9. Ingalls House, circa 1910
1213 Foothill Boulevard

The large Craftsman overlooks downtown from a prominent hillside location. Chaunce E. Ingalls worked for the Hercules Powder Company, improving dynamite.

10. The Oaks, circa 1920
2412 Foothill Boulevard

For Calistoga, this is a rare Tudor Revival. It has two-story bays with gambrel roofs on either side of a central entry bay. Small-paned windows, stucco siding, and contrasting wood trim enhance a picturesque image.

11. Kortum House, circa 1875
1004 Cedar Street

This vernacular Greek Revival house is only one example of the many early cottages of this type in Calistoga.

12. Augustus C. Palmer House, 1874
1300 Cedar Street

The Palmer House is contemporary with the stone Francis House at 1403 Myrtle Street, but here the Second Empire style is wood.

13. Brannan's Folly, 1862
1311 Cedar Street

The tiny cottage, one of Brannan's original resort cabins, was moved to this location in 1876. Its decorative scalloped trim is distinctive.

14. George Lillie House, circa 1870
1413 Cedar Street

Here is a wonderful example of a vernacular two-story Gothic Revival with the characteristic steep central gable. George Lillie's father, Leonard G. Lillie, built the overshot wheel for the Bale Mill; in 1852, he was the contractor for White Sulphur Springs Resort in St. Helena.

15. James H. Francis House, 1886
1403 Myrtle Street

Once Calistoga's most impressive house, the stone Italianate, with a mansard roof, arched windows, and quoins, is currently a ruin, but the excellent quality of the stonework is evident. Between 1918 and 1964, it served as Calistoga's hospital.

16. Holy Assumption Convent and Orthodox Church, circa 1945
1519 Washington Street

Reminiscent of the Orthodox chapel at Fort Ross, it has two faceted but different-sized cupolas with round windows on the spine of its tall hipped and gabled roof. Its unpainted vertical-plank siding blends with a lush garden overlooking the Napa River. A second Russian Orthodox Church, built in 1960, is located at 1421 Cedar and Berry Streets.

17. Frank House, 1887
1317 Washington Street

A. D. Rogers, builder

The Queen Anne has carved brackets with drop pendants over the front bay window. It now houses offices of the Sharpsteen Museum Foundation.

North (unmapped)

18. Chateau Montelena, founded 1882
1429 Tubbs Lane

Hamden W. McIntyre, architect

The winery was founded by Alfred Tubbs and called "Hillcrest." The stone winery building was constructed in 1888. Much of the winery is carved into the hillside; walls are said to be twelve-feet thick, and it sports turrets and battlements. In 1960, picturesque Jade Lake was created at the foot of the hill; a Japanese-style bridge leads to a small island where a Japanese-style pavilion stands.

South (unmapped)

19. Sterling Winery, 1973
1111 Dunaweal Lane

Martin Waterfield, architect

Set on an imposing solitary hilltop and approached via an aerial tramway, this stark-white Mediterranean/Moorish–looking edifice was the first prominent modern-style winery built in the Napa Valley and caused quite a splash at the time; over the years, trees and bushes have diminished the stark effect. There is a fee to take the tram lift to the winery.

20. Clos Pegase Winery, 1987
1060 Dunaweal Lane

Michael Graves, architect

The winery, designed to be a "temple to wine and art," is an interpretation of Classicism in ochre and burnt sienna, with a spare desert feeling. The choice of architect was the result of a competition sponsored by the San Francisco Museum of Modern Art; from ninety-six entrants, Michael Graves was chosen the winner. The large one- and two-story complex, located on a flat valley site, includes areas for winemaking and storage, a sculpture garden, a gallery, and, naturally, a tasting bar surrounding a courtyard.

VIII
Sonoma County

Marianne Rapalus Hurley, author & photographer (1–10)
Susan Dinkelspiel Cerny, co-author & photographer (10)

Sonoma County, thirty-five miles north of the Golden Gate Bridge, has rural scenic valleys, rich agricultural lands, redwood forests, a sizeable meandering river, fifty miles of rugged coastline, wineries, suburban cities, small picturesque towns, and rural homesteads. Nationally known residents have included horticulturist Luther Burbank, author Jack London, and cartoonist Charles Schulz.

The county extends from the Pacific Ocean to the Mayacamas Range bordering Napa County, and north from the Marin County boundary along San Antonio Creek to Cloverdale. Santa Rosa, the county seat, and the major population centers flank Highway 101, Sonoma's only freeway that was built parallel to both the Redwood Highway (the main artery from 1915 to 1957) and the historic railroad tracks.

The San Francisco & North Pacific Railroad, the first Sonoma County railroad, began operating in 1870. It met the ferries from San Francisco just south of Petaluma, with a line that stretched north eventually to Cloverdale. In 1875, a narrow gauge, the North Pacific Coast Railroad, linked Sausalito and the coastal communities along Tomales Bay. Farther east, the Sonoma Valley Railroad began operation in 1879. It was not until 1914, after most of the small lines had merged, that the Northwestern Pacific Railroad operated from Sausalito to Eureka in Humboldt County. The tracks remain although passenger service ceased in the 1950s, and the last freight trains ran until the 1990s.

European settlement began on the coast with the short-lived settlement at Fort Ross (1812–1841). With concern over the Russian presence, the Sonoma Mission was founded inland in 1823. After secularization, General Mariano Guadalupe Vallejo established the Pueblo de Sonoma in 1835, the first town in the county. For his services, Vallejo received a huge land grant that extended from Petaluma to Solano County.

During the Mexican era, adobe was the primary construction material, following Hispanic traditions while incorporating some Euro-American features. After 1850, both high-style and vernacular buildings followed regional and national trends, with wood commonly used, but later builders also used local stone and brick.

After statehood, logging along the coastal hills, cattle and dairy ranching, potato

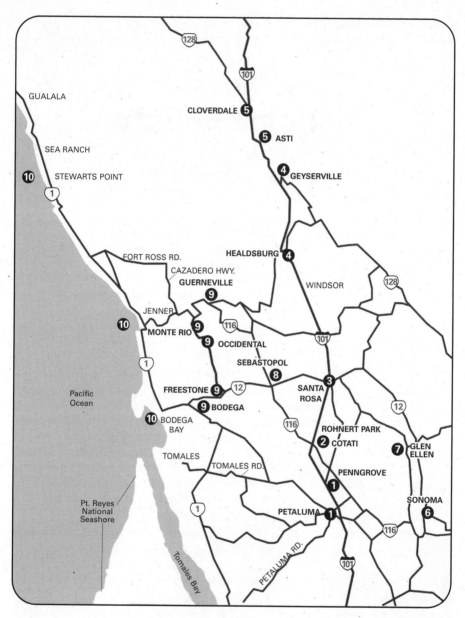

VIII • Sonoma County

farming, and viticulture supported the sparsely settled county. During the first half of the twentieth century, the poultry industry, fruit and fruit processing, and hops production enjoyed a brief but profitable time.

The county has doubled in population to 467,000 since 1980. Today, wineries and vineyards have replaced many of the ranches, farms, and fruit orchards. With the demand for housing and services, most poultry farms, apple orchards, and many dairy operations have relocated to the Central Valley or have closed. The Russian River area still caters to vacationers but on a smaller scale. Along the freeway, the cities continue to expand with subdivisions, business parks, and strip-mall shopping centers.

VIII • SONOMA COUNTY

Mission San Francisco Solano de Sonoma (Sonoma Mission)

1 · Petaluma · Penngrove

Petaluma

Petaluma, located at the head of navigation on the Petaluma River, began as a hunting camp but soon prospered as a shipping point to San Francisco for agricultural, poultry, and dairy products. A large grain elevator still dominates the skyline, a reminder of the importance that agriculture had played in the town's history since its incorporation in 1858.

By the 1880s, the downtown boasted ornate cast-iron and brick commercial buildings and industrial warehouses and factories along the river. Gracious residential neighborhoods were built west of downtown. Despite the loss of some important historic buildings—such as City Hall (1887; Newsom Brothers, architects), demolished in 1955 for a parking lot—Petaluma retains excellent examples from its past.

Petaluma became a major center of the poultry industry after the invention of the Petaluma Incubator in 1879. Later marketing claimed Petaluma to be the "Egg Basket of the World." After World War II, the poultry industry went into decline with the loss of a major poultry cooperative. Concurrent with this, new residential suburban subdivisions sprouted east of the freeway. Rampant growth in 1975 pushed the population to 30,000 and precipitated a community protest. The courts upheld "The Petaluma Plan," which limited growth to 500 units for a five-year period. Today the population is 55,000.

Petaluma's most prolific architect was Brainerd Jones (1869–1945), who designed nearly 75 percent of the historic downtown buildings. Jones grew up in Petaluma, worked for McDougall Brothers in San Francisco, and started his own practice in 1900. Other Bay Area architects who did work here include Julia Morgan, Albert Farr, and Ernest Coxhead.

1. Petaluma Adobe, 1836
*Adobe and
Casa Grande Roads*

General Mariano Vallejo built this U-shaped two-story adobe for his 66,000-acre ranch. A wood-shingle roof extends over the two-story porch that wraps around the entire building. In the Hispanic style, the building is one room wide, each room opening to the porch on the courtyard side. It became a state park in 1951.

2. Petaluma Community Center, 1988
320 North McDowell Boulevard

Roland Miller Associates, architect

This complex, which is constructed of textured and colored concrete block with a variety of cladding, has striking pyramidal roof forms, a colonnade, and a tower with an open framework.

3. Martin Ranch, 1908
1197 Washington Street

Brainerd Jones, architect

The stately shingled Craftsman is notable for the pergola that covers the front porch and for the prominent gabled dormers. The ranch house and tank house were part of a small family farm on what used to be the outskirts of town.

4. Old East Petaluma

The district includes vernacular cottages and former industrial buildings and factories near the railroad tracks and the river.

4a. Sunset Line and Twine Building, 1892
450 Jefferson Street

Charles I. Havens, architect

This distinctive and unique (for the West) brick textile mill with two prominent stair towers was built originally to manufacture silk, but it was adapted in 1940 for a cordage factory. The addition to the south is by Brainerd Jones (1906).

4b. 421 Washington Street, circa 1870

This early little-altered vernacular Gothic Revival house has a decorative balustrade above a full-width front porch.

4c. Western Refrigerating Company Building, 1898
East D and Lakeville Streets

This brick warehouse housed the Burdell Creamery, an egg-shipping depot, and a cold-storage plant where electricity for the town was first generated around 1900.

4d. Petaluma Passenger and Baggage Depots, 1914
East Washington and Lakeville Streets

D. J. Patterson, architect

This Mission Revival station is notable for its arcade, shaped parapets, and quatrefoil vents with decorative grillwork; the waiting room still has its original fireplace.

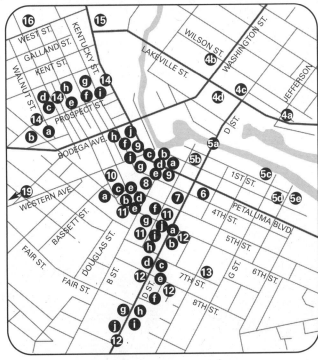

1 • Petaluma

5. Warehouse District

The area between the Petaluma River and Petaluma Boulevard once bustled with commercial activity. Metal warehouses, railroad tracks along First Street, and turn-of-the-century cottages create a distinctive neighborhood that reflects the area's past. Recent changes include a five-story parking garage (2005; Chong & Partners, architects) and the demolition of riverside warehouses.

5a. D Street Bridge, 1933
D Street at First Street

L. H. Nishkian, engineer

San Francisco Bridge Co., builder

This single-leaf steel bascule bridge allows large boats access into the turning basin adjacent to downtown.

5b. Petaluma Fire Station, 1938
198 D Street

Brainerd Jones, architect

PWA Moderne in its styling and detailing, the tower adds a sophisticated feature that for years was a visible point of reference for the neighborhood.

5c. First Street Warehouses, circa 1925

These buildings line the river, with their gable ends creating a distinctive pattern along the banks.

5d. 519 Second Street, 1928

This house is a former hatchery in brick, with a Mission Revival curved parapet.

5e. Foundry Wharf Business Park, 1987
625 Second Street

Richard Strauss, architect

An old foundry was incorporated into a complex of new commercial buildings clustered along the river.

6. Walnut Park, circa 1900
Fourth and D Streets

The Ladies Improvement Club planted this park around 1900; the bandstand was added in 1927, and the Moderne comfort station (Brainerd Jones, architect) in 1941. The large Italianate house (1871) across the street at **218 Fourth Street** retains its carriage house, iron fence, and tank house.

7. Post Office, 1932
120 Fourth Street

James Wetmore, architect

Five tall arched windows give this Mediterranean Revival a striking façade.

8. Petaluma Historical Museum, 1904
20 Fourth Street

Brainerd Jones, architect

The richly embellished Classic Revival former library has a temple-front portico where "Free Public Library" is proudly displayed. Built of buff-colored brick and locally quarried sandstone, the interior glows with varnished wood and a stained-glass dome.

9. Downtown Historic District

Particularly noteworthy is the ornate cast iron used in the storefronts and elevations on the south side of Western Avenue between Petaluma Boulevard and Kentucky Street.

9a. 13 Petaluma Boulevard South, 1917, 1923

Brainerd Jones, architect

This is a Mission Revival former automobile dealership with a tile base and shaped parapet.

9b. 6 Petaluma Boulevard, circa 1860s

Thomas Bayless, builder

This former mill complex has basalt-stone walls facing B Street.

9c. 22–34 Petaluma Boulevard North, 1920

Brainerd Jones, architect

The former Post Office, built of brick and glazed terra-cotta, curves to follow the alignment of the street.

9d. McNear Buildings, 1886, 1911
23 Petaluma Boulevard North

This 1886 iron front (O'Connell & Lewis Iron Foundry, San Francisco) is a delicate composition of closely spaced arched windows with ornamental heads used as keystones. The 1911 brick building (Brainerd Jones, architect) has simple classical detail; the Mystic Theater continues as a venue for live performances.

9e. Masonic Building, 1882
49 Petaluma Boulevard North

William Schrof, architect

The Seth Thomas clock on the corner tower of the Italianate Masonic Building still chimes. The façade is brick with a cast-iron framework.

9f. 101 Petaluma Boulevard, 1926

Hyman & Appleton, architects

This elegant Classic bank building is clad in terra-cotta with many decorative details, including open-winged eagles flanking the flagpole.

9g. 19 Western Avenue, 1885

John Curtis, architect

The iron-front Italianate Mutual Relief Building (O'Connnell & Lewis Iron Foundry, San Francisco) has an elaborate central bay with complex layers of ornament, including freestanding columns painted in faux marble. Across the street, **10 Western Avenue** (1910; Brainerd Jones, architect) is the first steel-framed commercial building in town.

9h. 145 Kentucky Street, 1870, 1901

Brainerd Jones, architect (1901)

S. H. Williams & Sons, builders (1870)

This Italianate Opera House building has cast-iron pilasters on the first floor and a painted pressed-metal façade on the second.

9i. 205 Kentucky Street, 1924

Frederick Whitton, architect

The five-story steel-and-concrete Hotel Petaluma is entered through a doorway framed by a molded Spanish Revival design. Across the street is **161 Kentucky Street** (1899), a commercial building with a projecting corner tower and tall transom windows of opalescent glass.

9j. 199 Petaluma Boulevard North, 1925–1926

H. H. Winner Co., architect

Prominently located on a busy corner, the Renaissance Revival former bank building is clad in terra-cotta and has a curved corner with a tall arched entry.

10. Saint Vincent de Paul Church, 1928

Liberty and Howard Streets

Leo J. Devlin, architect

This is a majestic Romanesque Revival of reinforced concrete with two prominent tile-domed bell towers. The stained-glass windows came from Munich, the marble altar from Italy.

11. "A" Street Historic District

This locally designated district exhibits a range of residences and institutional buildings dating from circa 1858 to the first half of the twentieth century.

11a. 15 Howard Street, 1903

Here is a late Queen Anne with a short corner tower.

11b. 423 A Street, 1908

Brainerd Jones, architect

The large shingled Craftsman has grouped exposed beam ends and a redwood paneled sunporch.

11c. 11 Fifth Street, 1911

Brainerd Jones, architect

This former school is a Classic symmetrical design with a modified temple front-entry portico.

11d. 15 Fifth Street, 1901

Brainerd Jones, architect

Gothic and Romanesque Revival characteristics are expressed in this vernacular church with a corner tower. Note trefoil pattern for vents and eave detail.

11e. Women's Club, 1913

518 B Street

Brainerd Jones, architect

Wide intersecting gable roofs have deep open eaves and simple square brackets; two tiers of grouped casement windows under the gable suggest both Craftsman and Prairie style for this Progressive Era women's clubhouse.

11f. Saint John's Episcopal Church, 1890

40 Fifth Street

Ernest Coxhead, architect

This is one of Coxhead's most successful Shingle-style churches. On both the exterior and interior, Coxhead manipulated classical and medieval elements. Note the entrance surround with Ionic columns and a fanciful pediment.

11g. 40 Sixth Street, circa 1858

A very early vernacular front-gable house has clapboard siding, six-over-six windows, and side-lights with a transom.

11h. 617 C Street, 1910

Julia Morgan, architect

Here is a Shingle-style house with a steeply sloping roof and shallow paneled projecting bay.

11i. 609 C Street, 1913

Brainerd Jones, architect

The shingled house has a symmetrical façade with a recessed entry under a projecting second-story bay.

11j. 100 Sixth Street, 1901

Albert Farr, architect

An unusual asymmetrical inter-pretation of Colonial Revival has rounded pediments.

12. D Street Neighborhood

D Street became the avenue of choice for those who benefited from Petaluma's prosperity between the 1870s and 1940s.

12a. 600 D Street, 1924
Albert Farr, architect

This elegant Mediterranean Revival has a symmetrical façade with a recessed entry surrounded by shallow molded stucco decoration.

12b. 625 D Street, 1929

Brainerd Jones, architect

Sheathed in brick, the graceful arcade gives this design a strong Renaissance Revival flair.

12c. 707 D Street, 1911

Julia Morgan, architect

The simplicity of this remarkable house predates Morgan's 1917

College Avenue Presbyterian Church in Oakland, which has similar elements such as the projecting front gable and simple half-timbering.

12d. 758 D Street, 1890

Walter Cuthbertson, architect

This grand Queen Anne with massive intersecting gabled roofs and a corner turret is covered with fishscale shingles.

12e. 201 Eighth Street, 1929

Albert Farr, architect

This Spanish Colonial Revival has thick textured stucco walls, plank shutters, and a second-story recessed porch.

12f. 15 Brown Court, 1925

Julia Morgan, architect

This shingled Colonial Revival is marked with a classic entrance surround.

12g. 900 D Street, 1930

Don Uhl, architect

This gracious Spanish Revival house takes full advantage of its corner lot with a prominent tower and arched entry.

12h. 901 D Street, 1902

Brainerd Jones, architect

Two colossal Ionic columns support this Colonial Revival's full-width two-story porch.

12i. 999 D Street, 1942

Mario Corbett, architect

This mid-century Modern has a shallow roof with deep overhang-ing eaves, continuous bands of windows, and strong horizontal lines.

12j. 1000 D Street, 1929

Warren Perry, architect

This is a shingled Colonial Revival with an expressed arched entry and an elegant swag frieze.

13. Former Must Hatch Incubator Co., 1926
401 Seventh Street
Brainerd Jones, architect

The importance of Petaluma's poultry business is evident in this elegant Renaissance Revival brick hatchery complex, once the largest in the world.

14. Oak Hill–Brewster Historic District

This local district is named for Oak Hill Park, an early city cemetery. Primarily residential, the houses range from early vernacular to high Victorian, Craftsman, and Period Revivals.

14a. Saint Vincent de Paul School, 1888
Howard Street at Union Street
Thomas J. Welsh, architect

St. Vincent's Academy, the oldest building on the campus, retains some of its former Italianate character, especially its elaborate covered front porch and its segmented paired windows. Across the schoolyard, the Spanish Revival grammar school was designed by Arnold Constable in 1937. The brick convent along Prospect Street was designed by John J. Foley and built in 1916.

14b. 245 Howard Street, circa 1870

Here is an early Greek Revival/Italianate with clapboard siding, carved brackets, and full-width porch.

14c. 301 Keokuk Street, circa 1895

Samuel Rodd, builder

This is a typical Queen Anne with gable-end decorative work and a variety of cut shingles.

14d. 319 Keokuk Street, 1912

Brainerd Jones, architect

This is Shingle style with a steep gable enveloping one and a half stories, a design often favored by Jones for many of his Petaluma houses.

14e. 226 Liberty Street, 1902

Brainerd Jones, architect

This Queen Anne with a tall tower was built for L. C. Byce, inventor of the chicken incubator.

14f. 200 Prospect Street, 1892

Samuel Rodd, builder

This commanding Queen Anne has a rounded three-story corner tower, a hipped roof, and gabled bays.

14g. 331 Keller Street, 1927

Brainerd Jones, architect

Formerly a school, this buff-brick building has a shallow portico supported by four octagonal columns decorated with shallow relief.

14h. 100 Prospect Street, 1885

Samuel and Joseph C. Newsom, architects

A straightforward house with a front-facing gable has a variety of siding material and frieze panels.

14i. 14 Martha Street, 1929

Julia Morgan, architect

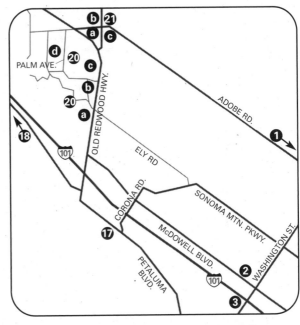

1 • Penngrove

Here is a Colonial Revival that uses gables and roof dormers as major features.

15. Poehlmann Hatchery, 1927

620 Petaluma Boulevard North

The distinctive brick building, with an emblem in the parapet displaying the date of construction, housed a prosperous hatchery until 1970.

16. A. Agius House, 1937

210 West Street

Julia Morgan, architect

Built on what was once the edge of town, this Mediterranean Revival has a recessed central balcony.

17. Bowles Estate, circa 1870

3175 Petaluma Boulevard North

The house, once part of a 200-acre farm, was remodeled into a Queen Anne in 1903 with the addition of a circular porch, bay windows, and a turret.

18. Washoe House, circa 1859 (unmapped)

Stony Point Road at Roblar Road

Robert Ayres, builder

The simple vernacular-style roadhouse with full-width front porch continues to provide meals for travelers between Petaluma and Santa Rosa.

19. Octagon House, circa 1860–1870 (unmapped)

3975 Spring Hill Road, at Purvine

This Italianate octagon house is similar to one illustrated in *The*

American Cottage Builder in 1869. Although it has lost its cupola and front porch, it retains its six-over-six light windows and paneled front door with arched transom.

Penngrove

Five miles north of Petaluma, Penn's Grove was a coach stop between Lakeville and Santa Rosa in 1857. With the arrival of the railroad in 1870, the major industry was basalt quarrying. After 1900, large farms were subdivided into small chicken ranches. Today the area is primarily a residential suburb with scattered remnants of dairies and chicken farms.

20. Old Redwood Highway, North

20a. 5433 Old Redwood Highway, circa 1896

The Denman Creamery complex with its commanding Queen Anne on the hill includes a concrete milking barn, a large cow barn, a silo, and vineyards.

20b. 5701 Old Redwood Highway, 1927

William McCarter, builder

The former brick Penngrove Hatchery with its corner diagonal entry was a pioneer in its use of electricity to run the incubators.

20c. 5865 Old Redwood Highway, 1934

A. Miriam Seeberg, designer

This Spanish Revival, part of the former Garzoli chicken ranch, exhibits a sophisticated design, embedded stones, and arched windows.

20d. 2386 Goodwin Avenue, circa 1880

This is a fairly intact nineteenth-century ranch complex with a stately farmhouse, a large barn, and a tank house.

21. Central Penngrove

A small business district developed where the railroad and Petaluma Hill Road intersect.

21a. 9595 Main Street, 1922
Charles Edwin Perry, architect

Here is a Neoclassic former bank building, with two-story pilasters capped with Ionic capitals.

21b. 10056 Main Street, circa 1910

This flatiron-shaped building was a former hotel.

21c. 365 Adobe Road, 1926

Al Herman, builder

Penngrove Grammar School exhibits an arched central bay. In 1968, additional classrooms were built in the rear.

2 • Cotati • Rohnert Park

Cotati

Dr. Thomas Stokes Page, a physician, purchased Rancho Cotate, a 17,000-acre Spanish land grant, and by 1869, he had established an extensive cattle ranch. In 1893, Page's son Wilfred, as manager of the Cotati Land Company, subdivided the ranch into five- to twenty-acre parcels for family farms, many of which became chicken farms.

Although the railroad serviced Cotati with two stops, it was the opening of the Redwood Highway along Cotati Boulevard in 1915 that spurred the commercial growth of roadside businesses. By the time the freeway bypassed the town in 1955, the town had lost much of its rural character, but it has remained a small community in contrast to the faster-growing Rohnert Park immediately north.

1. Downtown Plaza, 1893
Old Redwood Highway and East Cotati Avenue

Newton Smyth, designer

The Plaza has a hexagonal layout, one of only two in the United States (the other is in Detroit, Michigan). This was the site of Thomas Page's farm, and the streets radiating from the plaza are named for his sons.

2. Cotati Church, 1907
175 Page Street, at Sierra Avenue

This small frame church is embellished with spindle work in the belfry, pointed arched windows, and a pyramidal tower roof with flared eave ends.

3. Cotati City Hall, 1922
201 West Sierra Avenue

Norman R. Coulter, architect

This former school has a recessed entry bay with a distinctive parapet over a Tudor arched opening. It became City Hall in 1971.

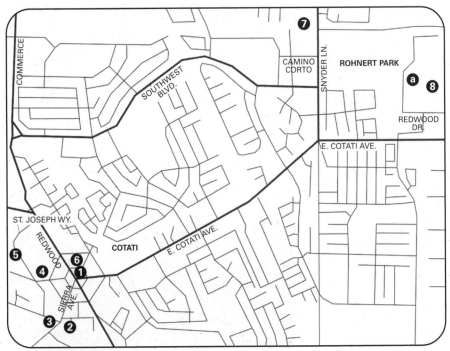

4. Former St. Joseph Catholic Church, 1908
81 West Cotati Avenue

Kearns and Shea, architects

This diminutive Spanish eclectic church is dominated by a central louvered bell tower bisecting a shaped parapet with Baroque-style coping.

5. St. Joseph Catholic Church, 1962
150 St. Joseph Way

Albert Hunter and Shig Iyama, architects

Recalling somewhat Dr. Thomas Page's hexagonal barn, which once occupied this site, the church has a similar spatial and design approach; its central tower is reminiscent of the barn's cupola. The draped roof soars 97 feet, creating an eccentric shape over the trapezoidal footprint. Six stained-glass windows from the 1908 church were reused in the side chapel.

6. Former Cotati Women's Improvement Club, 1910
85 La Plaza

The shingled Craftsman-style building has a central entry portico with heavy wood columns supporting a gabled roof.

Rohnert Park

Rohnert Park, located just north of Cotati, was primarily used for grazing until Waldo Emerson Rohnert bought 2,700 acres to expand his Hollister, California, seed company. The family ran the successful seed farm until 1955, when it was sold to developers for a planned community advertised as a "Country Club for the working class." When Rohnert Park was incorporated in 1962, it had a population of 2,775; today it exceeds 40,000.

7. Dorothy Rohnert Spreckels Performing Arts Center, 1991
5409 Snyder Lane

Glass Architects (Roland/Miller/Associates)

The board-and-batten-sided performing arts center, with two theaters, has a roof composed of oblique angles. The entrance façade is an expansive wall of glass under a separate gabled roof.

Rohnert Park Athletic Center (1987; Roland/Miller/Associates, architects) is next door to the arts center. It has a large landscaped pool and the roof is composed of multiple triangular forms.

8. Sonoma State University, 1966
1801 East Cotati Avenue

John Carl Warnecke, architect

Sonoma State College (now University) was established in 1961; the first campus buildings, **Stevenson and Darwin Halls,** are large concrete rectangular blocks with triple-height projecting piers.

8a. Jean and Charles Schulz Library, 2000
ED2 International, San Francisco, architect

The newest campus building has large colorful windows, open terraces, and a soft stucco exterior. A clock tower dominates the façade, and the building spreads out onto open terraces and patios.

8a

3 · Santa Rosa

Santa Rosa is the largest city in Sonoma County; it is the county's seat of government and its commercial, residential, and cultural center. Once considered the idyllic small town, the city has rebuilt and redefined itself several times since it was established. Rampant growth and urban renewal schemes have irreversibly changed the character of the city. Many of the civic and commercial buildings were replaced in the 1960s, resulting in designs that look inward and withdraw from the streetscape.

In 1837, the first non-native settler, Maria Carillo, built an adobe as part of the Rancho Cabeza de Santa Rosa. By 1854, a formal grid plan was established for what is now the center of downtown. During the nineteenth century and first half of the twentieth, the town's economy depended on the surrounding agricultural area. After the railroad arrived in 1870, the town assumed a major role as the hub of local commerce, replacing the water-based transportation hub in Petaluma.

The 1906 earthquake destroyed much of the downtown but spared most of the residential areas. The years after the earthquake were prosperous: the downtown was rebuilt and a large number of bungalows were constructed around the center of downtown. During the 1920s and 1930s, residential subdivisions were developed east of downtown; by 1940, the population was 12,000. After World War II, speculative houses marched eastward along Highway 12. In 2005, the population reached 155,000.

Urban renewal began shortly after Highway 101 was completed in 1949. The four-lane highway, bisecting the city just east of A Street, resulted in the relocation or demolition of buildings in its path. In 1969, Highway 101 was elevated and converted into a freeway, requiring the removal of more buildings. That same year, another earthquake severely damaged many downtown buildings, which were removed, and Santa Rosa Plaza, a downtown shopping mall, was constructed in that location. Despite this history, Santa Rosa has a good collection of buildings, many of them the work of local designers William F. Herbert, Clarence A. Caulkins, and J. Clarence Felciano.

1. Chapel of Chimes, 1938 (unmapped)
2601 Santa Rosa Avenue

The chapel is attributed to Julia Morgan because it is mentioned in some of Morgan's papers. The exterior is Spanish Revival while the interior is Arts and Crafts with an open-timber ceiling; it has murals by Camille Solon. Lazer, Nusbaum designed the Mausoleum to the south in 1941; a 1952 addition is by Aaron Green.

2. Veterans Memorial Auditorium, 1950
1351 Maple Street

Clarence. A. Caulkins, architect

The entrance bay of this large reinforced-concrete classic Moderne building is notable for its bold rectangular projecting piers and recessed narrow walls of glass topped with large shields.

3. Luther Burbank House and Gardens, circa 1875
200–204 Santa Rosa Avenue

This National Landmark property includes a bracketed barn with a cupola, a farmhouse, and a brick-and-glass greenhouse.

3a. Burbank Gardens Historic District
Santa Rosa and Sonoma Avenues, and Brown Street

Once part of Luther Burbank's property, this local district has a collection of turn-of-the-century cottages and Craftsman bungalows. The Park Apartment Building (circa 1895) at 300 Santa Rosa Avenue is one of the oldest multiunit frame buildings left in Santa Rosa.

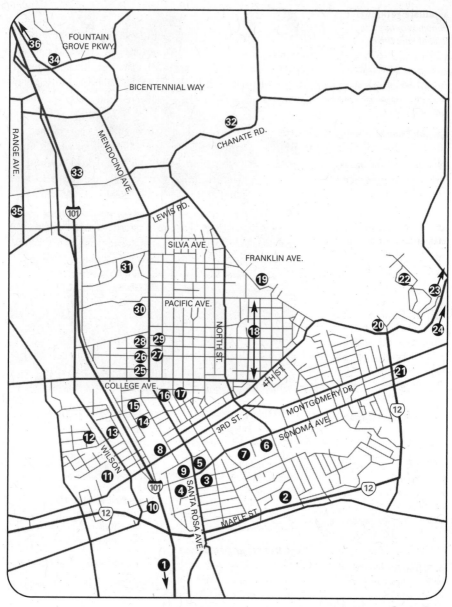

3 • Santa Rosa

4. Julliard Park, 1931
*Sonoma Avenue and
Julliard Park Drive*

This nine-acre city park was
once the Julliard estate; the
formal landscaping, pond,
and stone bridge were installed
with WPA labor.

4a. 488 Sonoma Avenue, 1873

The Gothic Revival church,
built from one redwood tree as
a publicity stunt, was moved to
Julliard Park in 1957.

4b. Luther Burbank Elementary School, 1940
203 South A Street

William F. Herbert, architect

The school incorporates "child-
centered" ideas such as built-in
furniture, activity areas, and
one-story wings with covered
corridors. The Streamline
Moderne styling is expressed
well in the curved corner of
the kindergarten with its own
fenced playground.

8a

5. Santa Rosa City Hall, 1969
100 Santa Rosa Avenue

*DeBrer, Bell & Heglund,
architects*

The clustered buildings are
geometrically arranged and
connected by open corridors
around a sunken courtyard.
The design is best appreciated
in the courtyard.

6. Bolton Residence, 1906
966 Sonoma Avenue

Brainerd Jones, architect

This stately Queen Anne has
a large round corner tower, a
smaller faceted tower, and
a porch that wraps around
two sides.

7. Residence, circa 1920
866 Sonoma Avenue

*Lew Meyer Tract Company,
builder*

This Craftsman, with a window
bay of grouped small-paned casement windows, is notable for its
quartz foundation, chimney, and
large terrazzo porch.

8. Downtown Santa Rosa
*B and E Streets, between
Third and Fifth Streets*

The downtown retains a few
examples of pre–World War II
commercial buildings. A large
shopping mall and undistin-
guished concrete buildings and
parking garages dominate the
streetscape.

8a. 217 Old Courthouse Square, 1906

*John Galen Howard and
J. D. Galloway, architects*

The former Santa Rosa Bank
building has Renaissance Revival
detailing with a rusticated arcade
on the first floor. A tall four-
sided clock tower overlooks
the square.

8b. 601 Fourth Street, 1921

*Styvain Schnaittacher,
architect*

The brick Rosenberg Office
Block was once the tallest building between San Francisco and
Portland. The mezzanine level
has arched windows, rusticated
stucco, and a narrow balcony.

8c. 404–414 Mendocino Avenue, 1907–1908

The Native Sons of the Golden West lodge, a Spanish Colonial Revival, was constructed using a steel frame with brick infill.

8d. 613–617 Fourth Street, 1931

John Fleming, architect

The Art Deco–style Kress Building has terra-cotta zigzag ornament at the cornice, low relief in the panels, and a basketweave pattern of bricks between the piers.

8e. 633 Fourth Street, circa 1907

Hoyt Brothers, builders

A decorative frieze, brick string-courses, and transom windows combine two buildings with one façade. The Classic Revival Doyle Building at **641–647 Fourth Street** (1911; Frank Sullivan, designer) has stone pilasters, modillions, and frieze decoration.

8f. 700 Fourth Street, 1937

Hertzka & Knowles, architects

A model of this Streamline Moderne building, formerly Rosenberg's Department Store, was exhibited at the 1939 Treasure Island World's Fair as an example of future architectural technology.

9. Prince Memorial Greenway, 2000
Santa Rosa Creek

Carlile Macy and RRM Design Group, designers

The restored Santa Rosa Creek features a linear park along the creek that will include pathways into the creek bed.

10. Olive Park Historic District
Orange and Laurel Streets at Olive Street

A locally designated district with good examples of late Queen Anne and Craftsman, this is the remnant of an 1888 development by contractor Thomas J. Ludwig.

11. Railroad Square Historic District
Wilson Street, between West Sixth and West Third Streets

Largely rebuilt after the 1906 earthquake, the brick and basalt-stone commercial and industrial buildings contribute to its character.

11a. Santa Rosa Railroad Station, 1904
Fourth Street at Wilson Street

William Peacock of San Francisco, builder

This basalt-stone Craftsman-style depot weathered the 1906 earthquake and continued to serve passengers until 1958. In 1995, architect Glenn David Matthews directed its rehabilitation.

11b. 24 Fourth Street, 1927

The Spanish Colonial Revival depot for the Petaluma & Santa Rosa Railway served the inter-urban electric line (established in 1904) that carried both freight and passengers.

11c. 100 Fifth Street, 1907
Peter Maroni and Massimo Galeazzi, builders

Constructed of dark gray rough-hewn stone, the three-story hotel is accented with light-colored stone stringcourses between the floors.

11d. 100 Block of Fourth Street

This is the district's main com-mercial block with good exam-ples that include the Jacobs Building (circa 1910) at **115 Fourth Street,** made of clinker brick, and Lee Brothers (1906) at **100 Fourth Street,** which has a metal colonnade.

12. West End Historic District
West Eighth and Donahue Streets

Many Italian emigrant laborers who worked in the mills, canner-ies, quarries, and farms lived in

this area known as "Italian Town." The neighborhood has excellent examples of Folk Victorian cottages and bungalows built between 1888 and 1913 of which **114 West Eighth Street** (circa 1890) is a good example.

12a. DeTurk Round Barn and Winery Building, circa 1880
819, 722 Donahue Street

Thomas J. Ludwig, builder

The round barn was built to exercise DeTurk's racehorse; his winery was the second largest in the state by 1890.

13. Former Lincoln School, 1923
709 Davis Street

William H. Weeks, architect

This Spanish Colonial Revival school is built of reinforced concrete and has interior ramps instead of stairs.

14. Sonoma County Museum, 1910
425 Seventh Street

James Knox Taylor, architect

This Italian Renaissance Revival design was the Santa Rosa Post Office and Federal Building before being moved in 1979. Faced with Indiana limestone, it is notable for its large portico with Corinthian columns.

15. Saint Rose Historic District
Morgan Street and Mendocino Avenue, between Lincoln and Seventh Streets

The city's first preservation district was designated in 1992. Residences range from large Italianate mansions to mid-size Queen Anne houses to Craftsman bungalows.

15a. Former Saint Rose School, 1931
560 Ninth Street

Henry A. Minton, architect

Here is a Spanish Colonial Revival with a central bell tower.

15b. 535 B Street, circa 1868
A. P. Petit, designer

This formal Italianate with a central gabled bay is similar to the Italianate at **537 B Street**, moved here in 1904. Both are impressive.

15c. Saint Rose Catholic Church, 1900
553 B Street

Shea & Shea, architects

This stone-faced Gothic Revival was the first stone building in Santa Rosa that was built with steel cables and a steel belt, enabling it to weather earthquakes. J. Clarence Felciano designed the addition in 1964.

15d. Thurlow Medical Building, 1940
576 B Street

Attributed to Clarence A. Caulkins, this dramatic reinforced-concrete Moderne building has a parabola footprint with the entrance door at the curved corner where it is topped with a large caduceus emblem.

16. Church of the Incarnation, 1873
550 Mendocino Avenue

This simple frame church with Gothic-arched windows is topped with a gabled bell tower. It was enlarged in 1893 and shingled in 1920.

17. Cherry Street Historic District
Cherry Street, between Mendocino Avenue and King Street

Located just north of downtown, this small district is notable for its handsome collection of late-nineteenth-century residences.

17a. James S. Sweet House, 1886
607 Cherry Street

Thomas J. Ludwig, builder

After the 1906 earthquake, the 1886 house was altered with the addition of a wraparound porch with Ionic columns and ornament in the gable ends. Sweet was a published composer, once the town's mayor, and proprietor of Sweet's Business College.

17b. 606 Humboldt Street, circa 1902

This is a late Free Classic Queen Anne with exotic ogee arches, clustered porch columns, and hooked eave brackets.

17c. 801 Cherry Street, 1888

A vernacular Gothic Revival, the former German Methodist Episcopal Church is without its steeple.

17d. 825 Cherry Street, 1888

A large Stick-style house with turned spindles in a cone shape creates a porch frieze that resembles a portcullis.

18. McDonald Historic District
College and Franklin Avenues, between Stewart and Helena Streets

In 1877, Col. Mark L. McDonald subdivided 160 acres of his land. McDonald built the first streetcar system and created the first water company. McDonald Avenue is the center of this elegant residential district lined with impressive homes.

18a. 718 McDonald Avenue, 1910

Brainerd Jones, architect

This beautifully shingled Craftsman with recessed front porch has an extended pergola and paired thick carved brackets under the eaves.

18b. 725 McDonald Avenue, 1931

Russell Guerne DeLappe, architect

A trim Period Revival with a turreted entrance tower, it has colorful glazed tile on the exterior and decorative brickwork on the chimney.

18c. 815 McDonald Avenue, 1878

Thomas J. Ludwig, builder

Elaborately embellished, the Queen Anne has friezes of spindle work over a recessed balcony.

18d. 824 McDonald Avenue, circa 1895

This Queen Anne was owned by Thomas J. Geary, author of the infamous national Chinese Exclusion Act of 1892.

18e. 904 McDonald Avenue, circa 1877

Here is a classic Italianate.

18f. 925 McDonald Avenue, circa 1880

Behind the Classic two-story portico is an older Italianate. **1104 McDonald Avenue** (circa 1877; Thomas J. Ludwig, builder) [18f] is another Italianate with a Classic portico addition.

18g. Mableton, 1869–1878

1015 McDonald Avenue

Mark McDonald, designer

Thomas J. Ludwig, builder

Secluded behind extensive landscaping, the former summer home of developer Mark McDonald (reconstructed after a fire in 1977) has wraparound porches, sawn-edge molding, a fan design in the porch railing,

and gabled dormers set within the tent-like hipped roof.

18h. First Presbyterian Church of Santa Rosa, 1949

1550 Pacific Avenue

Clarence A. Caulkins, architect

Tudor Revival details such as the diamond-window lights, "pegged" large timbers, and rustic half-timbering are well integrated into a Modern design.

19. Town and Country Village, 1948
1415 Town and Country Drive

Hugh Codding, developer

Santa Rosa's first shopping center is a rustic Ranch style with heavy wood posts supporting covered walkways; small, recessed board-and-batten storefronts face the off-street parking. Larger shopping centers followed: Montgomery Village (1950) at Montgomery Drive and Farmers Lane, and Coddingtown Mall (1965) at Cleveland Avenue and Steele Lane.

20. Flamingo Hotel, 1957
*Fourth Street and
Farmers Lane*

Hugh Codding, builder

Similar to one in Las Vegas, a revolving pink flamingo towers over the mid-century Modern design that uses a vocabulary of horizontal flat wall planes of stone and glass.

21. Carrillo Adobe, circa 1837
*Montgomery Drive and
Farmers Lane*

The adobe ruins stand east of St. Eugene's Cathedral (1950; J. Clarence Felciano, architect).

22. Thomas J. Proctor House, 1935–1936
2445 Sunrise Place

*William F. Herbert and
Clarence A. Caulkins,
architects*

Ellis Ahlstrom, builder

Built as the model home for the Proctor Heights tract, this impressive L-shaped Spanish Colonial Revival, perched on a hill, has a faceted tower and an entrance framed with colorful glazed tile.

23. Stonehouse Inn, 1912 (unmapped)
3555 Sonoma Highway

Massimo Galeazzi, builder

The basalt-stone building with a slate roof was constructed as the Rincon Hotel, offering room and board for the immigrant quarry workers. The central archway was once a passageway for carts and autos.

24. Hood Mansion, 1858 (unmapped)
7501 Sonoma Highway

William Hood built this two-story brick Greek Revival house for his bride as their summer home. In 1905, Senator Thomas Kearns of Utah added a second story to the one-story wings.

25. Lumsden Residence, 1901
727 Mendocino Avenue

Brainerd Jones, architect

The late Queen Anne has a prominent corner tower with scalloped belvedere and wrap-around porch.

26. Oates/Comstock Residence, 1905
767 Mendocino Avenue

Brainerd Jones, architect

This Shingle-style house has a deeply recessed front porch tucked under a large gambrel-roofed projecting bay.

27. Rosenberg Residence, 1937
824 Mendocino Avenue

Francis Nielsen, builder

The unusual entry bay of this Spanish Colonial Revival has a tall elaborately shaped parapet, with a shaped arched entrance trimmed with low-relief plaster.

28. St. Luke Evangelical Lutheran Church, 1949
905 Mendocino Avenue

Clarence A. Caulkins, architect

A mid-twentieth-century interpretation of English Gothic Revival, the square bell tower has a modern decorative band rather than traditional pinnacles. The complex includes a school and Family Activity Center (2000; Ken Coker, architect).

29. Wasserman House, 1907
930 Mendocino Avenue

Brainerd Jones, architect

The shingled Craftsman house has a porte cochere under an extended side-facing gable.

30. Santa Rosa High School, 1924
1141 Mendocino Avenue

*William H. Weeks and
William F. Herbert,
architects*

This is an impressive collegiate Gothic Revival with a central bay consisting of three slightly pointed, arched entrance openings and three tall Gothic-type windows above. Architect William Herbert began his career in Santa Rosa as Weeks' supervising architect during construction of the high school.

31. Santa Rosa Junior College, 1927
1501 Mendocino Avenue

*William F. Herbert and
Clarence A. Caulkins,
architects*

William F. Herbert designed Analy, Pioneer, and Garcia Halls; Clarence A. Caulkins designed Tauzer Gymnasium (1930) and Burbank

to this 56-acre park. The Administration Building (1957), the Fiscal Building (1960), Jail and Hall of Justice (1965–1967), and the Social Services Building (1968) all share similar materials (concrete), an emphasis on horizontal lines, and outdoor seating spaces.

34. Fountaingrove Round Barn, circa 1899
Mendocino Avenue and Fountaingrove Parkway

This faceted barn with small paired windows was part of an early California commune, the Brotherhood of the New Life, established here in 1874.

35. Charles M. Schulz Museum, 2002
2301 Hardies Lane

C. David Robinson, architect

The museum honors the work of cartoonist Charles Schulz (1922–2000). It is modest and low-key with an outdoor garden that includes a large labyrinth.

North of Santa Rosa
36. Windsor
(unmapped)

Incorporated in 1992, Windsor was named after the castle in England. Around 1900, the economy was based on hops and prunes. During the Second World War, an army base was built on the current site of the Charles M. Schulz County Airport. A prisoner-of-war camp was located north of town. Today, Windsor is home to a large live-work development built around a new town green.

Auditorium. All are collegiate Gothic Revival in style.

32. Former Sonoma County Hospital, 1936–1937
3325–3333 Chanate Road
John I. Easterly, architect

Built with WPA labor and PWA materials, the entrance of this Spanish Colonial Revival–style

hospital is surrounded by relief plaster ornamentation.

33. Sonoma County Administration Center, 1957
600 Administration Drive
J. Clarence Felciano, architect

The Sonoma County government offices were moved from downtown in the late 1950s

4 • Healdsburg to Geyserville

Healdsburg

In 1857, Harmon Heald laid out the town, setting aside land for a central plaza, school, cemetery, and churches. The town was incorporated ten years later; by 1871, it was served by the Northwestern Pacific Railroad.

From 1880 until 1920, Healdsburg was the center of the wine-producing region in Sonoma County. The agricultural base also included hops and prunes. By 1950, hops were no longer grown, and by the 1970s, the prune orchards had largely disappeared. Today, there are approximately sixty wineries in the Healdsburg area and the picturesque town has a population of 11,500.

1. Healdsburg Memorial Bridge, 1921
Healdsburg Avenue at Front Street

J. C. Lewis, engineer

The 400-foot-long steel-truss bridge crosses the Russian River onto palm-lined Healdsburg Avenue.

2. Healdsburg Railroad Station, 1928
Harmon Street near Fitch Street

Both the passenger and freight depots are stucco-sided Mission Revival examples with hipped roofs and square piers; there is a shaped parapet for the passenger entrance.

A lumber company, wine ware-house buildings, and railroad worker cottages comprise a small district. **444–448 Mason Street** (circa 1900) are among the tiny worker cottages built with a hall-and-parlor plan.

3. Tucker Street residences
Tucker Street retains good examples of middle-class nineteenth-century houses.

3a. 308 Tucker Street, 1871
This is vernacular Gothic Revival constructed in brick instead of the usual wood.

3b. 317 Tucker Street, circa 1865
This hall-and-parlor-plan cottage has clapboard siding and multi-light windows.

3c. 419 Tucker Street, 1895
502 Tucker Street, 1901
James W. Terry, builder

These are both Queen Anne, built by local builder James W. Terry. **502 Tucker [3c]** may be from a Wolfe & McKenzie catalogue.

3d. 411 Tucker Street, 1895
This Queen Anne cottage was built near grade to accommodate John Tucker and his wife, Mary, who were both blind. After

3a

3c

attending the Asylum for the Deaf, Dumb, and Blind (later the California Institute for the Deaf and Blind) in Berkeley, they ran a variety store in downtown Healdsburg from 1874 until 1929.

4. Sarah Cole House, late 1880s
204 Second Street

Framed by trees, the Italianate has paired brackets at the eaves, and paired and hooded segmented windows. The bowed front portico dates from circa 1900.

5. Matheson Street Historic District

This local district contains a range of styles; most have retained a high level of historic and contextual integrity.

5a. 439 Matheson Street, 1920

This building is in the Prairie style.

5b. 438 Matheson Street, 1914
Ed Guillie, builder

Here is an unusual Craftsman.

5c. 423 Matheson Street, 1905
W. H. Chaney, builder

This is a transitional Queen Anne that may also be from a Wolfe & McKenzie catalogue.

5d. 410 Matheson Street, 1921

Here is a stately Italian Renaissance Revival.

5e. 403 Matheson Street, 1895
James W. Terry, builder

This Queen Anne cottage has a corner tower.

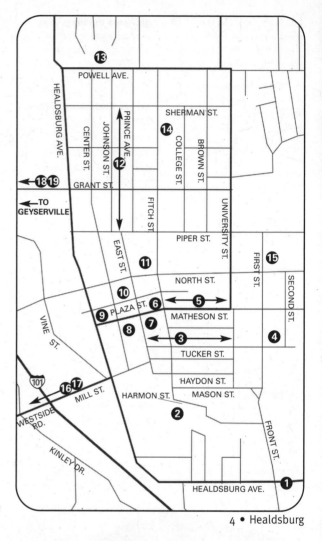

4 • Healdsburg

5f. 326 Matheson Street, 1903

The corner edges are curved on this Shingle-style building.

6. Carnegie Library/ Healdsburg Museum, 1910
221 Matheson Street

Brainerd Jones, architect

This elegant Neoclassic former library has a temple-like front-entry portico with two full-height Doric columns. The words "Public Library" are prominently displayed within the entablature.

7. St. John the Baptist Catholic Church, 1965
208 Matheson Street

Thomas Fruiht, architect

This mid-twentieth-century Modern uses conventions such as intersecting irregular volumes, punched small geometric window openings, full-height stained-glass walls, and a variety of curved copper roof forms.

8. Police Station, 1994
238 Center Street

Roland Miller Associates, architects

The modern police station has a bracketed trellis under the cornice, a large round window above the entrance, and a barrel-vaulted entrance porch.

9. Plaza Park, 1857, ongoing modifications

Like Sonoma, downtown Healdsburg is organized around Plaza Park, a public square that was included in the original plat for the town. Improvements over the years have included a band shell and exotic plantings. Surrounding the square, a number of early-twentieth-century buildings remains.

9a. Odd Fellows Building, 1905–1906
100 Matheson Street

Stanley & Sawyer, builders

The reinforced-concrete façade has understated Classic Revival detailing.

9b. Kruse Building, 1900
112 Matheson Street

A. J. Barnett, architect

Its second-story windows are original.

9c. 320 Healdsburg Avenue, 1920
Frederick H. Meyer, architect

This former bank building is an Italian Renaissance Revival design in brick and terra-cotta.

9d. 110 Plaza Street, 1908
Frank Sullivan, builder

Here is a former bank building that has a Neoclassic temple-front with double-height Ionic columns.

9e. Gobbi Building, circa 1880
318 and 312 Center Street

The Gobbi Building at 312 Center has a cast-iron storefront fabricated at the McCormick Foundry in San Francisco.

9f. Hotel Healdsburg, 2001
25 Matheson Street

David Baker + Partners, architects

This award-winning block-long hotel has projecting bays and a

scale compatible with the historic plaza. Its overhanging metal cornice and balconies accent the stucco walls. Described as "warm minimalism," the interiors were designed by Frost Tsuji.

10. Christian Bible Church, 1892
321 East Street

Simpson & Roberts of Santa Rosa, builders

Queen Anne and Gothic Revival are freely combined; decorative millwork includes spindle work in the belfry and geometric stick work in the gable ends.

11. First Baptist Church, 1908
429 Fitch Street

A large stained-glass window dominates the façade. There is a square corner entrance tower with pairs of arched windows and decorative shingles. The earlier 1868 building is attached to the rear.

12. Johnson Street Historic District

Located north of Plaza Park, Johnson Street is also known as "Nob Hill" for the elegant nineteenth-century homes. Interspersed are examples of earlier vernacular cottages.

12a. 607 Johnson Street, 1885

Here is a combination of Victorian elements that seems closest to Stick style.

12b. 619 Johnson Street, 1885
James W. Terry, builder

This stately Italianate has a symmetrical façade.

12c. 642 Johnson Street, 1900–1903
James W. Terry, builder

9f

Some Neoclassic elements are featured in this Queen Anne.

13. Joseph Priest House, 1871
201 Powell Street

This Folk Victorian has a full-width front porch with a spindle frieze, and was once home to the founder of the local Seventh-Day Adventist Church, Ellen G. White, who was instrumental in establishing the Adventist Healdsburg College in 1882 (later, Pacific Union College in Angwin, Napa County).

14. Frank Passalacqua House, 1914
726 Fitch Street

Brainerd Jones, architect

Marble steps lead to the two-story portico of this imposing Neoclassic mansion. A Palladian window opens to a small balcony above the front door.

15. Healdsburg Grammar School, 1935
400 First Street

John I. Easterly, architect

This is a Mission Revival design that incorporates arcades, a central tower, a clay-tile roof, and a rough white-stucco finish.

16. Madrona Manor, 1881
1001 Westside Road

J. Hooten, architect

Thomas J. Ludwig, builder

Known also as Madrona Knoll Rancho, this 240-acre property is one of the most extravagant estates in Sonoma County. John Alexander Paxton built the luxurious seventeen-room Second Empire mansion with money from mining, banking, and lumber.

17. Hop Kiln Winery, 1905
6050 Westside Road

Angelo Sodini built this large stone hop kiln on his 380-acre ranch. Also known as the Walters Ranch, it was a major producer of hops in the western United States.

18. Stryker Sonoma Winery, 2002
5110 Highway 128

Nielsen-Schuh Architects

The award-winning winery and tasting room has expansive views over the vineyards and hills beyond. Building materials include glass, stone, metal, and innovative horizontal terra-cotta screens that allow a semi-permeable wall surface.

Geyserville

North of Healdsburg, Highway 101 follows the Russian River and Alexander Valley vineyards. In 1847, pioneer William B. Elliott discovered the geysers, and within a few years, a stage road and overnight accom-

modations catered to tourists. Geyserville, founded in 1851, is a delightful remnant from the days when there was a railroad connection, a depot, and several large hotels.

19. Downtown

In the oldest remaining section of the small downtown are several buildings of note. Iron columns support the porch at the brick Odd Fellows Building at **21023 Main Street** (circa 1890). Farther down at **21043 Main Street** (1903) is a former bank building of brick with a large arched transom over the entry. The bank cages reputedly are salvage from the 1915 Panama Pacific Exposition. **21060 Main Street** (circa 1902) is a general store and a community gathering place. **21238 Main Street** (1904) is the Hope-Bosworth House, a Colonial Revival with narrow siding, unusual dormers, and decorative finials. **21253 Main Street** (circa 1880) was a stage stop at one time. This stately Stick-style house with square bay windows and vertical panels is further enhanced by a formal garden.

5 · Asti · Cloverdale

Asti

About five miles south of Cloverdale, San Francisco banker Andrea Sbarboro established Italian Swiss Colony winery in 1881. This was a cooperative venture for Italians who could work, earn shares, and then start their own vineyards. Here was the first "hospitality room" in the state, a precursor to the tasting room. Although the cooperative floundered, the winery was a success for many years.

1. Sbarboro Mansion, 1910
26150 Asti Road

Luigi Mastropasqua, architect

This large residence is visible from the parking lot of the former Italian Swiss Colony winery and is reputedly a replica of a villa in Pompeii.

2. Our Lady of Mount Carmel Church, 1960
26300 Asti Road

Albert Hunter and Shig Iyama, architects

A parabolic-shaped roof covers the large sanctuary space.

Cloverdale

Cloverdale was first settled in the 1850s. It was not only a resort destination but also the center of a fertile agricultural area. After Highway 101 bypassed the town in 1998, the town constructed a downtown beautification project in 2004. On the south side of town, Del Webb Corporation built Clover Springs (2000), a retirement community; its 650 residents constitute nearly one-third of the town's population.

3. Downtown
3a. 117 South Cloverdale Boulevard, 1923

This is the town's first fast-food restaurant.

3b. 119 South Cloverdale Boulevard, 1921

A Craftsman-style building, with a wall of windows on its north side, it served as the town's library until 1978.

3c. 124 North Cloverdale Boulevard, 1936

A WPA Moderne city hall has a tall central bay with piers, steel-sash windows, and rough stucco finish.

3d. 129 North Cloverdale Boulevard, 1907

Here is a Romanesque Revival brick bank building with large arched windows separated by a stringcourse of pressed brick with a delicate scroll pattern.

3e. 215 North Cloverdale Boulevard, 1864

A diminutive brick Gothic Revival house has delicate sawn details in the gable end.

4. United Church of Cloverdale, 1906
439 North Cloverdale Boulevard

Rev. Francis Reid, designer

This Shingle-style church is a good example of its style, further enhanced by river stones that extend up the walls of the bisecting gable-roofed wings. A bell tower with a tall pyramidal roof rises in the L created by the intersecting wings. The stained-glass windows include images of oranges, honoring the town's citrus groves.

5. Pinschower House, 1902
302 North Main Street

Brainerd Jones, architect

An elegant Queen Anne takes full advantage of its corner location with a round corner tower above the porch. During the 1920s, it served as Cloverdale's hospital.

6. Episcopal Church of the Good Shepherd, 1884–1886
120 North Main Street

Mr. Aston, architect

This small vernacular Gothic Revival church has retained its original art-glass windows along the side, but the tall panels were added in 1966. Next door is the vicarage (1905–1906).

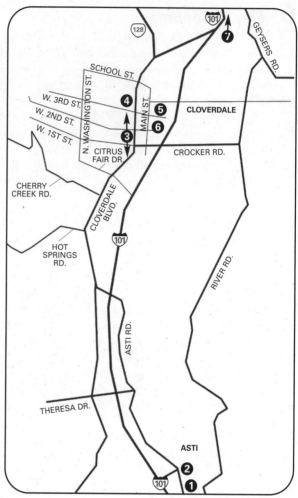

5 • Asti • Cloverdale

7. Preston, 1876
Northeast of Cloverdale

Frederick Rindge, builder

Madame Emily Preston, a charismatic faith healer, came here in 1876 and remained until her death in 1909. Many chronically ill people made the pilgrimage here for treatments, and those who stayed became part of the Free Pilgrims Covenant. In addition to the 1886 church building ("Church of Heaven on Probation") with its unusually large clock tower, there are four residences and a cemetery. To visit the site, contact the Cloverdale Historical Society.

6 · City of Sonoma

Sonoma is unique in the Bay Area because its buildings provide a physical history of California's early development, from Mexican occupation to the overwhelming American presence that culminated in statehood. Downtown is located around Sonoma Plaza, a National Historic Landmark District, which includes many Spanish Colonial adobe buildings that face the plaza.

Settlement began with the establishment of Mission San Francisco Solano in 1823. Ten years later, Mariano Vallejo established a pueblo and presidio for Mexican troops, and soon Sonoma became a major center of business and commerce. Mexico began losing control of California in 1846 with the Bear Flag Revolt, a small uprising centered in Sonoma. The city was incorporated in 1850 and briefly served as the county seat, which was moved later to Santa Rosa.

Shortly after statehood, dairies, fruit farming, wine, and basalt quarrying became important local industries. Resorts sprang up at the sites of natural hot springs north of town. After the train arrived in 1879, Fetters Hot Springs, Boyes Hot Springs, and Aqua Caliente catered to tourists on a large scale.

The mission and pre-statehood buildings illustrate the Hispanic tradition that used adobe brick for simple one-story buildings, fired clay tile for roofs, and an arrangement of rooms opening directly onto a covered porch. The later two-story Monterey-style adobes incorporated some Federal stylistic characteristics such as second-story narrow porches, wood-shake hipped roofs, small-pane windows, interior chimneys, sidelights, and center hall plans with wood floors.

During the past twenty years, Sonoma, with a population of 9,000, has experienced the same development pressures as elsewhere in the Bay Area as illustrated by the town's referendum election over a proposed shopping mall in 1987.

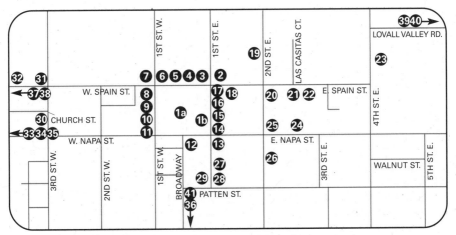

1. Sonoma Plaza, 1835
Central Sonoma

Mariano G. Vallejo, designer

Originally used as a military parade ground, structures began to appear in 1879 with a train depot at the north end. When City Hall was completed, the Women's Club financed most of the plaza's landscaping and fountain in 1909. The 1935 amphitheater was a WPA-funded project. The commercial and retail buildings facing the plaza retain a nearly cohesive nineteenth-century ambience.

1a. Sonoma City Hall, 1906–1908
Adolph C. Lutgens, architect

The beige-gray stone city hall is a proud interpretation of Mission Revival. Identical on all four sides, the elevations have a central triple-arched arcade on the ground floor with a shaped parapet above. There are tile hip-roofed pavilions at each corner and a central bell cupola with arched openings.

1b. Former Carnegie Library, 1913

Located in the Plaza at **453 First Street East,** the former library is built of buff-colored brick with a recessed arched entrance.

1c. Bear Flag Statue, 1914
John MacQuarrie, sculptor

The statue is placed in the northeast quadrant, and romanticizes the raising of the Bear Flag there on June 14, 1846.

2. Mission San Francisco Solano de Sonoma, 1840
114 East Spain Street

Mariano Vallejo built this Spanish Colonial adobe church on the site of the original wood-

frame mission. The former priests' quarters, or *convento* (1824), adjoining the chapel is the oldest building in Sonoma. Simple forms of whitewashed adobe bricks, hand-hewn timbers fastened with leather thongs, and a tiled porch roof supported by hand-hewn logs are examples of traditional Mission-era construction, restored and maintained after the state acquired it in 1906.

3. The Barracks, circa 1836–1840
East Spain Street and First Street East

Mark West, builder

This Monterey-style adobe exhibits a full-width cantilevered porch. This was the headquarters for the Mexican troops under Vallejo. In 1978, California State Parks seismically upgraded and rebuilt the adobe.

4. Toscano Hotel, circa 1855
20 East Spain Street

N. M. Nathanson, builder

By 1886, this vernacular Greek Revival provided lodging for the local Italian quarry laborers. In 1902, a kitchen and dining room were added in the rear.

Immediately adjacent, but set back from the street, is the adobe **Servants Barracks,** all that remains of Mariano Vallejo's 1835 Casa Grande, his elaborate townhouse that burned in 1867.

5. Sonoma Cheese Factory, 1945
2 West Spain Street

Pero D. Canali, architect

This Modern cheese factory, finished with large terra-cotta tiles, has projecting piers and steel-sash windows.

6. Swiss Hotel, circa 1840
18 West Spain Street

Built by Salvador Vallejo, Mariano Vallejo's brother, this two-story Monterey-style adobe became a hotel in the 1880s. Inside is a good collection of historic photographs.

7. Sonoma Hotel, 1879
110 West Spain Street

The first two floors are original; the third floor was added in 1934 by Samuele Sebastiani, who renamed it the Plaza Hotel.

8. Salvador Vallejo's Adobe, circa 1846
415–427 First Street West

This Monterey-style building began as a one-story adobe. In 1852, the second floor, constructed of redwood vertical boards, was added; the Greek Revival gable end was added in 1858. Around the corner at 143 West Spain Street is La Casita (1843), a small adobe.

9. Batto Building, 1912
453–461 First Street West

The classically detailed commercial building is finished with glazed brick for two of the bays and marble for the end that was designed for a bank.

10. Masonic Building, 1909
465 First Street West

The brick building has four shallow arched windows across the façade of the second story that is separated by flat pilasters extending to the parapet. A third-story addition is set back from view.

11. Leese-Fitch Adobe, 1841
487 First Street West

This two-story Monterey-style adobe is a heavily remodeled remnant of the original, which was the first building erected on the west side of the plaza.

12. Sonoma Valley Bank Building, 1891
500 Broadway

Remodeled after the 1906 earthquake, it has full-height flat pilasters on the sides of tall arched windows that flank the corner entrance.

13. Boccoli Building, circa 1896
101 East Napa Street

A handsome row of stone commercial buildings terminates at the corner with the Boccoli Building. Second-story bays use pressed metal that mimics rusticated stonework.

14. Sebastiani Theater, 1934, 1978
476 First Street East

Reid Brothers, architects

Samuele Sebastiani, builder

The Spanish Eclectic–style building with a seventy-two-foot clock tower is the oldest operating movie theater in Sonoma County; it was remodeled extensively in 1978.

15. Grinstead Building, 1911
466 First Street East

This small Spanish Revival commercial building has lovely low-relief plasterwork and a decorative canopy suspended from a molded "California" bear's head.

16. Pinelli Building, 1891
408–414 First Street East

Augostino Pinelli, builder

Here is a basalt-stone commercial building that has arched openings on one side, leaded-glass transoms over the storefront, and a metal cornice.

Behind the Pinelli Building and through a passageway is the **Hooker-Vasquez House,** built around 1855 and moved to this site in 1974. It is a simple, vernacular box with side-facing gables, full-width covered porch, clapboard siding, sidelights at the front door, and small windows under the eaves.

17. Former Sonoma Creamery, 1926–1930
400 First Street East

This is an interesting juxtaposition of a 1920s Mission Revival across the street from the Spanish Colonial Mission.

18. Blue Wing Inn, 1836, 1849
125–139 East Spain Street

The original two-room adobe was transformed into this two-story Monterey-style tavern and hostelry in 1849. It retains a high degree of historic integrity that clearly illustrates the Monterey style.

19. Vella Cheese Factory, 1910
315 Second Street East

Built of rubble from the Schocken Quarry located at the end of the street, the northeast corner of the factory is notable for its quoins and a handsome stone-arched doorway.

20. Ray Adobe, circa 1846–1851
205 East Spain Street

This Monterey-style adobe is distinctive and unusual for its wide hipped roof that extends out several feet beyond the walls to cover the ground-floor porch.

21. Cook/Hope House, circa 1852–1857
245 East Spain Street

This tiny frame house was constructed with wide horizontal redwood boards, small casement windows, and a low full-width front porch with square posts.

22. Trinity Episcopal Church, 1962
275 East Spain Street
Ian MacKinlay, architect

A tall sweeping, pointed gable roof is the main design feature, with art glass in the gable ends set apart with wood mullions.

23. Sebastiani Winery, 1903, 1913
389 Fourth Street East

Several historic quarry-faced stone buildings (the earliest dates from 1903) are part of a complex of more contemporary industrial structures. The 1913 winery building has oak doors carved by Earle Brown in 1967.

Samuele Sebastiani, who worked in the stone quarries before becoming a vintner in 1904, also became a building contractor and developer. Examples of his Craftsman bungalows are nearby at **344** and **356 East Spain Street.**

24. Sonoma Community Center, 1916
276 East Napa Street
Adolph C. Lutgens, architect

The former Sonoma Grammar School is Neoclassic with an impressive temple front entrance with tall Tuscan columns supporting a full pediment; the wings were added in 1926.

25. Ralph Murphy House, 1913
214 East Napa Street
Ralph Murphy, builder

This shingled Craftsman bungalow was the home of Ralph Murphy, a successful carpenter and contractor responsible for many Sonoma buildings. He also built the home at **230 East Napa Street** in 1914.

26. Duhring House, circa 1859; remodeled, 1927–1928
532 Second Street East
Bliss and Faville, architects (1928)
Thomas Church, landscape architect (1927)

This Greek Revival house was part of a three-acre estate called Pine Lodge. The west wing was added in 1890 and the property underwent a major remodeling in 1927–1928.

27. First Baptist Church, circa 1850
542 First Street East

Originally Methodist, this Gothic Revival church was moved in 1868 from nearby Napa Street, when the conical steeple was added to the square bell tower.

28. Julius Poppe House, circa 1858
564 First Street East

This tiny board-and-batten house is a restored mid-nineteenth-century Folk Victorian.

29. Nash Patten Adobe, circa 1847
579 First Street East
H. A. Green, builder

Hand-hewn redwood beams on the covered porch, simple square posts, and multiple door openings on the front are typical of these Hispanic-style adobe residences. It was restored in 1931.

30. Saint Francis Solano Church, 1923
469 Third Street West
Creston H. Jensen, architect

The focal point of this Spanish Revival church is an oversized quatrefoil window over the entrance portico. Large stained-glass clerestory windows light the open-beam interior.

31. Lacryma Montis, 1851 **Sonoma State Historic Park**
Third Street West and West Spain Street

Mariano Vallejo admired Yankee culture, as evidenced by his choice of this Gothic Revival house. The walls behind the wood siding are filled with adobe brick. A wine warehouse known as the chalet, built from precut and numbered timbers, was shipped to his country estate. Vallejo's estate also boasts remnants of his formal landscape, including fountains, the tree-lined Alameda, and olive trees.

32. Vallejo-Haraszthy House, 1878
400 West Spain Street

Vallejo's daughter lived nearby in this Folk Victorian with some simple Italianate elements such as eave brackets and segmented windows.

The following entries are unmapped:

33. Pensar Adobe, 1938
401 Fifth Street West

Frank Pensar, builder

A local high school teacher made his own bricks and constructed this modern adobe during his summer vacations. He added an asphalt emulsion to his soil mix and reinforced the walls with rods and cables.

34. Wells Fargo Bank Building, 1965
West Napa Street and Fifth Street West

John Carl Warnecke, architect

The simplicity of this bank building is a reinterpretation of Mission Revival that uses a broad enveloping gable roof with large tile vents and a shallow-arched arcade.

35. Sassarini Elementary School, 1952
652 Fifth Street West

Mario Ciampi, architect

The concrete-block classroom wings are oriented at right angles to the street, providing some privacy. Each outdoor corridor is sheltered by a roof overhang supported by steel beams, providing visual interest.

36. Sonoma Valley High School, 1922, 1953
2000 Broadway

William H. Weeks, architect

The original central entrance bay was retained when the upper floor and roof were removed and the windows replaced to create a Modern-era school building.

North of Sonoma

37. Sonoma Mission Inn, 1927
18140 Sonoma Highway

Joseph L. Stewart, architect

This Mission Revival design incorporates a pair of bell towers flanking the main entrance, arched openings, and generous wings to each side. The elevated tank is original and used for the hotel's pressurized water system.

38. St. Leo the Great Roman Catholic Church, 1968
601 West Aqua Caliente Road

McSweeney, Schuppel, and Kelley, architects

Resting on a broad wall of stone, the dominant hipped roof emphasizes the centralized plan of this contemporary suburban church.

East of Sonoma

39. Bartholomew Park Winery, 1988
1000 Vineyard Lane, off Seventh Street West and Castle Road

Victor Conforti, architect

Overlooking historic vineyards is a reconstruction of Agoston Haraszthy's villa at Buena Vista, originally built in 1857. It features stepped-back pavilions with prominent full-width porticos.

40. Buena Vista Winery, 1857
18800 Old Winery Road, off Seventh Street East and Lovall Valley Road

Two large stone buildings house a series of 100-foot-long tunnels dug by Chinese laborers for champagne cellars. Buena Vista Winery became the largest wine-growing estate in the world shortly after it was developed by Count Agoston Haraszthy, the father of California viticulture.

South of Sonoma

41. Cornerstone Festival of Gardens, 2004
23570 Arnold Drive, off Broadway

Peter Walker, landscape architect

This open-air gallery on a 9.5-acre site showcases imaginative garden installations and landscape art.

7 · Glen Ellen Area

As Arnold Drive skirts the eastern edge of the Valley of the Moon, it passes the Temelec subdivision, the eastern edge of El Verano, and then continues through the agricultural landscape dotted with farms and vineyards.

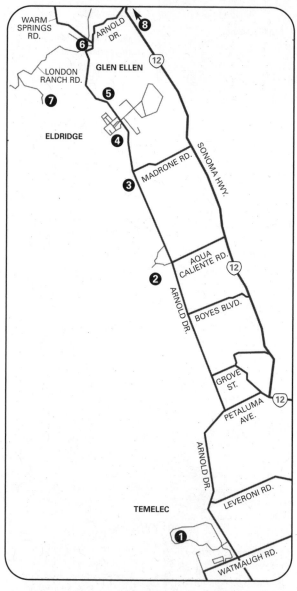

1. Temelec Hall, 1858
220 Temelec Circle, Sonoma

Granville Swift, builder

Built of quarried stone by a member of the Bear Flag Party, this elegant mansion incorporates a Greek Revival colonnade on both the first and second stories, but also uses Italianate elements as seen in its bracketed cornice. Across the street is its historic stone barn.

2. Hanna Boys Center, 1949
17000 Arnold Drive, Sonoma

Mario Ciampi, architect

Ruth Cravath, artist

This Catholic residential treatment facility for boys was an early project for Mario Ciampi, who designed the Modern-style chapel, school, dining hall, cottages, convent, gymnasium, pool, and priests' residence. Under the broken gable of the stone-faced chapel is a large relief sculpture by Ruth Cravath.

3. St. Andrew Presbyterian Church, 1992
16290 Arnold Drive, Sonoma

William Turnbull, architect

The board-and-batten contemporary church successfully uses the agricultural vernacular design idiom of a large barn.

1

4. Main Building at Sonoma Developmental Center, 1908
15000 Arnold Drive, Eldridge

George Sellon, architect

Sited at the end of a dramatic tree-lined approach, the former administration building is a handsome brick Tudor Revival with contrasting stone trim. The complex consists of additional buildings, many of which date from the 1920's, using an English Period Revival–style with steep gabled roofs. Established in 1883 as "The California Home for the Care and Training of Feeble-Minded Children," this was the first such facility in the state.

5. Eldridge Bridge, 1931
Arnold Drive, Eldridge

E. A. Peugh, engineer

This is a Parker-through-truss steel bridge.

Glen Ellen

The small woodsy town of Glen Ellen is best known for its association with Jack London, but many of the town's buildings bear the name of Chauvet, a French baker who arrived in the 1850s. In addition to the ranching and winemaking in the area, Glen Ellen became a tourist destination during the railroad years with two lines servicing the area.

At the intersection of the present Highway 12 and Arnold Drive, Charles Stuart built Glen Oaks ranch in the 1860s. Now part of the Sonoma Land Trust, glimpses of the stone house can be seen from Highway 12 beyond the white stone gateposts.

6. Central Glen Ellen

6a. 13760 Arnold Drive, 1905–1906

This Folk Victorian cottage with pyramidal roof and full-width porch was built for Joshua Chauvet, with bricks fired in Glen Ellen.

6b. 13756 Arnold Drive, 1906

The former Hotel Chauvet is a brick building with segmented arched windows, and is the last of five large hotels that were operating here in the early 1900s.

6c. 13750 Arnold Drive, 1906–1907

The store was originally built of stone, but after the 1906 earth-

quake, the second floor was rebuilt in wood.

Joshua Chauvet's name also appears across the street on the brick building with a full-width porch—the **Jack London Saloon** (1905).

7. Wolf House, 1911
Jack London State Historic Park
2400 London Ranch Road

Albert Farr, architect

Jack London's dream house, Wolf House, burned in 1913 just before he and his wife, Charmian, were scheduled to move in. Rising out of a battered base of stone, the large rambling Arts and Crafts design incorporated unpeeled redwood logs, volcanic stone, and a Spanish tile roof.

After the fire, London continued to live in the wood-framed "Cottage," which was his principal home on his 1860s property called Beauty Ranch, until his death in 1916.

The House of Happy Walls (1919) was designed for Charmian London by the cook's husband, Harry Merritt. She lived in the house until her death in 1955. This stone house resembles the destroyed Wolf House but on a smaller scale. It serves as the Visitors Center for this National Historic Landmark.

8. Kunde Estate Winery, 1990
10155 Sonoma Highway, Kenwood

Del Starrett, architect

The central winery building is an interpretation of an old cattle barn that was once located on the 1876 Kunde family ranch.

8 · Sebastopol

Fifty years ago, Sebastopol was the apple capital of the world with over 20,000 acres of orchards and related packing and processing plants. Today, about 3,000 acres of orchards remain, most along Pleasant Hill Road.

In 1855, Joseph H. P. Morris, the town's founder, created lots and offered them free to anyone starting a business. Soon, farmers moved to the area, growing hops, apples, cherries, grapes, and berries. In 1891, the Northwestern Pacific Railroad extended a branch line to the town, facilitating the movement of agricultural products. The town's economy was further bolstered by the opening of the Petaluma and Santa Rosa Railway in 1904, providing frequent service for both freight and passengers.

The town was incorporated in 1902 when many of the farms were subdivided, leaving a large legacy of cottages from the early 1900s; many neighborhoods in this town of 8,100 retain their turn-of-the-century character.

1. Llano Roadhouse, circa 1849, 1857 (unmapped)
4353 Gravenstein Highway, at Llano Road

Accounts claim the small clapboard one-story extension used redwood from Bodega's first sawmill in its timber construction. The two-story portion was added in 1857 and faced the early stage route.

2. Enmanji Buddhist Temple, 1932–1933
1200 Gravenstein Highway South

This temple was built of hand-carved Japanese wood for the Chicago Century of Progress World's Fair in 1933. It was dismantled and rebuilt here in 1934 for a local congregation of Buddhists. Designated a Historical Ethnic Site in 1988, it was closed during World War II when all local Japanese were interned in Colorado.

3. George Baxter House, 1892
876 Gravenstein Highway

This impressive Queen Anne has a tower at the cross gable and a sweeping curved porch.

4. Chamber of Commerce Building, 1923
6876 Sebastopol Avenue

Here is a nicely detailed, residentially scaled, Mission Revival building with a recessed entry arcade topped with a slender bell tower.

5. Downtown Industrial District

In addition to the apple-processing facilities located along Highway 116 north and south of town, similar buildings are located in this downtown area once known as "Applesauce Alley."

6. Sebastopol Cinemas, 1934
6868 McKinley Street

Brainerd Jones, architect (processing plant, 1934)

Vernon Avila, architect (theater, 1993)

The four-story concrete movie theater is housed in a former brandy warehouse that was originally part of the Speas Apple Vinegar Company.

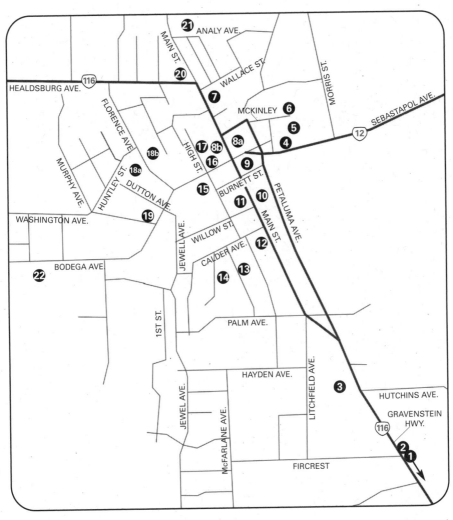

8 • Sebastopol

7. John Keating House, 1907
327 North Main Street

G. Lawrence and C. G. Sullivan, builders

Hidden behind dense vegetation, this elegant Queen Anne with a faceted tower roof once served as the town's first hospital.

8. Commercial buildings

8a. 149–153 Main Street, circa 1890

This is a double-bay store-front with corbelled brick cornice and a cast-iron façade by McCormick Bros. of San Francisco.

8b. 146 Main Street, early 1890s

This building has a wood upper-story with double-hung windows and a recessed storefront on the first floor.

8c. 138 Main Street, circa 1920

This has large transom windows and a mezzanine in the rear.

8d. 132 Main Street, circa 1895

Here is a building with three round-arched transom windows, the center one with leaded ribbed glass.

9. Former First National Bank of Sebastopol, 1910
6981 Sebastopol Avenue

Alfred Coffey, architect

Constructed of brick and steel, this small Neoclassic design has limestone cladding, tall Corinthian columns at the entrance, and a generous rooftop balustrade.

10. Sebastopol Train Depot, 1917
261 Main Street

Brainerd Jones, architect

A shallow hipped roof extends over a broad arcaded portico; local stone was used for its piers and base. The interior has original tile floors and redwood paneling. The depot served the Petaluma & Santa Rosa Railway until 1932 when passenger service was discontinued. The freight depot and electrical powerhouse (1904) at **258 Petaluma Avenue** is a stone-faced building.

11. Sebastopol Post Office, 1935
290 South Main Street

Robert McCarthy, contractor

This simple PWA Moderne post office retains the interior mural depicting an apple-orchard farm scene by Malette Dean for the Treasury Department Art Project of 1937.

12. Apartment building, 1903
408 South Main Street

This is beautifully detailed with many Neoclassical touches, including formal porticos with Tuscan columns.

13. Swain House, 1915
475 Vine Street

Located in a neighborhood of Craftsman houses, this example is larger than most in town and is notable for the stonework of the two chimneys and the gateposts.

14. Water Reservoir House, 1911–1918
463 Parquet Avenue

Originally the town's 500,000-gallon water reservoir, it was converted to a circular residence in the early 1980s by cutting doors and windows into the thirteen-inch-thick walls.

15. Office building, circa 1935
7203 Bodega Avenue

Clarence A. Caulkins, architect

This is a Moderne office building with corner glass-block windows and a vertical tower with glass detail.

16. Sebastopol Library, 1976
7140 Bodega Avenue

Lawrence Simons & Associates, architects

19. Park Side School, 1936
7450 Bodega Avenue

William F. Herbert and Clarence A. Caulkins, architects

This PWA Moderne school is notable for the dramatic three-story square tower rising above the one-story school.

20. United Methodist Church, 1915
500 North Main Street

Wilson Wythe of Oakland, architect

The Mission Revival church, with its prominent domed tower, sits dramatically on a hill that is on an axis with Main Street.

21. Analy Union High School, 1935
6950 Analy Avenue

Louis S. Stone & Henry C. Smith, architects

WPA funds financed this impressive two-story reinforced-concrete high school with expressed piers at the entrance. Notable are the colorful incised Art Deco zigzag pattern at the parapet and stylized Corinthian capitals used as decorative panels.

This redwood-and-brick contemporary box with vertical slats replaced an earlier Carnegie Library. Next door at **7120 Bodega Avenue** is the 1936 City Hall by William F. Herbert and Clarence A. Caulkins, hidden by a 1974 remodel.

17. Joseph H. P. Morris House, circa 1865
171 North High Street

A simple vernacular Gothic Revival is associated with the founder of the town. Morris owned more than 600 acres in the area; his son Harry became the first mayor of Sebastopol.

18. Florence Avenue houses

Florence Avenue was subdivided between 1892 and 1898 and is known locally as "the Art Street." Since 2001, Patrick Amiot and his wife, Brigitte Laurent, have created the whimsical sculptures found on many front lawns.

18a. 218 Florence Avenue, circa 1890

This Folk Victorian has a front-facing gable.

18b. 253 Florence Avenue, 1903
George Strout, builder

Here is a formal Queen Anne.

22. Gold Ridge Farm, 1906
7781 Bodega Avenue

Luther Burbank established his experimental gardens here in 1885 on eighteen acres.

9 · Russian River Area: Guerneville, Monte Rio, Occidental, Freestone, Bodega

The rustic Russian River resort area lies to the west of Santa Rosa. The lumber industry dominated the landscape and the economy in the nineteenth century, bringing two rail lines into the area by 1876. When the redwood forests were depleted, the area began marketing itself as a resort destination in 1897. Within a few years, there were camping sites, cabins, and large multistory hotels.

In the 1930s, the river towns hosted well-known "big bands," drawing large crowds, but by the 1960s and 1970s, most of the resorts experienced a decline in business. Today, the river still hosts vacationers under second-growth redwood forests, but on a smaller and quieter scale.

Small cottages, many with raised basements to avoid flooding, are typical year-round residences. Since the railroad years, many destructive floods have affected the towns, with the first recorded in 1879 and the most recent in 2005.

1. Korbel Champagne Cellars, 1876–1882
13250 River Road

The main winery building is visible from the parking lot, but the brick "Brandy Tower" tucked behind is the gem of the complex. An 1876 railroad station serves as the Visitors Center.

2. Rio Nido Lodge, 1919–1920
4444 Wood Road

This half-timber Tudor Revival lodge was once part of a popular resort complex with facilities that included an outdoor dance hall, cabins, bowling alley, and a grocery store. Landscape remnants and an underpass to the beach recall how extensive it was in its heyday.

3. The Willows, 1950
15905 River Road

Many lodges like this used to dot the Russian River area during the 1940s and 1950s. Balconies with log-pole railings and log-like siding were popular materials for these rustic lodges.

Guerneville

Guerneville is the largest town in the Russian River area, with several downtown blocks of remodeled vernacular commercial buildings from the 1920s through the 1930s. Main Street used to be the railroad right-of-way until passenger service stopped in 1935.

4. Guerneville Bridge, 1922
W. Lloyd Hook, engineer

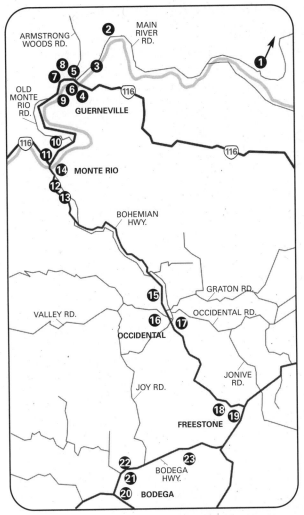

9 • Russian River Area: Guerneville, Monte Rio, Occidental, Freestone, Bodega

Formerly Guerneville School, it became a community center in 1949. Behind the arched entry is a handsome pedimented surround.

7. Congregational Church, 1904–1905
16355 First Street

James R. Watson, architect

This vernacular Gothic Revival church has two towers, one with short pointed arched windows and the other with a tall open bell tower above the primary entry.

8. Former Bank of Sonoma County, 1922
16290 Main Street

Miller and Warnecke, architects

This Neoclassical building is notable for its pilasters, arched windows along the side, and the recessed entry with a classical surround. Miller and Warnecke also designed the Mission Revival **Masonic Lodge** at 14040 Church Street in 1925.

9. Fife's Guest Ranch, 1923
16467 Highway 116

Miller and Warnecke, architects

Many of the Craftsman buildings, including the lodge and the small cabins, cluster around the inner courtyard and pool.

The removal of this steel-truss bridge was so controversial that Caltrans compromised by retaining it as a pedestrian walkway in 1998.

5. St. Elizabeth Church, 1938
14095 Woodland Drive

John J. Foley, architect

Perched on a steep hillside, this church with the simple Craftsman exterior utilizes log-like siding for a rustic camp appearance.

6. Veteran's Memorial Building, 1923
16255 First Street

Monte Rio

In 1876, the narrow gauge railroad arrived from Occidental. Most of the early hotels were located in this area, with the seven-story Monte Rio Hotel (circa 1901) nestled into the hillside on the south side of the river, where the fire station is today.

10. St. Andrew's Episcopal Church, circa 1930

20329 Highway 116

This small L-shaped Gothic Revival church presents a solid approach to the English period-revival design.

11. St. Catherine of Siena Mission, 1912

20355 Foothill Drive

Built for Bohemian Grove members, the design of St. Catherine's includes a portico with tapered posts, an open belfry, and a delightful zigzag path from the street below.

12. Rio Theater, 1946

20396 Church Street

*William B. David,
theater company designer*

Located near the Monte Rio Bridge, this large Quonset has a simple Moderne façade and a diminutive marquee. The historic Monte Rio sign arches over the road adjacent to the theater.

13. Monte Rio Bridge, 1934

Marshall M. Wallace, engineer

Judson Pacific Murphy Company fabricated this Pratt steel-truss bridge.

14. Highland Dell Inn, 1906

21050 River Boulevard

This shingled Craftsman-style resort has gable-roofed dormers. The Village Inn (1906) at 20822 River Boulevard was once a rambling shingled summer home.

Occidental

After leaving the Russian River, the Bohemian Highway travels south along the route of the railroad that serviced western Marin and Sonoma Counties from 1876 to 1935.

For most of the nineteenth century, the timber industry, ranching, and the railroad provided livelihoods for west county settlers, many of whom were Italian emigrants. After the railroad closed, the Italian restaurants that used to feed locals in the boardinghouses began catering to tourists. Today Occidental continues this tradition of family-style Italian meals.

15. Saint Philip the Apostle Church, 1902

3730 Bohemian Highway

Frank T. Shea, Shea & Shea, architect

This rustic Shingle-style church has a short square tower and windows with small diamond panes. The church refinished the

clear heart-redwood paneling on the interior and added the office and hall next door to celebrate its 100th anniversary.

16. Winding Rose Inn, circa 1905

14985 Coleman Valley Road

*Walter Lewis Proctor,
designer and builder*

Proctor, who also designed the house next door, is best known for his residential subdivisions in Santa Rosa.

17. Downtown

17a. 3703 Main Street, 1879

The vernacular front-gable Union Hotel continues to serve family-style Italian meals.

17b. 75 Main Street, 1906

The original 1886 general store was rebuilt with a full-width porch and balcony.

17c. Occidental Community Church, 1876

Second and Church Streets

Melvin "Boss" Meeker, builder

Perched along the hillside, this vernacular church was built by the town's founder shortly after he laid out the streets. The bell tower was added in 1888.

Freestone

Freestone was named in 1853 for the rock outcroppings and quarries in the area, but the town's building boom occurred in the 1870s when the railroad came through town.

18. Freestone General Store, 1876

500 Bohemian Highway

Still a store, this false-front building with covered porch sits alongside the road where railroad tracks used to be.

19. Freestone House, 1873
306 Bohemian Highway

This historic thirty-two-room vernacular Gothic Revival hostelry accommodated the railroad. With its symmetrical façade and pointed arched windows, it presents a handsome sight where the road takes a turn.

Bodega

Bodega, about seven miles inland from Bodega Bay, was laid out in 1863; by the 1870s, it was a small bustling community with two churches, several stores (**17190 Bodega Highway** was built in 1854), five saloons, a school, and an assortment of houses. Growth slowed when the train bypassed the town in 1876. Good examples of mid-nineteenth-century vernacular buildings remain, including an early 1868 board-and batten cottage at Bodega Highway and Bodega Lane.

20. Potter School, 1873
17110 Bodega Highway

L. C. Brooke, architect

The Italianate schoolhouse with distinctive cupola and arched windows was closed in 1961, but was used in the 1962 movie *The Birds.* Across the street at **132 Bodega Lane** is a former Druids Hall from the 1870s.

21. St. Teresa of Avila Church, 1861–1862
17120 Bodega Highway

This frame Gothic Revival church was built on land donated by Jasper O'Farrell, who also may have drawn the plans. In 1870, it was sawed in half and lengthened.

22. Murray House, 1860s
17135 Bodega Highway

This vernacular roadhouse with full-width covered porch is simply decorated with quoins at the corners.

23. Running Fence Commemorative
15017 Bodega Highway

A roadside park commemorates Christo and Jeanne-Claude's sculpture *Running Fence* (September 1976), a 24.5-mile-long billowing fence of white "curtains" that stretched from the ocean to Cotati Ridge. Watson School (1856) is a one-story, gable-roofed former schoolhouse next to the park.

10 · Sonoma Coast

The Sonoma Coast extends sixty-two miles along State Route 1, from Bodega Bay to Gualala Point. In addition to extraordinary views of ocean, rocky beaches, and steep forested mountains, the road passes barns, farmhouses, and related features that remain of nineteenth-century dairy, cattle, and sheep ranches.

Bodega Bay is the largest community on the Sonoma Coast and serves as both a vacation spot and a fishing harbor. Between Bodega Bay and Jenner are numerous sandy coves managed by the State Parks. Jenner, situated on the north side of the mouth of the Russian River, is a small community of hillside vacation homes and rental cabins overlooking the Pacific Ocean.

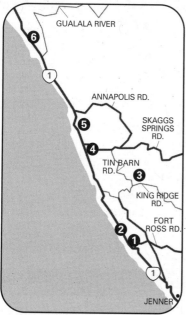

10 • Sonoma Coast

State Route 1

1. Fort Ross, Rotchev House, circa 1836
State Route 1, north of Jenner

A National Historic Landmark, Rotchev House is the only Russian-era building still standing in the continental United States. The buildings and stockade of Fort Ross (1812) are reconstructions of the original Russian buildings. They were rebuilt after the state acquired the property in 1906. The Rotchev House was constructed using a traditional system of interlocking logs; the roof consists of grooved planks. After the Russians left in 1841, the house was used as a residence; from 1878 until 1900, it housed the Fort Ross Hotel. In 1922, a restoration program (which continues today) was begun; the goal is to restore the house to the Russian period.

2. Peace Statue, 1962
Timber Cove Inn
State Route 1

Benjamin Bufano, sculptor

Benny Bufano named this seventy-two-foot-tall projectile-shaped statue *The Expanding Universe*. Images of the Madonna, the Universal Child, and the raised hand of peace are constructed of concrete and adorned with inlays of mosaic tile; it sits on the edge of a rocky outcropping facing the ocean. Bufano created his message of peace during the height of the Cold War.

3. Odiyan Tibetan Nyingma Country Center, begun 1975, ongoing construction
33755 Tin Barn Road, Cazadero

Nyingma Buddhist Community, designers and builders

Colleen Mahoney, architect (Padmasambhava Monument and Vajra Temple, 1992)

Improbable golden domes of a Buddhist Monastery can be seen in the distance when traveling from Stewarts Point to the Russian River by way of the old logging town of Cazadero. The monastery complex of four main buildings is part of the Tibetan Nyingmapa Meditation Center and Dharma Publishing founded in Berkeley in 1969. The countryside views are worth the winding trip.

4. Stewarts Point General Store, 1868
State Route 1

The two-story Classic Revival building had been in continuous use since it opened in 1868. In

2006, the store closed and the building was partially reconstructed. When the area was ranch land and there was still timber in the hills, Stewart's Point was once a larger town that included a school.

5. The Sea Ranch, begun 1963
State Route 1

*Lawrence Halprin,
landscape architect*

*MLWT (Moore, Lyndon,
Whitaker, Turnbull) &
Joseph Esherick, architects*

*Barbara Stauffacher,
graphic designer*

The Sea Ranch is mainly a residential subdivision on a ten-mile-long, 4,000-acre parcel south of the Gualala River. The property includes deeply forested hillsides east of Highway 1, and grassy meadows overlooking the Pacific Ocean. The property was purchased by Oceanic Properties (a subsidiary of Castle & Cook) in 1963. The company's project manager was Al Boeke, an architect who hired Lawrence Halprin to design the landscape plan.

Halprin believed that the project as a whole was more important than individual buildings: the buildings, he said, should be an "organic whole rather than just a group of pretty houses." By keeping the community's common open-meadow areas a dominant feature of the landscape, Halprin believed the natural setting would be preserved.

Halprin's drawings with notations are illustrated in Donlyn Lyndon and Jim Alinder's book *The Sea Ranch* (Princeton Architectural Press, New York, 2004). His handwritten notes contain the principles upon which a set of Covenants, Conditions & Restrictions (CC&Rs) were written.

The Sea Ranch opened in 1965 with a great amount of interest and press, especially in design circles. Five architects designed the first group of buildings, and set a design program that continues today; their design idiom also influenced domestic design well into the 1980s.

The first buildings completed in 1965 were open to the public for several months: the **General Store [5], Restaurant,** and **Sales Office** (Joseph Esherick, architect); Condominium I, consisting of ten housing units (MLWT: Moore, Lyndon, Whitaker, Turnbull, architects); and Hedge Row Housing, six single-family houses by Joseph Esherick.

The new buildings at Sea Ranch were unlike most of the post–World War II Bay Area residential architecture that emphasized an exposed post-and-beam structural system; wide overhanging flat, shed, or low gabled roofs; and regularly spaced and sized windows. At Sea Ranch, the architects turned the buildings inside out: the structure is hidden behind a skin of vertical board siding, or shingles; windows of different sizes and with minimal framing were placed wherever views and light were best; and, most strikingly, gone were the wide overhanging roofs. The buildings are geometric: right angles, rectangles, and squares with flat or sloping

The Sea Ranch, CA
POST OFFICE 95497

5

roofs that directly meet the walls, like wooden blocks or saltboxes.

On the interior, structural elements (unpainted timber framing, board siding, open plans, and raised sleeping lofts) were left mostly exposed; and window openings were arranged to capture the view from a dining room table or bed—cozy, secure, yet powerfully open to the drama of the site.

Over the past forty years, some design principles have been compromised (houses fill the north meadows), but overall, the development remains fairly true to its original concept. Sixteen-hundred lots have been developed (of 2,200 available), with houses between 800 and 3,000 square feet. Half the land will remain open space.

The Sea Ranch is not a gated community, but it is private. The store and sales office are open to the public, as is the chapel, and much can be seen from Highway 1 or the Coastal Access roads and pathways.

5a. The Sea Ranch Chapel, 1985
40030 State Route 1

James Hubbell, sculptor and architectural designer

Like the sheltering wings of a bird, this is a sculptural enveloping building. The chapel is set on a bed of stone, and the flared roof, which is the primary structure, is covered with shingles in a varied pattern, bisected by a wedge of stained glass and topped by pieces of metal like that of egret feathers. Beneath are strips of thin red-

wood that follow the shape of the curved roof. The entrance is under the upswing of a roof section. The sculpted interior is lit by colored glass. The walls are paneled with thin wood pieces and drops of white plaster. It is a spiritual place and is open to all.

Gualala

The Gualala River marks the boundary between Sonoma and Mendocino Counties. The town of Gualala is the main business and retail center for this part of the coast. It is not a particularly attractive town, filled with gas stations and supermarkets, but it does have an old two-story hotel that dates from 1906. Further north, the Mendocino coast is lovely and Mendocino City is a historic treasure.

6. Star of the Sea Catholic Community Church
East off State Route 1 (between Union 76 and Chevron gas stations, turn left at the Y)

Arkin Tilt, architect

Located on the first forested terrace above Highway 1, this small, forty-foot-square, wood-frame and glass sanctuary seems to merge with its wooded site. The copper roof rises from a low-ceiling entry to a nearly two-story apex behind the altar. Two walls of windows, divided into perpendicular sections with chevron-style divisions at the top, step up the rising wall to provide views of Gualala Point Regional Park to the south. The unpainted wood structural elements are left exposed.

IX
Marin County

Susan Dinkelspiel Cerny, author & photographer

Some places are simply blessed by their geography and Marin County is one of them. Surrounded by the Pacific Ocean on the west and San Francisco Bay on the east, the county is a peninsula composed of steep, mostly wooded hillsides separated by narrow valleys. From almost every vantage point, there is a breathtaking view of ocean, bay, mountain, or distant city skyline.

Mt. Tamalpais, believed to mean "west mountain" or "coast mountain" in the Native American Miwok language, is the county's dominating geological feature. It rises, without many intervening hills, to 2,600 feet. Its dramatic silhouette can be seen not only from almost everywhere in the county but also from the East Bay and the northern slopes of San Francisco.

Marin County has the largest percentage of parkland and open space preserves of the nine Bay Area counties. This is the result of a determined effort by residents of Marin County beginning in 1907, when Senator William Kent purchased a 285-acre grove of first-growth redwoods to preserve them and then donated the grove to the U.S. government. Muir Woods National Monument was dedicated in 1908. The two largest parks extend north from the Golden Gate Bridge to the tip of Tomales Point, approximately forty miles. The Point Reyes National Seashore was established in 1962 and dedicated in 1966; the Golden Gate National Recreation Area was established in 1972.

Marin was not settled by the Spanish until 1817, when Mission San Francisco de Asís built Mission San Rafael Archángel, a hospital mission and refuge. With the exception of the areas along the coast, which were reserved for the military, today's Marin County belonged to Mission San Rafael.

Beginning in 1834, the mission lands were subdivided into Mexican ranchos. According to Marin County historian Jack Mason, twenty-one ranchos containing from 740 acres (Angel Island) to 56,807 acres (Nicasio) were granted between 1834 and 1846. Many place-names reflect the history and pioneers of early Marin.

With the arrival of Americans in 1846, the fate of the Mexicans and their ranchos became tenuous, and after California became a state in 1850, Marin County was surveyed and divided into the townships of Saucelito (later Sausalito), Bolinas, Novato, and

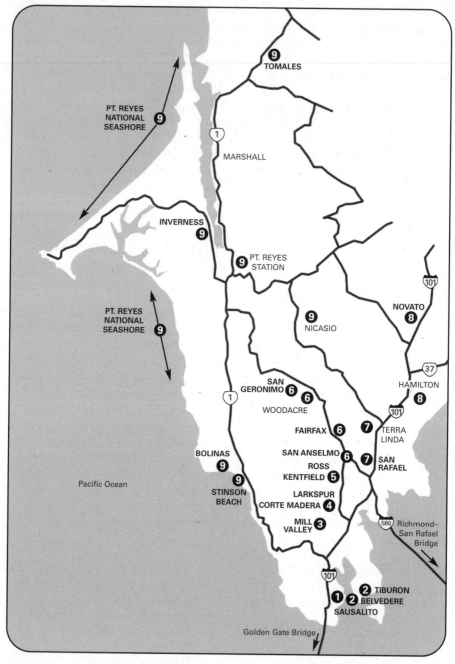

IX • Marin County

San Rafael. Numerous disputes arose over the ownership of the land, but by 1866, all of the early land-grant claims were resolved. Jack Mason commented that "the history of land in Marin is one of broken promises, litigation, and injustice nurtured on political expediency."

Ranching and lumber were the foundations of Marin's economy in the early days. John Reed built a sawmill in Mill Valley as early as 1834, and James Ross (for whom Ross Valley and the town of Ross are named) logged the area until his death in 1862. Logging on the west side of Mt. Tamalpais began in 1851, and the Bolinas Wharf was established to provide berthing for the sloops that would carry the lumber to San Francisco.

During the 1870s, railroads became an important factor in the economic development of Marin. The first railroad to operate in Marin County was the San Rafael & San Quentin Railroad, opened in 1870. The second railroad, the North Pacific Coast Railroad (later the Northwestern Pacific), opened in 1875. This was a narrow gauge line between Sausalito and Tomales. It was extended to Duncan Mills on the Russian River in 1877 and to Cazadero in 1886. In 1903, the line was electrified to San Anselmo and renamed the North Shore Railroad. The section between Pt. Reyes Station and Tomales was abandoned in 1930, as was the section between Fairfax and Pt. Reyes Station in 1933. In 1884, Peter Donahue completed the San Francisco and North Pacific Railroad between a ferry landing in Tiburon and San Rafael.

The Golden Gate Bridge was opened in 1937, but suburban commuter subdivisions did not grow and expand until after World War II. The filling, draining, and containment of the creeks, sloughs, and marshes on either side of Highway 101 have made development possible on formerly unbuildable land. The commercial developments and malls along Highway 101 first appeared in the 1950s, beginning with a shopping mall at Corte Madera and a smaller one at Strawberry Village. Northgate Mall was developed in the mid-1960s.

With few exceptions, the Highway 101 corridor has become an unappealing and eclectic combination of utilitarian buildings, big-box retailers, expedient tilt-up warehouses, stores, motels, and malls.

Dairy ranching, which dominated the landscape along Highway 101 until the 1960s, was also threatening to disappear in West Marin. A 1971 agricultural zoning ordinance reduced the number of houses per acre in West Marin to one house per sixty acres, but the A-60 zoning does not support agricultural use because the subdivided parcels are too small for grazing or farming. Land subdivided in this way only results in large country estates. With rising land prices and pressure for development, conservationists recognized

Marin County Civic Center, San Rafael

that agriculture could not be protected through zoning alone. In 1980, Marin Agricultural Land Trust (MALT) was founded to "permanently preserve Marin County farm lands for agricultural use . . . by acquiring development rights and creating a conservation easement and encourage public policies which support and enhance agriculture." As of 2005, conservation easements have been placed on 35,000 acres of agricultural land, but MALT considers 90,000 acres at risk.

Towns established along the spine of the early rail lines retain their traditional downtown main streets surrounded by walkable residential neighborhoods. Sausalito, Mill Valley, Larkspur, San Anselmo, Fairfax, San Rafael, and Novato have recognized their main streets as historic districts to be preserved and enhanced. In 1900, the population of Marin was about 15,000 with a spurt of growth after the 1906 earthquake and fire to 25,000. In 2000, the population was approximately 300,000.

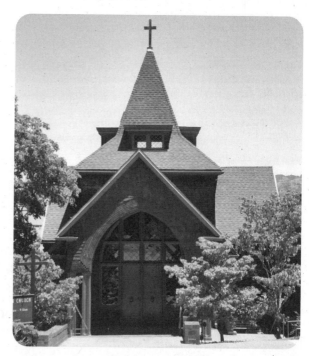

St. John's Presbyterian Church, Sausalito

1 · Sausalito

Nestled against steep hillsides overlooking San Francisco Bay, Sausalito lies northeast of the Golden Gate Bridge. In the mid-1820s, Captain William A. Richardson provided ships with fresh water and wood from a landing at Sausalito. Ten years later, after Richardson married the Presidio Commandant's daughter Maria Antonia Martinez in 1825, he was appointed Captain of the Port of San Francisco and helped establish the pueblo of Yerba Buena. In 1838, he was granted El Rancho del Saucelito (Sausalito), which consisted of 19,500 acres, where he built a port. When Richardson died in 1856, his land was quickly dispersed.

The hillside above the ferry terminal was subdivided in 1868 by the Sausalito Land & Ferry Company. After the North Pacific Coast Railroad began operating in 1875, Sausalito became the main rail and ferry route to San Francisco. Although the Golden Gate Bridge opened in 1937, ferries and trains continued running until 1941. Ferry service to San Francisco was reestablished in 1970.

Downtown Historic District

Bridgeway is Sausalito's "main street," and it retains the small-scaled, late-nineteenth- and early-twentieth-century ambience that makes strolling such a pleasure. It is a historic district listed on the National Register of Historic Places. Although most of the storefronts have been altered or modernized, the rhythm of "main street" remains. A building-by-building tour of the historic district can be found on the city's Web site at www.ci.sausalito.ca.us.

1. Plaza Vina Del Mar
Bridgeway Boulevard

The park site was given to the city by the North Shore Railroad in 1904 and is the center of downtown Sausalito. The fountain, designed by architect William B. Faville, came from the 1915 Panama-Pacific International Exposition. The elephants also came from the fair and were designed

by McKim, Meade & White. Across the street to the south is the 1915 Mission Revival–style **Sausalito Hotel.**

Residential

Above Princess Street, lined with early commercial buildings, residential Sausalito clings to steep wooded hillsides, where roads are narrow and homes are romantic retreats. The hillside provides many delightful walks. Through the verdant tangle of an overhanging bower of trees, over stone walls covered with moss and ivy, there are glimpses of rooftops, rounded corner bays, trellised porches, brown shingles, and the horizontal window grouping of mid-century Moderns.

2. St. John's Presbyterian Church, 1905
112 Bulkley Avenue

Ernest Coxhead, architect

The shingled church has an arched entry portico under a gable roof, subtly emphasized by a ribbon of tiny shingles. The pyramidal tower behind is

dramatic. The simple interior is paneled in unpainted wood.

Excelsior Lane is a steep pathway and staircase that leads to Bridgeway and Plaza Vina Del Mar below. The view as one descends is worth the climb.

3. Sausalito Woman's Club, 1913
120 Central Avenue, at San Carlos Avenue

Julia Morgan, architect

This simple brown-shingled building, with small-paned casement windows, is set in a lush garden, a building in harmony with nature.

4. Christ Church, 1882
Santa Rosa and San Carlos Avenues

Although begun as a Carpenter Gothic, alterations in the 1890s and 1912 have transformed it into a Shingle-style building. **Campbell Hall,** the church's parish hall across the street, was designed in 1967 by Henrik Bull. It has a wide trellised porch overlooking a spacious garden.

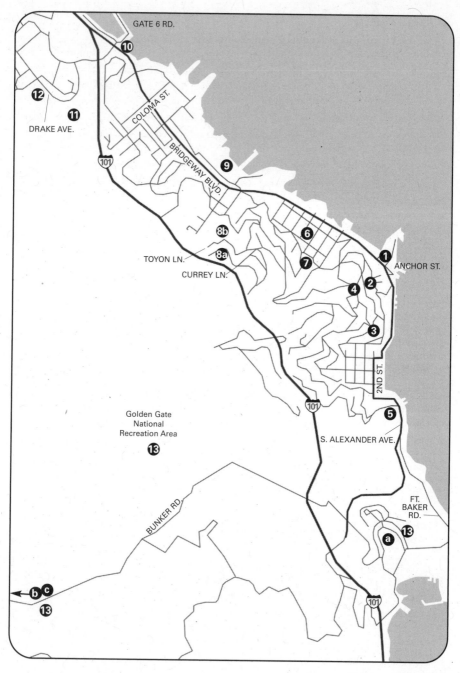

5. Dickinson House, 1890
26 Alexander Avenue

Willis Polk, architect

The house, sited below the street, has shingles laid in a wavy pattern.

6. Adolf Silva House, 1900
428 Turney Street

This two-story house is a transitional design displaying Italianate and Colonial Revival elements. It has bracketed hood moldings, prominent gabled dormers, Classic Revival details, and clapboard siding.

7. Gardner House, 1869
47 Girard Avenue,
at Turney Street

This is said to be Sausalito's oldest house. It is Gothic Revival with a steep central gable, a wide covered front porch held by split pillars, and bargeboards of lacy icicle design.

8. Toyon Terraces, 1950s
Currey and Toyon Lanes

When Bob Rose subdivided Toyon Terraces in the 1950s, he required that all houses be designed by an architect. The two streets are a showcase of excellent and mostly unaltered examples of mid-twentieth-century Modernism, sharing

similar design elements such as exposed post-and-beam construction, transparency, modular window units, flat or sloping roofs, and modest profiles set into naturalistic grounds and orientated toward views of the bay.

8a. Currey Lane homes

139 (1958; John Funk, architect).

244 (1953; Roger Lee, architect).

250 (1953; Charles Warren Callister, architect).

260 (1956; John Hoops, architect).

290 (1958; Henrik Bull, architect).

8b. Toyon Lane homes

66 (1956; George Rockrise, architect).

145 (1957; Mario Corbett, architect).

31 (attributed to Mario Corbett, architect).

121 (2004; Swatt Architects), a new house in the spirit of the 1950s.

9. Marinship,
1942–1947
2100 Block of
Bridgeway Boulevard

In 1942, after the bombing of Pearl Harbor, the U.S. Maritime Commission engaged the Bechtel Company to build ships for its Pacific fleet. By June 1942, 365 acres of mud flats, rail yards, and a residential neighborhood were redeveloped into a shipyard called Marinship. Its nearly 17,500 employees worked around the clock and had built ninety-three ships by late 1945. The first Liberty ship was named *William A. Richardson.* After the war ended, the shipyard closed as quickly as it had opened. Among Marinship buildings still standing are huge, connected, barrel-vaulted buildings in the 2100 block of Bridgeway that house the Army Corps of Engineers' **Bay Model,** a fascinating exhibit of how water flows in and out of the bay. Reused structures were given a new façade in 1980.

10. Waldo Point Harbor,
North Sausalito
House Boat Community
Gate 6 Road,
off Bridgeway Boulevard

Sausalito's harbors are filled with various types and styles of floating homes. Houseboat tours are held every year in the fall.

10a. 509 Bridgeway Boulevard

This is an original houseboat built in 1915.

10b. New houseboats

These come in all sorts of designs and sizes. The image on page 466 shows a variety of houseboats. Mt. Tamalpais is in the background.

8b

10b

Marin City

This was the site of temporary housing for employees of Marinship. In 1958, the wartime housing was replaced by permanent mixed-income housing consisting of rentals, cooperative apartments, and single-family homes.

11. Marin City Apartment Houses, 1958–1960
Cole Drive

John Carl Warnecke and Aaron Green, architects

There are eight four- to five-story apartment houses in this group. The buildings are widely spaced from each other and set at angles against the hillside so that all floors are accessible by car. Below are twenty-three one- to two-story apartment houses with balconies and gardens. Nearby is a group of single-family homes using log poles as the primary structural element (called "pole houses"), designed by DeMars and Reay.

12. Livermore/Brugess House, 1907
441 Drake Avenue

Marin City was built on a dairy ranch; its house and an 1880s carriage house are still standing. The gray-painted shingled house is Arts and Crafts in style. The property is now a private school.

13. Golden Gate National Recreation Area

From the days of Spanish rule, all the land on the water's edge on either side of the Golden Gate was reserved for the military. This use continued until 1972 when the Golden Gate National Recreation Area was established. The park initially consisted of 34,000 acres just north of the Golden Gate. Since then, the park has been extended to include the San Francisco Presidio and Alcatraz. Fort Baker is just south of Sausalito on the east side of the bridge, while Fort Barry and Fort Cronkhite are on its west. The three forts contain many historic buildings and structures.

13a. Fort Baker

The fort was established in 1866 and contains a nice group of

military housing, built between 1902 and 1903. They are set in a semicircle at the top of a former parade ground on Murray Circle. Most are large duplexes with gabled and cross-gabled roofs, and covered porches.

13b. Fort Barry and Fort Cronkhite

Located on the west side of Highway 101, both forts contain numerous military buildings that have been reused for a variety of purposes. The **California Marine Mammal Center** is located here, as is the **Headlands Center for the Arts** with interiors by David Ireland, and a youth hostel. Bunkers with gun emplacements dot the hillsides and a Nike site is open as a museum.

13c. Point Bonita Light Station, 1855, 1877

In 1877, the lantern and watch room of an 1855 lighthouse (built higher above the water) were reused when this lighthouse was built. It was extensively restored in 1993.

2 · Tiburon · Belvedere

Tiburon and Belvedere are often grouped together as if they are one place, but they are two separate incorporated towns with different histories. Tiburon is the larger of the two cities with a population of 8,600. Tiburon developed as a railhead and commercial district after Peter Donahue opened the San Francisco and North Pacific Railroad in 1884. Primarily used for freight, the railroad and ferry connected San Rafael with San Francisco by way of Tiburon. Belvedere, subdivided as a summer suburb, remains primarily residential with a population of 2,200.

Tiburon

1. Main Street

Main Street is only one block long and grew up after the railroad opened. Only 15 Main Street (1886) actually dates from the nineteenth century. After a fire destroyed most of downtown in 1921, an Old West theme was re-created. The ferry terminal to San Francisco and Angel Island is located just east of Main Street.

2. Corinthian Island

At the point where Main Street makes a sharp turn west, Corinthian Island rises abruptly. The Corinthian Island Company subdivided the island into ninety-seven building lots in 1907. Several large brown-shingle houses that date from 1909 and 1910 are located on Alcatraz Avenue.

3. "Ark Row"
104–122 Main Street

During the 1890s, floating summerhouses called "arks" bobbed in "Ark Cove," the inlet between Belvedere and Corinthian Islands. The arks

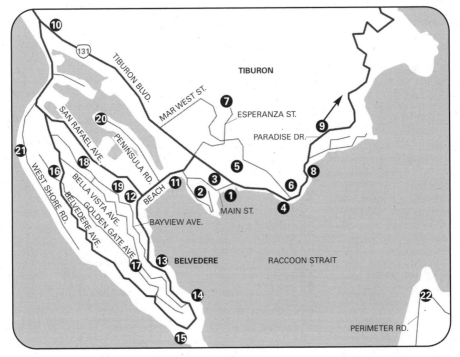

were tied up in a sheltered lagoon during the winter; now this is the parking lot behind "Ark Row." Only two arks remain; Ark #116 Main Street is the most original. A typical ark from Tiburon, the Lewis Ark, is on display at the Maritime Museum in San Francisco.

4. North Pacific Railroad Train and Ferry Terminal, 1882, 1884
1920 Paradise Drive

Constructed in Petaluma in 1882, the depot was moved to Tiburon in 1884. It is a simple, gable-roofed, two-story building with board-and-batten siding, and is now a museum. Freight trains stopped running in 1967.

5. Point Tiburon, 1986
Tiburon Boulevard and Main Street

Fisher-Friedman Associates, architects

This crisp development replaced the former railroad yard. It is a multiunit residential complex, sheathed in unpainted brown shingles, with 155 dwellings, gardens, pools, parking lots, a lagoon, a shopping area, and a public grassy space by the water's edge. In a crescent around the former freight yards are modest frame dwellings built in the 1880s for employees of the railroad. All have been altered, but their humble beginnings are evident by a few hipped roofs.

6. Tiburon Sewage Treatment Plant, 1962
Paradise Drive and Mar West Street

Kitchen & Hunt, architects

Subtle and unobtrusive, the walls are corrugated concrete and brick and partially covered with vines.

7. Saint Hilary's Roman Catholic Church, 1888
Esperanza Street, off Mar West Street

High on the hillside, this simple frame church has a gable roof, lancet windows, and a gable-roofed entry porch with Stick-style cross bracing. The interior is paneled with narrow boards of Douglas fir and redwood. The Landmarks Society has owned it since 1959.

8. Stone Tower, Lyford's Hygeia, circa 1890
2036 Paradise Drive

This failed utopian community called Hygeia is marked by the stone tower and contoured streets beyond. It was planned by Dr. Benjamin Lyford, son-in-law of pioneer John Reed.

9. Romberg Tiburon Center for Environmental Studies
3152 Paradise Drive

This thirty-four-acre site contains buildings and curious remnants of structures dating from 1906 to the 1940s. It's a deepwater port, and former users include a codfish curing and packing plant (1877–1904), a U.S. Navy Coaling Station (1904–1931), the forerunner of the California Maritime Academy (1931–1940), John Roebling & Sons Company steel-wire operation to make the cables for the Golden Gate Bridge (1930s), Tiburon National Marine Laboratory and Marine Minerals Center (1961–2001). The Center for Environmental Studies was established in 1978 and is part of San Francisco State University.

10. Benjamin Lyford House (Audubon Society), 1874
376 Greenwood Beach Road

This is a two-story Empire-style house with a mansard roof and an imposing three-story tower. Roof crestings on its gable ends and on the mansard window moldings are its only decoration. The house was barged across Richardson Bay from Strawberry Point in 1957 and restored by architect John Lord King.

Belvedere

In 1890, the Belvedere Land Company purchased the island from descendants of the John Reed family. Michael M. O'Shaughnessy, the civil engineer who later designed Hetch-Hetchy, designed the street layout; eucalyptus and pine trees were planted on the barren hillsides. Belvedere developed first as a summer town, attracting families from San Francisco.

Steep hillsides, narrow roads, a profusion of trees, and tall, well-tended hedges make it a challenge to clearly view the houses, even on foot. Many houses have been enlarged, such as architect Albert Farr's shingled F. L. Bridge House, "Land Fall" (1891), at 296 Beach Road, where only one wing appears to be original.

11. Social Saloon of the S.S. *China*, 1866
52 Beach Road

The sumptuous drawing room of the side-wheel

steamer S.S. *China* was salvaged when the ship was to be scrapped. Owned by the Landmarks Society, it is popular for special events.

12. Belvedere Land Company Building, 1905
83 Beach Road

Albert Farr, architect

The two-story shingle building provides a piece of urban sophistication. Gabled bays punctuate the broad side-facing gable roof, and grouped small-paned casement windows and an overhanging second story enrich its façade. The ground floor has been altered. At 80–88 Beach Road, Farr also designed shingled summer cottages in 1905.

13. Charles Crocker Summer House, 1900
228 Beach Road

Edgar A. Mathews, architect

This large stucco-sided house has many gables.

14. 246 Beach Road, 1946
Jack Heidelberg, builder

This romantic Period Revival has a wavy shingled roof and large stucco chimneys imbedded with clinker brick and stone. Heidelberg also designed 499 Bella Vista Avenue around the corner. Three impressive houses best viewed from Beach Road are **350 Bella Vista** (1893), a large four-story shingle with a rounded porch and balcony; **400 Bella Vista** (1895; John White, architect), a three-story shingle; and **460 Bella Vista** (circa 1893), a Queen Anne with Classic Revival decorations, including two-story Ionic columns and a balustrade around the upper floor.

15. House, 1930
423 Belvedere Avenue

Carr Jones, architect

Romantic and picturesque, this Medieval Revival house with half-timber and brick siding has a steeply sloping, interconnecting complex of slate roofs. Houses at **101 Belvedere** (Henry Hill, architect); **50 Cliff Road** (1950; Jack Hillmer, architect); **30 Cliff Road** (1957; George Rockrise, architect); **35 Belvedere** (1939; Henry H. Gutterson, architect); **19 Belvedere** (1956; Henrik Bull, architect); and **11 Belvedere** (1956; John Lord King, architect) are barely visible.

16. Belvedere Golf and Country Clubhouse, 1909
1 Britton Avenue

Albert Farr, architect

Built as a rustic, unpainted shingled clubhouse for the Belvedere Golf and Country Club, the club closed in 1933, the greens were subdivided, and the clubhouse was converted to a residence. It was enlarged by architect Clifford Conly in 1964.

17. Golden Gate Avenue

The avenue climbs to the crest of the island where the land is more level, the houses more visible, and views more spectacular.

17a. S. C. Peterson House, 1903
332 Golden Gate Avenue

Clarence Ward, architect

The shingled house has a pyramidal roof, hipped-roof dormers, and wide overhangs.

17b. House, 1904
334 Golden Gate Avenue

Albert Farr, architect

A three-story, double-gable-roofed, half-timbered house sits prominently on the edge of the hillside and is visible from various spots on the east side of the island.

17c. Howells House, 1915
339 Golden Gate Avenue

Walter H. Ratcliff Jr., architect

An impressively large eclectic mass of Mission Revival elements includes a tower and curved parapets.

14

17d. Stevenson House, 1928
345 Golden Gate Avenue
George W. Kelham,
architect

The huge French Revival, stucco-sided manor house stands out on the crest of the hill. Massive steeply pitched hipped roofs and gabled dormers are sheathed with flat clay tiles.

17e. Valentine Rey House, 1893
428 Golden Gate Avenue
Willis Polk,
architect

Located on a steep lot, the multi-storied house steps up and down the hillside. The pergola-covered entry is located in the middle of the house, on the south side, approached by a winding path. The house has stucco siding, a two-story polygonal bay, and carved brackets under the eaves. The different levels of the house are arranged around a dramatic two-plus-story central light well, which creates a remarkable interior space.

17f. Gordon Blanding House, 1895
440 Golden Gate Avenue

The Classic Revival house has a low one-story profile from the street, but from afar, it is an imposing edifice high above the water. It has a covered veranda with posts topped by Ionic capitals. Its clapboard siding is painted white.

18. House, 1890s
209 Bayview Avenue
McLean Builders

High above the street, this intriguing house has wraparound porches on two stories, an array of decorative spindles, and fish-scale and diamond-shaped shingles. Daniel McLean & Neil McLean built many Belvedere houses during the 1890s, including **140, 144,** and **160 Bayview** and **132 Bella Vista Avenues.**

19. First Church of Christ, Scientist, 1952
501 San Rafael Avenue
Charles Warren Callister,
architect

This small church is discreetly tucked into the hillside. It is a jewel of a building, built of reinforced concrete in a construction style typical of the period, and Callister has achieved a splendid and magical effect by filling the sections between the gray concrete with alternating vertical wood boards and narrow panels of stained glass. Concrete garden walls, pathways, and planting boxes create an integrated plan.

20. Belvedere Lagoon

Beginning in 1936, Belvedere Lagoon was created by dredging and filling silted wetland. By the 1960s, the lagoon development was a showcase of mid-twentieth-century Modernism. Today, only half of the original homes remains unaltered.

21. 27 West Shore Road, 1963
A. Quincy Jones, architect

This custom home, designed by Jones for Joseph Eichler, has a wide low profile with a high and dramatic gable roof over the entry.

22. Angel Island State Park

Angel Island is the largest island in San Francisco Bay; Mt. Livermore, its central peak, is 760 feet high. At water's edge, numerous coves are separated by gullies and ridges.

In 1863, during the Civil War, the U.S. military took control of the island, considering it an ideal location for coastal defense. By 1900, the entire island became the U.S. military base Fort McDowell. The island's use as a military installation is complex and varied. There was no master plan for the military installations; buildings and groups of buildings were constructed as needs arose.

The island contains 120 structures and landscape features listed on the National Register of Historic Places. The entire island and its buildings (most not open to the public) have been a state park since 1963. Ayala Cove, where the visitor ferry docks today, was the former **Quarantine Station**, which operated from 1891 until 1935. **Camp Reynolds**, a depot for new recruits, has vernacular frame residences (1864–1880s) that are the oldest on the island, creating a picturesque grouping along a former parade ground. The **Immigration Station** (1908; Walter J. Mathews, architect) operated from 1909 until 1940. **East Garrison** is notable for its World War I–era concrete Mission Revival buildings.

3 • Mill Valley

By 1856, entrepreneur Samuel Throckmorton had acquired most of James Reed and William A. Richardson's land-grant holdings in the area that would become Mill Valley. When Throckmorton died in 1883, his land passed through foreclosure to the Tamalpais Land and Water Company, whose investors included Joseph Eastland, Lovell White, Roger McGee, Louis Janes, and C. O. G. Miller.

The Tamalpais Land and Water Company extended a branch of the North Pacific Coast Railroad into Mill Valley in 1889, and hired Michael O'Shaughnessy to lay out the town. Mill Valley soon became a community of summer camps and cottages, and the trailhead for hikers to Mt. Tamalpais.

Downtown Mill Valley is a concentrated area with nearby residential neighborhoods within walking distance. Radiating beyond the central area, residential streets wind up steep hillsides and down deep canyons.

1. The Depot, 1929
87 Throckmorton Avenue, at Miller Avenue

This is the center of Mill Valley, and the plaza behind The Depot, now a coffee shop and bookstore, has become a community gathering place. The Mission Revival–style building, with a tile hipped roof and arched windows with drip moldings, was the fourth Mill Valley train station.

2. City Hall, 1936
26 Corte Madera Avenue

W. C. Falch & E. E. Jaekle, architects

The City Hall and Fire Station building is a picturesque two-story Tudor Revival with a bell tower. The bank building at **60 Throckmorton Avenue** is Classic Revival; the **Masonic Temple** (1903) at 23 Corte Madera Avenue was designed by architect Harvey Klyce.

3. Sequoia Theater, 1929
25 Throckmorton Avenue

Reid Brothers, architects

The former Art Deco theater is now filled with shops.

4. El Paseo, 1936–1948
11–17 Throckmorton and 35 Sunnyside Avenues

Gus Costigan, designer-builder

Edna Foster, owner-developer

Here is a small picturesque *paseo* that has vine-covered used-brick walls, heavy timbers, and brick paving.

5. Outdoor Art Club, 1904
1 West Blithedale Avenue

Bernard Maybeck, architect

Founded in 1902, the club is dedicated to preserving the area's natural environment. The clubhouse is a one-story wood-sided building with a tall gabled roof and a wall of French doors. The interior is notable for its redwood board-and-batten siding and for its unusual roof truss system. A massive stone fireplace dominates the north alcove.

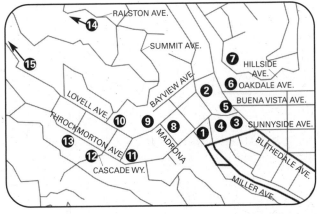

6. Our Lady of Mount Carmel Catholic Church, 1968

Corner of Oakdale and West Blithedale Avenues

Fred Howeling, architect

The dramatic spire of this unusual church, a true period piece, can be seen from downtown and rises behind the roof of the Outdoor Art Club. The base of the church contains concrete buttresses in-filled with panels of yellow concrete. A stringcourse of abstract patterns of stained glass, designed by Hogan Studios, separates the wall of the church from its huge roof.

7. Samuel Burt House, 1904

164 Hillside Avenue

Harvey Klyce, designer-builder

This is just one of a group of rustic Shingle-style houses located on Oakdale, Hillside, and Bolsa Avenues that were built during the first decade of the twentieth century. Klyce was a popular designer-builder here.

8. McInnes House, 1891

21 Lovell Avenue

The Queen Anne is cruciform in plan, with fishscale shingles and angled corner bays.

9. Mill Valley Carnegie Library, 1911

52 Lovell Avenue

This former library building, now a private residence, is Classic Revival in style, with redbrick walls and white trim.

10. Ernest Evans House, 1907

100 Summit Avenue

Louis Christian Mullgardt, architect

The three-story chalet-style house is located on a steep hillside. The first two stories slope inward like buttresses and are sheathed with horizontal wood siding; the third floor has stucco siding. The gable roof has wide overhanging eaves supported by brackets. A stepped row of leaded windows expresses the interior staircase.

11. Mill Valley Community Church, 1930

8 Olive Street, at Throckmorton Avenue

E. E. Wood, designer-builder

The Community Church, organized in 1925, first met at the Outdoor Club. E. E. Wood, a member of the congregation and principal at Tamalpais High School, was inspired by the spiritual atmosphere of Maybeck's clubhouse and had plans drawn up by the high school shop teacher. The shingle-sided church is paneled entirely in wood and has a large stone fireplace. The pews were built by the high school shop class. To the north, the Parish Hall, library, and chapel were built in 1953.

12. John Reed Sawmill, Old Mill Park, 1833–1834

Throckmorton Avenue and Cascade Way

The substantial wood framework marks the location of the first sawmill in Marin County.

14. Ralston White Retreat, 1912 (unmapped)

2 El Capitan Avenue

Willis Polk, architect

Located on a mountainside knoll far from the center of town, this reinforced-concrete house was built of material brought to the site by the old Mt. Tamalpais Railroad. It is a rectangular-shaped house with a symmetrical façade. The three-story central section has a wide gable roof and a recessed balcony above the recessed entry porch.

15. Mountain Theater, 1934–1936 (unmapped)

East Ridgecrest Boulevard, off Pan Toll Highway

Emerson Knight, landscape architect

Forty rows of rough stone seating were built by the California Conservation Corp (CCC) between 1934 and 1936. Emerson Knight, the designer, described the finished theater as having the "character of age-old ruggedness, thus preserving the spirit of the mountain." The first plays were performed here in 1913 in a natural amphitheater, and produced by Garnet Holme from the UC–Berkeley drama department. The land for the Mountain Theater was donated by Congressman William Kent in 1915. Farther up the mountain, **East Peak** lookout tower, constructed in 1937 by the CCC, provides a 360-degree view of the Bay Area.

13. Mill Valley Public Library, 1966

375 Throckmorton Avenue, at Elma Street

Wurster, Bernardi and Emmons, architects

This is an elegant essay in concrete and glass overlooking a creek and grove of redwoods. The interior has an open gable ceiling with dark-stained beams and sienna-colored paneling. Multipaned windows extend from the floor through the eave, bringing light into the reading rooms. An addition was designed by Turnbull, Griffin, Haesloop in 1998.

There are several historic houses dating from the 1890s farther up Throckmorton: **418** (1896); **448** (1894); **465** (1896; Willis Polk, architect); **501** (1900; Harvey Klyce, designer-builder); and **565** (1891).

4 · Corte Madera · Larkspur

The towns of Corte Madera and Larkspur were part of John Reed's Rancho Corte Madera del Presidio. A sawmill and logging operations were established in 1847; by 1851, the forests were gone and the land was used for farms and dairies. The North Pacific Coast Railroad came through in 1875. The flat low-lying land, where the freeway and most of the commercial businesses are now located, was once marshland.

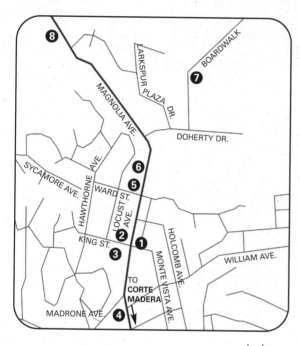

4 · Larkspur

In 1887, the land to the west of downtown was subdivided for housing, and engineer Michael O'Shaughnessy is said to have designed the sewer system. Initially, Larkspur was primarily a summer town with several hotels, cottages, and summer camps. Larkspur was incorporated in 1908; annexations have extended the city to include Greenbrae.

1. Larkspur City Hall, 1913
400 Magnolia Avenue

Charles O. Claussen, architect

The Mission Revival–style building has a symmetrical façade with twin towers rising above a curved Mission Revival–style false-front parapet. The towers have pyramidal tile roofs and arched openings. The Mission Revival fire station next door was built in 1939.

2. St. Patrick's Church, 1940
Corner of Magnolia Avenue and King Street

Henry A. Minton, architect

Here is a reinforced-concrete version of Spanish Colonial. The parish was established in 1896.

3. Patrick King House, 1890
105 King Street

Part of this house was constructed in 1870, but its most distinguishing features date from 1890 when it was enlarged

Corte Madera
(unmapped)

The town was initially settled on hillsides overlooking the marsh. Later, Meadowsweet Dairy was located on reclaimed marsh and operated until 1937, when it was subdivided. After World War II, more marshland was filled for Highway 101, shopping malls, and additional housing tracts.

Larkspur

Larkspur's old downtown, located on Magnolia Avenue between Madrone Avenue and Doherty Drive, owes its existence to the 1875 railroad and is a Historic District. Many downtown buildings have information plaques, and a tour of downtown can be found on the Internet. Before the freeway was built, Magnolia Avenue was the main road from Sausalito through San Anselmo to San Rafael.

in the Queen Anne style with a tower and a wide front porch.

4. Madrone Canyon

A creek lined with tall second-growth redwoods flows down from the hills. **Dolliver Park** is located at the intersection of Madrone and Magnolia Avenues; the upper canyon has been preserved as open space. Small houses built as summer cabins, some unaltered, line the canyon.

East of Madrone Canyon, Baltimore Avenue is lined with bungalows. The road is divided by a row of tall palm trees. **126 Magnolia** (1907) was built by local designer-builder Gustave Nagel, who was active here between 1888 and 1925.

5. Blue Rock Inn, 1895, 1910
507 Magnolia Avenue

Originally a wood-sided Queen Anne Victorian, the hotel was remodeled in 1910 by designer-builder Gustave Nagel, using locally quarried blue basalt rock. In 2004, it was again remodeled

and now has a corner "Victorian" turret and a third floor.

6. The Lark Theater, 1937
549–551 Magnolia Avenue

Here is a small Art Deco theater with a tall neon sign that has recently been meticulously restored.

7. Boardwalk #1
Doherty Drive

Until the 1960s, when the Army Corp of Engineers built a flood-control project along Corte Madera Creek to protect new housing tracts in the marsh, there were rows of small "arks" used as summer dwellings. Approximately thirty-eight floating homes remain on Boardwalk #1, where the homeowners' association dates from 1922. **Boardwalk #2** lies east of Highway 101 across the water from the Larkspur Ferry Terminal.

8. Escalle Winery, 1894
771 Magnolia Avenue

From 1879 to the late 1880s, this site was used by Claude

Callot for making bricks, raising cattle, and growing grapes. In 1887, he began to produce wine commercially. The distinctive redbrick building by the side of the road dates from 1894. The two-story brick and wood-frame building on the north side of the property dates from 1881.

9. Greenbrae Company Sales Office, 1946
500 Sir Francis Drake Boulevard

Albert Farr, architect

Marking the entrance to the first residential subdivision in Greenbrae, the miniscule French Chateau provides a degree of pretension for the California Ranch–style residential development.

10. Larkspur Ferry Terminal, 1976
101 East Sir Francis Drake Boulevard

Braccia, DeBrer & Heglund, architects

This triangular-shaped, 16,000-square-foot, steel-frame canopy

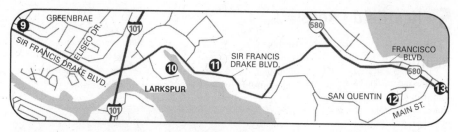

4 • Larkspur and Vicinity

is an open web of triangles standing on three pyramidal supports.

11. Remillard Brickyard Kiln and Smoke Stack, 1891, 1989
125 East Sir Francis Drake Boulevard

James Maxwell, architect (1989)

Pierre Remillard's brickyard included a self-contained village with workers' cabins, a cookhouse, a blacksmith's shop, a horse barn, and even pigsties, vegetable gardens, and orchards. The brickyard ceased operating in 1915, but it stood unused until 1989 when the kiln and smokestack were incorporated into a new development of offices and a restaurant.

12. San Quentin Prison, 1852 ongoing
Exit #880 (last exit before Richmond–San Rafael Bridge)

Maury Diggs, architect

San Quentin, California's oldest prison, opened in 1852. The 432-acre complex includes residences and other support buildings as well as cellblocks and guard towers built at different times over its 150-year history. It is highly visible from the bridge, the Larkspur ferries, and the Tiburon Peninsula. "The Stones," the first cellblock, was constructed in 1854 from granite quarried on the site. State architect Maury Diggs designed some of the buildings between 1920 and 1940. Since the prison opened, furniture for public buildings has been made here, most notably, the furniture for

Frank Lloyd Wright's Civic Center. This is the location of California's only "death row."

San Quentin Village, located just east of the prison, was established for prison employees. Some of the houses appear to date from the 1860s. The post office opened in 1859.

13. Richmond–San Rafael Bridge, 1953–1956
San Quentin Point

Ferry service to San Francisco began at San Quentin Point around 1860, and Marin's first railroad connected San Rafael with this ferry in 1870. An automobile ferry to Richmond opened in 1916 and continued to run until the five-and-one-half-mile-long Richmond–San Rafael Bridge was completed in 1956.

5 · Kentfield · Ross

Kentfield

The unincorporated town is named for Albert Kent, who settled near the intersection of Sir Francis Drake Boulevard and College Avenue (Kentfield Corners) in 1871. By 1872, Kent had moved to a large home in what would become the residential subdivision of Kent Woodlands.

1. Kent Woodlands

The subdivision was first laid out in the late 1930s, but only a handful of houses were built until after World War II, when Kent Woodlands became a popular place for custom homes on large lots.

From the mid-1940s and throughout the 1950s, a significant number of homes were designed by prominent Bay Area architects such as Charles Warren Callister, Joseph

Courtesy of House & House Architects

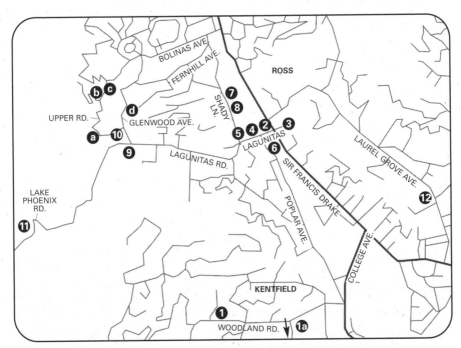

Esherick, Henry Hill, Jack Hillmer, Henry H. Gutterson, Fred Langhorst, Hans Ostwald, and William Wurster. Many were featured in magazines and guidebooks to Bay Area architecture. In the late 1980s, wonderful examples of Bay Area mid-twentieth-century Modern architecture were, and continue to be, demolished and replaced. A recent example is the 2005 demolition of the Esherick House at **10 Acorn Way** (1950; Rebecca Wood Esherick [Watkins] & Joseph Esherick, architects), noted in several publications for its dramatic and sheltering gable roof.

72 Ridgecrest Road (2004; House & House, architects) [1a] replaced a mid-century Ranch, but it embodies the sensibilities of mid-century Modern: careful siting, unpainted wood siding with accent colors that blend with nature, and low-profile massing.

Ross

The town is named for James Ross, who purchased Rancho Punta de Quintin in 1857. The post office was established in 1887 and the town incorporated in 1908. Ross is known for its large country estates and elegant homes. "Fernhill," its first impressive country estate, was developed by Albert Dibblee in 1870 and is now part of the Katherine Branson School.

Ross has beautiful late-nineteenth- and early-twentieth-century homes set in large lush

gardens. John White, Bernard Maybeck's brother-in-law, was active in Ross during the 1890s and early twentieth century. Architect Gardner A. Dailey designed a number of houses during the 1930s and 1940s.

2. Town Hall and Fire Station, 1927
31, 32 Sir Francis Drake Boulevard

John White, architect

City Hall is Mediterranean in style with red-tile roofs and stucco walls. The entry porch has a double-arched entry. A sculpture of a bear by Benjamin Bufano stands in front.

3. Marin Art and Garden Center, established 1945
Sir Francis Drake Boulevard and Lagunitas Road

The Marin Art and Garden Center is located on the site of "Sunnyside," the country estate of Annie Ross Worn, daughter of James Ross. The **Octagon House** [3a], now home to the Ross Historical Society, was built in 1864 and was moved to its present location in 1969. The **Marin Society of Arts Gallery** (1948; Gardner A. Dailey, architect) and the **Art Center** (1954; Wurster, Bernardi

and Emmons, architects) are simple frame buildings evocative of their time.

4. James Moore House, 1876
2 Lagunitas Road

This Victorian-era Gothic Revival with lacy bargeboards is in beautiful condition.

5. St. John's Episcopal Church, 1912, 1958
14 Lagunitas Road, at Shady Lane

Frederick H. Meyer, architect (1912)

Arnold Constable, architect (addition to nave, 1958)

A Gothic-inspired church with a crenellated bell tower sits on a corner lot in a prominent location across from Ross Grammar School.

6. Ross Post Office and Commons
Poplar Avenue and Lagunitas Road

The former train station that once sat on this site inspired the Mediterranean tile roof and triple-arched entry of the post office.

Shady Lane

Here was once a lush green tunnel of huge poplar trees, which are being replaced because of Dutch elm disease. A little less "shady" now, the street still provides a wonderful walk.

7. McNear House, circa 1900
32 Shady Lane

John White, architect

This is a massive two-and-one-half-story shingled Swiss Chalet, with an open recessed third-story balcony and wide gable roof. It was originally unpainted.

8. James T. Hoyt House, circa 1880
34 Shady Lane

This is an exceptional example of a lavish Victorian with a three-story turret and twenty rooms.

9. Lagunitas Country Club, 1909
Lagunitas Road, opposite Glenwood Avenue

John White, architect

The clubhouse is a rustic shingled building with a pergola-covered porch on two sides. Opening onto the porch are rows of French doors glazed with small panes of glass.

10. E. G. Schmiedell House, 1896
1 Upper Road

John White & George Howard, architects

A complicated composition of sections that step down the hillside, this large shingled house has many intersecting, steeply pitched roofs and dormers.

Architect John White also designed **7 Upper Road** (1906) [10a], a large shingled house of two, two-and-one-half-story, gable-roofed wings connected by a recessed two-story section with a cross-gable roof. **25 Upper Road** (1900) [10b] is a symmetrically arranged, two-and-one-half-story half-timber house with large gabled dormers in its slate roof. **40 Upper Road** (1903) [10c] is a two-and-one-half-story shingled house that has a shallow-pitched gable roof and an off-centered recessed entry. At **20 Glenwood** (1900) [10d] is yet another of White's large shingled houses.

11. Porteos House, 1894
End of Lagunitas Road, north side of Phoenix Lake

Page & Turnball, architects (restoration, 1986)

This is a rare Bay Area example of an Adirondack Queen Anne Victorian redwood log cabin with picturesque massing and even a log turret. It is notable for stick work made from small branch logs, and for window frames of curly burl wood. It was built for the manager of the Porteos family ranch. The fifteen-minute walk through Natalie Coffin Greene Park is worth the trip. It is located on Marin Municipal Water District property. The district was formed in 1913 and is the oldest publicly owned water district in the state.

12. Moya Del Pino House, 1937
160 Laurel Grove

Gardner A. Dailey, architect

The elegant simplicity of Dailey's early work is evident in this home for artist Moya Del Pino, a founder of the Marin Art and Garden Center.

8

11

6 · San Anselmo · Fairfax · San Geronimo Valley

San Anselmo

San Anselmo's growth from rural farmland into a small city began after the opening of the North Pacific Coast Railroad from San Rafael to San Anselmo in 1874, and the completion of the line from Sausalito through San Anselmo to Pt. Reyes Station in 1875. San Anselmo became an important crossroads or "hub" for these two lines, and the city was known as "Junction."

Settlement remained slow, and most houses were only used in the summer until the San Francisco Theological Seminary moved to San Anselmo in 1892. The population boomed after the 1906 earthquake and fire,

and the city was incorporated a year later.

1. San Francisco Theological Seminary, 1892
Bolinas Avenue and Seminary Road

Wright and Sanders, architects

The seminary was founded in San Francisco in 1871 and was moved to San Anselmo in 1892. Two Richardsonian Romanesque castle-like buildings are located on Seminary Hill, west of downtown, and are highly visible landmarks:

Scott Library Hall (1892) has two conical roofs and several intersecting gabled roofs; **Montgomery Hall** (1892) has

a tower, turrets, and an arched entry. Both are constructed of heavily rusticated blue-gray basalt stone with trim of a lighter sandstone from San Jose; the grounds were designed by John McLaren.

Also located on the hillside is **Geneva Hall** (1952), which is an eclectic combination of elements in white reinforced concrete inspired by the two earlier buildings, including a bell tower with arched loggia openings.

Montgomery Chapel [1], at the corner of Bolinas and Richmond Avenues, was also designed by Wright and Sanders. The cornerstone for the exquisite Romanesque-style stone chapel

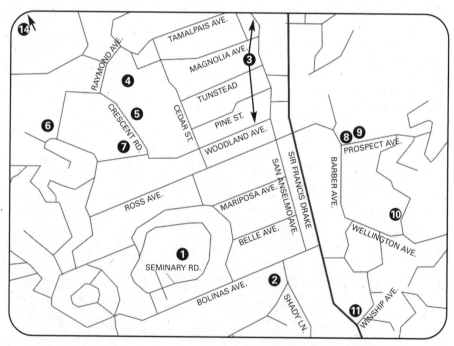

was laid in 1894, and the building was completed in 1897.
It is a memorial to benefactor Alexander Montgomery. It has a tall bell tower with an open loggia topped by a conical roof.

Other seminary buildings of interest include **47 Seminary Road** and **118 Bolinas Avenue**, both designed by Julia Morgan in 1921: 47 Seminary is a large brown shingle with a projecting second-story bay, and 118 Bolinas is smaller and boxier.

Known as the "twin houses," **134 and 138 Bolinas Avenue** (1892) are transitional examples of Colonial Revival. **15 Kensington Court** was designed by George Percy and Frederick Hamilton in 1895. **The Playhouse in San Anselmo** at Waverly and Bolinas, a large shingled building built for the seminary as a gym and theater, was designed by local architect Harris Osborn in 1928.

2. St. Anselms Catholic Church, 1908

67 Shady Lane

Frank T. Shea and John O. Lofquist, architects

The scale and massing of the Tudor Revival–style church are unusual. It has a wide-spreading gambrel roof with flared eaves and a large round window under the gable. The entry porch roof repeats the shape of the main roof and is set on heavy timbers with a timber-framed round window under its gable. It has two bays: a small round one has a conical roof and a larger polygonal bay is on the left. Half-timbering is perpendicular, with no diagonal pieces and only one continuous horizontal piece. The hexagonal, nearly

freestanding bell tower at the rear of the south side is now partially hidden behind a misplaced parish house built in the 1950s.

Downtown

3. Main Street

San Anselmo Avenue, between Bolinas Avenue and Bridge Street

This is an early-twentieth-century downtown of mostly one- and two-story buildings. In the center is **City Hall** (1991; W. Garden Mitchell, architect) and next door is the **Library** (1915; Mitchell & Hodge, architects). Both these buildings are vaguely Mission Revival. The **Cheda Building** (1911) is a two-story brick building with white trim; the **Mercantile Trust Building** (1926) across the street is also in brick. Both of these buildings create a formal entrance to downtown from Sir Francis Drake Boulevard.

West of Downtown

4. Robson-Harrington Park and House, 1906

Crescent Road and Raymond Avenue

The park is a pleasant walk from downtown through a residential neighborhood. The house, located at **237 Crescent Road,** was built by E. K. Wood, owner of the E. K. Wood Lumber and Mill Co. Essentially a Colonial Revival, the house has elaborate moldings and pilasters around the front door and windows. The interior is Craftsman style. Its raised basement is concrete scored to look like stone. The house (open occasionally) and its gardens (open daily) were donated to the city in 1979 by Kernan and Geraldine Robson.

5. Fred Croker House, 1906
245 Crescent Road

Harris Osborn, architect

This is an elegant Shingle-style home set in a large lush garden.

6. Arthur Wellington House, 1902
217 Crescent Road

Maxwell Bugbee, architect

The Wellington House and its neighbor, the Shatford House at **205 Crescent** (1907), were designed by Bugbee. Both are one-and-one-half-story brown-shingle houses with front-facing gabled roofs that dominate the façade. Closed eaves and simple thick bargeboards make a return at the gable end, emphasizing the large gable and suggesting a pediment.

7. Gallagher House, 1913
118 Woodland Avenue

The one-and-one-half-story Craftsman bungalow has a deeply recessed front porch that wraps around two sides of the house. The house has deep overhanging bracketed eaves, with a two-panel verge board design, twelve-over-one

sash windows, and a clinker brick chimney.

Winship Park

The neighborhood lies on the east side of Sir Francis Drake Boulevard and is partially in Ross. Two houses designed by Bernard Maybeck are obscured by trees: the **Hopps House** (1906) is on Winding Way, just south of Canyon Road, and the **Tufts House** (1904) is at 14 Entrata Avenue.

8. Curtis House, 1906
9 Prospect Avenue

Harris Osborn, architect

Harmonizing with its wooded location, the unpainted two-story shingled home has a two-story central gabled bay flanked by porches covered by trellises made of heavy wood posts and beams.

9. Grace Patterson Newell House, 1908, 1913
15 Prospect Avenue

Julia Morgan, architect

The wide horizontal-shaped shingled house has a tall side-facing gable roof with a shed roof dormer in the center; a central section is flanked by sunrooms. Clinker brick is used for entrance columns, pathways, foundation walls, and entry steps.

10. Beal House, 1904
160 Prospect Avenue

Ernest Coxhead, architect

Tucked behind ancient oaks, this Shingle-style house has a tall leaded window over the entry.

11. Barber House, 1890
73 Winship Avenue

Maxwell Bugbee, architect

The symmetrically arranged two-story façade has rounded corner bays.

Northwest of Downtown

12. 100 Alder Avenue, 1910
Maxwell Bugbee, architect

Although the house cannot be seen from the street because of a thick layer of shrubs, its remarkable (and rare) sixty-five-foot shingled water tower stands in full view.

13. Andrew Carrigan House, 1893
96 Park Drive

Ernest Coxhead, architect

The shingled house is distinctive for its enormous one-and-one-half-story gabled roof punctuated by bow-shaped dormers and massive chimneys. On the east side is a deep porch (now glassed in) covered by a shed roof and held by Tuscan columns.

14. Robert Berger House, 1950
259 Redwood Road

Frank Lloyd Wright, architect

Wide overhanging eaves and outstretching garden walls of embedded stone push the building horizontally into its natural setting. The only residential structure Wright designed in Marin County, it is a wonderful example of one of his Usonian houses. Robert Berger, the original owner, built the house, splitting stones, pouring concrete, and building fixtures and furniture. The house was almost complete when Berger died in 1973.

Sleepy Hollow

Sleepy Hollow is a residential subdivision begun in 1932. Architect Harold G. Stoner was the developer's architect who designed many of the California Ranch–style homes here. At the end of Butterfield Road is **San Dominico School,** designed by Schubart and Friedman (1966), with landscaping by Royston, Hanamoto, Mays and Beech. The school moved from Dominican Convent in San Rafael. On **Katrina Lane** off Butterfield is a small development by Joseph Eichler, consisting of seventeen houses designed by Claude Oakland in 1972. The hills on either side of Sleepy Hollow are public open space.

Fairfax

The town of Fairfax is named for Lord Charles Snowden Fairfax, tenth Baron of Cameron, Scotland. Fairfax came to California as a Gold Rush forty-niner, and by 1855, he was residing in what would become the town of Fairfax. Remnants of Fairfax's estate, the former **Town & Country Club,** still remain at the end of Pastori Avenue. Fairfax also was the location of **Arequipa Sanitarium** (1911) on Sir Francis Drake Boulevard west of town. Arequipa was a women's tuberculosis sanatorium that opened in 1911 and closed in 1957. Its rustic stone entry gates and retaining walls are visible from the road. The pottery made here between 1912 and 1917 provided meaningful work for the women, and has become internationally famous. **The Meadow Club** (1927; John White, architect) at 1001 Fairfax Bolinas Road is a rambling one-story shingled building overlooking a golf course.

15. The Red Pavilion, 1921
Elsie Lane, off Bolinas Road

This large Classic Revival building sits on the top of a knoll above the Civic Center and Park. It was built as a dance hall but now serves as an arts and sports center.

16. St. Rita's Church, 1912
2086 Sir Francis Drake Boulevard

The small wood-sided church, now used as the parish hall, has a high gabled roof with a clipped gable end over the entry and a distinctive pyramidal-shaped bell cupola.

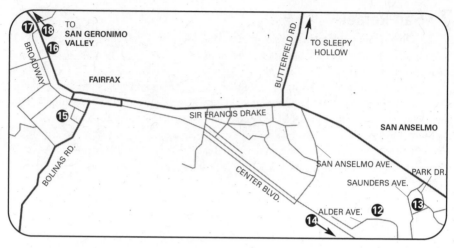

17. Fairfax Public Library, 1977

2097 Sir Francis Drake Boulevard

Bull, Field, Stockwell, Volkman, architects

Nicely nestled under the oaks, the shingle-style library has deep eaves held by pole posts and is well suited to its site.

San Geronimo Valley (unmapped)

San Geronimo Valley is "over-the-hill" (White's Hill), with four unincorporated rural communities. While Fairfax had Lord Fairfax, the San Geronimo Valley had Adolph Mailliard, the illegitimate grandson of King Joseph Bonaparte of Spain and Naples. It is said that Mailliard purchased 6,000 acres in the valley in 1867, sight unseen. After Adolph and his wife, Annie, died in the mid-1890s, their children began to subdivide the valley. In 1903, they created the community of **Lagunitas** and

built a store and several cottages facing the train station. In 1912, they sold the rest of their property to the Lagunitas Development Company, which created the communities of **Woodacre** and **San Geronimo** in 1913 and **Forest Knolls** in 1914. The 1920s Mission Revival–style San Geronimo School is now the **San Geronimo** Valley Cultural Center.

18. San Geronimo Train Station, 1875

Nicasio Valley Road and Sir Francis Drake Boulevard

This is the last of the original North Pacific Coast Railroad stations standing in Marin County. It dates from 1875, the year the railroad began operating. Although moved forty feet directly west, it remains on the berm next to where the railroad tracks were located. It is a Swiss-style train station with board-and-batten siding and a wide overhang-ing gabled roof supported by brackets. It is among the few pre-1880 train stations standing in the Bay Area.

7 • San Rafael

On a sunny south-facing hillside overlooking a fertile valley, Father Vicente de Sarria of Mission Dolores built a hospital mission in 1817. He named the mission San Rafael Archangel for the angel of healing.

After the mission closed in 1833, Timothy (Don Timoteo) Murphy was appointed accolade (mayor) of San Rafael and was granted 22,000 acres of land in 1844. Murphy's land grant stretched from San Rafael to Lucas Valley (named for John Lucas, Murphy's nephew). Today San Rafael encompasses most of that land grant.

In 1850, San Rafael was surveyed and laid out in a grid, with the streets conveniently, but unimaginatively, named numerically from south to north and alphabetically from east to west. San Rafael became the county seat in 1863. In 1870, Marin's first railroad began operating between San Rafael and a ferry at San Quentin Point.

San Rafael is a large spread-out city and has many distinct neighborhoods and cultural resources that date from various periods of its history.

1. Mission San Rafael Archangel, 1949
1104 Mission Avenue
Arnold Constable, architect

This is the site of the hospital mission built in 1817, eventually becoming a full mission and the twentieth in the chain of twenty-one California missions. The

mission grounds included a monastery, storehouses, a hospital, orchards, and a cemetery. The buildings were closed in 1833, gradually fell into ruin,

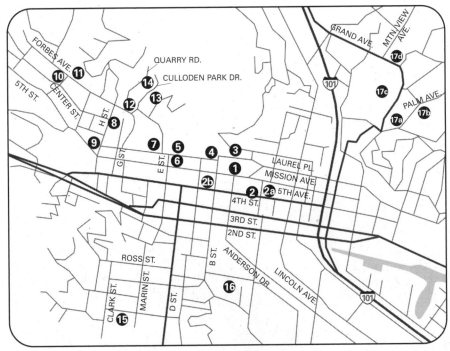

and were gone by 1861. The Mission-style chapel that stands today is said to have been copied from a 1902 painting based on written accounts. It is a simple one-story, L-shaped building with a gabled roof, white stucco walls, red-clay tile roof, and exposed rafter beams. The entry surround with two quatrefoil windows above are its only decorative elements.

St. Rafael's Catholic Church (1919; Shea & Lofquist, architects) replaced an 1870 parish church. Its tall Mission-style bell tower flanked by shorter ones is a prominent landmark. The bell tower once rose behind the cupola of the old 1873 County Courthouse that was demolished in 1971.

2. Fourth Street

Fourth Street has been important commercially since the 1850s, and it retains qualities of a traditional nineteenth-century main street. The redevelopment of Courthouse Square after the county completed its move to the new Civic Center in 1971 resulted in the erection of a box

of an office building that disrupts the scale of a cohesive downtown.

A group of two-story Italianates from the 1880s is located on the 700 and 800 blocks. They have original second stories, but ground-floor retail spaces have been altered. Plaques embedded in the sidewalk contain information about some of these historic buildings. Both the **Masonic Hall and Office Building** at 1010 Lootens, and the **Albert Building** at 1010 B Street (1924; Samuel C. Heinman, architect) are Moderne buff-colored brick with classically inspired terra-cotta window and door surrounds.

2a. Rafael Theater/ California Film Institute, 1919, 1938
1118 Fourth Street

The 1919 theater was remodeled in Art Deco style in 1938 and was reopened as the Film Institute in 1998 after being restored. The interior is noteworthy for its elegant curved staircase (1938) and Art Deco murals by Henry Martins.

2b. Mahon House Hotel, 1879
1330 Fourth Street

The three-story Second Empire–style building has a mansard roof inset with arched dormers. There are bracketed pediments over the second-story windows, cast-iron storefront surrounds, and stucco siding over brick. It is believed to be downtown's oldest building.

3. William T. Coleman House, 1849–1852, with later additions
1130 Mission Avenue

Believed to be the oldest building in San Rafael, it was purchased in 1866 by vigilante William Tell Coleman, an early developer in San Rafael. The original house is the two-story Gothic Revival section on the west side. It has a central gable, tall sash windows with drip hood moldings, a covered porch across the front, and painted wood siding.

Other nineteenth-century houses remaining on Mission Avenue include **1135** (1891; William Barr, architect); **907** (1880); **828** (1884); **823–825** (1881; Heatherton & Pelton, architects); **822** (1880s); and **820** (1885; T. J. Welsh, architect).

4. Boyd Gate House/ Marin County Historical Society, 1879
1125 B Street at Mission Avenue

This is an excellent and beautifully maintained Stick-style Victorian with scalloped bargeboards and lacy cresting over the porches and angled bays; there are carved brackets, cross gables, gabled dormers, covered porches on three sides, and narrow perpendicular pieces under the eaves and cross pieces used for the

railing of the porches. The house was originally the entrance lodge to Ira Cook's estate, "Maple Lawn." The house was moved to this location in 1924; it now serves as home to the Marin County Historical Society Museum and Library.

The **Ira Cook/John Boyd House** ("Maple Lawn") at 1312 Mission Avenue was constructed in the 1850s but has been enlarged and altered a number of times. Large gardens surround the house, now home to the San Rafael Elks Club. Boyd Park, once part of the estate, was donated to the city in 1907.

5. Robert Dollar Estate, "Falkirk," 1888
1408 Mission Avenue

Clinton Day, architect

An impressive and elegant Queen Anne Victorian has a multitude of elements, both decorative and structural, including a complicated arrangement of gable-roofed bays, one of which is rounded. The house retains much of its interior, original grounds, and landscaping. In 1974, the city of San Rafael, pressured by the community, purchased the property as a cultural center.

6. San Rafael Public Library, 1908
1100 E Street and Mission Avenue

Reid Brothers, architects

The square brick building with carved limestone trim, somewhat compromised with additions, was funded by the Carnegie Foundation.

7. O'Conner House/ Foster Hall, 1870
Mission Avenue

The former mansion, now covered with stucco, retains the characteristic profile of its Italianate style: rectangular shape, wraparound covered porch, hipped roof with flat central section, and brackets under the eaves. W. A. Foster donated the house and grounds to the San Rafael Military Academy in 1892; it is still a private school.

The Forbes District

Alexander Forbes was a major Marin County landowner who subdivided this area in 1867. It has a number of outstanding nineteenth- and early-twentieth-century houses.

8. Bradford Manor, 1883
333 G Street

The design of this large Stick/ Eastlake Victorian–era house is said to have come from a pattern book. It has an irregular roofline, shed dormers, gabled bays, stick-work brackets, and a variety of decorative siding. Its wraparound porch is partially glazed.

G Street has a number of historic houses: **115** (1908; C. M. Cook, builder); **301** (1881; William Wharff, architect); **313**, a Stick-style Victorian; and **346** (1917; Albert Farr, architect).

9. San Rafael Improvement Club, 1915
1800 Fifth Street

The square Neoclassic building has rounded corners and a distinctive copper dome. It was constructed for the Victor Victrola Company Pavilion at the Panama-Pacific International Exposition in 1915. It was re-erected here by the San Rafael

Improvement Club, and a restoration was completed in 2005.

10. Robert Dollar House, 1891
115 J Street

Newsom Brothers, J. E. Bundy, architects

This is a two-story Queen Anne Victorian. Around the corner on Center Street are two houses from the 1870s: the Gothic Revival at **12 Center Street** (1872) and the Italianate at **21 Center Street** (1879), both built by W. J. Dickson.

11. Lock House, 1889
230 Forbes Avenue

Samuel Newsom, architect

Here is a Victorian Queen Anne that has a multitude of carved decoration, including reclining lions in the circular recessed porch opening.

12. Judge F. M. Angelotti House, 1892
1 Culloden Park Drive

Percy and Hamilton, architects

A good example of the Shingle style (although painted), this house has a rounded corner bay, hipped roof dormers, and a sloping gabled roof.

13. Clarence Allen Thayer/ Babcock House, 1907
16 Culloden Park Drive

Maxwell Bugbee, architect

The large three-story Shingle-style house is set on a heavily rusticated stone foundation that has a wide arched opening in its center. A rounded corner bay, an angled central bay topped by a broken pediment, multiple roofs, and a three-part Palladian attic window enhance the large house. Thayer was in the lumber and shipping business; his schooner, the *C. A. Thayer,* is on display at the San Francisco Maritime Museum.

14. Tufts House, 1906
43 Culloden Park Drive
Bernard Maybeck, architect

Maybeck has exaggerated the scale and massing of this Tudor Revival; it has a prominent steeply pitched gable front and heavy wood pieces between the stucco panels.

15. Gerstle Park

The residential district south of downtown is named for the public park donated to the city in 1930 by descendants of Lewis Gerstle, who purchased a summer estate here in 1881. Louis Sloss, Gerstle's brother-in-law and partner in the Alaska Commercial Company, bought an adjacent property in 1883.

The neighborhood has a mix of buildings from different periods, but most of San Rafael's oldest vernacular nineteenth-century buildings are located here. There are some fine examples of Victorian-era houses (both large and small), Arts and Crafts bungalows, stucco bungalows, and Shingle-style houses mixed with a few post–World War II apartment houses.

The neighborhood may contain the largest group of unaltered raised-basement Italianate cottages from the 1860s through the mid-1880s in the Bay Area. They are rectangular- or cube-shaped with symmetrical façades: a front door flanked by one or two tall sash windows, covered porches across the front, and shallow hipped roofs. There is a good

example of an Italianate cottage at **806 E Street** off Third Street, even with its asphalt siding, and **127 San Rafael Avenue** (1883) is a grand Italianate Victorian with a gabled roof, angled bays, and many decorative details.

16. Wildcare
76 Albert Park Lane

The Terwilliger (formerly the Louise Boyd) Nature Education Center and Wildlife Rehabilitation Center is headquartered in a Gothic Revival building that dates from around 1870. Originally the parish house for St. Paul's Episcopal Church, it was moved with the church in 1923 to Center Street, and then moved again to this location in 1954. Although not in pristine condition, the building has lancet windows, a high-pitched open gabled ceiling, and interesting interior woodwork.

17. Coleman Park/ Dominican Area

William Tell Coleman subdivided this area in 1871. William Hammond Hall, a San Francisco civil engineer and first superintendent of Golden Gate Park, designed and laid out the curvilinear street plan. Coleman built Lagunitas Lake above Ross to bring water to Coleman Park, and his Rafael Hotel (burned in 1928) was built as an anchor for his subdivision. Coleman was also an early miner of borax, and Colemanite (a borax compound) is named for him. He is remembered also as a leader of the 1856 Vigilante Committee.

Grand Avenue leaves the grid at Mission Street and begins its curvilinear route through the Coleman Park neighborhood.

This was once an area of grand summer homes on large pieces of land, which have mostly been re-subdivided. A group of representative late-nineteenth- and early-twentieth-century homes are visible on Palm Avenue: **11** (1908) is a brown shingled house with an unusual angled façade embracing the front garden; **31** (1907) is a two-story brown shingle; **49** dates from 1896; **50** (1907) is a Tudor-style house with gray-painted shingles and diamond-paned windows; **122** (1895) and **130** (1890) were designed by architect Brainerd Jones; and **134** (1899, 1915) is an impressive Shingle-style home.

17a. Meadowlands, 1888, 1899
145 Palm Avenue
Clinton Day, architect

Built as a summer home for Michael de Young, cofounder of the *San Francisco Chronicle*, the house was remodeled in 1899 by Clinton Day. The rambling and picturesque front section of the shingled house is original even though marred by fire escapes. It has been used as a dormitory since 1918, and there are many additions on the back.

17b. John Lucas House, 1880s
160 Palm Avenue

The unpainted cube-shaped house has a hipped roof bisected in the front by a small gable and carved brackets under the eaves; an unusual stick-work veranda surrounds the house.

17c. Dominican Convent and Dominican University
1520 Grand Avenue

The Dominican Order moved from Benicia to this location in 1889. Their new home was a grand timber-framed Victorian-era building designed by T. J. Welsh. After a fire damaged the building in 1990, it was demolished. It was the last dramatic Victorian building of its type still standing in Marin County. All that remains are four Corinthian columns. A quiet group of one- and-two-story shingled buildings designed in 1996 by TWM Architects (Peter Walz, Ian McLeod and Dereck Dutton, architects) replaced the old convent.

Dominican College became Dominican University in 1997. Buildings of interest include **Fanjeaux Hall** (1926; Albert Cauldwill, architect) at 180 Palm, a Tudor Revival dormitory building; **Angelico Hall** (1922) and **Guzman Hall** (1930), designed by architect Morris M. Bruce; the **William Babcock House, "Edgehill"** (1887), at 25 Magnolia, an immense Victorian long used as a dorm; and **Santa Sabina** (1939; Arnold Constable, architect), a Gothic/Tudor with leaded-glass lancet windows. The **Dining Commons** (1959) and **Library** (1961) by architects Schubart and Friedman are good examples of wood-sided mid-century Modernism.

17d. "Ferndale," 1892
1 Locust Avenue, at the corner of Grand Avenue

Nathaniel Blaisdale, architect

Among many grand shingled houses in this area, this one is painted blue-gray, with multiple cross gables and covered porches.

18. Marin County Civic Center, 1962–1970
Junction of North San Pedro Road and Civic Center Drive

Frank Lloyd Wright, architect

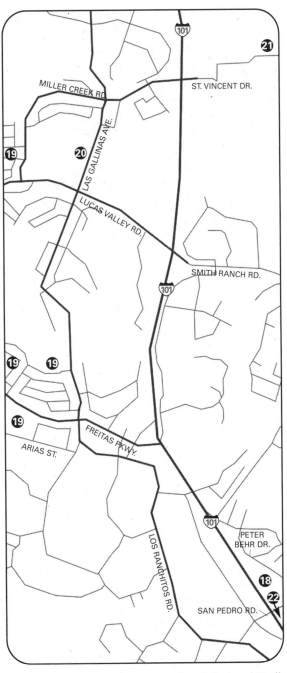

The Marin County Civic Center is the most architecturally significant building in Marin. Like a bridge, the wide horizontal, three- and four-story building spans the spaces between three hilltops, bringing together landscape and architecture. It is a remarkable design concept. The building also has a fully integrated interior design program that includes such elements as elevators, signage, light fixtures, furniture, and doorknobs.

The **Administration Building** (the south wing) was completed in 1962, and the **Hall of Justice** in 1970. The building contains the courthouse, government offices, and library. It is open to the public and has a decent cafeteria with outside seating; tours are given regularly.

Although the building can be clearly seen driving south on Highway 101, its once-pristine image between hillsides has been somewhat compromised by buildings at the base of the hill and the addition of a square-shaped, concrete-gray prison on the north hilltop in 2000.

19. Terra Linda, Eichler Homes, 1954–1972
Manuel Freitas Parkway and Lucas Valley Road

Anshen + Allen & Claude Oakland, et al., architects

There are several neighborhoods and hundreds of Eichler-built homes on or near Manuel Freitas Parkway and off Lucas Valley Road. Joseph Eichler (1900–1974) built thousands of mid-twentieth-century Modern-style houses in several hundred subdivisions in the Bay Area. His experience living in a

Usonian house designed by Frank Lloyd Wright inspired him to build houses for the middle class that incorporated modern design and construction concepts. Eichler's first subdivision (1947) was in Palo Alto; Terra Linda was begun in 1954, and he continued to build here until around 1972. Eichler did not discriminate in selling his houses; his goal was to build communities, not just houses.

A. Quincy Jones, Frederick Emmons, Robert Anshen and Stephen Allen (Anshen + Allen), and Claude Oakland were the principal architects who worked for Eichler. While simplicity and standardization saved construction costs, the house plans and details evolved over time. All featured modular, exposed post-and-beam construction set on a concrete slab with radiant heat. Floor plans were open but with a distinct separation of functions. The houses turn their backs on streets and open onto private gardens. The inner courtyard, or atrium, was first used in 1958 and soon became synonymous with the name "Eichler." The tall gabled roof was introduced in 1962.

20. Dixie School, 1864
2255 Las Gallinas Avenue

The Old Dixie Schoolhouse has a Gothic Revival profile with a steeply pitched central gable over the entrance and has Classic Revival decorative elements. It served as a schoolhouse until 1954 but is still owned by the school district.

21. St. Vincent's School for Boys
St. Vincent's Church, 1927

St. Vincent Drive,
4 miles north of San Rafael

Leo Mitchell, architect

The Sisters of Charity founded a school for orphans in 1855 on land donated by Timothy Murphy. The present buildings mostly date from the 1920s. The spires of the impressive Spanish Colonial–style church, which has a richly decorated façade, can be seen from the freeway.

22. R.A.B. Motors, 1985
Francisco Boulevard and Highway 101

Esherick Homsey Dodge and Davis, architects

Peter Dodge, principal architect

Sleek and silver with rounded corners and full-height windows, this showroom is the most distinguished on San Rafael's auto row.

8 · Novato

By 1850, Joseph B. Sweetser and Francis C. DeLong had gained possession of Fernando Feliz's Rancho de Novato and established orchards, dairy ranches, vineyards, and cheese factories. When the railroad arrived in 1879, DeLong subdivided 6,000 acres of his land.

Old "main street" Novato has been spruced up, repaved, and replanted; there are a few authentic historic buildings on Grant Street and nearby side streets. However, most of the incorporated city of 50,000 is spread out on both sides of the freeway, with six freeway exits, and many of its commercial and residential subdivisions are isolated enclaves that do not connect with one another.

1. First Presbyterian Church/City Hall, 1889
900 Sherman Avenue

This former Gothic Revival church is now the Novato City Hall and the beginning of "Old Town" Novato.

2. Novato History Museum, 1856
815 DeLong Avenue

This small Greek Revival wood-sided building has a gable roof and quoins painted white. It was Novato's first post office and was moved to this location in 1972.

3. Grant Avenue at Railroad Avenue

The train arrived in 1879 and there are still tracks, a signal light, and two train stations: the charred remains of one from the 1890s and an unused one in the Mission Revival style.

4. Holy Ghost Society Building IDESI, 1906
901 Sweetser Avenue, at Machin Avenue

This simple, almost-austere, two-story building has a front-facing gabled roof and a covered porch across the front and east sides.

5. Novato Branch of the Marin County Library, 1970
1720 Novato Boulevard

Marquis and Stoller, architects

The library is set into a grassy berm that contrasts nicely with the textured concrete-block siding and oversized gabled roofs sheathed with terra-cotta-colored concrete tile. The U-shaped plan creates an open courtyard. On the interior, the tall open-gable ceilings are dark above fluorescent lighting.

6. Delong House, circa 1870
50 Rica Vista

The two-story wood-frame house, now a retreat center, was once in the middle of a large farm and ranch. The gable ends of both the roof and its dormers have broken pediments. There is a covered veranda across the front.

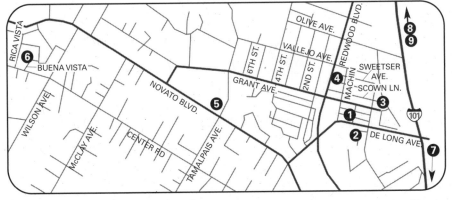

7a

7b

7. Hamilton Air Field,
1932–1935
(unmapped)
*Main Gate Road and
Highway 101
(exit Nave Drive)*

*Capt. Howard B. Nurse,
engineer-designer*

Captain Howard B. Nurse, a graduate of the Mechanics Institute in New York, designed and supervised the construction of the Spanish Colonial–themed air base between 1932 and 1935. The 1,776-acre site contains 108 buildings and 17 structures listed on the National Register as a Historic District. The base was decommissioned in 1975 and is being redeveloped; the old runways have returned to marshlands.

7a. Headquarter Building/ Novato Art Center

Inspired by California missions, the building has one-story arched loggias flanking a two-story gable-roofed section that has a richly decorated entry, tile roofs, and white stucco siding.

7b. Enlisted Men's Quarters

The block-long groups of reinforced-concrete three-story buildings are an unusual combination of utilitarian Moderne with Churrigueresque bas-relief decoration.

7c. Airplane Hangars

A stunning row of paired hangars have recently been gutted and redone. Two coast guard hangars on the south end are original and still have their small-paned industrial-steel windows.

7d. Officer Residences
Los Lomas Drive

On the hillside above the hangars is a row of Mediterranean-style houses, some with entrances surrounded by polychrome tiles. Palm trees and stone walls of blue chert line the streets. The houses are generously spaced, show views of the marsh, and have old oak trees in their yards.

8. Buck Center for Aging,
1998 (unmapped)
8001 Redwood Boulevard

I. M. Pei, architect

The angled sharp edges of the frankly contemporary buildings are prominent from Highway 101 and are quite a jarring contrast to the oak-studded grass of Mt. Burdell Open Space Preserve above. A building designed by architect Ieoh Ming Pei should generate interest here, but access is restricted.

9. Camilo Ynitia Adobe,
early 1830s (unmapped)
Olompali State Historic Park
*8901 Redwood Highway,
State Highway 101*

The adobe walls of the Camilo Ynitia Adobe lie within the charred ruins of the Burdell Mansion. Camilo Ynito received a U.S. Patent Title to his Mexican Land Grant, but he sold his land in 1852 to James Black, who gave this parcel to his daughter Mary and son-in-law Galen Burdell. The mansion they built around the adobe in the 1880s burned in 1969. Two barns are nearby: one is a square barn with a cupola in the center of its hipped roof and is believed to date from the 1850s, and the adjoining gable-roofed barn was built in 1882.

9 • West Marin County: Stinson Beach, Bolinas, Pt. Reyes National Seashore, Inverness, Tomales

Stretching north from the Marin Headlands just west of the Golden Gate Bridge to Valley Ford on the Sonoma County line, West Marin is a landscape of windblown cliffs plunging directly into the Pacific Ocean; wide, quiet grassy valleys and hills dotted with grazing cows; steep forested mountains, hills, and valleys; sandy beaches; and authentic small towns.

Intense development pressure beginning in the 1950s has been fought vigorously. Much of West Marin is parkland, watershed, or otherwise preserved. Muir Woods National Monument was dedicated in 1908; Mt. Tamalpais State Park was established in 1928; the Pt. Reyes National Seashore legislation was signed in 1962; the Golden Gate National Recreation Area was signed in 1972; seashore land acquisition funding began in 1970; and Marin Agricultural Land Trust was founded in 1980. The pressure for development continues, but West Marin has many watchful eyes.

Stinson Beach

The wide sandy beach, once called Easkoots and later Willow Camp, has been a popular resort since the early 1900s. In 1906, Nathan H. Stinson subdivided the land north of Willow Camp with *calles* (streets) perpendicular to the beach and named his subdivision Stinson Beach. A post office opened in 1916; Stinson Beach State Park began as a county park in the 1930s.

1. Tower House, 1971–1972
7655 Panoramic Highway

Val Agnoli, architect

1

Photo by Val Agnoli

The handcrafted three-story "tower" house is located on a steep lot overlooking the ocean. It is a post-and-beam ellipsoidal-shaped structure designed to have a very small footprint, with one twelve-by-fifteen-foot central room on each of its three floors. It is sheathed in unpainted shingles.

Val Agnoli's own house is located at 7100 Panoramic Highway. Constructed by the architect himself, it has a wide curved shape, like a bridge. Agnoli studied with Bruce Goff, who inspired Agnoli to design outside the confines of Classicism.

2. Seadrift
Calle Del Arroyo, at the end of the road

The sand spit was subdivided and the lagoon dredged in the 1940s. There are more than 300 houses behind the guarded gates of this private community, and prominent architects are well represented. Public access to the beach in front of Seadrift was won through numerous lawsuits; signs warn the public that they may walk but not sit or play there. Rooftops rise above the sand dunes, affording a glimpse of what lies beyond.

3. Audubon Canyon Ranch
4900 Shoreline Highway 1

The 1,000-acre Audubon Canyon Ranch was established in 1961 to protect the habitat of heron and egret nests. Its headquarters are in a Gothic Revival farmhouse (1875) that has clapboard siding and a steeply pitched cross-gable roof. Also on the property is a milking barn (1930) now used for displays and lectures, the Samuel P. Weeks ranch house (1875), and a carpenter's shop (1852).

4. Wilkens Ranch, founded 1868
Shoreline Highway and Bolinas Road

The two-story farmhouse dates from around 1869 and stands prominently on a rise above Bolinas Lagoon. The ranch was used as a farm until 2002, and includes the farmhouse, an exceptional horse barn, and other outbuildings. The National Park Service is in the process of converting it to a visitors' center.

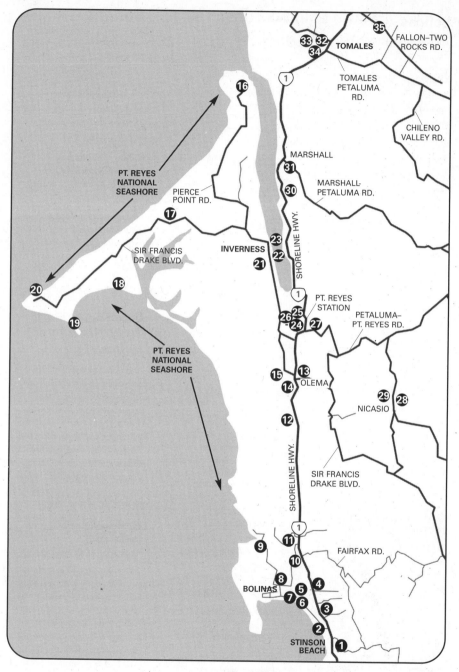

9 • West Marin County: Stinson Beach, Bolinas,
Pt. Reyes National Seashore, Inverness, Tomales

Bolinas

Timber from the Bolinas Ridge was cut and milled near here during the 1850s; the lumber industry created the town of Bolinas. When the post office was established in 1863, the population was more than 300. During the 1880s, Frank Waterhouse created building lots along Brighton Road and Park Avenue where summerhouses were built. The Little Mesa was subdivided in 1909 and the Big Mesa in 1927. On Wharf Road, the **Sharon Building, Smiley's Saloon,** and the grocery store have false-front façades. The **Gibson House** (1875) is a two-story Italianate Victorian with a cross-gable roof, and quoins at the corners.

5. Calvary Presbyterian Church, 1877
Brighton Avenue and Wharf Road

This Gothic Revival church that sits prominently at the entrance to town has a steeply pitched, double-sloping gable roof and, on the north side, a square bell tower with a steep pyramidal roof and flared eaves, carved brackets, and a lace-work balustrade.

6. Bolinas Museum
48 Wharf Road

Bolinas Museum, founded in 1982, is a complex of restored and reused late-nineteenth-century buildings. Its annual spring garden tours are an opportunity to visit private homes and gardens. The gallery building to the south dates from 1880, and next to that, the **Marin Marine Station** (1917) is a former Coast Guard Station.

7. House, 1860s
23 Brighton Avenue

This simple, unaltered, two-story Gothic Revival house dates from the 1860s. It has original two-over-two sash windows, a cross-gable roof, and a full-width porch covered by a shed roof supported by posts with curved brackets.

8. House, 1994
40 Mesa Road

Leddy Maytum Stacy, architects

This sleek contemporary house has a standing-seam metal roof and a low wide profile. The house is a contrast to the modest homes—woodsy and sometimes handcrafted—scattered on the mesa, and the older houses that line Brighton Avenue. Next door is a barrel-vaulted roofed house (2005; Arkin Tilt, architect).

9. Marconi/RCA Transmitting Station, 1914
451 Mesa Road

J. G. White Engineering Company, New York

The former wireless transmitting station was opened in 1914; it was connected to its counterpart in Marshall by a cable line laid underground and later by wires hung from poles. This complex includes two large multistoried concrete structures, several one-story cottages, as well as the former two-story Bolinas Hotel for workers and visitors.

10. Bolinas Grammar School, 1867, 1990
Bolinas-Olema Road

A Classic Revival schoolhouse has a square bell tower with

flared eaves, a recessed covered porch under a pediment, and simple columns. It was rebuilt twice (1908, 1990), each time replicating the original. Next door to the north is the former **Druid Hall** (1870) and on the south are two impressive, two-story nineteenth-century houses.

11. Mary Magdalene Catholic Church, 1877
Horseshoe Hill Road and Bolinas-Olema Road

This is a rectangular wood-frame building with a gable roof and a square enclosed bell tower. There are drip moldings above the windows.

Bolinas-Olema Road/Shoreline Highway 1

There are few buildings between Bolinas and Olema but the ten miles contain much history. **Dogtown** was the location of a bustling lumber mill, and in the hills to the east, there was once a copper mine. The **Randall Ranch House** (1875), a two-story bracketed Italianate once used as a stage stop, is now boarded up and unused.

12. Stewart Ranch House, 1864
8497 Shoreline Highway 1

This is an early, remarkably well-preserved Gothic Revival house with a projecting central gabled bay and a wavy patterned verge board. It has a covered porch across the front, and there are drip moldings above the four-over-four-light sash windows.

Olema

Olema (a Miwok word meaning Coyote Valley) was first settled in 1857 by Benjamin T. Winslow after he returned from the gold-fields. He gave the settlement its name, and built its first hotel, grocery store, saloon, and post office.

13. Olema Hotel, 1876
Sir Francis Drake Boulevard and Shoreline Highway

The prominent two-story struc-ture has a covered veranda across the front. **The Druid's Hall** (1881) is a two-story Italianate with a hipped roof and central gable. At **10045 Sir Francis Drake Boulevard** is a tiny false-front commercial building (1859) that served as the original post office.

14. James McMillan Shafter House/Vedanta Society Retreat, 1869
Shoreline Highway, 1/4 mile south of Sir Francis Drake Boulevard

Looking not unlike a Southern mansion, this remarkable two-story rectangular Italianate has a hipped roof with bracketed eaves, iron cresting, and a cov-ered porch that surrounds the house on three sides. It is the most impressive early West Marin house. The retreat is open to the public once a year.

Pt. Reyes National Sea Shore

On September 13, 1962, President John F. Kennedy signed the legislation creating Pt. Reyes National Seashore. The park is approximately twenty-seven miles long and averages four to five miles wide. It includes natural ecosystems, archeological sites, and historic buildings and structures. The archaeological sites contain remains of the Coast Miwok Native Americans, the possible site where Sir Francis Drake landed in 1579, and also the site of a 1595 Manila galleon shipwreck.

The Pt. Reyes dairy ranching industry that began in the 1850s is a cultural landscape of national significance. A few of the ranches are still in operation, and some of the hiking trails were once ranch roads. Other historic structures include a lighthouse, a coast guard rescue station, wireless receiving and transfer stations, ranch houses, and barns.

15. Bear Valley Visitor's Center, 1985
Bear Valley Road

Henrik Bull, architect

This large barn-like structure has board-and-batten siding and a corrugated metal roof. It was designed to reflect the dairy farming history of the Pt. Reyes Peninsula. Some of the buildings near the Visitors' Center date from before the park was created. This was the site of Bear Valley Ranch (the "W" ranch), and the large timber-framed Red Barn (1870s) is the education center and research library.

The Alphabet Ranches

During the Mexican period, the Pt. Reyes peninsula was used for grazing cattle as early as the 1840s. After 1858 and until 1919, most of the penin-sula was owned by the Shafter family, who leased ranches to tenant farmers. Around 1869, the ranches were brought up to the latest standards and then named for a letter of the alpha-bet, hence the nomenclature "Alphabet Ranches."

After the National Seashore was created, the ranches were pur-chased by the Park Service and leased back to the ranchers. Thirteen ranches are still operat-ing in the park. Along Sir Francis Drake Boulevard, there are signs indicating the date the ranches were first established.

14

16. Upper Pierce Point Ranches, 1850s
End of
Pierce Point Road

The Pierce Point Ranches (Upper and Lower Ranch) were not part of the Alphabet Ranches. Only the buildings at Upper Ranch are still standing, and they comprise a complex of eighteen buildings and structures that date from 1860 to 1933. The utilitarian wood-frame buildings display a straightforward simplicity and ordered arrangement around an open farmyard. It is an outstanding example of a nineteenth-century dairy ranch and is preserved by the park as a cultural and educational resource. **The Hay Barn** (1870) is a large exceptional example of the type of hay and milking barns built on Pt. Reyes. **The Ranch House** dates from 1859 with additions to 1869, the **Dairy** between 1862 and 1875, and the **Horse Barn** from the 1890s.

17. RCA/Marconi Wireless Transmitting Station, 1931
Sir Francis Drake Boulevard

The reinforced-concrete building is Classic Moderne in style with engaged columns. It is reached down a dark allée of Monterey Cypress—a tunnel of overhanging branches. The building and its adjacent fields of antennas (now mostly removed) eventually replaced the receiving communications center at Marshall. Together with the Bolinas station and the Marshall-Marconi receiving station, the three sites comprise what may be the last intact Marconi-era coast stations in North America. This ship-to-shore communication station was known as "KPH" and is open as a museum.

18. Drakes Beach Visitor's Center, 1967
Wong and Brocchini, architects

Here is an appropriate weathered-wood structure raised above the ground on post poles. It houses a visitors' center, a café, and restrooms. Two restroom structures by the same architects are located at North and South Beach.

19. Pt. Reyes Lifeboat Rescue Station, 1927
Chimney Rock Road, off
Sir Francis Drake Boulevard

A simple, two-story gable-roofed boathouse has a "marine railway" that is still operable, extending into the water for launching lifeboats. It is now an information center. On the hill above is a cottage-style residence.

20. Pt. Reyes Lighthouse, 1870
End of
Sir Francis Drake Boulevard
Phineas F. Marston, engineer

The U.S. Lighthouse Service built this station in 1870 on a rocky ledge way below the Pt. Reyes promontory, and the views are magnificent on a clear day. The light is kept in operation by the Park Service and is open to the public.

Inverness

Judge James McMillan Shafter subdivided 640 acres of his land as a summer resort in 1889 and named it Inverness. Many streets have Scottish names. Downtown consists of six buildings; one is a two-story commercial building with angled window bays and a false front, built in 1900 and restored after the 1906 earthquake.

Rustic summer cabins and cottages date from the first half of the twentieth century. Most have been maintained but not extensively altered. A typical rustic redwood summer cabin at 30 Argyle (1910, 1930; Thomas Kent, architect) has board-and-batten siding, one-wall construction, and a clinker-brick fireplace.

21. "The Gables," Jack Mason Museum, 1890
15 Park Avenue

This L-shaped cottage with a cross-gable roof is considered the oldest structure in Inverness. Jack Mason, "the authority on Marin County history," lived here after his retirement. The house was donated to the Inverness Association after his death in 1985. The Inverness Branch of the Marin County Library and the Jack Mason Museum are located in the former house, and the garden is maintained by the Inverness Garden Club.

22. Brock Schreiber Boat House, 1911–1914
12820 Sir Francis Drake Boulevard

This is a prominent landmark in Inverness because it is a large but simple wood-frame building set on pilings over Tomales Bay. A large black-and-white sign under the eaves announces "LAUNCH FOR HIRE."

St. Columba's Episcopal Church at 12835 Sir Francis Drake

Boulevard is a rambling English Cottage–style house (with additions) that was once a summer home. The large living room/chapel has a high, open gabled ceiling with exposed rafter beams. The grounds include rustic pathways between the Stations of the Cross.

23. Inverness Yacht Club, 1914
12845 Sir Francis Drake Boulevard

John Rasmussen, builder

A simple two-story building has a gable roof and some Classic details. At 12847 Sir Francis Drake, the Patterson House (1914) is a large three-story Shingle style.

Pt. Reyes Station

When the North Coast Pacific Railroad opened in 1875, the line was laid along Paper Mill Creek, bypassing the established town of Olema. Today it has a population of less than 700 but is the commercial and tourist center of West Marin.

The town has rural ambience. The Mission Revival brick **Grandi**

Building (1915; Louis Grandi, and sons Reno and Ennio, builders) is the largest and most prominent building; it has been vacant since 1978. The two-story **Western Saloon** (circa 1915) was built by Salvatore Grandi. On the blocks west of Shoreline are several small vernacular workers' cottages.

24. The Emporium Building, 1898
11315 Shoreline Highway

Pietro Scilacci, builder

A two-story false-front commercial building enhances the town's western look.

25. The Dance Palace Community Center, 1914, 1989
Fifth Street, at the corner of B Street

Jim Campe, architect (1989)

The Dance Palace is an important community center located in a former Catholic church.

26. Foresters Hall, 1914
505 Mesa Road

This is distinctive Mission Revival, a two-story clapboard-sided building with a raised

22

basement and twin hip-roofed towers at the corners extending above the roof. The entry bay, set back from the towers, has a curved parapet.

27. Presbyterian Church of Pt. Reyes, 1986
Shoreline Highway

Ray Zerbe, architect

The small brown-shingled building has a large, round stained-glass window, crafted by artist Elizabeth Devereaux, beneath its wide gable.

Nicasio

The village of Nicasio contains just a few buildings around the Will Lafranchi baseball field and village square. Two important historic buildings, plus some scattered nineteenth-century structures and homes, provide a "sense of place" and rural charm.

28. Old St. Mary's of Nicasio Valley, 1867
Nicasio Square

This is a small, simple wood-frame church with a stepped spire rising from the entry porch. Its interior is surprisingly beautiful with redwood paneling and a choir loft; an altar is set back and framed like a proscenium.

29. Nicasio School, 1871
5249 Nicasio Valley Road

The crisply painted former schoolhouse is an excellent example of an Italianate cross-gable-roofed building with broken pediments and carved brackets. It sits on a raised basement and has a cupola with flared eaves.

Marshall

30. Marconi Wireless Receiving Station, 1914
Highway 1, south of Marshall

J. G. White Engineering Company, New York, architects

Guglielmo Marconi's Wireless Company of America transmit-

31

ted its first wireless message across the Atlantic in 1901. In 1914, a transmitting station was built west of Bolinas, and a receiving station, offices, and a hotel were located at Marshall. These two installations were the final link in wireless communication around the world. In 1920, the Marconi Company became the Radio Corporation of America (RCA). Although the transmitter towers and actual station were relocated to a site on the Pt. Reyes Peninsula in 1929, this location was used by RCA until 1947.

The former Marconi Hotel, the largest building of the complex and currently unused, is a two-story reinforced-concrete structure with a raised basement, a tile roof, and a balcony that wraps around three sides. There are also four smaller, one-story concrete buildings with tile roofs. In the 1970s, a group of buildings was constructed higher on the hillside; these have been operated by the State Parks Department as the Marconi Conference Center since 1990.

31. St. Helen's Catholic Church, circa 1906
Marshall-Petaluma Road, just above Highway 1

This tiny shingle church has an arched recessed entry, diamond-paned windows, and little buttresses.

Tomales

The unincorporated town of Tomales has a population of about 250 and approximately 100 buildings. The North Pacific

Coast Rail Road opened here in 1875, but the town was established as a shipping center in the 1850s when agricultural products were shipped by schooner from Walker Creek. The post office opened in 1852. It has a "main street" (State Highway 1), many nineteenth-century houses, and two splendid churches.

32. Church of the Assumption of Mary,
1860, restored 1906
State Highway 1

Here is a Gothic Revival building that has painted shingles, lancet windows, stepped buttressing, and a square bell tower with simple geometric stick work; the entry is accented by a large lancet-shaped stained-glass window framed by an elongated ogee arch above the entrance.

Also on the grounds are a water tower (1887) and a white one-story shingled bungalow with a covered porch on two sides.

33. Tomales Presbyterian Church and Cemetery, 1868
11 Church Street

Here is a simplified Greek Revival temple with a closed gable end and engaged square columns at the corners. Flanking the entry are tall arched windows with pedi-

mented hood moldings. The square bell tower has arched louvered openings.

34. Tomales Regional History Center
26701 Highway 1

The center preserves the history of North Marin County.

Northwest Marin County

Between Tomales and Petaluma, there are a few nineteenth-century ranch houses, barns, and three one- and two-room schoolhouses. **2401 Tomales-Petaluma Road** (1860s), a former school, is now a home, but its bell tower is still in place; **Laguna School** (1906) on Chileno Valley Road is still a two-room schoolhouse with a bell tower; it does not have

a bell because it was donated to the World War II effort. **Lincoln School** (1872) on Hicks Valley Road still functions as a school. 5105 Chileno Valley Road, the **Gale Ranch House,** dates from the 1880s; the two-story Victorian has been restored and remodeled a bit but is noteworthy as being the best maintained of the older houses in this area.

35. Nicholas Turkey Breeding Farm
2400 Fallon Road

The former turkey farm includes a two-story Italianate house that dates from the 1870s or possibly earlier. On the surrounding fields are unusual long-and-narrow turkey coops, some that curve over the contours of the hills.

BART
Bay Area Rapid Transit

When the first section of the Bay Area Rapid Transit system (BART) opened in mid-1972, it was with great relief and celebration. After more than twenty years of planning and construction, the transit system was finally going to run.

Construction began on June 19, 1964, with the groundbreaking for a four- and one-half-mile research test track between Concord and Walnut Creek. Parsons-Brinkerhoff-Tudor-Bechtel, an engineering consortium, designed the system and managed construction. They also were responsible for hiring the architects, landscape architects, and graphic artists who designed the stations.

The Fremont to MacArthur Station was the first section to open in 1972 and the first phase was completed in 1974. The system was extended to Bay Point in 1996, to Dublin/Pleasanton in 1997, and to the San Francisco Airport in 2003. Plans for further expansion into Santa Clara County, Antioch, and Pleasanton are in progress.

More than fifty years after BART's formal planning process began, and more than thirty years after it began operating, the enormous effort by numerous public agencies, engineers, architects, planners, and citizens, as well as extensive press coverage have all but receded into history. This was a huge undertaking. The issue, for example, of placing BART underground through Berkeley was a major and controversial consideration but, in retrospect, it was the best decision.

Each BART station was designed by prominent local architects and landscape architects. Many stations are enhanced with artwork as well. The overall signage was designed by Ernest Born. Don Emmons, and then Tallie B. Maule, coordinated the process.

Stations Completed by 1974

Architects

Glen Station and Balboa Park
Corlett & Spackman/Ernest Born

**El Cerrito Del Norte,
El Cerrito Plaza**
DeMars & Wells

*Test Track & Building,
Oakland: 19th and 12th Street,
Daly City*
Gerald McCue & Associates

*Concord, Pleasant Hill,
Walnut Creek, Lafayette,
Orinda, San Leandro, Bay Fair*
Gwathmey, Sellier & Corsby/
Joseph Esherick & Associates

16th and 24th Mission Street
Hertzka & Knowles

*Oakland West, South
Hayward, Union City,
Fremont, north Berkeley*
Kitchen & Hunt

*Richmond, Berkeley, Ashby,
MacArthur, Rockridge*
Maher & Martens

Civic Center and MUNI at Van Ness Avenue, Church and Castro Streets
Reid & Tarics

Fruitvale, Coliseum
Neil Smith/
Reynolds & Chamberlain

Montgomery and Powell Streets
Skidmore, Owings & Merrill

Embarcadero
Tallie B. Maule/
Hertzka & Knowles & Associates

Hayward
Wurster, Bernardi and Emmons

Lake Merritt
Yuill-Thronton,
Warner & Levikov

Landscape Architects

Glen Park and Balboa Park
Douglas Baylis

Concord, Pleasant Hill, Walnut Creek, Lafayette, Orinda, Coliseum, San Leandro, Bay Fair, Hayward
Anthony Guzzardo

South Hayward, Union City, Fremont, Oakland West
Robert Kitchen

16th and 12th Mission Streets
Theodore Osmundson

Richmond, El Cerrito Plaza, North Berkeley, Berkeley, Ashby, Mac Arthur, Rockridge
Royston, Hanamoto,
Beck & Abby

Test Tracks, Del Norte
Sasaki, Walker and Associates

Works of Art

MacArthur Station
Mark Adams (mosaic)

Embarcadero
William Cullen (relief sculpture)

Barbara Shawcroft
(woven rope sculpture)

Stephen De Staebler
(sculpture)

San Leandro
Joseph Esherick (mural)

Fremont
Tallie B. Maule (mural)

Lake Merritt
William Mitchell (plaster relief)

16th Street
William Mitchell (sculpture)

24th Street
William Mitchell (sculpture)

Orinda
Win Ng (mural)

El Cerrito Del Norte and El Cerrito Plaza
Alfonso Pardinas (mosaics)

12th Street
Harold Paris (sculpture, 1974)

Diana Pumpelly Bates
(steel sculpture: 17-foot-long streetscape, 2003)

Union Station
Jean Varda (mural)

Coliseum
John Wastlhuber (mural)

Lafayette
Helen Webber/
Alfonso Pardinas (mosaics)

Stations Completed after 1974

North Concord/Bay Point Extension, 1996
1. North Concord/Martinez
IDG Architects

2. Pittsburg Bay Point
Gannett Fleming, Inc./
Finger & Moy Architects

Castro Valley Dublin Line, 1997
1. Dublin/Pleasanton
Stone Marraccini & Patterson (architects)

2. Castro Valley
Group 4/Architecture Research and Planning, Inc. ICF Kaiser Engineers Ca. Corp (architects)

San Francisco Airport Extension, opened 2003

Four new stations were constructed that extend BART service from Daly City to the San Francisco airport: **South San Francisco, San Bruno, Millbrae, and SFO Station.**

The stations were constructed using the Design-Build method. Several architects participated in different aspects of the design at various stages of the design development.

Warm Springs Extension, scheduled for completion 2009

This extension will add 5.4 miles of new tracks from the existing Fremont Station, south to a new station in the Warm Springs District of Fremont.

Architectural Styles

An architectural style is a synthesis of form, plan, structure, material, siting, and decorative detail resulting in a recognizable and easily described set of design characteristics particular to a period in time. Defining a building as a certain "style" is a shorthand method of describing what a building generally looks like and the period of time it was built.

Although many buildings do not fit neatly into an abbreviated description, familiarity with architectural styles enhances an appreciation of the built environment by providing a clue to the age of a building, neighborhood, or town. During the past 200 years, more than two-dozen architectural styles have been popular in the San Francisco Bay Area.

While the majority of schools, churches, and large apartment and commercial buildings were professionally designed, the majority of residential buildings were designed by builders inspired by work published in books and magazines. Only a small percentage of residential buildings are designed by architects. As early as 1850, popular publications such as Andrew Jackson Downing's *Architecture of Country Houses* and, later, the Newsom Brothers' *Picturesque California Homes* (1884) were the principal means by which architectural styles were articulated and disseminated.

1. Spanish/Mexican Period, 1776–1849

Characteristics: thick walls of sundried adobe bricks covered by a whitewash of lime, with gabled roofs and simple rectangular shapes. Until the 1820s, most dwellings were one-story; the later two-story adobes with second-story balconies across the front are called "Monterey Colonials."

Monterey has the largest, most concentrated examples of adobes in both styles.

Spanish/Mexican— 36501 Niles Boulevard, 1842
Fremont, Alameda County

2. Early Greek Revival, 1850s–1870s

Characteristics: rectangular footprint, gable roofs with eave returns, and commonly a symmetrical "temple" front with a gabled pediment. Often there are quoins at corners, a full porch with lathed balusters,

and boxed posts resembling classical columns.

Early Greek Revival—
Tomales Presbyterian Church, 1868
*11 Church Street
Tomales,
Marin County*

3. Gothic Revival,
1850s–1870s

Characteristics: steep gable roofs often intersecting, varied façades, windows with pointed arches, drip moldings, and spidery wood trim. Most early examples mixed Gothic elements with Greek symmetry.

Gothic Revival—
627 Hamilton Street, 1860
*Redwood City,
San Mateo County*

4. Octagon Houses,
1850s–1870s

The octagon-shaped house is a minor but curious type promoted by Orson Squire Fowler in *A Home for All* (1849). There are only five octagon houses in the Bay Area.

Octagon—
House, 1864
*2645 Gough Street
San Francisco,
San Francisco County*

5. Victorian Era,
1860s–1900

San Francisco is known for residential streets lined with highly decorated Victorian-era row houses. Narrow, regularly spaced city lots and the use of wood balloon-frame construction contributed to their distinctive character. Thousands built by developers between the 1870s and 1890s used pattern-book plans and lavish decorative wood elements supplied by machine shops and found in catalogues.

Victorian-era houses flourished in California in the last third of the nineteenth century and fall into three stylistic categories: Italianate, Stick, and Queen Anne.

5a. Italianate,
1860s–1890

Characteristics: rectangular form with low-pitched hipped roof or false-front parapet, and heavy closed cornices with brackets. Forms and façades varied between a free mix of Classical, and non-Classical, motifs. Windows and doors were often arched; angled bays and formal covered porticos were common. During the 1870s, most stylish residences for merchants, professionals, and prosperous farmers and ranchers were Italianate. There was also a one-story vernacular version and a sub-type with a mansard roof called Second Empire. Octagon-shaped houses from this period have Italianate features.

Italianate—
Peralta House, 1871
*2465 Thirty-Fourth Street
Oakland,
Alameda County*

5b. Stick Style, 1870s–1890s

Characteristics: an emphasis on angularity, square bay windows, and an overlay of milled stick work such as batten friezes. The suburban form was likely to be L-shaped with a front-facing gable, a wing with a side-facing gable, and a covered veranda.

Stick—
O'Connor House, 1891
*1001 Grand Street
Oakland,
Alameda County*

Charles S. Shaner, architect

5c. Queen Anne, 1880–1900

Characteristics: asymmetrical façades with bay windows, patterned shingling, wraparound porches, and profuse displays of jigsaw and lathed ornament; on more elaborate examples were towers with conical roofs. Queen Anne was the Romantic style of the era, and there are many variations within the style.

Queen Anne—
220 West Third Street, 1890s
Antioch,
Contra Costa County

6. Romanesque, 1880s–1890s

Characteristics: rugged stone construction, rounded arches, circular towers with conical roofs, picturesque massing that was primarily used for institutional buildings. The style is associated with the work of architect Henry Hobson Richardson and is often called Richardsonian Romanesque.

Romanesque—
Montgomery Chapel, 1893
San Francisco Theological
Seminary
Bolinas Avenue and
Seminary Road
San Anselmo,
Marin County

Wright and Sanders, architects

7. Colonial Revival Styles, 1890s–1910

Two Colonial Revival styles coexisted between the mid-1890s and 1910s: the classic Colonial Revival style and the Shingle style.

7a. Colonial Revival

Characteristics: rectangular footprint, usually a hipped roof with a dormer, closed eaves, plain lap siding, and understated ornament in the form of classically inspired porch columns, fluted pilasters, modillion-like brackets, and dentil molding. There were two versions. The Classic Box style (San Francisco versions are called Edwardian) was the prevalent residential style at the turn of the nineteenth century and was mostly designed by builders in symmetrical, asymmetrical, and one- and two-story versions.

Classic Box—
1179 Washington Street,
1905
Santa Clara,
Santa Clara County

Louis Theodore Lenzen,
architect

The Classic Revival style was more elaborate and usually larger with a one- or two-story temple-style portico.

Classic Revival—
726 Fitch Street, 1914
Healdsburg,
Sonoma County

7b. Shingle Style

Characteristics: uniformly sheathed with unpainted shingles or board-and-batten siding; window trim and closed eaves; unemphasized balustrades, bargeboards, and posts; painted, or left unpainted to blend with the natural wood shingles. On the interior, unpainted walls of redwood paneling were common. Early shingled houses had the complex massing and romantic picturesque profiles of late Queen Annes; later examples had the boxy profiles of Colonial Revivals; and when the Shingle style merged with Tudor Revival, half-timbering and small-paned windows were present. The Shingle style had its roots in the English Arts and Crafts movement that sought a preindustrial "natural" aesthetic; it was less popular than the classic Colonial Revival style, but more romantic and free flowing.

Shingle—
United Church of Cloverdale, 1906
*439 North Cloverdale Boulevard
Cloverdale,
Sonoma County*

Rev. Francis Reid, architect

Shingle—
Mouser-Parsons House, 1888
*21 Mosswood Road
Berkeley,
Alameda County*

*John Hudson Thomas
(alterations, 1910)*

8. Craftsman Style,
circa 1905–1930

Shingle style and Craftsman style, though both derived from the same philosophy embedded in the English Arts and Crafts movement, did not share the same stylistic attributes.

Characteristics: one-story or one- and two-story split-level rectangular shape, layers of shallow gabled roofs with wide projecting open eaves, and large covered or recessed front porches. In contrast to the Shingle style, there is an emphasis on the contrast between wall surfaces (wood, shingle, or stucco) and the simple, large wood rafter ends, bargeboards, angled brackets, and porch posts. The Craftsman Bungalow was the preeminent house type between about 1910 and 1930 and came in many sizes and variations.

Craftsman—
Blair House, 1911
*1145–1147 Martin Avenue
San Jose,
Santa Clara County*

*Louis T. Lenzen,
architect*

9. Prairie Style, 1900–1930

Characteristics: emphasis on wide rectangular shapes, flat roofs or horizontal parapets, horizontal window groups, and stucco siding. Inspired by the early work of Frank Lloyd Wright in Chicago, the style is noteworthy for eschewing decorative detail inspired by the past. Almost contiguous with the emergence of the Period Revival style and overlapping with the Craftsman Bungalow, the Prairie style was not widely popular in the Bay Area.

Prairie—
Charles S. Allen House, 1916
*901 Plaza Drive
San Jose,
Santa Clara County*

*Frank D. Wolfe,
architect (attributed)*

10. Period Revival, 1905–1935

As early as the 1890s, work by the major Bay Area architects used references to historic precedents, but by the end of the First World War, popular residential architecture was deeply entrenched in historic revivalism. The Period Revival came in many forms: English Tudor, English Cottage, Mediterranean, Italian Renaissance, French Chateau, Spanish Colonial, Mission, Classic Revival (again), Southwest Pueblo, and variations of all.

Although the Period Revival style is often dismissed as a backward step in the march towards modern architecture, innovations were being made under the safety of traditionalism: floor plans became more fluid and open, the shape of the house became wide U, L, and T shapes; a garden or patio formed by the sheltering enclosure of the wings was the precursor to the California Ranch.

Period Revival:
English Tudor—
141 Pepper Avenue, 1895
*Hillsborough,
San Mateo County*

A. Page Brown, architect

**Period Revival:
Mediterranean —
900 D Street,** 1930
*Petaluma,
Sonoma County*

Don Uhl, architect

**Period Revival: Mission —
1085 Ralston Avenue,** 1905
*Belmont,
San Mateo County*

11. Classic Revival Institutional and Office Buildings, 1890–1940

Design inspired by historic Classical buildings, both Greek and Roman, was never abandoned but was augmented from time to time by new interpretations. Classic Revival buildings were divided into symmetrical three-part compositions consisting of base, shaft, and capital, like a Classic column.

**Classic Revival —
YMCA,** 1910
*2001 Allston Way
Berkeley,
Alameda County*

*Benjamin G. McDougall,
architect*

Classic decorative details included pediments, entablatures, triglyphs, coffers, dentils, egg and dart, bead and reel, acanthus leaves, and all their hundred's of variations. The most prominent examples are bank buildings with Classic temple fronts. Bay Area architects who studied at the École des Beaux-Arts in Paris incorporated the Classicism of the Renaissance and the decorative Classicism of the Baroque into their work; this is referred to as Beaux-Arts Classicism.

**Beaux-Arts Classicism —
Wheeler Hall,** 1907
*University of California
Berkeley,
Alameda County*

*John Galen Howard,
architect*

12. Classic Moderne, 1925–1950

Toward the end of the 1920s, the Classic idiom flattened, becoming less plastic and sculptural. The resulting style is called Stripped Classic, Classic Moderne, and sometimes WPA Moderne.

**Classic Moderne —
Analy Union High
School,** 1935
*6950 Analy Avenue
Sebastopol,
Sonoma County*

*Louis S. Stone &
Henry C. Smith,
architects*

13. Art Deco, 1925–1940

The Art Deco style was inspired by the 1925 Exposition Internationale des Arts Décoratifs et Industriels Modernes in Paris, which showcased new machines, automobiles, airplanes, and ocean liners. The streamlined angular, curvilinear, and zigzag forms that developed are absent of historical or classical references. New building techniques such as reinforced concrete made traditional cornices, pitched roofs, window moldings, and emphatic corners obsolete.

Art Deco—
George Hein Building, 1936
1660 Laurel Street
San Carlos,
San Mateo County

14. International Style, 1930–1960

Characteristics: rectangular shapes (often like layers of stacked boxes), repetitive-sized window openings, grouped windows, flat roofs, and cream-colored or white stucco siding. Between the mid-1910s and 1920s, the International Modernist movement was introduced to Southern California through the early work of Irving Gill and Rudolf Schindler. By the mid-1930s, work by Richard Neutra was being built in the Bay Area.

International—
House, 1954
775 San Diego Road
Berkeley,
Alameda County
Donald Olsen, architect

15. Mid-twentieth-century Architecture, 1935–1960s

The California Ranch house and the mid-twentieth-century Modern are not the same style although they are often confused. While they are parallel styles that occasionally overlap, there are distinct philosophical and idiomatic differences.

15a. California Ranch House

Characteristics: a wide U- or L-shaped one-story building directly connected to the garden or patio from a major room. Commonly there is a low-pitched hipped or gabled roof covered with wood shakes or composition shingles and horizontal or board-and-batten wood siding that is painted. The California Ranch house had its roots in the Period Revival and Bungalow styles of the 1920s and 1930s. It became the dominant vernacular style after World War II.

California Ranch—
House, circa 1958
Residential Subdivision
Los Gallinas Road at
Elvia Court
Marinwood,
Marin County

15b. Mid-twentieth-century Modernism

Characteristics: post-and-beam construction with walls of glass that reveal structure and commonly built on slab-on-grade concrete. The low single-story profile is usually sheathed with unpainted redwood siding and freely opens to a pebble-imbedded patio and garden of native California plants. It was discreet, unassuming and hidden in lush gardens. Mid-twentieth-century Modernism is a fusion of ideas that include Frank Lloyd Wright's Usonian houses and the International Style. Like the shingle style, Mid-twentieth-century Modernism was the less popular but more avant-garde mid-century style, although vernacular versions were also built.

Modernism—
House, 1950
106 Forest Lane
Berkeley,
Alameda County
John Funk, architect

15c. Flamboyant or Expressionistic Moderne, 1946–1960

Characteristics: a combination of Streamline Moderne exuberance and Art Deco with angled or curved forms. It was a popular style for drive-in restaurants and gas stations and a few houses and residential subdivisions.

Expressionistic Moderne—
Mel's Drive-In, 1954
1701 San Pablo Avenue,
at Seventeenth Street
Oakland,
Alameda County
William B. David, architect

15d. Mid-twentieth-century Stucco Apartment, 1946–1980

Characteristics: rectangular and flat roofed, with a grid of evenly spaced window openings or bands of windows across a flat façade; usually stucco-sided with accents of wood or concrete-block latticework. Central courtyards or balconies are often present, and some were raised on slender pipe posts above open parking "garages." More-sophisticated designs provided closed parking discreetly tucked under the units. In suburban settings, the parking might be behind the building in detached carports. The proliferation of the stucco apartment was due to the sudden increase in the Bay Area's population after World War II.

Stucco Apartment— Fuji Towers, 1976
690 North Fifth Street
San Jose,
Santa Clara County
Yuzuro Kawahara, architect
Carl Swenson, builder

16. New Form, 1950–1980
16a. Concrete Brutalism, 1960–1975

Characteristics: raw, unpainted reinforced concrete; boldly expressed structure; sculptural emphasis. The style produced some truly sculptural work as well as repetitive modular walls and screens of precast concrete.

Concrete Brutalism— Sumitomo Bank/ Family Court, 1979
170 Park Center Plaza
San Jose,
Santa Clara County
Cesar Pelli & Associates, Inc., architects

16b. Minimalism & Experimental Forms, 1950s–1980

Characteristics: cubes, rectangles, and squares with sloping roofs that directly meet the walls, windows of different sizes with minimal framing, a skin of vertical board siding, shingles and, later, stucco. Often structural elements are exposed on the interior but are not expressed on the exterior. The period also saw the rise of experimental forms such as geodesic domes, A-frames, and butterfly roofs.

Experimental Forms: Domed Roof— Our Lady of Mount Carmel Church, 1960
26300 Asti Road
Asti,
Sonoma County
Albert Hunter and Shig Iyama, architects

Experimental Forms: A-frame— Hope Lutheran Church, 1955
55 San Fernando Way
Brisbane,
San Mateo County
Mario Corbett, architect

16c. High-rise Office and Apartment Shafts, 1950–1980

Characteristics: bold and simple rectangular shafts sheathed in a visually thin skin of repeating patterns of glass, metal, and/or concrete. Like a repetitive pattern on fabric, these buildings have a minimalist quality.

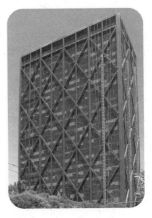

High-rise Office Shaft—
Alcoa Building, 1964
1 Maritime Plaza
San Francisco,
San Francisco County

Skidmore, Owings & Merrill,
architects

17. 1990–present

New architectural forms are created as a response to the immediate past, the availability of new building materials, and advances in engineering, as well as economic conditions. During the 1990s, a building boom in the Bay Area has transformed the skyline, altered older industrial areas, and intensified suburban sprawl.

17a. Housing Trends

Two current housing trends are entirely at odds with one another: **neo-traditionalism** in the form of Period Revivals, Bungalows, and Colonial Revivals are popular in most suburban subdivisions.

Period Revival—
Neo-traditional Housing
Development, 2005
Merrydale and
San Pedro Roads
San Rafael,
Marin County

Industrial Modern with cubist shapes and frankly expressed industrial materials is the

prevailing style for multi-unit inner-city projects and high-end, architect-designed single-family homes and apartment buildings.

Industrial Modern—
119 Strathmore, 1994
Oakland,
Alameda County

Jim Jennings Architecture

17b. Non-Residential
Buildings

A sculptural approach to designing the high-rise building has resulted in breaking up the smooth-skinned shaft to produce a more varied profile accentuated with color and texture.

Non-residential—
Rincon Annex High-rise,
1989 addition
101 Spear Street
San Francisco,
San Francisco County

Scott Johnson; Fain & Pereira
Associates, architects

Airports as well as sports and convention pavilions tend toward exposed structure and transparent roofs.

Non-residential:
Pavilion—
Milbrae BART & Train
Station, 2003
200 North Rollins Road
Millbrae,
San Mateo County

Eli Naor, VBN Architects

A breaking up of the massing, and introduction of multiple building materials has become popular for institutional buildings such as schools and city halls.

Non-residential:

Institutional—
Ernesto Galarza
Elementary School, 2001
1619 Bird Avenue
San Jose,
Santa Clara County

Bill Gould Design,
architect

Further Reading

Most of the cities and towns listed in this guide have resources that are available in city planning departments, history rooms of public libraries, and local historical societies. During the past fifteen years, comprehensive historic surveys of cities, towns, and neighborhoods have been conducted. To find a city's Web site in California, type the following: ci.[name of city].ca.us. Historical societies usually can be found by conducting a Web search with key words; berkeleyheritage.com has many links.

Copies of cultural surveys, landmark applications, and reports are usually available in planning departments; monographs and articles on towns and neighborhoods are commonly published by historical societies or local newspapers and are available at local history museums.

The major archival sources for the Bay Area are found in the Bancroft Library and the Documents Collection of the College of Environmental Design Library, both are at the University of California–Berkeley. Good collections are also found in the history rooms in the main public libraries of San Francisco, San Jose, Oakland, and Marin County.

The Architect and Engineer, San Francisco: 1905– is the premier journal covering California architecture in the twentieth century; and *California Architect and Building News, San Francisco: 1879–1900* is the primary journal covering San Francisco architecture in the nineteenth century. Gary Goss compiled an *Index to The Architect and Engineer, Volume 1–95, 1905–1928.* Both journals and the Goss index are located in the Environmental Design Library, University of California–Berkeley.

General

Adamson, Paul, and Marty Arbunich. *Eichler: Modernism Rebuilds the American Dream.* Salt Lake City: Gibbs Smith, Publisher, 2002.

Benet, James. *A Guide to San Francisco and the Bay Region.* New York: Random House, 1963.

Boutelle, Sara Holmes. *Julia Morgan: Architect.* New York: Abbeville Press, 1988.

Cardwell, Kenneth H. *Bernard Maybeck.* Salt Lake City: Peregrine Smith Books, 1983.

Crowe, Michael F. *Deco by the Bay: Art Deco Architecture in the San Francisco Bay Area.* New York: Viking Studio Books, 1995.

Dunlap, Carol. *California People.* Salt Lake City: Gibbs M. Smith, Inc., Peregrine Smith Books, 1982.

Federal Writers' Project. *The WPA Guide to California* (1939). Reprinted with an introduction by Gwendolyn Wright. New York: Pantheon Books, 1984.

Freudenheim, Leslie, and Elizabeth Sussman. *Building with Nature: Roots of the San Francisco Bay Region Tradition.* Santa Barbara and Salt Lake City: Peregrine Smith Books, 1974; revised, Salt Lake City: Gibbs Smith, Publisher, 2005.

Gebhard, David, Robert Winter, and Eric Sandweiss. *Architecture in San Francisco and Northern California*. Salt Lake City: Gibbs Smith, Inc., Peregrine Smith Books, 1985.

Gudde, Erwin G. *California Place Names*. Berkeley, Los Angeles, London: University of California Press, 1949; revised and enlarged edition, 1969.

Hart, James D. *A Companion to California*. Berkeley, Los Angeles, London: University of California Press, 1987.

Hess, Alan. *Ranch House*. New York: Harry N. Abrams, 2004.

Hoover, Rensch, Abeloe. *Historic Spots in California*. Stanford: Stanford University Press, 1932; revised, 1966.

Images of America. San Francisco: Arcadia Publishing. This series uses historic photographs and long captions to convey the history of smaller cities and neighborhoods. More than one-hundred titles have been published for the Bay Area (www.arcadiapublishing.com).

Jenkins, Olaf P., editor. *Geological Guidebook of the San Francisco Bay Counties*, Bulletin 154. State of California, Division of Mines, 1951.

King, John. "Places," *San Francisco Chronicle*, 2000– , ongoing series.

Lloyd, Peter. San Francisco *Houses after the Fire*. Köln, Germany: Könemann Verlagesellschaft, 1997.

Lloyd, Peter. *San Francisco: A Guide to Recent Architecture*. London: Ellipsus London Limited, 1997.

Longstreth, Richard. *On The Edge of the World: Four Architects in San Francisco at the Turn of the Century*. Boston: MIT Press, 1983.

Lowell, Waverly. *Conducting Architectural Research in the San Francisco Bay Area*. Berkeley: University of California, 1988.

Markinson, Randell L. *Greene & Greene: The Passion and the Legacy*. Salt Lake City: Gibbs Smith, Publisher, 1998.

McAlester, Virginia and Lee McAlester. *A Field Guide to American Houses*. New York: Alfred Knopf, 1984.

McCoy, Ester. *Five California Architects*. New York: Reinhold Publishing, 1960.

Olmsted, Roger, and T. H. Watkins. *Here Today*. San Francisco: Chronicle Books, 1968.

Reiff, Daniel D. *Houses from Books, Treatises, Pattern Books, and Catalogs in American Architecture, 1738–1950: A History and Guide*. University Park: Pennsylvania State University Press, 2000.

Richards, Rand. *Historic San Francisco: a Concise History and Guide*. San Francisco: Heritage House Publishers, 1991.

Rifkind, Carole. *Field Guide to American Architecture*. New York: New American Library, 1980.

San Francisco Museum of Art. *Domestic Architecture of the San Francisco Bay Region*. San Francisco Museum of Art, 1949.

Sardar, Zahid. *San Francisco Modern: Interiors, Architecture & Design*. San Francisco: Chronicle Books, 1998.

Shay, James. *New Architecture San Francisco*. San Francisco: Chronicle Books, 1989.

Starr, Kevin. *Americans and the California Dream*. Santa Barbara and Salt Lake City: Peregrine Smith, Inc., 1981.

Temko, Allen. *No Way to Build a Ball Park*. San Francisco: Chronicle Books, 1993.

Treib, Marc, editor. *An Everyday Modernism: The Houses of William Wurster*. San Francisco Museum of Modern Art. Berkeley, Los Angeles, London: University of California Press, 1995.

Treib, Marc. *The Houses of Joseph Esherick*. Environmental Design Archives at the University of California–Berkeley. San Francisco: William K Stout, 2005.

Waldhorn, Judith Lynch, and Sally Woodbridge. *Victoria's Legacy, Tours of San Francisco Bay Area Architecture*. San Francisco: 101 Productions, 1978.

Whiffen, Marcus. *American Architecture since 1780: A Guide to the Styles*. Cambridge, MA: MIT Press, 1992.

Weingarten, David, and Alan Weintraub (photographer). *Bay Area Style: San Francisco Bay Region Houses*. New York: Rizzoli, 2004.

Weinstein, Dave. *Signature Architects*. Salt Lake City: Gibbs Smith, Publisher, 2006.

Winter, Robert, editor. *Towards a Simpler Way of Life: The Arts and Crafts Architects of California*. Berkeley: Norfleet Press, University of California, 1997.

Wollenberg, Charles. *Golden Gate Metropolis: Perspectives on Bay Area History*. Berkeley: University of California, Institute of Governmental Studies, 1985.

Woodbridge, Sally. *Bernard Maybeck: Visionary Architect*. New York: Abbeville, 1992.

Woodbridge, Sally, editor. *Bay Area Houses*. New York: Oxford University Press, 1976.

Woodbridge, Sally, John M. Woodbridge, and Chuck Byrne. *San Francisco Architecture*.

San Francisco: Chronicle Books, 1992; Berkeley: Ten Speed Press, 2005.

I San Francisco City and County

Alexander, James Beach, and James Lee Heig. *San Francisco: Building the Dream City.* San Francisco: Scottwall Associates, Publishers, 2002.

Baird, Joseph Armstrong Jr. *Time's Wonderous Changes: San Francisco Architecture 1776–1915.* San Francisco: California Historical Society, 1962.

Caen, Herb. *Herb Caen's Guide to San Francisco.* New York: Doubleday and Company, 1957.

Corbett, Michael. *Splendid Survivors.* San Francisco: California Living Books, 1979.

Delehanty, Randolph. *In the Victorian Style.* San Francisco: Chronicle Books, 1991.

Delehanty, Randolph. *San Francisco: The Ultimate Guide.* San Francisco: Chronicle Books, 1989; revised, 1995.

Kostura, William. *Russian Hill: The Summit, 1853–1906.* San Francisco: Aerie Publications, 1997.

McGrew, Patrick. *Landmarks of San Francisco.* New York: Harry N. Abrams, 1991.

Muscatine, Doris. *Old San Francisco: The Biography of a City from Early Days to the Earthquake.* New York: G. P. Putnam's Sons, 1975.

Myrick, David F. *San Francisco's Telegraph Hill.* Berkeley: Howell-North Books, 1972.

Radford, Warren and Georgia. *Outdoor Sculpture in San Francisco.* Gualala, CA: Helsham Press, 2002.

Richards, Rand. *Historic Walks in San Francisco.* San Francisco:

Heritage House Publishers, 2001.

Stich, Sidra. *Art-sites San Francisco.* San Francisco: art-SITES Press, 2003.

Wiley, Peter Booth. *National Trust Guide: San Francisco.* New York: John Wiley and Sons, 2000.

II San Mateo County

Numerous surveys, monographs, and walking tours available through the San Mateo County Historical Society.

III Santa Clara County

Butler, P. F. *The Valley of Santa Clara, Historic Buildings, 1792–1920.* San José: Junior League of San José, 1975.

Espinola, G. *Cottages, Flats, Buildings and Bungalows: 102 Designs from Wolfe & McKenzie, 1907.* San Jose: Bay Valley & Valley Publishers, 2004.

Joncas, R., D. J. Neuman, and P. V. Turner. *Stanford University: The Campus Guide.* New York: Princeton Architectural Press, 1999.

Regnery, D. F. *An Enduring Heritage: Historic Buildings of the San Francisco Peninsula.* Stanford: Stanford University Press, 1976.

IV Alameda County

Alameda

Buildings of the Edwardian Period, City of Alameda, 1905 to December 31, 1909. Researched and compiled by George C. Gunn. Alameda, CA: Alameda Historical Museum, 1988.

Documentation of Victorian and Post Victorian Residential and Commercial Buildings, City of Alameda, 1854 to 1904.

Researched and compiled by George C. Gunn. Alameda, CA: Alameda Historical Museum, 1985; revised, 1988.

Berkeley

Berkeley Historical Society. *Exactly Opposite the Golden Gate.* Berkeley: The Berkeley Historical Society, 1983.

Cerny, Susan Dinkelspiel. *Berkeley Landmarks.* Berkeley: Berkeley Architectural Heritage Association, 1994. Revised, 2002.

Helfand, Harvey. *University of California, Berkeley: the Campus Guide.* New York: Princeton Architectural Press, 2002.

Keeler, Charles. *The Simple Home.* Berkeley: The Hillside Club, 1904. Republished with an introduction by Dimitri Shipounoff, Santa Barbara and Salt Lake City: Peregrine Smith Books, 1979.

Willis, Burl. *Picturing Berkeley: A Postcard History.* Berkeley Historical Society & Berkeley Architectural Heritage Association, 2002. Republished, Salt Lake City: Gibbs Smith, Publisher, 2004.

Woodbridge, Sally. *John Galen Howard and the University of California.* Berkeley: University of California Press, 2002.

Emeryville

Behind the Boomtown, Growth and Urban Redevelopment in Emeryville. East Bay Alliance for a Sustainable Economy, Center for Labor Research and Education, Berkeley: University of California, May 2003.

Early Emeryville Remembered, Historical Essays and Photographs. Emeryville Historical Society, 1996.

Oakland

Bagwell, Beth. *Oakland, The Story of a City.* Oakland: Oakland Heritage Alliance, 1982, 1994.

Hildebrand, George H. *Borax Pioneer: Francis Marion Smith.* San Diego: Howell-North Books, 1982.

Thompson & West. *Official and Historical Atlas of Alameda County, California.* Oakland: Thompson & West, 1878. Bicentennial reprint, Fresno: Valley Publishers, 1976.

Piedmont

Pattiani, Evelyn Craig. *Queen of the Hills, The Story of Piedmont, a California City.* Oakland: Yosemite-DiMaggio, 1982.

South Alameda County

Historical monographs are available for Dublin, Washington Township, Sunol, Livermore-Amador Valley, Hayward, Newark, Pleasanton, San Leandro, and architect W. H. Weeks.

The Rancho of Don Guillermo, Volume 1: Years 1843–1890: A History of Hayward, Castro Valley and San Lorenzo. Hayward, CA: Mt. Eden Historical Publishers, 1991.

Sandoval, John S. *Mt. Eden: Cradle of the Salt Industry in California.* Hayward, CA: Mt. Eden Historical Publishers, 1988.

Wood, W.M. *History of Alameda County, California.* Reprint. Oakland: Holmes Book Co., 1969.

V Contra Costa County

Emanuels, George. *Contra Costa County: An Illustrated History.* Fresno, CA: Panorama West Books, 1986.

Leighton, Kathy. *Footprints in the Sand.* City of Brentwood and East Contra Costa Historical Society. Ann Arbor, MI: Sheridan Books, Inc., 2001.

VI Solano County

Arnold, Anthony. *Suisun Marsh History; Hunting and Saving a Wetland.* Marina, CA: Monterey Pacific Publishing Co., 1996.

Bruegmann, Robert. *Benicia: Portrait of an Early California Town,* 2nd edition. Fairfield, CA: James Stevenson, Publisher, 1997.

Heritage Society of West Central Solano for the City of Fairfield. *The Heritage Collection—Sites, Structures and History of Fairfield and Vicinity.* Vallejo, CA: Wheeler Printing, Inc., 1999.

History of Solano County. San Francisco: Wood, Alley & Co., 1879. Reprinted, with a Preface by Mary Higham and an Index prepared by Solano County Genealogical Society, Fairfield: James Stevenson Publisher, 1994.

Keegan, Frank L. *Solano: An Illustrated History.* Northridge, CA: Windsor Publications, 1989.

VII Napa County

Heintz, Willliam F. *California's Napa Valley.* San Francisco: Scottwall Associates, 1999.

Verardo, Denzil, and Jennie Dennis Verardo. *Napa Valley: From Golden Fields to Purple Harvest.* Northridge, CA: Windsor Publications, Inc., 1986.

Weber, Lin. *Old Napa Valley: The History to 1900.* St. Helena, CA: Wine Ventures Publishing, 1998.

VIII Sonoma County

Finley, Ernest L. *History of Sonoma County, California: Its*

People and Its Resources. Santa Rosa, CA: Press Democrat Pub. Co., 1937.

Griffin, L. Martin. *Saving the Marin-Sonoma Coast: the Battles for Audubon Canyon Ranch, Point Reyes, and California's Russian River.* Healdsburg, CA: Sweetwater Springs Press, 1998.

Historical Atlas Map of Sonoma County, California. Compiled, drawn, and published from personal examination and actual surveys by Thos. H. Thompson & Co. Oakland: Thos. H. Thompson & Co., 1877.

An Illustrated History of Sonoma County, California. Salem, MA: Higginson Book Company, 1999.

Rosenus, Alan. *General Vallejo and the Advent of the Americans: a Biography.* Berkeley: Heyday Books/Urion Press, 1999.

Wilson, Simone. *Sonoma County: the River of Time: an Illustrated History.* Sun Valley, CA: American Historical Press, 1999.

IX Marin County

Livingston, Dewy. *A Good Life: Dairy Farming in the Olema Valley, A History of the Dairy and Beef Ranches within Point Reyes National Seashore, 1834–1992.* National Park Service, 1993. Revised, 1994.

Mason, Jack. *Point Reyes, The Solemn Land.* Point Reyes Station, CA: DeWolfe Pringin, 1970.

———, and Helen Van Cleave Park. *The Making of Marin.* Inverness, CA: North Shore Books, 1975.

Teather, Louise. *Discovering Marin.* Fairfax, CA: The Tamal Press, 1974.

Tracy, Jack. *Sausalito, Moments in Time.* Sausalito, CA: Windgate Press, 1983.

Index

Index Key

SAN JOSE {III}, iv, 26, 85–99. *See also* Naglee Park; San Jose State University
  SAN JOSE = main city, area, or county
  {III} = San Jose is located in Santa Clara County
  iv, 26, 85–99 = San Jose is listed on pages iv, 26, and 85 through 99
  See also Naglee Park; San Jose State University = San Jose has additional entries

Morgan, Julia, 45, **63, 83-84, 145 (2),** 346, **510**
  Morgan, Julia = name of architect, designer, or landscape designer
  63, 83–84, 145, 510 = Julia Morgan's architecture is listed on these pages
  145 (2) = Julia Morgan has two buildings on page 145
  45, 346 = Julia Morgan is mentioned on pages 45 and 346

Temple of Wings, Berkeley {IV}, 314–15
  Temple of Wings = numbered entry also appears on a map,
        or the name of another building appears in the entry
  Berkeley = Temple of Wings is located in Berkeley
  {IV} = Berkeley is located in Alameda County
  314–15 = Temple of Wings is listed on pages 314 and 315

Corners, The, Walnut Creek {V}, 355, 410
  Corners, The = area of a larger city or county mentioned in the text
  Walnut Creek = The Corners is located in Walnut Creek
  {V} = Walnut Creek is located in Contra Costa County
  355, 410 = The Corners is listed on pages 355 and 410

Chateau Chevalier Winery, St. Helena {VII}, 391
  Chateau Chevalier Winery = this winery mentioned in the text
  St. Helena = Chateau Chevalier Winery is located in St. Helena
  {VII} = St. Helena is located in Napa County
  391 = Chateau Chevalier Winery is mentioned on page 391

A

"A" Street Historic District,
Petaluma {VIII}, 421–22
ABAG. *See* Association of Bay
Area Governments
Abel, Arthur, 268, 274
**Abrams, Millikan and Kent,
334, 335**
Academy of Science,
Golden Gate Park {I}, 107
**Ace Architects, 244, 264 (2),
280 (2), 281 (3), 330**
Aced, Steve, 184
Adams, C. C., 292
Adams, Charles, 88
Adams, Edson, 262
Adams, Henry, 89
Adams, Mark, 195, 502
Adobes. *See* Altamirano Adobe;
Alviso Adobe {IV}; Alviso
Adobe {III}; Berryessa Adobe;
Brown Adobe; Castro/
Alvarado Adobe; Hacienda
Cottages; Juarez Adobe;
Leese-Fitch Adobe; Pensar
Adobe; Peralta Adobe–
Fallon House Historic Site;
Petaluma Adobe; Ray Adobe;
Roberts-Sunol Adobe; Salvio-
Pacheco Adobe; Sanchez
Adobe; Santa Clara Women's
Club; Sonoma Mission;
Southern Pacific Passenger
Station; Vaca-Pena Adobe;
Vallejo Adobe; Vallejo's
Adobe; Salvador; Ynitia
Adobe
Adrian William, 102
Aetna Springs,
Pope Valley {VII}, 410

*African American Museum and
Library at Oakland (AAMLO)*
{IV}, 246
Agnoli, Val, 493
Aidlin, Joshua, 88
Ainsley House, J. C.,
Campbell {III}, 194
Aitken, Robert I., 24, 74, 108
ALAMEDA, Central,
293, 295–96
ALAMEDA, City of, 229,
288–99. *See also* Alameda,
Central; East End; Gold
Coast; Northside;
Waterfront; West End
Alameda Civic Center, 289,
290–91
ALAMEDA COUNTY {IV},
xi, 6, 229–38, 339, 340, 353.
See also Alameda, City of;
Alameda County, Southeast;
Alameda County, Southwest;
Berkeley, Castro Valley,
Dublin, Emeryville, Fremont,
Hayward, Livermore,
Newark, Oakland, Piedmont,
Pleasanton, San Leandro, San
Lorenzo, Sunol, Union City
Alameda County Courthouse,
Oakland {IV}, 252–53
Alameda County, East, 231
ALAMEDA COUNTY,
Southeast, 231–33.
See also Dublin; Livermore;
Pleasanton
ALAMEDA COUNTY,
Southwest, 234–41.
See also Castro Valley;
Fremont; Hayward; Newark;
San Leandro; San Lorenzo;
Sunol; Union City

ALAMO {V}, 341, 353
Alamo Square Park,
Western Addition {I}, 69
Alaska Commercial Company,
389, 488
Alavi, Seyed, 207
Albro, Maxine, 162
Alcalanes Union High School,
Lafayette {V}, 352
Alcatraz, GGNRA {I}, 113, 466
Alcoa Building,
Financial District {I}, 12
Alden, Herbert O., 292
Alexander, Christopher, 212
Allen, F. E., 261
Allen, Harry B., 112
Allen, Stephen, 490
Allied Arts Guild,
Menlo Park {II}, 162
Almaden Valley, 169.
See also New Almaden
Alphabet Ranches,
Point Reyes National
Seashore {IX}, 494, 496–97
Alta Plaza,
Pacific Heights {I}, 63
Altamirano Adobe,
Martinez {V}, 360
Altamont Pass, xiv
Altimira, Padre, 365
Alvarado, Union City {IV},
229, 237–38, 241
ALVISO {III}, 166, 220
Alviso Adobe,
Pleasanton {IV}, 232
Alviso Adobe, Milpitas {III}, 221
Amador {IV}, 232
American Conservancy Theater
(ACT), 29
Amiot, Patrick, 451
Anderson Brule Architects, 207

Authors
·
Photographers

SUSAN DINKELSPIEL CERNY is an architectural historian who has published numerous articles on Berkeley and the Bay Area's architectural history for various publications. She is the author of *Berkeley Landmarks,* a contributing author of *Picturing Berkeley: A Postcard History,* the essayist on architect Henry H. Gutterson for *A Simpler Way of Life,* a past president of the Berkeley Architectural Heritage Association, and a former chair of Berkeley's Landmarks Preservation Commission.

Cerny is a fourth-generation San Franciscan, and has made her home in Berkeley since her graduation from the University of California, where she earned a degree in art and architectural history.

San Francisco Bay and Mt. Tamalpais

Contributors

BETH A. ARMSTRONG has been with the Oakland Cultural Heritage Survey for ten years and participated in compiling the Historical Resources Inventory (2002) of Fremont, California.

ANTHONY BRUCE is executive director of the Berkeley Architectural Heritage Association. His degree in art is from the University of California–Berkeley. He has conducted extensive research and written numerous articles about Berkeley and is a contributing author of *Picturing Berkeley: A Postcard History.*

CHARLENE DUVAL is a public historian and executive secretary of the Sourisseau Academy for State and Local History, San Jose State University. Her co-authors are associated with the firm of Archives & Architecture: **Leslie Dill,** a preservation architect and historian, is the principal of Dill Design Group; **Franklin Maggi** is an urban development historian; **Bonnie Montgomery** owns Bay & Valley Publishers, specializing in books on local history and architecture.

WARD HILL received a master's degree in architectural history from the University of Virginia, with an emphasis in American architecture and historic preservation. From 1979 to 1983, he worked for the Foundation for San Francisco's Architectural Heritage and later as staff architectural historian for the architecture/planning firm Page & Turnbull. Since 1990, he has been the principal in his own firm—Ward Hill, Architectural Historian—specializing in architectural history and historic preservation.

MARIANNE RAPALUS HURLEY is an architectural historian and historic preservationist. She is currently a field historian for the California State Parks, but has also worked for the California Department of Transportation and the private sector. She served on Petaluma's Historical and Cultural Preservation Committee.

JUDY IRVIN is a semi-retired historic architect living in Vallejo, California.

WILLIAM KOSTURA has been active as a San Francisco historian since 1981. He is the author of *Russian Hill: The Summit, 1853–1906,* and many articles on other San Francisco subjects. He lives in Oakland and works as an architectural historian.

GAIL G. LOMBARDI is an architectural historian who has worked for the Oakland Cultural Heritage Survey for Oakland City Planning since 1985. She is a board member of the Piedmont Historical Society, editor of their newsletter, and writes articles on Piedmont's history.

BETTY MARVIN is a historic preservation planner with the Oakland City Planning Department, where she has worked on the Oakland Cultural Heritage Survey since 1983. She has also worked on surveys in Berkeley and Santa Rosa.

WOODRUFF MINOR is a Bay Area native from Alameda. He has a degree in history from the University of California–Berkeley and a master's degree in urban planning from the University of Oregon. Since 1977, he has worked in the Bay Area as a preservation planner, an architectural historian, and a freelance writer. Among his many articles and books is *The Ratcliff Architects,* a centennial history of the architectural firm, published in 2006.

MITCHELL P. POSTEL has been executive director of the San Mateo County Historical Association since 1984. He oversees the association's archives and library, exhibits and education programs, and manages the operation of three museums. He teaches California history at San Mateo County Community College. Postel's latest publication is *San Mateo: A Centennial History.* He sits on the San Mateo County Historic Resources Advisory Board and the Leadership San Mateo Board.

SHELBY SAMPSON earned a master's degree in cultural geography from the University of California– Davis. She is a life-long resident of the East Bay, now living in Richmond.